Marketing Decision Making:
Concepts and Strategy

Marketing Decision Making:
Concepts and Strategy

DAVID W. CRAVENS, D.B.A.
GERALD E. HILLS, D.B.A.
ROBERT B. WOODRUFF, D.B.A.

all of
The University of Tennessee

1976

RICHARD D. IRWIN, INC.   Homewood, Illinois   60430
Irwin-Dorsey International   Arundel, Sussex   BN18 9AB
Irwin-Dorsey Limited   Georgetown, Ontario   L7G 4B3

First Printing, March 1976

ISBN 0-256-01799-9
Library of Congress Catalog Card No. 75–35090
Printed in the United States of America

To Sue

To Michele

To Dottie

Preface

The unprecedented societal, economic, and technological changes that have occurred in our nation and throughout the world in the last half-decade provide a clear challenge to contemporary marketing management practice. During this period and the preceding decade substantial progress has been made in applying marketing management concepts, analytical tools, and skills in a variety of business firms and other institutions. The impact on and importance of marketing decisions to the corporate mission as well as all areas of the enterprise have been clearly demonstrated. Marketing management is broadly viewed as an activity of the enterprise, rather than being restricted to the marketing organization. Decisions concerning choice of markets and related marketing actions must be guided by the corporate purpose, and integrated into overall corporate strategy. Therefore, those studying and practicing business management in functional areas other than marketing require a basic understanding of the marketing management function.

This book has been designed for use in marketing management core courses for MBA students and in advanced undergraduate marketing management courses. It should also provide business executives with an operational examination and synthesis of contemporary marketing practice. Our objective is to focus upon marketing management from a decision-making perspective in seeking to provide an operational framework for decision analysis, strategy design, and management control. Marketing management decision making is based on three major types of managerial activities: (1) managerial analysis of the marketing environment; (2) market opportunity analysis leading to the selection of market targets; and (3) marketing strategy design, implementation, and control. The marketing management task is viewed as moving through these three stages of management analysis and decision making.

A key concept underlying the development of the book is that marketing decision making consists of a set of basic processes which can be applied in any type of firm as well as in nonbusiness organizations, providing the processes are used in a manner that recognizes the factors relevant in a specific organization. The book provides decision process frameworks for the various decision activities involved in the marketing management task. These should prove useful to both marketing practitioners and students in gaining an understanding of marketing management, in applying it to marketing activities, and in integrating future contributions to marketing thought and practice. There is a clear emphasis throughout the book on *how* marketing management decisions should be made. In responding to this focus, a major effort has been made to synthesize the myriad contributions from contemporary marketing thought and practice, with extensive use of examples in illustrating marketing management decision processes.

A major premise which extends throughout the book is that in order to understand and practice the marketing management function relevant decision areas must be identified and their interrelationships recognized. Thus, considerable attention has been given to the sequence and interrelationships of the various chapters that comprise the book. Marketing management is viewed as an integrated set of decision activities, which work together in accomplishing the marketing task in a particular organization.

The central thrust of the book is analytical rather than descriptive. Emphasis is placed on marketing decision-making concepts, analysis and the role of information, and the design of strategy. Simply describing marketing practice in the absence of a conceptual orientation contributes little to the understanding and application of marketing management knowledge and skills. Yet, we have tried to avoid overly complex and mathematical discussions. Complex concepts and approaches to decision analysis are conveyed in a manner that does not require specific knowledge of behavioral or management science concepts and methods.

A corollary to effective decision making is acquisition and use of information. Thus, substantial attention has been given to the role of information, both internal and external, in marketing decision making. This perspective spans the entire book with a focus upon the *user* of information rather than information specialists (marketing researchers, for example). The critical role of information is largely neglected in most marketing management texts, other than superficial discussions of marketing research functions. A perspective relevant to the marketing decision maker must focus on his role as a user of marketing information.

It is becoming increasingly clear that marketing decision makers in the years ahead must recognize and understand the relationships of marketing activity to all levels of society. The issues of consumerism, pollution, energy shortages, minority groups, and international politics provide evidence of the acceleration and increasing relevance of changes in the marketing environment to marketing management. This book pays careful attention to environmental analysis as an input to marketing decision making in the organization.

Recognizing the pivotal role that the market plays in marketing decision making, a systematic and comprehensive approach to market opportunity analysis has been developed utilizing traditional methods in combination with the newer contributions from segmentation and buyer behavior research. This integrated approach to market analysis seeks to overcome the fragmented treatment of markets, buyer behavior, and segmentation found in many marketing management textbooks.

The book is organized into six parts. In Part I the marketing management function in the organization is examined and linked to the marketing process in society. Part II deals with managerial analysis of the marketing environment. Appropriate concepts of and approaches to environmental analysis are explained for use in monitoring and forecasting social, economic, technological, and governmental changes of relevance to marketing decision making.

Part III examines the important task of market opportunity analysis. An operational approach to market analysis is presented and illustrated, utilizing a process of narrowing down market opportunities to select those target markets that best mesh with the corporate mission. Concepts and methods of market segmentation are discussed within an overall framework of market opportunity analysis. Buyer decision processes are considered in the context of an operational approach to analysis of buyer behavior for use in market analysis and strategy development.

In Part IV concepts and methods for design of marketing strategy and for guiding decision making in the various marketing mix areas are considered. The concept of marketing strategy positioning is developed to provide an operational framework for planning the marketing program. Specific attention is given to relevant decision making concepts and models, approaches to analysis, and the important task of marketing information planning. Guidelines for design of the marketing program are examined to provide a foundation for considering decisions for the various elements which comprise the marketing program.

In Part V the marketing decision areas which together comprise the marketing program are examined. These marketing mix components, including product or service, channel of distribution, pricing, advertising, and personal selling, must be assembled into an integrated effort for use in seeking favorable response from the organization's target markets. Concepts, decision analysis approaches, and evaluation and control guidelines are reviewed and illustrated for each of the marketing decision areas. Finally, in Part VI, the application of marketing management concepts and practice in the nonbusiness sector is discussed and illustrated.

February 1976   DAVID W. CRAVENS
                                                    GERALD E. HILLS
                                                    ROBERT B. WOODRUFF

Acknowledgments

This book is based upon the contributions, insights, and experiences of innumerable people who have had a variety of impacts upon the development of marketing thought and practice over the past half century, as well as upon our personal development. Our colleagues at the University of Tennessee and at various other institutions influenced the development of this book in many important ways. While we regret that space does not permit acknowledgment of every contribution provided by these people, we want to specifically indicate our sincere appreciation for the assistance provided by several individuals. Robert Robicheaux of the University of Tennessee made substantial contributions to the pricing chapter. Gilbert A. Churchill, Jr., of the University of Wisconsin, Andrew C. Ruppel of the University of Virginia, and Arch G. Woodside of the University of South Carolina, who reviewed the manuscript at various stages, made invaluable suggestions and observations critical to moving the book toward its present form. Students in several classes served as important sources of suggestions during the use of chapter drafts. Also, student assistants provided helpful types of support and we are indebted to each of them. While the typing of many drafts and the final version of the manuscript was accomplished by several, we particularly thank Ramona Taylor for her superb dedication to preparing the manuscript. We are also greatly appreciative of the support and encouragement provided by our dean, John B. Ross, and by Gary N. Dicer, our department head, without whose help, the development of the book would have been impossible. Similarly, we want to express appreciation for the support provided by the Alcoa Foundation. Finally, but most importantly, the encouragement and understanding of our wives and children were vital to completion of the book, and we deeply appreciate their involvement and dedication.

We are indebted to all of these people, and to the many publishers who allowed us to use their materials. While we are responsible for the final result, the opportunity to plan and produce this book would not have been possible without the rich base of contemporary marketing thought and practice provided by marketing scholars and practitioners, past and present.

D.W.C.
G.E.H.
R.B.W.

Contents

ment. Environmental Forces and Decisions. Illustrations of Environmental Influences. Monitoring and Forecasting Environmental Change.

Product Use Tests. Market Testing. Overview of Demand Analysis. New Product Introductions: *Introduction Timing Alternatives. Management of New Products after Introduction.*

part one

The Marketing Process

The marketing process plays a central role in society and influences in various ways the lives of everyone. Marketing management is responsible for guiding the decision making processes in business firms that are aimed at linking customers in the marketplace with goods and services. Non-business organizations such as government agencies, hospitals, and universities are also faced with performing marketing management functions.

In Chapter 1, "Marketing in the Organization," the role and scope of marketing management are examined and a perspective is developed toward this essential organizational activity. The relationship between marketing and organizational strategy is illustrated and assessed. The marketing concept as a guiding philosophy for the marketing management function in an organization is presented, and the nature and scope of the marketing management task are discussed. A decision making framework is developed to serve as a guide to the marketing manager in carrying out the management task. This framework provides a basis for integrating the various areas examined throughout the book.

Chapter 2, "A Macro-marketing Perspective," moves beyond the organization in seeking to consider marketing from the point of view of society. The objective is to provide a rationale for the marketing function and to examine its societal implications. The interrelationships between managerial and societal perspectives toward marketing are considered. The marketing system within which a particular business organization functions is discussed. The system, comprised of various marketing organizations including manufacturers, wholesalers, retailers, end users, and facilitating firms, provides the institutional structure for fulfilling the marketing function in society.

1

Marketing in the Organization

While marketing is a central part of the daily experience of nearly everyone, it is one of the least understood activities of business, and perhaps the most criticized. The pervasiveness of marketing processes in our society is demonstrated by the variety of ways consumers of products and services come into contact with the marketing activities of businesses and other institutions. Consider, for example:

The unbreakable concentration of a nine-year-old girl during a T.V. commercial featuring a new fashion combo for Mattel, Inc.'s "Barbie" doll (who has over 12 million "sister" Barbies throughout the country).

The smug purchaser of a new automobile who has negotiated a 10 percent discount off list price.

A frustrated and angry purchasing agent who has been unable to locate a late shipment of electrical switches ordered from a supplier; the shipment is delaying manufacturing of a large appliance order.

An anxious and nervous newly-wed couple, who both have good jobs, waiting on approval of a bank loan for the purchase of a new home.

A housewife thumbing through a trading stamp catalog in attempting to identify a product choice for which she can exchange the ten books of stamps she has accumulated.

A block-long line of people waiting to gain admittance to an "X" rated movie, paying nearly double the usual ticket rate (for a movie with production costs under $25,000).

These are but a few of the many ways people come into contact with marketing activities in their daily lives. Although many experiences are favorable, some are not. Moreover, what most consumers do not recog-

3

nize is that their exposure to advertising, for example, or to negotiating with a salesman is only part of a larger program of marketing effort carried on by a successful business firm. Through integrated marketing effort the firm seeks to serve its customers effectively in the marketplace, and at the same time, to generate profits for use in expanding the company and in payment of a competitive return to those who have invested their capital in the enterprise.

The underlying objective of this book is to examine the marketing activities of business firms and other organizations with a primary focus on: (1) identifying concepts that guide marketing decision making in the organization; (2) developing effective approaches to analyzing marketing opportunities and problems; and (3) formulating appropriate marketing strategies for serving customer needs and achieving organizational goals.

In this chapter, we first illustrate the relation of marketing to the success of overall organizational strategy. In seeking to establish a proper perspective concerning marketing management, the marketing concept is presented and the nature of the marketing management task is outlined. A framework for guiding marketing management decision making is discussed and the key variables within the framework are examined. The chapter is concluded with an overview of the remainder of the book.

MARKETING AND ORGANIZATIONAL STRATEGY

Marketing is an integral part of organizational strategy. The impact of marketing decision making on corporate results can be illustrated by examining a marketing success story, and an example of certain of the problems encountered in designing an effective marketing strategy. Building on these illustrations, observations are presented concerning the pervasive role of marketing in corporate strategy.

The examples demonstrate the importance of starting with the marketplace in designing and implementing business strategy. A customer orientation should cut across the entire organization. Design of an organizational strategy involves determination of the corporate mission or purpose; selection of objectives to be achieved (e.g., profit, market share, return on investment); determination of types and levels of resources (people, money, and materials) needed to accomplish the objectives; and formulation of policies for guiding the use of organizational resources. The firm's marketing efforts should consist of an *integrated* strategy aimed at providing customer satisfaction. Marketing is the process through which the firm identifies and satisfies customers in the marketplace. In achieving this task the firm has certain demand influencing instruments available for use which are characterized as the "marketing mix."[1] The resources that comprise the marketing mix include the product (or service) offered by the firm, the distribution channels used (e.g., wholesalers, retailers) to make the product available to customers, the price charged for the product, advertising activities, and personal selling efforts.

A Marketing Success

One fascinating business success story of the past decade is McDonald's Corp., the fast food hamburger retailer. By the end of 1972, the firm's outlets numbered nearly 2,300 and total sales of company-owned and independently-operated units were over $1 billion, thus surpassing the U.S. Army as the largest dispenser of meals in the United States.[2] Marketing strategy plays an important role in this significant business success. McDonald's began its ascent to corporate success with top management's eyes focused clearly on customers and their needs and wants. The customer provides the restaurant chain's basic guide to business strategy.

The firm began franchise operations in the mid 1950s in California. In 1961 Ray A. Kroc purchased the interests of the McDonald brothers for $2.7 million (which Kroc indicates ended up costing him $14 million), and as chief executive officer of the firm, he provided the management leadership for advancing the firm to the position in the marketplace it occupies today.[3] Regardless of how high the cost of purchasing the firm was at the time, the investment has paid off handsomely. Profits increased from less than $0.5 million in 1962 to $52 million in 1973; an investment of $5000 in common stock in 1965 would in 1973 have grown to a value of $320,000!

What was responsible for McDonald's tremendous and profitable growth pattern over the past decade? Certainly the strong customer orientation in combination with the use of an integrated marketing strategy (product/service, price, advertising and selling, and outlet location) were central to the overall management thrust of the firm. More specifically:

1. Careful attention has been given to providing operators of individual outlets with complete management assistance and operating guidelines (unlike many of the short-lived, fast food ventures that failed in the early 1970s).

---

[1] Neil H. Borden, "The Concept of the Marketing Mix," *Journal of Advertising Research*, 4 (June 1964), pp. 2–7.

[2] "The Burger That Conquered the Country," *Time* (September 17, 1973), p. 84. Refer to this article for a more detailed discussion of the McDonald "hamburger empire."

[3] Ibid., p. 89.

2. Corporate headquarters has developed a competent store location staff group, and location decisions are carefully controlled.
3. McDonald's follows a practice of locating several outlets in a trade area to spread various operating costs (e.g., local advertising) over more than one retail unit (their store location network concept is used by several successful retail chains where operating costs are prohibitive for a single unit).
4. Retail units are supported by national advertising and sales promotion campaigns including the development of a strong brand image using the "Ronald McDonald" theme.
5. Continuous monitoring of product and service quality assures customer satisfaction and the maintenance of a strong and consistent image throughout the country, thus linking the production function to customer needs and wants.
6. Considerable effort has been directed toward the "technology" of hamburgers and supporting food items. Equipment in each unit is highly automated, thereby enabling managers to train operating personnel relatively quickly, maintain high quality, and cope with the high operating employee turnover rates typical in the fast-food industry.
7. Careful movement has been made into diversification of food items in contrast to the trend by some fast-food retailers to offer hamburgers, fried chicken, roast beef, etc. (The "Egg McMuffin" breakfast item introduced in the early 1970s comprised one of the first major additions to the basic line of food items.)
8. The importance of making a new venture successful for a franchise operator has been central to McDonald's management strategy, thus recognizing the important fact that a channel of distribution is only as strong as its weakest link.

These are several of the ingredients in McDonald's management strategy, many of which are important elements of an integrated marketing strategy. Perhaps most important, they demonstrate the close relationship which should exist between marketing and management strategy. A strong social role is also reflected in the management philosophy of the firm: ". . . each McDonald's licensee is expected to utilize a reasonable portion of profits for contributing to community service."[4]

Difficulties in Strategy Design

The importance of marketing in organizational strategy can also be demonstrated by examining the marketing strategy of The Great Atlantic & Pacific Tea Co. The firm has encountered significant corporate

---

[4] Ibid., p. 90.

problems in recent years due, at least in part, to inappropriate marketing decisions.[5]

A&P's "WEO" (Where Economy Originates) discount strategy launched in 1972 is a clear example of a non-integrated marketing strategy that resulted in a major negative impact on corporate profits, and adversely affected the entire retail food industry. A&P lowered prices, pruned their merchandise lines, and renamed their over 4,000 stores in 35 states "WEO's," seeking to convert to a super-discount image. The move was made in an attempt to try to regain their image as a price leader, fight increasing competition (e.g., Safeway and other chains), and counteract a leveling sales trend and shrinking profits.[6] The strategy did produce increased sales ($860 million increase in the year of conversion) but the profit penalties were significant with a loss of over $50 million in the fiscal year ending in February 1973. A&P management placed too much reliance upon price as a single instrument of marketing strategy, apparently not recognizing that price is but one element in an integrated marketing strategy. One analyst of the strategic management error observed:

> Its competitors are convinced that A&P's assault with WEO was doomed from the start. Too many of its stores are relics of a bygone era. Many are in poor locations—and a lot are small, ugly, and cluttered. They are just not big enough to support the tremendous volume that is needed to make a discounting operation profitable. Furthermore, these small stores lack shelf space for stocking general merchandise items, such as housewares and children's clothing, that attracts customers while commanding higher gross profit margins than most grocery items.[7]

Attempting to salvage the situation, in 1973 A&P's management increased prices and accelerated efforts at closing small, unprofitable, and poorly located supermarkets while openings of new giant size stores were expanded. These actions resulted in profit improvement: In the fiscal year ending February 1974 profits were $12 million. In the following 12 months A&P closed 325 stores and opened 113 units. Yet, whether they can regain the dominant market position held in the early 1960s still remains to be seen. A&P lost its position as the largest food retailer to Safeway in 1973. Profit margins on sales continue to be well below the traditional penny on the dollar (last achieved in 1968). A new chairman and chief executive officer assumed top management leadership of the firm in early 1975, with a primary goal of turning A&P around

---

[5] For an interesting analysis of several other firms whose marketing strategies contributed problems, see Thomas L. Berg, *Mismarketing: Case Histories of Marketing Misfires* (Garden City, N.Y.: Doubleday & Co., 1971).

[6] Eleanor Johnson Tracy, "How A&P Got Creamed," *Fortune* 88 (January 1973), pp. 103–44. This article contains a detailed account of the A&P WEO story.

[7] Ibid., p. 104.

toward new growth.[8] Closing of old stores and development of new supermarkets and superstores will be rapidly moved forward under his direction. As many as one-third of the chain's 3500 stores were being considered as candidates for closing during 1975–76.[9] Losses in fiscal 1975 exceeded $150 million, due, in part, to the retrenchment effort underway.[10]

Corporate and Marketing Strategy

These illustrations of effective and ineffective marketing efforts provide important insights into the role of the marketing function in the success of the enterprise. The marketing function must assemble the customer influencing resources (the marketing mix) of the organization into an integrated marketing strategy as illustrated by the McDonald's Corp. example. Perhaps most important is the central role of the market in influencing corporate success or failure. Drucker succinctly defined the basic entrepreneurial functions over two decades ago: "Because it is its purpose to create a customer, any business enterprise has two—and only these two—basic functions: marketing and innovation."[11] While one must acknowledge the various important activities that must be performed in a business firm (e.g., finance, manufacturing, distribution, etc.), Drucker's statement provides strong emphasis to the market as the essential focus of overall corporate strategy.

Marketing is the primary means by which the organization links itself with the external environment. Each customer, and the combination of customers that comprise a market for a product or service, must be satisfied if an enterprise is to survive. Marketing must perform the task of identifying specific customer targets in the marketplace and formulating and implementing effective marketing mix strategies for reaching these targets.

Top management of the enterprise must coordinate all business functions toward the objective of meeting the needs of the market place, and through this process, achieve corporate goals. Marketing alone cannot design and produce a product or service or assure that its quality and performance meet customer expectations. Nor can marketing raise financial capital for new plants, distribution outlets, and various other

---

[8] "Who Did the Housecleaning at A&P," *Business Week* (December 21, 1974), p. 29.

[9] "A&P's Big Close-Out," *Time* (March 24, 1975), p. 56.

[10] For an analysis of A&P's problems and actions taken to overcome them, see "Can Jonathan Scott Save A&P?" *Business Week* (May 19, 1975), pp. 128–31, 133, 134, and 136.

[11] Peter F. Drucker, *The Practice of Management* (New York: Harper & Row, Publishers, 1954), p. 38.

needs. The organization must function efficiently and the many other important tasks that comprise a viable business venture must be accomplished. Top management is responsible for combining these various business activities into an overall business strategy and for providing each area with the necessary resources to do its assigned job. Marketing can make a major contribution to top management by identifying market needs and ways of meeting them (e.g., new products), by communicating the availability of products and services, and by making products and services available in the market place. Thus, the design of corporate strategy should start with the customer and should utilize the perspective and expertise provided by the marketing manager and his staff.

THE MARKETING CONCEPT

Having examined the role that marketing plays in corporate strategy, it is important to develop a perspective toward managing the marketing functions in a given organization. The *marketing concept* provides a basic philosophy for guiding marketing planning, action, and control.

Development of a Marketing Orientation

The contemporary perspective toward the marketing function in a business firm gained initial emphasis in the 1950's. In moving toward a corporate focus on producing goods and services *wanted* by customers rather than selling what products or services were available, American business institutions moved through four eras of emphasis:

1. *Production orientation.* Up until the first quarter of the 20th century, industry preoccupation was on producing goods and services. Manufacturing processes were developed and refined. Customers tended to be viewed as recipients rather than guiding elements in business strategies.
2. *Sales orientation.* In the 1930s, increasing competition and growing complexity of markets (size, location, composition, differing needs, etc.) caused business attention to shift toward the selling function. Efforts were made to analyze markets and to develop sales and distribution organizations.
3. *Marketing orientation.* A significant impetus for pulling together various customer influencing activities came about in the early 1950's. Markets had grown large and complex, competition was keen, and choice of appropriate markets for particular firms became much more difficult. Firms rapidly recognized their dependence upon the marketplace. Business firms began to pull together the separate corporate activities of selling, advertising, marketing research, pric-

ing, and product planning into a new integrated function called "marketing."

4. *Marketing control.* A decade ago top management of leading business firms began to stress the important focus provided by the market as a guide to overall company policy and strategy. The need for a customer orientation throughout the organization was recognized. The market knowledge and experience of marketing executives was recognized as an important influence on corporate planning.[12]

The development of a marketing orientation in business firms emerged as a basic philosophy characterized as the marketing concept. Moreover, a top management executive with The Pillsbury Company predicted the following trend over a decade ago:

> . . . marketing will become the basic motivating force for the entire corporation. Soon it will be true that every activity of the corporation—from finance to sales to promotion—is aimed at satisfying the needs and desires of the consumer.[13]

The marketing concept is comprised of three key elements as shown in Figure 1–1. Initial focus is upon customer needs and wants as a basis for directing existing products or services and for developing new products or services. Yet, to be complete, the marketing concept must go beyond recognition of the market place as a starting point. An integrated marketing effort must be developed by the firm to meet the identified needs and wants of customers. Finally, through the process of accomplishing customer satisfaction the firm in turn seeks to achieve its organizational objectives. One of the leaders in adopting and implementing the marketing concept in the late forties was the General Electric Company. The concept as expressed by a GE executive begins with the customer:

> . . . the principal task of the marketing function in a management concept is not so much to be skillful in making the customer do what suits the interests of the business as to be skillful in conceiving and then making the business do what suits the interests of the customer.[14]

Beginning with the customer's needs and wants in directing the organization's marketing efforts is really nothing more than common

---

[12] Based upon Theodore N. Beckman, William R. Davidson, and W. Wayne Talarzyk, *Marketing*, 9th ed., Copyright © 1973, The Ronald Press Company, pp. 40–42. For a description of the movement of The Pillsbury Company through the four eras by an executive vice president of the firm see Robert J. Keith, "The Marketing Revolution," *Journal of Marketing* (January 1960), pp. 35–38.

[13] Keith, "The Marketing Revolution," p. 38.

[14] Reprinted from J. B. McKitterick, "What Is the Marketing Management Concept," in Frank M. Bass (ed.), *The Frontiers of Marketing Thought and Science,* 1957, p. 78, published by the American Marketing Association.

FIGURE 1–1

Elements of the Marketing Concept

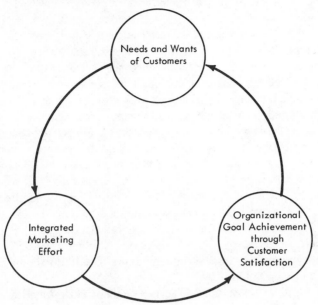

sense. This philosophy has been practiced intuitively by successful firms for decades. Nevertheless, as we saw in the experience of A&P, failure to assess market needs and wants carefully before designing corporate and marketing strategies can adversely affect achievement of objectives.

Implications of the Marketing Concept

Several implications of the marketing concept should be recognized. An initial focus upon the marketplace suggests the need for identification and assessment of markets as a part of the marketing management function. Implied by the marketing concept is the determination of which preferences can (and should) be met by a particular firm, since few businesses have the skills and resources to be "all things to all people." A business enterprise should seek to meet customer preferences that will contribute to corporate goal achievement. A key element in the process is the identification of those preferences which a given organization is best equipped to serve and which are likely to provide the organization with the most favorable advantage over its competition. Thus, it seems appropriate to view selection of target customers as an integral part of the philosophy suggested by the marketing concept. Sorting out particular groups of customers to cater to is called selection of target markets. The concept does not imply or suggest unfair or deceptive exploitation of the customer, although consumer spokesmen have forcefully argued that firms have neglected their social responsibilities in pursuit of profits.

The concept further indicates that the firm should assemble its customer influencing resources into an integrated marketing strategy that will satisfy its customers and also meet the organization's goals. This integrating task recognizes that the customer's responsiveness to a firm's offer in the marketplace is influenced by the product as well as advertising, personal selling, price, and distribution approach (e.g., purchase in a retail store versus catalog ordering). Designing this integrated "offer" (marketing mix) for the customer is the essence of marketing strategy. The creative role that the firm must play in moving from a knowledge of the market to the selection of products or services and formulation of marketing strategies for effectively utilizing the organization's skills and resources represents a major challenge to the marketing manager.[15] The major premise underlying the development of this book is that concepts, strategies, and decision making approaches can be learned and applied by marketing managers to enable them to respond effectively to this challenge.

Another implication of the marketing concept is the need for information about a firm's existing and potential customers, and their probable responsiveness to alternative marketing strategies. Adoption of the marketing concept places substantial demands upon the firm's information gathering and analysis capabilities. Choosing appropriate target markets and marketing mix strategies to direct toward these customer groups requires a variety of information. The rapid growth in the marketing research function over the past decade in many firms provides clear evidence of the recognition of the role of information in aiding marketing decision makers. For example, the General Electric Company has developed a consumer information system to provide attitude and preference information about consumer appliance needs, response to new products, product use experience, and other information useful in defining target markets, developing new products, and guiding marketing mix decisions.[16]

Finally, the adoption of marketing concept has significant implications regarding organizational design. Development of an integrated marketing strategy requires a suitable organizational design for ac-

---

[15] Andrew G. Kaldor, "Imbricative Marketing," *Journal of Marketing*, 35 (April 1971), pp. 19–25.

[16] Robert W. Pratt, Jr., "Using Research to Reduce Risk Associated with Marketing New Products," in *Changing Marketing Systems*, Reed Moyer (ed.), (Chicago: American Marketing Association, 1967), pp. 98–104.

FIGURE 1–2

Bank Organization Chart with Marketing Concept

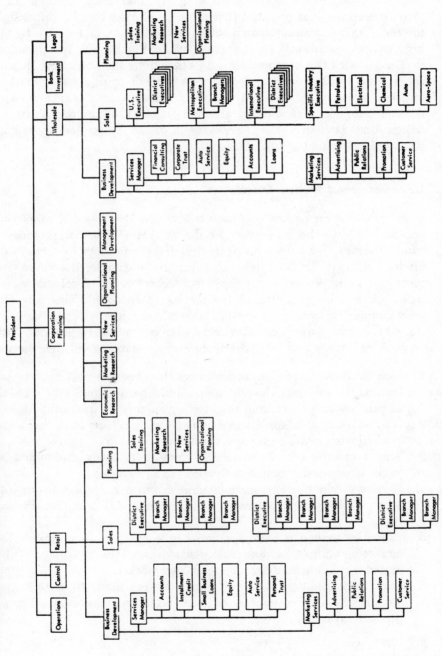

Reproduced by permission from Harper W. Boyd, Jr. and Robert T. Davis, *Marketing Management Casebook* (Homewood, Ill.: Richard D. Irwin, Inc., 1971), p. 576.

complishing this objective. While there is no single organizational approach to assembling and coordinating the marketing function in a given enterprise, it is essential that a top level executive be responsible for the firm's marketing management activities. As shown by the illustrative organizational chart for a bank in Figure 1–2, the president is charged with this responsibility. In other firms the marketing organization may be assembled under a vice president or director of marketing. The key consideration is that the various functions associated with the marketing mix should be grouped together in an organizational design that facilitates the development of an integrated marketing strategy for serving the firm's target markets.

Customer versus Product Orientation

An examination of how a business firm has developed a marketing approach within the framework of the marketing concept provides a good illustration of how a firm can shift from a product to a customer oriented strategy. In 1970 Reliance Electric Co. completed a three-year restructuring of its marketing approach to serve its customers which was a clear implementation of the marketing concept.[17] This specialty manufacturer of industrial motors, drives, and measuring equipment shifted toward a strong customer orientation in contrast to past emphasis on product quality and limited attention to its markets and their needs:

1. New products were designed to meet the needs of customers rather than as the designer thought they should be designed (thus a shift in primary emphasis from engineering quality to user utility).
2. New markets and applications where the firm's expertise could be applied were searched for and identified.
3. The company's broad capabilities were aggressively communicated to customers and potential customers via advertising.
4. Certain product groups were combined into one division to provide a broad offering to markets served, thus following a market orientation.
5. 12 *market* managers were appointed to integrate and coordinate the marketing efforts aimed at particular markets, thereby using an integrated marketing strategy for each target market.
6. Sales force additions and re-alignments were made to focus better on markets and customers, as opposed to past concentration on product coverage.

---

[17] For a more detailed discussion of Reliance Electric's implementation of the marketing concept, see "Putting Customer Demands First," *Business Week* (November 28, 1970), pp. 62–63.

7. Marketing research efforts were expanded to provide needed information for more effective, market-oriented decision making.

The result of these various changes in Reliance's marketing approach has been significant in contributing to improved operating results. Annual growth surged from a four percent to an 8–10 percent rate. Both sales and earnings reflected clear upturns; in 1974 record sales ($580 million) and earnings were achieved.

Firms that are customer oriented are more likely to use the marketing concept as a basis for guiding their strategies than are firms that are product oriented. For example, when a product orientation dominates corporate strategy, assessment of the market tends to follow after development of a new product. Consider the following illustration:

> A manufacturing firm with annual sales of $40-million invested approximately $300,000 on a new fluid measurement instrument during a two year period. In advance of development efforts management selected the natural gas industry as its target market. No marketing research was conducted. Moreover, in advance of market introduction, the firm had not developed an integrated approach to accomplishing its marketing efforts. About four months before the firm planned to introduce the product into the market, responsibility for developing a marketing program was assigned to a member of the technical staff who had participated in the technical development of the product. His efforts consisted primarily of developing a brochure and identifying sales personnel within the firm's field sales force who would handle the sales of new products along with existing products. Most of the salesmen had not been calling upon individuals that would be responsible for recommending purchase of the new instrument. Nearly two years later the product was dropped from the firm's line due to inadequate sales and increasing marketing costs. When sales personnel began calling upon prospects in the natural gas industry they learned that measurement standards for natural gas had been established for existing measurement instruments and were not applicable to the new instrument. Thus, in this firm a product orientation dominated management's decision making efforts and led to a major financial loss for the firm.

Several illustrative characteristics of product oriented firms are contrasted with those of market oriented firms in Table 1–1. Firms that approach the marketing task with a primary focus upon their products often give inadequate attention to customer needs and wants and to integration of marketing efforts. Organizational design tends to be dominated by product considerations rather than market consideration; use of marketing information and research is often limited to sales and cost analysis. While the product is an important element in the design of marketing strategy, the fundamental importance of the marketing con-

TABLE 1–1

Illustrative Characteristics of Product versus Customer Oriented Firms

	Product Orientation	*Customer Orientation*
Markets	Focus is upon finding markets for products New product emphasis and priorities are likely to be dominated by technical rather than marketing management Markets tend to be defined on a relatively general basis	Focus is upon developing products for identified customer needs and wants New product development activities are guided by market needs in combination with the firm's technical capabilities Market targets are defined in terms of specific end user groups
Marketing mix approach	Primary emphasis is upon selling rather than the complete marketing function Customer influencing efforts frequently are not assembled into an integrated marketing mix	Marketing mix efforts are integrated and coordinated to serve the firms target markets Marketing mix strategies are modified over time to respond to changing conditions
Organizational implications	Marketing offer efforts, when integrated, are centered around products rather than markets Product managers may be used to coordinate particular lines of products	Marketing organizational design is based upon the target markets the firm serves Firms serving several market targets may utilize market managers to coordinate marketing efforts within a given target market
Use of marketing information and research	Marketing information efforts concentrated largely upon sales and cost analysis Limited emphasis placed on researching the needs and wants of end-user customers and potential users	End user research is likely to receive strong emphasis for use in guiding marketing decisions Information collection and analysis expenditures typically higher than for comparable firms with product orientations

cept as a guiding philosophy for both corporate and marketing strategies cannot be overemphasized. Drucker has captured the essential distinction between a product orientation and a customer orientation based on the philosophy of the marketing concept in the following:

> True marketing starts out the way Sears starts out—with the customer, his demographics, his realities, his needs, his values. It does not ask, "What do we want to sell?" It asks, "What does the customer want to buy?" It does not say, "This is what our product or service does." It says, "These are the satisfactions the customer looks for, values, and needs."[18]

[18] Peter F. Drucker, *Management: Tasks, Responsibilities, Practices* (New York: Harper & Row, Publishers, 1974), p. 64.

Progress during the past twenty years in the application of the marketing concept in business firms has been favorable, although implementation has required a major management commitment. For example, results of a survey of 225 business executives (55 percent response) and 142 marketing educators (72 percent response) suggest that in principle it is accepted as a powerful concept and that problems center primarily on implementation, particularly on a day-to-day basis as compared to disagreement with the overall philosophy.[19] Eighty percent of survey respondents agreed that the marketing concept has contributed to improved organizational arrangements of marketing activities. Yet nearly sixty percent agreed that there are frequent conflicts between a customer orientation and profit goals.

Some have observed that the concept may be faltering because there is a conflict in the relative roles perceived by businessmen and consumers as to implementation of the concept. In resolving this conflict, it has been suggested that as an integral part of the marketing concept "company managements include the consideration of social implications in their decision processes and their management control procedures."[20] While this explicit acknowledgment of increased responsibility for consumer welfare is perhaps implied in the traditional statement of the marketing concept, the rise of consumerism issues and related areas of social concern clearly accentuate its importance. Dawson offers a convincing argument in favor of broadening the marketing concept into the "human" concept which seeks to respond to the various societal challenges and issues facing business firms and other institutions in the contemporary environment. The major elements of the human concept are described by Dawson as follows:

> A managerial philosophy centered upon the continuous search for and evaluation of opportunities for the mobilization, utilization, and control of total corporate effort in: (1) achieving a genuine internal social purpose in the development of organization members to their fullest potential; (2) generating the necessary profit input within the proximate environment by devising solutions to selected consumer problems; (3) achieving a genuine external social purpose within the ultimate environment by contributing to the identification and fulfillment of the real human needs of our time.[21]

The importance of the firm's societal role and the need for management's development of an understanding of environmental issues and influences

---

[19] Hiram C. Barksdale and Bill Darden, "Marketers' Attitudes Toward the Marketing Concept," *Journal of Marketing* (October 1971), pp. 28–36.

[20] Martin L. Bell and C. William Emery, "The Faltering Marketing Concept," *Journal of Marketing* (October 1971), p. 42.

[21] Leslie M. Dawson, "The Human Concept: New Philosophy for Business," *Business Horizons*, 12 (December 1969), p. 37.

are considered in Part II of the book, and in certain other chapters, where appropriate.

Adoption of the marketing concept has not progressed at equal rates in all business firms. Variations exist by size of firm, industry, channel level (manufacturers, middlemen, retailers), and by type of customer (consumer and industrial). For example, consumer goods firms appear to be utilizing the marketing concept more extensively than industrial producers, and larger firms (over $150 million annual sales) have adopted and implemented the concept to a greater degree than have small and medium-sized firms.[22]

FRAMEWORK FOR MARKETING MANAGEMENT

We have gained an understanding of the role and relationship of marketing to organizational strategy, the important guidelines provided by the marketing concept, and insights as to the scope and challenge of marketing management. The final task in this chapter is to pull together the description of marketing management into an analytical framework for more systematically viewing the major marketing decision areas. As a basis for guiding the development of this framework for marketing management, certain essential definitions of key marketing management terms and activities are shown in Figure 1–3, illustrated below.

FIGURE 1–3

Definitions of Marketing Management Terms and Activities

Marketing Management Task

> The analysis and planning leading to selection of one or more *target markets*—the design, implementation, and control of an *integrated marketing strategy* to reach selected target markets and achieve the organization's marketing objectives.

Target Markets

> Through the process of analysis of market opportunities selection of the types, location, and numbers of end-user customers for which the organization has (or can develop) the capabilities to serve their identifiable needs and wants, and in turn accomplish the organization's goals.

Integrated Marketing Strategy

> Determination of marketing objectives for selected target markets, selection of the kinds and levels of marketing resources (marketing mix) needed to achieve specified objectives, and formulation of the policies appropriate for guiding the acquisition and use of marketing resources.

[22] Carlton P. McNamara, "The Present Status of the Marketing Concept," *Journal of Marketing* (January 1972), pp. 50–57.

FIGURE 1-3 (continued)

Programming the Marketing Mix
Selection of the most effective combination and levels of marketing resources for achieving objectives for specified target markets. The resources for use in assembling the marketing mix consist of the firm's products (or services), channels of distribution, prices, advertising, and personal selling.

Marketing Management Decisions
The choices made among alternative courses of action for the various decision areas (e.g., market targets, products, pricing) necessary to accomplish the marketing management function in an organization.

Marketing Management Framework

The framework in Figure 1-4 provides a basis for linking together the various decision making areas that, in combination, comprise the marketing thrust of the firm. It will play an essential and integrating role in the book and the reader may find it helpful to refer back to this chapter in moving through the book. Moreover, the reader is encouraged to use this framework as an aid to developing and organizing his understanding of marketing management. A major premise underlying the framework is that it will provide a guide to action regardless of size or type of firm. The relevant variables in marketing decision making are similar throughout all kinds of businesses, although their relative importance will typically vary from firm to firm, as will the external influences operating upon the firm. The real value of a decision framework is to focus attention on relevant variables, thus facilitating problem and opportunity identification, analysis and action.

The marketing management task is shown in Figure 1-4 as a sequence of decision activities, guided by the corporate mission and the objectives of the firm. Marketing management decisions should be formulated within an overall framework of the corporate mission. Underlying the process of goal determination is the assessment of the basic purpose of the enterprise; identification of relevant external constraints (economic, social, technological, governmental, and competitive); and consideration of available resources and capabilities. Analysis of this information provides guidelines for establishing specific operational goals for the organization in such critical areas as profitability, physical and financial resources, market position, innovation, development, and worker performance and attitude.[23] Corporate objectives must also be used to establish essential guidelines and boundaries within which functional (mar-

---

[23] Peter F. Drucker, *The Practice of Management* (New York: Harper and Row, Publisher, 1954), p. 63.

FIGURE 1–4

Marketing Management Framework

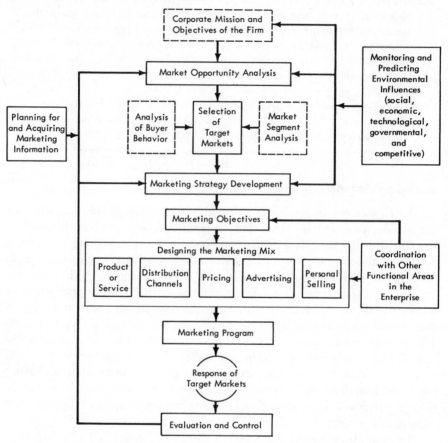

keting, production, finance, etc.) goals can be formulated. The hierarchy of objectives for the Interstate Telephone Company shown in Figure 1–5 illustrates the linkage of corporate to marketing objectives.

Upon establishing corporate goals, the management task involves the sequence of interrelated decisions shown in Figure 1–4:

1. Monitoring and predicting environmental influences upon market opportunity analysis and marketing strategy.
2. Analysis of market opportunities leading to the selection of market targets.
3. Marketing strategy development including determination of marketing objectives and designing the marketing program.
4. Implementing and managing the resulting marketing program in seeking to obtain favorable response from the firm's target markets.

5. Evaluation and control of marketing activities to keep the gap between desired and actual results as small as possible.

In the process of accomplishing the above marketing management task it is essential that needed marketing information be planned for

FIGURE 1–5

Hierarchy of Objectives for the Interstate Telephone Company

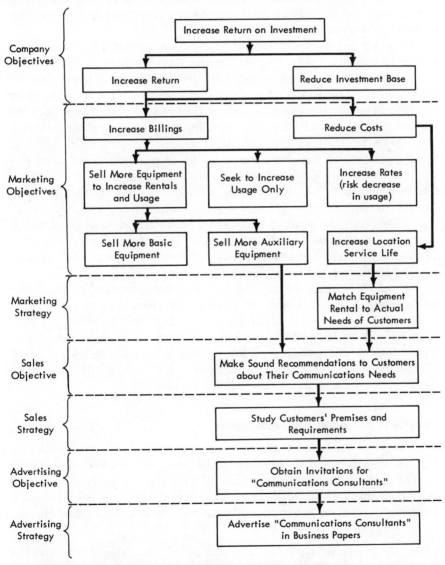

Reprinted from Leon Winer, "Are You Really Planning Your Marketing?" *Journal of Marketing* 29, January 1965, p. 3, published by American Marketing Association.

and acquired, and that marketing management decision activities be coordinated where appropriate with other functional areas of the enterprise.

Decisions made at a particular stage of the process shown in Figure 1–4 may require revision at subsequent stages because of the various interrelationships involved. For example, market opportunity analysis must give explicit attention to product/service and distribution channels open to the enterprise. The framework should not be viewed as a detailed, step-by-step procedure; rather it should serve as a general frame of reference for identifying and relating the major marketing management decision areas.

Marketing management decision processes should be viewed as a system of activities operating within the total decision making system of the enterprise. Similarly, marketing decisions include those that are made jointly by decision-makers from various areas in the firm (product, pricing policy, distribution) as well as those made primarily within the marketing area (advertising and sales force). It is important to recognize these interrelationships of decision activities between different functional areas of the organization. A firm's products or services provide the focal point within which corporate strategy and associated marketing strategy are formulated. Inadequacies of existing products tend to precipitate new product activities and/or diversification strategy.[24] Decisions concerning long-range product and market planning, new products, product modification, and elimination of products affect all functional areas (production and distribution, finance and accounting, and marketing) of the enterprise.

Each of the major decision making areas that comprise the marketing management framework are examined in the remainder of the chapter to provide a more detailed perspective toward the marketing management task. Parts II–V of the book are devoted to development of concepts; strategy and policy guidelines; approaches and methods of decision analysis; and illustrative applications for each of the marketing management decision areas shown in the framework.

Analysis of the Marketing Environment

Managerial analysis of the environment identifies opportunities as well as constraints and provides guidelines for market opportunity analysis and marketing strategy design. This type of analysis is largely focused within the societal environment and concerns social trends, economic conditions, governmental influences, and technological change.

---

[24] R. Hal Mason, Jerome Harris, and John McLoughlin, "Corporate Strategy: A Point of View," *California Management Review* (Spring 1971), p. 8.

FIGURE 1–6

Levels in the Marketing Environment

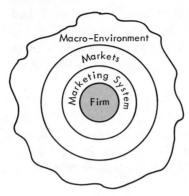

In addition markets, the marketing system (including competition), and the internal environment of the firm should be assessed in the process of analyzing market opportunities and designing marketing strategy. The different levels of the marketing environment are shown in Figure 1–6. A description of each of these environments is provided below:

1. *Macro-Environment*—Social, economic, governmental, technological, and natural changes within a society (among societies) that may create both opportunities and problems for individual firms.
2. *Markets*—The various domestic and international consumer, business, and institutional end-users that comprise markets for goods and services.
3. *Marketing System*—The various types of organizations (e.g., manufacturers, wholesalers, retailers, banks, transportation firms, etc.) that perform the marketing function necessary to provide markets with goods and services, including both competiting and cooperating firms.

In support of environmental analysis as an input to managerial planning one authority has observed that:

> Social expectations and changing environment are and will continue to alter top management practice and structures. Increased emphasis on strategic planning and identification of opportunities and threats in the environment will put a company in a better position to exploit the opportunities and avoid the threats.[25]

[25] George A. Steiner, "Changing Managerial Philosophies," *Business Horizons,* 14 (June 1971), p. 10.

The environmental processes that occur at the different levels (e.g., technological change) influence the marketing management function for an individual firm in a multitude of ways. Consider, for example:

The impact wash and wear fabrics have had upon the market for laundry and dry cleaning markets (technological change).

"No-bra look" which gained momentum in the early 1970s and its associated influence upon the market for women's foundation garments (social change).

Social acceptance of long hair styles for males leading to a substantial reduction in the size of the market for hair cuts (social change).

1971 boom in the bicycle market resulting from greatly increased adult interest in the recreational and exercise benefits of bicycle riding as well as gasoline conservation (combination of economic and social change).

Elimination of cigarette advertising on television by the federal government (legal change).

Wage-price freeze imposed by President Nixon in the early seventies which directly constrained marketing strategists in using price as a variable (combination of economic and governmental change).

These are but a few of the many ways that changes in the environment have recently affected business firms, groups and organizations, and individuals operating within the societal environment.

The dynamic nature of changes in markets and in the competitive environment force the marketing manager continually to appraise and attempt to forecast changing conditions and their probable impact upon marketing strategy. Two examples illustrate the dynamics of the marketplace:

Twenty years ago 90 percent of total annual turkey sales fell in November and December of each year. Through promotion and product improvement, today over 25 percent of households serve turkey at least six times a year.[26] Over half of sales occur in the period of January through October.

Needlepoint, a popular activity several decades ago, has developed into a $30 million market with estimates of large increases over the next few years. Estimates of users are as high as 25 percent of the population including substantial participation by men![27]

The socio-economic system generates various forces or influences which can affect a business firm in general and its marketing strategy.

---

[26] "The Turkey Carves a Year Round Market," *Business Week* (November 21, 1970), p. 30.

[27] "Who Makes the Money in Needlepoint," *Business Week* (December 16, 1972), p. 30.

While the particular approach taken by a business firm in seeking to identify, respond to, and possibly influence these forces will vary, certain factors should be considered:

1. Identification of those influences of primary relevance to a particular firm.
2. Determination of the particular groups associated with each force and assessment of their goals and interrelationships.
3. Assessment of the nature and types of potential impact of each influence on the firm's markets and marketing strategy.

Certain external influences have developed over a long timespan such as the various laws and regulations at national, state, and local levels of government. In contrast, the multitude of actions relating to the pollution of the environment are more recent developments. In certain types of business enterprises external influences may not be relevant to short and intermediate range strategy. For example, technological change in retail institutions typically occurs over a long time horizon compared to relatively rapid technological changes in the electronics manufacturing industry.

Market Opportunity Analysis

An essential part of implementing the marketing concept is to analyze the marketplace as a basis for designing an effective marketing program. Customer needs and wants should be the starting point. Market Opportunity analysis is concerned with identification and evaluation of one or more market targets. Rapid technological change tending to shorten the lives of products, differences in buyer wants and needs, and limited marketing resources demand that marketing decision makers carefully analyze and evaluate market opportunities in advance of designing product/service strategies for reaching markets. While consumer marketing has led the way in market opportunity analysis, there is also evidence that industrial goods firms must identify target market segments in which they can achieve a competitive advantage.[28]

The marketing manager is confronted with a number of questions in seeking to assess market opportunities. Various types of information are needed. Illustrative of the questions faced in seeking to identify and evaluate market opportunities are:

1. What environmental influences and constraints are relevant to each of the markets of interest?

---

[28] Richard N. Cardozo, "Segmenting the Industrial Market," in Robert L. King (ed.), *Marketing and the New Science of Planning* (Chicago: American Marketing Association, 1968), pp. 433–40.

2. What generic need does the firm's existing or planned product/ service offering serve in the marketplace?
3. What characteristics best describe the variations that exist in each aggregate market (e.g., income, age, location, etc. of potential buyers) of interest to the firm?
4. How can the aggregate market be broken down into strategically useful parts or segments?
5. What types of distribution channels have been (or should be) developed to serve each market?
6. What is the competitive situation in each market?
7. What is the relative economic and strategic worth of each segment in the market?
8. What particular strengths and weaknesses does the firm have in the segments of interest?
9. Which segments should be selected as market targets?

As shown in Figure 1–7, market opportunity analysis consists of assessments at several levels of market aggregation. At the highest level is an industry market assessment. If meaningful industry boundaries can be identified, typically by customer end use (e.g., outdoor cooking market) or by general product/service type (e.g., contract packaging), then an overall assessment of entire industries may be attempted. Information on trends in industry sales volumes, gross margins, costs, size of firms, and merger activity can be gathered through appropriate information

FIGURE 1–7

Market Opportunity Analysis

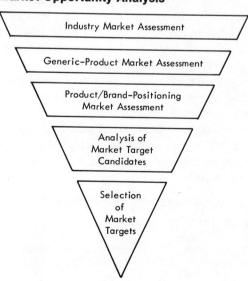

sources to estimate profit and return on investment ranges that can be expected in alternative industry markets. In addition, if customer characteristics can be determined, then trends in customer populations may be forecasted as a check against financial and competitive structure trends.

Within specified industry boundaries there are typically a number of different generic product categories (e.g., at a minimum, the outdoor cooking market consists of grills, fuels, and accessories). Analysis of opportunities at this level of market aggregation is critical because there can be substantial differences in the opportunities available in each generic-product market even within the same industry. Again, firms can turn to information sources to collect the same kind of trend information on financial and competitive structures as well as on customer characteristics for each product category. The market assessments at both of these levels are useful for firms analyzing currently entered markets and for identifying diversification opportunities.

To take advantage of opportunities identified in industry and generic-product markets, firms must design product/service and supporting strategy offerings to meet customer needs and wants. In doing so, both industrial and consumer-goods firms are increasingly aware of the fact that customers comprising markets are heterogeneous in terms of a variety of characteristics including desired product/service features.[29] Market segmentation analysis represents an important and potentially useful approach to the positioning of a firm's brands and appeals against arrays of customer wants and needs.

The identification of market opportunities has been strengthened by improved understanding of markets gained through use of buyer behavior concepts and research findings. In the last decade significant progress has been made in the formulation of models of buyer behavior for use in guiding research efforts and marketing strategy. Substantial diffusion of the concept of market segmentation (breaking down markets into specific market targets) throughout business has also contributed to improved market opportunity identification since the concept first emerged in the mid-1950s.[30]

In the final stages of market opportunity analysis, candidate market targets must be evaluated to determine which ones offer the most promising opportunities for the organization. An attempt must be made to establish priorities or rankings of the target markets. Completion of this

---

[29] "Selling to the Hottest Market Ever," *Business Week*, October 17, 1970, pp. 124 and 131; "Picking Customers Out of the Mob," *Business Week*, June 5, 1971, p. 71; and Elmer P. Lotshaw, "Industrial Marketing: Trends and Challenges," *Journal of Marketing*, vol. 34, no. 1 (January 1970), p. 23.

[30] Wendell R. Smith, "Product Differentiation and Market Segmentation as Alternative Marketing Strategies," *Journal of Marketing*, 21 (July 1956), pp. 3–8.

evaluation process should result in selection of one or more target markets.

Marketing Strategy Development

Having analyzed market opportunities and selected target markets, the next marketing management task consists of determining objectives to be achieved for each target and assembling an integrated marketing mix (specific decisions on product/service, channel of distribution, price, advertising and personal selling) for meeting the needs and wants of each target market.

Marketing Objectives. Objectives should be consistent with corporate objectives and should be stated for each target market. Specific objectives may be expressed in terms of sales, market share, profit contribution (net of marketing costs), and various other performance targets (e.g., strengthening brand image). Objectives provide a basis for designing a marketing mix appropriate for each target market. For example, a firm seeking to increase sales by six percent in target market A for the coming year would very likely make limited changes in the allocation and levels of marketing resources compared to the past year. Alternatively, if management desires to gain a substantial increase in sales (say 35 percent), changes in the components of the marketing mix may be needed as well as increases in the resources used for each component (e.g., size of the sales force).

Designing the Marketing Mix. The success of Hamm's beer in the West Coast market in the 1950s compared to the failure of Rheingold beer illustrates the importance of developing and implementing an integrated marketing mix for a firm's target markets.[31] Both beers dominated a major metropolitan market before moving into the West Coast market (Hamm's—Chicago and Rheingold—New York). Each had a quality image and did not vary its brewing formula in different regions. Yet, the marketing mix strategies pursued by the two firms were quite different. Hamm's proceeded systematically to develop acceptance for its product by recognizing and building upon existing cultural and distribution patterns in the region. Rheingold apparently blindly attacked the West Coast with essentially the same marketing mix which had been successful in New York City. Hamm's worked through beer wholesalers while Rheingold went direct to retailers in opposition to local practice. Rheingold failed to use appropriate advertising media for the West Coast market such as broadcast and outdoor media and

---

[31] This account is based on *Mismarketing: Case Histories of Marketing Misfires* by Thomas L. Berg. Copyright (c) 1970 by Thomas L. Berg. Reprinted by permission of Doubleday & Company, Inc.

instead focused on printed media. Moreover, their message designs were quite similar to those used in the East. Hamm's carefully designed a marketing mix recognizing that different markets require the development of marketing programs to mesh with each market's particular characteristics. They recognized that gaining a profitable position in a new target market requires a well designed and carefully implemented plan of action as opposed to a large and poorly planned blast into the marketplace.

The design of the marketing mix involves three interrelated decisions with respect to the firm's specified target markets: (1) determining the magnitude of the total marketing effort (dollars to be expended); (2) allocating marketing resources to the controllable marketing mix variables of the firm (product/service, price, advertising, personal selling, channels, and information activities); and (3) selecting the most appropriate use of resources that are allocated to the marketing mix variables (as for example, Hamm's use of broadcast and outdoor sign media compared to Rheingold's use of printed media). Assembling the marketing mix consists of determining the proper use of the following marketing variables for gaining desired responses from one or more target markets:

1. Selection of new products (or services) to be developed, needed product improvements, and elimination of products that are not contributing to corporate goals.
2. Determination of the proper combination of marketing intermediaries (e.g., agents, brokers, wholesalers, distributors, retailers) or use of direct approach for reaching end user target markets. The result of this decision is the selection of one or more channels of distribution for use by the firm.
3. Selection of appropriate pricing levels and policies consistent with selected target markets and the role of price in the marketing mix.
4. Development of an advertising and sales promotion program designed to accomplish the marketing mix objectives assigned to the advertising function (e.g., creative appeals and media to be used).
5. Formulation of sales force goals, determination of needed resources (types, number, and location of sales people), and sales force management policies (e.g., method of compensation).

The assembly of a proper marketing mix presents a major challenge to marketing management. In practice, mix decisions are complicated by the large number of possible combinations that may be used, and by the difficulty of estimating the revenue and cost impact of each combination. The crux of the decision is determining what level and combination of marketing resources will yield the most favorable profit contribution level net of marketing costs. Estimating the responsiveness (sales levels) of target markets for possible marketing mixes is a major uncertainty associated with the mix decision. A major portion of the book (Parts IV and V) is devoted to developing concepts, methods of analysis and guidelines for determination of the marketing mix and deployment of resources within each mix area (e.g., advertising).

A basic premise that spans the entire book is that decision making in marketing can be more effective if management intuition, judgment, and experience are combined with appropriate marketing concepts and methods for systematically assessing problems and evaluating decision alternatives. While marketing decision making is far from being a science, considerable progress has been made over the past twenty years in the development and application of more analytically oriented approaches to decision making. Research aimed at gaining a better understanding of the marketing mix variables in combination with advances in the management and behavioral sciences and computer technology have led to more analytical approaches to marketing decision making in business firms. Concurrently the essential role of information in guiding decisions is being acknowledged by firms, thus resulting in allocation of more resources to information gathering and analysis activities. Increased use has been made of the concepts and methods of management science to supplement decision maker's judgment and experience. As shall be illustrated in subsequent chapters, encouraging results have been obtained by business firms in applying analytical methods for decision analysis in the areas of new products, pricing, advertising, sales force, and distribution channels.

Moreover, growth of the marketing research function has occurred to provide needed information for decision analysis in advance of marketing action, although corporate expenditures have been relatively modest compared to allocations in other areas such as advertising and new product development. Yet, marketing management is increasingly recognizing the important role that information can play in decision making. Developments in computer technology (both hardware and software) have contributed to supporting more analytical approaches to marketing decision making. Using these capabilities, several leading firms have developed information systems to provide marketing management with a significant information data base for use in a variety of decision making activities. Marketing information systems promise to develop even more rapidly in the decade ahead.[32]

Marketing mix decisions are made by executives of the firm or organization in seeking to identify, create, and serve market opportunities

---

[32] See for example Valerie H. Free and Thomas E. Neman, "Market Research Matches Products to Consumers," *Computer Decisions* (May 1972), pp. 12–16.

with products or services. There are many diverse kinds of decisions as illustrated by the following:

A decision to survey a sample of households to determine brand preferences for instant coffee (marketing research decision).

Selection of appropriate advertising media (television, radio, magazines, and other media) for an advertising campaign to introduce the Ford Motor Company's 1975 automobiles (advertising decision).

An industrial valve manufacturer's decision to shift from independent manufacturers' representatives for selling its industrial products to a company sales force (channel of distribution decision).

The elimination of software services as a part of the purchase price of IBM Corporation computers resulting in adjustments in prices of their equipment (product and price decision).

Discontinuation of the manufacture and marketing of general-purpose computers in 1971 by the RCA Corporation (product drop decision).

Design and implementation of an incentive plan for a firm's salesmen (sales force decision).

These examples provide an insight as to the nature and scope of marketing mix decisions which confront different types of business organizations. Since the various decisions are interrelated, it is essential that marketing mix activities be managed as a combined and integrated effort aimed at favorably influencing target customers.

Strategic and Tactical Decisions. The marketing manager and staff are confronted with a variety of strategic and tactical decisions as shown in Table 1–2 on the following page. Strategic decisions provide a broad framework for marketing action. They tend to be longer term (a year or longer), and, as illustrated by the examples in Table 1–2, strategic decisions are broader in nature and scope. Tactical decisions occur more frequently as a part of the process of implementing the marketing program, and managing marketing activities on an on-going basis. In sum, strategic and tactical decisions structure and guide marketing management activities in the organization.

Evaluation and Control

Implementation is guided by the plan specifying how the marketing program is to be carried out. The purpose of evaluation and control is to bring the actual results of the firm's marketing efforts as close as possible to marketing objectives. Control accounts for a substantial portion

TABLE 1–2

Illustrative Marketing Management Strategic and Tactical Decisions

Decision Area	Strategic	Tactical
Product (or service)	Development and introduction of the "Trac II" razor by the Gillette Co. Discontinuation of production and marketing of vacuum cleaners by a large appliance manufacturer.	Increases in planned production levels of compact and intermediate size automobiles during the 1973–74 oil embargo. Adjustment in field warehouse inventories of insulation materials in response to changing market conditions.
Channel of distribution	Conversion by a manufacturer of industrial control valves from company salesmen to independent sales agents. Decision by a metropolitan bank to install 24 hour automated banking facilities throughout its trade area.	Shifting from one health and beauty aids rack jobber to another by a convenience store retailer. Conducting an opinion survey of retail customers to identify problems and needed changes in services.
Pricing	Increase in warranty period provided a manufacturer of television sets from one to two years. Determination of the selling price of a new industrial water treatment chemical.	Before Christmas sales by retailers in 1974 to stimulate lagging sales resulting from the recession, inflation, unemployment, and general consumer pessimism. Use of "cents off" coupons by food manufacturer to encourage trial of a new breakfast cereal.
Advertising	Reduction of trade journal advertising expenditures by a medium size producer of small motors, and use of the funds for a direct mail product information program directed to existing and potential accounts. Selection of an advertising program theme for a line of products (e.g., Samsonite's "A New Bag Named Sam").	Modification of advertising message in magazine advertisements to stress product features unrecognized by respondents to a recently conducted marketing research study. Change in the color of printing on a food package intended to increase package visibility on supermarket shelves.
Personal selling	Decision to shift from use of salesmen specializing on certain products to selling of the entire product line by each salesman. Design and implementation of an incentive compensation plan in a firm that has been using a straight salary basis of compensation.	Sales contest offered to appliance salesmen by a distributor to stimulate off season sales of air conditioners. Splitting a sales territory handled by one machine tool salesman into two territories due to expanding sales potential and workload.

of the marketing manager's activities in many organizations. Planning and implementation are typically more demanding during the initial stages of a business venture. Control on the other hand is a continuing process, and provides the guidelines for needed modification in planned marketing strategies. Of course, a comprehensive understanding of the marketing strategy planning process provides a necessary framework for performing the control function. Briefly, the control process consists of these activities.

1. Determination of the aspects of marketing strategy that the marketing manager wants to focus attention upon (e.g., total marketing program, sales force, advertising program, etc.).
2. Determination of standards or benchmarks against which to monitor actual performance or results.
3. Development of formal and informal information gathering and analysis processes.
4. Evaluation of results to identify gaps in performance.
5. Planning and implementing strategy and tactics designed to eliminate or reduce performance gaps.

Thus, control is an integral part of the marketing management task. While making decisions is a critical task of the marketing manager, once made the actions defined by decisions must be implemented, evaluated, and controlled toward desired performance levels.

OVERVIEW OF THE BOOK

In this chapter we have described the marketing management function in the organization and its relationship to corporate strategy. The logic of the marketing concept as a guiding philosophy has been developed and illustrated. A decision making framework for use in gaining an understanding of and applying marketing management concepts, methods, and practices was presented and its major parts described. The remainder of the book is devoted to comprehensive examination of each of the decision making areas of marketing management which comprise the framework. In the next chapter the societal system within which an individual firm operates is considered.

Part II is concerned with managerial analysis of the marketing environment. The objective of these chapters is to guide the development and understanding of the nature and scope of external influences which may create both opportunities and problems for marketing management in a particular firm. In Part III the task of analyzing market opportunities and the selection of target markets is considered. An analytical approach is developed for identifying, evaluating, and selecting market opportunities which best mesh with the firm's chosen mission and purpose. Part IV presents important concepts and guidelines for the design of marketing strategy. Essential decision analysis approaches are developed and illustrated to provide a necessary framework for use in considering the various marketing mix decision areas. In Part V the decision variables that comprise the marketing mix are examined. Analytical frameworks to guide analysis and decision making regarding products, channels of distribution, pricing, advertising, and sales force are developed. Relevant decision making concepts in each marketing mix area are examined and useful decision making approaches are presented and illustrated. Finally, in Part VI the marketing management challenge in non-business institutions is considered, building upon the basic foundation for marketing management practice developed in the book.

EXERCISES FOR REVIEW AND DISCUSSION

1. The Colgate-Palmolive Company produces and markets a broad line of consumer packaged goods (soap, detergents, toiletry, drugs, cosmetics, etc.) including certain products produced by other firms whereas the Wm. Wrigley, Jr. Co. produces and markets primarily chewing gum. Discuss the influence of the corporate mission upon the marketing management function in each of these firms.

2. Assume you have been asked by the president of a medium size manufacturer of outboard motors and boats, lawnmowers, and ski-mobiles to assess the firm's marketing activities and to make appropriate recommendations for improvement. What are the major areas you would assess and why?

3. How would you explain the marketing concept to a government official interested in applying marketing concepts and methods to mass transit systems in urban communities?

4. Compare and contrast marketing decision making for a potato chip manufacturer with a department store chain.

5. "Marketing management is a decision making process that is primarily useful for firms involved in the manufacture and distribution of consumer goods (e.g., television sets, clothing, processed foods, beer, etc.)." Comment upon this statement.

6. Discuss the interrelationships between the corporate mission, analysis of the marketing environment, market opportunity analysis, and marketing strategy design. How might the importance of these areas vary for an electronics manufacturer compared to a grocery wholesaler?

7. If the widespread shortages. in energy, raw materials, and productive capacity experienced in the mid-1970s persist for several years, what should be the role and scope of the marketing management function in those business firms affected by imbalances in supply and market demand caused by shortages?

2

A Macro-marketing Perspective

Marketing and business activities in the United States have played a large role in developing the most affluent society in history. American consumer affluence is unsurpassed worldwide with 1973 median family income reaching $12,051. This abundance is translated by consumers into many forms of satisfaction—travel, finely produced music, wine-tasting, skiing, and numerous other experiences reserved only for the wealthy in most nations. Yet a Harris poll in the early 70s concluded that between 1966 and 1972 the percentage of the public with "a great deal of confidence" in the heads of major companies dropped from 55 percent to 27 percent. An earlier Opinion Research Corporation survey reported that on the average, the public believed after-tax corporation profits (during the period covered) were close to 28 percent of sales. In reality, profits represented only four cents of each sales dollar (for the nation's 1,000 largest industrial concerns) and to place these figures in perspective, the average citizen considered 10 percent a "fair" return.[1]

The gap between the public's perceptions and reality was sensed by E. Mandell deWindt, Chairman of Eaton Corporation, in speaking with students at a midwestern college. Faced with skepticism and hostility, he decided to develop a special communications program at Eaton. He noted: "The woeful lack of understanding of business by students and the public led us to a high-priority program to develop the means of telling the business story to the public."[2] This realization and reaction was no exception. *Business Week* magazine reported that the public opinion polls hold a blunt warning: "Corporations are under severe

---

[1] "America's Growing Antibusiness Mood," *Business Week,* June 17, 1972, pp. 100–102.

[2] William S. Hieronyms, Jr., "Worried About Image, Business Makes Effort to Sell Itself to Public," *Wall Street Journal,* June 12, 1973, p. 1.

pressure to dispel the public distrust that threatens their prosperity."[3] The courts also seemed to reflect this public sentiment. The Supreme Court in 1973 for example, confirmed the right of the Food and Drug Administration to exercise sweeping authority to force ineffective drugs off the market, issue stringent rules governing products' effectiveness, deny manufacturers hearings on contested actions and proceed against entire product classes rather than move case by case against individual drugs.[4] Consistent with this decision was a 1972 poll indicating that the U.S. citizens wanting more product-related health and safety laws had increased to over 75 percent.[5]

By 1975, recession conscious consumers seemed less vocal. But as a staff member of General Electric's Business Environment Research Section observed:

> . . . we should note the differences between the current public mood toward corporations and the 1968–72 outbursts against business. First, the criticisms do not come just from the alienated . . . but from "middle America." Second, dissatisfaction is concerned not just with "social-responsibility" issues, but with performance of business's basic role.[6]

This suggests that marketing and society issues may be even more pervasive influences today than in recent years. A continuing public re-examination of business has demonstrated that marketing cannot be studied in isolation from the many groups, organizations and larger systems from which it derives its justification and sustenance.

This chapter studies the larger context within which marketing functions by (1) distinguishing a macro from a micro perspective, (2) illustrating the evolution of marketing in response to human needs, (3) outlining the basic marketing relationships to the economic, governmental as well as, generally, the social system, and finally, (4) discussing the evolutionary nature as well as the current structure of marketing institutions. The chapter is unique because it is non-managerial in perspective—even though this material provides a base for subsequent managerial discussion of consumer values and social issues (Chapter 5) and, in the last chapter, social marketing.

MACRO VERSUS MICRO MARKETING

It is important to examine how the firm relates to the marketing process from the point of view of society. We assume we are on the "out-

---

[3] "America's Growing Antibusiness Mood," p. 101.

[4] *Wall Street Journal,* June 19, 1973, p. 4.

[5] "America's Growing Antibusiness Mood," p. 102.

[6] Ian H. Wilson et al. "What the Future Holds for Today's Managers," *Managers Forum,* vol. 2 (January 1975), p. 4.

side looking in," or, in the context of Figure 2–1, at the top looking down. Looking at the decisions of marketing management through the eyes of society (downward in Figure 2–1) rather than through the eyes of the manager (upward) means adopting a *macro* perspective as opposed to a *micro* or managerial perspective.

FIGURE 2–1

Societal versus Managerial Perspective

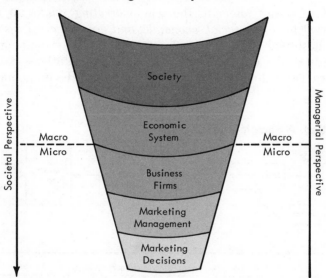

It may be seen that micro levels include business firms which, of course, encompasses marketing management. The macro levels extend beyond the firm to the economic and societal systems. Grashof and Kelman use an analogy of a biologist who, with his microscope, begins with a low-powered lens and can only see the broad outlines of the earth.[7] As increasingly powerful lens are used, he gradually focuses on society, then the economic system, the firm, and finally, on marketing management. "It is imperative to remember, however, that because part of the subject under study disappears from our field of vision, it does not cease to exist."[8] Management has sometimes forgotten the societal context in which it operates.

The meaning of marketing is largely dependent on one's perspective from a given level. As Bartels writes,

[7] John F. Grashof and Alan P. Kelman, *Introduction to Macro-Marketing* (Columbus, Ohio: Grid, Inc., 1973), p. 2.

[8] Ibid.

From one standpoint, marketing is an activity: consumers purchasing provisions or 'doing their marketing'; businessmen selling products; the economy effecting distribution of goods and transfer of their title. However, marketing is more than a mere business practice; it is a pattern of the way of life which society has adopted. It is a social institution, an economic function, a business undertaking, a consumer-oriented service.[9]

MACRO-MARKETING

Macro-marketing refers to the way *marketing relates to its larger context; that is, to the social, economic, and governmental systems.* The process illustrated in Figure 2–2 interrelates key evolutionary stages from needs to the development of marketing institutions and decision techniques. Paralleling these stages is reference to the economic, govern-

FIGURE 2–2

Macro-marketing: A Societal Perspective

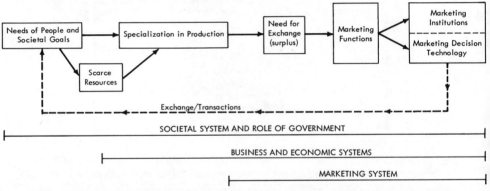

Note: For related concepts, see Daniel J. Sweeney, "Marketing: Management Technology or Social Process?" *Journal of Marketing*, vol. 36, no. 4 (October 1972), pp. 3–10; Robert Bartels, *Marketing Theory and Metatheory*, 1970, pp. 155–91, 243–53, published by the American Marketing Association; John F. Grashof and Alan P. Kelman, *Introduction to Macro-Marketing* (Columbus, Ohio: Grid, Inc., 1973), inside cover.

mental and social systems. Marketing is a need fulfilling activity which exists in some form in nearly all societies. By way of overview, the needs of people, given scarce resources, are better met through use of specialization. Specialization increases output from available scarce resources (inputs). But people specializing (rather than working to meet all of their own needs) develop surpluses and must exchange their output with others—thus the need to perform marketing functions (e.g., selling and distribution) to accomplish exchange. Finally, over time, institutions (e.g., wholesalers) evolve that specialize in performing marketing

---

[9] Reprinted from Robert Bartels, *Marketing Theory and Metatheory*, 1970, p. 156. Published by the American Marketing Association.

functions. Or, in reverse in Figure 2–2, marketing institutions exist because of the need to perform marketing functions; these functions are performed because exchange must be carried out; exchange is necessary because of surplus resulting from specialization; specialization exists because of the desire to fulfill as many needs as possible from a given set of resources. Thus, marketing clearly evolved as a need-fulfilling activity. Let us examine each of these stages in greater detail.

Societal Needs and Goals

The *raison d'etre* for a social system is to serve the needs of the people. This is also the justification for marketing. Society's needs, in turn, serve as the basis for societal goals. Although it is not immediately operational, a basic goal of a society may be to contribute to the "happiness" of its people or, a highly related concept, to the "quality of life." Immediate complications arise in striving for these types of goals because, (1) with limited resources, there is inherent conflict in attempting to satisfy the desires of all people, (2) allocating resources is an imperfect process and is not perfectly related to the creation of happiness—no matter what the nature of this process, and (3) this goal requires a clear understanding of what is satisfying (or happiness generating) for different people. The means to happiness for different people varies greatly so this impedes implementation of a happiness type of goal. The associated problems, nevertheless, do not preclude using happiness as a normative guideline for societal level decisions while recognizing that the harsh realities of social and governmental processes do not always allow for the maximization of this objective.

If we accept this general norm, marketing activity, as part of society, should be consistent with upgrading the quality of life. As part of the social system, marketing must fulfill its role in the larger community. "Social system may be defined as the patterned normative order through which the life of a population is collectively organized."[10] Key terms include "patterned," "order," and "collectively organized" because these all suggest an interdependence, certain rules of behavior, and, implicitly, some assumptions as to what is desirable. The normative order of a society is based on the values of people and the existing culture, mores, and folkways. Basically, the question becomes, "How should a society be "ordered" (or organized) to achieve what is considered desirable (i.e., societal needs)? How should marketing assist in meeting societal needs?

During the past few decades, the U.S. population moved from farms to urban areas. Family farms were largely self-sufficient (nonspecial-

---

[10] Talcott Parsons, *Politics and Social Structure* (New York: The Free Press, 1969), p. 11.

ized) and provided for their own needs. There was less need for exchange and, thus, the role of marketing was less than today. This same rationale helps to explain why marketing plays a lesser role in virtually every other country in the world than in the United States. Less economic development typically requires less exchange.

The specific needs of a people at a given time may be cast in a need hierarchy from basic to less basic: (1) physiological (e.g., hunger), (2) safety, (3) belongingness and love, (4) esteem and status, and (5) self-actualization.[11] People are first motivated to satisfy basic needs such as hunger (physiological) but, once these needs are partially met, there is a tendency to move up the need hierarchy. As each need stage is reached and partially satisfied, the next higher level becomes increasingly important. Underdeveloped countries concentrate on the satisfaction of basic needs such as physiological and safety and security, whereas most people in the United States are concerned with higher level needs. Similarly, the frontier days in the United States represented an era with very different needs than those which exist for most U.S. consumers today. Shifting needs require business and marketing activity to change from providing basic, undifferentiated food, shelter and self-protection items to provision of products and services which help to satisfy even subtle psychological needs. The types of needs dominant at a given stage of development have direct implications for the specific role of marketing. Analyzing market needs, for example, becomes increasingly difficult as more and more consumers seek to satisfy higher level needs.

As consumers seek a higher "quality of life," greater attention has been given to actually measuring the phenomenon. The measures, called "social indicators" are imperfect but they assist in defining the goals for society as well as for business.[12] Assuming that marketers have a broader role to play than promoting products for profit, they must be sensitive to the ways they potentially affect society. To ignore their duty to the larger community is to forget their reason for existence. Use of social indicators in corporate goal formulation and in performance measurement would serve to enhance societal contributions and minimize conflict.

Scarce Resources, Specialization and Exchange

Viewing marketing as a need-fulfilling social process requires more understanding of the conditions leading to exchange (Figure 2–2). In

---

[11] A. H. Maslow, "A Theory of Human Motivation," *Psychology Review*, vol. 50, no. 4, July 1943.

[12] Robert L. Clewett and Jerry C. Olson (eds.), *Social Indicators and Marketing* (Chicago, Ill.: American Marketing Association, 1974); Polia Lerner Hamburger, *Social Indicators—A Marketing Perspective* (Chicago, Ill.: American Marketing Association, 1974).

the simplest and smallest primitive communities, every family may satisfy nearly all of its needs itself. Yet, over a period of time, people recognize the advantage of cooperation and, eventually, some people perform certain tasks while others engage in different tasks for the sake of efficiency as well as enjoyment. Given limited human and physical resources, specialization provides for greater satisfaction and economic well-being (output) than would otherwise be produced with the same amount of input (productivity). In explaining the nature of profit in a now classic letter to his grandson in 1941, Fred I. Kent, a former director of the Federal Reserve Board referred to an example of specialization:

> Our primitive community, dwelling at the foot of a mountain, must have water. There is no water except at a spring near the top of the mountain: therefore, every day all the 100 persons climb to the top of the mountain. It takes them one hour to go up and back. They do this day in and day out, until at last one of them notices that the water from the spring runs down inside the mountain in the same direction that he goes when he comes down. He conceives the idea of digging a trough in the mountainside all the way down to the place where he has his habitation. He goes to work to build a trough. The other 99 people are not even curious about what he is doing.
>
> Then one day this 100th man turns a small part of the water from the spring into his trough and it runs down the mountain into a basin he has fashioned at the bottom. Whereupon he says to the 99 others, who each spend an hour a day catching their water, that if they will each give him daily production of 10 minutes of their time, he will give them water from his basin. He will then receive 990 minutes of the time of the other men each day; this arrangement will make it unnecessary for him to work 16 hours a day in order to provide for his necessities. He is making a tremendous profit—but his enterprise has given each of the 99 other people 50 additional minutes each day.
>
> The enterpriser, now having 16 hours a day at his disposal and being naturally curious, spends part of his time watching the water run down the mountain. He sees that it pushes along stones and pieces of wood. So he develops a water wheel; then he notices that it has power and, finally, after many hours of contemplation and work, he makes the water wheel run a mill to grind him corn.
>
> This 100th man then realizes that he has sufficient power to grind corn for the other 99. He says to them, "I will allow you to grind your corn in my mill if you will give me ¹⁄₁₀ the time you save." They agree, and so the enterpriser now makes an additional profit.[13]

This example clearly illustrates the advantages of specialization in an enterprising context and it also suggests the rudiments of marketing in

---

[13] Fred I. Kent, "What is Profit," pp. 95–97. Reprinted with permission from the June 1961 *Reader's Digest*. Condensed from a publication of the New York State Economic Council. Copyright 1943, 1961, by The Reader's Digest Assn., Inc.

that *exchange* becomes necessary as specialization is initiated (see Figure 2–2). The entrepreneur trades his "creative time" for a proportion of the output resulting from the efforts of others. Specialization and exchange are not necessarily tied to the profit motive, as is evidenced by communistic economies. Yet wherever specialization exists, there must be some form of exchange.

Prior to the development of markets and modern marketing systems, other forms of distribution existed. Societies fulfilled their needs by other systems:[14]

> *Reciprocity* is that conduct of society whereby one gives from the harvests of his production, not for immediate material benefit in exchange, but for the approbation which society places on good husbandry and fine citizenship. . . . Social values are paramount; the economic effect is secondary. . . .
>
> *Redistribution* is the principle employed in societies of a territorial character, under a common chief, whereby a substantial part of production is delivered to village headmen who keep it in storage. Redistribution of the provision is made according to a plan of differentiated rations to both producing and nonproducing parts of the population and to members of other distant communities on ceremonial and festival occasions . . .
>
> *Householding* is that principle of economic organization whereby production is carried on by a closed group, such as a family, a village settlement, or a political unit, for supplying the needs of the group.
>
> In these three forms of the economy, there is no instance of trade or markets, where equivalencies are determined and expressed as a price. Where there is no market, there obviously is no marketing. However, before markets developed, trade existed and was widely carried on. The development of markets antedated the rise of the market economy. And the existence of the market economy was prerequisite to the modern conception of marketing.

Some might argue, based on their conception of marketing, that even exchange as just noted represents marketing. Whether the above are viewed as *stages* of marketing or as *pre*-marketing-methods of satisfying needs is not as important as an appreciation of the evolutionary process.

Marketing Functions

To accomplish the exchange process brought about by specialization, various marketing functions must be performed. As outlined in the first

---

[14] Bartels, *Marketing Theory and Metatheory*, pp. 159–60; also see Karl Polanyi, Conrad M. Arensberg and Harry W. Pearson (eds.), *Trade and Market in the Early Empires: Economies in History and Theory* (Glencoe, Ill.: Free Press, 1957); Cyril S. Belshaw, *Traditional Exchange and Modern Markets* (Englewood Cliffs, N.J.: Prentice-Hall, 1965).

chapter, basic marketing mix variables such as product, price, distribution and promotion represent marketing functions. But the classic statement of marketing functions by McGarry include:[15]

Contactual .... the searching out of buyers and sellers.

Merchandising ...... fitting the goods to market requirements.

Pricing .... selection of a price high enough to make production possible but low enough to induce users to accept the goods.

Propaganda .... conditioning of the buyers or of the sellers to a favorable attitude toward the product or its sponsor.

Physical Distribution . the transporting and storing of the goods.

Termination .... the consummation of the market process (agreement on at least the quantity, quality and the price of the services to be exchanged).

The contactual and termination functions refer to the exchange itself whereas physical distribution relates more to functions which resolve the spatial and temporal discrepancies between buyers and sellers. Merchandising resolves the differences between large homogeneous quantities provided by producers and the small, heterogeneous assortments demanded by consumers. Propaganda, as a facilitating function, serves to "oil the wheels" by assisting in the fulfillment of the other functions. Advertising, for example, helps build awareness of products and provides information which is used by consumers prior to exchange. The performance of marketing functions is necessary to accomplish exchange which is, in turn, necessary to serve the needs of consumers efficiently. As Sweeney has suggested, marketing is not merely something that *is done*—a management technology; but something that *is*—a social process. The process of exchange occurring in society *is* the marketing process and not just the technique employed to execute the exchange process.[16]

Creation of Utility. Of what value is the performance of marketing functions? Economics has long stated that three forms of satisfaction arise from these processes; time, place, and possession utility. These utilities are largely conceived on the distribution part of marketing. The utilities (satisfactions) are illustrated by shoppers who may conveniently travel to food stores near their home any time during the day (and possibly all night) to purchase, for example, coffee for immediate use. Marketing has created time utility by making the coffee available

---

[15] Adapted from Edmund D. McGarry, "Some Functions of Marketing Reconsidered," reprinted in *Theory in Marketing*, eds., Reavis Cox and Wroe Alderson (Homewood, Ill.: Richard D. Irwin, Inc., 1950), pp. 263–79.

[16] Sweeney, "Marketing: Management Technology or Social Process?" p. 7.

when it was needed, place utility by making it available *where* it was needed (a convenient location) and possession utility by providing the mechanism for transfer of title (termination) at the checkout counter. It is natural to underestimate the satisfaction created by marketing activities unless one estimates the tremendous inconvenience if marketing activities were abolished. The cost of consumers individually obtaining coffee from Brazil, for example, would render nearly all consumers tea drinkers (unless, of course, consumers also had to obtain their tea individually from China!).

In considering time, place, and possession utility, the performance of the marketing functions creates these forms of satisfaction. In addition, in a modern marketing era, some marketing communications and products extend beyond the traditional product concept and contribute to

TABLE 2–1

Marketing Cost for Selected Farm Food Products

		Percent of Retail Value	
Product	*Farm Price*	*Marketing and Processing Cost*
Bakery and cereal..............	21	79
Meat........................	52	48
Fruits and vegetables..........	25	75
Dairy.......................	47	53
Poultry and eggs..............	53	47

Source: U.S. Department of Agriculture, *Agricultural Statistics* (Washington, D.C.: U.S. Government Printing Office, 1968), p. 463.

psychological utility. The promotion of a Cadillac may, for example, contribute to the prestige of owning the automobile, and for many, represents a significant source of satisfaction. This form of utility goes beyond the processes which deliver the car at an appropriate time and place with a mechanism for obtaining possession. As consumers seek the satisfaction of even higher level needs in the future, this utility has even greater potential significance.

Utility not primarily created by marketing activity has been termed "form utility"—this is typically attributed to the production process. Marketing contributions to product design, however, may guide production decisions and thus contribute to even form utility. Form utility is the transformation of things into more satisfying states.

As one measure of utility, the "value added" by marketing is estimated to average about 50 percent of the consumer's dollar. The cost of marketing, of course, varies greatly from product to product as shown in Table 2–1.

Marketing Technology and Institutions

The final stage of viewing marketing as a social process (Figure 2–2) requires attention to marketing technology (tools or techniques) and marketing institutions. Much of this text discusses marketing concepts and technology from a managerial perspective. The methods and practices have evolved as efficient means to perform marketing functions.

Over time, the performance of a set of functions by certain methods gains general acceptance which, in turn, leads to the established methods and corollary structure eventually being considered as "institutions." Marketing institutions represent a proven set of efficient arrangements which have stood the test of time. Institutions are modified and new institutions arise due to competitive and environmental pressures—consider, for example, the advent of the discount store and the suburban shopping mall and the demise of the general store. Managerial approaches and techniques as well as marketing institutions change in response to the changing needs of people in society. They also change because, as other uncontrollable factors change (e.g., technology—the rise of the computer), new and better approaches for serving the needs of people are developed. Thus the final stages of institutions and techniques in Figure 2–2 are likely to change.

Economic System

First, however, let us look specifically to marketing within the economic system. Although marketing exists in some form in virtually all societies, the specific role of marketing in a given society is dependent on the prevailing type of economic system. Centralized vs. market economies exist with many gradation of mixing. The key differences between these economies concern (*a*) who makes the decisions as to what needs exist, and (*b*) how the needs will be satisfied.

Centralized Economy. In a centralized economy, central planners rather than customers make many of the decisions concerning consumer needs, the priority of need satisfaction (e.g., capital vs. consumer goods), as well as production decisions and the allocation of resources and production output. Despite the role of central planners, however, marketing *functions* still have to be performed—*marketing is not eliminated.*

Marketing activities may be performed in somewhat different ways and through different types of institutions. Fundamentally, however, the same functions are performed to varying degrees in both types of economies. In a centralized economy, for example, there may be less emphasis on advertising with consumers expected to search more for information on their own. Consumers may wait in lines outside the stores to, in effect, perform part of the advertising function by finding out what is available. But marketing functions are still being performed. This is especially evident in Yugoslavia, a country which has increasingly gravitated to use of the market system.

Market System. The market system places much of the allocation responsibility on individuals. The degree of decentralization becomes apparent when one considers the millions of daily decisions made by individual consumers in the U.S. These decisions collectively spell success or failure for products, companies and even industries. The "votes" cast every day by customers ultimately determine how resources are allocated to the satisfaction of various needs. Realizing this, it becomes apparent that a central planner's task in other economies is of tremendous magnitude and complexity. Further, the task becomes increasingly difficult as a nation develops beyond satisfying the basic needs of its citizenry to satisfaction of more subtle needs. The market system allows consumers to directly cast their "votes" for and against *specific* products. In a centralized economy, even if central planners are elected by the people, the planners undoubtedly hold some product preferences that a voter would approve and others that a voter would oppose—but the voter has only *one* vote. In the market system, each consumer "votes" daily on the future of specific products and services.

Reliance on markets and the "market mechanism" underscores the importance of marketing activity. As illustrated in Figure 2–3, the market mechanism is the means for resolving the allocation of scarce resources to producers given the demands of consumers. Customers, via the market mechanism, lead to production decisions which, in turn, results in the utilization of resources. It may be seen that the managerial marketing variables (discussed in Chapter 1) of product, price, promotion and distribution are shown in Figure 2–3, although from a very different perspective than that for designing marketing strategy. *Product* sales are sustained because the products are valued as need satisfiers by customers. This is insured as long as the consumer has alternative product choices—that being the value of competition between firms. Business competition in combination with free consumer choice is the crux of the market system. In Figure 2–3, the *prices* of the goods cover costs in the long-run and, most importantly, price is a measure of the *value* of goods to consumers. Lest we forget, consumers may normally pay a given price or allocate their income elsewhere. Also in Figure 2–3, distribution and *communication* (promotion) are necessary to match the needs of customers with production decisions. The free flow of reliable information is prerequisite to the effective functioning of the market system because consumers must make their purchase decisions on the basis of available information. Finally, the *distribution* of goods and services in the quantities demanded by cus-

FIGURE 2–3

Marketing and the Market Economy

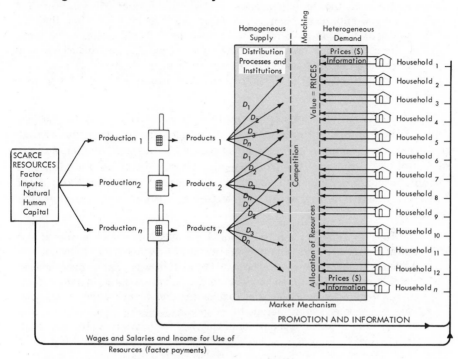

tomers requires collecting, sorting and dispersing of goods to match demand and supply.

A key characteristic of the free market system is reliance on the *profit motive* as an incentive for people to contribute capital and human resources to the production process. The returns to investors and laborers (profits, wages, etc.) for the use of their resources provides the dollars ("votes") that consumers expend in the marketplace. Individuals are allowed to accumulate capital and resources and provide these for the production process in return for compensation. These factor inputs and factor payments are shown in Figure 2–3.

The value of the monetary incentive as a motivator is provided by an extension of the earlier "water trough" example:

> But suppose that, when the 100th man had completed his trough down the mountain and said to the other 99, "If you will give me what it takes you 10 minutes to produce, I will let you get your water from my basin," they had turned on him and said, "We are 99 and you are

only one. We will take what water we want. You cannot prevent us and we will give you nothing." What would have happened then? The incentive of the most curious mind to build upon his enterprising thought would have been taken away. He would have seen that he could gain nothing by solving problems if he still had to use every waking hour to provide his living. There could have been no advancement in the community. Life would have continued to be drudgery to everyone, with opportunity to do no more than work all day long just for a bare living.[17]

In contrast with this example, centralized economies tend to remove some of the immediate monetary incentive in return for the *promise* that the greater and longer run good will be served. Despite the tremendous merits of the profit motive, we must also be cognizant of potential disadvantages. The profit motive may, of course, be taken too far as Bartels indicates in reviewing the historical development of the U.S. economy:

> Between the development of national markets and the later rise of the market economy, prevailing concepts of the relationship between the economy and society were changed. Production was carried on primarily for sale on the market; incomes were derived from sales on the market; personal gain became the principal motivation of exchange; and social values become subordinated to economic value . . . In their early stages, the market economy and market society were fraught with commercial tyranny and social depredations . . . Then social resistance to predatory business practices began to express itself in legislation and in other ways intended to improve trade and market practices.[18]

In every society there is some degree of balancing between the social good and use of individual incentives recognizing that some inherent conflict exists. The balance at a given time varies and is the basis for continual debate (Chapter 6).

Governmental System

Two roles occupied by government in any society are (1) to provide organization for the direct satisfaction of certain needs, and (2) to determine the appropriate *means* of satisfying other needs (e.g., free enterprise). Government complements the private marketing system by *directly* satisfying certain needs in addition to shaping the form and operation of the marketing system by laws.

Regarding the satisfaction of collective needs, it is generally recognized as beneficial for joint efforts to be used for the production of certain "public goods." The maintenance of an army, accumulation of

---

[17] Kent, "What is Profit," p. 97.
[18] Bartels, *Marketing Theory and Metatheory*, p. 161.

weaponry, building of bridges, and compensation of teachers are examples of goods and services which are necessary for the functioning of society. These areas are either (a) too important to trust to control by individual or private interests or (b) too large in magnitude for private interest to muster the resources required to provide the good. Providing for the direct satisfaction of needs and setting rules for private enterprise requires only a minimal involvement of the central leadership. This was suggested by Abraham Lincoln when he said, "The function of government is to do for the people what needs to be done, but what they cannot do for themselves, or do so well."[19]

The second role of government, that of determining the appropriate *means* for satisfying noncollective needs, requires the central leadership to decide what role individuals should play in *determining* societal goals as well as the individual's role in actually meeting these goals. This is related to the existing political system with a greater role given to individuals in a democratic form of government than in a more centralized form. Heavy reliance on the market system serves to decentralize decision-making to producers and, ultimately consumers. The more power is centralized, the greater the temptation for leaders to assert their judgment as to the needs of the society. Even using the market system, however, requires passage of guides (e.g., antitrust legislation) to insure its continued workability.

Marketing Today

It may be argued that marketers are more responsive to society than ever before—but the standards of conduct set by society seem to be shifting upward at an even greater rate—resulting in a widening gap between societal expectations and marketing practices. Yet most would agree that marketing has its faults and that significant change has transpired since business and marketing evolved in its primitive form to satisfy needs. As business and marketing institutions evolved, they became organisms, growing in size and complexity, and became increasingly difficult to manage. In a market economy, the profit goal of firms combined with competition serves to encourage efficiency and generally reconcile the interests of business firms with the interests of society. Those who make profit are typically responding to the needs of customers. Yet it is plausible to reason that, over time, the emphasis and focus on the profit motive grew to the point that profit became businesses' total rationalization of their activities. In the late 1800s there was ample evidence of business people in this country going to extreme lengths to circumvent the underlying justification for business and mar-

---

[19] Cited in John H. Ferguson and Dean E. McHenry, *Elements of American Government* (New York: McGraw-Hill Book Company, 1962).

keting. Some of the largest business empires were built to insure that very little would block the pursuit of profit. This was possible, in part, because of the great amount of good (e.g., economic development and employment) which typically paralleled the pursuit of profit. In the early 1900s, however, government began to move against the largest firms via antitrust actions, beginning a new era with government playing a larger and more restrictive role.

By the mid-1950s business people were once again talking of serving the needs of people under the caption of the "new marketing concept" (Chapter 1). This was partially due to increased competition following the depletion of accumulated demand after World War II. Since that time there appears to have been an increasing tendency to recognize what was obvious and immediate to people in the earliest days of marketing—that the justification for business and marketing emanates from the social system. The justification for marketing is one of need satisfaction. This was reflected in the 1973 Annual Report of Xerox in the statement, "Simply stated, we consider that Xerox Corporation is a social institution, as well as a business."

Yet, current practices indicate there is still some distance between a full adoption of this perspective as opposed to the lower system level consideration of business survival and profit. The perspective of the larger society is increasingly recognized as a valuable input to marketing decision-making although several factors impede returning to the exchange concept of marketing as in the primitive village example. These factors include:

1. Size of Firms. The size of firms and the powerful role of business in the United States will help to insure that businesses are not *totally* subservient to serving the needs of people in the event of profit conflict. Business will remain a powerful force capable of changing the environment as well as adapting to it.

2. Complexity of Business Organizations. The sheer complexity of business firms contributes to a loss of understanding by many people in the firm as to *why* they are performing certain functions. The size of firms combined with a high degree of specialization contributes to employees seeking only to satisfy their own economic needs rather than identifying with the goals of the firm. Thus, even if the firm's goals are consistent with those of society, they may be difficult to convey to employees except by managerial incentives.

3. Distance from Societal Goals. Business people today have several generations of ancestors who deemphasized the true justification for business and marketing within society. It may be unrealistic to believe that the profit goal can be substantially compromised in the event of profit-societal conflict due to the profit goal's promi-

nent role in our culture. A managerial vs. societal perspective in Figure 2–1 suggests the distance between the profit and societal orientation. In addition, the acceptance of the Protestant ethic as part of our culture encourages independence and self-serving rather than societal serving activities (although this may be changing).

4. Modern Role of Marketing. Marketing will never return to performing only exchange functions. Although most marketing activities center about the exchange process, the role of marketing in an affluent society is inevitably complex and sophisticated. As observed by one, "Marketing societies, as anthropologists distinguish them, are far more complex. The United States, having moved furthest beyond the simple goods-for-prestige, goods-for-goods, or goods-for-money trading mechanisms, is thus the world's most complete marketing society. Here the exchange process takes on such nuances as quantity discounts, credit cards, multilevel distribution channels, perfumed newspaper pages, and computer selected market segmentation."[20]

Marketing may have deviated somewhat from its original and clearly stated justification. Yet social forces (even in the mid-seventies recession) suggest that the pendulum may be swinging back toward a new recognition of the role marketing should play in a highly-developed society. These issues are explored in greater depth in Chapter 5 and at the end of this volume. The current structure of marketing which has evolved over the years concludes our analysis of macro-marketing.

MARKETING SYSTEMS AND STRUCTURE

The nature of marketing has evolved from simple one-to-one exchange to today's complex arrangements of highly specialized institutions. Marketing has changed in response to its environment, especially to changing consumer needs and wants and the advent of new technologies for serving customers. Ecology, the study of the relation between organisms and the environment, provides a perspective for viewing marketing over time as well as cross-culturally.

The marketing system is characterized by its "openness." The system is bombarded by external influences such as consumer preferences, competitive pressures, public opinion, and governmental actions. Marketing is constantly modified and altered to fit the many demands placed upon it.

There is greater pressure for efficiency in the marketing system. Pres-

---

[20] Quote only from Richard H. Brien, Betsy D. Gelb and William D. Trammell, "The Challenge to Marketing Dominance: Will Social Responsibility Be Recognized?" *Business Horizons*, vol. 15, no. 1 (February 1972). p. 245.

sure is directly felt from competition; the efficient performance of functions is necessary for the survival and profitable operation of the business. If customers can buy competitive products for less (due to greater marketing efficiency and lower costs), they typically will. This simple but critical mechanism within the *market* system provides constant pressure for efficiency in the *marketing* system. This constant pressure is why marketing changes. Thus, the macro question concerning marketing systems is this: Given an understanding of consumer needs and desires, *how can the most efficient arrangement of marketing components be developed for the performance of marketing functions?*

The starting point for understanding a marketing system is to understand the functions it must perform. In recognition of the tasks at hand, a system would ideally be developed with the most appropriate institutions (sets of arrangements) interrelated in the most effective manner. Partly because of different emphasis on functional requirements, IBM has a different system for marketing computers than Procter and Gamble has for "Pringles Potato Chips." Based on the tasks to perform, differing numbers and types of marketing institutions (or system components) may be involved (e.g., retailers and wholesalers). Other less obvious parts of the system include manufacturers and customers. Manufacturer's branch houses are marketing organizations. Consumers play an active part in the marketing system as they search for information and alternative products, negotiate sales, and make payments. Consumers who engage in self-service are actually assuming marketing tasks previously performed by retailers. Consumers may even assume *most* of the functions typically performed by retailers—by, for example, buying directly from a wholesaler or a manufacturer or by forming a consumer buying cooperative. Therefore, the customer is part of the marketing system as well as producers and various middlemen because they perform marketing functions. In addition, institutions such as financial, insurance, and transportation firms are critical to system functioning. Employment in marketing and facilitative firms is estimated to be between one-quarter and one-third of the entire labor force.

To have a system requires more than components. The components are engaging in processes which result in flows between retailers, wholesalers and consumers. The flows, in turn, represent interrelationships. Important flows include information, goods and services, negotiation, risk, money and manpower. Traditionally, attention has been on the physical flow of goods as well as the flow of title from manufacturers to the customer. But the systems viewpoint recognizes no end point. In Figure 2–4, for example, the marketing system for canned goods (e.g., vegetables) is shown with special attention to the flows of negotiation, financing and risk. The food canner typically negotiates with the wholesale grocers, who negotiate with retail grocers who, in turn, deal with

FIGURE 2–4

A Marketing System: Selected Flows

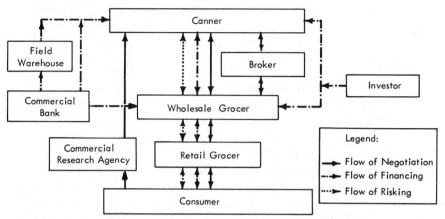

Source: Roland S. Vaile, E. T. Grether, and Reavis Cox, *Marketing in the American Economy.* Copyright 1952, The Ronald Press Company, New York.

consumers. Arrangements for negotiation are often set up by a broker. Financing is important due to the seasonality of canned foods and the resulting need for inventories.

The funds can flow into the system from commercial banks or from individual investors (Figure 2–4). Financing may flow backward as well as forward; for example, when a wholesaler advances funds to a canner during processing. Risks typically flow forward with each new link assuming its share of risk as it takes title. Yet, exceptions exist as when a wholesaler agrees in advance to pay a canner a specified price for future shipments. Generally, Figure 2–4 demonstrates the interactive nature of the marketing system as middlemen and others perform essential functions. The remainder of this chapter analyzes the role of marketing distribution or channel institutions.

A Rationale for Marketing Middlemen

To pose some commonly asked questions, why do manufacturers use middlemen? Do consumers really benefit from use of middlemen? Doesn't the price necessarily go up as middlemen are added? To approach this sensitive area, one may ask what alternatives exist to the use of middlemen. For manufacturers, the alternative is to distribute directly to the consumer. For consumers, the alternative is to buy as directly as possible from the manufacturer.

Given that the marketing functions have to be performed by *someone,* it is then a matter of determining who can perform them most efficiently. Assessing efficiency, in turn, requires attention to (*a*) scale economies, (*b*) expertise due to specialization, and (*c*) the sheer number of contacts in the exchange process.

Scale Economies.   Consider for a moment a manufacturer of household brooms. Would it make sense for that manufacturer to distribute directly to the doors of consumers—or, alternatively, to invite consumers to buy directly at the door of the manufacturer? Using the labor of employees to sell door-to-door, one broom at a time, would be grossly inefficient. An alternative is for the manufacturer to add a middleman who handles complementary household goods (e.g., mops) and have him add brooms to his line. In this way, the middleman can spread the cost of his time and expenses over the sales of several products—not just brooms. Further, the agent, rather than sell directly to the consumer, may sell the brooms (and his other goods) to retailers. Another middleman? Scale economies enter here as well because brooms may be only one of five-thousand products in the retail store. The costs of selling each broom as part of a large assortment of goods is much less than if a separate broom store were set up with, in all likelihood, a lesser number of customers (and sales) over which to spread the retailing costs. The net effect of adding middlemen in this example is to *lower* distribution costs drastically for each broom. Thus consumers are served better and the manufacturer can be more competitive because middlemen were added and unit costs were lowered.

Specialized Expertise.   Manufacturers also often recognize that they have no real distribution expertise. By contrast, established wholesalers and brokers have experience and knowledge in performing wholesaling functions—understanding which could take a manufacturer years to accumulate. Knowledge of the distribution structure, the nuances of the trade, and possession of personal contacts in the distribution channels can contribute substantially to efficiency of operation. Although large businesses today are assuming a greater role in vertically integrating their distribution channels, these moves are sometimes taken with at least a short term loss in efficiency.[21]

The consumer, like the manufacturer, may take over part of the distribution process. Here the question of relative inefficiency is even more striking. Consumer food cooperatives, for example, are designed to provide consumers with lower prices. Consumers perform the marketing (retailing) functions (run the co-op). Co-ops usually deal in much lower volume than the average food market so they are unable to spread their costs or capitalize as much on scale economies. Further, consumers who run the cooperatives are seldom as knowledgeable and efficient as

---

[21] Forms of channel integration are discussed in Chapter 16.

established "middlemen" would be. One may, therefore, wonder how the consumer could save money. The "savings" result in large part due to donated time from consumers who perform the retailing functions. Consumers also may donate such things as garage space for inventory storage. In addition, the service level which consumers normally receive in food markets may be grossly reduced in a food co-op by inconvenient location, drab facilities, or limited assortments. Retail food stores could also lower their service levels and, of course, lower their prices! This discussion is not to ridicule consumers who wish to engage in "eliminating the middleman"—but simply to recognize that, in fact, the retailing functions are *not* being eliminated and that savings usually arise only from not counting the value of the consumer's time (and facilities) and by lowering the service level. The prices to consumers may, in fact, be less via a cooperative if they place a low value on their discretionary time (or on the space being used in the back of their garage). Savings, however, do not result from more efficient performance of marketing functions. Profits of chain supermarkets (in good times) are less than two cents for each sales dollar.

Number of Contacts. Middlemen also contribute to the marketing process by reducing the number of contacts required in the exchange process. Consider, for example, three processors or manufacturers of soap, bread, and candy in Figure 2–5. Also note the three consumers representing their market. To distribute directly as shown in Figure 2–5A requires nine contacts or exchanges whereas with a middleman (as in 2–5B), the number of required exchanges is only six. Applying this concept to our modern economy with hundreds of thousands of producers and millions of consumers convinces the skeptic of the importance of this factor. The number of transactions necessary to carry out decentralized exchange (Figure 2–5A) is $\dfrac{n(n-1)}{2}$ where n is the number of producers and each makes only one article. Since the number of transactions required is only n if the central market is operated by a dealer, the ratio of advantage is $\dfrac{n-1}{2}$. Thus, if the number of producers is raised from 5 to 25, the ratio of advantage in favor of an intermediary increases from 2 to 12. With 125 producers the ratio of advantage is 62.[22]

Reducing the number of transactions increases efficiency and benefits

---

[22] Wroe Alderson, "Factors Governing the Development of Marketing Channels," in *The Marketing System: Organization and Dynamics,* vol. 2, edited by Donald H. Granbois, Bert C. McCammon, Jr., and William C. Panschar, Bureau of Business Research, Indiana University, September, 1966, pp. 6.1–4. Originally in Richard M. Clewett, ed., *Marketing Channels for Manufactured Products* (Homewood, Ill.: Richard D. Irwin, Inc., 1954).

FIGURE 2–5

Exchange Reduction by Middlemen

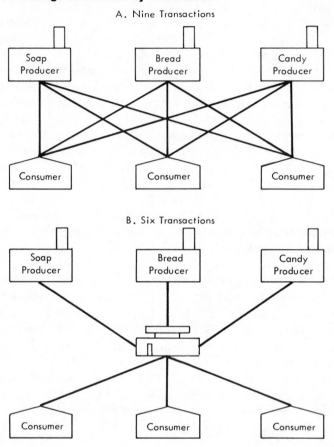

A. Nine Transactions

B. Six Transactions

both producers and consumers. Consider for a moment consumer Betty X. If all of the marketing middlemen were eliminated, she could take eight hours a day (or more) to obtain the many products that are needed to sustain her life style. Just obtaining various food items from processors would be an insurmountable task. If all the Betty Xs in the United States were charged with going direct to producers, imagine the mass confusion that would result! This type of thinking serves to remind the consumer that an average supermarket with 10,000 items is, in fact, worth its small profit margin.

In summary, middlemen exist because of unique expertise, a reduction in the number of transactions and from scale economies. In addition, many manufacturers could not own their own distribution system due to limited financial resources. Even if a producer *could* financially afford to own all its distribution outlets, it would not be justified unless it were the best investment from available alternatives. Thus, middlemen play an essential role in efficiently meeting consumer needs. Now, what are the characteristics of distributive middlemen?

Marketing Institutions

The institutions which serve consumers are transient even though the functions they perform are not. Institutions do not "change with the wind" but, as Figure 2–2 illustrates, are largely the result of other changing factors.

Institutional Change. In the frontier days, the *general merchandise store* met the needs of small communities when consumers were largely self-sufficient and had limited financial abilities. As the population became concentrated into urban areas, the *specialty shop* became economically feasible with large numbers of people available to support the limited-lines. The later rise of the *department store* was due partly to rising land values in downtown areas and, in effect, the realization that several specialty shops could be jointly owned under one roof. In the food area, the advent in the 1930's of the *supermarket* is usually associated with penny pinching consumers during the depression and their need for low prices. The demise of the corner grocery store was also hastened by the mobility provided by the automobile. The supermarket concept in turn was the basis for the *discount* house in the fifties and somewhat later, the development of *suburban shopping centers,* as consumers moved from central city areas. Today, in part due to computer technology and changing life styles, retail food warehouses are being experimented with where consumers may order groceries by telephone and expect efficient home delivery. Vending machines and other non-store retailing are also increasing as consumers accept machines in trade for convenience. It may be seen that as consumers and factors within the environment changed, retailing institutions have changed. The same has been true for wholesaling.

Types of Marketing Institutions. The components of the distribution system may be classified by ownership of goods and by level in the distribution system.

Classified by *ownership of goods,* establishments which take title to goods they handle are termed merchant middlemen. Retailers are typically merchant middlemen since they take title to the goods. An exception is when retailers take goods on consignment and sell the goods on commission (without taking title). Firms which do not take title to the goods are called functional middlemen and are common in wholesaling. Non-merchant or functional wholesalers include brokers, selling agents, manufacturers' agents and commission merchants (Figure 2–7). Functional middlemen are compensated by commission and may or may

FIGURE 2-6
Marketing Channels

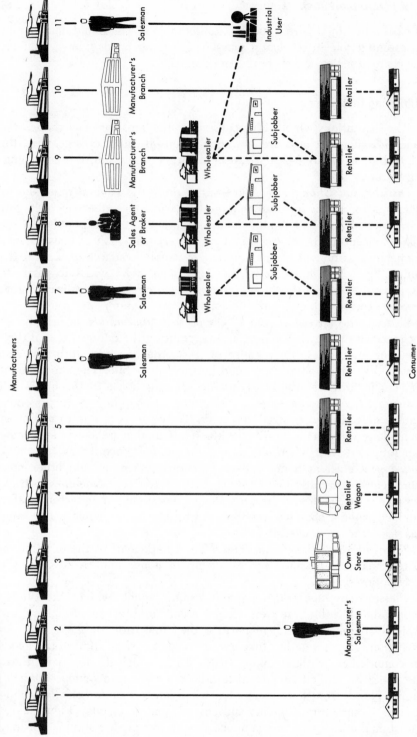

Source: G. E. Larson and M. N. Poteat, *Selling the United States Market: A Marketing Guidebook for Manufacturers and Distributors, Domestic Commerce Series No. 29 (New series)* (Washington, D.C.: U.S. Government Printing Office, 1951), p. 28.

not actually take physical possession of the goods. Because they do not take title, they do not assume market risk (the risk of price fluctuations).

Middlemen may also be classified as to their *level in the channel.* Alternative vertical channels may be seen in Figure 2–6 with six levels from manufacturer to consumer. Closest to the consumer are retailers as well as the manufacturers' own arrangements (channels 1, 2, and 3) for performing the retail functions. The next higher level in Figure 2–6 includes subjobbers, who in turn, work under wholesalers. Manufacturers sometimes employ salesmen for contacting wholesalers or they sometimes own their own offices and branches. If such sales personnel cannot be economically justified by sales volume and profits from their activities (e.g., due to a limited product line), an agent or a broker could be used on a commission basis. Figure 2–6 illustrates common arrangements of institutions for economically distributing different types of products. The nature and functions of various channel members are described in Figure 2–7. An appreciation of the structure of marketing is

FIGURE 2–7

Marketing Institutions

Middlemen. A business concern that specializes in performing operations or rendering services directly involved in the purchase and/or sale of goods in the process of their flow from producer to consumer. Middlemen are of two types: merchants and agents. The essence of the middleman's operation lies in the fact that he plays an active and prominent part in the negotiations leading up to transactions of purchase and sale. This is what distinguishes him from a marketing facilitating agent who, while he performs certain marketing functions, participates only incidentally in negotiations of purchase and sale.

Facilitating agencies in marketing. Those agencies which perform or assist in the performance of one or a number of the marketing functions, but which neither take title to goods nor negotiate purchases or sales. Common types are banks, railroads, storage warehouses, commodity exchanges, stock yards, insurance companies, graders and inspectors, advertising agencies, firms engaged in marketing research, cattle loan companies, furniture marts, and packers and shippers.

Merchant. A business unit that buys, takes title to, and resells merchandise. The distinctive feature of this middleman lies in the fact that he takes title to the goods he handles. Wholesalers and retailers are the chief types of merchants.

Agent. A business unit which negotiates purchases or sales or both but does not take title to the goods in which it deals. The agent usually performs fewer marketing functions than does the merchant. He commonly receives his remuneration in the form of a commission or fee. He usually does not represent both buyer and seller in the same

FIGURE 2–7 (continued)

transaction. Examples are: broker, commission merchant, manu-facturers agent, selling agent, and resident buyer.

Broker. An agent who does not have direct physical control of the goods in which he deals but represents either buyer or seller in negotiating purchases or sales for his principal. The broker's powers as to prices and terms of sale are usually limited by his principal.

Retailer. A merchant, or occasionally an agent, whose main business is selling directly to the ultimate consumer.

Voluntary Group. A group of retailers each of whom owns and operates his own store and is associated with a wholesale organization or manufacturer to carry on joint merchandising activities and who are characterized by some degree of group identity and uniformity of operation. Such joint activities have been largely of two kinds: co-operative advertising and group control of store operation.

Retailer Cooperative. A group of independent retailers organized to buy cooperatively either through a jointly owned warehouse or through a buying club.

Wholesaler. A business unit which buys and resells merchandise to retailers and other merchants and/or to industrial, institutional, and commercial users but which does not sell in significant amounts to ultimate consumers. In the basic materials, semi-finished goods, and tool and machinery trades merchants of this type are commonly known as "distributors" or "supply houses." Generally these mer-chants render a wide variety of services to their customers. Those who render all the services normally expected in a few of the wholesale services are known as Service Wholesalers; those who render only a few of the wholesale services are known as Limited-Function Wholesalers. The latter group is composed mainly of Cash-and-Carry Wholesalers, who do not render the credit or delivery service; Drop-Shipment Wholesalers, who sell for delivery by the producer direct to the buyer; Truck Wholesalers, who combine selling, delivery, and collection in one operation; and Mail Order Wholesalers who perform the selling service entirely by mail.

Jobber. This term is widely used as a synonym of "wholesaler" or "distributor." The term is sometimes used in certain trades and lo-calities to designate special types of wholesalers.

Manufacturer's agent. An agent who generally operates on an extended contractual basis; often sells within an exclusive territory; handles noncompeting but related lines of goods; and possesses limited au-thority with regard to prices and terms of sale. He may be authorized to sell a definite portion of his principal's output.

Selling agent. An agent who operates on an extended contractual basis, sells all of a specified line of merchandise or the entire output of his principal, and usually has full authority with regard to prices,

FIGURE 2–7 (concluded)

> terms, and other conditions of sale. He occasionally renders financial aid to his principal. This functionary is often called a "sales agent."
>
> Commission house (sometimes called Commission merchant). An agent who usually exercises physical control over and negotiates the sale of the goods he handles. The commission house usually enjoys broader powers as to prices, methods, and terms of sale than does the broker, although it must obey instructions issued by the principal. It generally arranges delivery, extends necessary credit, collects, deducts its fees, and remits the balance to the principal.
>
> Branch House. An establishment maintained by a manufacturer, detached from the headquarters establishment and used primarily for the purpose of stocking, selling, delivering, and servicing his product.

Source: *Marketing Definitions: A Glossary of Marketing Terms*, compiled by the Committee on Definitions of the American Marketing Association, Ralph S. Alexander, Chairman, 1960, published by the American Marketing Association.

essential prior to the managerial approach in the remainder of the book. There are also important horizontal relationships between marketers at a given level of distribution. Voluntary groups and retailer cooperatives (Figure 2–7) are examples of marketers joining together for mutual advantage. Pooled buying groups are, for example, comprised of independent grocers working cooperatively to lower the costs of goods from wholesalers. Partial horizontal integration of independent retailers to enable buying in larger quantities has allowed the independent stores to receive better prices from wholesalers and better compete with chain stores. Shopping centers also illustrate horizontal channel relationships with the combination of perhaps 100 stores creating a greater customer attracting force than the sum of its parts. Spreading expenses such as advertising across all the stores is also advantageous.

Retailing Structure. The retailing structure is comprised of institutions such as department stores, supermarkets, discount houses, shopping centers, and franchises. But because of public awareness of retail establishments, sales are instead presented by product grouping in Table 2–2 on page 62. In 1972 there were over 1.9 million retail establishments, a somewhat greater number than in 1963 although retail sales rising from $244 billion (1963) to $459 billion (1972). Sales volume per store continued to rise significantly. Food stores in 1972 continued to represent the largest single chunk of retail sales (23.4 percent) although as shown in Table 2–2, because of larger and higher volume stores, the number of food stores shrank from 18.7 to 14.0 percent of all retail establishments. Attention to Table 2–2 should yield a fuller understanding of the current retail structure as well as retailing trends.

Wholesale Structure. Evidence is presented on the wholesaling

TABLE 2–2

Retail Establishments: Number and Sales Volume

	1963				1972			
Type of Retailer	*Number of Establish- ments*	*Percent of Total Number*	*Aggregate Sales (in millions)*	*Percent of Total Sales*	*Number of Establish- ments*	*Percent of Total Number*	*Aggregate Sales (in millions)*	*Percent of Total Sales*
All retailers	1,707,931	100.0	244,202	100.0	1,912,871	100.0	459,040	100.0
Food Stores	319,433	18.7	57,079	23.4	267,352	14.0	100,719	21.9
Eating and drinking places	334,481	19.6	18,412	7.5	359,524	18.8	36,868	8.1
General merchandise	62,063	3.6	30,003	12.3	56,245	2.9	65,092	14.2
Apparel and accessory	116,223	6.8	14,040	5.7	129,201	6.8	24,741	5.4
Furniture and home furnishings	93,649	5.5	10,926	4.5	116,857	6.1	22,533	4.9
Automotive	98,514	5.8	45,376	18.6	121,369	6.3	90,030	19.6
Gasoline service stations	211,473	12.4	17,760	7.3	226,459	11.8	33,655	7.3
Lumber, mobile home, and hardware	92,703	5.4	14,606	6.0	83,842	4.4	23,844	5.2
Drug and proprietary	54,732	3.2	8,487	3.5	51,542	2.7	15,599	3.4
Other retail stores	244,868	14.3	21,309	8.7	338,359	17.7	34,391	7.5
Nonstore retailers	79,792	4.7	6,204	2.5	162,121	8.5	11,568	2.5

Source: U.S. Department of Commerce, Social and Economic Statistics Administration.

TABLE 2–3

Wholesale Establishments: Number and Sales Volume

Type of Wholesaler	1963				1972			
	Number of Establishments	Percent of Total Number	Aggregate Sales (in millions)	Percent of Total Sales	Number of Establishments	Percent of Total Number	Aggregate Sales (in millions)	Percent of Total Sales
All wholesalers...............	308,177	100.0	$358,386	100.0	369,791	100.0	$695,224	100.0
Merchant wholesalers...............	223,107	72.4	167,212	46.6	278,697	75.4	343,665	49.4
Manufacturers' sales branches.......	28,884	9.4	116,443	32.5	33,112	9.0	232,615	33.5
Merchandise agents and brokers.......	25,313	8.2	53,245	14.9	32,449	8.8	85,586	12.3
Petroleum bulk plants and terminals.......	30,873	10.0	21,485	6.0	25,533	6.8	33,358	4.8

Note: Changes in census classifications between 1963 and 1972 necessitated adjustments to derive comparable data.
Source: U.S. Department of Commerce, Social and Economic Statistics Administration.

structure in Table 2–3. In 1972, there were nearly 370,000 wholesale establishments totaling over $695 billion in sales. Basic types of wholesalers are cited with merchant wholesalers comprising 75 percent of the establishments and about 49 percent of total wholesale sales. Conversely, manufacturer's sales outlets represent only 9 percent of the establishments but make up one-third of all wholesale sales. A careful review of Table 2–3 should yield insights into the existing structure as well as into wholesaling trends. It should be kept in mind that several variations exist within each classification. Merchant wholesalers, for example, include wholesale merchants, rack merchandisers, import-export merchants, cash and carry wholesalers, truck wholesalers, drop shippers, and mail-order wholesalers. Also, merchandise agents include brokers, commission agents, purchasing agents, auction companies, export-import agents, selling agents, and manufacturers' agents.

Wholesaling versus Retailing. In 1967, it may be seen in Tables 2–2 and 2–3 that wholesale sales were roughly 1½ times as great as retail sales—$695 billion as compared to retailing's $459 billion. It will be recalled that the relative number of establishments is in the opposite direction with 1,912,871 retail establishments and only 369,791 wholesale establishments. Sales per wholesale establishment are much higher than for retail establishments. The public probably perceives retail sales to be higher because retail prices are higher. Wholesale sales are higher because about 39 percent of wholesale sales is to industrial and other institutional users, 17 percent to other wholesalers, 4 percent as exports, and 1 percent to consumers and farmers. Only the remaining 39 percent of wholesale sales is to retailers.

SUMMARY AND CONCLUSIONS

This chapter builds a perspective for viewing the role of marketing within society. Marketing may be viewed in a macro-context as a social process—one in which institutions and techniques continually evolve to meet the needs of consumers. It is important in this setting to understand the relation of marketing to governmental and economic processes and to appreciate their interdependence. Government directly provides for the collective needs of the populace with business and marketing responding to other needs. Although marketing *functions* are performed in centralized economies, marketing plays a more active role in a market system. Marketing is particularly significant in the United States because of the existing degree of specialization and the advanced stage of economic development.

Marketing institutions (accepted sets of arrangements for performing marketing functions) provide the structure of marketing and it is important to understand the structural system within which management operates.

EXERCISES FOR DISCUSSION AND REVIEW

1. Independently study the institutions and processes of food distribution and then relate these processes to Figure 2–2. Starting with marketing institutions and decision technologies, show how these exist *because* of marketing functions which, in turn, exist *because* of exchange, and so on until you reach the needs of people in society. Do historical trends in food distribution illustrate a similar, evolving process (as in Figure 2–2)?

2. As a society evolves, it often goes through a process with more and more emphasis on the later stages in Figure 2–2. Discuss in this context the largely agrarian society in the U.S. prior to 1900 versus that of today. Are there international marketing implications as well (e.g., marketing in India versus the U.S.)?

3. Marketing activity provides both food as well as rock music to consumers. How might these products relate to Maslow's hierarchy of needs, and in this context, how could the general mix of needs in India compare to the U.S.?

4. What functions does government play, with respect to need-fulfillment and, therefore, with respect to marketing? Could government be considered a "competitor" to the marketing system? How?

5. How are the advantages of specialization and exchange illustrated by the 100th man in the primitive community? Exactly how did all benefit because of the profit motive and what represented "profit"?

6. Marketing *creates* as well as *responds* to social change. Discuss.

7. Joe comments to his friend Myron, a marketing major at XYZ State, that the price of food is exorbitant. He goes on, "If we could only do away with the middlemen, we would all be better off." Assuming you are Myron, respond in detail to Joe, explaining the reasons for middlemen, the advantages they offer and why, in the case of food, it could be better for consumers to have three middlemen rather than two.

8. In reference to the chapter tables on retailing and wholesaling, identify and assess trends with respect to retail and wholesale sales and establishments. Compare and contrast retailing and wholesaling on these dimensions.

part two

Managerial Analysis of the Marketing Environment

Effective marketing decision making is dependent on an understanding of numerous uncontrollable or environmental factors. Success is significantly related to marketing management's ability to develop plans that coincide strategically with the environment.

Chapter 3, "The Marketing Environment: Concepts and Analysis," defines the managerial environment and examines marketing's organizational environment, task environment (competition and markets), and the macro-environment (social, technological, governmental, economic, and natural). Macro-environmental forces are usually felt through the task environment—too often as a surprise. It is essential to forecast environmental forces so as to provide for planning to minimize negative impacts.

"The Technological Environment," Chapter 4, is devoted to a basic understanding of an important but little understood environmental sector. An unprecedented rate of technological change has created a new awareness of its presence. Marketers need to guide new technological development toward meeting consumer needs and, generally, interact with research and development (R&D) people to foster communication and exchange. Technology affects every marketing decision area, not just product decisions, and it is essential to closely monitor and forecast changes in the technological environment.

Chapter 5, "Societal Change and the Consumer" examines the changing characteristics of consumers including socioeconomic shifts of marketing significance and changes in values. Values, in effect, place weights on different forms of need satisfaction. They must therefore be understood and interpreted for planning purposes by marketers. Consumer characteristics also help explain the rise of social issues such as consumerism. The issues, although transient, often generate powerful forces via public opinion and resulting legislation.

"The Governmental Environment," Chapter 6, examines the rationale for legislation, regulation and other governmental activity. Specific statutes are reviewed as they relate to key marketing decision areas. Monitoring of the macro-governmental environment is essential as governmental activity increases.

3

The Marketing Environment: Concepts and Analysis

Major determinants of success or failure of marketing strategy include the uncontrollable factors within the environment. Marketing decision-makers are continually adapting to new information and external influences. The firm is like a stellar satellite; always moving and adapting —yet attached to a larger system and environment. Marketing management must respond to environmental changes such as the following:

Average family incomes should increase in the current decade from less than $10,000 to nearly $14,000 (and even faster given the prevailing rates of inflation)!

The Federal Trade Commission is challenging the truthfulness of advertising; the Food and Drug Administration is requiring more information be made available about the nutritional value of food products; and the Consumer Product Safety Commission is establishing increased constraints upon business decision making.

Technological change is increasing at a fantastic rate. The number of inventions in the next 10 years will equal the number of inventions in the past 30 to 50 years. The number of new products staggers the imagination.

The voice of the consumer has impact and significance, unprecedented in history. According to some, the age of *caveat emptor* is ending and is being replaced by an age of *caveat venditor*.

A survey of college students at the end of the sixties revealed that 28 percent did not believe that competition encourages excellence. By 1971, 38 percent of the students cited this belief. Furthermore 15 percent said they did not believe business is entitled to make a profit.[1]

---

[1] *The Changing Values on Campus: Political and Personal Attitudes of Today's College Students,* A survey for the JDR 3d Fund by Daniel Yankelovich, Inc. (New York: Washington Square Press, Pocket Books, 1972), pp. 40–41.

Energy shortages are creating imbalances in supply and demand in various industries. The dominant societal and economic role of the automobile is being questioned.

Environmental changes have far reaching implications for vast numbers of marketers. Retailers, wholesalers, brokers, advertising agencies, and other marketing institutions are affected as are marketers within manufacturing enterprises. This chapter explores the relationship of environmental changes to marketing decision making in the following sequence: (1) the nature and complexity of the marketing environment are examined; (2) the relevance of various environmental influences to marketing management decision making is considered; (3) marketing decision making is assessed from an environmental perspective; and (4) the task of monitoring and forecasting environmental change is described to provide a frame of reference for more detailed consideration in subsequent chapters. The remainder of this part of the book will present detailed information on the technological, social, and governmental environments of marketing. This four-chapter unit assumes a managerial perspective and is a central input to decision making in marketing.

THE MARKETING ENVIRONMENT

Marketing Environment Defined

The environment of something is as big or small and as simple or complex as one defines it. The marketing environment is purely a matter of what and how much is abstracted from an infinite variety of factors. Most would agree, however, that the above examples of rising incomes, increasing technological innovation, changing governmental agencies and different consumer attitudes are all part of what might be construed as the marketing environment. A few decades past, people in a prosperous buggy whip industry laughed at the "horseless carriage," a technological innovation underestimated by numerous firms that were doomed to failure. Management of American railroads, only a few years ago, would have thought it preposterous to suggest some were on a downhill slide to bankruptcy. Yet, in part, insensitivity to a changing environment contributed to the current problems faced by rail carriers. At this moment, other firms are initiating bankruptcy proceedings because they failed to comprehend changing wants and needs of customers, evolving technology or competitive moves. Marketing successes, on the other hand, typically exhibit a close sensitivity to environmental changes. Consider, for example, the success of denim leisure clothing manufacturers in the mid-70s as a result of their responding to the changing lifestyles of both young and old.

The example illustrates the following characteristics of the marketing environment:

External.

Potentially relevant.

Uncontrollable.

Changing.

Constraining.

Uncertain.

External, in our context, means beyond the *marketing* management function within the firm because the *organizational* environment within the firm may play a large role in influencing the decisions of marketers. Factors external to the marketing function which are largely *uncontrollable,* yet are *potentially relevant to marketing plans and decisions* represent part of the operational marketing environment. Although electronics technology is potentially relevant to the office equipment industry, it would normally not be part of the marketing environment of a food processor. Thus, various companies will define their environment very differently according to the external influences that are relevant. Those factors outside the marketing management function are uncontrollable, in varying degrees. Attempts to significantly change consumers or government, for example, are typically exercises in futility. Factors within the firm (but external to marketing) are somewhat amenable to change. Marketers are primarily *adapters* rather than fundamental agents of change.

Other characteristics of the environment include its *changing* as well as *constraining* nature from the standpoint of marketing decision making. Acting as a constraint, environmental factors at a given point in time often define the "straight and narrow path" within which decisions must fall. The Flammable Fabrics Act, for example, creates a constraint on certain product decisions in the apparel industry. But special attention must be given to *change* within the marketing environment—changes which present *new* rules for carrying out marketing plans, and, due to this changing nature, these are variables in a decision-making context. Predicting new legislation, for example, is an important function which needs to be carried out meticulously. Marketing decisions are often dependent on predictions of the future state of variables; this is the source of *risk or uncertainty* in decision making. Uncontrollable or environmental variables present a real challenge to marketing management because the success of decisions depends on management's understanding of uncertainties associated with such groups as customers, governmental agencies, and new innovations.

Considering all of these dimensions the marketing environment may be defined as: "all factors external to the marketing function and largely uncontrollable which are changing or constraining in nature, and are potentially relevant to marketing decision making."

Increasing Environmental Complexity

Alvin Toffler in his book *Future Shock*, maintains that the rate of change in society is becoming so great that people may suffer "future shock"—a state of disorientation similar to cultural shock. The victim of culture shock suffers from an inability to cope with the new environment in which he or she is placed.[2] Future shock, on the other hand, is said to result from being unable to cope with the rate of environmental changes in a *given* culture. In the case of culture shock the person moves; in future shock the environment "moves"—but in both the rate of change is troublesome to the persons involved. More and more we witness obsolescence: obsolescence of college training, obsolescence of managerial tools, obsolescence of products, obsolescence of previously accepted concepts and institutions.

The role of the housewife-consumer changes; black consumers have become a significant factor in the marketplace; and the needs of the educated young seem to differ from past generations. Management cries for information about the many changes which are occurring—changes which a few years ago were improbable if not impossible. These changes cause many of the stresses as well as create many of the opportunities for the marketing community. Stresses within the governmental sector, fueled by demands of consumers, contributed to changes in the governmental environment of marketing in the early seventies. Uncertainties within the economic environment have also contributed to environmental complexity with problems such as record high interest rates, declining value of the U.S. dollar, and unacceptable inflation rates. Improved communications and data processing technology may contribute to a new *awareness* of environmental change and that part of an apparent acceleration of change may be more a matter of perception than real. Undoubtedly this view has merit although it is difficult to attribute current rates of change totally to changes in perception.

Other than the *rate* of environmental change, new *types* of change have become increasingly significant to marketing. Group demands by consumers and changing values of young consumers are fairly new types of considerations to marketing decision makers. Economic factors represent the core of business activity and have historically been important to marketing management, as has competition. Until around 1900, economic factors and competition virtually equalled the marketing environment.

---

[2] Alvin Toffler, *Future Shock* (New York: Random House, Inc., 1970).

At the turn of the century, governmental and legal forces became increasingly significant environmental factors as evidenced by antitrust suits and other government actions. The significance of legal forces has increased substantially to the anguish of many business people and there is no evidence of abatement. The emerging importance of legal forces to marketing at the turn of the century was a significant pivotal point because, until then, the free enterprise system was literally free. Abuses by business management at that point in history led to further restriction of their discretionary decision making power—in addition to restrictions emanating from the economic system.

Kelley has theorized that another turning point occurred in the marketing environment in the 1930s when the advent of political power, or the power of groups and coalitions, further affected the decision making realm of business management.[3] This may be construed as a form of social change, particularly as evidenced by unionization of labor during that period. More recently and of immediate concern to marketing management, consumers have collectively organized with use of similar tactics. Both the organization of labor and the new voice of consumers highlights a trend toward an increasingly pluralistic and interdependent society with business recognized as but one component. Business today is faced with demands from not only stockholders and government, but also from employees, consumers, citizens (in communities where they are located), as well as from special interest groups. The result is the advent of many more types of relevant environmental change than existed only a few decades ago.

Further, economic factors, competition and legal considerations have *not* diminished in importance but have increased in magnitude. These forces remain as the most significant environmental factors to marketing management even though other parts of the environment have risen to new levels of importance. The net effect for marketers is a requirement that more time be used to understand and cope with various external influences. Marketing decision making will become more and more dependent on factors beyond the control of the firm—a trend which is vital to understand and appreciate.

Levels of the Environment

In order to sort out the myriad of environmental factors important to marketers, it is useful to classify them using the different levels shown in Figure 3–1. The immediate environment for the marketing decision maker (3–1A) is that of the organization itself; the other units or func-

---

[3] Eugene J. Kelley, "From the Editor," *Journal of Marketing*, vol. 33, no. 1 (January 1969), pp. 1–2.

FIGURE 3–1

Environmental Levels

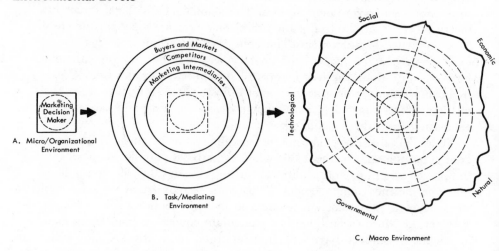

A. Micro/Organizational Environment

B. Task/Mediating Environment

C. Macro Environment

tions within the business firm. Surrounding the marketing management function is the task environment (3–1B), or the day-to-day operating environment of marketing management which in turn is surrounded by the macro-environment (3–1C). These, when placed together, conceptually portray levels and types of uncontrollable factors surrounding the marketing decision maker. Dividing the environment into layers facilitates the identification of uncontrollable factors at differing levels of immediacy and, to some extent, differing levels of contact frequency.

Surrounding the micro-environment are levels of immediate concern to management (Figure 3–1B). For the manufacturing enterprise (and all organizations which do not distribute direct to consumer, or industrial end-users), the link to markets is provided by marketing intermediaries such as distribution members, advertising agencies, and marketing research firms. Moving outward from marketing intermediaries, competitors are shown as the next level. The three layers (marketing intermediaries, competition, and buyers and markets) represent traditional concerns of marketing and top-level management and, therefore, provide the *task/mediating environment* for marketers. Coping with changing consumers, competitors' strategies, and working with external intermediaries present immediate and often daily challenges.

The task environment may also be thought of as the *mediating* environment because these levels typically serve as the interpreter and filter for macro-environmental changes (Figure 3–1C). The effects of changes in the social, technological, economic, governmental, and natural environments are usually felt by the decision maker through the mediating levels of the task environment. The effects, for example, of government on competitors, social changes on consumers, and technological changes on distributors are felt most directly through the task or mediating environment. It should be noted, however, that macro-environmental changes may, as discussed later, also impact *directly* as forces on marketing management. Changes in the macro-environment are usually, but not always, mediated through the task environment.

In defining the environment of marketing decision makers, Figure 3–1 attempts to build a perspective which has the following implications for management.

a.   Marketing decision makers are subject to influence from their peers within the marketing management organization as well as from other subsystems within the firm (Figure 3–1A). Inherent conflicts with other functional areas in the firm, for example, point up the necessity to recognize organizational influences on the decision maker. Secondly, it is important to conceive of not only managers coping with the environment but also the organization itself as an organism relating to the environment.

b.   Management (and this book) tends to focus on the development of strategy and related decisions. Figure 3–1B highlights the immediate dependence of these decisions on an understanding of the task environment including intermediary firms, competitors, and buyers.

c.   Management should find it useful in accordance with Figure 3–1C to group various macro-environmental factors relevant to the firm into the five categories shown. Each has commonalities which should facilitate use of similar approaches to analysis and, in some cases, even common strategic responses.

d.   Management should be aware of a continuing need to interpret task environment changes in the context of broader macro-environmental changes. To focus only on the task environment is to ignore the basic changes in society which *cause* the task environment to change; and, to not understand the causes of macro-environmental change ignores the means of predicting future shifts.

Within the various environmental levels, there are many specific organizations and individuals which engage in activities contributing to a dynamic and changing environment. The interaction of these many "components" such as research organizations, consumers, businesses and governmental agencies determines the task environment of marketing. Changes within the environment are the results of what might be termed "environmental processes." A process has been defined as a set of activities related to a particular goal or result.[4] The generation of environ-

---

[4] John W. Buckley, "Goal-Process Systems Interaction," *Business Horizons*, vol. 14, no. 6 (December 1971), pp. 81–91.

mental changes such as new technology, legislation, and gross national product is largely the result of processes engaged in by groups and organizations. The concept of processes is important for without the identification and understanding of the goals and activities of change generators (such as competitors or the Food and Drug Administration), marketing management is not in a position to *predict* changes that might be forthcoming. The processes which comprise the macro-environment have been characterized as economic, technological, social, governmental and natural. Similarly, the task environment may be thought of as various goal-oriented activities carried out by marketing intermediaries, competitors, and buyers whereas the micro-environment consists of processes within the firm. The individuals and organizations, therefore, within the micro, task and macro-environments of marketers, engage in goal-oriented processes (i.e., activities) which result in environmental change.

ENVIRONMENTAL INFLUENCES ON MARKETING DECISION MAKING

Both the micro and macro-environments influence marketing management decisions. The macro-environment is almost totally uncontrollable whereas the environment within the firm itself is usually uncontrollable only in the short-run. First each part of the macro-environment is discussed and then the micro or organizational environment is briefly examined.

Social Environment

The social environment in a sense encompasses the governmental, economic and technological environments because the common denominator of the social system, people, determines the nature and direction of all forms of environmental change except natural. The social system is more than the sum of the others. The social environment is comprised of characteristics of people, their culture, their social class, values, and life styles. The social environment affects the functioning of virtually everything in a democratic society and implicitly sets the priorities as well as the directions for change.[5]

For marketers, there are several aspects of the social environment of immediate relevance. Anything in the social system which is related to the needs of consumers is of interest to marketers. Socio-economic and demographic characteristics, such as incomes, educational levels, and age are related to needs and therefore to demand for luxury products, airline

---

[5] For an extended discussion, see Alfred Kuhn, *The Study of Society: A Unified Approach* (Homewood, Ill.: Richard D. Irwin, Inc., and The Dorsey Press), 1963.

tickets, books, and medicine. Shifting consumer values have been described by an executive of a major company as the single most important factor to the future of business and marketing. The values, social classes, and lifestyles of people are critical for marketing management to decipher. Companies such as Whirlpool Corporation have committed significant resources toward predicting and interpreting social trends.[6] As consumers change, their needs change, and then there is a need for marketing to change. New marketing opportunities appear and existing marketing strategies need to be modified.

The social environment also ultimately determines the role of marketing within society (Chapter 2). Social pressures from the news media and the "codification" of pressures into law by government loom as increasingly important factors. Social issues concerning such things as product safety, advertising truthfulness, wasted natural resources and conditions within the ghetto marketplace are major challenges currently facing marketing management.

As already suggested, it is difficult to consider the social system separately from other parts of the macro-environment. As shown in Figure 3–2 on page 78, the social system tends to guide priorities assigned to different technologies. This is illustrated, for example, by less emphasis in recent years on the space program and not developing the supersonic transport (SST), but rather placing higher priorities on new pollution-control technologies. In a democratic-system, the people guide the functioning of government and, in the shorter run, the government has significant effects on economic and technological development. The values of people determine the role of economic advancement as it relates to an increasingly broad concept of the quality of life. Consumers no longer accept economic and technological advancement for its own sake. Various dimensions underlying social change and the consumer are presented in Chapter 5 with attention to demographic factors, value change and current social-marketing issues.

Technological Environment

Technology is the application of knowledge and encompasses the related concepts of science, innovation, invention, and discovery. The manifestation of technology may be a physical item like a computer, but the essence of technology is new understanding. Technology is a pervasive influence within society as shown in Figure 3–2. New technology

---

[6] William Lazer and John E. Smallwood and others, "Consumer Environments and Life Styles of the Seventies," *Michigan State University Business Topics*, vol. 2 (Spring, 1972), p. 1. Also see John F. Mee, "Profiles of the Future: Speculation about Human Organization in the 21st Century," *Business Horizons*, vol. 14, no. 1 (February 1971), pp. 5–16.

FIGURE 3–2

Macro-environmental Interrelationships

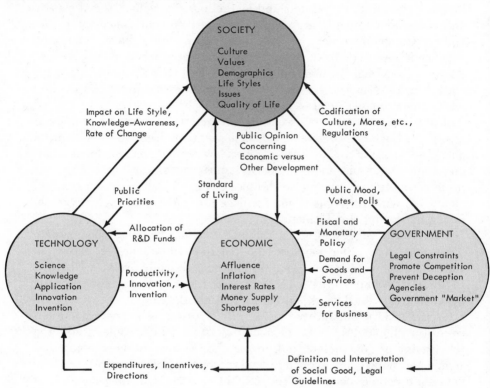

fuels the economic system with direct effects on productivity, the standard of living and the buying power of all consumers. Although estimates are tenuous, one study reported that between 1929 and 1957, the "advance of knowledge" contributed about 40 percent of the total increase in national income per person.[7] Technology is the basis for a trillion-dollar U.S. economy.

Technology also directly impacts the social system with effects on the rate of social change, consumer values and life styles (Figure 3–2). New knowledge and innovation create strains in the social system. Management fights to keep up with new developments and to update its skills. Consumers select from a confusing array of new and increasingly complex products and complain because product service facilities are inadequate and the rate of product obsolescence increases. Sophisticated news media technology has contributed to a new public awareness of

---

[7] E. Mansfield, *The Economics of Technological Change* (New York: Norton Publishing Co., 1968), p. 9.

the world, including a heightened awareness of consumer problems. The exponential growth rate of technology has led social critics to attack technological growth as evil although, at the same time, others see technology as the solution to existing problems. Alvin Toffler sees technology as the fuel for an unprecedented rate of social change with which increasing numbers of people will be unable to cope.[8] The advent of television, birth control pills, the computer, and the automobile serve only as examples of inventions with tremendous social impacts. Yet, ultimately, the social system reigns. People in society, as indicated by the SST decision, will slow or redirect the rate of technological change if it is deemed undesirable. Public reaction often lags undesirable trends but redirection typically occurs. Today, for example, politicians speak of a "humanized" and redirected technology for curing cancer and solving pollution woes.

Marketing decision makers feel the effects of technology as it is mediated through the task environment as well as directly. The effect of technologically created social change is seen on consumers. More aware and more demanding, consumers have new needs created by technology. Consider for example, the housewife who has a virtual "factory" of labor-saving machines at her fingertips. What of her leisure activities? Market opportunities have abounded recently in meeting these needs with such things as arts and crafts products. In addition, the continual opportunity exists to develop new technologies to meet existing needs better. The development of radically new products also opens the way for auxiliary support products and services. Technology has a pervasive influence on marketers and this is discussed in the next chapter.

Economic Environment

The economic environment is probably the best understood of all the parts of the macro-environment. The very existence of econometrics for predicting economic changes, for example, indicates a better understanding of the variables and flows within the economic system than, for example, the social system. Yet, in the mid-seventies economists were having greater problems understanding the system than at any time in recent economic history. As reported by *Business Week* magazine, "Economists will remember 1974 for many things: for the squeeze on energy, for the breathtaking rise in prices, and perhaps for events yet to come. But mainly they will remember 1974 as the year the forecasters blew it."[9]

The economic environment with all its uncertainties permeates the

---

[8] Toffler, *Future Shock.*

[9] "Theory Deserts the Forecasters," *Business Week* (New York), June 29, 1974, p. 50.

business system. Macro-economic conditions are of interest to every top level business manager—marketing or otherwise. Inflation, supplies of basic materials, economic growth rates, interest rates, the money supply and the devaluation of the dollar are of critical interest to marketers.

Governmental Environment

Government is directly related to economic conditions through the exercise of monetary and fiscal policies. The powers of government affect the state of the economy, expenditures on various new technologies, as well as the social state of the country (Figure 3–2). In a democratic form of government, as discussed in Chapter 2, the government has less autonomy and is influenced more by the social system than in more centralized political systems. In the United States, government is comprised of the various local and state governments as well as the federal level. Marketers use lobbying efforts to inform, and sometimes influence, legislative bodies. Marketers also use the courts, particularly the appeal process. Of special importance also is an understanding of the executive branch of government, with its hundreds of offices and agencies, which are charged with carrying out existing legislation.

Governmental activities are oriented toward: (1) maintaining healthy competition within the business system; and (2) preventing deceptive or fraudulent marketing practices. Laws pertaining to the anti-trust area as well as those addressing specific problem areas in the marketing-society interface define the limits of legality for marketing activity. Laws such as the Sherman Anti-Trust Act and the Federal Trade Commission Act, for example, are fundamental to understanding the relationship of government to marketing.

In addition to laws, business has long recognized the need to understand the political processes within the governmental structure. Identification of key legislators and regulatory agencies (such as the Food & Drug Administration) is part of an intelligent approach to strategy relative to government actions. Marketing decision makers also recognize the many government services of value, such as secondary data and information services. Finally, government represents the nation's single largest purchaser of goods and services, so firms such as Xerox Corporation view government markets as a very significant part of their task environment. The governmental environment is discussed in Chapter 6.

Natural Environment

For a discussion of the macro-environment to be complete, the natural or physical environment needs attention. Natural resources, climate, physical barriers and terrain are examples of factors which relate to the role of marketing in a given geographic area. The planet earth has finite resources but increasing numbers of people seem to exhibit almost infinite needs and wants. This natural conflict is aggravated by the pollution and degradation of scarce resources by the production, distribution, and use of products. With a new awareness of these interrelationships, government has moved in recent years toward forcing reduction in pollution levels and better conservation of resources. The relationship of marketing to this social issue is discussed in Chapter 5.

Other relationships to marketing include such things as the effects of different physical environments on consumer needs (e.g., climate and air conditioners) and natural barriers to distribution (e.g., mountains). Yet the natural environment is probably less of a day-to-day factor in marketing decisions than the previously discussed parts of the macro environment and it is therefore less emphasized.

Micro Environment

The micro or organizational environment is more controllable than the macro-environment but it also has a more immediate impact. Corporations which today dominate the business scene are comprised of hundreds or even thousands of specialists within finance, production, accounting and other functional areas. Marketing is one area of specialization within the firm and within marketing several sub-functions exist such as sales, advertising, product planning, marketing research, and distribution. The marketing sub-system should complement the larger management system of the firm although numerous areas of potential conflict exist. Management of the production function, for example, may strive for efficient production runs which conflict with making desirable delivery dates to customers; management of the credit function may wish to incur few if any credit losses whereas assuming more risk could lead to new customers; and engineers may prefer to use costly materials and a functional new product design that is inconsistent with consumer preferences. Resolution of such conflicts is no easy task. It is fundamentally a task of implementing the marketing concept.

Marketers, as well as other managers, are continually faced with an organizational environment that is not entirely supportive of their functions and activities. Decisions are often modified by forces from within the company and even from within the marketing organization itself (e.g., sales vs. advertising). Good decision-making hinges on identifying the uncertainties within the firm as well as from outside. It requires an ability to understand and communicate with other management personalities. Managers are continually developing strategies, often unconsciously, to cope with the internal environment—to gain acceptance of ideas, to convince other management of the value of a marketing program, or to resolve conflicts. The finest marketing program will go unfunded without support from within the firm. It is, therefore, imperative for marketing management to analyze the micro-environment and to formulate appropriate strategies for coping with other functional areas and personalities—just as is required for the environment beyond the firm.

MARKETING DECISION MAKING AND THE ENVIRONMENT

In this section, attention is given to (1) the role of the decision maker at the interface between the organization and the environment, (2) the concept of environmental forces and their relation to the marketing decision process and, (3) specific relationships of the macro-environment to traditional as well as crisis management situations.

The Organization and the Environment

In addition to the environment within the firm, management needs to have some conception of how the organization actually copes with changes in the task and macro-environments. As an organization and institution, business has an admirable record in adapting to external influences. For example, few nonbusiness organizations have demonstrated the flexibility of retailing which has yielded numerous new institutions in response to greater numbers of people, shifts to the suburbs, and other environmental changes. Government and churches serve as examples of organizations which have undergone considerably slower rates of change despite recent cries that our institutions are no longer "relevant" to the needs of the day.

Much of the change within business organizations is undoubtedly due to the fight for survival in a competitive system. Few organizations have this incentive to adapt continually. The survival of the business enterprise is partially dependent on maintaining an organizational structure which allows for continuous input and provides flexibility for adapting. This is increasingly important as the rate of environmental change rises and as new forms of change occur. Yet, organizational structure is but one factor in adapting to change. J. M. Ewell, Vice President-Manufacturing and Employee Relations at Procter & Gamble emphasizes the challenges of change and concludes it is the people comprising the organization that make the difference:

> There is no reason to review the details of the numerous recent and ongoing societal changes which have had dramatic impact, some almost on an overnight basis, on business organizations. Whether it be technological change, structural changes in society as a whole, or the

emergence of powerful new social forces, a business organization is affected. The pressure for change is sometimes subtle but more often obvious, and it shows no tendency to ease off.

Whether we proceed in Procter & Gamble to initiate change voluntarily or whether we have to react to change forced by others, we know we will succeed only to the extent that our organization is properly geared to handle the difficult problems associated with either situation.

And this essential need brings us back full circle to people. It is only with an organization filled with people who see change as desirable and necessary—a way of life—that constructive change can be brought about in an orderly and gradual fashion through self-initiative. And it is only with an organization of people already change-oriented—people who even welcome the challenge of *unanticipated* demand for change— that we can maintain our corporate equilibrium and come back strongly if knocked off balance by a "blind side" blow.[10]

Within the business organization, marketing functions are frequently located at the interface between the firm and the environment and directly feel the rate of change. Within manufacturing enterprises, marketing shoulders the uncertainties associated with consumer or industrial markets. The continued existence of marketing institutions, such as wholesalers, retailers and/or advertising agencies, depends on their ability to interpret and cope with the environment. Marketing is a function which must attract employees who will deal effectively and creatively with uncertainties. Salesmen, market researchers, advertising personnel, and marketing executives span the distance at the interface between one organization and another and between the firm and its customers. In Figure 3–1A imagine placing individual decision makers diagrammatically on the outer border of the figure—because it is people at this organizational boundary that determine how well the firm relates to the environment.

The people who exist at this interface have been termed "boundary agents" and they play a critical role given the rate and importance of environmental change:

. . . There is a growing suspicion that the more relevant criterion of organizational effectiveness is not, as it used to be, that of efficiency, but rather that of adaptability to changes in the environment. . . . To the extent that organizations depend on other organizations for survival and growth, they must establish linkages, or mechanisms of some kind, with those organizations in order to reduce the threats of uncertainty posed by dependence. Ultimately, of course, such linkages take the form of organizational roles, acted out by "boundary agents" who fill these roles. It is not really organizations which interact—it is people. It is such

---

[10] J. M. Ewell, "The Effect of Change on the Organization," reprinted from a speech before the Society for the Advancement of Management by the Procter and Gamble Company (Cincinnati, Ohio), September 1971.

roles, as salesman, purchasing agent, labor negotiator, credit manager, liason personnel, lobbyist, and so forth that constitute the interorganizational linkages.[11]

Although little is known about the traits of good marketers (acting as boundary agents), it could be hypothesized that this person would have characteristics such as above average communication skills, creative abilities, a pleasant personality, an ability to respond quickly to new situations and, generally, a tolerance for uncertainty. This is an area deserving of study. This brief discussion will hopefully be thought-provoking for the student contemplating a boundary-agent type of career such as marketing.

Environmental Forces and Decisions

"AUTO INDUSTRY PUSHED TO MEET STANDARDS" reads the newspaper headline. "CONSUMERISM THREAT TO BUSINESS SYSTEM" says a company president. "BLACKS WIN VICTORY IN FOOD CHAIN DISPUTE." These types of headlines and statements seem almost commonplace today in an era when many businesses continually struggle to cope with changes in the environment. One of the most dramatic examples of environmental change in recent years was offered by the energy crisis that emerged in the mid-1970s. Unanticipated environmental forces severely hit oil companies, automobile makers, and independent auto dealers. The effects were also strongly felt in other industries dependent on large quantities of fuel or on materials such as plastics which are fuel derivatives. The crisis precipitated from the governmental environment, specifically the political oil embargo, as well as from overestimating the availability of scarce resources within the natural environment. In addition, it is felt by some that U.S. oil companies underinvested in refining capacity due, in part, to economic pressures from legislation designed to protect the physical environment.

The one certain thing was the impact. At one point, approximately 60,000 auto production workers were laid off, 16 of the 44 auto plants in the nation were either closed or partially shut down and major plans were altered such as General Motors deferring a major expansion of its Oldsmobile division.[12] For the 25,000 U.S. make, independent auto dealerships, the impact was also sharply felt. Shortage of gasoline at higher prices caused consumers either to delay car purchases or to buy smaller, more economical cars. The effects were largely filtered through

---

[11] Dennis W. Organ, "Linking Pins Between Organizations and Environment," *Business Horizons,* vol. 14, no. 6 (December 1971), p. 74.

[12] This example adapted from Charles B. Camp, "Plunge in Big-Car Sales Leaves Some Dealers With Serious Problems." Reprinted with the permission of *The Wall Street Journal,* © Dow Jones & Company, Inc. (January 30, 1974).

the task environment (Figure 3–1) by changes in consumers and competition. Competitors offering supplies of small, economical cars gained a significant edge over dealers whose inventory was dominated by larger, gas-guzzling autos. By the end of January 1974, the slump in big-car sales turned from a steep 25 percent year-to-year drop of a few weeks previous to an unprecedented rout, with sales running more than 50 percent behind a year earlier. After three good years, the collapsed big car market forced many dealers into a crisis situation. The adjustment process will be felt well into the decade of the seventies as higher gasoline prices become a way of life and consumer preferences stabilize.

What are the implications of this example? First, and most obviously, the dependence of the firm on uncontrollable, environmental variables becomes crystal clear. Although this is an extreme example, knowledgeable observers of the business environment warn that uncontrollable disruptions will likely increase, rather than decrease in the future. Secondly, the case illustrates the concepts presented earlier—the effects from the governmental, natural and economic environments as mediated through the task levels, including effects on marketing intermediaries (dealerships of the automakers), competitors (e.g., foreign car dealers) and buyers (consumers). Finally, it sets the stage for considering the concept of an "environmental force." The Arab governments, the U.S. government, U.S. oil companies and Israel represented key components engaging in processes which ultimately precipitated environmental forces—forces of greater magnitude than many U.S. businesses had felt for at least several decades.

In a marketing context, an "environmental force" may be defined as a *change emanating from the environment with the potential of impacting on marketing opportunities or strategies.* The word "force" denotes the dynamic nature of the concept. Forces are changes which affect decisions and pose opportunities as well as threats to marketing management. As already emphasized, system components (such as government representatives, auto makers and dealers, oil companies, and consumers) engaging in processes (or activities) comprise the environment. To reach the stage of *forces* impinging on decision making, however, the concept of flows must be added. Flows represent the output of individuals, groups and organizations pursuing their goals by engaging in activities. The output of some groups, of course, is the input to others. *If* such flows potentially impact on marketing decision making, either directly or by creating a changed state within the environment, they are environmental forces. Schematically, the process is as follows:

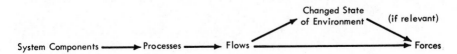

This process contains essential elements necessary to understand environmental forces. Flows during the energy crisis, for example, included political influence, news information to consumers, reduced monetary flows (sales) to dealers, reduced order flows to Detroit, restricted flows of small cars from Detroit to the auto dealerships, and, in the short run, delivery of large cars which were not in demand to dealerships. Certain flows such as reduced revenue impact *directly* as forces on marketing whereas others may be better considered as contributors to a *changed state* in the environment (e.g., large big-car inventories). The important point, however, is that environmental *changes* often require corollary changes within the firm.

In order to understand potential forces, the components, processes and interrelated flows must be understood. Forces (output) occur because of changes in components or processes or because of changes in the inputs they receive. The energy crisis, for example, might have resulted in less disruptive forces (output) upon the automobile industry if the changes in inputs (e.g., less oil) had occurred with less rapidity or if people within government or the oil companies could have somehow changed their activities to reduce the impact. Government, of course, did engage in allocation efforts to try to ameliorate the situation. Yet, firms were still forced into decisions such as curtailing expansion and developing strategies for survival.

Illustrations of Environmental Influences

Various examples of relationships of the macro-environment to marketing decisions (typically mediated through the task environment) are shown in Table 3–1 on pages 88–89. These should be largely self-explanatory although they will be discussed in subsequent chapters which examine the different decision areas. It is evident from Table 3–1 that numerous interrelationships exist which are traditionally mediated via consumers and competitors.

In certain instances crisis management situations arise because environmental forces are not adequately predicted. The scope of analysis may be overly restrictive, the understanding of groups and processes inadequate, or the real relevance and priorities of change to marketing may have been underestimated. Crisis management situations also arise, however, because some forces are simply extremely difficult to predict. Examples of crisis situations precipitated by environmental forces abound. Consider the forces which built up around such products as micro-wave ovens, cyclamates, and pornography, the highlights of which are illustrated in Tables 3–2 on page 90.

In June of 1973, the following report appeared in *Business Week* magazine. It describes attacks and counterattacks of Consumers Union and Amana, Inc. over the safety of the micro-wave oven. As abstracted in Table 3–2, the news media played a prominent role in processing flows of information that became "forces" to management.

Amana Puts the Heat on the Oven Critics

Despite the occasional critical reports on microwave ovens in the five years they have been on the market, sales of the home appliance are expected to top 800,000 units this year. To make sure that forecast does not fall flat, Amana Refrigeration, Inc., a leading manufacturer of the ovens, this week increased its unusually aggressive campaign against *Consumer Reports,* the latest critic of the oven's safety. Amana contends that the magazine's story rating the ovens unacceptable was inaccurate and published only to boost circulation, not help consumers.

The verbal brawl between Amana, a Raytheon Co. subsidiary, and *Consumer Reports,* which now has a circulation of 2.3 million, began last April when the monthly carried a 10-page article headlined: "Microwave Ovens—Not Recommended." The authors contended that they could not find any data establishing "to our satisfaction" what level of microwave radiation emission could be called "unequivocally" safe, although they acknowledged that the 15 ovens tested, including Amana's, met federal safety standards. Even so, they concluded, no oven would receive its "acceptable" rating, because each oven tested leaked a small amount of microwaves.

Retail setback. George C. Foerstner, Amana's president, said that stores carrying the company's microwave models stopped promoting them after the *Consumer Reports* article appeared, thereby stalling the "upsurge" in sales expected during the first half. But, Foerstner says, this will not delay plans to expand production from 12,000 units per month to 20,000 per month.

At a company-sponsored news conference this week, Amana presented Channing H. Lushbough, who worked 21 months as associate director for Consumers Union, the magazine's publisher, until he quit on May 1. Lushbough criticized the magazine's testing procedures and termed the results "speculation." In addition, he said: "There was an editorial slant made to increase sales of the magazine. Reference to consumer safety was a sham."

Lushbough denied that he was a "disgruntled" employee, or that he was being paid for his statement by Amana, which has also submitted them to the Federal Trade Commission as part of their request that FTC make the magazine back up its story with data. "I just don't see how *Consumer Reports* can hold itself out as being objective, when they also try to be advocates for consumers," Lushbough said.

Warren Braren, an associate director of Consumers Union, sharply denied Lushbough's charges and claimed that the former employee was in no position to make them. He had "nothing whatsoever to do with preparation of the *Consumer Reports* article on microwave ovens, or their testing," says Braren.[13]

---

[13] "Amana Puts the Heat on the Oven Critics," *Business Week,* June 16, 1973, p. 30.

TABLE 3-1

Marketing Decisions—Macro-Environment Relationships

Marketing Decision Areas	Macro-Environment				
	Economic	Technological	Governmental	Social	Physical/Natural
Market opportunity analysis	Effects of affluence on markets Demand for services given value of consumer's time	Means of fulfilling opportunities/needs Obsolesence	Government purchases as a market Effects of government action; e.g., pollution equipment industry Legality of opportunities	Qualitative shifts in values and preferences Socio-economic trends Subcultures Needs and wants of people Life styles, classes	Effects on economic status of areas Needs related to physical environment changes (e.g. climate). New substitute products, given shortages
Marketing information systems/research	Economic conditions and effects on research expenditures Research costs Buying power index	Information processing approaches, methods, computer Technological forecasting	Invasion of privacy laws Provision of secondary data, projections, etc.	Social issues of data banks-individual privacy Better information facilities, better serving of needs Social trends (predictions)	Effects on communications systems
Strategy Product	Demand for luxury items Production costs	Required servicing of increasingly complex products New and better products, innovations, inventions	Technology transfer from defense/space programs Product safety legislation Product Safety Commission Food and Drug Administration Patent laws	Materialism vs. purchasing "experiences" Fads Convenience products	Product materials and costs—wood vs. plastic; e.g., solid waste problem Product-related pollutants

Pricing	Inflation psychology Consumer ability to pay prices Price elasticity—effect on volume by price changes	Costs of better technology Productivity increases and lower costs Costs of research and development	Illegal pricing constraints Executive branch "jawboning" against higher prices Price ceilings and regulatory pricing	Perceptions of pricing fairness—social issue Behavioral dimensions of pricing Effects of demographic changes on price elasticity	Costs of materials/resources given scarce supplies
Promotion	More important variable in economically advanced countries Promotion costs—efficient use of media.	New techniques, media such as color TV, etc. Information about products more complex	Laws, e.g., Wheeler-Lea Act, cooling-off legislation Federal Trade Commission Federal Communications Commission	Shifts of promotional themes, in response to social changes Truth in advertising Social desirability of promotion (advertising, personal selling)	Billboards—bad for environment
Distribution	Consumer willingness to pay for nicer outlets, more services Costs of distribution facilities	New marketing institutions Physical distribution methods New transportation modes (BART)	Legal constraints Regulation of transportation industry	Location decisions related to geographic mobility Efficiency of distribution system—social issue Ghetto marketplace structure	Land, water and other natural barriers to transportation Weather, acts of God

TABLE 3–2

Environmental Forces and Crisis Management

	Components ⟶	Processes ⟶	Flows ⟶	Forces and Impact
Micro-wave ovens: (Social/ Technological)	*Amana, Inc.*	Production and distribution of micro-wave ovens	Products, payment, etc.	Sales drop
	Consumers Union	Investigation/ evaluative process	Information on radiation/ safety	Magazine report
	Consumers	Purchasers use	Payment, products	Stop buying
	News media	Reporting	News	Negative publicity
Cyclamates: (Social/ Governmental)	*Abbott Laboratories*	Production and marketing cyclamates Petitioning FDA to resume	Product/ payments	$16 million sales loss
	Food and Drug Administration	Investigation	Legal orders Continuing research	Ban of cyclamates
Pornography: (Government)	*Traditional publishers, film makers*	Production and distribution of sex-related products Court appeals	Books, pay- ments, etc.	Increased uncertainties
	Supreme Court and local courts	Evaluation and interpretative processes	Legal orders Local standards	Stricter limits
	Consumers	Purchasing	Flows of payment, etc.	Cease buying— no supply

Amana was being impacted with environmental forces of significant magnitude. The example illustrates an attempt to reduce the impact by questioning the credibility of the information generated by Consumers Union. Product safety issues are likely to increase in number in the future, particularly with the new Consumer Product Safety Commission to address such problems specifically. Manufacturers will be increasingly required to monitor trends in the social and governmental environment and to meet the expectations of the public.

Another safety related issue which directly pertains to the governmental environment is the case of cyclamates, the artificial sweetener that was banned from the market in 1970.[14] They were the largest sell-

---

[14] This example adapted from Richard D. James, "Remember Cyclamates? Maybe They Weren't So Harmful After All." Reprinted with the permission of *The Wall Street Journal,* © Dow Jones & Company, Inc. (July 21, 1973).

ing artificial sweeteners with sales of $34 million in 1969. Abbott Laboratories, whose cyclamate sales prior to the ban totaled $16 million a year, conducted additional research which suggests the earlier research findings may have been misleading. In the original research, 8 out of 80 rats fed high dosages of cyclamates developed bladder cancer although current research reportedly does not support this. Abbott Labs never completely abandoned their cyclamate facilities and Abbott is planning to petition the FDA for a reversal of its earlier decision. In early 1974, the Food and Drug Administration began a public review of its ban. Quality research prior to releasing the product could have possibly averted the environmental forces which "hit" the drug-industry. Because of the publicity associated with the cyclamate issue, consumers may not buy now even if cyclamates are shown to be safe.

The final example in Table 3–2 concerns the impact of the 1973 Supreme Court decision against pornography on traditional publishers and filmmakers. As reported in the *Wall Street Journal:*

> "The decision wasn't supposedly aimed at the serious filmmaker," said Jack Valenti, president of the Motion Picture Association of America, a trade group. "But already the Georgia supreme court has declared obscene 'Carnal Knowledge,' " a serious film made by Mike Nichols.

> ❖ ❖ ❖ ❖ ❖

> The book and magazine publishers and the movie companies have formed an ad hoc coalition to seek to mitigate the impact of the decision on their industries. The coalition plans to petition the court to clarify its decision, to propose model obscenity legislation for states and localities and to amass legal defense funds for expected court fights by booksellers and filmmakers.

> ❖ ❖ ❖ ❖ ❖

> United Artists has been taking a special approach to marketing the film because of its subject matter and has shown it to district attorneys, prosecutors, mayors and church officials in many cities before opening the film in local theaters.

> ❖ ❖ ❖ ❖ ❖

> Mr. Bernstein, the Random House president, says the decision will cost the publishing industry "millions of dollars" and "hours and hours of effort." Monitoring the 50 state legislatures to see what obscenity laws will be passed "will run into six-figures with fees to attorneys in capital cities alone," Mr. Bernstein says.[15]

---

[15] Earl C. Gottschalk, Jr., "Pornography Ruling Causing Confusion and Chaos, Many Traditional Publishers and Filmmakers Say." Reprinted with the permission of *The Wall Street Journal,* © Dow Jones & Company, Inc. (July 16, 1973).

This example illustrates plans to cope with environmental forces by (1) monitoring interpretation of laws at the local level, (2) attempting to work with district attorneys and Mayors (components) in order to predict the outcome of selling films and materials that could be questioned, and (3) developing strategies for modifying and/or adapting to the forces. Prediction is the key to avoiding crisis management situations as well as the mitigation of more traditional forces.

MONITORING AND FORECASTING ENVIRONMENTAL CHANGE

Avoiding crises is dependent on anticipating events within the marketing environment in time either to change the operation of the firm or to develop effective counterstrategies. Attempting to peer through the haze into the future social, technological and other environments is a difficult task. Some changes are largely unpredictable because they occur with such rapidity or because of too little understanding of the underlying processes. Yet with the environment changing more and more rapidly, it becomes increasingly incumbent upon management to attempt to forecast the future. The necessary scope and components of any environmental forecast include:

1. For the environmental processes of interest, develop an understanding of relevant variables and interrelationships.
2. Identify the nature of relevant change processes and related flows. Obtain information for use in analysis and projections.
3. In conjunction with (2), select one or more suitable forecasting methods for generating estimates of future trends and values.
4. Analyze and interpret forecast results.
5. Attach importance measures and priorities to environmental forces, based on the probability of impact, magnitude, and timing.
6. Determine appropriate management strategy and tactics based on (5).

The first two components cited above are necessary to *monitor* the environment, not to forecast it. Many marketers are having difficulty even monitoring the environment, much less forecasting it. The relative stage of development varies by the type of environmental process. Economic processes, as noted earlier, are better understood than social or technological processes and, consequently, forecasting in economics utilizes the full approach above as a matter of course. Forecasting social changes, on the other hand, is rudimentary because the processes themselves are not well understood. As stated by one group:

> Prevalent thinking about [social systems] tends to characterize them as static and fixed in contrast to engineering systems, which have well-

founded scientific "principles" that can be used to comprehend and/or guide change occurring in them. No such laws of social behavior are at hand. They are not likely to be available in the near future. Nevertheless, we must be able to come to grips with our changing social system in ways that enable us to deal with its ramifications in an intelligent and flexible fashion. . . .

✿ ✿ ✿ ✿ ✿

In short, the current state of the art does not provide a vehicle for continued monitoring. As a result, there is no effective early warning system for predicting future social change and emerging social problems.[16]

Although directed toward city management, this is equally applicable to marketing management in the business firm. Environmental forecasting for much of the social as well as technological environment is intuitive and judgmental, and compared to forecasting the economic environment, relatively unsophisticated. Forecasting attempts in the governmental sector also fall into the "monitoring and judgmental" stage of development although the processes are simpler than, for example, the social system with typically fewer components (e.g., agency directors and legislators) than in the social system (masses of people). Governmental processes are specified in the constitution (and modified and refined by precedent) which greatly facilitates monitoring. Furthermore by, for example, pooling the anticipated votes of legislators on specific bills, prediction may be simple. Yet attempts to identify general trends, the effects of various influences on legislators, and other uncertainties still leave governmental forecasting an undeveloped area.

Several categories of forecasting techniques are shown in Table 3–3 (page 94) in conjunction with macro-environmental sectors. Monitoring is included in addition to forecasting techniques such as extrapolation methods, models (including descriptive, predictive, normative), and subjective/judgmental techniques. For each part of the macro-environment (excluding natural), examples and observations are presented.

Descriptive (as opposed to predictive) modeling tends to dominate all but the economic cell which, consistent with the above discussion, leaves forecasting attempts for the other environments largely within the monitoring, extrapolation or subjective approaches. Each of the approaches will be given additional attention in the technological, social, and governmental chapters (Chapters 4, 5, and 6).

---

[16] Charles Eastman, Normal J. Johnson and Kenneth Kortanek, "A New Approach To An Urban Information Process," *Management Science,* vol. 16, no. 12 (August 1970), pp. B733–34.

TABLE 3-3

Monitoring and Forecasting Environmental Change

	Social	Technological	Economic	Governmental
Monitoring (continually assessing position currently)	Social indicators Yankelovich social trends monitor Census data	Assessing current state of the art Government publications	Economic indicators Government and industry reports	Lobbying activities Government reports News media
Extrapolation Methods (time series and other methods utilizing historical data)	Intuitive extensions of social trends (e.g. values) into future Socio-economic projections (e.g., population, divorces)	Projections of gross technological change Projections in specific areas (e.g., trend extrapolation of aircraft speeds)	Long-range extrapolations of economic progress Macro-economic projections (e.g., housing starts, capital expenditures, personal consumption expenditures	Trend analysis of expenditure levels in certain areas (e.g., defense) Energy projections Regulatory trends
Models (describing components and interrelationships)	Descriptive, static models of social systems Pioneering computer simulations at task-level Consumer behavior models	Correlative and dynamic modeling	Econometrics Existence of several simulations of U.S. economy Regional economic development	Legislative processes and flows of power and influence
Subjective-Judgmental Methods (intuition, brainstorming, delphi approach)	"Think tank" approaches to future social environment Forecasting future of cities, crime, leisure, education, values, institutions Use of "experts"	Forecasting scientific breakthroughs Predicting economical applications of existing technologies, technology transfer Industry task force study of technological trends	Economic forecasts by a panel of experts	Collective opinions, predictions of trade associations, lobbyists Use of "experts" in government

SUMMARY AND CONCLUSIONS

The marketing environment includes more types of changes than only a few decades ago and the rate of change continues to move upward. Environmental factors require that marketing management be fully cognizant of its dependence on uncontrollable or environmental variables in decision-making. This chapter provides a framework and perspective for viewing the myriad of factors important to marketing management and also provides the basis for defining environmental forces. Forces are the end result (or output) of economic, social, technological, governmental and natural processes. It is, therefore, critical to understand the activities, or goal-oriented processes carried out by individuals and organizations in order to understand the environment. Forces from the macro-environment may be flows which impact on the decision-maker or forces may be changed states within the environment, the end result of dynamic processes, including flows. Forces from the macro-environment are often mediated by the task environment of marketing intermediaries, competitors, and buyers. Environmental forces may impact with such force and/or rapidity to precipitate a crisis management situation. The key to coping with the environment is anticipating or forecasting potential forces before they are imminent although at our current level of understanding, it is an ambitious task for marketers even to effectively monitor most parts of the environment. The remaining chapters in this section examine the technological, social, and governmental facets of the macro-environment as they relate to marketing decision-making.

EXERCISES FOR DISCUSSION AND REVIEW

1. Select a corporation or nonbusiness organization that you are familiar with and identify several of the specific types of micro, mediating, and macro-environmental influences of potential importance to management of the organization.

2. Assume you are a marketing executive in a firm of your choice. Using the marketing management decision framework presented in Chapter 1, discuss the nature and scope of environmental analysis as it relates to the corporate mission and each of the various marketing decision areas (e.g., market opportunity analysis and product, channel, promotion and pricing decisions.

3. Suppose you are the chief marketing executive for a large steel company and you have been asked by the president to develop a plan for managerially analyzing the marketing environment over the next decade. Develop an outline of how you would proceed with the formulation of the plan. Be as specific as possible and make any assumptions that are necessary.

4. Chrysler Corporation in the early 1970s launched a major product development effort for their full size and intermediate size automobiles. The new automobiles reached the marketplace in the mid-1970s concurrent with high gasoline prices, double digit inflation, and world-wide recession. These environmental forces had a major impact upon Chrysler sales and profit performance. Based on your knowledge of the environmental analysis task from this chapter, develop an argument either for: (1) supporting Chrysler management's inability to forecast relevant environmental changes or (2) showing how the firm's present problems could have been avoided or at least reduced in impact. As part of this analysis, carefully define selected "environmental forces" within the framework suggested in the chapter.

5. Why is marketing (as one function within the firm) more likely to find it necessary to cope with the environment than other organizational functions such as finance, accounting, and manufacturing? Recognizing the regular interaction between marketing and the external environment, how might the role of boundary agents be consciously integrated into the marketing function?

6. In contemporary society, business has been more responsive to environmental change than many other institutions such as churches, government, and universities. What characteristics of business firms enable them to adjust to change more rapidly? Does the marketing function play a special role in the adapting process?

7. Are there any reasons to anticipate an easing of environmental pressures in the future (both with respect to the *type* of forces as well as their *magnitude*)? Why or why not?

8. Differentiate the "micro" or managerial viewpoint that pervades this chapter from the "macro" perspective in Chapter 2. Is this chapter also based on an "environmental" view of marketing and business? Discuss.

9. During the 1970s, inflationary pressures and shortages of basic materials created severe business problems. Select either inflation *or* shortages and identify several effects this condition could have on marketing activity. Then engage in a limited review of the literature to check your reasoning abilities.

4

The Technological
Environment

The very lifeblood of many firms is dependent not only on an awareness but on an understanding of technological processes. Consider, for example, events during the early seventies. DuPont wrote off $100 million on corfam, General Electric and Radio Corporation of America lost millions in the computer business, and Rolls Royce went bankrupt over jet engines. At the same time, Xerox, Polaroid, and Texas Instruments continued sensational growth with new technologies. Although these failures and successes cannot be attributed solely to technological change, understanding and anticipating technological change promises to be one increasingly significant aspect of corporate strategy.

For marketers, the technological environment is important in several ways. As part of the marketing macro-environment, technological impacts are felt both in the influence that technology has on other parts of the macro-environment as well as by the direct effects of technology on the task and organizational environments of marketing (Figure 4–1). Technological change directly affects the economic and social environments for marketing as well as, to a lesser degree, the governmental and natural environments. Technology in Figure 4–1 affects decision making by its impact on marketing intermediaries, competition, and buyers and markets (the task environment), as well as through its effects on the organizational environment. Threats as well as opportunities bridge the various levels of the task environment (Figure 4–1). Market response as well as innovation forged the success of the "horseless carriage," solid state color television, and the polaroid camera. Entire industries emerged from such technological developments as the computer, office copiers, and air conditioning.

But the impact of technology on marketing goes far beyond new products. Technology affects the social and economic environment for doing business. American consumers benefit from the most labor-free

97

FIGURE 4–1

Technology and Marketing Decision Making

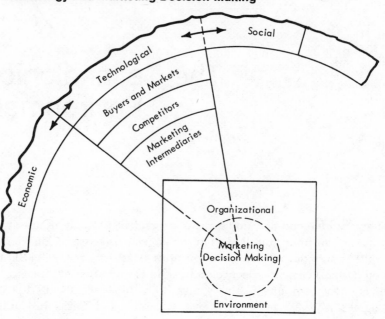

and leisure oriented society the world has even known. At the same time, consumers become confused by thousands of technological influences that confront them daily. Illustrative of these stimuli are sophisticated mass communications technology, an onrush of increasingly complex products and services and, generally, a rate of change unprecedented in the history of the world. As society changes, consumers and markets change: thus, the effects of technological change are often

FIGURE 4–2

Technology and Marketing

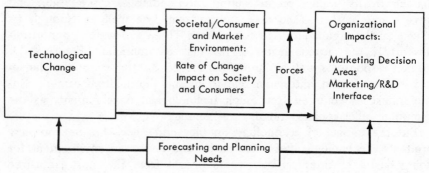

mediated through the consumer and market environments which directly impact the marketing organization (see Figure 4-2). Technological processes may also impact *directly* on the firm (Figure 4-2). These processes generate *flows* of new methods, equipment, products, processes, tools and techniques—that is, new applications of knowledge, which extend the existing level of technological development, or "state of the art." Direct effects of relevant changes, or forces, may be seen as they alter the tools and concepts used by management and as they impact on marketing decision areas such as products, pricing, distribution, promotion, and marketing research. Understanding and capitalizing on innovations relating to these decision areas requires the best talents of marketing management.

RATE AND SIGNIFICANCE OF TECHNOLOGICAL CHANGE

From a historical perspective, marketers have devoted little time to understanding the technological environment. So why the interest now? First, the redefinition of marketing within more and more firms has expanded the scope of marketing beyond just the "selling" function (Chapter 1) to encompass product and other decision areas and, secondly, the sheer rate of technological change today requires a closer monitoring of potential threats and opportunities. Although the *existing* state of technological development poses constraints on decision situations, increasingly attention is focused on the *dynamic* nature of technology and its impact throughout the marketing environment.

First, what is technology? To many, technology represents a machine. Although machines (such as computers) are manifestations of technology, this is an inadequate conception of this powerful and pervasive influence. Technology is applied science, and encompasses both the physical and social sciences. Technology can be broadly viewed as a process of extending human capability, and thus may include tools, techniques, products, processes, and methods.[1] The results of technology include for example, fiber optic devices for examining the interior of a human stomach; micro-wave ovens; management science analytical models; and communications satellites.

As illustrated in Figure 4-3, technological change is a complex process (even when oversimplified!). Although industry plays an important role in the *inventive* process, business plays an increasing role as we proceed from invention to innovation, adoption and diffusion. Marketing is particularly influential at the diffusion stage, that is, the spreading of innovation throughout society. Marketing activity is often designed to facilitate and to increase the rate of diffusion both by communicating

---

[1] Donald A. Schon, *Technology and Change* (New York: Delacorte Press, 1967), p. 1.

FIGURE 4–3

Technological Change

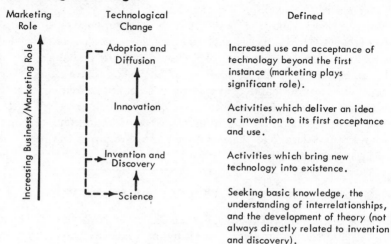

Marketing Role	Technological Change	Defined
	Adoption and Diffusion	Increased use and acceptance of technology beyond the first instance (marketing plays significant role).
	Innovation	Activities which deliver an idea or invention to its first acceptance and use.
	Invention and Discovery	Activities which bring new technology into existence.
	Science	Seeking basic knowledge, the understanding of interrelationships, and the development of theory (not always directly related to invention and discovery).

the availability of products as well as through identifying the existing needs of consumers to guide the development of new technology (products and services).

Rate of Change

At least four generalizations may be made about the current rate of technological change. First, *all the technological development experienced by humankind has occurred within a mere moment of history.* As expressed by Toffler:

> . . . if the last 50,000 years of man's existence were divided into lifetimes of approximately sixty-two years each, there have been about 800 such lifetimes. Of these 800, fully 650 were spent in caves.
>
> Only during the last seventy lifetimes has it been possible to communicate effectively from one lifetime to another—as writing made it possible to do. Only during the last six lifetimes did masses of men ever see a printed word. Only during the last four has it been possible to measure time with any precision. Only in the last two has anyone anywhere used an electric motor. And the overwhelming majority of all the material goods we use in daily life today have been developed within the present, the 800th, lifetime.[2]

If we were to equate the earth's history to the distance around the world, the last 50 years, the period of most rapid technological development,

---

[2] Alvin Toffler, *Future Shock* (New York: Random House, 1970), p. 13.

would equal *one foot*.[3] There is no question that recent decades have witnessed an unprecedented acceleration in technological change; for that reason, people are today experiencing a unique chapter in human history. Consider for example, the projections made in the late 1940s concerning the development of electronic computers:

> While the computer was a "major scientific revolution," everybody "knew" that its main use would be science and warfare. As a result, the most extensive market research study undertaken at that time reached the conclusion that the world computer market would, at most, be able to absorb 1,000 computers by the year 2,000. Now, only twenty-five years later, there are some 150,000 computers installed in the world, most of them doing the most mundane bookkeeping work.[4]

Secondly, to understand this rate of change one must recognize the nature of technology—*it feeds on itself*. A given level of technological development provides the ideas and concepts for additional development. Major new inventions combine in multiplicative ways with other technologies to advance technology even further—and on and on. Technology gives rise to new technology.[5]

Thirdly, *various determinants of technological change, such as the number of scientists, expenditures on research and development, and growth of "knowledge industries," point toward more technological change.* It is often estimated that nine out of every ten scientists who ever lived are alive today. As shown in Figure 4–4, R&D outlays increased from about $5 billion in 1953 to over $30 billion in 1973. In 1973 R&D spending was split about evenly between federal and non-federal areas but because government transfers monies to industry, industry actually carries out nearly three-fourths of the nation's R&D effort. Besides industry, universities and other non-profit organizations receive some government monies and accomplish about 17 percent of the total R&D effort. Despite a short-term reduction in real dollar expenditures in the early seventies, by 1975 it was predicted that U.S. R&D would rise to over $35 billion with significant increases in real dollar expenditures.[6]

Also fueling technological changes, the so-called "knowledge industries," producers and distributors of ideas and information, have grown

[3] Frank K. Shallenberger, "Management and the Challenge of Change," in Robert J. Holloway and Robert S. Hancock, eds., *The Environment of Marketing Management* (3d ed.; New York: John Wiley and Sons, 1974), pp. 144–45.

[4] Peter F. Drucker, *Management: Tasks, Responsibilities, Practices* (New York: Harper & Row, Publishers, 1974), p. 331.

[5] W. Jack Duncan, *Decision Making and Social Issues* (Hinsdale, Ill.: The Dryden Press, 1973), p. 20; Toffler, *Future Shock*, p. 24.

[6] "Research and Development Appears to Escape the Recession," *The Wall Street Journal*, February 6, 1975, p. 1; Lawrence Lessing, "Why the U.S. Lags in Technology," *Fortune*, vol. 86, no. 4 (April 1972), pp. 69–71, 150.

FIGURE 4–4

R&D Funding Trends, 1953–73

| | Average Annual Rate of Growth | | | | | |
| | Current | | | Constant | | |
Year	Total	Federal	Non-federal	Total	Federal	Non-federal
1953–61......	13.7%	16.3%	10.1%	11.3%	13.9%	7.8%
1961–67......	8.4	7.7	9.6	6.3	5.6	7.5
1967–73......	4.1	1.7	7.4	−.1	−2.4	3.1

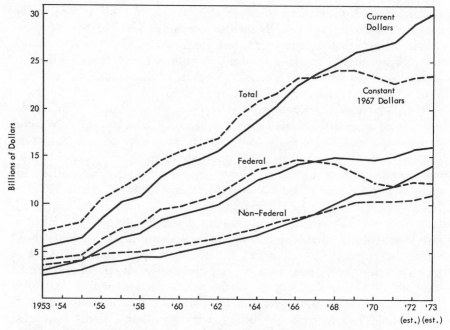

Note: The GNP implicit price deflator was used to convert from current to constant dollars.
Source: National Patterns of R&D Resources, 1953–1973 NSF 73–303 (Washington: National Science Foundation, February 1973).

dramatically; they accounted for one-quarter of U.S. GNP in 1955, one third in 1965 and by the late 1970s will account for one half of the total national product.[7]

Fourthly, *the long-run trend of technological advance will continue upward, despite occasional cycles and redirection of priorities.* Because

---

[7] Peter F. Drucker, *The Age of Discontinuity* (New York: Harper and Row, 1969), p. 263.

technology feeds on itself and because the long-run outlook for R&D expenditures appears strong, there is little reason to expect a downturn. Methods of measuring technological change are admittedly crude, however. As an adjunct to economics, technological change has been roughly measured by studying changes in productivity per worker. A more direct measurement is reported by Lynn where twenty major innovations from different historical periods were studied to determine the amount of time taken from "incubation" to "diffusion."[8] Over the past 60 to 70 years, he concludes that the incubation period (from technical feasibility to apparent commercial potential) has been cut from an average of 30 to 9 years, the commercial development phase from an average of 7 to 5 years, and with accelerated diffusion, lapsed time required for technology to produce widespread effects on the economy and society decreased by a factor of four or more. Although these results have limitations, this quantitative measure supports more casual observations of technological trends.

Technology and Social Change

Perhaps the least immediate but most important effect of changing technology is its impact on consumers and on the social environment. Although social change is examined in the next chapter, it is important to note the close interrelationship between technology and society. Technology has been defined in terms of extending human capability and, as this capability is extended, the lives of people are changed. Imagine the effects on lifestyles if the automobile were banned! Eliminate air conditioning, television, wash n' wear fabrics, computers, telephones, and jet travel, and even more dramatic social changes would occur. A culture may be changed in one of two ways: by diffusion, including borrowing traits or patterns from other cultures—or by the invention or discovery of new cultural elements within the society.[9] The addition of new traits or patterns will, in turn, produce changes in the social structure. For example, the changing role of women is one of the most significant social developments in recent history—and there is no question that technology helped to encourage that change. In the kitchen cupboards are instant potatoes, cake mixes, and dinner mixes. In the freezer are instant pies, sea food, snacks and even complete dinners. Consider the wide array of time and labor saving appliances. Is it any

---

[8] Frank Lynn, "Our Accelerating Technological Change: Its Impact and Effect," *Management Review,* vol. 67 (March 1967), pp. 65–70; condensed from *Automation and Economic Progress* (Englewood Cliffs, N.J.: Prentice-Hall, 1966).

[9] Kimball Young and Raymond W. Mack, *Sociology and Social Life* (New York: American Book Company, 1962), p. 455.

wonder that the role of the housewife has been revolutionized, that more and more women are entering the labor force and that women want and expect liberation? The effects are pervasive—including the impact on markets and marketing.

Also consider the societal impact of communications technology. The family, as a social institution, has been altered with even the family life style being formed around television. Television may replace family discussion during the evening meal, if not the evening meal itself, and preferences for different television programs contributes to parents and children viewing TV in different rooms. Various media have made contemporary America the best informed, although not necessarily the most satisfied, nation in the world. Important events broadcast "live" from the other side of the earth or from the moon help to insure that the general functioning of society will accelerate by speeding information feedback. Decisions and actions of people in all parts of society depend on feedback from across the country or from another continent—which, until recent decades, was painfully slow.

While technology dramatically affects the social behavior and structure of a society, the debate continues as to which is the more fundamental—the social system or technology. Is new technology the cause of social change, is social change the cause of new technology, or both? Technology speeds social change—but is technology uncontrollable (as social critics suggest), or does society ultimately determine the rate and direction of technological change and its effects? One must conclude that, *although the effects of technology on society are sometimes random and too often unanticipated, people within society ultimately dictate the rate and direction of technological change.* Allocation of research and development funds by government and industry as well as legislation affecting technological development, at least over the long run, reflect the will of the citizenry in a free society. In recent years, for example, technology has actually lagged new social values concerning pollution abatement and the physical environment. Clean air and water are only possible at great cost—cost which will likely diminish with new technology. New social values also surfaced and prevailed in the fight against the supersonic transport (SST) (Chapter 3). *Business Week* magazine, at the turn of the decade, referred to a ". . . dawning recognition that technology's contribution to good living, albeit enormous in totality, has been fragmentary, undirected, and unanalyzed." They go on to conclude that, "There are signs that the nation is awakening from its technological trance in time to reassert its right to make rational choices."[10] Anticipating the social (and other) costs and benefits

---

[10] "Human Needs Gain the Top Priority," *Business Week* (December 6, 1969) pp. 150, 154.

of anticipated technologies (i.e., technology assessment) is receiving new emphasis as government requires more attention to social/technological relationships.[11]

Technology Changes Consumers

Consumers are in a position to purchase a vast number of satisfactions in the marketplace. Product choice is truly phenomenal. Thousands of different retail stores are stocked with millions of products, models, and brands. In the early stages of economic development, highest priority is given to providing for the basic needs of the population—and few consumers complain when products meeting their general needs are inexpensively mass produced and mass marketed. But as affluence has increased in the United States, more and more people have become less and less satisfied with standardized products. Contemporary American consumers seek an identity of their own, evidenced particularly by the young, and mass marketing has decreased substantially in importance.

Instead there has been increasing splintering and segmenting of markets based on the needs and wishes of smaller and smaller groups of consumers. It is sometimes overlooked that *better satisfaction of consumer needs is made possible not only by consumer affluence, but perhaps more importantly, by technology.* As production and marketing technology becomes more sophisticated, the cost of introducing variations declines.[12] Thus consumers have greater opportunity than ever before to satisfy their individual needs—and the trend continues.

The effects of technology on consumers are not all positive, however. Some consumers purportedly feel overburdened by too much choice, product complexity, and information—some of which is useless for sound consumer decision making. *Overchoice* has been called "the point at which the advantages of diversity and individualization are cancelled by the complexity of the buyer's decision making process."[13] Also, as more and more new products are introduced, more and more products become obsolete, an experience which is aggravating to many consumers. Obsolescence may result from (1) physical deterioration, (2) new and better ways to perform the functions carried out by old products, as well as from (3) the "keeping up with the Joneses" and related socio-psychological type of phenomena. New technological variations of products may lead consumers to believe they have been tricked and

---

[11] Emmanuel G. Mesthene, *Technological Change: Its Impact on Man and Society* (Cambridge: Harvard University Press), 1970, pp. 42–43.

[12] Alvin Toffler, *Future Shock*, p. 228.

[13] Ibid., p. 231.

that planned obsolescence is a scheme (although building a longer-lasting product could require prohibitively higher product costs).

It may be argued that obsolescence and the "throw-away society" contributes to *transcience,* or a sense of impermanence in people's lives.[14] Obsolescence contributes to a rate of change surrounding the individual that may lead to *future shock,* a state of disorientation (see Chapter 3) caused by a lag between the pace of environmental change and the limited pace of human response.[15] In his fascinating and well-documented book, Alvin Toffler advanced the thesis that the rate of technological change and its effects on society are creating severe problems for people in all roles, including consumers. Although product technologies impinge directly on the consumer, changes in advertising and mass communications and innovations in distribution also have many of the same positive as well as negative effects.

TECHNOLOGY AND MARKETING MANAGEMENT

The technological environment surrounds and permeates the marketing organization, affecting decision areas of promotion, distribution and pricing. Yet the greatest single interface between technology and marketing is the product decision area. The relevance of technology to a given firm is highly influenced by the company's products: whether they are "high technology" in nature or if they are vulnerable to a rapidly changing technology.

Technology and the Marketing Concept

Marketing and technology are inexorably interrelated by the customer orientation dictated by the marketing concept. Marketing is the link between product R&D and customers—and without a customer orientation, this link becomes superfluous. In the now classic article "Marketing Myopia," Levitt argued against a product orientation and encouraged firms not to view themselves as goods producers but as customer-satisfiers.[16] Short-sighted or "myopic" focus on specific product technologies as opposed to the generic needs of customers is a certain path to failure. In integrating the marketing concept and technology, it has been observed that:

> If science is knowledge about man and his environment; if technology is the application of this knowledge to achieve desired results; and if

---

[14] Ibid., pp. 46, 59–62.

[15] Ibid., p. 3.

[16] Theodore Levitt, "Marketing Myopia," *Harvard Business Review,* vol. 38 (July–August, 1960), pp. 45–46. © *Harvard Business Review.*

marketing is concerned with matching the needs and wants of potential buyers with profitable want-satisfying products and services through market transactions, then clearly, it is in the general interest of mankind everywhere to seek integration of science, technology, and marketing.[17]

It is the role of marketing to channel "want-satisfying products and services" to customers and so management must continually engage in the "creative destruction"[18] of its existing products by seeking new and better ways to meet market demands. Modern management is predicated on marketing as an important link between technology and markets.

A case illustrating a product vs. a marketing orientation surfaced in the mid-seventies with the electric automobile reported to have everything except a market.[19] A University of Wisconsin study concluded that people buy for their maximum needs rather than their average needs and that, therefore, electric cars would be attractive only to ecologically inclined urban and suburban families earning more than $10,000. Battery technology limited the outlook. Speeds were generally limited to below 50 miles per hour, temperature extremes adversely affected battery efficiency and the batteries were costly. Despite these hurdles, several small firms were making plans to market electric cars. Instead, Ford Motor Co., which reportedly has the largest investment in the electric car of the big auto makers, was pessimistic about market acceptance. Ford was hoping to perfect a sodium-sulfur battery with a 20-year life before introducing the car to the market. As stated by a Ford spokesman, "We could start making a lousy product now, but would there be a market for it?" Other smaller firms disagreed as to product quality and are proceeding with production and marketing plans. Although the circumstances are not completely clear, the smaller firms appear to be less market and more product technology oriented than Ford Motor. The related success or failure story has yet to be written but the common story of ignoring markets and pushing products appears clear.

Differences between marketing and R&D people require special organizational efforts to insure communication and interchange. General Electric, in the earliest days of the marketing concept, established a product planning unit within marketing to help bridge the distance between technical researchers and customers. R&D often represents a

---

[17] Robert L. Clewett, "Integrating Science, Technology, and Marketing: An Overview," *Proceedings of the Fall Conference of the American Marketing Association,* 1966, p. 11, published by the American Marketing Association.

[18] Levitt, "Marketing Myopia."

[19] This example abstracted from, Thomas Failla, "Electric Autos Have Everything—Except a Market," Associated Press Newstory, in *The Times-Union,* Rochester, New York, August 3, 1974, p. 8A.

line function[20] and, along with marketing, reports directly to the highest level corporate management. To facilitate cooperation within the organization therefore, most large firms have such mechanisms as new product departments, product committees, venture analysis groups or long-range planning departments (see Chapter 14). For example, the Carborundum Company has a new product branch in the R&D division which is charged with advancing new products from the laboratory to existing or new operating divisions. Each product group is responsible for all aspects of developing and marketing the new product, including R&D, market research, engineering, production cost studies, and pricing. In many instances, the research people move with the product from the laboratory into production and sales.[21]

Ultimately, top management, in charting the course of the enterprise, must monitor and incorporate a changing technological environment into decision making. In assessing who should plan for change, Levitt writes:

> Certainly the marketing people are in a good position to keep their eyes peeled. But the things that are at stake for the company are too important for the highest level of management *not* to get seriously involved in. It is the unique and inescapable job of top management itself to assure the direction and destiny of the company. This means that top management must turn on its radar sets and put up its antenna more systematically than anyone else in the company.[22]

Significant technological innovation takes place in organizations of any size *only* when top management is personally involved and lends its full support.[23] The experiences of the Magnavox Co. in the early 1970s illustrate the adverse affects of management's incorrect assessment of technology and market trends. This well-known manufacturer of television, radio-phonographs, and other appliances and parts as well as of specialized electronic equipment has, for many years, held a strong reputation for quality and profitability in its industry. During the years of growth in sales of color television sets, Magnavox reached a point where about one-third of its total sales were contributed by this product group. The firm ranked third after RCA and Zenith in sales of TV sets. In 1971 top management acknowledged that an incorrect assessment was made of the need to shift to the use of all solid-state electronics in

---

[20] Keith Davis, and Robert L. Blomstrom, *Business, Society, and Environment: Social Power and Social Response*, 2d ed. (New York: McGraw-Hill Book Company, 1971), p. 61.

[21] Victor J. Danilov, "Bridging the R&D and Marketing Gap," *Proceedings of the June Conference of the American Marketing Association*, 1967, p. S–64.

[22] Theodore Levitt, *Innovation in Marketing* (New York: McGraw-Hill Book Company, 1962), pp. 35–36.

[23] Donald R. Schoen, "Managing Technological Innovations," *Harvard Business Review*, vol. 47 (May–June, 1969), p. 167.

FIGURE 4-5

Market/Technology Interdependence

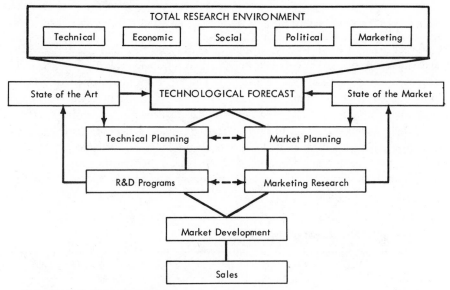

Source: Battelle Memorial Institute.

their TV sets.[24] Management decided to delay conversion to 100 percent solid state sets until 1973. Competitors that had already made the conversion were able to persuade consumers to buy all solid-state sets through aggressive promotion coupled with demonstrated reductions in service calls. Magnavox lost sales, market share, profits, and dealer confidence (Magnavox has for years followed a strategy of direct distribution to a limited number of carefully selected dealers). Management recognized the strategic error quickly. Yet, due to the design and production lead time required to develop a complete line of solid-state TV receivers, conversion could not be immediate. The firm lost third place in sales, allowing Sears and Motorola to move up in the ranks. In 1974 the firm's weakened profit position plus the impact of a depressed stock market caused their shares to decline to such a low level that purchase of the firm became attractive to other firms. The North American Phillips company acquired a controlling interest in Magnavox. While the delay of the decision to convert to full solid state technology was not the only factor that contributed to Magnavox's problem in the early 1970s, it was clearly a very significant element. The need for high-level interdependent ties between marketers and technologists is illustrated in Figure 4-5. *Technical* planning and research must be coordinated with

[24] "Magnavox Tries for a TV Comeback," *Business Week* (April 14, 1973), pp. 49-59.

market planning and research for successful market development and, of course, sales.

Sources of Technological Innovations

Given the risk of payoff from basic or "pure" research, companies instead tend to concentrate their R&D monies in relatively short-run development of existing technologies. Due to anti-trust problems, companies cannot pool their resources to work on high risk development nor does the government consistently support basic research. Further, it is well known that many of the truly significant technological developments of the past few decades have come from industries where one would *not* have logically expected them. Table 4–1 pointedly illustrates this fact. In addition, this was true of xerography, frozen foods, and the

TABLE 4–1

Sources of Technological Innovations

Concept	Logical Concept Source	Actual Concept Source	Initial Commercial Support
Synthetic fiber (nylon).	Textile industry	Chemical industry	DuPont
Diesel locomotive.	Railroad equipment industry	Automobile industry	General Motors
Numerical control for machine tools.	Machine-tool industry	Small control manufacturer	U.S. Air Force
Ball-point pen.	Fountain pen manufacturer	Hungarian sculptor and chemist (Biro brothers)	Individual
Polaroid film.	Photographic industry	Independent scientist (Dr. Land)	Independently financed
Color film.	Photographic industry	Two musicians (Godowsky and Mannes)	Eastman Kodak
DDT insecticide.	Insecticide or agricultural chemicals manufacturer	Synthetic dye manufacturer	Same as source
Computer.	Business machine manufacturer	Universities	U.S. government
Hydrofoil boats.	Major shipbuilder or U.S. Navy	Inventor of the telephone	Italian businessman

Source: James R. Bright, "On Sources of Technological Innovations," *Research, Development, And Technological Innovation: An Introduction* (Homewood, Ill.: Richard D. Irwin, Inc., 1964), p. 380.

jet engine. As Levitt has written, "The inability or refusal of companies to see the opportunities produced by change often seems to be a peculiar affliction of big, well-organized companies!"[25] The pressure in large firms is for profitable output and this is most easily found by squeezing existing technologies instead of developing fundamentally new ones. As *Fortune* pointed out:

> As time goes by, improvements become smaller and increasingly trivial. A point in time is finally reached, as the industry ages and agglomerates into a few big units, when the research becomes mainly "defensive," i.e., designed mainly to protect the established product and the industry's heavy capital investment in it. This stage occurs, according to one of Parkinson's satiric laws, when research is moved into huge, new, handsomely accoutered and magnificently outfitted laboratories, seemingly designed to keep out revolutionary new ideas, or at least to slow them down to a evolutionary crawl.[26]

Thus, despite the rational appearing R&D process, major breakthroughs often result from random appearing processes carried out by the "garage inventor." Despite heavy R&D expenditures by many firms, there appears surprisingly little relation between expenditures and output. The large organization too often seems to inhibit major breakthroughs and provides a sterile environment for the truly creative mind. There is ". . . widespread agreement that 'entrepreneurs,' 'innovators,' 'product champions,' or some similarly committed individuals are essential to innovation in organizations. But there is no real agreement on what makes an individual such a person, how you find him, whether he can be developed, or how you encourage him in an organization."[27] Thus, the R&D and innovative process is by no means fully understood—but the increasing relevance of the technological environment to product decisions is generating more study of these phenomena.

Technology and the Marketing Mix

The impact of technology upon a firm's products or services has already been illustrated and one might be tempted to conclude that this is the major area of influence upon the marketing mix. Yet, as shown in Table 4–2 on page 112, technology may also affect other marketing mix components. Thus, the potential impact of technology upon the marketing mix is pervasive.

Consider for example the impact of technology on the advertising function in business and industry. Changes in the mass media have

---

[25] Levitt, *Innovation in Marketing*, pp. 35–36.
[26] Lessing, "Why the U.S. Lags in Technology," p. 72.
[27] Schoen, "Managing Technological Innovations," p. 160.

TABLE 4–2

Illustrative Influences of Technology on Marketing Mix Decisions

Marketing Mix Component	Types of Influence	Examples
Product/Service	Source of new products	birth control pill
	Improvement in product performance	transistors
	Patent protection over competition	Xerox process
	Customer convenience	microwave ovens
Channels of Distribution	Increase speed of distribution	air freight
	Increase capacity of distribution	super tankers for oil
	Monitoring and control of distribution	computers
	Increased storage capabilities	freeze drying of foods
Pricing	Lower product cost	synthetic fabrics
	Efficiency of order processing	optical readers
	Computation of prices	airline information systems
Promotion	Improved communications capabilities	communications satellite
	Access to customers	cable TV, video phone
	Scheduling of advertising media	management science models
	Information on customer preferences	marketing research methods

revolutionized the advertising industry. Developments during the past 40 years include talking motion pictures, television, teletype setting, offset printing, communications satellites, and audio and video tape recording.[28] Such innovations as computerized typesetting and photocomposition, laser based communications technology, and complex systems of information retrieval promise to continue the revolution. The "mass" media will likely become more and more individualized, allowing the receiver wide latitude to select the specific information and programming of interest.

The home information system of the future may have its visual center in a large mirror on the wall, a mirror which at our command will present an illuminated reproduction of any kind of information we want. This information may take the form of written language—letters and words as they now appear on the daily newspaper or magazine page. We can summon up these messages to our command by predesignated codes which will yield the particular kind of information we are interested in. Through another system of controls . . . we might get pictures to illustrate the words which interest us, just as we might be able to get the full story if the headline is intriguing. . . . Another

---

[28] This discussion partially based on Leo Bogart, "Mass Media in the Year 2000," *Gazette*, vol. 13, no. 3, 1967, pp. 221–35.

control might bring us the sound of the speaker's voice or the filmed visual record.[29]

Although this system is not now economical, most of the technology is already available. What would happen to advertising as we now know it if this were to become reality?

COPING WITH TECHNOLOGICAL CHANGE

Marketing decision makers of today, much less tomorrow, must learn to cope with change—both technological as well as other changes fueled by new technology. Marketing within the organization must both adapt and react to technological forces as well as actually *generate* innovative technologies for serving markets. To do this requires an eye to the horizon, particularly as long-range plans are developed. The challenges to management are real. As Henry Boettinger, Assistant Controller at AT&T wrote:

> In the relevant future, organizations will experience a flood of sensory data and information. Their ability to think through—and about—this information in order to discern patterns of opportunity and potential harm will be taxed to their limits. Decisions and choices will be required in greater numbers. In addition, they will be more varied and far reaching in a world demanding transcience, novelty, and diversity for its desired qualities of life and the products needed to support a myriad of life styles.[30]

In facing a changing technological environment, management must anticipate and predict, to the extent possible, technological forces of interest. During the past decade, the importance of monitoring and forecasting external technological change has become generally recognized and considerable attention has been devoted to developing forecasting techniques.

Technological Forecasting: Nature and Limitations

Because the future is obviously unknown, any forecast must rely on intuitively or explicitly seeking relationships in the past and present which help us to anticipate the future. This includes projecting historical trends, predicting future technology from related current events, or basing a forecast on variables thought to actually cause future technological events. There is some disagreement as to what should qualify

---

[29] Ibid., p. 29.

[30] Henry M. Boettinger, "Technology in the Manager's Future," *Harvard Business Review,* vol. 48, no. 6, November–December, pp. 4, 165. © *Harvard Business Review.*

as a "technological forecast" (TF). Some assert that a TF has to be reproducible, others that it must be quantitative, while others point up the fact that some are really resource allocation techniques or serve only to structure the task (e.g., cross-impact matrices, networks, trees). Still, basically, a technological forecast is a forecast of the invention, innovation, and/or diffusion of some technology.[31] Four elements of the forecast susceptible to specifications include (1) the time period, (2) the nature of technology, (3) the characteristics to be exhibited by the technology, and (4) the probability associated with the characteristics.[32] As noted by Martino, the time period may be general or specific, the nature of the technology may be broadly defined or refer to a particular technique or thing, the characteristics may be generally described or cited in quantitative values, and the probability of occurrence might be generally cited as high or low or placed in numerical form. A forecast encompassing each of the required components is: "An increase of 20 percent in the tensile yield strength of carbon fiber composite materials can be achieved in three years, with 50 percent likelihood that the time required will be between $2\frac{1}{2}$ and four years."[33]

The most widely used classification scheme for TF approaches is by exploratory and normative techniques. The distinction between them rests on two differing assumptions about technological change. Respectively, the ontological view is that ". . . invention and innovation are visible manifestations of a self-generating process or an institution having a dynamism and a life all its own." In contrast, the teleological view is ". . . that invention and especially innovation are actually impersonal social processes determined by social or military needs or by the existence of an effective economic demand."[34] The latter view holds considerable merit, that "need is the mother of invention." Yet there are obviously needs such as the eradication of cancer, which still await sufficient technological capability. Thus, exploratory forecasting is oriented toward the future with particular attention to technological *capability* whereas normative methods look to future *needs* on the premise that need will breed the technology.

Technological forecasts do have limitations.[35] It is difficult to predict

[31] H. W. Lanford, "A Penetration of the Technological Forecasting Jungle," *Technological Forecasting and Social Change,* vol. 4, no. 2, 1972, p. 208.

[32] Discussion of these elements from Joseph P. Martino, *Technological Forecasting for Decisionmaking* (New York: American Elsevier Publishing Co., 1972), p. 3.

[33] Ibid.

[34] Views from Robert U. Ayres, *Technological Forecasting and Long-Range Planning* (New York: McGraw-Hill, 1969), pp. 29–31.

[35] Based on James Brian Quinn, "Technological Forecasting," *Harvard Business Review,* vol. 45, no. 2, 1967, pp. 101–03; and Ayres, *Technological Forecasting and Long-Range Planning.*

major scientific breakthroughs where wholly new phenomena are discovered. The randomness of scientific discovery contributes to a low batting average although some evidence does usually exist prior to a major invention. Secondly, despite government and research group attempts to accumulate technological information, there is a paucity of secondary data; this necessitates the collection of expensive primary data, thus limiting the use and quality of technological forecasting. Thirdly, interaction between simultaneous technological advances may create totally unexpected potentialities which can render forecasts useless. Quinn, for example, cites the decision after WWII to emphasize manned bombers instead of missiles as not anticipating the multiple development of compact, higher powered nuclear weapons, smaller and more reliable solid state devices, the guidance and control capabilities of computers, and the impact of new heat resistant materials. In combination, these spelled *missiles.*

Within a given company, there may be other limitations, such as inadequate resources, an inappropriate organization or poorly qualified personnel. In a 1971 study, Bayne and Price found that technological forecasting is an important input to formal planning in R&D in 50 percent of the companies reporting, to engineering in 28 percent of the companies, to marketing in 15 percent of the companies, to manufacturing in 25 percent of the companies, and to corporate planning (financial, staff, aquisitions) in 25 percent of the companies.[36] Even recognizing that all companies are not in a dynamic technological environment, it is nevertheless evident that technological forecasting is in the early stages of diffusion, particularly for marketers!

Drucker indicates that management attention should be placed upon monitoring existing technologies rather than trying to predict the impacts of totally new technologies:

> Technology monitoring is a serious, an important, indeed a vital task. But it is not a prophecy. The only thing possible with respect to *new* technology is *speculation* with about one chance out of a hundred of being right—and a much better chance of doing harm by encouraging the wrong, or discouraging the most beneficial new technology. What needs to be watched is "developing" technology, that is technology which has already had substantial impacts, enough to be judged, to be measured, to be evaluated.[37]

Marketing managers need to be familiar with the nature of technological forecasting techniques. Several of these techniques may be

[36] C. D. Bayne and W. Price, "Summarization of Technological Forecasting Questionnaire," July, 1971, communication cited in Lanford, "A Penetration of the Long-Range Forecasting Jungle," p. 225.

[37] Peter F. Drucker, *Management: Tasks, Responsibilities, Practices,* p. 333.

used for general environmental forecasting (Chapter 3) with the following discussion actually an extension of the last chapter on environmental analysis. Depending on the classification scheme used and attention to minor variations, the number of different TF techniques vary from 10 to perhaps 30.[38] Special attention is given to monitoring, subjective-judgmental, and extrapolation methods.

Monitoring

Technological monitoring is based on the well documented premise that most technological innovation is visible long before widespread use. A young IBM marketing man, for example, noted Chester Carlson's patent on Xerography in the *New York Times* in 1940, but failed for over a year and a half to interest IBM management. The xerography patent was also abstracted in an Eastman Kodak publication in 1943, but was ignored.[39] "Monitoring" as used in the TF literature, goes well beyond scanning. It includes four activities:[40]

1. Searching the environment for signals that may be forerunners of significant technological change;
2. Identifying the possible consequences (assuming that these signals are not false and the trends that they suggest persist);
3. Choosing the parameters, policies, events, and decisions that should be observed and followed to verify the time, speed and direction of technology and the effects of employing it; and
4. Presenting the data from the foregoing steps in a timely and appropriate manner for management's use in decisions about the organization's reaction.

As steps 1 and 3 suggest, the key is to identify the appropriate parameters or "signals" to monitor. The signals go beyond technical considerations and include attention to the social, governmental, and economic environments (Figure 4–5).[41] Signals from all these non-technical areas are essential, for example, in assessing the future of the pollution control equipment industry, the internal combustion engine, and various forms of energy. Economic feasibility, the level of government support, and potential production economies are typically factors to consider. The

---

[38] For the first comprehensive American textbook on these techniques, see Martino, *Technological Forecasting for Decisionmaking*.

[39] James R. Bright, "Evaluating Signals of Technological Change," *Harvard Business Review*, vol. 48, no. 1 (1970), p. 66.

[40] Ibid., p. 64.

[41] A good discussion of information sources and the state of corporate development regarding surveillance of the changing environment is contained in Kenneth R. Andrews, *The Concept of Corporate Strategy* (Homewood, Ill.: Dow Jones-Irwin, 1971), pp. 69–77.

social and governmental priority (or demand) for new technologies are also signals with other clues including population trends, social conditions, shifting attitudes, formation of special interest groups, the delivery of speeches, the publication of books, actions of government committees, appointment or election of certain personalities, or the occurrence of certain political conflicts.[42] All of these considerations could be related to demand and support for new forms of technology.

Specifically monitoring the technological environment may include such signals as the formation of new firms, patent literature, competitor's announcements on new products, increased research staffs, trade literature and governmental research. In an excellent illustration of monitoring, Utterback and Brown present the case of developing non-silver technology for photographic processes.[43] Photography, a growing avocation, is the major use of silver, annually consuming over one-quarter of available silver. Establishing a need for monitoring was based on numerous observations pointing toward a silver shortage—such as an analysis of the limited silver supply and actions by the government to remove silver from coinage and from backing currency. Study of the announcements and activities of several firms including DuPont, Technicolor, CBS, and OptoGraphics led to an identification of signals to monitor such as (1) reductions in the size, complexity, and difficulty of use of videotape and other electronic media, (2) increases in the speed of photopolymeric and photochromic materials and, (3) improvements in resolution and color fidelity, particularly in electro-photographic techniques. These signals each relate to alternative directions that could develop such as the use of more efficient silver-based films, the use of non-silver processing substances, or the advent of competitive media such as in electronics. Monitoring is continuing, but at the date of this writing, it appeared that a variety of techniques might replace those based on silver, depending on the application. Except with 20–20 hindsight, selecting the appropriate "signals" is a difficult task. Yet monitoring efforts are essential to effective long-term planning, often in combination with actual forecasting approaches.

Subjective-Judgmental Forecasting

These approaches typically rely upon individual experts or groups of experts, where judgment and experience provide the basis for forecasting the nature and direction of technological trends. Consider the uncanny genius displayed by Jules Verne in his novels about future

---

[42] Bright, "Evaluating Signals of Technological Change," pp. 67–68.

[43] James M. Utterback and James W. Brown, "Monitoring for Technological Opportunities," *Business Horizons* (October 1972), pp. 5–15.

technologies.[44] Various uses are made by business and other organizations of individual experts in projecting future trends. Also, role playing games or scenarios have received some attention by the military and a few business firms to gain insights regarding future environments and technological requirements.[45] One of the more promising subjective-judgmental approaches is the Delphi method. Since this method provides a systematic means of collecting and analyzing expert opinion we shall examine it to gain an understanding of its characteristics and potential.

Developed several years ago at the Rand Corporation, Delphi procedures provide a method of systematically questioning a panel of experts concerning some future event or trend.[46] Figure 4–6 shows the major stages in the Delphi process. Each expert is independently questioned and then responses from all panel members are combined, summarized, and returned to participants. Based on questions raised by participants, modifications may be made in the questionnaire before sending it to panel members. The process continues for three or more rounds until an acceptable degree of consensus is achieved or until responses stabilize. The intent of the Delphi procedure is that responses of participants will converge over several rounds toward the true value of the event or trend being estimated.

Several applications of the Delphi method have been made in the areas of technology forecasting, corporate planning, and other areas where traditional forecasting methods could not be used due to lack of data:

TRW, Inc., in assessing space, aircraft, electronics, defense, automotive, and industrial product markets was seeking information to aid corporate executives in their perception of the need for, and feasibility of new products and services.[47]

Smith, Kline, & French, the pharmaceutical firm, has used Delphi methods to study the long-range future of medicine.[48]

The Rand Corporation in the early 1960s using a panel of over 80 experts developed estimates of probable dates for 30 areas of tech-

---

[44] Also see Arthur B. Bronwell, ed., *Science and Technology in the World of the Future* (New York: Wiley-Interscience, 1970).

[45] See Ayres, *Technological Forecasting and Long-Range Planning*, pp. 146–47.

[46] See for example, Norman C. Dalkey and Olaf Helmer, "An Experimental Application of the Delphi Method to the Use of Experts," *Management Science*, 9 (April 1963), pp. 458–67.

[47] Harper Q. North and Donald L. Pyke, "Probes of the Technological Future," *Harvard Business Review*, vol. 47, no. 3, 1969, p. 29.

[48] "Forecasters Turn To Group Guesswork," *Business Week* (March 14, 1970), p. 132.

nology development including ocean farming, growth of new organs and limbs, and intelligence drugs.[49]

The Delphi approach is not limited, of course, to technological forecasting or even to environmental forecasting. The Bell System, with the Institute for the Future, conducted a wide-ranging Delphi study, "to examine the future of communications, both from the point of view of the public interest and that of the long-range corporate goals of the Bell System."[50] Identification of information needs were first formalized

FIGURE 4–6

Major Stages in Delphi Forecasting

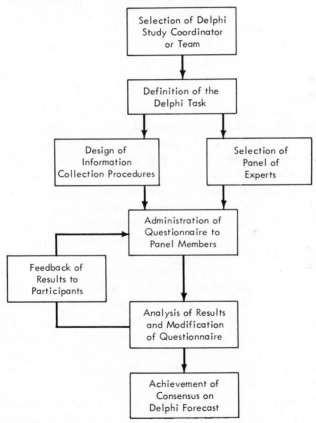

---

[49] D. D. Wilmot, "A Comparison of the Methods of Technological Forecasting," *Industrial Marketing Management,* 1 (September 1971), p. 97.

[50] D. K. Conover, "Bell System Sponsored Delphi Studies," delivered at the Annual Marketing Conference of the Conference Board, New York, October 17, 1973, p. 3.

through the use of a "relevance tree." At each branching point (going from the general to the specific), the question was asked, "What percentage of the total effort at this node should be assigned to each branch?" The results were summarized in a chart—Figure 4–7—which illustrates that 67 percent of the effort was to be allocated to external factors. This, then, served as the basis for forming five panels, and proceeding with the Delphi approach.

Delphi offers marketers and other decision makers a systematic approach for predicting change that is too little understood or too nebulous for more objective forecasting approaches. The composite of expert opinion is considered more reliable than one opinion and the anonymity of response (which is fundamental to the Delphi method) contributes to less biased results than brainstorming or committee meetings. Its greatest benefit may be the process itself, involving key decision-makers in a creative, future oriented assessment, the type of task too often ignored because of other pressures.

Trend Extrapolation

The main objection to Delphi forecasts, their intuitive nature, has undoubtedly contributed to continued use of extrapolation, a "black box" approach. With extrapolation, there is no attempt to identify causes of technological change as the basis for the forecast. Instead, extrapolation projects the historical trend forward on the assumption that factors affecting the advance of a technology in the past will not change significantly in the future. Shifting priorities and a reallocation of government monies could, for example, render a forecast useless. Yet, there is evidence that many technologies can be forecast using trend analysis.

Similar to trend analysis, progression of technological advance is plotted over time using some consistent definition of increased technological capability that will allow comparison of different advances. Selecting this measure is a challenging task. In the case of illumination sources, the trend could be efficiency as measured by lumens per watt. A remarkably consistent trend may be seen in Figure 4–8 (page 121) despite the fact that most of the technological advances are quite unrelated to the previously accepted light source (trend line fitted by least squares). Statistical regression analysis yields a regression formula which may be used to project the trend. This is an example of the use of trend extrapolation on a semi-log graph (i.e., exponential growth is involved). Evidence suggests that exponential growth is a more common case than simple linear growth—as hinted earlier in noting that technology "feeds on itself." This consistency in the nature of technological advance is the very justification for using trend forecasts.

FIGURE 4–7

Distribution of Effort for Institute for the Future Delphi Study on the Future of the Telephone Industry

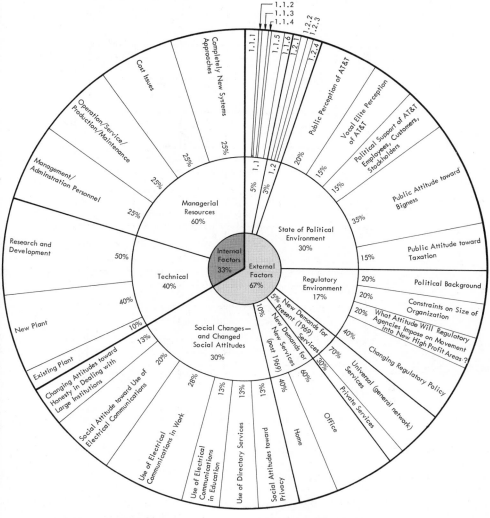

1.1 State of population distribution relative to Bell plans—demography	1.1.5 Mobility 30 percent
	1.1.6 Transportation (local) 20 percent
	1.2 Affluence 25 percent
1.1.1 Change in character of cities 35 percent	1.2.1 Distribution 25 percent
1.1.2 Suburbs 5 percent	1.2.2 Distribution 25 percent
1.1.3 New cities: where? when? 5 percent	1.2.3 U.S. position relative to world 20 percent
1.1.4 Age 5 percent	1.2.4 Financing 30 percent

Source: D. K. Conover, "Bell System Sponsored Delphi Studies," Annual Marketing Conference of the Conference Board, New York, New York, October 17, 1973.

FIGURE 4–8

Trend Extrapolation of Efficiency of Illumination Sources

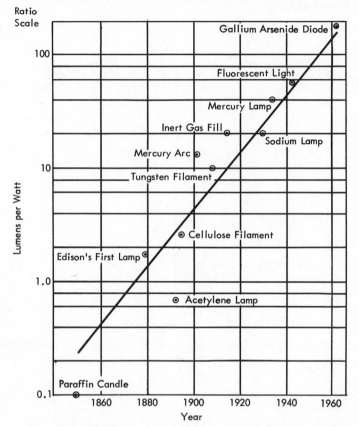

Source: Joseph P. Martino, *Technological Forecasting for Decision-making* (New York: American Elsevier Publishing Co., 1972), p. 133.

SUMMARY AND CONCLUSIONS

A changing technological environment poses threats and offers opportunities to marketing decision makers. Technological change (an extension of the existing level of technology) has become an important part of the marketing environment in recent years as the rate of technological change has increased, affecting consumers, organizations, and society in general. Technology tends to underpin much social change; thus, its role within the marketing environment is pervasive. In addition, technology impacts directly on marketing decision areas, with the greatest effects on product decisions. It is important to bridge the gap that frequently exists between the functions of R&D and marketing. Acceptance of the marketing concept, or a customer orientation, by both groups is essential although marketers must be especially aware that the processes of technological research are not always subject to rational planning and timetables, particularly basic research.

Technological change becomes increasingly relevant to marketing decision making as it advances into the latter stages of the technological process which includes science, invention, innovation, adoption, and diffusion. This fact facilitates anticipating changes of importance to marketers through monitoring, subjective-judgmental methods, trend extrapolation and by use of analytical models. Monitoring and forecasting technological change are essential to the long-range planning activities of marketers.

As Roberts has noted, economic forecasting seemed to progress through five developmental stages including wisdom or genius forecasting, "naive" models, simple correlative models, complex multivariate econometric forecasts, dynamic causally-oriented models and, in the future, a sixth stage, learning models.[51] He goes on to conclude that exploratory technological forecasters should move as quickly as possible to dynamic modeling efforts. Although this is an appropriate goal, it is unlikely that vast strides with dynamic modeling will be seen soon, partly because the causal variables underlying much technological change are not entirely identified much less specified. There is no question, however, that increasing attention will be given to the actual *causes* of changes in technological capability. This will pave the way for more sophisticated and, hopefully, more accurate forecasting.

EXERCISES FOR DISCUSSION AND REVIEW

1. The birth control pill has clearly had a pervasive impact upon contemporary society. As a technological innovation, the pill has stimulated a variety of environmental changes, and it illustrates the close relationship between social and technological change. Identify and discuss the nature and scope of related impacts upon the various levels of the environment (Chapter 3) and identify several tentative implications for marketers.

2. Top management of the Hewlett-Packard Co. (electronic instruments, calculators, and small computers) in the mid-1970s adopted a corporate strategy focusing on the development of innovative products that provide a distinct competitive advantage. What implications does this strategy have for technological monitoring and forecasting?

3. Video telephones (visual display and voice) have been commercially available for the past few years. Assume that this mode of communica-

---

[51] Edward B. Roberts, "Exploratory and Normative Technological Forecasting: A Critical Appraisal," *Technological Forecasting*, vol. 1 (Fall 1969), p. 116; also, A. Wade Blackman, "Forecasting Through Dynamic Modeling," *Technological Forecasting and Social Change*, vol. 3, no. 3 (1972), pp. 291–307.

tion gains widespread acceptance by both commercial and consumer telephone users and then identify and discuss several potential impacts that this product could have on marketing practices.

4. You have been assigned responsibility for planning and implementing a technology monitoring and forecasting program for a manufacturer of outboard motors and other motorized recreational equipment. Outline an approach to this task, including in your discussion: (1) relevant factors to be assessed; (2) specific types of information needs; (3) potential sources of information; and (4) major problem areas that you anticipate in carrying out your assignment.

5. Examine the process of food distribution (including the network of marketing intermediaries such as brokers, wholesalers, retailers, and transportation firms) with respect to the nature and types of technologies that facilitate the distribution process. Based on the idea that "need is the mother of invention," speculate concerning possible technological advances that could significantly improve the effectiveness and efficiency of the food distribution process.

6. Within the business firm, potential conflict exists between marketers and the research and development (R&D) people. Explain why this is understandable and suggest means for minimizing such conflict.

7. Research and development activities commonly concentrate on new products and the production function within business. Is there a need for *marketing* R&D? What would be the nature of this process?

8. It is possible to overconcentrate on a firm's products and lose sight of the market needs they fulfill. But it is also possible to understand shifting market needs without comprehending the different technologies required to meet these needs—that is, "technological myopia." Discuss with examples.

5

Societal Change and the Consumer

Facing more demanding consumers and increased competition, marketers continue efforts to understand consumers better. In recent years, the consumer behavior discipline has blossomed and a later chapter overviews this study of individual consumers. This chapter instead looks at broad consumer/social shifts within society that impinge on marketer decisions. Although it is impossible to draw an exact line between social and other macro-environmental changes, social change typically involves broad-based shifts involving many people. In a sense, social change is changing people. More formally, social change is ". . . the occurrence of an alteration in the form or functioning of a significant group, institution, or social order."[1] Such "alterations" discussed in this chapter include (1) changing population characteristics (demographic and socio-economic), (2) changing consumer values and life styles, as well as (3) the increasing importance of social issues concerning consumerism, the natural environment, and the ghetto marketplace. From the perspective of analyzing environmental forces (Chapter 3), social processes and flows of potential relevance to marketers are overviewed and analyzed.

The impact of social forces (part of the macro-environment) is usually mediated through the task environment including effects on competition and marketing intermediaries. The portion of the task environment of special significance here however, is that of consumers and markets. The chapter sections tend to build on each other with the sequence on the next page.

---

[1] Philip Kotler, "The Elements of Social Action," in *Processes and Phenomena of Social Change,* Gerald Zaltman et al. (New York: John Wiley and Sons, 1973), p. 171.

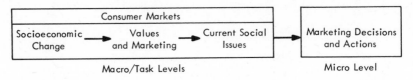

Attention to socio-economic change in the first section provides an overview of changing population characteristics such as age, income, educational levels and mobility. This discussion contributes to understanding why consumer values change (second section) and both of the two initial sections help to explain why social issues arise. Finally, social changes are brought into focus as they pertain to marketing decision-making.

It should first be noted, however, that social change may be incorporated into at least four marketing decision areas. First, identifying *market opportunities* requires attention to social change because factors such as shifting population characteristics and consumer values may determine consumer needs and wants and, ultimately, the success or failure of new products. Clothing designers decided the midi dress (below the knee) was to be the fashion at the end of the 1960s, but they ignored social change and changing consumers. Increasingly liberated women not only rejected the midi but threatened the brassiere industry as well. In contrast, changing life styles and higher incomes have presented numerous market opportunities for the leisure products industry. Even the general social climate may affect consumer needs and wants. Declining demand for hard rock music in the early seventies, for example, was purportedly associated with the end of the Vietnam War, an era of protest.

Selecting specific market segments with an eye to consumer needs also requires monitoring social factors such as demographics and values that are related to consumer needs. Markets for different types of music and sound equipment, for example, are related to age and educational characteristics. Narrowing in on the needs of specific groups is essential for the development of marketing strategy and monitoring social change is important both for identifying changes within existing market target groups as well as for detecting new groups with market potential.

Designing and controlling marketing programs must also be based on an understanding of society. Consumerism, for example, brought to the limelight issues concerning advertising truthfulness, selling techniques, pricing practices and product safety. Consumerism demands have been felt as direct social pressure as well as through the marketplace and via government. Marketing strategies may be designed that capitalize on the opportunity of responding to consumer problems better than competitors. Whirlpool Corporation, for example, was the first company to establish an effective direct communications link (toll free "cool line") with consumers. Beyond the design of strategies, monitoring marketing effectiveness hinges on understanding consumers as they change with society.

Perhaps most important, social change must be anticipated as an input to *long range corporate planning and goal formulation*. Social pressures are requiring marketers to seek a better understanding of consumer expectations, assess internal operations accordingly, and realign the corporate mission in accordance with the dictates of society.

SOCIO-ECONOMIC CHANGE AND CONSUMERS

Socio-economic change refers to *social* as well as *economic* change but much of this is the study of *demographics;* that is, the statistical study of human populations. The changing composition or "form" of society is partly measured by factors such as income, race, age and education.

Use of Socio-economic Information

In recent years, middle and higher-income consumers migrated to suburban areas, working wives and higher family incomes created the two-car family, and, with college education available to the masses, college towns boomed. Marketers who anticipate these types of socio-economic changes often gain strategic advantages over competitors and are able to capitalize on related market opportunities.

The most obvious use of socio-economic information therefore is for delineating markets. If consumer needs correlate with such variables as age, income, and education as evidenced, for example, by the youth market and the senior citizen market, socio-economic characteristics may be very useful. The relationships must be as follows for demographic information to be of use:

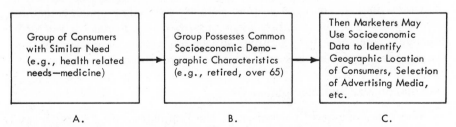

A. B. C.

In breaking down markets, marketers have traditionally relied on socio-economic data, often making gross, unsupported assumptions as to the relationship of the data to consumer needs and product or brand preferences. In other words, the relationship between (a) and (b) above has too often been assumed rather than known as fact. Yet the needs of consumers *are* often related to socio-economic characteristics and, where this relationship exists, socio-economic analysis may be useful. Geritol, for example, has historically been advertised in media that reached older age groups. More recently, Geritol has also been advertised to women. Similarly, medicine for skin blemishes is marketed to teenagers using appropriate media and messages. Socio-economic characteristics are important if they serve to group consumers with similar needs or desires, that is, consumers with related preferences for certain products, brands, and/or stores.

As more and more people gain significant amounts of discretionary income, however, it is anticipated that consumer preferences will be less related to age, sex or education and it will become more important to look beyond demographic data to such factors as attitudes and the subtleties of differing life-styles. As incomes rise, consumers will have greater latitude for satisfying subjective needs via whimsical *appearing* purchase decisions. In reality, consumers are increasingly difficult to understand and with competition forcing firms to "tune in" to specific groups of consumers, demographic data usually serves as only a first stage, albeit an important one, in market analysis. Most firms place considerable emphasis on these data yet recognize the need for additional information.

Demographic data are often inexpensive as well as readily available, so it is desirable to use them. Also, because advertising media such as television and magazines typically have a socio-economic profile of their audience, use of demographics for allocating the advertising budget is very common. It is no accident that new food products are advertised on afternoon television shows viewed by housewives, and Mennen's after-shave is advertised on sports telecasts. Another function of socio-economic data in connection with marketing research surveys is in selecting a sample of consumers.

Other than use of demographic data by marketing management for market analyses, these data may be used to help explain basic social changes. Affluence, for example, affects the values of consumers and rising educational levels seem to lead to more demanding consumers.

Population Size and Distribution

The gross size and distribution of the population affect the size and nature of markets. Key generalizations of significance to marketers are shown in Figures 5–1 and 5–2 and include:

The population of the U.S. will continue to grow in *numbers* until at least the year 2020. Between 1974 and 2000, for example, the population will increase by about 50 million people.

FIGURE 5–1

United States Population Trends

U.S. Population (millions)		Projections-Series			
			I	*II*	*III*
1900	76				
1920	106	1980	226	223	220
1940	132	1990	258	245	235
1960	181	2000	287	262	245
1970	205	2010	322	279	250
1974	212	2020	362	294	252
		2025	382	300	250

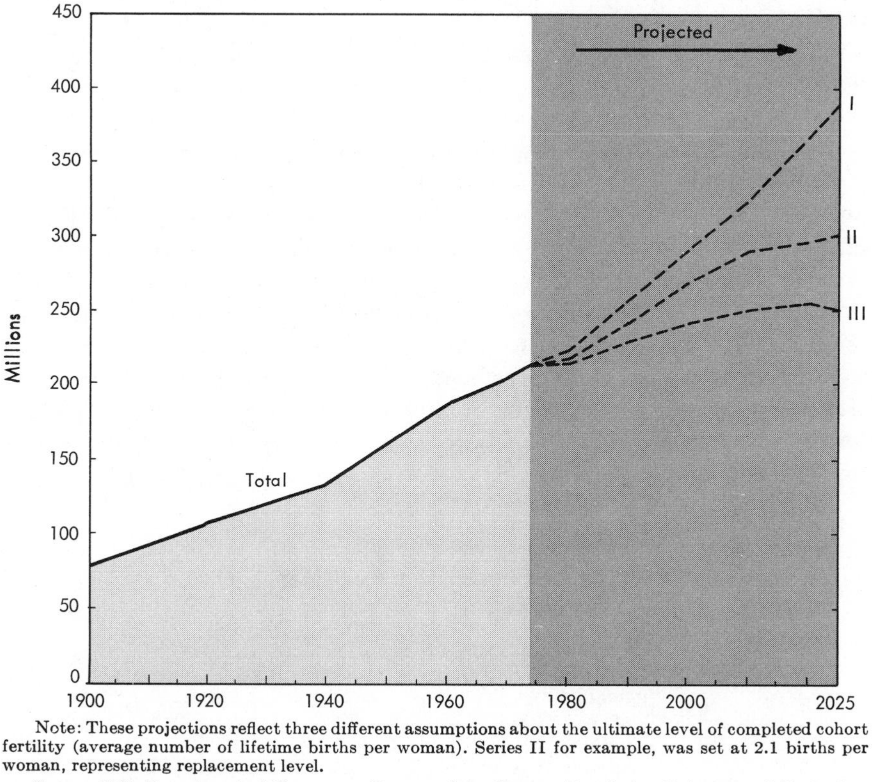

Note: These projections reflect three different assumptions about the ultimate level of completed cohort fertility (average number of lifetime births per woman). Series II for example, was set at 2.1 births per woman, representing replacement level.

Source: U.S. Department of Commerce, Bureau of the Census, *Population Estimates and Projections* (Series P–25, No. 541), February 1975, p. 1.

The *rate* of growth has continued to decline in recent years although the increase in the number of women of child-bearing age has more than offset this decline.

Forty percent of the total U.S. population resides in only six states.

Some find it surprising that with all the discussion of a zero growth rate, the U.S. population is likely to grow beyond the year 2020. To understand growth projections, one must consider not only birth rates and death rates (and immigration and emigration) but *also* the actual number of women of child-bearing age. During the seventies, the large number of women born in the post World War II "baby boom" were having their *own* children. Although the U.S. growth *rate* dropped well below long-term replacement levels, the population continues to grow in actual numbers. The net increase just during 1974, for example, totaled 1.6 million people.

The number of families will also be increasing. The influence of the family unit on purchasing decisions as well as the reliance of many families on one paycheck makes family formations of special interest to marketers. Despite publicity about communes and dissatisfaction with the marriage contract, in reality family formations remain high. There were about 68 million households in 1973 including 54 million families.

Lower growth rates will eventually contribute to fewer consumers and, at first glance, declining markets. But counteracting this thesis, economists see (1) increases in productivity due to an older and more experienced work force and greater use of technology; and (2) a rising standard of living because of this productivity combined with smaller families and more women workers.[2] Although some predict a higher savings rate, others believe that consumer expenditures will continue to rise as consumers seek greater quality in the goods they buy. Overall, lower birth rates should contribute to a higher quality of life with no great threats to marketing activity.

FIGURE 5–2

Distribution of Population by States

Population, by Size of States: 1972

Population Size of States	Number of States	Population	
		Total (millions)	Percent of U.S.
Total*........ 51		208.2	100.0
Over 10 million...... 6		84.4	40.6
5–10 million......... 6		40.0	19.2
3–5 million.......... 12		47.8	23.0
2–3 million.......... 7		17.2	8.3
1–2 million.......... 7		10.4	5.0
Under 1 million*..... 13		8.3	4.0

* Includes District of Columbia.

[2] "The Burgeoning Benefits of a Lower Birth Rate," *Business Week* (New York), December 15, 1973, pp. 41–42.

FIGURE 5–2 (continued)

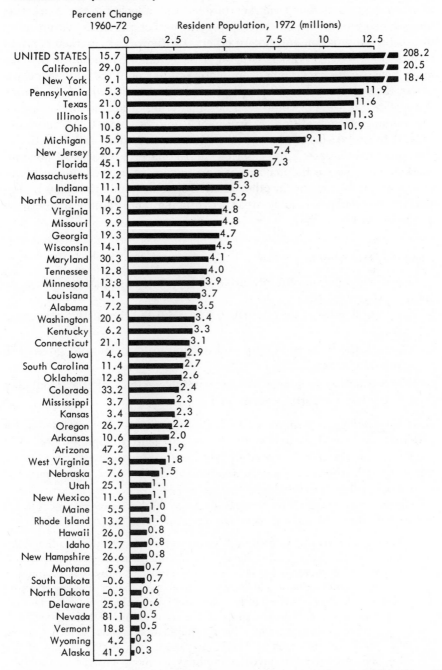

Source: U.S. Department of Commerce, Bureau of the Census, *Pocket Data Book USA 1973*, p. 40.

The geographic distribution of the population may be of importance to marketers in defining market targets and allocating the marketing budget geographically. It is tempting to market products within areas of greatest population and ignore others. In Figure 5–2, marketers might choose to ignore Nebraska, Oregon, Utah, Idaho, Montana, and Wyoming because their combined populations total only 6.6 million people —less than the number of people in New York City alone. To ignore these states, however, would overlook many important factors including the amount of competition. A firm which ignores competition and looks only at the total size of the consumer market may have fallen victim to the "majority fallacy." By catering to the largest and most obvious markets (i.e., where the majority is), management may encounter heavy competition not present in other areas. Yet total population may be important, particularly if some areas are growing more rapidly than others, as shown in Figure 5–2.

Changing Age Structure

One of the most important variables for analyzing markets is age. As shown in Figure 5–3:

The largest growth between 1970 and 1980 will be in the age group 25–34.

Although the 0–14 age group will decline in total, the 0–4 group will increase in size.

The population is generally young with over half of the population in 1970 under thirty years of age.

It is interesting to witness promotional activity in various media for products and services and note the relationship to age groups. The youngest and the oldest age groups will both increase in size over coming years contributing to a combination of toddler play equipment and retirement village advertising.

Although baby product companies have had to lower expectations somewhat, they are nevertheless facing some good years.

> With fewer mouths to feed and fewer bottoms to powder, leading companies in the baby market have already embarked on an aggressive effort to widen their market. The major producer of baby care products is currently conducting a television advertising campaign showing a young mother who has switched to her daughter's baby shampoo and a he-man cop who discovers the pleasures of a cooling douse of baby powder.
> . . . Having kept close tabs on the population trends of recent years, the marketing planners at Hamilton Cosco, Inc., which is one of the top five producers of juvenile products in the country, . . . hold an encouraging outlook regarding the future effects of Z.P.G. [zero population growth] on Cosco . . . For the next few decades, the juvenile

FIGURE 5–3

Population Growth By Age Group

	Millions of Persons		
Age	1970	1980	1985
0–4.........	17.2	18.6	20.6
5–14........	40.7	34.4	35.8
15–19.......	19.3	20.2	17.7
20–24.......	17.2	21.2	20.4
25–34.......	25.3	36.9	40.8
35–44........	23.2	25.3	31.1
45–54........	23.3	22.4	22.1
55–64........	18.7	21.1	21.3
65 and over.........	20.1	24.1	25.9
Total	205.0	224.1	235.7

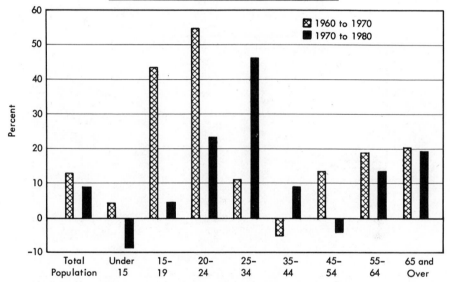

Source: Helen Axel (ed.), *A Guide to Consumer Markets 1974/1975* (New York: The Conference Board, 1974), pp. 14, 18.

products industry will benefit from a rise in . . . [births] among the largest potential parent group in our history . . . With increased family formations, purchases for the first baby are likely to skyrocket.[3]

Education, Occupation, and Incomes

These three interrelated factors continued on an upward trend during the past decades as partially shown in Figures 5–4 and 5–5, pp. 134–37.

[3] "Hamilton Cosco, Inc.," *The Stock Market Magazine*, vol. 12, no. 11 (December 1973), pp. 11–12.

FIGURE 5–4

Educational Attainment (years of school completed, persons 25 and over)

	Percent Distribution (millions)	
	1975	*1985*
Elementary or Less............	22.8	14.4
Some High School.............	16.9	15.4
High School Graduate..........	36.2	38.9
Some College.........	11.3	13.7
College Graduate..........	12.8	17.5
	100.0	100.0
Total Number	118.2	139.9

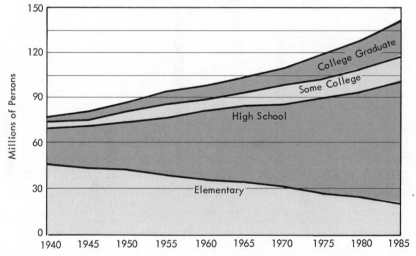

Source: Helen Axel (ed.), *A Guide to Consumer Markets 1974/1975* (New York: The Conference Board, 1974), p. 80.

By 1975, almost one in every four persons (25 years older and over) had attended *or* graduated from college with this figure expected to approach one in three by 1985.

In 1972, over half of all families earned over $10,000 per year.

In 1972, white-collar workers represented the largest occupational category with nearly half of the 81 million work labor force so classified. The number of blue collar workers trailed white collar (by 11 million) and although the number of service workers expanded at a rapid rate, they remained a distant third in total employment.

The number of families with an annual income of over $15,000 continues to grow, despite cycles of recession and inflation. By 1972, three out of every ten families exceeded this level. By 1975, about one-third of all families possessed supernumerary income (income over $15,000/yr. in constant dollars) that, in total, represented over 17 percent of all family personal income. Despite general affluence, one of every six families had an annual income under $5,000 in 1972.

Rising educational, occupational and income levels appear to foster consumerism and more astute and demanding consumers. Although business benefits from increased consumer purchasing power and growing markets, it seems more difficult to satisfy consumers than ever before. Again, with increasing numbers of families spending income on non-necessities, consumers are even more difficult to understand and predict. Some have noted that while income still dictates the consumer's capacity to spend, it is the consumer's general confidence or mood that determines whether the consumer spends or saves.[4] Increasingly, businesses are truly at the mercy of the consumer, despite growing markets.

Sex and Race

Because of the importance of the head of the household to many family purchase decisions, it is noteworthy that 11 percent of all families have females as the head of household, and among black families this figure is 28 percent. Women in the labor force (age 16 and over) increased from 27.4 percent in 1940 to 42.5 percent by 1971, and further, 63.1 percent of these women were married. These trends are related to the success of such products as convenience foods which complement the changing role of women. Understanding this changing role, however, requires going beyond statistics to attitudinal measures and efforts to assess the impact of the "new woman" on marketing strategy. Virginia Slims was one of the earlier products catering to "liberated" women and one may easily note numerous advertising campaigns that reflect the changing roles of men and women in the family. Although a minority of women are actively engaged in "liberation" activities, the effects are pervasive and have altered the role of most women. It is likely that with fewer boundaries about this role, marketers will find greater heterogeneity within female markets in future years. Reliance on stereotypes will become increasingly dangerous and no one role will be dominant.

Many of the effects of racism and sexism are similar, even though the

---

[4] "What Makes the New Consumer Buy," *Business Week*, April 24, 1971, p. 53.

FIGURE 5–5

Income Classes and Supernumerary Income

A. Families by Income Class
(based on 1971 dollars)

	Percent of Families by Income Class, 1972
Under $5,000............	16.6%
$5,000– 7,000............	10.2
7,000–10,000............	16.8
10,000–15,000............	26.1
15,000 and over..........	30.3

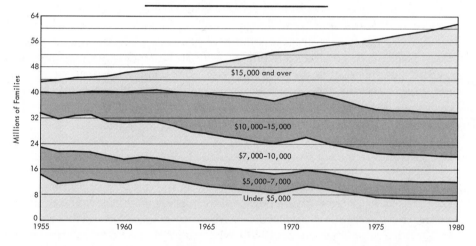

impact on minorities has been more severe in the economic realm. Although women could rely on the family paycheck, minorities often had no way to tap the economic mainstream. Twenty-six million people (12½ percent of the population) were members of minority races in 1970 and blacks comprise approximately 92 percent of all minorities. With increasing amounts of attention being given to Afro-American markets, it is significant that the size of the black population increased 20 percent during the sixties relative to a general increase of 13 percent. Other minority races (e.g., Mexican-Americans) jumped 78 percent! Although average incomes of black families are only about 60 percent that for whites, they are increasing at an above average rate, and total black purchasing power exceeds $40 billion per year, larger than the entire Canadian consumer market. Although 30 percent of black families have an income level of under $4,000 per year, nearly 10 percent

FIGURE 5–5 (continued)

B.   Supernumerary Income
(all figures in 1970 dollars)

	Percent of all Families with Supernumerary Income
1970.............	22.3%
1975.............	33.5
1980.............	42.0

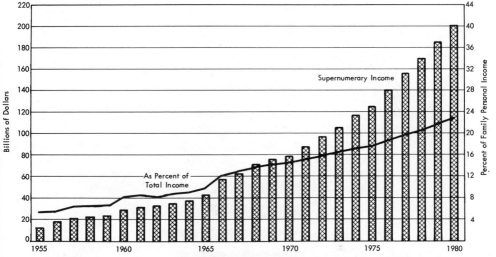

Source: Helen Axel (ed.), *A Guide to Consumer Markets 1974/1975* (New York: The Conference Board 1974), p. 126, 130, 144.

earn over $15,000 per year. For a given company the question becomes, "Would a differentiated marketing effort seeking black consumer patronage more than pay for the additional effort?" For most types of products, the answer is probably "no" because in comparing blacks and whites of comparable incomes, only 6.6 percent of the income of blacks was allocated to different product categories than that of whites.[5] Yet, for some products, it is definitely "yes" as, for example, with above average expenditures by blacks on clothing and scotch. Beyond products, this may be even more true of certain brands and stores. The "green power" of the minority consumer must be recognized and the complexity and increasing heterogeneity of black markets must be understood as a

---

[5] Raymond A. Bauer and Scott M. Cunningham, "The Negro Market," *The Journal of Advertising Research*, vol. 10, no. 2 (April 1970), pp. 3–12.

basis for designing strategies.[6] Marketers should not assume a priori that differences exist, however.

Product/Market Growth and Lifestyles

One may readily relate changing demographic characteristics to the growth and decline of product markets. As illustrated in Figure 5–6, food continues to represent the largest single portion of consumer expenditures, but food continues to decline as a proportion of total spending. Consumer life styles involve more and more non-essentials and certain of these product sectors exhibited well above average growth while others grew only modestly. American consumers have more flexibility than ever before in selecting the life style most suited to their needs and wants. Although deviant life styles (e.g., "hippie") receive

FIGURE 5–6

Consumer Expenditures and Product/Market Growth

A. The Distribution of Consumer Expenditures (total expenditures, 1972 = 100%)

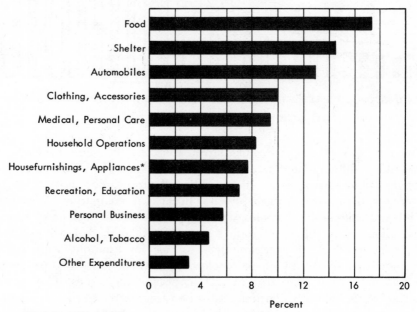

* Includes radio and TV.

---

[6] Gerald E. Hills, Donald H. Granbois, and James M. Patterson, "Black Consumer Perceptions of Food Store Attributes," *Journal of Marketing*, vol. 37, no. 2 (April 1973), p. 56, published by the American Marketing Association.

FIGURE 5–6 (*continued*)

B. The Rate of Growth by Sector (average annual growth rates, 1960–1972, based on constant dollars)

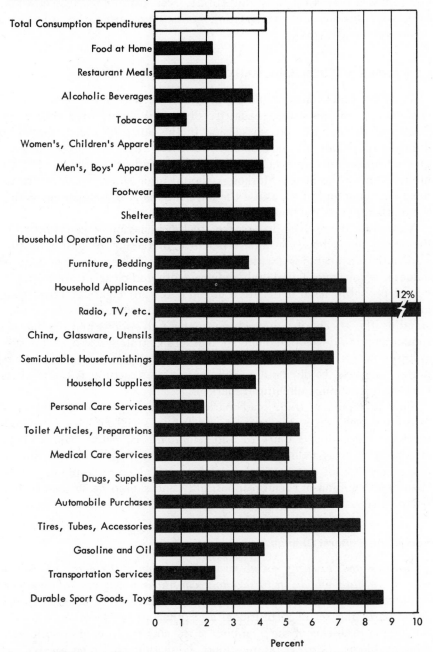

Source: Helen Axel (ed.), *A Guide to Consumer Markets 1974/1975* (New York: The Conference Board, 1974), pp. 163, 171.

the greatest press coverage, less recognized is a tendency for most families to fall into a mode of living that can be partially characterized by the types of products and services purchased. More and more life styles encompass a means for satisfying subtle, even psychological needs, and even yoga lessons and wine-tasting courses are often the subject of commercial endeavors.

CONSUMER VALUES AND MARKETING

In recent years considerable attention has been devoted to such social changes as new life styles, sexual freedom, and a purported shift away from materialism. Campus dissension in the late 1960's contributed to radical predictions of value change but more recently, campuses have quieted and observers even parallel current student apathy to that exhibited during the fifties. Marketers should understand if values are indeed changing and, if so, assess the implications of these changes within the marketing task environment.

Values by themselves do not dictate the behavior of consumers but they help shape how consumers perceive marketing programs. Values also underpin attitudes (with attitudes often defined as even part of values). A consumer who highly *values* health and clear air, for example, would probably have a negative *attitude* toward cigarette advertising and might *perceive* only negative aspects of an advertisement. Understanding the effects of values on consumer perceptions and attitudes is fundamental to developing effective marketing strategy. Also, ethnic subcultures possessing differing values are increasingly recognized as important markets. Understanding different value structures is essential for effectively reaching subcultural markets.

Beyond inputs to traditional marketing strategy decisions, values of consumers help shape the current and future social and legal environment for marketing. Failure to understand the collective values of society and the way values underpin social issues (e.g., consumerism) is to risk the rise of devastating social forces. Values underpin the ever-changing definition of social responsibility and should be studied in that perspective.

Social and Cultural Change

Culture and existing social structures provide the base on which values are built which, in turn, affect consumer needs and related perceptions, attitudes and purchasing patterns. The culture of any country is the particular set of institutional and other arrangements which exist for solving problems of the members of the society. In coping with common problems, (e.g., obtaining food, educating children) people try various solutions and some become firmly established and are transmitted to later generations as culture. Patterns which are well established and accepted as a fundamental part of culture are termed "institutionalized ways." The family, schools, government, and the economic system, for example, are institutions; and specific to marketing, retailing and wholesaling are marketing institutions. The transmittal of these "arrangements" from generation to generation contributes to the newer members accepting these as the "approved" way or, possibly, the only "decent" way. Thus, culture may be defined as *the peoples' ". . . modal patterns of behavior and the underlying regulatory beliefs, values, norms, and premises."*[7] To elaborate:[8]

A belief system includes all of the cognitions (ideas, knowledge, lore, superstitions, myths, and legends) shared by most people.

Cultural norms are the rules and standards accepted by members of a society. Norms may be split into *folkways* which are not clearly enforced, whereas *mores* are enforced by social sanction or law.

Cultural values represent an especially important class of beliefs shared by the members of a society concerning what is desirable or "good" or what ought to be.

In bridging culture and values, it may be seen that values represent an important set of beliefs and that both values and norms are important parts of culture.

Consumers in the U.S. seem to be increasingly questioning certain beliefs, values, and, therefore, norms in addition to certain very basic premises of our culture. To the extent that these are altered, marketing must adapt. Marketing, for example, is currently coping with consumerism legislation, social pressures, and the shifting values of consumers.

Causes of Value Change

A statement emanating from the Business Environment Section of the General Electric Company cited shifts in peoples' basic values as the single most important element in forecasting the environment of business.[9] Partially accepting that thesis, it is important to build a framework for predicting value change. In the case of values, this requires attention to changing social structures such as the family, schools, and church as well as numerous *lifetime experiences.*

---

[7] David Krech, Richard S. Crutchfield, and Egerton L. Ballachey, *Individual in Society* (San Francisco: McGraw-Hill Book Co., 1962), pp. 341–53.

[8] Ibid., pp. 349–51.

[9] Ian Wilson, "Socio-Political Forecasting: A New Dimension to Strategic Planning," *Michigan Business Review,* July 1974, p. 22.

It appears that differences between the values of younger and older consumers may be partially explained by younger people taking affluence and fulfillment of lower level needs for granted. The fulfillment of basic needs such as hunger are assumed away by young, affluent consumers with attention instead given to craft projects, the arts and other creative outlets. Older consumers may be perceived by the young as materialistic. Other lifetime experiences such as technological changes are basic factors contributing to social and value change. We are now witnessing the first generation to have "grown up on television." Television contributes to the perceptions and beliefs that the young have of society—certainly supplementing if not even replacing to some extent the role of other institutions as a source of learning. Also, consider the impact on values of the "pill," smaller families, and a white-collar society with more college graduates than ever experienced. Consider mobility, its relation to awareness, and the possible impact on values. Another form of experience relating to value change is interaction with changing peer (or reference) groups:

> People are influenced by and tend to accept as their wants and goals the values shared by members of their reference groups and, less directly, the values of the larger society. . . . but the values of a society do change, and they change because of the actions of individuals . . . What the person recognizes as desirable—his values—are not necessarily his desires. As people grow up and become "culture broken," the desirables tend to become desires—values become goals—Because of his particular life experiences, an individual may acquire new values and goals which dominate his life.[10]

All of these experiences undoubtedly help to insure that today's consumer values are different than tomorrow's.

Fundamental social structures such as the family, the church and educational institutions also affect values through socialization processes.[11] As societal institutions, they tend to be stable and, in many ways, are more fundamental influences on values than life experiences.

But the increasing role of women outside the home, divorce rates, as well as increasing competition from schools and television have all contributed to change in the family. Although still important, the family has probably declined in influence as a value-transmitter. The church has historically had a dramatic influence on the values of consumers as sug-

---

[10] Krech et al., *Individual in Society,* pp. 80, 351.

[11] William Lazer and John E. Smallwood, "Consumer Environments and Life Styles of the Seventies," *MSU Business Topics,* vol. 2 (Spring 1972), pp. 5–17. Reprinted by permission of the publisher, Division of Research, Graduate School of Business Administration, Michigan State University; Kimball Young and Raymond W. Mack, *Sociology and Social Life* (New York: American Book Company, 1962), pp. 323–32.

gested by the terms "puritan ethic" and "Protestant ethic." But over the past several decades there is little question that the church has declined in influence. Although in the mid-seventies this decline stabilized, 56 percent of the respondents to a Gallup poll still felt religion was losing its influence on American life. With the increasing length and intensity of the educational experience, there is evidence that the schools, unlike the family and the church, have become *more* important as value transmitters. The formal educational experience today starts earlier and lasts longer. Education has also contributed to an atmosphere of questioning which has contributed to the values and institutions within society being challenged.

Although government reflects the will of the people and is not as fundamental an influence on values as the family, church and schools, government as a primary social structure also influences values. Governmental activity permeates the life styles of consumers by its effects on the economy, taxes, legislation, and assistance programs. Governmental positions on credit, birth control, pollution and consumer deception influence as well as reflect the perceptions and attitudes of the people. Thus, a cursory glance at changing social institutions and life experiences as causal factors underlying value change intuitively confirms their relationship. Unfortunately, we do not understand the relationships sufficiently for modeling—but it is a beginning to identify related factors.

Value Trends

The composite value structure of the United States is changing although not as dramatically as anticipated at the end of the 1960s. *Fortune* magazine for example, using Yankelovich, Inc. studies of the young (18–24 years), reported in 1969 and 1973 that changes are occurring; although in 1973 they wrote, "Underneath all that hair, young Americans exhibit many of the same qualities their predecessors did ten or fifteen years ago. Yet, the 'youth revolution,' . . . has left a permanent imprint on the young people who passed through their formative years while it was under way. Middle-class values were challenged in basic ways, and a broad residuum of change in style and viewpoint remains."[12] About one out of every nine Americans were between the ages of 18–24 at the turn of the decade and 25 percent of them were on college campuses. Of those on campuses, even in 1969, three-fifths of the students were "practical" in orientation with rather traditional values.[13] The others were best characterized by their lack of concern about mak-

---

[12] Edmund Faltermayer, "Youth after the Revolution," *Fortune,* vol. 87, no. 3 (March 1973), p. 145. Also see Daniel Seligman, "A Special Kind of Rebellion," *Fortune,* vol. 79, no. 1 (January 1969), pp. 67–69, 172–80.

[13] Seligman, "A Special Kind of Rebellion," p. 68.

ing money—certainly a tidbit of interest to marketing management, both from the standpoint of employee motivation as well as of product development (e.g., related anti-materialism). By 1973, it was concluded that "tolerance" best characterized the viewpoint of college students.[14] This included respecting the rights of others and also extended to sexual freedom. The roles of men and women were reported to be blurring and artificial barriers (e.g., rigid dating formalities) between the sexes on campus were virtually gone. The majority of students had career goals, were "pretty satisfied" with their upbringing, but did not accept things at face value. They tended to lack respect for impersonal institutions, although they respected the rights of the "little guy."[15] *Fortune* concludes:

> It would seem, then, that reports from the campus, whether of continuing revolution or of counter-revolution, have been exaggerated. A distinct youth culture has spread from a trend-setting minority to the majority, but in the process of assimilation has lost most of its ideological content.[16]

A study group commissioned by Whirlpool Corporation to study social change seemed to go even further. From the group, John Smallwood, Director of Economic and Marketing Research at Whirlpool and William Lazer of Michigan State University concluded:

> Despite the attention given to changes and technological developments, studies of the probable trends during this decade suggest that life styles and values of various social classes will demonstrate great stability. Life styles will continue to highlight the dominant characteristic of the existence of core values, of permanence, stability, and, in general, a lack of change in *basic* belief and value systems.[17]

The authors point out that some value change may be attributed to consumers ascending into higher social classes which have always exhibited somewhat different values and purchase behavior. They also emphasize they are referring to a lack of change in *basic* values which, of course, is difficult to define except by degree.

There is considerable agreement among several studies as to the following value-related trends:

1. Delayed Gratification to Instant Gratification
2. Materialism to Purchase of "Experiences" and New Symbols
3. Artificial Behavior to Naturalism

---

[14] Faltermayer, "Youth after the Revolution," p. 146.

[15] Ibid., pp. 145–48, 152, 158.

[16] Ibid., p. 158.

[17] Lazer *et al*, "Consumer Environments and Life Styles of the Seventies," p. 5.

4. Work Ethic to Hedonism
5. Sexual Chastity to Sexual Freedom
6. Self-Reliance to Institutional/Governmental Reliance
7. Husband-Dominated Family to Greater Role Equality
8. Thrift to Credit
9. Object Accumulation to Utilization Orientation
10. Purchases Becoming More a Form of Self-Expression and Identity

These shifts are occurring faster within some groups than others, and, generally, they are not changing significantly on a monthly or probably even a yearly basis. Yet one analyst concluded that we today witness

FIGURE 5–7

Profile of Significant Value-System Changes: 1969–1980 as seen by General Electric's Business Environment Section

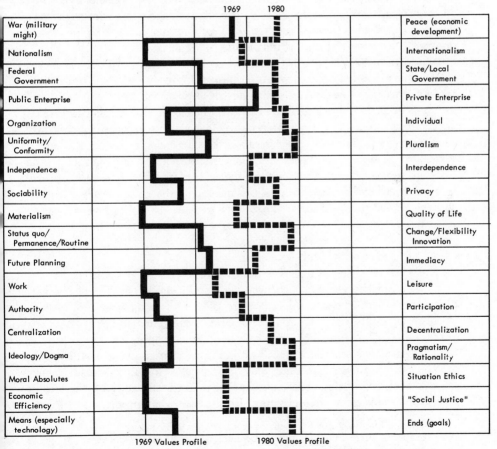

Source: Ian H. Wilson, "Socio-Political Forecasting: A New Dimension to Strategic Planning," *Michigan Business Review*, July 1974, p. 24.

about the same change in values in seven or eight years that used to occur in every twenty years.[18] In attempting to systematize analysis of value change, General Electric uses a "value profile" shown in Figure 5–7 above. Although not intended as a precise, foolproof instrument, it nicely illustrates trends of significance to business and marketing. Each major value trend could be interpreted in terms of its implications for various product/markets. This task is left to the reader and it is instead emphasized that values set the stage for understanding social issues.

SOCIAL CHANGE AND SOCIAL ISSUES

The very process of socialization prohibits rapid change in basic values. Marketing management can therefore monitor and attempt to predict values with assurance that they change over a period of years. Consumer attitudes and perceptions are much more volatile and must be monitored more closely than values. Anticipating consumer perceptions and attitudes toward new as well as ongoing marketing programs represents an essential part of marketing management.

In addition to collecting information on traditional consumer responses to the market offering, management must increasingly determine consumers' attitudes toward the social desirability of the offer. As discussed in Chapter 2, consumer attitudes toward business and marketing are at an all-time low and it is no longer sufficient for business to pursue only economic goals. Instead, the effects of business decisions on the social system must be gauged and incorporated into marketer planning. The rules of the business game are changing and marketing managers are recognizing they have responsibilities not only to stockholders but to consumers, to the communities where they live, to their employees, and to socially disadvantaged groups. Societal expectations are rising with respect to marketing activities and social issues such as consumerism demand the attention of high-level management.

The idea of a "social issue" is based on the concept of conflict resolution. Whether the issue be consumerism, pollution or the ghetto marketplace, its nature is captured in Figure 5–8. The *expectations* of people in society (notably consumers in our case) sometimes *conflict* with their *perceptions of reality*. The "reality" here is the actual performance of the marketing system. Consumer's *perceptions* of marketing performance, if divergent from *expectations*, may lead to the advent of social issues. If consumer perceptions are inaccurate, the net result may be the rise of unjustified consumer social issues. Because of the importance of con-

---

[18] Florence Skelly, "Life Style and Social Values in Future Planning," presentation at Spring American Marketing Association Conference (Chicago: American Marketing Association, 1973).

FIGURE 5–8

Marketing and Social Issues

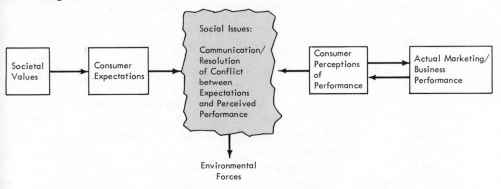

sumer perceptions, Figure 5–8 illustrates social issues as evolving from the gap between perceived marketing performance and expectations.

Marketing-related social issues, therefore, *represent conflict between consumer expectations and consumer perceptions of marketing performance including the related processes of communication and resolution.* It is in this context that marketing management must attempt to anticipate and cope with environmental forces. Marketing management within different business firms will not be equally affected by different social issues. The relevance of a given social issue is determined not only by the company's products, promotional efforts and pricing policies but also by its philosophy of social responsibility. A company may (1) focus entirely on profits (and a profitable firm is typically serving society well); it may (2) *explicitly* incorporate social responsibility into its day-to-day marketing decisions to minimize negative effects on society and to enhance positive effects; and/or (3) a firm may go even further and engage in social projects unrelated to corporate mission and even detrimental to profits (which might not be socially desirable!). In analyzing social changes or potential social forces, management must determine whether social issues concerning the ghetto[19] marketplace, consumerism, and pollution of the environment are relevant, and therefore potential forces, as they pertain to their specific business. Unless a company markets its products within the ghetto, consideration of social issues in the ghetto marketplace might be deemed irrelevant. An exception would exist if management accepted the third category of social responsibility—that of contributing to the resolution of social problems unrelated to profit.

---

[19] Ghetto is used herein to refer to a geographical concentration of blacks in an urban area.

Unlike the ghetto marketplace, both the natural environment and consumerism issues are commonly recognized by firms as relevant "environmental forces" with the potential of affecting profits.

Ghetto Marketplace

As an area for social concern as well as an example of market failure, the marketplace within urban inner-city areas is noteworthy. Issues concern price discrimination against the poor, exorbitant credit charges and unethical merchant practices. In the context of Figure 5–8 the primary reasons for the rise of social issues in the ghetto marketplace were, first, the changing awareness, perceptions and attitudes of people both inside and outside the ghetto marketplace and, secondly, the actual conditions themselves. Blacks became increasingly dissatisfied with conditions in the inner cities (including retail services), expectations were raised and the resulting gap contributed to frustration and violence. The violence, in part, awakened the conscience of the nation and contributed to a much greater awareness by the general community of deplorable conditions in the ghetto marketplace. Concern spread beyond the inner cities and the expectations of the general public vs. the actual performance of marketing and business in these areas did not match. Thus, during the 1960s and early seventies, considerable attention was devoted to delineating the problems in these areas.[20] These problems relate to business practices, the market structure and the behavior of consumers. These, in combination, determine the performance of the retail system in these areas.[21]

Studies have identified a higher incidence of fraudulent *business practices* in the ghetto marketplace such as price discrimination, exorbitant credit charges, high pressure salesmanship and trickery. Concerning credit, for example, a study in Washington, D.C., found that eleven retailers reported 2,690 judgments in one year against delinquent debtors; these resulting in 1,568 wage garnishments and 306 repossessions.[22] These results, although not conclusive, point toward too much easy credit being aimed at naive consumers. Another study reported credit charges at interest rates as high as 82 percent with 20 to 30 percent rates being

---

[20] Frederick D. Sturdivant, ed., *The Ghetto Marketplace* (New York: The Free Press, 1969). Also see, Gerald E. Hills and Gerald E. Nichols, "Business and the Minority Community," *Tennessee Survey of Business,* vol. 7, no. 9 (May 1972), pp. 3–6, 16; Alan R. Andreason, ed., *Improving Inner-City Marketing* (Chicago: American Marketing Association, 1972).

[21] Frederick D. Sturdivant, "Distribution in American Society: Some Questions of Efficiency and Relevance," in *Vertical Marketing Systems,* ed. by Louis P. Bucklin (Glenview, Illinois: Scott, Foresman and Company, 1970), pp. 94–115.

[22] Federal Trade Commission, "Economic Report on Installment Credit and Retail Sales Practices of District of Columbia Retailers," in *The Ghetto Marketplace,* ed. by Frederick D. Sturdivant (New York: The Free Press, 1969), pp. 76–107.

common.[23] In some cases, economic principles help to explain retailer practices. The Washington study (above), for example, concluded that inner-city retailer *profits* were not higher despite higher prices. Although some studies conflict, prices do tend to be somewhat higher in inner city areas for both food and durables. It is important to recognize, however, that such costs as insurance, pilferage and labor turnover are often higher for inner-city retailers and, as importantly, that the 'mom and pop' scale of operation prohibits the economies which large retail chains take for granted. Further, studies show that many inner city consumers in certain cities travel to the suburbs to shop and therefore pay no more than suburban residents. Yet, as a generalization, the poor do tend to pay more than their higher-income counterparts. Furthermore, it is clear that economic justification for the practices of some retailers does not exist, and, indeed, that some merchants do take unfair advantage of area consumers.

Also affecting retail system performance, the retail *market structure* of the ghetto has been described as "atomistic," that is, composed of tiny, often inefficient, poorly managed retail businesses. Mass merchandising and discount stores are usually underrepresented or non-existent. Also, until recent years, whites often owned most of the area businesses but did not reside in the area with the resulting loss of multiplier effects (from the spending of owner income within the ghetto area). Finally, serious barriers to entry have retarded entry of mass merchandisers into the marketplace. Large retailers have pressed Congress for tax incentives and investment guarantees to make ghetto investments more attractive, but with little progress. Other efforts have included attempts to develop more minority-owned enterprises by, for example, the Office of Minority Business Enterprise (in the U.S. Department of Commerce) and the Small Business Administration. Also, Community Development Corporations, involving widespread community investment, have been formed in some areas to promote the redevelopment of the retail sector.

Perhaps the most basic problem of the ghetto marketplace is not the retailer practices or the retailer structure, but concerns the *consumers* themselves. Unethical merchants tend to be attracted by naive consumers and, to some extent, an atomistic retail structure (small stores in close proximity to one another) is necessitated by consumers who search less and are relatively immobile. Research findings indicate that, relative to middle-income consumers, lower-income consumers tend to search less for information before making purchase decisions, are less mobile shoppers, rely more on personal contacts and friendly merchants, and generally engage in behavior which is less consistent with the

---

[23] Frederick D. Sturdivant and Walter T. Wilhelm, "Poverty, Minorities, and Consumer Exploitation," in *The Ghetto Marketplace,* ed. by Frederick D. Sturdivant (New York: The Free Press, 1969), pp. 108–17.

"economic man" type of consumer. Less comparative shopping tends to reduce competition between retailers and the often fatalistic shopper tends to prolong the existence of marginal retailers. Attempts to alter consumer behavior patterns which are entrenched in a basic life style is difficult except over the long run. Yet it is probably the most fundamental problem area in the ghetto marketplace and, thus, deserves research and action.

The social problems within the inner city marketplace remain a challenge to the social conscience of marketers throughout the nation. But other social problems such as the physical environment and consumerism are closer to the heartbeat of marketing operations and confront marketers more frequently.

Natural Environment

Marketing ultimately ties back to the use of scarce resources for the fulfillment of human needs. Actions which serve to upset the ecological balance by either harming or unnecessarily using scarce resources have become the object of social and governmental criticism.[24] To understand the relation of marketing, an overview of the material flow process within the economic system is shown in Figure 5–9. Attention on this figure is twofold: (1) the effects of the four processes and related residuals (in the upper part of the model) on the environmental media of air, water and land as well as (2) the extraction of scarce natural resources. Consumer-oriented firms today provide goods and services which meet consumer needs—but often without considering related social costs to society. The expectations of consumer/citizens have risen and, at the same time, people have come to perceive the effects of marketing on the physical environment. Whereas a smokestack used to be a sign of prosperity, due to different values and expectations, it is now a sign of degradation. Although business probably pollutes less today than ever before, the expectations of consumers appear to be at an all-time high. The result is a gap between expectations and business performance with resulting conflict.

Marketing management subscribing to the second level of social responsibility (above) are cognizant of the social effects of their decisions; especially product-related decisions.[25] Marketing management influences what is produced and indirectly affects (a) the natural resources and

---

[24] George Fisk, *Marketing and the Ecological Crisis* (New York: Harper & Row, 1974), pp. 1–19.

[25] For related reading, see Dale L. Varble, "Social and Environmental Considerations in New Product Development," *Journal of Marketing*, vol. 36 (October 1972), pp. 11–15.

materials used, (b) the amount of energy required in the production process, as well as (c) the residuals (e.g., wastewater) which result from production (Figure 5–9). Product decisions also affect (d) the consumption process. Consumers, for example, may have to consume resources and energy to use the product (e.g., air conditioners); the *use* of the product may generate additional pollutants (e.g., automobiles); there may be substantial packaging material to be discarded or the product itself may be designed to become obsolete (e.g., plastic, non-refillable cigarette lighters); or finally, the materials may not be bio-degradable or sufficiently valuable to provide an incentive for recycling (e.g., most plastics will not disintegrate nor will aluminum—but aluminum is sufficiently valuable to encourage recycling). In addition to product decisions, the physical distribution and transportation of products may incur social costs (such as air pollution) not fully reflected in the profit and loss statement.

Marketing management is increasingly being pressured to consider various social costs in their decision making, both by ecology groups (often via the news media) as well as by government (Chapter 6). Yet, it must be recognized that not all consumers, or perhaps even a majority, have been willing to pay higher prices for products which conserve resources or pollute less. If marketers attempt to alter consumers' product preferences by limiting their choice (either by dropping existing products or not offering new products), a question of consumer freedom arises. Supporters of the free market system argue that consumers should be cognizant of social costs associated with the production and use of products and then *consumers* should decide whether or not to purchase. Because the actions of individual consumers impact on the lives of *other*

FIGURE 5–9

Material Flow Process in the Economic System

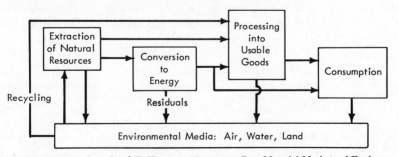

Source: Taken from Jared E. Hazelton, "Impact on Raw Material Markets of Environmental Policies," *Technological Forecasting and Social Change*, no. 3 (1972), p. 354. Also, Harold W. Henry, College of Business Administration, University of Tennessee, for modifications to the original schema.

people, however, many cannot accept this mode of resolution including, it seems, many in government.

Although marketing may contribute to the degradation of the environment, marketing techniques may also help to resolve the problem. Marketing may be used both by business and social organizations to better inform and educate the public as to the effects of their consuming decisions. Also, in an age of scarce resources, management may even engage in demarketing, encouraging consumers to consume less as with electricity and gasoline during the energy shortage.[26] Marketing knowledge may also facilitate efficient recycling because recycling is, in effect, a *reverse* channel of distribution. Consumers become the *de facto* producers with middlemen channeling these resources back to be used again (e.g., returnable bottles), to be reprocessed into a different product, or to be reused as a raw material.[27] The major portion of the cost of most recycled products is their collection, sorting, and transportation. Marketing probably relates more directly to the 3.5 million tons of solid waste generated annually than to air and water pollution, so it would be appropriate for marketing technology to facilitate recycling as well as to market new, recycled "products."

In defense of marketing, Mr. Judd Alexander, Vice President, Marketing-General Packaging, American Can Company, said "We know that packaging composes less than 14 percent of collectable solid waste. But the consumer will often estimate packaging's share at 40 to 80 percent."[28] While acknowledging that some excess packaging exists, Mr. Alexander outlined numerous ways in which packaging reduces costs—in the shipping process, in facilitating self-service, in contributing to less spoilage, in reducing pilferage and by facilitating efficient use of display space.[29] The average U.S. citizen generates about 1,800 pounds of solid waste annually and it is tempting for consumers to generalize from the household wastebasket which contains a disproportionate amount of consumer goods packaging. The packaging industry is attempting to cope with social pressure (environmental forces) for national legislation similar to Oregon's law banning cans with pull-tab openers and requiring refund values on all beer and soft-drink containers.

---

[26] Philip Kotler and Sidney Levy, "Demarketing, Yes Demarketing," *Harvard Business Review*, vol. 49 (November–December 1971), pp. 74–80; David W. Cravens "Marketing Management in an Era of Shortages," *Business Horizons*, vol. 17, no. 1 (February 1974), pp. 79–85.

[27] William G. Zikmund and William J. Stanton, "Recycling Solid Wastes: A Channels-of-Distribution Problem," *Journal of Marketing*, vol. 35, no. 3 (July 1971), pp. 34–39, published by the American Marketing Association.

[28] Judd H. Alexander, a speech, "Packaging . . . The Silent Servant . . . Silent Too Long," delivered to the Packaging Institute's 33rd Annual Forum in New York, October 4, 1971.

[29] Ibid.

Consumerism

According to a consumerism publication published by E. I. Dupont Company:

> Of the vital issues facing business today, few, if any, rank higher than consumerism. Recent surveys indicate that consumerism is the nation's No. 1 business issue and that its problems are for business—not the public—to solve. Consumerism is potentially the most damaging problem business faces, and it is going to be around a long time.[30]

Ms. Virginia Knauer of the Office of Consumer Affairs defined consumerism as simply, "Let the *seller* beware" but, more descriptively, consumerism is ". . . *a social force within the environment designed to aid and protect the consumer through the exertion of legal, moral, and economic pressure on business.*"[31] This definition first recognizes that consumers, politicians, and various groups engage in actions to stir public opinion and generate public pressure—thus making consumerism a *social*-environmental force. Consumer activity is oriented toward the *protection* of the consumer (e.g., product safety and fraudulent sales practices) as well as toward *aiding* the consumer (e.g., better information for consumer decisions). The definition also recognizes the tactics employed; generating pressure for new legislation (in 1974 there were about 400 consumer related bills in Congress), appealing to the conscience of corporate executives, as well as through economic pressure from boycotts and negative publicity. Consumerism activity is often directed toward a better functioning market system (Chapter 2). For the market system to function, consumer rights and responsibilities must be exercised as in Figure 5-10. Consumerism activities of educating, providing information and consumer protection may foster the exercise of consumer rights essential to the preservation of the market system.

Consumerism is an issue because rapidly rising consumer expectations have outpaced business performance. Increasing incomes, higher educational levels, and changing values have all contributed to a more demanding consumer. Add the impact of mass communications on consumer awareness, such catalysts as Ralph Nader, the increasing visibility of the low-income consumer, inflation, political activity, and, generally, an atmosphere of cynicism regarding institutions (including marketing) and one may begin to understand the rise of consumerism. The causes of consumerism, therefore, go far beyond the failure of marketing and business.

---

[30] Virginia Knauer and Frank McLaughlin, a private interview, "Consumerism Is Good for Business," *Dupont Context*, no. 1 (1973), pp. 16–18.

[31] David W. Cravens and Gerald E. Hills, "Consumerism: A Perspective for Business," *Business Horizons*, vol. 13, no. 4 (August 1970), pp. 21–28.

FIGURE 5–10

Consumer Policy and Consumer Rights and Responsibilities

Consumer Policy	CONSUMER RIGHTS			
	1. Choose Freely	2. Be Informed	3. Be Heard	4. Be Safe
A. Education	Decision-making, budgeting; nature of market economy; rights and responsibilities	Generic product and materials data; information sources	How to assert consumer rights	Importance of health and safety; user manuals and training
B. Information	Buying criteria; buying advice	Models and brands data; independent consumer information programs	Market research, two-way market dialogue	Safety certification; care and maintenance data
C. Protection	Maintain open markets, antitrust; stop high-pressure and deceptive tactics	Truly informative advertising; product claims substantiation	Complaints handling machinery	Minimize health and accident risks
	Choose Wisely	Keep Informed	Sound Off	Safety First
	CONSUMER RESPONSIBILITIES			

A third dimension of the matrix would show the makers of consumer policy. These policy-makers include *consumer organizations, other citizen groups, business, government, educational institutions and the mass media.* (copyright: H. B. Thorelli)

Source: Hans B. Thorelli, "A Concept of Consumer Policy," *Proceedings of Annual Meeting* (Association for Consumer Research, 1972), p. 195.

But at the same time, business failed to implement the marketing concept to the extent desired by consumers. With self-service, retailing became "depersonalized" as the age of mass marketing truly matured, products became increasingly complex without related service and information, and generally, the gap between marketing and consumers widened despite more "efficient" marketing than consumers had ever known. Yet, if business has failed, it has failed in communicating with consumers. Consumers grossly misperceive how the business system operates; and they also misjudge the actual level of business profits.

For many reasons, therefore, marketers are having to cope with over 200 consumer organizations in the U.S., consumer offices in nearly all state and several city governments, and with over thirty different federal departments and offices. The issues (and related forces) are wide-ranging and impinge on every marketing decision area.

Relating to *product decisions,* issues arise concerning quality, safety, planned obsolescence, packaging, product differentiation as well as warranties and, very basically, the alleged effects of marketing on materialism in society.[32] *Promotion decisions* relate to consumerism issues including personal selling techniques, deceptive advertising, the cost of advertising, promotion directed to vulnerable groups (such as children and lesser educated consumers), and the use of advertising to foster "unreal" perceived differences between products. *Distribution decisions* relate to social issues concerning the cost of distribution, the level of service in disadvantaged areas as well as the impact of large shopping centers on the community. *Pricing decisions* have historically been more circumscribed by law than many marketing decision areas. Pricing collusion and unfair price discrimination are examples of illegal pricing practices. Finally, *marketing research* is being challenged by those who see it as an invasion of privacy. Many of these issues are discussed in the next chapter on the governmental environment.

In a survey of the American Marketing Association membership, only 16 percent agreed with the statement that: "The 'consumer movement' is likely to result in more harm than good for society."[33] Also, the responses of businessmen and educators were similar. Such results suggest, despite early resistance, that the vast majority of marketers have come to view current social changes as a legitimate call for different "rules" for doing business.

---

[32] See, for example, Frederick E. Webster, Jr., *Social Aspects of Marketing,* (Englewood Cliffs: Prentice-Hall, 1974), pp. 29–72.

[33] Conducted by R. Lavidge & Associates, Chicago, Illinois and reported in *The Marketing News,* American Marketing Association.

SOCIAL CHANGE AND MARKETING DECISIONS

Until recently, many marketers viewed social changes with interest, but not of direct relevance to marketing management. Today, more and more attention is being given to incorporating social changes into marketing decision-making—both from (a) the perspective of traditional marketing strategy as well as (b) in response to new social responsibility requirements. The remaining portion of this chapter emphasizes the latter. For social change to be incorporated into the decision environment of marketers, three things must occur. Marketers must (1) understand the "rules of the game" as dictated by society, (2) assess marketing operations as they relate to the rules (social audit), and (3) respond.

Social Environment: Rules of the Game

Considerable resources are being directed by companies to various methodologies for identifying social trends. Daniel Yankelovich, Inc., a New York research firm, was among the first to confront the challenge, and in recent years several companies have purchased the Yankelovich Social Trends Monitor. The Monitor is used both for traditional marketing tasks as well as for monitoring the social climate:

> There is a lot going on in the country today. We read about it in the press; we know about it from our own contacts with younger people. We see it in the streets around us. Are these things going to have an effect on my business? Are there some opportunities that I am missing —opportunities for new products; for product-line expansion; for changes in distribution—which would give me a better competitive position? . . .[34]

Not surprisingly, firms in the clothing, financial services, and leisure time industries were particularly interested in the Monitor for obtaining hard data on social trends. The Monitor is an extensive longitudinal data collection program that periodically measures approximately 35 social/ value trends such as materialism, sexual freedom, hypocrisy, religion, hedonism and personalization.

Also, "social indicators," measures of the quality of life, are "statistics and forms of evidence that enable us to assess where we stand and where we are going with respect to our values and goals, and to evaluate specific programs and determine their impact."[35] A current challenge is to

[34] Florence R. Skelly, "Development of Social Trends Measurements," *Spring New York Conference on Research Methodology* (Chicago: American Marketing Association, 1970), pp. 1–2.

[35] Definition by Raymond Bauer, cited by Harry A. Lipson, Eugene J. Kelley and Seymour Marshak, "Integrating Social Feedback and Social Audits into Corporate Planning," in *Social Marketing*, ed. by William Lazer and Eugene Kelly (Home-

operationalize social indicators as a context for business and marketing goal formulation. Measuring consumer values, for example, would help define appropriate marketing goals and techniques.

Corporations are also working, "in-house" to analyze and predict social changes. General Motors, in its Societal Analysis Department, combines the talents of demographers, economists, social psychologists, mathematicians, psychologists, sociologists, physicists and engineers on projects concerning public attitude change, modeling and simulation of social systems, recycling and reclamation, energy, natural resources, and quantification of social costs. Similarly, Whirlpool Corporation commissioned a multidisciplinary group to interpret social changes of importance.

In addition to assessing social change implications for market opportunities and strategy, firms also use research information to provide direction in the social responsibility arena. For example, attention in recent years to actually measuring consumer satisfaction is related to profit-oriented strategy but also provides direction for assessing consumer expectations. New and better research objectives need to be devised as suggested, for example, by Scott and Lamont in calling for a better definition of consumerism by distinguishing alienation, hostility, frustration and satisfaction.[36] Oriented toward forecasting, a 1974 Delphi study involving several companies (contributing $10,000 each), used the services of 150 experts in various fields of study to predict, among other things, the corporate impacts of the energy crisis and the future of the world.[37] Better information on the nature and the causes of social change will enable future marketers to better monitor and forecast as well as strategically respond to both market shifts and a changing social climate.

Social Audit: How Do We Measure Up?

If the expectations of society and social changes relevant to marketing strategy are understood, marketers may assess current corporate strategies and social posture against the backdrop of societal expectations. Because decisions as they pertain to market opportunities and to market-

wood, Ill: Richard D. Irwin, Inc., 1973), p. 177; also see Robert L. Clewett and Jerry C. Olson, eds., *Social Indicators and Marketing* (Chicago: American Marketing Association, 1974).

[36] Jerome E. Scott and Lawrence M. Lamont, "Consumerism: A Theoretical Framework for Analysis," *Marketing and Social Issues: The World Around Us*, ed. by Boris W. Becker and Helmut Becker (Chicago: American Marketing Association, 1972), p. 241.

[37] Harold W. Henry, "Distinctive Features of the Long-Range Strategies Planning Systems in Six Large U.S. Corporations," presented at the International Conference on Corporate Planning, San Francisco, May 22, 1975.

ing strategy are discussed later, attention here is limited to evaluating the social posture of the corporate marketing function. It has been proposed that a "social audit" might be instituted by companies to assess a firm's effects on society and to measure, not unlike financial statements measure financial progress, the degree to which *social* goals have been met. Without attention to *measuring* corporate social progress, the concept of social responsibility remains nebulous and impossible to implement. Only a few companies are currently experimenting with the social audit, so it may be premature to consider a specific *marketing* social audit. Attention here is on the marketing component, however. A corporate social audit is a ". . . systematic assessment of and reporting on some meaningful, definable domain of a company's activities that have social impact."[38] Although at least one accounting scholar foresees a distant day when externally verified social audits will be commonplace,[39] they are currently in the embryonic stages. Essential stages of a marketing social audit include to (1) identify the positive and negative social impacts of the firms' marketing activity on its various constituencies; (2) develop measures of these effects; and (3) measure impacts and draw implications for management.

Social impacts often taken for granted such as employment and employee training must be included. Although some firms have attempted to find a common denominator for measuring social effects (Abt Associates has used dollars), only a few firms have yet attempted to develop a "Social Balance Sheet."[40] Dayton-Hudson Corporation, a diversified retail organization headquartered in Minneapolis, began by attempting to define and measure social impacts relevant to the entire industry but soon found the enormity of the task overwhelming. They then formed four task forces on consumerism, human resources, environmental impact, and community development; and rather than measure impacts precisely, they chose to respond to areas of apparent social need.[41] Measurement will become increasingly important once marketers have responded to readily apparent problems in the marketing society interface; but it is a challenge to measure such impacts better so as to assign priorities to areas of greatest need and/or social threat. One objective is to have a basis for intelligent business response, so as to defuse social

---

[38] Raymond A. Bauer and Dan H. Fenn, Jr., "What *Is* a Corporate Social Audit?" *Harvard Business Review*, vol. 51, no. 1 (January–February 1973), pp. 37–48; Raymond A. Bauer and Dan H. Fenn, Jr., *The Corporate Social Audit* (New York: Russell Sage Foundation, 1972), pp. 15–42.

[39] Norton M. Bedford, "New Dimensions in Corporate Accountability," a lecture delivered as part of the Visiting Distinguished Scholars Series, the University of Tennessee, Knoxville, January 19, 1973.

[40] "The First Attempts at a Corporate 'Social Audit'," *Business Week*, September 23, 1972, pp. 88–92.

[41] "The Social Audit Begins to Move," *Industry Week*, August 20, 1973, p. 45.

issues in their early stages, or, better, remove the causes of such issues before they arise.

Business/Marketer Response

Many firms such as Dayton-Hudson and the Quaker Oats Company have been concerned with how to change internally to respond to external social changes. Business response may be grouped into three categories including (a) shifting goals, (b) organizational changes and (c) participation in new activities.

Goals of marketers have begun to shift in recognition of new consumer demands which, in large part, represent an expanded definition of the marketing concept. It has been noted that:

> Firms devoted to the marketing concept have taken a narrow viev of the consumer's needs and have focused almost exclusively on dis covering typical product usage patterns and developing products which best serve these needs. Other needs, such as the need for information for decision-making have been largely ignored.[42]

> In consideration of the issue of marketing philosophy, it has become increasingly apparent that the marketing concept, as commonly conceived, is not sufficiently adequate to reflect a subtle and yet fundamental transition now underway in the discipline. The transition in question is that of marketing changing from being mostly concerned with the firm's relationship to the customer to being concerned with the organization's . . . relationship to the societies in which it operates . . .[43]

This requires consideration of more than "consumers"—because the satisfaction of a group of consumers (e.g., wanting high performance autos or guns) *may* be to the overall detriment of society. Increasing recognition that the marketing concept must encompass a wider definition of societal needs has come about in an atmosphere of expanding corporate goals. As noted by Stanley J. Goodman, Chairman, May Department Stores,

> I believe . . . that the American corporation has come to a moment of change, of fundamental rethinking of where it is going and what it is all about. As a nation, we must integrate social and economic goals; and as business managers, we must assume the responsibility to meld social and economic achievement, so that the national yardstick can evolve from gross national product to gross social product, and business be

---

[42] Robert O. Herrmann, "The Marketing Profession and the Consumer Interest," *The Journal of Consumer Affairs*, vol. 5, no. 1 (Summer 1971), p. 86.

[43] Leonard L. Berry, "Challenges for Marketing in the Age of the People," *MSU Business Topics*, Winter 1972, p. 8. Reprinted by permission of the publisher, Division of Research, Graduate School of Business Administration, Michigan State University.

judged not just for the quantity but for the quality of profits . . . "What's good for the people is good for business."[44]

Although some business leaders might consider this an extreme stance, there is a trend toward goal-sets which respond to societal expectations. Quaker Oats called a "Social Progress Assembly" in 1973 of senior, middle-level and entry-level employees to evaluate new social needs and appraise national trends. This innovative approach yielded several ideas that altered the social objectives of the company. These goals, in turn, are reflected in organizational changes.

Organizational changes of direct relevance to consumerism and marketing are seen in over two-hundred companies that now have high-level organizational positions to deal with consumer problems; mostly titled "Director" but including even "Vice-President" for Consumer Affairs. The positions are designed to respond to consumer problems and to identify problem areas within the firm. To be successful, the occupants of these coordinative types of positions must have the full support of top management and, many, in fact, report directly to the President. For responsive efforts to be effective, however, they should also involve middle-management. This requires meaningful communications from top management tied to the incentive system. As Phillip Drotning, Director of Corporate Social Responsibility, Standard Oil of Indiana, has stated:

> Social policies will remain placebos for the tortured executive conscience until they are implemented with the same iron-fisted management tools that are routinely employed in other areas of activity to measure performance, secure accountability, and distribute penalties and rewards.[45]

Response to social-environmental forces requires that related goals be translated into new areas of accountability within the organization. Also, in the early seventies, the number of chief executive officers (CEO's) with marketing backgrounds came to exceed those with finance and production backgrounds. This was attributed in part to the rise of consumerism, although CEO's with production backgrounds were reported on the rise partly because of plant modernization required to meet pollution-control standards.[46] Thus, organizational structure and personnel change as the social environment changes.

Responsive activities of marketers may be placed into at least three groupings. First are changes in marketing strategy due to a changing

---

[44] "Raising the Fallen Image of Business," address before the National Retail Merchants Association meeting (January 7, 1974), p. 9.

[45] Phillip T. Drotning, "Organizing the Company for Social Action," in *The Unstable Ground: Corporate Social Policy in a Dynamic Society*, ed. by S. Prakash Sethi (Los Angeles: Melville Publishing Company, 1974), p. 259.

[46] "More Room at the Top for Marketing Men," *Business Week*, August 12, 1972, p. 27.

society. This includes removing sources of problems which create consumerism and other issues and also includes responding to new market opportunities arising from social change. Secondly, management must increase efforts to solicit consumer feedback on specific problems and high level management must become involved. This should include, for example, consumer-executive panel discussions, instituting direct communication lines with consumers (Whirlpool's toll free, telephone "cool line") as well as moves toward self-regulation. Although coordinated self-regulation within an industry is fraught with antitrust uncertainties, some progress is seen by, for example, the National Advertising Review Board under the Council of Better Business Bureaus. Activities should also include efforts to inform and educate the public so as to reverse the trend of lower and lower confidence in business. Public relations by itself is insufficient but carefully developed communications to consumers are essential to the future of marketing and business. Enlightened and responsive management must not only act but also communicate with their constituencies.

SUMMARY AND CONCLUSIONS

For marketing decision-makers, there are significant social changes occurring in consumer markets including socio-economic and demographic shifts as well as the changing values of consumers. These, in turn, provide some understanding of current social issues and social forces confronting marketing management such as consumerism, the natural environment and the ghetto marketplace. These changes must be placed in an operational context by a three-stage process including (1) interpreting the current social environment and delineating the "rules of the game," (2) an internal marketing social audit, and (3) marketer response to gaps in social performance. This perspective provides a framework for viewing social change into the future, and is therefore the most lasting section of a chapter inevitably threatened by the very changes discussed within it.

EXERCISES FOR DISCUSSION AND REVIEW

1. Based on an understanding of major socioeconomic trends, explain their relationship to the growth of selected industries and product markets. (Please use both the information in the chapter as well as your reasoning ability).

2. Joe recently received an unexpected promotion and an increase in salary from $13,000 to $17,000 a year. After the immediate impact of this change dissipates, would you as a marketer anticipate being *better* able to predict his behavior as a consumer than before? How does your answer

    relate to an economic state of generally rising real incomes throughout the country?

3.   Based on an awareness of several significant value trends in America, try to explain their relationship, if any, to the rise of selected marketing-related social issues (e.g., consumerism). What other societal changes represent fundamental causes underlying increased attention to the natural environment, ghetto marketplace and consumerism issues?

4.   Several large firms during the past few years have appointed corporate officers to posts with assigned responsibilities for consumer affairs. Most of these companies already had chief marketing executives (e.g., vice-president of marketing) with responsibility for managing the firm's marketing programs. Examine the implications of these consumer affairs appointments in terms of the interrelationships and possible conflicts with the responsibilities of the marketing executive.

5.   The social environment of marketing has risen significantly in importance during recent years. Looking back to the discussion of environmental forecasting in Chapters 3 and 4, discuss the current relevance of different types of forecasting methods to the social environmental area. Cite barriers that would impede their implementation.

6.   Numerous social issues are encompassed by the consumerism "umbrella." Several were alluded to in the chapter such as truthful advertising, product safety, unfair pricing methods, personal selling tactics, and planned obsolescence. Select one such issue and analyze the pros and cons of related practices to society and to management (a limited library search would aid in the task).

7.   As this book goes to press, interest appears to be growing in attempts to measure "consumer satisfaction" specifically. Although the marketing concept (Chapter 1) is two decades old, little need was seen until recently to go beyond the most general measures of satisfaction. This is a simple task on the surface but limited analysis demonstrates its complexity. Assume you are employed by a consumer goods company and you are charged with developing a set of measures for this purpose. Outline the major issues you must face and then make any necessary assumptions in order to facilitate suggesting possible measures.

8.   In consideration of causal factors underlying increased attention to the social responsibilities of business, would you anticipate this concern to be a "fad"? If not, what *degrees* of commitment might a corporation make (i.e., are there stages of increasing involvement)? Finally, to whom do business and marketing have responsibilities?

6

The Governmental
Environment

The small beginnings of marketing legislation at the turn of the century have mushroomed into a myriad of complex laws and enforcement mechanisms impinging on virtually every decision area within marketing. The trend is not abating. By the beginning of the 1970s, over 400 consumer-related bills were in various stages in Congress and, even assuming most of these will fail, the trend is toward more, not less, interdependence between government and marketing. Marketing management literally cannot afford to ignore the governmental environment—whether it be legislative activities, regulatory trends, interpretations by the courts or even the services offered to marketers by government. Consider, for example:

The establishment of a National Product Safety Commission that in 1975 held vast authority which was still unexercised.

Supreme Court decisions in 1973 and 1974 which gave the Federal Trade Commission and the Food and Drug Administration the authority to issue regulations on an industry-wide basis (versus case-by-case) and also added power for the agencies to operate with even less chance of court reversals.[1]

A vast increase in the number of suits filed by private and other interests against companies. In Federal District Court, for example, antitrust filings between 1966 and 1972 nearly tripled.[2]

The number of consumer protection laws enacted between 1966 and

---

[1] Lawrence E. Hicks, *Product Labeling and the Law* (New York: AMACOM-American Marketing Association, 1974), preface.

[2] Eleanor Carruth, "The 'Legal Explosion' Has Left Business Shell-Shocked," *Fortune*, vol. 39, April 1973, pp. 65–69, 155–57.

1972 exceeded the number passed in the previous eight decades—the entire history of such legislation in this country.[3]

These developments clearly illustrate the importance of understanding governmental processes as an incentive for preventive measures as well as for coping with the processes themselves. It is essential that business decision makers be cognizant of (1) the nature of and rationale for governmental activity; (2) major legislative and regulatory activities affecting marketing decisions; and (3) the means for monitoring, predicting and coping with the governmental environment. Each of these areas is explored in this chapter.

RATIONALE FOR LEGISLATION AND REGULATION

Government may be seen as a *structure* of organizational units such as congressional committees, government agencies and elected and appointed offices. Or, government may be equated to its *output,* particularly legislation and regulatory activity which affects marketing. But of greatest value is to view government as a set of *processes* and as a system, comprised of agencies, committees, courts and other organizations which generate output affecting the task environment of marketers. Our concept of environmental forces (Chapter 3) provides a perspective for examining the *dynamics* of governmental activity. Decision makers must incorporate macro-environmental considerations into their planning by systematically monitoring and forecasting potentially relevant environmental change.

An illustrative overview of U.S. governmental processes is shown in Figure 6–1. Structurally, special attention is given to federal governmental agencies and activities which pertain to marketing and business. In a democratic government, over the long run, government acts at the discretion of its citizens. Despite lags and imperfections, the dramatic political events of the early 1970s demonstrated the continued responsiveness of government to the will of the majority. Government (*a*) interprets the needs of the people and *directly* provides for the satisfaction of certain collective needs (e.g., transportation/roads) as well as (*b*) determines the appropriate *means* for satisfying other needs (Chapter 2). The "means" in our society is through a mixed economy, relying on the market system. Much of this chapter deals with continuing governmental guidance over this system.

The structure in Figure 6–1 is comprised of the public, information intermediaries (in recognition of the powerful role of the news media),

---

[3] *Safety in the Marketplace,* National Business Council for Consumer Affairs, U.S. Department of Commerce (Washington, D.C.: U.S. Government Printing Office), April 1973, p. xiv.

governmental participants (legislature, executive branch, court system) and, finally, marketer/business decision makers. Based on the previous chapter, the values and expectations of consumer/citizens, when contrasted to their perceptions of the actual state of affairs, provides the framework for understanding "issues" (e.g., consumerism). The listing of governmental participants in Figure 6–1 emphasizes the important role of key subgroups such as committees and staff members. The usual process of governmental activity is illustrated with the House of Representatives and the Senate introducing legislation (often at the request of the executive branch or pressure groups) and then forwarding the bills to the President for evaluation and signature. The executive branch is charged with implementation giving rise to "administrative law" via the regulatory bodies. Operating between consumer/citizens and the various branches of government are "information intermediaries" such as the press, the pollsters, and lobbyists. The rapid processing and transmission of public opinion polls, reporting practices of the press and lobbying activities all affect the decisions of citizens, legislators and other parties.

What is the rationale for governmental influence over marketing? The U.S. economy is permeated with marketing activities which may or may not contribute to the upgrading of the quality of life of con-

FIGURE 6–1

Governmental Processes and Marketing

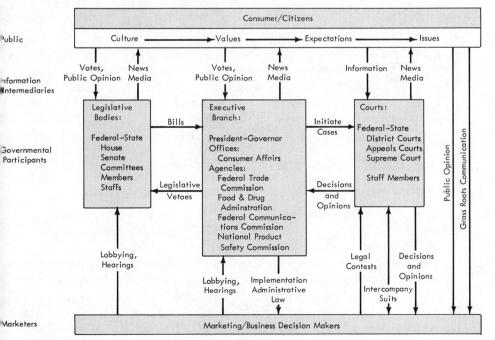

sumer/citizens. For the market system to effectively allocate resources and contribute to a higher quality of life, it is required: (1) that the consumer have different product choices available from independent sources (i.e., competitors); (2) that the consumer have freedom of choice and financial resources; (3) that a sufficient amount of reliable, timely information be available for consumer decision making; and (4) that consumers themselves be capable decision makers. These are minimal conditions for the market mechanism to work effectively. Deceptive advertising (information) contributes to consumers misallocating their incomes and sustaining undeserving marketers and producers; collusive actions between firms restrict consumer choice and artificially support high prices; and uneducated consumers thwart the functioning of the market system. *The objective of much government activity is to promote "workable" competition in recognition of the destructive potential of cutthroat competition as well as the dangers of monopoly.* Workable competition is maintained by satisfying the above four conditions. Specifically, government over the years has (1) maintained competition and consumer choice through antitrust enforcement; (2) curtailed use of deceptive practices and information in the sale of products; and (3) required that useful product information be available for consumers. Consumer education programs have also received some support. These various activities have been pro-competition and pro-economic system in nature, a higher societal priority than pro-business.

Other governmental activity exists not to maintain the market system but, in a sense, to create less dependence on it. The government has actually *restricted* consumer choice by banning the sale of dangerous products and by specifying the features (e.g., car seat belts) of products. This activity moves decision making from consumers to government officials and such action is clearly not in support of the market system (the pros and cons are, of course, widely debated). The following pages serve to illustrate in greater detail the role of government in maintaining the market system as well as shifting selectively from it.

MAJOR LEGISLATION AFFECTING MARKETING

Antitrust Law

Several legislative "pillars" have been passed over the years with the intent of maintaining and promoting healthy or workable competition. Most significant in this regard is antitrust or trade law.

The Sherman Act, passed to curtail the "robber barons" from forming trusts and cartels, had little impact until Theodore Roosevelt aggressively joined in trust-busting efforts and, in 1904, the Supreme Court reversed its previously lax orientation in the Northern Securities case. Other major antitrust victories (1911) included American Tobacco and Standard Oil Company. But in the latter case, the "rule of reason" was introduced leading to the requirement that each case had to be evaluated as to whether it represented an "unreasonable" restraint of trade. This rule created vagaries which were not clarified until the Clayton Act was passed in 1914. The Clayton Act made it clear that an actual monopoly did not already have to exist but that corporate activities which would have the effect of *"substantially* lessening" competition or *"tending* to create a monopoly" could be attacked. This provided for the prevention of monopoly rather than only punishment after the fact. Several practices were outlawed by the Clayton Act, as cited in Figure 6–2.

FIGURE 6–2
Major Antitrust Laws

The Sherman Act (1890)

Section 1:

Every contract, combination . . . or conspiracy, in restraint of trade or commerce among the several States, or with foreign nations, is hereby declared to be illegal. Every person who shall make any such contract or engage in any such combination or conspiracy, shall be deemed guilty of a misdemeanor . . .

Section 2:

Every person who shall monopolize, or attempt to monopolize, or combine or conspire with any other person or persons, to monopolize any part of the trade or commerce among the several states, or with foreign nations, shall be deemed guilty of a misdemeanor.

The Clayton Act (1914)

Specifically outlawed price discrimination, tying contracts, exclusive dealing, and intercorporate stockholdings and interlocking directorates among directly competing companies, where the effect is to "substantially lessen competition or tend to create a monopoly."

Section 2:

Forbids sellers to discriminate in price between purchasers of commodities of like grade, quantity, or quality where such discrimination results in a substantial lessening of competition or tends to create a monopoly in any line of commerce. Price discrimination is permitted where there are differences in costs incident to serving different customers, or where lower prices are granted in "good faith" to meet competition. (Amended by Robinson-Patman Act).

Section 3:

Forbids sellers to lease, sell, or make a contract for the sale of goods on the condition that the purchaser or lessee agree not to use or sell the goods of a competitor (tying contract) where the effect of such an agreement is substantially less competition or a tendency toward monopoly in any line of commerce.

FIGURE 6–2 (continued)

Section 7:
Forbids any corporation engaged in commerce to acquire the stock of a corporation or to acquire the stocks of two or more competing corporations where the effect is substantially less competition or a tendency toward monopoly. (Amended by Celler-Kefauver Act)

Section 8:
Forbids the same persons from serving on the boards of directors of two or more competing corporations where one of the corporations has assets of more than one million dollars and where the elimination of competition between them would violate any of the provisions of the antitrust laws (interlocking directorates).

The Federal Trade Commission Act
(1914)

Established the Federal Trade Commission to enforce the provisions of the Clayton Act.

Section 5:
Forbids "unfair methods" of competition as defined by the FTC and gives the FTC the power to prosecute. (Amended by Wheeler-Lea Act)

The Robinson-Patman Act (1936)

Section 2(a):
Prohibits the granting of different prices to different buyers of commodities of like grade and quality where the effect of such discrimination would be a reduction in competition between the seller and his competitors, between a buyer and the buyer's competitors, or between the customers of a buyer.

The price differences between different customers are permitted if they do not exceed differences in the costs of serving them.

FTC was given the power to establish maximum limits on quantity discounts granted to any customer or class of customers, regardless of differences in the costs of serving them.

Section 2(b):
The "good faith defense" in the Clayton Act was to continue to apply.

Section 2(c):
Prohibits the granting of brokerage allowances by a seller to a buyer or a brokerage firm owned by the buyer.

Section 2(d and e):
Sellers must make any supplementary services or allowances to all purchasers on a proportionately equal basis.

Section 2(f):
It is illegal for a buyer knowingly to induce a discriminatory price from a seller.

FIGURE 6–2 (concluded)

Celler-Kefauver Antimerger Act
of 1950

Amended Section 7 of the Clayton Act to include the purchase of assets as well as stock.

Wheeler-Lea Act (1938)

Broadened Section 5 of the FTC Act to include the prohibition of practices which might *injure* the public without affecting competition. Also extended FTC's authority over the false advertising of food, drugs, cosmetics, and therapeutic devices.

Fair Trade Laws (1931)—
California

State laws which provided for vertical price fixing in channels of distribution. "Non-signers clause" provided that once a manufacturer obtained the agreement of *one* dealer in a state to resell his product at a given price, no other competitors in that state could sell it lower. Miller-Tydings Act (1937) exempted interstate resale price-fixing contracts from the antitrust laws when both the states involved recognized the legality of such contracts. McGuire Act (1952) established the legality of the nonsigners clause for interstate commerce. (Actually exemptions from the antitrust laws.)

Based on Louis W. Stern and John R. Grabner, Jr., *Competition in the Marketplace* (Glenview, Ill.: Scott, Foresman and Company, 1970), pp. 69–78.

Concerning interlocking directorates, for example, the Federal Trade Commission (FTC) reached a settlement in 1975 with several energy producing firms which had Board of Director members in common.[4] Based on Section 8 of the Clayton Act, the companies agreed to end the interlocking directorates and to set up information mechanisms to insure overlap would not occur again. Section 7 of the Clayton Act warns corporations against acquiring the stock of other companies and, in 1950, was amended by the Celler-Kefauver Act which added the "purchase of assets" to stock acquisition. The effects are seen in greater caution being exercised in horizontal and vertical mergers while, in effect, encouraging corporate growth through diversification. This is of special significance to marketing channel decisions because it limits the acquisition of distribution members where the effects could be anticompetitive.

The Federal Trade Commission Act (1914) established the Federal Trade Commission for enforcing the Clayton Act and also, in Section 5, gave the FTC the power to define and prosecute "unfair

---

[4] "Twelve Firms End Director Interlocks, Sign FTC Consents," *The Wall Street Journal*, April 23, 1975, p. 5.

methods" of competition. The FTC was empowered to carry out investigations and issue cease and desist orders. The Wheeler-Lea Amendment later expanded the Federal Trade Commission Act by charging the FTC with protecting consumers from "unfair or deceptive acts or practices" even if competition is not the issue (this expanded the limits from an earlier court decision allowing the FTC to only deal with "injury to competition"). The significance of this amendment has been demonstrated in recent years with a much more active FTC posture regarding deceptive advertising. The Robinson-Patman Act and Fair Trade laws are discussed below in conjunction with pricing decisions.

Thus, in summary, the Sherman Act was made more specific and strengthened by the Clayton Act and the Federal Trade Commission Act. The Clayton Act was expanded by the Celler-Kefauver Act (which included control over market power created by mergers). Finally, the Federal Trade Commission Act was broadened by the Wheeler-Lea Act (which gave the FTC responsibility for consumer protection and monitoring of false advertising). The Justice Department usually administers the Sherman Act, shares enforcement of the Clayton Act with the FTC except for Section 2 (the FTC usually assumes this) and the FTC administers Section 5 of the FTC Act.[5]

Several major antitrust cases were pending in the mid-70s involving such companies as IBM, Xerox, American Telephone and Telegraph as well as several oil industry firms. In recent years the number of antitrust cases as well as the severity of penalties have contributed to more and more companies initiating in-house educational campaigns to sensitize employees to the "dos and don'ts" of antitrust. Criminal felony charges may now be placed against individual executives as well as fines of up to $1 million per violation.[6] *Business Week* magazine reports, "Salesmen are the employees most likely to slip inadvertently into antitrust hot water, but company education programs are being expanded to cover personnel in almost every aspect of corporate life."[7]

Consumer Legislation

Selected examples of consumer legislation are shown in Figure 6–3. The separation of laws between Figures 6–2 and 6–3 is consistent with the reorganization of the FTC which included forming two major operating bureaus, the Bureau of Competition and the Bureau of Consumer Protection. Antitrust laws probably do more to assist consumers (through promoting competition) than the laws in Figure 6–3. But there

---

[5] Louis W. Stern and John R. Grabner, Jr., *Competition in the Marketplace* (Glenview, Ill.: Scott, Foresman & Co., 1970), p. 76.

[6] "How to Avoid Antitrust," *Business Week*, January 27, 1975, p. 84.

[7] Ibid.

FIGURE 6–3

Selected Consumer Legislation

Mail Fraud Act of 1872

To make it a federal crime to defraud through the use of mail.

Food and Drug Act of 1906

To regulate interstate commerce in misbranded and adulterated foods, drinks, and drugs.

Federal Trade Commission Act
(1914)

To set up the Federal Trade Commission which, among other responsibilities, is to be concerned with "unfair methods of competition," such as deceptive advertising (See Figure 6–2).

Federal Food, Drug, and
Cosmetic Act of 1938

To strengthen the Food and Drug Act of 1906 by extending coverage to cosmetics and devices; requiring predistribution clearance of safety on new drugs, providing for tolerance for unavoidable or required poisonous substances; and authorizing standards of identity, quality, and fill of container for foods.

Wheeler-Lea Amendment (1938)

To amend the Federal Trade Commission Act of 1914 by making it possible to prosecute for deceptive advertising or sales practices (See Figure 6–2).

Flammable Fabrics Act (1953)

To prohibit the shipment in interstate commerce of any wearing apparel or material which could be ignited easily (amended 1967 to include household products).

Automobile Information Disclosure
Act (1958)

To require automobile manufacturers to post the suggested retail price on all new passenger vehicles.

Food Additives Amendment
(1958)

To amend the Food and Drug Act by prohibiting use of new food additives until promoter establishes safety and FDA issues regulations specifying conditions of use.

Textile Fiber Products
Identification Act (1959)

To cover the labeling of most textile products not covered by the earlier Wool or Fur Products Labeling Acts.

FIGURE 6–3 (continued)

*Kefauver-Harris Drug
Amendments (1962)*

To require drug manufacturers to file all new drugs with the Food and Drug Administration; to label all drugs by generic name; and to require pretesting of drugs for safety and efficacy.

*Fair Packaging and Labeling Act
(1965)
(Truth-in-Packaging)*

To regulate the packaging and labeling of consumer goods and to provide that voluntary uniform packaging standards be established by industry.

*National Traffic and Motor Vehicle
Safety Act (1966)*

To authorize the Department of Transportation to establish compulsory safety standards for new and used tires and automobiles.

Child Safety Act (1966)

To strengthen the Hazardous Substances Labeling Act of 1960 by preventing the marketing of potentially harmful toys and permitting the Food and Drug Administration to remove inherently dangerous products from the market (amended 1969).

Cigarette Labeling Act (1966)

To require cigarette manufacturers to label cigarettes: "Caution: Cigarette smoking may be hazardous to your health."

Wholesome Meat Act (1967)

To require states to upgrade their meat inspection systems to stringent federal standards and to clean up unsanitary meat plants (Poultry Act added in 1968).

*Consumer Credit Protection (1968)
(Truth-in-Lending)*

To require full disclosure of annual interest rates and other finance charges on consumer loans and credit buying including revolving charge accounts.

Fair Credit Report Act (1970)

To regulate credit information reporting and use, provide consumer access to credit files, limit consumer liabilities from lost or stolen credit cards to $50.

*Consumer Product Safety Act
(1972)*

Created the Consumer Product Safety Commission.

are fundamental differences between the nature and administration of antitrust law as compared to consumer law. In 1971, the President's Advisory Council on Executive Organization concluded that antitrust cases sometimes require changes in industry structure whereas consumer protection violations typically involve lesser sanctions. Antitrust law normally requires a case-by-case approach whereas consumer protection problems are more amenable to resolution by rules and regulations. Finally, antitrust cases are usually long and complex with consumer protection disputes being less complicated.[8] The antitrust laws are fundamental to the basic functioning of the economic system whereas consumer laws are often limited to specific problems. Yet this does not diminish the importance of consumer legislation to companies whose product/markets are directly affected. Many of the consumerism activities that gained momentum during the sixties (Chapter 5) are today being "institutionalized" into law. According to one analysis, 18 consumer protection laws were passed in the seventy years prior to 1960 with the next 12 years netting 29 laws, 19 of those passed in the 5 years through 1973.[9] A total of 47 laws were cited.

Some of the more significant laws in Figure 6–3 include the Food and Drug Act of 1906 (as amended in 1938), The Federal Trade Commission Act (Section 5—with the Wheeler-Lea Amendment), the 1965 Fair Packaging and Labeling Act, the 1968 Consumer Credit Protection Act, and the 1972 Consumer Product Safety Act.

The Food and Drug Act created the Food and Drug Administration (FDA) which is today the largest consumer agency. The Act was the first significant piece of consumer legislation—forbidding the adulteration and misbranding of food sold in interstate commerce.[10] A 1938 amendment better defined adulteration and misbranding; extended coverage to cosmetics and therapeutic devices; set standards for the identity, quality, and fill of goods containers; and required clearance of drugs prior to distribution. The 1965 Fair Packaging and Labeling Act and the 1968 Consumer Credit Protection Act, known as the "truth-in" laws were enacted to provide consumers with more and better information (despite the dissatisfaction of consumerists with these statutes). The Consumer Product Safety Act established the Consumer Product Safety Commission. Other significant consumer-related laws not shown in Figure 6–3 include environmental protection laws, especially the 1970 Clean Air Act Amendments and the 1972 Clean Water Amendments, both giving the

---

[8] Dorothy Cohen, "Abolish FTC—Proposal of President's Advisor Group," *Marketing News*, June 1, 1971, published by the American Marketing Association.

[9] *Safety in the Marketplace*, p. xiv.

[10] Barbara B. Murray, "Major Federal Consumer Protection Laws, 1906–1970," in Barbara B. Murray (ed.), *Consumerism: The Eternal Triangle* (Palisades, Calif.: Goodyear Publishing Co., 1973), pp. 78–79.

Environmental Protection Agency general standards and deadlines for environmental improvement. Also, in 1970 the Council on Environmental Quality was established in the Department of Interior to conduct studies on environmental impact. Finally, a major consumer bill pending in 1975 was to establish an Agency for Consumer Advocacy—an organization to represent consumer interests in government formally.

GOVERNMENT IMPACT ON MARKETING DECISIONS

The laws in Figures 6–2 and 6–3 have specific implications for marketing decisions concerning pricing, distribution, products, promotion and also marketing research. Although large companies have in-house legal counsel for management, marketers must be sufficiently aware of legal ramifications to *know when to seek* counsel.

Pricing Decisions

The following practices are important as they interrelate pricing and the law: (*a*) horizontal price fixing (price collusion between competitors); (*b*) price discrimination (charging different customers different prices); (*c*) vertical price fixing (specifying the prices of distributors); and, more recently, (*d*) decisions concerning the form and availability of price information (for consumers).

Horizontal Price Fixing. This refers to joint or collusive price setting between competitors at a given level of distribution (e.g., retailers) and is illegal per se. Whether at the manufacturer, wholesaler, or retailer level within the channel, it is indefensible for competitors to jointly establish prices. Under the Sherman Act, Clayton Act, and FTC Act (Figure 6–2), attempts "to monopolize" or to "substantially lessen competition" are prohibited. Fostering price competition requires maintaining a market structure sufficiently distant from monopoly to insure independent pricing decisions. An illustrative price-fixing case in the mid-70s involved 6 sugar-refining companies charged with fixing prices across markets in 23 Western and Midwestern states.[11] The Justice Department initiated criminal antitrust charges in addition to several civil suits filed. Another example concerned the automobile industry which ended a bitter eight-year pricing war in 1970 over discounts to big fleets, leasing and rental customers. In May 1972 General Motors and Ford were indicted on criminal charges of price-fixing, ostensibly to "gang-up" on Chrysler which was gaining an increasing share of the then $2.5 billion fleet market.[12] Although these cases are not settled, there was clearly a new

---

[11] Mary Bralove, "Four Sugar Firms in East Asked for Data in New Inquiry of Alleged Price-Fixing," *The Wall Street Journal,* January 30, 1975, p. 12.

[12] Seth Lipsky, "How GM and Ford Allegedly Ganged Up to Slap Down Chrysler," *Wall Street Journal,* February 1, 1973, p. 1.

sensitivity to price-fixing practices—partly because of high inflation rates and consumer dissatisfaction at the time.

Price Discrimination. The environment in the mid-1970s was also conducive for a new attack on the Robinson-Patman Act that in 1936 expanded the types of activities defined as constituting price discrimination (Figure 6–2). In the 1930's, the large grocery chain store organizations, capitalizing on scale economies and special prices (discounts) from suppliers were able to offer consumers low prices and were viewed as a threat to smaller grocery stores. Such firms as A&P were able to exercise great bargaining power to obtain special price concessions from food processors. Because the Clayton Act required that a firm be proven to have "substantially" lessened competition, the Robinson-Patman Act was enacted to outlaw price discrimination which would only "injure" competition. It also outlawed price discrimination if it lessened competition at *any stage* of the distribution network. The courts have interpreted this Act largely in terms of injury to *competitors* (e.g., small grocers) rather than to *competition,* contributing to a continual debate as to whether the Act does more good than harm—it may restrict price competition and protect inefficient firms from head-on price competition.

But not all price discrimination is illegal. For marketing management, the main defense for charging different customers different prices for goods of "like grade and quality" is cost-based (Figure 6–2). If costs can be shown to be lower for serving one group of customers than another, then price differences are usually not illegal (e.g., quantity discounts). In building a cost defense, allocating costs to serving specific customers is usually arbitrary and difficult to defend (especially overhead costs) with the net result that companies often feel compelled to "play it safe" with less pricing freedom than would otherwise exist. Other than a cost defense, if it can be shown that a company is meeting (but not exceeding) price cuts by competitors in good faith or if merchandise is sold under distress sale circumstances, different prices may be allowed. In addition to price advantages, the Robinson-Patman Act prohibits giving selected customers special treatment with respect to advertising allowances and special support services—these are subject to the same defenses. Again, if "injury to competition" cannot be established, special allowances and price discrimination are not illegal. In summary, price differences may *not* be illegal if (1) the price difference is based on actual cost differences in serving particular types of customers; (2) if price discrimination can be shown to have *not* injured competition; (3) if the goods sold to different customers are actually not of "like grade and quality"; and/or (4) if the price was set in "good faith" to, for example, meet a competitor's price or to sell merchandise under distressed conditions.

A landmark case (1958) involving Borden Company concerned the legality of charging different prices for private versus national brands (or labels). A series of battles over the years finally culminated with the Supreme Court upholding the FTC's decision that, in determining whether products are of "like grade and quality," labels are *not* sufficient to differentiate products. Thus, Borden's policy of higher prices for nationally branded products was not upheld but the case was sent back to the Court of Appeals to determine if there was "injury to competition." The Court found no such injury because the buyer had the option of buying the private label from Borden as well as the Borden brands. While a clear decision still does not exist, the safe way to charge different prices for a good is to have actual physical differences (in addition to the label).

Resale Price Maintenance. The Miller-Tydings Act and the McGuire Act (Figure 6–2), in combination with state "fair-trade" or resale price maintenance laws, allow manufacturers to vertically fix prices—that is, set the prices which distributors must charge. The Miller-Tydings Act (1937), like Robinson-Patman, was passed in the depression with protecting small businesses in mind. Interstate resale price fixing was exempted from the federal antitrust laws and manufacturers were allowed to force retailers to sell a branded or trademarked product at a given price. The large chain retailers again lost a potential advantage. In 1941 there were 45 states with resale price maintenance laws, most with a "nonsigner clause." If the clause is signed by one retailer in the state, all others are required to sell the product at a stated price. Because the Supreme Court held the nonsigner clause to be unconstitutional, Congress passed the McGuire Act (1952) to specifically legalize it. But in 1975, only 9 states had full-fledged fair-trade laws although another 16 states permitted vertical price fixing, but without benefit of the non-signer clause. Several states were considering repeal, some companies were rescinding such pricing programs (partially because of costly enforcement difficulties), and in May 1975, the Senate Judiciary subcommittee voted unanimously to ban all state fair-trade laws, reflecting the apparent sentiment in both Houses of Congress.[13] Although repeal would reduce the option of a manufacturer to maintain a high-price, quality image for a product (except by charging distributors a high price), opponents argue that repeal could save U.S. consumers around $2 billion per year. Research evidence cited by opponents also suggests no clear negative impact on small businesses. Thus, by the next edition of this book, vertical price fixing may again be illegal.

Other Developments. Other governmental actions in recent years concerns "unit pricing" and consumer credit. Unit pricing refers to providing consumers with the price per unit (e.g., per fluid ounce, lb., etc.)

---

[13] "Senate Unit Votes to Ban State Laws on 'Fair Trade,'" reprinted with permission of *The Wall Street Journal,* © Dow Jones & Company, Inc. (May 6, 1975). All rights reserved.

on grocery food items to facilitate price comparisons between different brands. Certain states (e.g., Oregon) have passed laws requiring such information to be available in grocery stores for consumer use although no federal statute has been enacted. Also, laws concerning the "price" of credit (i.e., interest rates) include the 1968 "Truth-in-Lending" statute which specifies required consumer information. Also related, the Fair Credit Reporting Act (Figure 6–3) guaranteed consumers greater access to their credit records.[14]

Aside from legislation, government seems increasingly tempted to "toy" with the economic system by price regulation. The early 70s witnessed the establishment of wage and price controls to constrain inflationary price increases and, although it was a largely unsuccessful attempt creating supply-demand distortions, many governmental representatives seem to remain naive about the use of such controls and the associated dangers. The complexity of the economic system and the costs and difficulty of monitoring wages and prices provide major obstacles to attempts at central control. Nevertheless, marketing management may experience direct control over certain pricing decisions in the future.

Channel Decisions

Decisions concerning the relationships between manufacturers, wholesalers, retailers, and other channel members are also subject to legal constraints. Previously cited practices such as price discrimination and vertical integration relate to channel decisions but additional legal considerations include refusals to deal, exclusive dealing, tying contracts and exclusive territories.

Refusals to Deal. According to the Colgate Doctrine put forth by the Supreme Court in 1919, a trader or manufacturer may exercise his "independent discretion as to parties with whom he will deal" as long as no intent exists to create or maintain a monopoly. More scrutiny, however, is usually directed at plans to *drop* distributors than to add new ones. Franchised automobile dealers, for example, are protected by legislation passed in 1956 which specifically cites their right to legal recourse if an auto manufacturer acts to terminate the dealer without sufficient cause. Manufacturers and distributors must act in good faith in order to terminate a customer (dealer) and, specifically, cannot cut off a dealer who refuses to engage in questionable arrangements such as exclusive dealing or tying contracts.

Exclusive Dealing. Exclusive "dealing" refers to a seller requiring that distributors *not* handle competitors' products (but only carry the

---

[14] "Consumer Credit Reports' Content, Distribution Put under New FTC Rules," *The Wall Street Journal*, February 26, 1973, p. 16.

one company's products). This goes beyond "exclusive distribution" where a distributor is given exclusive rights to sell a manufacturers' products but is also allowed to also sell other brands. Exclusive dealing is not illegal per se but, according to Section 3 of the Clayton Act, is outlawed where the effect is to "substantially" lessen competition (Figure 6–2). Exclusive dealing arrangements may be mutually beneficial because a *manufacturer* has a dealer concentrate sales efforts solely on his brand and the *dealer* is usually assured of a source of supply and often gains exclusive rights to handle the product in a given market area. Yet because competitive brands are excluded from the dealer's assortment, the practice may also serve to lessen competition. A major question concerns where the courts and the FTC draw a line between "lessening" and "substantially lessening" competition. For example, franchise contracts which require the franchisee to purchase *all* products and supplies from the franchisor are considered suspect.[15] The negative effects of such franchising arrangements are receiving increased attention although no clear answer now exists. Generally, if a manufacturer holds a dominant share of the market (and therefore may hold considerable power over distributors), exclusive dealing will be considered illegal.

Tying Contracts. Also, it is typically illegal to require a customer to purchase a product that is not wanted as a condition for obtaining a product that is wanted (Clayton Act, Section 3). Sales of desired products which are "tied" to the purchase of other products is an illegal practice if competition is substantially lessened. "Full line forcing," a form of tying agreement, refers to a requirement that a dealer purchase an entire product line when only part of the line is really wanted. A firm usually must possess considerable power over a customer for this to occur. Predictions of continuing material shortages in the future may increase the potential for illegal tying contracts. Unless a tying device is used by a small firm in an attempt to break into a market, a tying arrangement is likely to be declared illegal.

Exclusive Territories. Franchisees and exclusive distributors are almost always given a specific territory for distributing a manufacturer's brand. Yet recent cases indicate that the Supreme Court expects not only *inter*brand competition to be maintained (between different manufacturers' brands) but also within a given market area, *intra*brand competition (competition between distributors of a given brand).[16] It may be necessary for a manufacturer actually to own their distributive outlets in order to control restricting intrabrand competition between outlets in a given market. It appears at least necessary to use an agency-consignment

---

[15] "FTC to Study Purchasing Requirements Imposed by Fast-Food Franchise Firms," *The Wall Street Journal*, February 25, 1975, p. 4.

[16] Louis W. Stern and John R. Grabner, Jr., *Competition in the Marketplace* (Glenview, Ill.: Scott Foresman & Co., 1970), p. 135.

goods arrangement with the manufacturer retaining ownership of the products. If the manufacturer retains no ownership interest in the distribution network, control over intrabrand competition may be largely lost. If interbrand competition is so strong that intrabrand competition is not required to maintain the general level of competition, then intrabrand competition may be legally restricted by the manufacturer. Generally, however, a manufacturer cannot limit the freedom of independent distributors to dispose of the products they purchase in any way they see fit. The desire to maintain channel control may cause increased vertical integration in the future.[17]

Product Decisions

Governmental influence on product and packaging decisions is growing dramatically. The earlier noted Supreme Court decisions in 1973 and 1974 gave the FDA and the FTC the right to issue regulations on an industry-wide basis without serious challenge from judicial review.[18] As one observer noted, "The expansion in government power to regulate consumer goods as a consequence of these decisions can only be termed revolutionary."[19] FDA's regulations and guidelines, for example, now have virtually the same effect as law.[20] Also, the Consumer Product Safety Commission (in the mid-70s) was still organizing and planning without having exercised much of its vast authority. The net result was an unprecedented governmental role (actual and potential) relative to product information and safety. As for legal dimensions of product decisions, expanding product lines by mergers and acquisitions (as already noted) may be subject to governmental scrutiny. Additional management considerations include (a) patents and trademarks; (b) product labeling; (c) product safety; and (d) product liability.

Patents and Trademarks. Under U.S. patent laws, a company may gain a monopoly over the production and marketing of a specific product or process for a seventeen year period. Polaroid, for example, has been protected from direct competition for many years, giving their marketing management people added flexibility in pricing and other decisions. Justification for this legalized exception (allowing monopoly power) comes from a rationale of encouraging invention by giving the inventor protection from competitive infringement on potential profits. The patent gives the holder power to prevent others from offering an identical product unless the holder chooses to sell the patent or license others to

[17] Ibid., p. 138.

[18] "Justices Rebuff Oil Companies' Challenge to FTC's Use of Industry-Wide Trade Rules," *The Wall Street Journal,* February 26, 1974, p. 9.

[19] Hicks, *Product Labeling and the Law,* preface.

[20] Ibid., p. 30.

use the patent. Restrictive licenses, however (for example, requiring a licensee to sell the product for a specified price), are illegal under the Sherman Act because of price-fixing and restraint of trade ramifications. Also, patent holders are not allowed to harass potential or existing competitors by the threat of a patent infringement suit. The net effects of patents on the public are often debated—but with no changes or resolution.

Trademarks, like patents, allow the owner to file suits against unauthorized users. Trademarks or trade names may be registered with the U.S. Patent Office to ascertain evidence of ownership (Lanham Act, 1946). Trademarks, often a key part of product differentiation and brand image, are registered for twenty years with renewal possible. If the name becomes the *generic* term for the product, however, the name may become available for general use. Thus, a company may wish to avoid having a trade name (such as "Xerox") become *that* well accepted!

Product Labeling. Product label information is highly related to safety since: (*a*) the information may provide warnings against misuse and hazards, and (*b*) legally required safety labeling statements, in order to be factual and therefore legal, in effect require products to meet the stated safety standards. The Federal Food, Drug, and Cosmetics Act of 1906 was the first attempt to outlaw false labeling statements concerning product composition but the Supreme Court soon held that the Act did not make false *therapeutic* claims illegal. The Act as amended in 1938 therefore required drugs to be "safe and effective" and also required directions for use. Following the thalidomide drug experience in 1962 (causing the birth of deformed babies), drug effectiveness and safety standards were further raised to require that related claims be supported by "substantial" evidence.

A second function of labeling is to assist consumers in evaluating alternative products (e.g., weight, grade labeling, nutritional content labeling, and ingredient labeling). The above safety-related labeling is required by the Consumer Product Safety Act, whereas information to assist in evaluating products is usually required by the Fair Packaging and Labeling Act. The Food, Drug, and Cosmetic Act has also led recently to FDA regulations that require nutrition information on packages (as a percent of the U.S. Recommended Daily Allowance) and dictate the location and size of labeling information on packages (effective 1975).[21] In addition to food and drugs, labels citing cosmetic ingredients were recently required for the first time and the Treasury department is considering ingredient labeling for alcoholic beverages, effective in 1977. At the state and local level, numerous labeling laws have been passed that are inconsistent with each other or with federal legislation. With

---

[21] Ibid., p. 9.

87,000 local governments, lack of uniformity can create havoc for national distributors, so attempts to guide consistency are underway through a National Model for Packaging and Labeling Regulation.[22]

Product Safety. The Consumer Product Safety Act (see Figure 6–3), enacted at the recommendation of the National Commission on Product Safety (1968–72), established an independent agency to reduce consumer, product-related injuries. The five-member Consumer Product Safety Commission administers the Federal Hazardous Substances Act (as amended), the Poison Prevention Packaging Act, the Flammable Fabrics Act (and its 1967 amendment) and the Refrigerator Door Safety Act.

The Federal Hazardous Substances Act is designed to provide labeling information (such as cautionary statements, instructions for safe use and first aid instructions) but it may also be used to ban some substances entirely.[23] The Flammable Fabrics Act and the Poison Prevention Packaging Act (PPPA) are primarily product safety *standard* laws instead of *labeling* laws. For example, they were used (respectively) to raise standards reducing the flammability of children's sleepwear and to require that packages containing a toxic or harmful substance be difficult to open by children under five years of age. Concerning the latter, aspirin bottles were among the first changed and thousands of drugs and household substances (e.g., furniture polish) were later affected.

The attention to product safety arose because it is estimated that every hour household hazards in America kill 3 victims—and for every one killed, more than 1,000 suffer injuries.[24] The laws have proven inadequate without enforcement machinery. The National Commission on Product Safety estimated that 20 million Americans are injured and 30,000 killed each year by consumer products, excluding automobiles, with a related cost of $5.5 billion in medical care and economic loss.[25] In 1973–74, for example, the CPSC reported defective TV sets ignited 196,000 house and apartment fires and appliances were blamed for 3.5 million fires.[26]

It is not clear whether the Commission will rely heavily on warning statements to consumers or on labeling which, again, actually requires that standards have been met. The Commission has authority to issue safety standards and require specific label instructions and warnings for

---

[22] Ibid., p. 9.

[23] Ibid., p. 18.

[24] From condensation of the final report of the National Commission on Product Safety (Washington, D.C.: Superintendent of Documents, June 1970), in Norman Kangun (ed.), *Society and Marketing, An Unconventional View* (New York: Harper and Row, Publishers, 1972), p. 58.

[25] *The Wall Street Journal*, October 1, 1973, p. 5.

[26] *ACCI Newsletter* (Columbia: University of Missouri, American Council on Consumer Interests), vol. 23 (January 1975), p. 1.

an estimated 43,000 consumer products (excluding tobacco products).[27] The Act also requires manufacturers to have a "reasonable" product safety testing program and *may* require notification of purchasers if a product is found to be defective.[28] By the mid-70s the agency was expected to have approximately 1,200 employees.[29]

The Commission's activities include pinpointing problem products. A CPSC "hot line" was established to facilitate consumer reporting of product injury related accidents; a 119 hospital information network called the National Electronic Injury Surveillance System (NEISS) monitors product-related consumer injuries to alert the Commission to problem products; and manufacturers, importers, distributors and retailers must notify the Commission within 24 hours of obtaining information which "reasonably" supports the idea that a product defect could create a substantial risk of injury to consumers.[30] Between 1970 and 1975, just for toys and children's items, the Commission banned 1,770 products and through 1,000 volunteer "Consumer Deputies," assisted in finding 1,200 banned toys still on the shelves of 1,400 stores during a one-year period.[31] A court appeal to a CPSC decision banning a baby crib produced by the Simmons Company (1974) was rejected, indicating few, if any, challenges to the regulatory authority of the Commission would be upheld. Simmons Co. wished to sell its remaining inventory of baby cribs (purportedly with slats sufficiently far apart for infants to get their heads caught).

Product Liability. Product liability refers to the legal liability of manufacturers, retailers, and other distributors who produce and/or distribute defective or unsuitable merchandise that causes injury to consumers.[32] Sellers may be liable because of (*a*) negligence, (*b*) breach of either an express or implied warranty, (*c*) fraudulent misrepresentation of the product or, more recently, (*d*) simply because a defective product was sold which was unreasonably dangerous to the user or consumer. This latter concept of *strict liability* does not require proof of negligence, warranty or misrepresentation.

The Supreme Court in 1916 first held a manufacturer liable for con-

---

[27] Thomas Caruso, *Marketing News,* vol. 6 (May 1973), p. 1.

[28] Walter Jensen, Jr., Edward M. Mazze, and Duke Nerdhinger Stern, "The Consumer Product Safety Act: A Special Case in Consumerism," *Journal of Marketing,* vol. 37 (October 1973), pp. 69–70, published by the American Marketing Association.

[29] Ibid., p. 18.

[30] *ACCI Newsletter* (Columbia: University of Missouri, American Council on Consumer Interests), vol. 22 (October 1974), p. 1.

[31] *ACCI Newsletter* (Columbia: University of Missouri, American Council on Consumer Interests), vol. 22 (December 1974), p. 1.

[32] Mahlon Lynn Townsend, "Product Liability," *Tennessee Survey of Business,* May 1971, p. 13.

sumer injuries resulting from *negligence* in producing a product despite no privity of contract (a requirement for a contractual relationship— direct manufacturer contact with the consumer). In the case of an *implied warranty*, however, the manufacturer until recently would normally *not* be held liable because of lack of privity (this was not true for an express warranty) although the retailer could be held liable. The increasing acceptance of the concept of "strict liability" makes it possible for a seller (including the manufacturer) to be held responsible for injury caused by a defective product even if due care was exercised in its preparation and sale. Privity of contract and proof of negligence are not normally considered and it must only be shown that the product was defective when it left the manufacturer and that the damage was proximately caused by the defect.[33] There are few defenses and, when combined with the trend of public opinion and court decisions, it has been predicted that we will, at least for a time, see the concept of absolute liability applied: that is, liability imposed on a producer of goods irrespective not only of the standard of care used but also without regard to proof of the existence of the defect.[34] It seems clear that firms must take actions such as increasing quality control, improving in-plant inspections, emphasizing safety in product design, keeping accurate records, increasing insurance protection and adding to legal capacity— in addition to developing a more positive orientation by expanding the marketing concept to include postpurchase (after sale) satisfaction and by using safety and quality marketing appeals.[35] Also, improving product warranties may be viewed as an integral part of the marketing mix[36] and, significantly, the FTC may now set rules for manufacturers to disclose the terms and conditions of warranties voluntarily given on products costing more than five dollars.[37]

Promotion Decisions

Promotion activities, encompassing advertising, personal selling, sales promotion (e.g., product demonstrations), and publicity are very visible marketing activities that are particularly subject to consumer criticism. A market-based economy, premised on consumers having sufficient in-

---

[33] Lynn J. Loudenback and John W. Goebel, "Marketing in the Age of Strict Liability," *Journal of Marketing*, vol. 38 (January 1974), p. 63. Also, David L. Rados, "Product Liability: Tougher Ground Rules," *Harvard Business Review*, vol. 47 (July–August 1969), pp. 144–52.

[34] Loudenback and Goebel, "Marketing in the Age of Strict Liability," p. 64.

[35] Ibid., pp. 64–65.

[36] See discussion in George Fisk, "Guidelines for Warranty Service after Sale," *Journal of Marketing*, vol. 34 (January 1970), pp. 62–67.

[37] "Magnuson-Moss Warranty Improvement Act," *ACCI Newsletter* (Columbia, Mo.: American Council on Consumer Interests), vol. 23 (January 1975), p. 1.

formation to make "rational" choices, has too often been provided with inadequate or misleading advertising, thus hindering the market system. Section 5 of the Federal Trade Commission Act was amended by the Wheeler-Lea Act (1938) to prohibit practices which might "injure" the public but not affect competition (Figure 6–3). It also extended authority over the false advertising of food, drugs, cosmetics, and therapeutic devices. More recently FTC interpretations and various court decisions have broadened the original meaning of "false" to "deceptive," and to even "unfair." Determining the meaning of these terms is the task of the Federal Trade Commission (FTC) and, as shown in Table 6–1, the FTC is responsible for pursuing violations of the Wheeler-Lea Act in all media for nearly all products and services except prescription drugs (FDA's domain). The Federal Communications Commission (FCC) works with the FTC to encourage good advertising in the broadcast media. Also, by 1974, 44 states had deceptive and unfair trade practice laws.

False, Deceptive, and Unfair Advertising. The reorganization of the Federal Trade Commission in 1970 significantly expanded its focus beyond antitrust. A new Bureau of Consumer Protection was established and greater attention was given to collecting and interpreting information about consumer problems.[38] Actions taken by the Commission, in combination with support from the courts, have had a major impact upon corporations as well as on Madison Avenue advertising agencies.[39] The "rules of the game" and the standards of advertising acceptability have shifted sharply upward. Although a Truth-in-Advertising Act (1971) and a proposed "Institute of Advertising, Marketing and Society" (for the FTC) were not passed by Congress,[40] the FTC has proceeded to implement many of the proposed provisions such as requiring factual substantiation of advertisements.

Advertising Substantiation. The days are largely gone when shaving cream commercials can "shave" plexiglass and sand and call it sandpaper or when a soup company can put marbles in its soup to push the vegetables to the top (actual cases). But advertisements which are clearly *false* like these are less of a problem currently than advertising falling into a constantly changing "grey area." The current paucity of

---

[38] "The FTC Builds a Model Informer," *Business Week*, March 11, 1972, p. 94; "FTC Call for Comment Program," *ACCI Newsletter*, vol. 22 (November 1974), p. 1.

[39] "Madison Avenue's Response to its Critics," *Business Week*, June 10, 1972, pp. 46–54; "Those Throbbing Headaches on Madison Avenue," *Fortune*, February 1972, pp. 103–6, 197–206.

[40] "Senator Moss Proposes Creating an Institute of Advertising, Marketing and Society," *The Marketing News*, vol. 4 (Mid–August 1971), p. 1; John G. Myers, "The Truth-in-Advertising Act of 1971," in *Public Policy and Marketing Practices*, Fred C. Allvine (ed.), 1973, pp. 121–40, published by the American Marketing Association.

TABLE 6-1

Product Jurisdiction of Federal Agencies and Departments

Agency	Products
Food and Drug Administration.............	Labeling of food, drugs, cosmetics and medical devices Advertising of prescription drugs
Federal Trade Commission.................	Labeling of household products (non-safety labeling) Advertising of all products except prescription drugs
U.S. Department of Agriculture.............	Labeling of meat and poultry
Treasury Department.....................	Labeling of alcoholic beverages and tobacco products
Consumer Product Safety Commission........	Labeling of hazardous products—(safety information)

Source: Abstracted from Lawrence E. Hicks, *Product Labeling and the Law* (AMACOM, American Management Association, 1974), pp. 42–43.

clearly false advertisements is undoubtedly related to the FTC's advertising substantiation program initiated in 1971. Numerous firms and industries have been required to submit data to support their advertised claims. To evaluate companies' substantiation data requires a definition of "deceptive and unfair," a definition which is still very nebulous.[41] The deception criterion adopted by the FTC is called the "reasonable basis" standard. If *performance claims* are even implied in an advertisement, a company should have substantiating data. The support, where possible, should be based on testing procedures with "scientific underpinnings" and should be extensive and well-documented.[42] The test requirement also seems to apply to *uniqueness claims* with the FTC recently questioning such purported brand differences as "accu-color," "instamatic," and "total automatic color" or the uniqueness of Crisco cooking oil in creating "less greasy" tasting food.[43] *Subjective claims* (whether performance or uniqueness) are particularly difficult to work with. The FTC, for example, challenged an advertisement saying that "Vega is . . . the best handling passenger car ever built in the U.S. . . ."[44] Such previously accepted "puffery" (although the Vega ad was based on a report in a leading auto magazine) is increasingly under attack. This may

---

[41] David M. Gardner, "Deception in Advertising: A Conceptual Approach," *Journal of Marketing*, vol. 39 (January 1975), pp. 40–46.

[42] Robert E. Wilkes and James B. Wilcox, "Recent FTC Actions: Implications for the Advertising Strategist," *Journal of Marketing*, vol. 38 (January 1974), p. 56, published by the American Marketing Association.

[43] Ibid., p. 57.

[44] Ibid., p. 56.

be especially true for subjective claims where consumers rely on questionable "indicators." Chevron F-310 gasoline, for example, was advertised as
creating less air pollution with commercials showing a bag of colorless
exhaust fumes; the Commission also considered ordering "Profile" bread
to change its *name* because it was not lower in calories than other
breads; and, finally, the endorsement of toy Mattel race cars by famous
race-car drivers was questioned because of the driver's lack of related
expertise. Each of these cases provided a potentially misleading "surrogate indicator" which, understanding the behavior of many consumers,
was seen as potentially misleading.[45] Special regulatory attention is often
given to children, the poor, the elderly and/or the uniformed due to a
higher incidence of consumer problems within these groups.

   Other Deception. In addition to inspecting advertising claims, the
FTC is charged with prohibiting other deceptive practices such as "bait
and switch" advertising, fictitious bargains, or the "You have been specially selected" tactic. Bait and switch refers to advertisements which
"bait" consumers with tempting product prices—but once the consumer
arrives in the store, sales tactics are used to get the consumer to "trade-
up" to a more expensive model. Sears, Inc. at the date of this writing is
facing an unresolved FTC charge of using "bait and switch" tactics. Fictitious bargains are sometimes offered by unethical business people when
the price is not actually reduced. The "specially selected" ploy uses flat-
tery and the presentation of a unique opportunity to con consumers into
buying merchandise which is actually available to anyone for as good a
price. Other problems including deceptively large packages and misleading guarantees are also subject to FTC action.

   Personal Selling Practices. Deceptive selling practices are also subject to prosecution although little FTC action has occurred to date.
Exceptions include action in 1974 against several encyclopedia companies to require salespersons to identify their actual intent in the sales
situation rather than using a misleading sales approach. Also, a "cooling-
off period" for door-to-door sales became effective in 1974 which
allows a buyer the right to cancel a purchase from a door-to-door salesman anytime prior to midnight of the third business day after the date of
the transaction, if the purchase price is $25 or more.[46]

   FTC Procedures and Remedial Actions. The approach typically
taken against companies suspected of deceptive or anticompetitive practices is shown in Figure 6–4.[47] To speed up FTC case handling, the Com-

---

   [45] Dorothy Cohen, "Surrogate Indicators and Deception in Advertising," *Journal
of Marketing*, vol. 36 (July 1972), pp. 10–15.

   [46] *ACCI Newsletter* (Columbia, Mo.: American Council on Consumer Interests),
vol. 22 (February 1974), p. 1.

   [47] Abstracted from "FTC Adopts 2 Rules to Speed up Cases on Unfair Practices,"
The Wall Street Journal, February 21, 1975, p. 6. Reprinted with permission of *The
Wall Street Journal*, © Dow Jones & Company, Inc. (1975). All rights reserved.

FIGURE 6–4

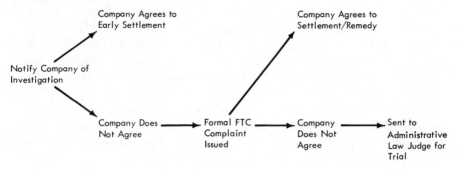

mission dropped a "proposed complaint" stage (preceding the formal complaint) and will also require less evidence from its staff prior to issuing a formal complaint—as long as the staff has "reason to believe" a company has violated the law.[48] A firm may voluntarily acquiesce or it may fight the action. If challenged and an administrative judge then finds against the firm, the firm may appeal through a federal Circuit Court of Appeals and the Supreme Court, although such appeals have not generally been fruitful in recent years.

Voluntary compliance prior to the complaint stage may be facilitated by a "Trade Practice Conference" (TPC) where an industry seeks interpretative rules from the FTC regarding its problems.[49] Industry members discuss as well as propose needed rules and, then the FTC staff obtains preliminary approval from the five-member Commission, releases the rules for a public hearing and, after the hearing, the Commission issues rules. "Industry Guides" are sometimes issued that are limited to a particular problem area—but they may go beyond a single industry. If an industry is hostile to an idea, an Industry Guide is normally issued instead of using the TPC. Also, "advisory opinions" were issued beginning in 1962 at the request of companies. They are typically binding upon the Commission. A firm, for example, might submit proposed advertising (or a proposed merger) to the Commission for approval and the advisory opinion provides an advance evaluation for the firm. Finally, "Trade Regulation Rules" are issued which represent conclusions of the Commission after appropriate hearings as to the illegality of particular practices. Once the final ruling is issued, the FTC may rely upon the rule to resolve any issue in an adjudicative proceeding.

As for remedies, the FTC has historically issued "cease and desist" orders and, when a case was not settled by negotiation, it has been pursued at length in the Courts. The J. B. Williams Company, maker of

---

[48] Ibid.

[49] This paragraph abstracted from *Here Is Your Federal Trade Commission* (Washington, D.C.: U.S. Government Printing Office, 1969–0–334–889), pp. 17–20.

Geritol, lost a 13-year battle in federal court in 1973 and was ordered to pay an $812,000 penalty for ignoring an FTC order to stop advertising Geritol as a "surefire pick-me-up for people with tired blood." The only longer case was a 16-year effort to stop Carter's Little Liver Pills from claiming that the pills could overcome lethargy. Because of the problems associated with the cease and desist order, it is understandable that the Commission has increasingly used other remedies as cited in Table 6–2.

It is evident that existing proposals combined with judicial and regulatory interpretations in recent years have already drastically altered the freedom of the advertising decision-maker. Slowing down this regulatory trend will likely hinge, in part, on the effectiveness of self-regulation efforts of the advertising industry (e.g., the National Advertising Review Board and the Better Business Bureau) as well as increased sensitivity to consumer needs by all advertisers.

Marketing Research Decisions

Marketing research has greatly expanded over recent decades and accompanying this growth has been increased attention to related ethical consequences.[50] Issues include consumer irritation over such abuses as (1) coercing respondents into an interview situation, (2) use of "deceptive" methods such as use of one-way mirrors and disguising the purpose of studies, (3) respondents feeling "used" and, generally, researchers not being sensitive to respondent needs and (4) invasion of privacy, particularly concerning confidentiality of respondent answers given to interviews.[51]

Although these are "ethical" as opposed to "legal" issues, some attention has also been given to the law of privacy in this context. Four related types of tort action (a civil wrong which will support an action for damages) include (1) intrusion (the act of intruding upon an individual's private affairs, his solitude, or his seclusion), (2) disclosure (the act of making public embarrassing private facts about an individual), (3) false light (the act of publicizing misrepresentative statements about an individual) and (4) appropriation (using an individual's name or likeness for the appropriator's advantage).[52] As long as no *individual* data is released and publicized, the latter three types should not pose a significant threat to marketing researchers. The threat in the future could

---

[50] For an interesting presentation of issues, see C. Merle Crawford, "Attitudes of Marketing Executives toward Ethics in Marketing Research," *Journal of Marketing,* vol. 34 (April 1970), pp. 46–52.

[51] For related discussion, see Alice M. Tybout, and Gerald Zaltman, "Ethics in Marketing Research: Their Practical Relevance," *Journal of Marketing Research,* vol. 11 (November 1974), p. 359.

[52] Charles S. Mayer and Charles H. White, Jr., "The Law of Privacy and Marketing Research," *Journal of Marketing,* vol. 33 (April 1969), pp. 1–4.

TABLE 6–2

Settlement Mechanisms of the FTC

Remedy	Procedure
Cease & Desist Order	A final order to cease an illegal practice —often challenged via the courts.
Consent Decree	Business consents to stop the questionable practice without admitting illegality.
Affirmative Disclosure	Requires advertiser to provide additional information about products in their advertisements.
Corrective Advertising	Requires advertising to "correct" the past effects of misleading advertising (e.g., 25 percent of media budget to FTC approved advertisements or FTC specified advertising).
Restitution	Require refunds to consumers misled by deceptive advertising. According to 1975 Court of Appeals decision, cannot be used except for practices carried out *after* the issuance of a cease-and-desist order (still in appeal).
Counteradvertising	FTC proposed that FCC permit advertisements in broadcast media to counteract advertising claims (also proviso for free time under certain conditions).

Sources: Robert E. Wilkes and James B. Wilcox, "Recent FTC Actions: Implications for the Advertising Strategist," *Journal of Marketing*, vol. 38 (January 1974), pp. 58–60; Dorothy Cohen, "FTC Orders Corrective Ads: Restitution Waiting in Wings," Legal News Section, *Marketing News*, October 1, 1971; Dorothy Cohen, "Court Decisions Weaken FTC's Public Interest Power," Legal News and Views Section, *Marketing News*, February 14, 1975, p. 4, published by the American Marketing Association.

come from "intrusion" *if* research were defined to encompass "mental or psychological" intrusion. Even though a respondent's right is waived by consent, it is not clear that consenting to be interviewed would include consent, for example, to use disguised questioning.[53] In these instances, the law of misrepresentation could also enter. Perhaps most importantly, if consumers are generally offended by marketing research activities, the potential of new legislation will increase as marketing research increases. Paradoxically, understanding consumer needs and implementing the marketing concept requires use of marketing research.

MONITORING AND FORECASTING THE GOVERNMENTAL ENVIRONMENT

As the *rate* of governmental action increases, and as the *nature* of regulation and legislation becomes more relevant to marketers (e.g.,

---

[53] Ibid., p. 3–4.

consumer legislation), it is incumbent upon marketers and other corporate officials to become attuned to potential governmental forces. With corporate diversification in recent years contributing to diverse product mixes, the task of identifying "potentially relevant" governmental action is no small task. Moreover, governmental activity increasingly requires day-to-day attention, bringing it closer to the "task environment" of management (Chapter 3), along with other environments such as markets and competition.[54]

Who Monitors

The corporate lobbyist, despite a sinister and "influence-peddling" image, is the primary "middleman" between companies and the federal government. While recognizing that abuses are sometimes associated with lobbying, representation for business is essential to the democratic process. Sometimes referred to as the "fourth branch" of government, lobbying is legitimized by the First Amendment to the Constitution which refers to ". . . the right of the people . . . to petition the Government for a redress of grievances." Some of the most effective lobbyists are reportedly former congressmen. A thorough understanding of governmental processes and access to offices of former associates make them valuable liaisons.[55] A negative "influencing" orientation too often characterizes the lobbying approach rather than a positive and systematic information gathering approach. Taking a positive stance, Kennecott Copper Corporation emphasizes information monitoring through a "listening post"—that is, a position of "Director of Washington Services" established at the end of the 60s.[56] B. F. Goodrich Company hired its first full-time Washington lobbyist in 1972. As expressed by a corporate vice president:

> My feeling was that so many regulatory activities were burgeoning in Washington, and the whole matter of relations with government becoming so complex, that I recommended that we needed somebody who knew Washington well.[57]

An American University Professor estimated in the early seventies that some 80 percent of the 1,000 largest U.S. companies had Washington offices or used law firms, public relations agencies and consultants to represent them full-time.[58] Food companies such as General Foods,

---

[54] William R. King and David I. Cleland, "Environmental Information Systems for Strategic Marketing Planning," *Journal of Marketing*, vol. 38 (October 1974), pp. 35–40, published by the American Marketing Association.

[55] Kerry North, "Old Lawmakers Don't Fade Away but Come Back on Another Day," *The Wall Street Journal*, July 23, 1973, p. 1.

[56] "The Corporate Lobbyist: Why He Is Necessary," *Business Week*, March 18, 1972, p. 64.

[57] Ibid., p. 62.

[58] Ibid., p. 63.

General Mills and H. J. Heinz, spurred by consumerism activity, have established Washington offices.[59] There is also a trend toward top-level corporate officers serving as occasional Washington representatives, rather than relying totally on trade associations, legal staffs or even professional, full-time lobbyists.[60] Line management is becoming increasingly involved. Smaller firms usually rely on one or more of the estimated 2,000 trade associations in Washington for information and assistance with government agencies.[61] Spending reported by registered lobbyists in 1973 totaled over $9.4 million (business expending $3.3 million) although this is commonly assumed to be but a fraction of actual spending (due to weak lobbying laws).[62]

Despite the importance of federal governmental activity, state government is viewed by many firms as of even greater importance. This is particularly true for industries which are primarily regulated at the state level, such as insurance. According to one source, ". . . experts say that it is in the nation's 50 state capitals that many industries are most active and potent."[63] Corporate emphasis on state-level activity is partly because of industry's greater freedom to operate in state capitals with less press coverage and fewer rules. Also, state legislators often have small staffs and therefore rely more on lobbyists for information.[64] Finally, particularly in the case of consumer-related legislation, states sometimes pass laws in advance of federal action. In sum, state government action may be more important than federal to many marketers.

The Monitoring Process

The starting point for monitoring is identifying key legislative bodies, agencies, and offices that potentially relate to marketing operations. Selected regulatory agencies of interest to marketers are shown in Table 6–3. Within legislative bodies, understanding the committee and subcommittee structure is essential given their powerful role in drafting legislation.

Beyond an identification of components, understanding dynamic processes requires a comprehension of personalities, the role of staff members, the relevance of given bills to congressional districts and many other

---

[59] Ibid.

[60] Ibid., p. 62.

[61] William Smith, "Lobby Isn't Always a Dirty Word," *The MBA* (October 1971), pp. 12–14, 72.

[62] Congressional Quarterly, *The Washington Lobby*, 2d ed. (Washington, D.C.: Congressional Quarterly, Inc., 1974), p. 43.

[63] Laing, J. R. and F. C. Klein, "Industry Lobbies are Active and Powerful at the State Level," *The Wall Street Journal*, June 6, 1974, p. 1.

[64] Ibid., p. 1.

TABLE 6–3

**Budget Requests by Agencies for Consumer Concerns
(millions of dollars)**

	1975 Estimate	1976 Estimate	Change
Office of Consumer Affairs	1.5	1.5	0
Food and Drug Administration	200.9	203.5	+2.6
Federal Trade Commission	39.0	45.6	+6.6
Consumer Product Safety Commission	35.7	36.6	+ .9
Consumer Information Center	1.0	1.1	+ .1

Source: *ACCI Newsletter* (Columbia, Mo.: American Council on Consumer Interests), vol. 23 (March) 1975), p. 1; Also see *United States Government Organization Manual 1972–73* (Office of the Federal Register, National Archives and Records Service, General Services Administration, U.S. Government Printing Office, 1972).

matters. Despite the relatively small number of "components" in the governmental system, the complex interdependencies and processes still make governmental action difficult to understand and forecast.

It is possible, however, to identify certain "governmental indicators" which often help to anticipate governmental action. Although any one is insufficient by itself, factors such as the following may signal the future:

1. Changes in the membership of legislative and regulatory bodies.
2. Changes in agency budgets (Table 6–3).
3. Organizational changes (e.g., office to independent agency status).
4. Actions by one agency may signal future developments over other products regulated by different agencies.
5. Required attention of governmental bodies to other issues (e.g., impeachment processes in the early 70s).
6. Rulings and legislation not yet implemented and/or enforced.
7. Actions by states that are leaders in governmental action (e.g., California, Oregon, New York).
8. Previously introduced bills which continue to receive congressional priority.

Although other indicators could be cited, it is clear that similar to economic indicators (e.g., new housing starts), these factors must be judiciously combined and interpreted. Yet they provide a beginning for monitoring governmental action.

Forecasting

As is true of social forecasting, governmental forecasting is at a rudimentary stage. An early pioneer in General Electric's Business Environment Studies unit, Ian Wilson, noted ". . . sociopolitical forecasting lacks the armory of analytical tools and techniques possessed by older forecasting disciplines. Trend projections, Delphi forecasting, scenarios, and 'cross-impact analysis' are useful starts on forecasting methodologies, but the need for more tools remains great."[65] The importance of anticipating governmental action was underscored by GE's Public Issues Committee (of the Board of Directors) that in 1972 identified the following high priority concerns for the future:

> Problems and opportunities of business-government partnership—including a redefinition of the private sector in public problem-solving.
>
> "Politicizing" of economic decision-making—the growing government involvement in corporate decisions through consumerism, environmentalism, industrial reorganization, inflation control, etc.
>
> Constraints on corporate growth—a spectrum of issues ranging from national growth policy through economic controls and environmental protection to questions of antitrust policy and industrial structure.[66]

In addition to these issues, two other concerns (from a total of six) were heavily intertwined with governmental influence. This priority list was used to allocate GE's forecasting efforts. Although governmental processes are not sufficiently understood to identify and specify the causes of governmental action, conscious efforts need to be made in developing causal models. General Electric, for example, monitors consumer values and other social changes as inputs to predicting governmental action. Social issues logically serve as causal-type variables in judgmental analyses even if the exact relationship cannot be specified. Use of the Delphi method (Chapter 4) offers potentially good results. Also of value to many firms are subscriptions to information services which monitor business-related government action.

SUMMARY AND CONCLUSIONS

An awareness of the many anti-trust and consumer laws as well as administrative guidelines and regulations is essential in this age of burgeoning governmental influence. Marketers must relate these influences to marketing decisions concerning pricing, channels, product and promotion as well as to marketing research. The governmental environment for marketers is changing at a rapid pace. It is no longer sufficient to expect corporate legal counsel to respond to all governmental issues facing marketing. Line management must be aware of legal requirements relevant to their activities and should actively participate in coping with governmental processes. This requires attention to legislative actions,

---

[65] Ian H. Wilson, "Socio-Political Forecasting: A New Dimension to Strategic Planning," *Michigan Business Review*, July 1974, p. 21.

[66] Wilson, "Socio-Political Forecasting," p. 17.

court decisions, as well as administrative law developed by agencies in the executive branch. Also important in understanding the processes are public opinion, information intermediaries (e.g., news media), and the social changes and issues that often lead to new regulation and legislation. Monitoring governmental processes and, ideally, forecasting future directions is today an essential task. Positive lobbying is an important part of this overall task—involving both information gathering as well as dissemination—although business must recognize "healthy competition" as a higher level goal than the protection of business. This requires a pro-competition, not just a pro-business perspective.

EXERCISES FOR DISCUSSION AND REVIEW

1. Identify a recently passed law (e.g., National Product Safety Act) that impinges on marketing management and (*a*) trace and analyze the processes preceding its passage (in Figure 6–1) and, (*b*) carefully identify potentially negative consequences of this legislation to society (if any). Would an understanding of this process assist management in future monitoring of legislation?

2. Certain conditions must be met for the market system to function effectively. Review these conditions (early in this chapter) and (*a*) identify new legislation that could be passed to help insure these conditions are met and (*b*) identify any possible negative effects of implementing such legislation.

3. Peruse your campus libraries (including the law library, if separate) and identify key sources of information for assessing both *proposed* as well as newly *enacted* legislation and regulatory actions. Assess the potential value of each source to business management.

4. "Fair trade legislation is unfair." Discuss.

5. ABC Company manufactures small electrical appliances for a 10-state area. An employee in the quality control department informs her supervisor that uninsulated wire was inadvertently included in the assembly of several hundred hair dryers. The product case is plastic and it is unlikely that users would suffer an electric shock in normal use. It is conceivable, however, that severe shock or even death could result if the wire slipped downward to the inside of the metal switch plate. For this to happen, the product would probably have to be dropped or severely jolted several times.

   High-level executives in the company are informed of this development at a hastily-called meeting. Assume you are present at this meeting as Vice President of Marketing for ABC. What is your considered opinion as to appropriate action(s) to take, if any? Carefully detail potential legal violations as well as possible consequences. Second, how would the actions taken differ if the case were evaluated from an ethical as opposed to a legal viewpoint?

6. XYZ Company has for years sold merchandise to CBA Retailing Company. CBA orders on a regular basis and continues to be one of XYZ Company's largest customers. Because of this relationship, CBA Retailing is given a special 7 percent discount. Exactly what would you need to know to determine if this practice is legal?

7. A television advertisement for electric shavers includes a statement that the shaver is the "finest available." In fact, the manufacturer has no data to back this up. Is this misleading advertising? Why or why not? Should the practice be dropped?

8. Monitoring and forecasting the governmental environment is essential to the future of marketing. Based on a review of forecasting in Chapters 3 and 4, discuss the relevance of each of the forecasting techniques to predicting the governmental environment. To the extent that certain methods are inappropriate, explain why.

part three
Market Opportunity Analysis

The previous part provided a perspective on the various, largely uncontrollable factors that influence the success of corporate/marketing strategy and tactics. Part III continues the examination of managerial analyses for marketing decision making by discussing the analysis of market opportunities. This task prepares management for the critical decision of selecting market targets on which to concentrate marketing effort and provides the essential understanding of market behavior needed for designing and controlling marketing programs.

Chapter 7 leads off by providing the conceptual and procedural foundation for market opportunity analysis activities of firms. The chapter begins by defining market opportunity analysis and discusses its essential role in corporate decision making. Then, a framework for systematically guiding analyses of market opportunities is developed and examined. Moreover, kinds of information needed as well as appropriate information sources are suggested. The intent is to provide a highly operational approach to market opportunity analysis for any kind of product/market situation. The final part of the chapter overviews frequently-used forecasting procedures and techniques.

Chapter 8 follows with a discussion of market segmentation concepts and procedures. Market segmentation is presented as a strategic approach to decisions on market targets and marketing programs. Thus, market segmentation overlaps with market opportunity analysis in the assessment of market demand and competitive positions, but extends beyond it into key marketing decisions. After defining market segmentation, the chapter examines the requirements for applying segmentation by firms. Then, the key tasks necessary to implement a market segmentation strategy are examined. The chapter ends with two illustrations of segmentation approaches.

Chapter 9 concludes the section with a discussion of buyer decision processes. At the core of both market opportunity analysis and market segmentation is the analysis of demand. Thus, marketing managers must be familiar with the factors, relationships, and processes describing buyer decision making in order to analyze markets. The first part of the chapter presents a comprehensive consumer behavior model to serve as a framework for marketing management. The model is then applied in the analysis of a potential market target of a company. This is followed by a brief assessment of the "state-of-the-art" in buyer behavior research. Finally, industrial buying behavior is discussed and contrasted with consumer buying behavior.

7

Analysis of Market Opportunities

One of the most difficult challenges facing marketing managers is to ensure that corporate decision making is based upon a sound understanding of the customers comprising target markets. Under the marketing concept, marketing is the major link between internal operations and the external markets upon which the organization is dependent. Marketing managers must develop and maintain considerable knowledge about both present and future markets to assure that corporate market target and offer decisions are consistent with the wants, needs, and unique characteristics of customers.

This chapter discusses the concepts, procedures, and information needed for analyzing market opportunities. First, market opportunity analysis is defined, and its role in corporate decision making is examined. Then, an operational framework for systematically conducting a market opportunity analysis is presented and explained. Finally several demand forecasting procedures and techniques are discussed.

UNDERSTANDING MARKET BEHAVIOR

Barriers to Managerial Development of Market Expertise

Owners and managers of small firms can often develop an understanding of their markets through frequent contact with customers. For example, the president of a small lumber mill equipment distributor spends more time visiting mill operations than he does in the office. As the top manager of the firm, this executive is intimately familiar with his customers and relies on this knowledge to direct the activities of the firm. However, as organizations grow, managers become more and more immersed in an organizational hierarchy which typically inhibits direct contact with customers. Moreover, growth causes firms to hire professional managers who may be quite unlike their customers due to differences in social class, educational training, values, goals, and attitudes. These managers cannot automatically rely on personal introspection (e.g., "What would I look for in the product if I were the buyer?") and experiences to predict market wants and needs. Even the more successful large companies such as General Motors have suffered from this isolation from customers:

> GM has been noticeably tardy in recognizing some emerging market segments. Ford's Mustang had the sporty car market to itself for 2-½ years before GM countered with the Camaro. Cynics wonder if GM has missed the market on occasion because the world a GM executive sees from this pinnacle can be distorted. Says a man who was once close to the pinnacle: "The top executives tend to be too isolated from what goes on in the marketplace."[1]

Management's understanding of customers may also be hindered or outdated by changes occurring in markets. Consider the major shifts in consumer preferences that occur because of long-run changes in population structural characteristics. For example, while considerable attention has been focused on the "youth market," the "over-65 market" may be even more important to many organizations in the 1970s and 1980s. People are retiring earlier, having fewer children to drain income during their working years, receiving larger retirement incomes, and living longer. The result is a rapidly growing over-65 proportion of the U.S. population representing an important source of demand for many products including retirement villages, hobby and sporting equipment, specialized medical care, and entertainment.

Market Opportunity Analysis Defined

Since managers cannot rely solely on personal experiences and first-hand knowledge of buyers, effective procedures for obtaining information concerning market behavior must be developed. Market opportunity analysis (MOA) is the primary activity by which marketing managers develop and maintain this understanding of market demand. More specifically, *MOA is the systematic collection and analysis of information about end users and the organizations serving them to determine the potential demand within end-user groups that can be tapped by a marketing offer.* MOA involves much more than sales forecasting, though forecasting is an essential part of the total activity. Typically, a wide variety of information is collected about customers and other firms which enables marketing managers to determine who

---

[1] "Mighty GM Faces Its Critics," *Business Week,* July 11, 1970, p. 72.

customers are, to understand their needs and wants, and to assess how well they are being currently served by other firms.

The focus for MOA should be on end users (who may be ultimate consumers or business and industrial organizations) of a corporation's product. Admittedly, some firms concentrate their analysis on intermediate customers in a channel of distribution. For example, a food flavoring manufacturer viewed its customers as wholesalers and large-scale retailers. Management knew very little about the consumers using their product nor why they were using it. In effect, this manufacturer had turned over considerable responsibility and control for the performance of its product to other firms. The product was being used as a loss-leader by retailers and was receiving almost no selling support. This was not consistent with the manufacturer's objectives, but little could be done to change retailers. Management did not know enough about end users to recommend or implement a selling strategy to more comprehensively develop demand. Clearly, end users' demand ultimately determines the degree of success (or failure) experienced by all firms in a channel of distribution. So, to maintain at least some control over a marketing offer as well as to be prepared for inevitable market changes, firms even several levels removed from end users in a channel of distribution should use MOA to develop an understanding of end-users markets. Intermediate customers should also be assessed, not as markets, but as an *access* to selected market targets.

Finally, the collection and analysis of market information for a MOA should pertain to some marketing offer, either existing or proposed. Markets exist because some group of potential customers has a need that can be satisfied by a product or service. Thus, preparing management for decisions concerning a product and/or its supporting strategy and tactics should be the justification for conducting analysis of market opportunities. Other information gathered by a firm may concern the behavior of people, but unless it is directly related to potential customer behavior for a product, service, or other component in a marketing mix such information is not part of a MOA. For example, some companies employ "soothsayers" to study a variety of phenomena such as the changing relationships among U.S. family members. This information is not part of any MOA activity unless it is used to help management make decisions concerning marketing offers and markets. Otherwise, it is part of broader environmental analyses with no assurance of being included in a future MOA.

Role of MOA in Corporate Decisions and Activities

Figure 7–1 shows the link between MOA, analysis of the marketing environment, and key marketing decision areas in which a MOA

FIGURE 7–1

Market Opportunity Analysis in Corporate Decision Making

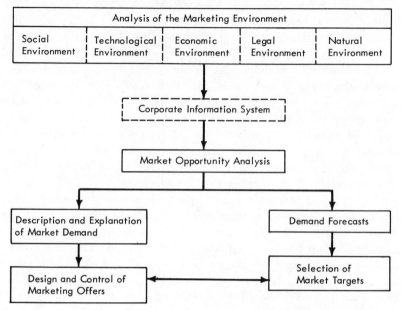

can contribute. A firm's analysis of the marketing environment can provide an important input into a MOA and in some cases may even trigger the need for an analysis of a particular market opportunity. For example, an environmental analysis of census and other data showing population age structure changes may cause a bank to become interested in the over-50-years-of-age portion of the U.S. population. Management would then request a MOA to assess the opportunity for bank services or investment opportunities (such as in retirement villages) directed toward this group.

The output of a MOA can benefit marketing management in both the design and control of marketing strategy and the selection of market targets. Understanding market demand enables marketing managers to supplement and improve judgment concerning marketing strategy decision alternatives. As an illustration, a wine distributor recognized the desirability of adding a premium brand of wine to its line by relying on a MOA to better understand customer wine selection decisions. Management learned that many customers are introduced to wine by trying a "pop" wine such as Boone's Farm. This typically generates enough interest to try inexpensive table wines, and eventually to move up to premium table wines. The distributor had a very popular brand of "pop" wines and several brands of inexpensive, high-volume table wines. To complement these brands, a premium brand of table wine was needed. Thus, improved understanding of customers through a MOA can substitute, at least in part, for direct contact with customers by management.

Marketing managers must also predict how and to what extent customers will respond to marketing strategy and tactical decision alternatives. This requires selecting market targets and forecasting their reaction to decisions made by management. While cost and other considerations are needed to select market targets, demand forecasts based on a MOA are key inputs. Returning to the wine distributor example, management had to estimate the number of consumers in their market area who were moving toward the premium brand stage in the wine decision process. Moreover, an estimate of the average quantity that each user could be expected to buy was needed. Combined, these estimates allowed management to assess the size of the opportunity for a new premium wine brand which was pivotal in the eventual decision to add such a brand.

A MARKET OPPORTUNITY ANALYSIS FRAMEWORK

What Is a Market?

Since a MOA is designed to help management understand and predict demand within markets, a key task is to determine the boundaries that identify the particular market to be analyzed. Thus, both managers and analysts involved in a MOA must have a clear understanding of the concept of a market. Otherwise, conflicting notions of a market can hinder the usefulness of information gathered and analyses performed. For example, if a manager considers youth as a single market (i.e., the so-called youth market), a MOA may not uncover important differences in the buying behavior of young people. To avoid these kinds of difficulties, the following definition of a market is offered: *A market is a group of people who are potentially able and willing in some designated future time period to decide to purchase a product or service for end-use purposes.*

Markets are comprised of people. Companies design marketing strategies and tactics to influence buying decisions, and it is people who decide whether or not to buy a product or brand. In those situations where people are not users of a product, a MOA may have to analyze more than markets to assess demand. For example, consider the market for dog food. Clearly, dogs do not decide how much and what brand of dog food to buy. People who own or care for dogs buy dog food. So, companies such as Purina should define their markets as comprised of dog owners and handlers (e.g., veterinarians, kennels, etc.). Dogs would be considered a demand factor to be analyzed since characteristics such as nutrition needs, taste preferences, and quantity intake influence the decisions of people buying dog food. Similarly, for industrial products, buying firms are the users rather than people. Yet, people employed by these industrial buyers decide what to purchase. The marketing efforts of sellers are directed toward purchasing agents, engineers, and other employees who are responsible for buying decisions. So, industrial markets should also be defined in terms of selected people. The characteristics of organizations would be analyzed as a demand factor, since industrial buyers must consider the needs and resources of their organization when making buying decisions.

To determine which people to include in a market, firms should assess both the *ability* and *willingness* of people to buy. Those who do not have sufficient resources (income, assets, borrowing power, etc.) to buy during the time period under analysis cannot be considered part of a market. Given present technological development of atomic power, for instance, purchasers for electrical utilities in smaller towns cannot be included as part of a market for atomic reactors due to the very high cost of this product. Moreover, typically only some portion of those who are able to buy are also willing to buy. Those who are not willing to buy, nor can be influenced to be willing to buy should be excluded from a market for a product regardless of their resources. For example, strong religious convictions will exclude some people from being in a market for alcoholic beverages or X-rated movies even though they could afford to buy these products.

Markets are comprised of future or potential buyers of products or services. Marketing managers use market analyses to aid in making marketing decisions which are intended to influence people to buy. Thus, management is primarily concerned with what people will decide to buy in some future time period as a result of the marketing decisions. This is true even though much of market analysis focuses on the past buying behavior of people. For example, a camera manufacturer might be very interested in the demographic characteristics of those who have been heavy buyers of camera equipment. This data on past buyers is only useful to management if the same kinds of people will also be heavy buyers in the future.

Markets include only those people who buy for end-use purposes. This excludes intermediate buyers from being included in a company's market. It also insures that the concept of market is consistent with the focus for market opportunity analysis. Again, intermediate buyers represent an access to markets not part of a market and should be analyzed as such.

Finally, markets should be defined in terms of some product or service. People buy to obtain the need-satisfying functions of a product. A product's supporting strategy facilitates buying and even enhances the value of these functions, but it is the use of a product that is the reason for existence of demand. Thus, a definition of a market must specify the product demanded to be a useful concept to a firm's management. The so-called youth market, for instance, is a rather vague use of the term market, since youth are neither able nor willing to buy all products. Youth may be included in some markets, but will be excluded from others. Certainly youth are not in a market for retirement villages, and so "youth" market has no meaning or significance for a contractor in the business of developing these villages.

Levels of Market Aggregation

The task of identifying a particular market for analysis is complicated by having to define some product or product concept for which a market is believed to exist. Most products can be described in varying degrees of detail depending on what and how many attributes, features, and functions are included in the description. For example, stating a product as an "appliance" involves far less description than if the product was defined as a "refrigerator." A refrigerator is an appliance, but it is described by many more specific features. An appliance runs on electricity and is a mechanical aid for household tasks, while a refrigerator has an electrical motor, a coolant, storage space, a thermostat, shelves, and preserves food for later consumption. Correspondingly, markets differ according to the product or product concept description. The market for appliances is not the same as the market for refrigerators since during any time period there will be people who buy some appliance, but who do not buy a refrigerator.

In general, as a product is defined in more detail, fewer people can be included in the corresponding market. Adding more attributes, features, and functions to a product description causes the market to become less aggregate because some people cannot afford or do not want to buy these product characteristics. Again, going from appliance to refrigerator excludes all those potential appliance buyers who are either unable or unwilling to buy a refrigerator in the time period under analysis. Thus, markets have different levels of aggregation depending upon the degree of product description specified. A market opportunity analysis should recognize this fact when boundaries are formed for the market or markets that management wants assessed.

Interrelationship of MOA Activities

Figure 7–2 shows the interrelationships between the activities that comprise a market opportunity analysis. The central activity is *demand*

FIGURE 7–2

Market Opportunity Analysis Activities

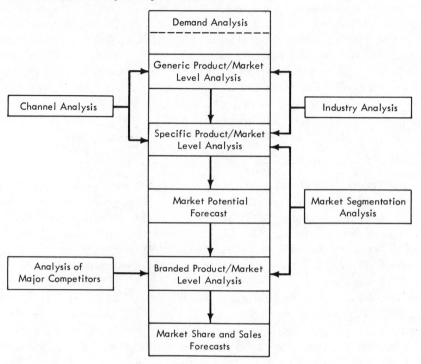

analysis which focuses on the nature and extent of demand that exists within markets. Market demand (D) is essentially a function of two factors: the number of people who are included within market boundaries (N) and the average usage rate of the product that can be expected by these people (R). Thus, demand within a market for a designated time period (t) can be characterized by:[2]

$$(1) \qquad D_t = N_t \times R_t$$

For example, if 10 million people in the United States are expected to consume an average of 6 bottles of wine next year, the demand for wine for that year could be quantified as: 60 million bottles = 10 million people × 6 bottles per person.

Demand analysis attempts to provide estimates of N_t and R_t by systematically collecting and analyzing information about end users for a specified product. Determining *quantitative* estimates of D_t is a fore-

---

[2] A similar function is discussed in G. David Hughes, *Demand Analysis for Marketing Decisions* (Homewood, Ill.: Richard D. Irwin, Inc., 1973), pp. 1–7.

casting task, and so, forecasting is a part of demand analysis. However, management may want more understanding of demand than a numerical forecast provides. Then, demand analysis would also include information and analyses that describe the *nature* of demand including descriptive characteristics of those comprising N_t, their needs related to the product, their attitudes toward competitive products, influences of others on their buying decisions, and so forth. These kinds of information are more qualitative, but "flesh out" demand by allowing management to better understand who comprises a market and why they want to buy. For example, a wine distributor may improve marketing decisions by knowing that demand is generated primarily by middle to high income, well educated people from the East, North and Far West regions of the United States who typically serve wine at social functions, yet know very little about the characteristics of the wines being served.

Demand analysis can be conducted at more than one level of market aggregation for most, if not all products. Figure 7–2 identifies three different levels that are frequently of interest to marketing managers: generic product/markets, specific product/markets, and branded product/markets. Essentially these levels refer to the markets that correspond to the same product described in three different degrees of detail. A generic product is very broadly defined; a specific product is defined in greater detail, but is constrained to be a specific type of generic product; and a branded product is the offering of a specific product by a particular company, and so includes those characteristics that identify it as a company's brand. Examples of products at each of these levels are shown in Figure 7–3. For each level, there is a different size market (N_t) and probably a different usage rate (R_t).

The implication of these product/market levels is that demand analysis can be viewed as a process of funneling toward the nature and extent of demand opportunity for a company (branded product/market) by initially analyzing more aggregate demand to determine what opportunity is available for all firms. By studying demand at more aggregate levels, management gains an improved perspective on the nature of market needs and characteristics. As an illustration, the management of Wilson Sporting Goods company can benefit by understanding the more aggregate trends affecting the generic sporting goods product/market such as the increasing desire of many to have and use leisure time for pleasure. Moreover, assessing the extent of demand at more aggregate levels helps management place an upper limit on the opportunity that can be tapped. Wilson's ability to sell increasing volumes of golf equipment is constrained by the size of the market for all golf equipment.

Market segmentation can make an important contribution to demand analysis. This activity recognizes the potential for a generic and/or

FIGURE 7–3

Illustrative Product/Market Levels of Aggregation

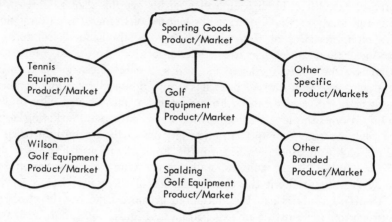

A. Generic, Specific, and Branded Product/Markets for Golf Equipment

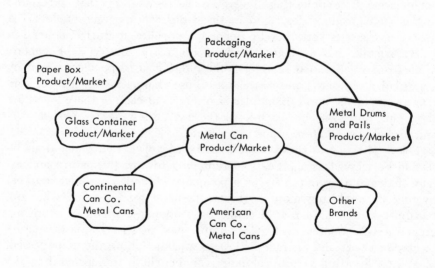

B. Generic, Specific, and Branded Product/Markets for Metal Can Packages

specific product/market to be comprised of people with substantially different preferences. For example, there are likely to be both heavy users and light users of wine in the same specific product/market. If a heavy user consumes 15 bottles a year and a light user consumes only 2, management may want to design different marketing offers to appeal to these two groups or segments. Market segmentation is a managerial approach to decisions on market targets and on marketing offers and so, extends beyond demand analysis. The nature and size of demand is only one of several factors to consider in these decisions. Yet, segmentation requires the identification of market segments and the analysis of demand within these segments which are demand analysis tasks. Demand analysis utilizes a segmentation approach by recognizing that total demand in a market (D_t) is comprised of the sum of demand in individual segments $(i = 1, 2, \ldots, n)$:

$$(2) \qquad\qquad D_t = \sum_{i}^{n} N_{it} \times R_{it}$$

The nature and extent of demand available in a market does not completely determine market opportunity for a company. This opportunity is also dependent on how well demand is being served by other firms. A market may have a considerable demand potential, but if customers are being satisfied by existing firms, there may be little opportunity for another firm in that market. Or if competition is intense for market demand, as occurs in the maturity stage of a product life cycle, companies may actually be squeezed out of markets. So, a MOA must assess the firms that are serving a particular market to fully evaluate market opportunity.

At more aggregate levels of a market (generic and specific) there are too many firms to analyze individually. However, an *industry analysis* can be conducted to determine how well all firms as a group are serving a market. An industry is considered here to be all firms that are selling to the market under analysis from the same level in a channel of distribution as the firm doing the MOA. The relevant industry for Continental Can Company when performing a MOA for metal pails, for instance, would be all other manufacturers of metal pails since Continental is a manufacturer. Similarly, an industry can be all wholesalers, all distributors, or all retailers for firms at these levels in a channel.

The purpose of an industry analysis is to determine how well direct competitors as a group are satisfying demand as well as to identify operating practices (in marketing, production, distribution, etc.) that are required to serve a market. Due to the length of time an industry has existed, the quality of marketing offers, and other factors, industries differ in the extent to which demand has been developed in their markets. For example, the automobile industry has been quite successful in developing demand for autos by generating high sales volume relative to the total number of potential auto buyers. This is reflected by the high percentage of all U.S. households that own cars. In contrast, the public transportation industry has very low penetration (percent ridership on public transportation vehicles out of all trips taken by people) suggesting that demand has not been very well developed. The opportunity for a firm to enter these industries is entirely different even though the size of demand is quite large in both of the corresponding markets.

Typically, an industry develops certain practices, used by all or most firms, that experience has shown are successful approaches for a particular market. For example, contract packagers for aerosol products (firms that contract for the packaging of consumer aerosol products such as hair spray and deodorant) must have very effective quality control procedures since an error in aerosol packaging also ruins the product. Thus, an industry analysis can help management identify such marketing offer practices that are essential for achieving sales in a market.

At the branded product/market level, an *analysis of individual competitors* can be conducted. Typically, there are a relatively few firms that are or will be most directly competing for the same customers. Here, a MOA should assess the strengths and weakness of these firms in terms of their ability to satisfy customers. The analysis, being restricted to a small number of firms, can be a more indepth assessment of operational practices and marketing programs than is feasible during an industry analysis. A competitor analysis is essential for estimating the portion or share of market demand that a firm can reasonably expect to generate with a particular marketing offer as opposed to the share that will be captured by these competitors.

Finally, evaluating how well demand is being served also requires doing a *channel analysis*. This involves assessing types of firms and individual firms at other levels in channels that are used to reach end-user markets. The focus should be on describing the channel arrangements (i.e., the number of levels used, the types of firms at each level, and the number of firms at each level) characteristic of an industry's effort to reach markets. The results of the analysis should provide management with a better understanding of requirements for channels that will most successfully serve demand. As an example, a channel analysis for a food product revealed that typical channels at the specific product/market level included a large number of different types of wholesalers and retailers including hardware distributors, large chain stores, food chain stores, food brokers, gas stations, and independent food stores. This was necessary since consumers would not search for the product very extensively, and so, it had to be made available in many different stores to generate demand.

The remainder of the chapter discusses each of the MOA activities in more depth. The focus is on describing demand, industry/competition, and channel analyses at each of the three market levels of aggregation.

GENERIC PRODUCT/MARKET ANALYSIS

Generic Product/Market Definition

Generic product/markets represent the broadest delineation of market boundaries that an organization might define. *A generic market would include all people who are potentially able and willing in a designated future period to decide to purchase a class of products for end-use purposes.* A generic product is not a single product, but a group of products that all serve the same general customer need or want. The corresponding generic needs would also be very broad categories of more specifically defined needs. For example, Table 7–1 shows the generic needs and defining product characteristics that correspond to selected product classes. Notice that a generic need such as "convenience in performing household chores" summarizes convenience in performing a variety of specific chores (e.g., washing, drying, and ironing clothes).

While there is very little in the way of established, sophisticated techniques for determining generic product/market boundaries, analysts can use (1) managerial judgment, (2) definitions apparent in available secondary sources, and/or (3) marketing research. Marketing managers may be able to provide sufficient guidance by relying on their experience with similar products and understanding of product functions. For example, an executive of a food-flavoring product was able to define the relevant generic market as the "outdoor cooking" market. He reasoned that the product would have to be used while cooking outside the home due to the amount of smoke generated by the product when heated.

When managerial judgment is not sufficient, generic product/market definitions may be available in various secondary sources. For example, as a service the U.S. Bureau of the Census and hundreds of trade associations define generic product/markets in order to collect a variety of statistical data. Food and beverages is a Census definition, while the "outdoor cooking" market is a definition used by several trade associations (e.g., the Charcoal Briquet Institute). If a particular product

TABLE 7–1

Corresponding Generic Products and Needs

Generic Product	*Defining Feature*	*Generic Need*
Appliances..............	Electrically powered	Convenience in performing household chores
Food and beverages.......	Edible	Nutrition, health
Fuels.................	Combustible	Energy
Transportation..........	Powered mechanically	Mobility

concept being evaluated by a firm appears to fit into a predefined product/market, then the analyst has, simultaneously, a generic product/market definition and an available pool of information about that product/market. As an illustration, Table 7–2 shows some of the Census data that is available for the Food and Beverages generic product/market.

In some cases, management may have to use marketing research to define generic product/market boundaries. One interesting procedure is to analyze the use of a product by customers. This research technique assumes that how a product is used will reflect the generic needs for that product. Called consumption system research, the data describes the total consumption system for a product including related products.[3] For example, research might show that people who frequently paint their houses also spend considerable time doing yard work (cutting grass, planting flowers, trimming trees, etc.). This might suggest to a paint manufacturer that the relevant generic need served by paint is "pride in home appearance."

Generic Product/Market Information Needed

Once a generic product/market has been defined at least in terms of product characteristics and generic need, market opportunity analysis can begin to assess the opportunity existing at this market level. Consistent with the MOA framework, the focus should include demand, industry and channel analyses.

Demand Analysis. Demand analysis at this level should describe who are the most likely customers for the generic product and identify and assess relevant demand factors. Temptation to include everyone in the generic product/market should be resisted since some people are more likely to be potential customers than are others. Thus, characteristics of the *most likely* customers are needed. For industrial generic products, such characteristics as size of buying firm (sales, assets, production capacity, etc.), geographic concentrations, type of products sold, or use of the class of products are commonly used to describe market customers. For consumer end users, demographic and socioeconomic characteristics are most widely used. For example, the outdoor cooking market can be adequately described by three such characteristics: age (25–55), income (primarily middle income categories), and residential location (suburban areas).

With such characteristics, management can estimate the size of generic markets within selected geographic areas. Census data is gathered

---

[3] Harper W. Boyd, Jr., and Sidney J. Levy, "New Dimension in Consumer Analysis," *Harvard Business Review*, vol. 41 (November–December 1963), pp. 129–30.

TABLE 7–2

Food and Beverages: Projections 1973–1980

SIC Code	Industry	1973	Percent Increase 1972–73	1974	Percent Increase 1973–74	1980 Low	1980 High	Percent Increase 1973–80 Low	Percent Increase 1973–80 High
20............	Value of shipments	126,930	16	135,930	7	188,710	200,860	5.8	6.8
20............	Total employment	1,560	–.5	1,558	0	n.a.	n.a.	n.a.	n.a.
20............	Value of imports	4,400	9	4,800	9	7,000	7,500	6.9	7.9
20............	Value of exports	3,300	12	3,575	8	5,000	5,500	6.1	7.6

Source: Adapted from table in *U.S. Industrial Outlook with Projections to 1980* (Washington, D.C.: U.S. Department of Commerce, 1974), p. 175.

that shows the number (N_t) having these characteristics. Moreover, by projecting this number into the future, management can assess growth potential. For example, the outdoor cooking market appears to have substantial growth potential since census forecasts show large population growth in the young-to-middle ages, middle income, and suburban residence portions of the U.S. population. (See Table 7–3 for population trend data for each of these characteristics).

TABLE 7–3

U.S. Population Trends for Age, Income, and Residence

U.S. Population Age Projections (000,000)—Young to Middle Ages

Age	1960	1970	1975	1980	1985
20–24	11.1	17.2	19.2	20.9	20.9
25–29	10.9	13.9	17.3	19.3	21.0
30–34	12.0	11.5	14.0	17.4	19.4
35–39	12.5	11.1	11.5	14.0	17.4
40–44	11.7	11.9	11.1	11.5	14.0

U.S. Population Distribution of Income
(percent of total income)—Middle Incomes

Income Categories	1970	1975	1980
$10,000–$15,000 per year	30.0	27.5	23.0
15,000–$25,000 per year	27.5	34.5	40.0
25,000 and over per year	14.5	17.5	21.0

U.S. Population by Residence Area (000,000)

Residence	1950	1960	1969
Metropolitan areas	89.2	112.9	129.2
In central cities	52.2	57.8	58.6
Outside central cities	37.0	55.1	70.6
Nonmetropolitan areas	61.4	65.6	71.1

Source: *A Guide to Consumer Markets 1971/1972* (New York: The Conference Board, Inc., 1971), pp. 16, 33, 111.

Selected demand factors may have to be identified and assessed. A demand factor is any variable that is believed to influence either the number of people in a market (N_t) or their decisions to buy and use a generic product (R_t). As an example, a demand factor affecting the size and usage rate of the outdoor cooking market was the introduction of gas grills. These grills can be easily installed on apartment balconies to bring the possibility of cooking outside to urban apartment dwellers. The increasing installation of gas grills in apartment houses will substantially expand this generic product/market. Other demand factors affecting the outdoor cooking market and factors for the food and beverage market are shown in Table 7–4.

Industry Analysis. A MOA should also identify general trends occurring within the industry to assess how well demand is being satisfied.

TABLE 7–4

Selected Demand Factors for Two Generic Product/Markets

Generic Product/Market	Demand Factors
Food and beverages	1. Population growth 2. Attitudes toward desired diets 3. Economic conditions such as inflation
Outdoor cooking	1. Population growth 2. Movement to suburbs 3. Apartment construction 4. Increase in leisure time 5. Family size trends

Industry sales in dollars and in units are often available to provide some insight into the growth (or lack of it) being experienced. Moreover, estimates of the number of firms, rate of increases or decrease in firms, number of firms by size categories (sales volume, assets, output capacity), ownership and merger trends, gross margin trends, and cost trends will help management assess the directions and causes of growth.[4] Of particular importance is to obtain this kind of data for several past time periods so that trends or patterns of growth can be assessed and then projected into the future. Consider the data in Table 7–2 again. No insight into growth can be gained by only noting the value of food and beverage shipments in a single year, say 1974. The data is considerably more meaningful when shipments are compared for 1973, 1974, and 1980 where a growth trend is evident.

The analysis of industry information allows management to assess key opportunity indicators including the stage of the industry life cycle, operating practices common to industry firms, and barriers to entry into the market.[5] One industry analysis for the contract packaging industry revealed the following information: (1) the number of total contract packaging firms was stable to declining; (2) there was considerable merger activity occurring between firms; (3) the number of smaller contract packagers was declining; (4) the number of larger firms was stable, but not growing; (5) the more successful firms were older firms with established reputations; (6) there was intense price competition among firms; (7) there was a movement by many larger con-

---

[4] When census or trade associations do not provide this kind of information, there are a number of marketing research agencies that sell standardized industry reports. Such firms include Predicasts, Inc., Economic Information Systems, Inc., and Frost and Sullivan, Inc.

[5] Many products go through a set life cycle in terms of both sales and profits. This cycle includes the stages of introduction (low sales, often negative profits), growth (most rapid increase in sales and profits), maturation (leveling of sales, downturn in profits), and decline (declining sales and profits). The life cycle concept is discussed in more detail in Chapter 10.

sumer-goods manufacturers to set up in-house packaging operations; (8) these in-house operations contracted with other firms to utilize excess capacity; (9) long time contract packager-customer relationships were characteristic of more successful firms. This information caused a firm to drop their plan to enter the contract packaging industry in spite of a favorable growth in packaging demand. For example, the intense price competition, stable number of total firms, merger activity, and declining number of smaller firms indicated that the industry was in the maturity to decline stages of a life cycle. Moreover, there were serious barriers to entering this industry including large size (more successful firms were large), established reputation (successful firms were older with long relationships with customers), and extreme efficiency (to compete on price).

Channel Analysis. Serving every generic market will be existing channel arrangements. No attempt can be made to describe every channel arrangement due to the large number of arrangements that typically exist. Yet, an analysis of channel designs may yield some commonalities that are characteristic of the industry. These suggest what must be done to make the firm an attractive addition to an existing channel or what must be built into a new channel. For example, in the packaging industry, independent packagers must have warehouse facilities to receive and store products in bulk form until packaging runs can be scheduled. After packaging, products are shipped to distribution points for allocation to retailers. Figure 7–4 shows the typical channel arrangement in-

FIGURE 7–4

Channel Arrangement for Contract Aerosol Package Services

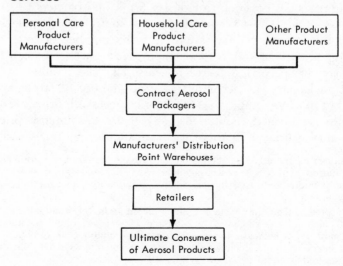

cluding contract packagers that was constructed from a channel analysis at the generic product/market level. Thus, packagers provide a warehousing and shipping service in the channel for many consumer goods, and so performing these functions is an entry requirement for prospective packaging firms.

Uses of Generic Product/Market Analyses

A generic product/market analysis can be used to quickly evaluate the potential opportunity available in alternative markets for new product candidates. Usually, a firm has limited resources for a MOA at early stages in a new product decision process and must identify which of several potential markets appear most promising without expending substantial amounts of time, manpower, and money. So, a generic product/market analysis helps management decide whether to drop a new product candidate or to allocate more resources for a MOA at the specific product/market level.

In addition, MOA at the generic level ensures that the firm takes a sufficiently broad look at the potential markets for a product by analyzing all markets having a common generic need. It is too easy to lock in on the most obvious or most immediately accessible groups of potential customers when the analysis is restricted to specific product and branded product/markets. By assessing the class in which a product is included other important groups that may have essentially the same generic need may be uncovered. As an example, consider the benefit management gained from performing an analysis at the generic product/market level in the following MOA:

A specialty paper company was considering the opportunity for introducing a new product called fiber reinforced film (FRF). This was a well-defined product concept that was being considered for use in construction projects. Its industrial application would be to keep construction and foundation materials dry. Consequently, the market for the product was felt to be construction firms. However, by performing the MOA at the generic product/market level, it was apparent that the construction industry did not comprise the total generic market. FRF was considered to be part of a class of products called moisture vapor barriers. The corresponding generic need for this class of products is to keep moisture in or away from materials. When viewed in this way, other types of organizations have essentially the same generic need as contractors. For instance, the large pest control organizations (e.g., Orkin) also provide a moisture control service for houses having an open crawl-space underneath the flooring. Part of this service involves laying a moisture vapor barrier over the ground to keep moisture from rising to the wood frame causing rotting. Also, various packagers may have need for effective moisture vapor barriers for use in packaging of products that could be damaged from moisture or that must retain moisture in the product.[6]

Finally, a generic product/market level analysis may help management uncover demand factors that might not be discovered if the MOA focus were restricted to less aggregate levels. Frequently, secondary sources such as business and general interest periodicals discuss entire industries and trends affecting these industries, which correspond to generic product/markets. Thus, a search for MOA information at this level increases the likelihood of discovering those trends that will affect specific products and brands within the generic class. As an example, the early 1970s spiraling food prices led to discussions and analyses of changes in Americans' eating habits and diets.[7] These reports typically referred to impact upon the entire food industry and so may be overlooked if a MOA focused only on one specific product within the food industry.

Analysis of generic product/markets offers these benefits at relatively low cost. Frequently, needed information can be gathered and analyzed for a few thousand dollars, or less, due to heavy reliance on existing information from secondary sources and expert opinion. So, the net benefits over costs can often make the generic product/market level analysis a very attractive step in a MOA. In some situations, this level analysis is not possible. For example, when a MOA is being conducted for a radically new product concept, there is unlikely to be a generic market that is sufficiently developed to be included in various secondary information sources.

SPECIFIC PRODUCT/MARKET LEVEL ANALYSIS

Specific Product/Market Definition

All generic product/markets include several different specific product/markets. These are identified by defining product concepts in more detail in terms of product attributes, features, and/or functions performed. Table 7–5 shows some of the specific products that are included in selected generic product/markets.

The bond that links specific products together within a generic class is that all are serving essentially the same generic need of customers. For instance, all specific products comprising the appliance generic

---

[6] "New Era Specialty Paper Company," in Edward C. Bursk and Stephen A. Greyser (eds.), *Advanced Cases in Marketing Management* (Englewood Cliffs, N.J.: Prentice-Hall, 1969), pp. 27–30.

[7] For example, see "Changing Eating Habits Spurs $87 Billion Grocery Field," *Advertising Age*, November 1, 1971, pp. 21, 125, and "How Three Families Buy Their Food," *Business Week*, November 25, 1972, pp. 86–88.

TABLE 7–5

Specific Products Included in Selected Generic Product/Markets

Generic Product/Markets	Specific Products
Appliances.............	Washers, dryers, refrigerators, stoves, blenders
Packaging..............	Aerosol, box, can, glass, flexible packages
Outdoor cooking........	Grills, fuels, accessories

product/market satisfy consumer needs for convenience in performing various household tasks. There may also be other commonalities between specific products in terms of product components, production processes, distribution networks, and so forth. All appliances are powered by electricity, for example.

Specific product/market analyses may be complicated by the fact that more than one degree of descriptive detail is possible. In these cases, there are multiple levels of specific products within the same generic product/market. For example, Figure 7–5 shows that within the generic

FIGURE 7–5

Two Layers of Specific Product/Markets within the Generic Outdoor Cooking Product/Market

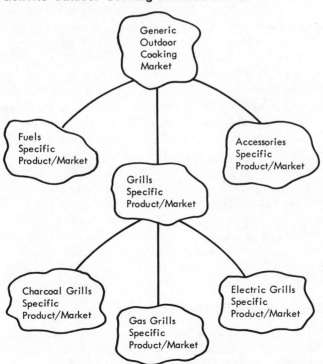

outdoor cooking market the specific product, grills, can be further classified into gas grills, electric grills, and charcoal grills depending on type of fuel required. Thus, by adding type of fuel to the product description for grills a new level is created. The markets for each of these types of grills is different. Consequently, the experience and judgment of management is needed to determine appropriate specific product concept descriptions when conducting a MOA at this level.

In general, *a specific product/market is comprised of those people within a generic product/market who are able and willing in a designated future time period to decide to purchase a specific product for end-use purposes.* In most cases this will be a smaller market than the correspondent generic market since specifying a product concept in greater detail will usually eliminate some customers who do not want or need a particular specific product. How much the specific product/market will differ from the generic product/market depends on why specific products break out within the aggregate market.

Specific products can break out because more than one product is required to satisfy the same generic need. As an illustration, in the outdoor cooking market, consumers require some kind of cooking surface (grills), a heat source (fuels), and various utensils and flavorings (accessories) in order to satisfy their desire for this kind of food preparation. Since the specific products are complementary in use, much of the generic demand analysis will also describe markets at the specific product level. For example, people who cook outdoors are largely the same as those who use grills, fuels, and accessories.

Alternatively, there can be a diversity of ways in which various customers want to satisfy a generic need. For example, a generic need for packaging is the protection of products. However, there are several types of protection that can be provided including protection during the handling of products in a distribution system, protection from natural forces (e.g., moisture), protection from deterioration over time, and so forth. Depending on the type of protection needed, protection qualities of various types of packages, and the costs of these packages, buyers in organizations demand different types of package material. Here, the aggregate market will break out into several smaller market segments for different specific products. Moreover, the description of customers at the aggregate level will probably not be sufficient to identify customers in each of these different specific product/markets.

Specific Product/Market Information Needed

The analyses for a MOA at the specific product/market level are essentially the same as for generic product/market analyses: demand analysis, industry analysis, and channel analysis. However, because the focus is on predicting market reaction to specific products in order to make market target and marketing offer design decisions, the information will be considerably more varied and detailed. In addition, there will probably need to be greater reliance on marketing research as an information source.

Demand Analysis. A MOA should describe and distinguish customers of a specific product from those who are not very likely prospects. If specific products are complementary in use, then customers may be largely the same as generic market customers. However, if there are customers who do not all want to satisfy generic needs in the same way, a MOA should be directed toward identifying market segments. A market segment at the specific product/market level is a grouping of customers who will respond in a similar way toward a specific product offer.[8] For example, in Figure 7–5 those people who are included in the gas grill specific product/market comprise a segment since they all will respond similarly to a gas grill product offer (they want a gas grill, will respond favorably to gas grill advertising, etc.). Moreover, these people will not respond favorably toward a charcoal grill specific product which appeals to a different specific product/market segment. For segmentation to be operationally useful, management must know who segment customers are and be able to predict how they will respond (e.g., purchase, change attitudes, evaluate product features, etc.) to a specific product offer. In addition, the demand potential must be great enough to justify the use of resources to serve that segment. The task for a MOA, then, is to identify and describe market segments so that marketing managers can analyze market opportunity in each one. The understanding of customers developed from this analysis is the basis for designing marketing offers that will closely match the needs and wants of segment customers. Moreover, since a segment's customers have similar response tendencies, more efficient use of corporate resources is achieved by designing the same offer for all customers within the segment.[9]

At the specific product/market level, managers need to develop an understanding of *why* customers will behave in a certain way in response to marketing offer decisions. Since marketing management must predict how customers will respond to their marketing offer decisions, developing this understanding of markets will improve confidence in the ac-

---

[8] For a discussion of the meaning of market segments and segmentation, see Henry J. Claycamp and William F. Massy, "A Theory of Market Segmentation," *Journal of Marketing Research,* vol. 5 (November 1968), pp. 388–94.

[9] A more in-depth discussion of the concept, methods, and approaches to the strategy of market segmentation is contained in the next chapter (Chapter 8). For purposes of this chapter, it is only necessary to recognize the role of market segmentation in an overall market opportunity analysis.

curacy of these predictions. Clearly, providing information that *explains* market behavior will greatly aid in this task.

Since there may be differences among generic market customers in the way they want to satisfy generic needs, managers should understand what these variations are. Therefore, a MOA at the specific product/ market level should provide information about *customers' specific needs and wants*. Information intended for this task concerns customer evaluative criteria. Evaluative criteria are the characteristics or dimensions of a specific product that buyers use to compare alternative products or brands. While these criteria are usually measured in terms of benefits or functions that a product performs for customers, they generally correspond to various parts of the marketing mix controlled by a firm. For example, criteria typically used by consumers to evaluate alternative transportation modes and the corresponding controllable service components are shown in Table 7–6. Consumer evaluation of a specific mode (e.g., taxicabs, conventional transit, dial-a-ride services) can be influenced by designing service features into the total offer as well as by use of promotion to inform customers of these features.

In addition, a variety of *customer decision influences* help to explain customers' future product/brand purchase decisions. These influences are not the same for every purchase situation, so it is impossible comprehensively to catalog all important influences a marketing manager might encounter. However, several *kinds* of influences are typically worth assessing. A marketing manager should understand customers current purchase and use behavior. This information reflects the experi-

TABLE 7–6

Selected Consumer Evaluative Criteria for Transportation Modes and Corresponding Controllable Service Features

Evaluative Criteria	*Corresponding Controllable Service Components*
Punctuality	Schedules, number of vehicles, routes
Comfort	Seat design, seating configuration, climate control
Simplicity	Pick-up locations, routes, number of transfer points
Safety	Promotion of safety record, driver training, driver rules and regulations
Modernity	Vehicle styling, promotion of new and unique service features
Cost	Fare rates, method of payment, area covered
Reliability	Control of service performance, number of vehicles, driver training, schedules

ence built up by buyers as well as the patterns of need and want satisfaction that already exist. For example, General Foods has gained valuable insight into the current meal preparation behavior of housewives, including important changes occurring in this activity:

> In looking at the same housewife as a food buyer, General Foods Corporation wants to know how she runs her "meal situation." Says one General Foods executive: "In the more traditional household, you have three meals a day, and if you're not there, you don't eat. But more and more, you have a household where the kids pop in after school and are gone again, and mom may have her own outside activities. This housewife wants convenience and single-service foods that are quick to prepare and eat." No doubt this housewife is one reason that frozen food sales, up 70 percent in the last five years, now run nearly $4 billion a year and represent more than 5 percent of total food store sales. "Then there is the permissive mother who feels she has to bribe her young ones to drink milk," says the same executive. "So she uses a chocolate additive. We don't make these additives, but we still want to know this because it tells us a lot about her."[10]

Another kind of influence consists of psychological variables describing individual buyers' makeup. A large number of factors are included in this category such as attitudes, personality, interest and opinions, motives, and values.[11] When combined into a profile, these factors give the marketing manager considerably more understanding of what target market buyers are like than do the more traditional demographic and socioeconomic profiles. As an illustrative example, compare in Table 7–7 the understanding gained about two groups of automobile drivers with psychological profiles as opposed to just having demographic descriptions.

Finally, management should be interested in understanding *buyer decision processes*. For instance, a manager should know who comprises the relevant decision making unit. For consumer products, this unit may be a single consumer, or may include several members (husband, wife, children, etc.) of target market households. Similarly, for industrial products, several people (purchasing agent, buying committee, users, functional managers, technicians, etc.) within buying organizations may have some role in the purchase decision process. Other relevant decision process information might include (1) relative importance of various sources of product information, (2) intentions to purchase a product in the future (3) preferences for alternative products or brands, and (4) the product or brand information that is desired by customers to evaluate alternatives.

---

[10] "What Makes the New Consumer Buy," *Business Week,* April 24, 1971, p. 56.

[11] These factors are discussed in greater detail in Chapter 9 in the context of a buyer behavior model.

TABLE 7–7

Demographic and Psychological Profiles of Automobile Drivers

The Dependent Driver		The Active Driver	
Demographic Profile	*Psychological Profile*	*Demographic Profile*	*Psychological Profile*
1. Older	1. Knows little about cars	1. Younger	1. Knows a lot about cars
2. Better educated	2. Uninvolved in cars, driving, maintenance	2. Middle-class income	2. Involved in cars and maintenance
3. Higher incomes	3. Apprehensive about cars	3. Middle-class education	3. Enjoys driving
	4. Needs reassurance that car will run well		4. Is power-oriented in driving
	5. Gets pleasure from appearance of car		5. Wants to be in control when driving
	6. Car make and dealer important		6. Believes in differences between makes

Source: Adapted by permission from Ruth Ziff, "The Role of Psychographics on the Development of Advertising Strategy and Copy," in William D. Wells (ed.), *Life Style and Psychographics,* 1974, pp. 145–46, published by the American Marketing Association.

In summary, a comprehensive description of customers within specific product/markets should include, but go beyond demographic-socioeconomic characteristics. Marketing managers must try to obtain and combine information, often from different sources, into a total profile of the customer including who they are, their psychological makeup, their needs and wants relative to the product concept, and their current behavior patterns satisfying these needs and wants.[12] Where segmentation is possible at the specific product/market level, profiles will also show major differences between customers in different segments.

Industry Analysis. Industry analysis at the specific product/market level does not differ greatly from the same kind of analysis performed at the generic product/market level. The focus should be on determining how well customers are already being served by the group of firms at the same level within a channel. Information such as the number of competitors; rate of increase or decrease in number of competitors; size of competitors in terms of sales, assets, and production capacity; ownership and merger trends; prices charged and policies; and cost trends are all highly useful to managers in assessing competition.

A major difference in the information and analysis at this level is the

---

[12] In the field of consumer behavior, the linking together of these kinds of buyer profile information is the objective of a relatively new type of study called psychographics. For a comprehensive treatment of psychographics, see William D. Wells (ed.), *Life Style and Psychographics* (Chicago: American Marketing Association, 1974).

degree of detail. Particularly when the generic product/market has been segmented by specific products, a generic product industry is partitioned into different specific product industries. For example, the generic transportation industry is comprised of two subsets: the auto industry including all automobile manufacturers and the public transportation industry. Trade association studies, financial analysis publications such as Moody's, periodicals, required Security and Exchange Commission reports, and expert opinion are typically sufficient for the analysis.

Another difference is the desirability of obtaining information on customer perceptions of existing products. This information provides the marketing manager with customers' assessment of competitive effectiveness. For example, when conducting a MOA for a new public transportation service (e.g., carpooling) it is important to determine how well potential users feel existing transportation modes (bus, private automobiles, rail, etc.) are meeting their transportation needs. This usually requires use of attitude and opinion surveys of representative customer samples.

Channel Analysis. MOA at the specific product/market level also includes a closer examination of existing channel arrangements. There are often important differences in channels for different specific products. So, the analysis should concentrate on identifying linkages between firms handling each specific product included in a MOA. Moreover, measures of channel effectiveness are needed to aid management in the design and evaluation of alternative channels that might be used.

Channel arrangements differ considerably in complexity. For more complex channels, search for appropriate information can be quite tedious and lengthy, involving numerous informal interviews with managers in channel firms. Figure 7–6 shows the result of a channel analysis description of a typical specific product channel for a food-flavoring product included with the generic outdoor cooking market.

Uses of Specific Product/Market Analyses

Specific products within the same generic product/market will usually not present equally attractive opportunities for a firm, even when the overall opportunity for a given generic market is favorable. For example, analysis of U.S. population trends in age, income, and residence suggested a growing outdoor cooking market. Yet, the opportunity for entry into this market with grills varied considerably depending upon the type of grill. Electric grills were in the introductory stage of a life cycle where sales were very low, few firms were producing them and the opportunity was, at best, highly uncertain and risky. Gas grills were in the growth stage with expanding sales, few producers, and a very attractive market opportunity. Finally, charcoal grills were at

FIGURE 7–6

A Channel Arrangement for a Food-Flavoring Product Included within the Generic Outdoor Cooking Market

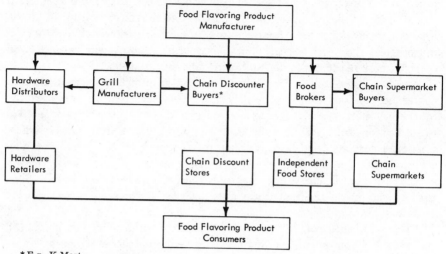

* E.g., K-Mart.

the saturation-decline stage of a life cycle with declining sales, many producers, and an unattractive market opportunity.

Since a firm must enter a market with a specific product offer, a MOA at this level provides a further screening of potential market opportunities. Information collected can be used to estimate market potential, and provide much of the detailed understanding of customers necessary for managers to put together a total marketing offer.

Market potential is the *total volume of end-user purchases that is potentially available to all firms offering a specific product within a given geographical area and time period.* Thus, market potential is the upper limit on the magnitude of demand that can be tapped by a firm. When assessing market potential, it is usually possible to forecast the volume of end user purchases in terms of the number of physical units. Moreover, if average price estimates can be made, then market potential should also be forecasted in terms of dollar volume. This is shown in the following relationship:

(2) $$\text{Market Potential Dollars} = N_{g,t} \times R_{g,t} \times AP_{g,t}$$

where:

N = number of people in a specific product/market
R = Average quantity purchases per person
AP = average price per specific product unit
g = geographic area
t = time period

As a supplement to managerial judgment, more formal approaches to forecasting market potential include: (1) projections of industry sales trends; (2) summation of customers; and (3) correlations with existing indexes. Each of these is briefly discussed.

Industry Sales. Historical industry sales data are often available, for existing industries, from secondary sources such as trade association reports. By plotting these industry sales figures over time, marketing managers can assess the industry's pattern of growth (or decline), and project this trend into the future. An example of this forecasting approach is shown in Figure 7–7. The data for the years 1967–70 represent actual shipments of commercial flexible packaging (a specific product within the generic packaging service/market) reported by the U.S. Department of Commerce. The dotted line connecting 1970–71 was the projected market potential for flexible packaging for 1971 based on an adjusted extension of the industry sales trend.

Past industry sales data shows the historical collective efforts of all firms that are serving a specific product/market to develop demand. In contrast, market potential is the volume of end-user purchases potentially available to all firms. Thus, to the extent that the marketing efforts of all firms have not been completely successful in developing this entire opportunity, industry sales trend will understate true market potential.

FIGURE 7–7

1971 Estimate of Commercial Flexible Packaging Market Potential Using Projection of Industry Sales

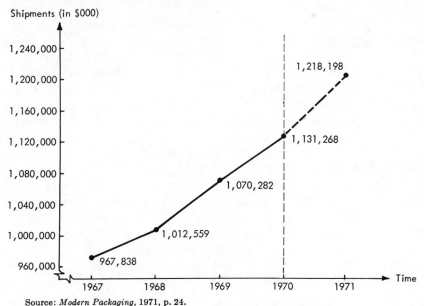

Source: *Modern Packaging*, 1971, p. 24.

Therefore, in projecting market potential from industry sales data it is essential to temper the estimate with a judgmental evaluation of the total effort put into the specific product/market by all firms.

Summation of Customers. Market potential can also be forecasted using MOA information to obtain estimates of the key variables on the right-hand side of equation (2) presented earlier in the chapter. This procedure begins with the identification of key descriptive characteristics of customers, and then requires counting the number $(N_{g,t})$ of customers having these characteristics in each geographic area. For example, for aerosol packaging, customers are typically classified by geography and type of product sold: personal products, household products, and all other products. The task, then, would be to count the number of organizations handling these kinds of products in the geographic areas of interest. Finally, management also needs to estimate the expected growth (decline) trend in the number of customers.

Average purchase per customer $(R_{g,t})$ is a judgmental estimate based on managerial experience and available market information. MOA information on customer needs and wants, current purchase and use behavior, product preferences, and purchase intentions is quite useful for this task. Average price per unit $(AP_{g,t})$ is also an estimate, but can be facilitated by current industry pricing practices.

Correlations with Existing Indexes. Some firms use various indicators and indexes to estimate market potential. These indexes are comprised of factors that are felt to be correlated with or causes of market potential. Management must be able to forecast change more easily in the indexes than to forecast market potential directly. Moreover, the relationship between a selected index and market potential must be established, generally through judgment and/or correlational analyses of historical relationships. If there is a consistent relationship between past levels of the index and market potential, the forecast of market potential is made by projecting the selected index into the forecasting period. For example, Figure 7–8 shows how a forecast of market potential might be made using an index. The curve was developed from historical data showing past market potential and the corresponding level of the index in each of several past periods. Then, a forecast is made of the index (e.g., 10.9) for the future period and is projected on this curve to forecast market potential ($3.4 million). A widely used index for consumer goods market potential forecasts is Sales Management's Buying Power Index (BPI). This index is regularly calculated for both counties and metropolitan areas in the United States by use of surveys to measure basic components of an area's ability to buy goods and services. The components are (1) population, (2) effective buying income (personal income minus federal, state, and local taxes), and (3) retail sales, and

FIGURE 7–8

An Illustrative Market Potential Forecast Using a Historical Relationship between Past Levels of an Index and Market Potential

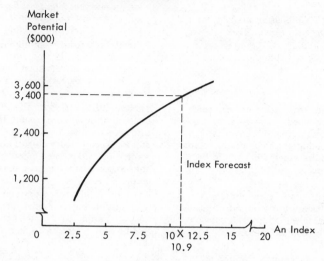

are weighted in a 2:3:5 ratio to form a single number index for each area.[13]

A MOA at the specific product level can also aid tremendously in the design of marketing programs. Decisions on product features, promotional themes and media, price, customer services, and channels are facilitated by the understanding developed concerning customer wants, unique characteristics and degree of satisfaction with existing industry and channel offers. For example, Procter & Gamble's analysis of the potato chip specific product/market showed that housewives were "getting 25 percent of the product crumbled or broken."[14] This led to the development of a new production technique and package design for Pringles, a recent P&G entry into this market, that virtually eliminated product damage. As a more comprehensive illustration, consider the implications for marketing strategy and tactics of a wine distributor derived from a specific product/market MOA for wine shown in Table 7–8.

The cost of a MOA at the specific product/market level varies considerably depending upon the extensiveness of the analysis and amount of reliance on marketing research. Expenses for this level analysis can

[13] "Explanation of Terms Used in the Survey," *Sales Management*, July 23, 1973, pp. cs–11, cs–12.

[14] "The Spectacular Rise of the Consumer Company," *Business Week*, July 21, 1973, p. 48.

TABLE 7-8

Implications of a Specific Product/Market MOA for Wine for a Wine Distributor's Marketing Strategy and Tactics

Selected Results of an MOA for Wine in a Urban Area	*Corresponding Implications for a Wine Distributor's Marketing Strategy*
1. Wine drinkers were found to be not very knowledgeable about wine.	Educate potential wine buyers about wine types, brands, and taste characteristics through advertising, newspaper articles on wine, brochures and displays in retail stores.
2. Important evaluative criteria that customers used to choose between types of wine (e.g., red versus white) included flavor, aroma, color, situation in which wine would be served, price, and brand image.	Include information on these characteristics of wine in advertising, brochures, and sales promotion displays in retail stores. Also, feature stories on selecting wine for various kinds of social gatherings and meals were submitted to newspaper.
3. Wine drinkers rely on retail liquor store salesmen for wine information, yet these salesmen are not very knowledgeable about wine.	Educate retail store salesmen through visits by distributor salesmen, brochures, and general wine literature. Add a new salesman to help in this task.
4. Wine drinkers move through an adoption process from "pop" wines to inexpensive table wines to premium table wines.	Develop a full line of wine by handling popular brands for each of these wine types. This required adding a premium brand to the distributor's line.
5. A high proportion of heavy wine users were concentrated within one geographic area.	Reallocate greater distributor salesmen time to visits at retail stores selling wine in this area of the city.

run from several thousands of dollars up to $100,000 or more. Consequently, management should carefully evaluate the cost/benefit value of such a detailed analysis.

BRANDED PRODUCT/MARKET LEVEL ANALYSIS

Branded Product/Market Definition

A corporate brand will only be able to capture a portion of total market potential. So, a MOA at the branded product/market level must assess the proportion or share of market potential for a specific product that can be captured by a company's marketing offer. This requires a forecast of the *brand's market which includes only those people in a specific product/market who are potentially able and willing in a designated future time period to decide to purchase a company's brand for end-use purposes.*

Brands may compete for the same specific product/market when there is little variation in the specific wants and needs of customers or when firms have made no attempt to identify and serve existing specific product/market segments. For example, the first brand to enter a specific product/market may attempt to appeal to the entire market during the introductory and growth stages of the specific product life cycle. In this case, a brand market is identical to the entire specific product/market. For example, a taxicab company appeals to an entire specific product/ market since cab companies in general have not significantly differentiated their offers to appeal to brand segments.

A firm may choose to have its brand compete for segments within a specific product/market. Increasing competitive pressures often lead firms to look for "market niches" where they can gain a stronger competitive advantage. Thus, corporate attempts to identify branded product/market segments, if not done earlier, are likely to occur during the later part of the growth stage and maturity stage of a life cycle. In this case, the brand market is a segment within the total specific product's market (which, in turn, may be a segment of the generic product/ market).

Branded product/market segments may be found when specific products have multiple attributes and/or functions that can be offered. Segments arise when customers attach differing relative importance to these attributes and functions for satisfying their needs and wants. For example, toothpaste is a specific product within the larger generic dentifrice product/market. There are several dimensions to toothpaste that are not equally desired by all toothpaste customers. These might include a toothpaste's taste and appearance, ability to prevent tooth decay, ability to brighten teeth, and price.[15] By emphasizing one of these features in product design and promotion, toothpaste brands can appeal to a particular segment in the specific product/market. Crest toothpaste, for instance, has been designed to appeal to those people who are most interested in preventing decay, while Ultra-Brite's brand market segment is comprised of those people who are primarily concerned with having white teeth (see Table 7–9).

Similarly, industrial markets for a specific product may be segmented by branded products or services. For example, within the generic packaging service market, independent contract aerosol packages have further divided the aerosol product/market segment into two major brand segments. These segments exist because manufacturers of aerosol products place different importance on price vs. quality control reputation. The small-to-medium sized manufacturers segment that sell primarily

---

[15] Russel I. Haley, "Benefit Segmentation: A Decision Oriented Research Tool," *Journal of Marketing*, vol. 33 (October 1969), pp. 37–43, published by the American Marketing Association.

TABLE 7-9

An Illustrative Analysis of Toothpaste Market Segments

Toothpaste Market Segments Based on Benefits Desired	*Existing Brands Serving Each Segment*
Economy benefit.............................	Private brands, sale brands
Medicinal benefit............................	Crest
Cosmetic benefit.............................	Ultra-Brite, Macleans, Plus White, Close-Up, Gleem
Taste, appearance benefit.....................	Colgate, Aim, Pepsodent

Source: This table was adapted from material in Russel I. Haley, "Benefit Segmentation: A Decision Oriented Research Tool," *Journal of Marketing*, vol. 33 (October 1969), pp. 37–43, published by the American Marketing Association.

regional and/or private brands are most interested in economy from contract aerosol packagers. In the other segment are the large manufacturers selling national brands that are most concerned with quality control due to their considerable investment in a national brand reputation.

Branded Product/Market Information Needed

Marketing management's information needs at the branded product/ market level include the identification and description of customers, assessment of major competitive strategies, and analysis of key channel arrangements.

Demand Analysis. If a brand strategy is aimed at an entire specific product/market, managerial information needs for demand analysis are identical to those previously discussed for a specific product/market level demand analysis. However, if a segmentation strategy is to be pursued, then the task is to search for customer differences in terms of profiles, needs and wants, and/or decision processes. Since the next chapter (Chapter 8) is devoted entirely to the approaches, procedures, and tools for implementing a segmentation strategy, further discussion of segmentation at the branded product/market level is deferred until then.

Assessing Major Competitors. A total industry analysis beyond that performed at the specific product/market level is not necessary. However, a MOA at the branded product/market level should analyze key competitors providing direct competition for the firm's target market customers. The analysis begins by assessing the financial strengths of competitors in order to evaluate their "staying power." This is a particularly important competitive characteristic during periods of intense competition between firms such as at the later stages of a product life cycle, during a recession, and when shortages are prevalent. Competitor financial strength can be indicated by data on profitability, price/earning ratios, sales trends, cost trends, inventory size and other performance measures. Such data is readily available in company annual reports, standardized services such as *Moody's Manuals*, Securities and Exchange Commission reports, and in business publications such as *Business Week*.

Analysis of financial strength should be followed up with an evaluation of the strengths and weaknesses each competitor has in serving markets. This involves assessing competitors' marketing programs to determine how well customer needs are being met. For example, if customers in a brand segment for a restaurant are known to want a menu with assorted meals, table service, a family atmosphere, moderately fast service without being rushed, ample parking, and alcoholic beverages served, an analysis should evaluate how well each competitor restaurant provides these services.

Information on competitors' strengths and weaknesses can help management differentiate a marketing offer from these competitors as the basis for attracting target market customers. By appropriate marketing offer design, competitor weaknesses may be turned into the firm's strengths. For instance, upon discovering a competitive retail store's salespersons were not considered a very helpful or knowledgeable source for fashion merchandise information, a department store put its own salespersons through a special fashion merchandise training program to ensure that this service was a strong part of their marketing program.

A competitor's marketing offer can be described and assessed by management using their experience and judgment. For example, competitive products can be purchased and analyzed for strengths and weaknesses, advertising themes and media used can be assessed by seeking and reading advertisements, company salesmen and channel members can be interviewed to evaluate competitor channel strategy and tactics as well as pricing policies, customer services offered, and use of sales personnel. The analysis can also be supplemented with discussions of competitors in such secondary sources as *Fortune, Business Week, Time,* and *The Wall Street Journal.* This approach is relatively inexpensive and takes advantage of management's familiarity with products and markets. Yet there is a danger that management's evaluation will not coincide with that of market customers. A manager's perspective from "behind a desk" in a firm may not be adequate to fully determine how well customers are satisfied with a competitor's marketing offer.

An important perspective for competitor analysis is that of customers. Data can be obtained on customer attitudes, opinions, and preferences toward existing competitors and their products or services. An illustration of this kind of data is shown in Figure 7–9. A sample of potential customers for a department store was asked to rate two competitors on

FIGURE 7–9

Consumer Ratings of Competitive Department Stores on Important Evaluative Criteria

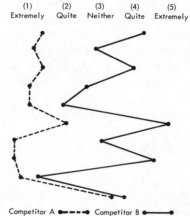

	(1) Extremely	(2) Quite	(3) Neither	(4) Quite	(5) Extremely	
Pleasant Store Interior						Unpleasant Store Interior
Easy to Shop in Store						Hard to Shop in Store
Many Services Offered						Few Services Offered
High Merchandise Quality						Low Merchandise Quality
Wide Variety of Merchandise						Limited Variety of Merchandise
High Prices Relative to Other Stores						Low Prices Relative to Other Stores
Friendly Salespersons						Unfriendly Salespersons
Helpful Salespersons						Unhelpful Salespersons
Convenient to Other Stores						Inconvenient to Other Stores
Convenient to Home						Inconvenient to Home

Competitor A ●– – –● Competitor B ●———●

selected evaluative criteria. The results allowed management to determine the areas in which customers were most dissatisfied with competitive offers. Of course, customer evaluations of competitors should be reconciled with management's knowledge of a competitor's strategy and tactics. For example, a poor customer rating of a major competitor's product may be due to ineffective promotion rather than a product weakness when assessed in light of a technical evaluation that reveals a competitor's product to be of high quality.

Determining the potential for new competition entering a particular market is often a much more difficult task than assessing the effectiveness of current competitors. Corporations are extremely secretive concerning their plans, particularly for entering new markets. So, marketing managers must develop sources of competitor information that can aid in this task. Salesmen can be used as information gathering agents by training them to carefully monitor competitive activity in their territories.[16] For example, a salesman may provide advance warning of a new product being evaluated by a major competitor by noting that a market test is being conducted in his territory. Other information sources might include informal interviews with channel members who have information about changes in competitive activity, or publicity (e.g., an announcement of a new technology development) in various secondary sources.

---

[16] See for example, Frederick E. Webster, Jr., "The Industrial Salesman as a Source of Market Information," *Business Horizons,* 8 (Spring 1965), pp. 77–82.

Channel Analysis. The analysis of channel arrangements at the specific product/market level must be continued at the branded product/market level. The focus should be on a detailed analysis of channels used by key competitors. Information sources include interviews with key corporate and channel personnel and the same secondary sources used to assess competitors. Also, customers can be interviewed concerning their degree of satisfaction with the channel members with which they come in contact in a market area (e.g., for ultimate consumers, these members would be retailers), though customers may not be well informed about other channel members and, in particular, about channel linkages.

Uses of Branded Product/Market Level Analysis

Application of market opportunity analyses at the branded product/market level include determining the opportunity for positioning or repositioning corporate product offers, and determining sales forecasts. These applications are necessarily highly interrelated since future sales depend, in part, on the detailed brand strategy and tactics developed to generate sales. Thus, the sales forecasting process must begin with a marketing program designed to appeal to potential customers.

Product Offer Positioning. Analysis of market opportunities at the brand level can be done for existing brands in a corporation's product mix. A MOA would be an input into the corporate management control process by providing information on the market reaction to previous marketing decisions. Moreover, the analysis should try to discover possible changes in customer wants, needs, and unique characteristics, as well as competitive strategy changes, in order to provide the maximum lead time possible for corporate response.

MOA at the branded product/market level can also be used to uncover market opportunities for positioning new brands or repositioning current brands. This requires the use of both market description and competitor strategy-tactics information to search for "holes" in the marketplace. A hole in the marketplace exists when there is at least one sufficiently large market segment that is not adequately being served by competitors. Returning to the toothpaste example, suppose Table 7–9 shows a match between market segments within the toothpaste product/market and existing toothpaste brands.

To explore the opportunity for entry into the toothpaste product/market, a marketing manager might begin by assessing the demand potential in each brand segment and evaluate how well the demand is being tapped by competitors. Suppose all four segments were of approximately equal size. At first glance, a partial "hole" appears to exist in the medicinal benefit segment since it is supporting only one brand, while the others are supporting three or more brands. Yet, it is possible that Crest is so effectively serving this segment's needs that entry here would be difficult. Thus, the existence of an opportunity would hinge on a new brand's ability to capture a share of the medicinal benefit segment from Crest.

Suppose further that analysis of the toothpaste market at the brand level uncovered a fifth segment comprised of customers seeking a breath freshener benefit. Since no other brands are seeking to satisfy this particular segment, these customers have been buying other brands that do not closely match their primary want. This fifth segment would then constitute a "hole" in the toothpaste market. To fill this hole, a current brand might be repositioned to appeal to the breath-freshener wants of customers by reformulating the product and/or use of promotional appeals. Or, a totally new brand could be introduced and positioned to serve this segment. In either case, the positioning strategy requires the design of a product offer that will closely match target market wants (i.e., position *toward* selected markets) and at the same time be sufficiently differentiated from competitive offers to give customers a reason to select it over other brands (i.e., position *away* from major competitors).

Sales Forecasting. Sales forecasts estimate the *share of total specific product/market potential that can be captured by a brand strategy* as shown in the following relationship (where g = geographic area and t = time period):

(3)   Sales Forecast$_{g,t}$ = Market Potential$_{g,t}$ $\times$ Market Share$_{g,t}$

Using this relationship, company sales for a brand can be forecasted by first forecasting market potential and then multiplying this volume by an estimated market share percentage. As an illustration, if the market potential for wine in an urban area for the next year was estimated to be 100,000 bottles and a distributor judged that their share of this potential would be 25 percent, the sales forecast for the firm is 25,000 bottles. Market potential forecasting has already been discussed in the specific product/market level analysis section of this chapter. Expected market share for a particular brand is necessarily a judgmental estimate that must ultimately be made by management. Management must judgmentally assess how well their offer meets customer needs and wants as objectively as possible. Moreover, a brand strategy must also be evaluated against the strategies of major competitors to determine how successfully the firm's brand can compete for the same customers. These two evaluations must then be combined into an estimate of the percentage of the total market that can be captured by the brand. An important guideline in performing this task is to compare the brand strategy to customer wants and needs and to competitive brands on a feature-by-feature basis. MOA analyses at both the specific product and branded product/market levels should be relied upon to identify the most important customer evaluative criteria so that comparative brand assessments can focus on brand strategy dimensions designed to satisfy these criteria. To guard against being too optimistic, it is often useful to determine the effect on the sales forecast of a optimistic, most likely, and pessimistic market share estimate. This will help managers assess the risk inherent in the brand strategy decision.

When management feels particularly uncertain about making a market share estimate, additional forecasting procedures and analyses may be used.[17] Market share/sales forecasts can be determined by relying on the *opinions of key corporate personnel*. For example, salesmen may have considerable insight into what customers will buy due to their frequent contacts with them. So, management may ask salesmen to estimate sales and/or market share that a brand can achieve in their territories. An important advantage with use of salesmen is that forecasts are broken down by geographic areas. Managerial opinions can also be solicited by pooling the judgment of those executives who have relevant experience and expertise with the brand. Some method must be used to reconcile opinion differences, but several procedures are available including a numerical averaging of estimates, face-to-face discussion and reconciliation of differences, or a non face-to-face reconciliation using the Delphi method.[18]

When forecasts are being made for existing brands where historical sales and market share data are available, *time series analyses* may be quite useful. These analyses determine the historical patterns of brand sales/market share over several past periods as the basis for extrapolating into future periods (see Figure 7–7 for an example). However, managerial judgment is required to assess how much the future will be like the past periods in which the data was generated. The extrapolation of past sales/market share must be adjusted for new market conditions and significant changes in brand strategy and/or tactics.

Sales forecasting for existing brands may go beyond time series analyses by exploring *correlational relationships* between historical sales/market share data and other factors (e.g., level of company advertising, disposable personal income, or GNP). Statistical techniques are used to build a mathematical model showing how selected factors are related to brand sales/market share. Then, if these relationships are found to be

---

[17] For an overview of sales forecasting techniques, see John C. Chambers, Satinder K. Mullick, and Donald D. Smith, "How to Choose the Right Forecasting Technique," *Harvard Business Review*, July–August 1971, pp. 45–74.

[18] For a discussion of the Delphi method, see Alan R. Fusfeld and Richard N. Foster, "The Delphi Technique: Survey and Comment," *Business Horizons*, 14 (June 1971), pp. 63–74.

sufficiently strong, and if the factors can be readily forecasted, sales/ market share for the forecast period can be obtained by plugging factor forecasts into the model. Of course, the resulting forecasts must be tempered by management's judgment concerning new market conditions and brand strategy/tactic changes.

Finally, when historical data is not available or considered to be outdated, needed information can be gathered through *marketing research*. One technique is to survey prospective customers concerning their intentions to purchase the company's brand. This information would then be used to supplement managerial judgment in estimating sales and market share. Yet, the accuracy of the survey results is difficult to determine since some customers may be reluctant to state intentions or be unable to predict their own future purchases.

Another marketing research technique, used primarily by larger firms, for forecasting sales/market share is test marketing. This technique involves trial testing the brand strategy in a few market areas selected to be representative of market targets. For example, a company might introduce a new product into several urban areas to determine what sales/market share can actually be obtained. Then, if the test areas have been properly chosen, management can gain considerable understanding as to how much sales/market share the brand strategy will capture on a full scale basis.

The cost of conducting a MOA at the branded product/level varies widely depending upon the extensiveness of information collection and analysis beyond the specific product/market level. For example, should a segmentation strategy be pursued at this level, the cost may run into the tens of thousands of dollars. But if the marketing offer is intended to appeal to the entire specific product/market, then very little may be needed beyond what has already been done.

SUMMARY AND CONCLUSIONS

This chapter has developed a framework for conducting market opportunity analysis, and identifying needed information. An analysis can be done at different levels depending on the degree of specificity of a product offer. Moreover, information and analyses at each more aggregate level provide useful guides for analysis at the next lesser aggregative level. Finally, since MOA is primarily an information activity comprised of multiple stages, management must be prepared to apply an information planning process, including cost/benefit analyses, to determine how extensive the total analysis should be.

Only limited attention was given to the making of marketing decisions requiring market opportunity analyses: selection of market targets, design of marketing offers, and control of current product offer performance. Marketing decisions invariably require more than MOA information to estimate whether a decision will be likely to achieve corporate and marketing objectives (e.g., costs, legal restrictions, ethics, other uses of resources, etc.). Thus, a MOA is one of several important analysis activities designed to provide essential information for marketing management decision making.

The next chapter, "Market Segmentation Strategy," continues the discussion of market opportunity analysis, by concentrating on one important approach to the selection of market targets and design of marketing offers. The focus will be on understanding the approaches, procedures, and tools that are available to implement a segmentation strategy. Part IV concludes with Chapter 9, "Buyer Decision Processes," which discusses the new, but rapidly developing field of buyer behavior. No doubt it is clear by now how important understanding buyers is to marketing decision making. This chapter provides the foundation for the skills required by management to apply the discipline of buyer behavior effectively to marketing decisions.

EXERCISES FOR REVIEW AND DISCUSSION

1. Suppose you are analyzing the market opportunity for a new home-use minicomputer. Your boss believes that the product will be sold through large chain retailers. He proposes to focus the market opportunity analysis on these retailers. Evaluate the desirability of following this proposal.

2. "The elderly market is becoming increasingly important due to increases in buying power of people over 65." Carefully evaluate the appropriateness for marketing managers of the concept of *market* used in this statement.

3. For one or more of the following specific products, define the corresponding generic product/market in terms of attributes, features, functions and needs: wine, tennis racquets, minicomputers, shotguns, and furniture.

4. Suppose you were asked to recommend a MOA approach for the analysis of a new kind of tennis racquet. Would you include a generic product/market level analysis? Why or why not?

5. Choose two or three brands within one of the specific products listed in Exercise 3 above and analyze the marketing positions taken by the firm marketing each brand as evidenced by the themes and messages in each company's advertising.

6. Choose an existing generic or specific product industry and use secondary information sources to identify the life-cycle stage characteristics of that industry. Support your result with description of appropriate industry characteristics.

7. Suppose that your colleague has made the statement that to analyze a market opportunity is essentially the same as forecasting sales in that market. How would you respond to this statement to ensure that she

clearly understood market opportunity analysis and the role of sales forecasting?

8. Choose any specific product in Exercise 3 and develop a procedure for estimating market potential for that product. Include in your discussions the specific types and sources of information that would be used to develop your estimate of market potential.

8

Market Segmentation Strategy

The previous chapter developed a framework for conducting analyses of market opportunities. This chapter continues the discussion of market opportunity analysis by developing in greater depth the strategy of market segmentation. The first section presents market segmentation as a managerial process of analysis and decision making and discusses its relationship to market opportunity analysis. In addition, requirements for successful segmentation applications are presented. The next three sections discuss the key steps in a segmentation decision process and assess the current level of sophistication of tools and procedures. Finally, alternative operational approaches to the timing of segmentation analyses with respect to product decisions are reviewed.

MARKET SEGMENTATION AS A MANAGEMENT STRATEGY

Market Segmentation Defined

Market segmentation involves considerably more than dividing some total market into separate customer groups or segments. Fundamentally, segmentation is a managerial approach to organizational decision making on market targets and on marketing offer strategies/tactics. Therefore, a successful segmentation strategy must link the forming of customer segments with the efficient use of organizational resources to influence market demand. This is apparent in the following definition of market segmentation: *Market segmentation is the process by which an organization's managers attempt to match more precisely a marketing mix strategy and tactics to significant differences in the way one or more customer groups will respond to specific and/or branded product-offer alternatives.*

241

Market segmentation is essentially a process beginning with the search for customer groupings within an aggregate market. Each segment should be comprised of customers who have similar preferences for marketing offer alternatives, while customers in different segments should have different preferences. Upon identifying customer groups, managers can use information about customer preferences and descriptive characteristics to determine marketing offer alternatives required to match segment preferences, and to analyze the opportunity for achieving performance goals in each group. This analysis, in turn, provides the rationale for selecting market targets.

Relationship to Market Opportunity Analysis

Recall from Chapter 7 (see Figure 7–2) that there are three market levels at which a MOA can be conducted: generic product/market, specific product/market, and branded product/market levels. Consistent with these levels, segmentation processes can be used to determine whether each more aggregative level can be partitioned into separate customer groupings. Thus, market segments may exist at the specific product/market and/or at the branded product/market levels. For example, industrial purchasing of packaging services (a generic product/market) can be divided into segments at the specific product level according to the type of packaging preferred (e.g., box, glass, aerosol, etc.). This occurs because manufacturers of consumer products have differing needs for protecting and handling their products during distribution. So, different types of specific packages have been developed to serve these need variations. Similarly, segments may be identified at the branded product level when preferences for the same specific product offer differ in some way among customers. Continuing the packaging example, segments for aerosol packaging exist because of varying price elasticity and preferences for quality control among buying firms. Individual contract packaging firms have designed their offers to appeal to one or the other of these needs by emphasizing low price or quality. These relationships are shown in Figure 8–1.

The distinction between market segmentation at the specific and the branded product/market levels has considerable significance for marketing management. Identifying segments at the specific product/market level is likely to be an easier task than at the branded product/market level. This is because customer preference differences at the branded level will typically be more subtle. Here, segments may be formed based on differences in the relative importance of the same attributes rather than on preferences for entirely different attributes as would be the case at the specific product/market level. Consider Figure 8–1 again. The segment for box packaging is based on essentially dif-

FIGURE 8–1

Market Segments at Specific and Branded Product/Market Levels

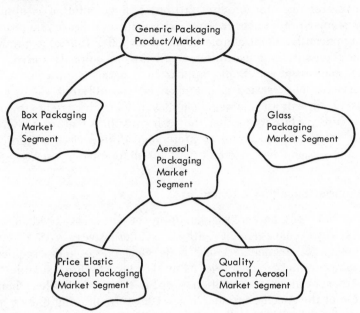

ferent product attributes than the segment for aerosol packaging. Yet, both the price and quality control branded product/market segments want the same product attributes. The difference between these segments is that the price elastic firms weight low price heavier in their supplier decisions than quality control while the quality control segment does just the opposite. The greater difficulty in segmenting at the branded product/market level means that segmentation may occur sequentially at these levels. During the earlier stages of a product life cycle, firms concentrate efforts on segmenting at the specific product/market level. However, as the number of competitors increase in each specific product/market segment, there is pressure for firms to differentiate their offers. So, the search for segments then moves to the branded product/market level to determine if there are differences in preferences among customers for the same specific product. Discovery of branded segments allows a firm to compete more effectively in the same specific product/market by tailoring a product directly for one or more branded segments. For example, Procter & Gamble gained substantial competitive advantage with Head & Shoulders over competitive shampoos by emphasizing the dandruff fighting attribute of its product. This appealed directly to a shampoo segment that believes the dandruff control ability of a shampoo is a very important consideration in its brand purchase decision.

The potential for segmentation at either level does not have to depend only on preferences for product attributes. Segmentation is applicable when customer preferences for any component in a firm's marketing mix differ significantly. For example, a firm may offer the same product to different segments, but use different advertising appeals and/or media to reach each segment. Banks appear to use this approach for credit card services. The service is not changed for different segments, but advertising appeals to one segment may discuss the credit advantages of using cards, while to another the cash substitute feature is touted. In this case, segments exist due to preference differences for information since each segment uses a credit card for different purposes.

Market Target Selection Alternatives

Application of market segmentation at different product/market levels provides management with two alternatives to the selection of market target segments. A firm may select one or more segments at the specific product/market level as market targets. For example, urban public transportation organizations appear to go no further than segmentation at the specific product/market level by offering one of several mode alternatives (bus, rail, taxicab, etc.) to different ridership segments. There is little differentiation among firms (e.g., taxicab companies) in services offered within the same mode. In general, all firms serving segments only at this level will have very similar marketing offers.

A firm may choose to carry its segmentation strategy to the branded product/market level by selecting brand segments as market targets. Toothpaste manufacturers, for instance, appear to have gone this far by designing appeals around different specific product attributes (fluoride, teeth brighteners, taste and appearance, etc.). Crest is differentiated from Ultra-Brite by emphasizing its tooth decay prevention ability rather than being positioned as a teeth brightener. Segmentation at the branded product/market level is usually more difficult than at the generic product/market level since the bases for customer variations are not easily identified. Correspondingly, the cost of researching and serving brand segments is greater. However, the competitive advantage gained by carrying segmentation to the brand level can justify the additional effort and expense.

As an alternative to market segmentation, an organization may decide to serve an entire aggregate market with the same marketing strategy and tactics. This is a mass market strategy since the market target is all customers who have a generic need for a product. An example of mass marketing is the "variety strategy" used by some firms. This strategy depends on one or more preferences being held in common by potential customers within a mass market. For instance, a consumer goods manufacturer may have several brands in the product line because mass market customers have in common the desire to try something new and are constantly switching brands. A variety strategy is implemented by appealing to the entire mass market with several brands. Thus, buyers switch within the company's product line, remaining customers of the firm, rather than switching to a competitor's brand. This market target strategy probably characterizes the approach taken by manufacturers of consumer soap products.[1]

Marketing strategy design and implementation is substantially different depending upon whether a mass market or market segments are selected as market targets. Under a market segmentation strategy, a different marketing mix is used to appeal to each market target segment. By offering several market mixes, each matched to a particular segment's unique preferences, the total demand generated should be greater than if the same marketing mix were used for all selected segments. In contrast, the mass market strategy involves the design and implementation of a single marketing mix appealing to the "average" or "typical" customer in a generic product/market. Management believes that the commonalities between customers are more important in influencing product and brand purchase decisions than are any differences. Moreover, implementing a single marketing mix is less costly than offering several marketing mixes due to economies of scale of production, distribution, and selling achieved by having only one offer.

Mass markets were the central targets for much of marketing effort in the 1930s and 1940s. Major improvements in communication, storage, and transportation technologies during this period allowed firms to reach large numbers of customers in widespread geographic locations. Mass market strategies enabled firms to expand volume and reduce per unit costs through scale economies. However, many marketers now argue that mass markets are becoming less prevalent in the United States.[2] A number of changes are occurring that cause mass markets to break into segments. For example, greater affluence allows customers to increase discretionary spending as well as satisfy a greater number and variety of wants and needs. Firms have advanced their technical ability to generate modified and totally new products to satisfy expanding new wants and

---

[1] William H. Reynolds, "More Sense about Market Segmentation," *Harvard Business Review*, vol. 43 (September–October 1965), pp. 107–14.

[2] For example, see Steven C. Brandt, "Dissecting the Segmentation Syndrome," *Journal of Marketing*, vol. 30 (October 1966), p. 23; Ronald E. Frank, William F. Massy, and Yoram Wind, *Market Segmentation* (Englewood Cliffs, N.J.: Prentice-Hall, 1972), pp. 4–5; and Russell I. Haley, "Benefit Segmentation: A Decision Oriented Research Tool, *Journal of Marketing*, vol. 32 (July 1968), p. 30.

needs. Finally, increasing intra- and inter-industry competition has led firms to search for market "niches" by identifying customer segments to serve.

MARKET SEGMENTATION DECISION PROCESS

Segmentation Decision Process Framework

Figure 8–2 presents a decision process framework for market segmentation applications. Segmentation begins when a firm seeks bases upon which generic and/or specific product/markets can be segmented. These bases are one or more characteristics of potential customers that allow the marketer to classify them into segments for further analysis. Bases should be selected so that each segment is comprised of customers who will respond to marketing offer alternatives in a similar way, while customers in different segments will respond differently. For example, if

FIGURE 8–2

Market Segmentation Decision Process

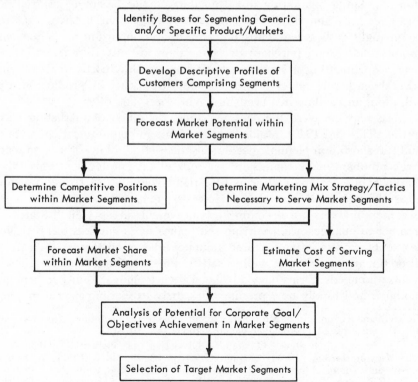

Procter & Gamble decides to market Crest to a segment comprised of large families, then management should be confident that most large families are interested in preventing tooth decay so that they will be similarly receptive to the Crest marketing offer.

Once segments have been formed, managers should seek to understand customers comprising each segment. Segmentation bases provide some insight into the nature of customers, but typically not enough for decisions that marketing managers must make. Sufficient description of customers is needed to enable managers to match needs with marketing offers rather precisely. This requires understanding those characteristics that explain the similarity between customers within each segment as well as account for differences between segments. Thus, the task for this stage is to develop profiles of the typical customer in each segment. For example, a profile for a segment might include demographics, attitudes toward brands, brand preferences, product use habits, and so forth.

In the next stage, market segmentation and market opportunity analysis continue to coincide in the forecast of market potential within each segment. Market potential sets the upper limit on the demand that can be expected from a segment, and so, determines the maximum opportunity available. This stage should be a decision point for management since it must be determined whether or not the available opportunity in each segment is sufficient to justify further analysis. Some segments will be screened out because of insufficient potential demand, while others will be sufficiently attractive to continue assessing.

Once market potential has been estimated, the proportion of demand that can be captured by the firm must be determined. This requires a forecast of probable market share. As discussed in Chapter 7, market share forecasts depend upon both an analysis of competitor's positions in segments and on the specific marketing strategy and tactics designed to serve these segments. These two activities can be performed simultaneously. Moreover, design of marketing strategy and tactics determine the expected level of resources (i.e., costs) that will be necessary to tap the demand potential in segments.

Finally, the information, analyses, and forecasts accumulated throughout the process allow management to assess the potential for the achievement of corporate goals and objectives in each segment. For example, demand forecasts when combined with cost projections are used to determine the profit and return on investment that can be expected from each segment. Also, analysis of marketing strategy and tactics will determine the degree of consistency with corporate image and reputation goals as well as with unique corporate capabilities achieved by serving a segment. These assessments will, in turn, determine the selection of specific segments as market targets by management.

Requirements for Segmentation Application

The key to segmentation is that a significant difference must be found between at least two customer groups in terms of their responses toward marketing mix alternatives. With this in mind, segment differences are considered to be operationally meaningful to management when (1) customer differences do, in fact, exist; (2) these differences can be identified and matched with customer descriptions; (3) segment preferences can be translated into marketing offer decisions; (4) at least one segment has sufficient demand potential to justify selection as a market target; and (5) market target segments must be sufficiently stable to allow adequate lead time for design and implementation of a marketing strategy.[3]

Existence of Customer Response Differences. An underlying premise of market segmentation is that all potential customers do not have the same response elasticities to possible marketing offer alternatives. Response elasticity refers to the degree of reaction that customers show to all or some component of a marketing mix. High response elasticity occurs when a customer responds very favorably to a marketing mix decision, while low elasticity is demonstrated by little or no response that is favorable. Response elasticity is most easily illustrated by a demand curve showing how customers change their buying decisions in response to changes in price. Similarly, customers will be more or less responsive to all other components of a marketing mix including product features, advertising messages, media, product availability, personal selling appeals, customer services, and so forth.

When differences in response elasticities exist, a firm can design unique marketing offers that are tailored to match selected segment preferences. However, if response elasticities are not very different among customers, then the design of a single marketing mix for the entire mass market is a more appropriate strategy. For example, customers do not appear to have very different response elasticities for commodities such as soap, salt, and sugar. So, firms handling these products have applied mass marketing strategies.

Identifying Customer Response Elasticities and Characteristics. For market segmentation to be operational, it must be technically and economically possible to identify response elasticity differences between customer groups. Information is needed concerning probable customer reactions to alternative marketing offer designs. In addition, customers

---

[3] Requirements for successful segmentation applications are also discussed in Ronald E. Frank, "Market Segmentation Research: Findings and Implications," in Frank M. Bass, Charles W. King and Edgar A. Pessemier (eds.), *Application of the Sciences in Marketing Management* (New York: John Wiley and Sons, 1968), pp. 41–43; and Philip Kotler, *Marketing Management: Analysis, Planning, and Control* (Englewood Cliffs, N.J.: Prentice-Hall, 1972), pp. 167–68.

with each response variation must be described so that management understands who is to be included in each segment. Managerial judgment and experience may be sufficient to provide this information. More often, though, managerial judgment must be supplemented with marketing research. Here, the technical and economic constraints refer to the costs and feasibility of obtaining market information directly from customers. One barrier to meeting this requirement may be the lack of valid or reliable measurement techniques for use in marketing research. For example, management may believe that consumer personality is an appropriate basis for segmenting automobile markets. Yet, the development of measurement techniques for personality is not far enough along to easily identify people with different personalities.

Even if appropriate measures exist, a firm may not have personnel who know how to use them. This is a real problem for smaller firms with less educated or sophisticated management. Finally, management must consider the cost of extensive segmentation research. Finding appropriate segmentation bases is often a trial-and-error kind of process. A firm may have to conduct several research projects to find a workable way of forming segments, and then use research periodically to monitor any changes that might occur. All of these efforts can add up to a considerable cost.

Translating Customer Response Elasticities into Marketing Mixes. Since market segmentation is a competitive strategy, management must design and implement marketing offers that are tailored to appeal directly to target segments. Consequently, knowledge of market segments must enable management to choose marketing mix combinations that will satisfy customer preferences in each target market segment. Meeting this requirement, even when customer response elasticity differences have been found, is not always easy. For instance, a firm may not have appropriate marketing offer alternatives to respond to a segment's unique characteristics and preferences. Consider the plight of a department store in a small city trying to reach market segments with differential advertising appeals by using community media (local newspapers, radio, television, etc.). Local media typically have rather broad audiences, and so, reach customers in different segments. Thus a department store cannot tailor media to efficiently reach each target market segment. As another illustration, lack of technology can prevent the design of products or product variations that will satisfy known segment preferences. Calculator manufacturers may have been aware of consumer segments for different calculator models, but had to wait for the MOS circuitry developments before being able to design models at prices that would attract consumers.

Finally, a marketing mix designed for one segment may cannibalize a product offer designed for another segment. Consider the experience of Ford Motor Company after introducing the Falcon. The Falcon was intended for an economy car segment, but also cannibalized the standard size Ford by attracting buyers who would have bought the larger car if the Falcon were not available. This was particularly undesirable since profit margins were greater for the standard-sized car.

Sufficient Demand Potential. At least one identified segment must have sufficient demand potential to justify the costs of implementing a market segmentation strategy. Costs of research, of designing unique offers, and of controlling performance in segments rise as segments get smaller and more numerous.[4] For example, offering lines of color television that vary in price to segments that differ in price elasticity will cause RCA to sacrifice economies of scale in product design, manufacturing, distribution, and selling over what could be achieved by offering only one television model to everyone. Therefore, an operational segmentation strategy must select target segments that will provide sufficient demand potential to offset increased cost from sacrificing scale economies. A statement of sales and costs for a company's segments in one geographical territory is shown in Table 8–1 to illustrate the kind of profit analysis that is needed to determine whether segments have enough demand potential to justify being selected as market targets.

Sufficient Stability Over Time. Management must have adequate lead time to design and implement a marketing strategy for market target segments. Moreover, the match between marketing offers and segment preferences must remain unchanged long enough for the firm to achieve performance objectives. What constitutes sufficient lead time will differ considerably between firms depending upon such factors as the speed with which decisions are made, the amount of resources required to tap segments, and the commitments that must be made to implement a strategy. For example, in the toy industry fads such as the hula hoop do not seem to require much stability beyond a few months. On the other hand, automobile manufacturers need years of stability, since so much time is required to design, produce, and distribute a new automobile model. One reason usually given for the failure of Ford's Edsel is that

---

[4] In theory, determining market segments should be viewed as an aggregative process of building market segments by grouping customers together. The reason for this is that to maximize demand, an optimal segmentation would involve treating individual customers as segments. Yet, the costs of doing this are usually prohibitive. So, segmentation should continue to group customers into larger and larger segments until the marginal decline in revenue from a more aggregative segment is just equal to the reduction in the costs of researching and serving the segment. See Henry J. Claycamp and William F. Massy, "A Theory of Market Segmentation," *Journal of Marketing Research*, vol. 5 (November 1968), pp. 388–94. However, using the market opportunity analysis framework developed in Chapter 7, the end result of market segmentation is a partitioning of generic and/or specific product/markets into smaller market groupings.

TABLE 8–1

A Contribution Analysis of Segments for a Manufacturer of Computers, Calculators, and Adding Machines

	Company Total	Full Keyboard		Deluxe 10-Key		Basic 10-Key
		Bank Seg.	Nonseg.	Mfg. Seg.	Nonseg.	Retail Seg.
Net sales......................	$10,000	$3,750	$1,250	$2,550	$450	$2,000
Variable manufacturing costs......	5,100	1,875	625	1,169	206	1,225
Mfg. contribution.........	$ 4,900	$1,875	$ 625	$1,381	$244	$ 775
Marketing costs						
Variable:						
Sales commissions...........	450	169	56	115	20	90
Variable contribution......	$ 4,450	$1,706	$ 569	$1,266	$224	$ 685
Assignable						
Salaries—salesmen..........	1,600	630	140	420	210	200
Salary—marketing manager..	100	38	12	19	6	25
Product advertising.........	1,000	670	–0–	200	–0–	130
Total.................	$ 2,700	$1,338	$ 152	$ 639	$216	$ 355
Segment contribution......	$ 1,750	$ 368	$ 417	$ 627	$ 8	$ 330
Nonassignable						
Institutional advertising.....	150					
Marketing contribution....	$ 1,600					
Fixed-joint costs						
General administration.......	300					
Manufacturing..............	900					
Total.................	$ 1,200					
Net profits...........	$ 400					

Source: Leland L. Beik and Stephen L. Buzby, "Profitability Analysis by Market Segments," *Journal of Marketing*, vol. 37 (July 1973), p. 52, published by the American Marketing Association.

the target market segment had substantially changed by the time the Edsel was ready for sale.

Benefits from Applying the Market Segmentation Process

While the concept of market segmentation has been widely accepted, the experience from actual attempts to apply the process has been mixed. There are numerous successful applications by firms including Timex watches, Honda motorcycles, Ford Mustang, Pampers disposable diapers, and time sharing computer services. But, there have also been difficulties reported.[5] The five requirements for a successful market segmentation strategy have proven quite demanding for firms to meet. When diffi-

[5] Ronald E. Frank and Paul E. Green, "Numerical Taxonomy in Marketing Analysis: A Review Article," *Journal of Marketing Research*, vol. 5 (February 1968), p. 83, published by the American Marketing Association.

culties are encountered, they are most likely to involve the inability to satisfy the second (identifying customer response elasticities and characteristics) and/or the third (translating customer response elasticities into marketing mixes) segmentation requirements. These difficulties have caused marketers to continue to seek out and test improved procedures and techniques for implementing segmentation processes.

A market segmentation decision process forces management to carefully assess market opportunities in depth. The improved understanding of markets can aid management in making successful marketing decisions regardless of whether segments are discovered and selected as market targets. Managerial experience and judgment is focused on analyzing which portions of mass markets are likely to provide the greatest opportunities for achieving corporate goals and objectives. In addition, management usually gains considerable understanding of markets. For example, prior to an MOA and segmentation study of demand for housing in a southeastern city, a firm's management believed demand from certain middle and upper income groups existed for a multi-family unit located near the downtown area. The study showed, however, insufficient demand from these groups as well as intense competition from a large number of existing and planned housing units. These results caused management to delay plans for construction in order to reevaluate the use of the land originally allocated to this project. Also, in a study of wine demand for a distributor, there were no strong indications of separate wine consumer segments. However, the study did provide management with considerable understanding of wine drinkers and how they differed from nondrinkers. Moreover, several weaknesses in past marketing strategy were uncovered that led to several marketing mix changes including the addition of a premium brand of wine to their product line.

The remainder of the chapter discusses the "state of the art" for market segmentation decision processes. Particular attention is given to some of the most recent procedures and techniques that offer considerable promise in advancing the sophistication of market segmentation applications.

IDENTIFYING SEGMENTATION BASES

An Ideal Segmentation Basis

To identify market segments, potential customers must be classified into separate groups. A segmentation basis is the means by which a firm accomplishes this task. For a particular application, a basis may be a single variable or may be some combination of variables that describe characteristics of potential customers. For example, one basis for determining segments of industrial customers is the type of application of the seller's product. Each segment would consist of buying firms having similar uses for the product, while firms in different segments would use the product differently. Aircraft manufacturers appear to use this segmentation basis to develop and sell planes to the airlines and cargo lines for commercial use and to the U.S. government for military use.

The ideal segmentation basis, according to the concept of market segmentation, is a measure of potential customer response elasticities to one or more components of a firm's marketing offer. If such a measure could be obtained, segments would easily be formed by grouping customers with similar elasticity scores. In some cases, particularly for industrial segmentation applications, managerial experience and judgment may be sufficient to classify customers according to response elasticities. For example, a packaging firm may be able to segment industrial packaging users by relying on management's extensive experience to identify firms having different packaging needs. A difficulty arises, however, when management's judgment is not sufficient to classify customers into segments, and more formal segmentation analysis is required. Unfortunately, a methodology for obtaining response elasticity measures directly from customers is not widely available at the present time, though progress is being made in this direction. Consequently, marketers must use other bases that will serve as *indicators* of customer response elasticities. For instance, household income might be used as a segmentation basis by RCA if management believes that households with high income will be more likely to buy color televisions than low-income households. These substitute or proxy segmentation bases usually have the advantage of being easily measured characteristics of potential customers. However, since bases should classify customers into segments that meet the five requirements for a successful segmentation strategy application the search for the most appropriate substitute bases can be quite time consuming and difficult.[6]

Consumer Segmentation Bases

Different bases have been used to segment consumer markets than to segment industrial markets. Moreover, considerably more attention has been given to the kinds of analyses and procedures needed for consumer market segmentation. Much of this effort has concentrated on identifying appropriate bases for consumer segments which indicates the difficulty encountered at this stage in the process. A large number of variables have been suggested as useful bases, but these can be classified into three

---

[6] John C. Bieda and Harold H. Kassarjian, "An Overview of Market Segmentation," in Bernard A. Morin (ed.), *Marketing in a Changing World* (Chicago: American Marketing Association, 1969), p. 249.

general types: (1) purchase/use behavior variables; (2) customer descriptive characteristics; and (3) product characteristics desired by customers. Figure 8–3 shows examples of segmentation bases in each of these categories.

FIGURE 8–3

Market Segmentation Bases

Purchase/Use Behavior:
Specific product purchased, media usage, brand purchased, brand loyalty, volume of product purchased, volume of brand purchased, deal proneness, proportion of income spent on a product, store shopped in, store loyalty, frequency of purchase, degree of planning for product purchases, timing of product adoption, and private brand proneness.

Customer Descriptive Characteristics:
Geographic location of customer, demography (age, sex, race, number of adults, family size, etc.), socioeconomic characteristics (education, income, occupation, social class, etc.), family life cycle, AIOs (activities, interests, and opinions), personality traits, cultural values and beliefs, and attitudes.

Product Characteristics Desired by Customers:
Attitudes toward products, attitudes toward brands, brand preferences, perceived product similarities, perceived brand similarities, desired product attributes, and relative importance of desired product attributes.

Purchase/Use Behavior Variables. Purchase and use behavior segmentation bases measure behavior at the purchase stage of buying decision processes, though a very few (e.g., media usage) are more concerned with prepurchase stages. Moreover, the tendency has been to use single, rather than multiple variables to classify customers into segments. For example, suppose a firm wanted to segment customers into heavy and light buyers. The usual approach is to ask customers a single question on a survey concerning their frequency of buying rather than to ask a series of questions about both buying and use behavior.

The major difficulty in applying these bases has been the inability to distinguish between customers in different segments. Typically, product or brand purchase/use data on customers are collected in a survey so that customers can be divided into segments. Then, regression or discriminant analysis is used to determine whether these segments contain consumers with unique descriptive characteristics. Unfortunately, the results too often show very weak relationships between behavior and customer descriptions, particularly when the descriptions are restricted to geographic, demographic, socioeconomic and personality trait characteristics.[7]

This approach is illustrated by the analysis of household grocery product consumption. For many food products a large proportion of total sales is accounted for by a relatively small percentage of all households. These households are the "heavy users" of grocery products. If they could be identified using socioeconomic and demographic descriptive characteristics, a segmentation strategy would be possible. So, data were obtained from a sample of households measuring their purchase volumes for each grocery product of interest and their socioeconomic and demographic characteristics. Then, multiple linear regression was used to determine whether any of the descriptive characteristics was related to differences in household purchase volume. Essentially regression models estimate whether there is a consistent tendency for households identified by certain characteristics (e.g., high income, large families, middle aged, etc.) to also have similar purchase volumes. In this study, these tendencies or relationships were all very weak showing that it was not possible to identify which consumers were heavy users in terms of demographic and socioeconomic characteristics.[8]

Several reasons probably account for poor results in the regression type of study using behavioral and demographic variables. Inappropriate interpretation of statistical test results by analysts may account for some of the difficulty. The weak relationships found in these segmentation studies mean that there is considerable variability across people on the selected descriptive characteristics in the same segment. At first glance this seems to be contrary to the requirement that people within segments be similar. Yet, for *managerial applications,* substantial variability within segments on the descriptive characteristics can be tolerated as long as there are significant differences in buying behavior between the segments.[9] For example, this reasoning was used to identify demographic and socioeconomic characteristics of light versus heavy buyers of several specific products shown in Table 8–2. Note the substantial differences between the purchases made by buyers in each segment.

---

[7] William Wilkie, "Market Segmentation Research: A Conceptual Analysis," paper no. 324, Institute for Research in the Behavioral, Economic, and Management Sciences (Lafayette, Ind.: Purdue University, 1971).

[8] Ronald E. Frank, William F. Massy, and Harper W. Boyd, "Correlates of Grocery Product Consumption Rates," *Journal of Marketing Research,* vol. 4 (May 1967), pp. 184–90, published by the American Marketing Association.

[9] For discussions of this reasoning see, Frank M. Bass, Douglas J. Tigert, and Ronald T. Lonsdale, "Market Segmentation: Group verus Individual Behavior," *Journal of Marketing Research,* vol. 5 (August 1968), pp. 264–70; and Henry Assael, "Segmenting Markets by Group Purchasing Behavior: An Application of the AID Technique," *Journal of Marketing Research,* vol. 7 (May 1970), pp. 153–58.

TABLE 8–2

Customer Descriptions of Segments Based on Volume Purchased

Specific Product	Description of Volume Segments		Average Purchases in Volume Segments	
	Light Buyers	Heavy Buyers	Light Buyers	Heavy Buyers
Frozen orange juice......	Under 35 or over 65; income less than $10,000; not college grads; 2 or less children.	Between 35 and 65; college grads; income over $10,000.	1.12–2.24 cans per month.	3.53–9.00 cans per month.
Cake mix............	Not married or under 35; no children; income under $10,000; TV less than 3½ hours per day.	35 or over; 3 or more children; income over $10,000.	.55–1.10 boxes per month.	2.22–3.80 boxes per month.
Beer............	Under 25 or over 50; college educated; nonprofessional; TV less than 2 hours per day.	Between 25 and 50; not college graduate; TV more than 3½ hours per day.	0–12.33 bottles per month.	17.26–40.30 bottles per month.

Source: Bass, Tigert, and Lonsdale, "Market Segmentation: Group versus Individual Behavior," *Journal of Marketing Research*, August 1968, p. 267, published by the American Marketing Association.

In addition, the measures used so frequently by firms may be over-simplistic. Most studies use a single behavioral variable to define segments. Yet, it is generally accepted that buyer behavior is a complex process influenced by multiple factors. A single measure of purchase or use behavior may not adequately reflect the total buying behavior of customers. It is likely that stronger customer description-behavior linkages can be found if multiple measures of behavior are used to classify potential customers into segments.[10]

Also, inappropriate descriptive variables may have been used to identify which customers comprise each segment. The rationale for using demographic, socioeconomic, and personality measures as descriptive variables is that people with the same enduring characteristics ought to have the same product/brand needs and wants. For example, a furniture manufacturer may expect middle income families with two or more children living in suburban areas to have similar furniture needs. While such an assumption is intuitively appealing, particularly at the specific product/market level, there is no strong evidence to support it for a wide variety of products.[11] Thus, demographic, socioeconomic and personality variables may not be the most appropriate factors for explaining intra-segment similarities and inter-segment differences to management.[12]

Finally, neither the traditional description variables nor the purchase/use behavior segment bases may have adequately reflected customer reactions to alternative marketing mixes.[13] Consider the following possible situations:

"*Situation 1.* Suppose that two brands, A and B, were essentially appealing to one set of needs and two other brands, C and D, were essentially appealing to another set of needs. If information on the marketing strategies of the four brands were not incorporated prior to using regression or discriminant analyses then the buyers of each of the brands would be considered a separate group . . . This being the case, the regression or discriminant function would not be able to distinguish between the buyers of brands A and B nor between the buyers of brands C and D. In this situation we would probably conclude that the results were negative because we could not predict which brand consumers would buy based on the independent variables.

---

[10] For an example of this approach see Daniel W. Greeno, Montrose S. Sommers, and Jerome B. Kernan, "Personality and Implicit Behavior Patterns," *Journal of Marketing Research*, vol. 10 (February 1973), pp. 63–69.

[11] Bieda and Kassarjian, "An Overview of Market Segmentation," p. 251.

[12] Frederick Wiseman, "Methodological Considerations in Segmentation Studies," in Fred C. Allvine (ed.), *Marketing in Motion and Relevance in Marketing* (Chicago: American Marketing Association, 1971), p. 307.

[13] Wilke, "Market Segmentation Research," p. 15; and Brieda and Kassarjian, "An Overview of Market Segmentation," p. 252.

"*Situation 2.* Suppose that one brand was appealing to several segments using different marketing mixes for each segment. If this were the case then we would expect to find the brand satisfying a unique set of needs for buyers in each of the segments. When one or more companies follow this practice a discriminant or regression analysis would not be able to identify purchasers for the different brands because the buyers for each brand are aggregated even though they may belong in different market segments."[14]

The negative findings and possible explanations concerning the traditional use of behavioral variables as segmentation bases should not be viewed as a rejection of the strategy of market segmentation. Behavioral variables were the initial attempts to identify managerially useful segmentation bases, and are only one of several alternative approaches to operationalizing this stage in the market segmentation decision process. In fact, the disappointing results have served as an impetus to the search for more managerially useful segmentation bases.

Consumer Descriptive Characteristics. Consumers can be classified into market segments by using consumer descriptive characteristics as a segmentation basis. Here, multiple characteristics of consumers are measured, and customers are classified into segments according to similarities and differences on the composite "score" on all descriptive variables. The task is then to explore buying behavior similarities within segments and differences between segments. Thus, the sequence of analysis is just the opposite of the first approach which begins with behavioral variables as segmentation bases, and then attempts to match segments with consumer descriptive characteristics. The underlying rationale is that there are consumer "types" comprising a market and each type buys differently than other types.

Life style segmentation is a recent development that is characteristic of this approach.[15] Consumers' life styles refer to the pattern or mode of living that have been adopted as their approach to life. The marketer is interested in the way in which products and brands are used to facilitate and enhance life style patterns characteristic of segments. To identify life style segments, firms typically measure consumers' activities, interests, and opinions (AIO variables). Table 8–3 illustrates the kinds of variables that are combined into a segmentation basis.

Once appropriate segments have been formed based on consumer AIO profiles, the analysis turns to examining buying behavior characteristics of consumers in each segment. In particular, such buying di-

---

[14] Bieda and Kassarjian, "An Overview of Market Segmentation," p. 252.

[15] For a comprehensive discussion of life style segmentation see William D. Wells (ed.), *Life Style and Psychographics,* (Chicago: American Marketing Association, 1974); and Joseph T. Plummer, "The Concept and Application of Life Style Segmentation," *Journal of Marketing,* vol. 38 (January 1974), pp. 33–37.

TABLE 8–3

Variables Used in Determining Life Style Segmentation Bases

Activities	Interests	Opinions	Demographics
Work	Family	Themselves	Age
Hobbies	Home	Social issues	Education
Social events	Job	Politics	Income
Vacation	Community	Business	Occupation
Entertainment	Recreation	Economics	Family size
Club membership	Fashion	Education	Dwelling
Community	Food	Products	Geography
Shopping	Media	Future	City size
Sports	Achievements	Culture	Stage in life cycle

Source: Plummer, "The Concept and Application of Life Style Segmentation," p. 34.

mensions as (1) usage of specific products (2) frequency of use of these products; (3) brand usage and frequency and (4) product/brand attitudes and use patterns, are typically measured to identify the most important segments.[16] The end result is life style segments matched with their buying and use behavior.

Experience so far suggests considerable potential for life style segmentation applications. One major reason is the richness or depth of understanding of customers that management gains from the variety of variables used to form and describe segments. Table 8–4 shows a portion of the results of a life style study for commercial bank credit cards. Life style questions on which there was a significant difference in answers between credit card users and non users were pulled out of a questionnaire. Notice the detailed insight into the people who are users that could be gained by a bank's management. Moreover, since AIO variables reflect reasons for products usage, management typically gains a better understanding of what potential consumers are seeking in products and brands. This, in turn, can reflect the nature of customers' response elasticities to marketing offers.

Consumer Desires for Product Characteristics. A final approach to determining segmentation bases (refer again to Figure 8–3) uses customer desires for product characteristics. The thrust is to seek segmentation bases that more nearly approximate the response elasticities of consumers toward specific attributes or dimensions of product offers. Appropriately, such approaches are called benefit[17] or product[18] segmentation.

---

[16] Plummer, "The Concept and Application of Life Style Segmentation," p. 35.

[17] Russell I. Haley, "Benefit Segmentation."

[18] Norman L. Barnett, "Beyond Market Segmentation," *Harvard Business Review,* January–February, 1969.

TABLE 8–4

Life Style Segmentation of Bank Credit Card Users

Statement	Card Users Definite and General Agreement (percent)	Noncard Users Definite and General Agreement (percent)
I enjoy going to concerts............................	25	17
A woman's place is in the home......................	27	41
In my job I tell people what to do...................	53	21
I am a good cook.....................................	36	26
My greatest achievements are ahead of me............	56	42
I buy many things with a charge or credit card.......	39	22
We will probably move once in the next five years..	46	37
Five years from now the family income will probably be a lot higher than it is now...............	71	60
Good grooming is a sign of self-respect..............	52	71
There is too much advertising on TV today...........	59	70
Women wear too much make-up today...............	43	51
My job requires a lot of selling ability..............	51	37
I like to pay cash for everything I buy...............	26	67
Television is a primary source of our entertainment...	25	40
Investing in the stock market is too risky for most families...	47	56
To buy anything other than a house or car on credit is unwise..................................	29	47
Young people have too many privileges today........	52	64
I love the outdoors..................................	54	76
There is too much emphasis on sex today............	52	64
There are day people and there are night people; I am a day person............................	58	69
I expect to be a top executive in the next ten years..	44	27
I am or have been president of a society or club...	51	36
I would like to have my boss' job....................	42	33
A party wouldn't be a party without liquor...........	29	17
I would rather live in or near a big city than in or near a small town..............................	46	34
I often bet money at the races.......................	18	8
I like to think I'm a bit of a swinger.................	38	26
I stay home most evenings...........................	62	71
Advertising can't sell me anything I don't want...	55	68
I often have a cocktail before dinner.................	36	20
I like ballet...	26	16
When I must choose between the two, I usually dress for fashion, not comfort.................	19	10
Liquor is a curse on American life....................	34	49
Movies should be censored..........................	41	57
I read one or more business magazines regularly..	34	18
I am active in two or more service organizations..	28	17
I do more things socially than most of my friends......	19	10

TABLE 8–4 (continued)

Statement	Card Users Definite and General Agreement (percent)	Noncard Users Definite and General Agreement (percent)
We often serve wine with dinner.....................	30	16
I buy at least three suits a year.....................	25	11
Playboy is one of my favorite magazines..............	25	16
I spend too much time talking on the telephone...	31	17
It is good to have charge accounts...................	33	21
Hippies should be drafted..........................	48	61
When I think of bad health, I think of doctor bills...	31	46
My days seem to follow a definite routine............	47	58

Note: All differences are significant above the .05 level based on Chi-square tests of significance.
Source: Joseph T. Plummer, "Life Style Patterns and Commercial Bank Credit Card Usage," *Journal of Marketing*, vol. 35 (April 1971), p. 38, published by the American Marketing Association.

The data used to form benefit segments are either customers' preferences for specific product attributes or their attitudes toward specific product or brand dimensions. Such measures are usually multivariate since customers are grouped into segments based on their preferences or attitudes toward *several* product attributes. Essentially, the underlying rationale is that segments exist because consumers are looking for different *combinations* of attributes:

> Each segment is identified by the benefits it is seeking. However, it is the *total configuration* of the benefits sought which differentiates one segment from another, rather than the fact that one segment is seeking one particular benefit and another a quite different benefit. Individual benefits are likely to have appeal for several segments. In fact, the research that has been done thus far suggests that most people would like as many benefits as possible. However, the *relative* importance they attach to individual benefits can differ importantly and, accordingly, can be used as an effective lever in segmenting markets.[19]

Conceptually, benefit segmentation is quite straightforward and consistent with the notion of using consumer response elasticities as segmentation bases, at least more so than the other two approaches. However, the data and analytical techniques (e.g., multidimensional scaling, multiple discriminant analysis, cluster analysis) are rather complex. Moreover, data gathering and analysis methods have only recently been adapted to market segmentation analysis. Thus, the approach is still too

---

[19] Haley, "Benefit Segmentation," p. 32.

new to evaluate its applicability to a wide variety of markets and organizations. The results of a benefit segmentation study are highly product-specific and cannot be generalized to other products. This is shown in Table 8–5 which presents illustrative results of an application for toothpaste. On the other hand, the reported successful applications by firms suggest that this approach has considerable promise. A detailed application of benefit segmentation is discussed in the next section.

Industrial Segmentation Bases

If published literature is an indication, considerably less attention has been given to the segmentation of industrial markets than consumer markets.[20] While industrial goods firms may be just more reluctant to discuss their segmentation efforts, it appears more likely that industrial sellers have not attempted to apply market segmentation as explicitly or in as much depth as consumer goods sellers.[21] The reason may simply be that there is less pressure to conduct the necessary market analyses due to the greater and more regular contact between buyers and sellers and the often comparatively small number of customer organizations that must be served.

Most attention has been concentrated on determining appropriate bases for segmenting industrial markets. Thus, it appears to be equally, if not more difficult to decide how to classify organizational buyers as it is to classify consumers. Conceptually, the ideal industrial market segmentation basis is a measure of buyer response elasticity to sellers' marketing offers. Yet, there is no such direct measure available for industrial buyers. So, industrial sellers must also use indicator or proxy variables to measure variations in response elasticities.

Bases used in available studies correspond to the purchase/use behavior variables applied by many consumer-goods marketers. For instance, the most common basis is the *choice of suppliers* by industrial buyers, which is similar to classifying consumers by brand purchased. A much less used basis is *decision making style* which classifies industrial buyers according to the decision rules used by purchasing managers to choose a supplier.[22] For example, one study classified industrial buyers as either normative or conservative decision makers based on whether they

---

[20] For a review of published literature on industrial segmentation see Richard N. Cardozo, "Segmenting the Industrial Market," in Robert L. King (ed.), *Marketing and the New Science of Planning* (Chicago: American Marketing Association, 1968), pp. 433–40.

[21] Ibid., p. 433.

[22] See, for example, David T. Wilson, H. Lee Mathews, and Timothy W. Sweeney, "Industrial Buyer Segmentation: A Psychographic Approach," in Fred C. Allvine (ed.), *Marketing in Motion and Relevance in Marketing* (Chicago: American Marketing Association, 1971), pp. 327–31.

TABLE 8-5

Benefit Segmentation of Toothpaste Market

	Segment Name			
	The Sensory Segment	*The Sociables*	*The Worriers*	*The Independent Segment*
Principal benefit sought..............	Flavor, product appearance	Brightness of teeth	Decay prevention	Price
Brands disproportionately sought.......	Colgate, Stripe	McLeans, Plus White, Ultra-Brite	Crest	Brands on sale

Source: Adapted from Haley, "Benefit Segmentation," p. 33.

used an expected monetary value criterion in selecting between alternative suppliers. Conservative industrial buyers used other criteria to select suppliers in high risk buying situations while normative decision makers consistently used expected monetary value of a purchase.

There is little indication that the customer-characteristics or customer-demand-for-product-attributes approaches now gaining so much attention in consumer segmentation applications have been applied in the industrial field. Yet, there is no particular reason why these approaches would not work as well for classifying industrial buying organizations as for classifying consumers. This indicates a substantial potential for advancing the sophistication of industrial market segmentation by transferring the developing knowhow from consumer segmentation approaches to industrial market analysis.

DEVELOPING CUSTOMER PROFILES

Nature of Customer Profiles

Once segments have been formed, managers must have a sound understanding of what the typical customer is like in each segment. Thus, the second step in the market segmentation process is to develop customer profiles. *A profile is comprised of all variables, including segmentation basis variables, that describe characteristics possessed by a large proportion of the customers within a segment.* Not all segment customers must have each profile characteristic, nor will this likely be the case. How large the proportion must be before a variable should be included in a profile is a judgmental decision that must be made by a firm's analysts and management.

Development of customer profiles may require no more than managerial experience and judgment when management has extensive familiarity with customers. This might be the case for industrial sellers servicing a relatively few purchasing organizations or for small firms selling in a limited geographic area. When managerial judgment must be supplemented with a more formal analysis of customer profiles, there are a number of statistical tools that can be used. All of these tools essentially search for relationships between segmentation basis variables and descriptive characteristic variables. Strong correlations between the way customers score on segmentation basis variable(s) and on a descriptive characteristic support the inclusion of that descriptive characteristic in the profile. Many of the available statistical tools allow the analysis of correlations between multiple descriptive and the segmentation basis simultaneously. This enables management to assess how well each profile variable and the profile in total describes segment customers.

Management is interested in both within-segment similarities and in between-segment differences. So, an analysis should include comparisons of customer profiles across segments. However, each segment's profile may not be entirely unique. While a segmentation basis should unambiguously classify customers into segments, customers in different segments do not have to "score" differently on every profile variable. The fact that more than one segment has a concentration of customers having one or a few of these characteristics will not lessen the value of the composite profile. For example, the consumer profiles for television show segments shown in Table 8–6 have some common variables across

TABLE 8–6

Consumer Profiles for Canadian Television Program Segments

Male Singers (Cash, Martin, Williams, Campbell)	Television Movies	Variety—Comedy (Gleason, Burnett, Lucy, Skelton)
Lower education	Lower income	Very low education
Slightly lower income	Lower education	Older
Pro-National Guard	Strong on traditional conservatism	Lower income
Brand loyal	Compulsive TV viewers	Strong on cooking
Strong on uncertainty, distrust and worry	Home cleanliness	Positive towards advertising
		Compulsive housekeepers
Care and pride in home	Care of and pride in home	Anti-youth, drugs
Affectionate, tender and loving	Nonrisk takers	Weight and health conscious
Permissive on female use of cosmetics, cigarettes	Very security conscious	Religious, non permissive
	Homebody, not socially active	Pro-TV
Worried about youth, drugs, and responsibility	Financially dissatisfied	Fashion and personal appearance conscious
Big on health aids (deodorant, mouthwash)	Price conscious	Homebody
		Security conscious
		Self-conscious
		Self-disciplined
		Belief in salvation
		Want an enjoyable leisurely life

Source: Douglas J. Tigert, "Life Style Analysis as a Basis for Media Selection," in William D. Wells (ed.), *Life Style and Psychographics*, pp. 197–98.

segments (e.g., education and income). If total profiles are rather similar across segments, however, management will gain little additional insight on how to serve segments differentially beyond that provided by the segmentation basis variables.

Consumer Profiles. Most of the variables that are used to develop consumer profiles have already been discussed in this and the previous chapter and are summarized in Figure 8–4. Quite a few of these variables have also been used to form segmentation bases, as a comparison of Figures 8–3 and 8–4 demonstrates. Though the variables in Figure 8–4 are probably more inclusive than would be measured in a single segmentation study, understanding customers as persons requires information on quite a wide variety of aspects of customers and their buying behavior. Tables 8–6 and 8–7 illustrate consumer profiles for Canadian television program audiences and for toothpaste market segments, respectively.

Industrial Customer Profiles. Profiles of industrial customers in market segments can be as extensive as consumer profiles in terms of the number of variables needed to give management an adequate understanding of purchasers. However, since industrial customers are organizations with individuals doing the buying, variables are needed to describe the nature of the organizations as well as the kind of individuals involved in the buying process. Figure 8–5 shows variables that might be included in industrial customer profiles.[23]

ANALYZING AND SELECTING TARGET SEGMENTS

Forecasting Segment Potential

The previous two stages in the segmentation process defined market boundaries (market segmentation bases) and described customers within markets (customer profiles). The task now is to estimate the potential demand available to all firms deciding to serve each segment. Market potential and sales forecasting tools and approaches were presented in the previous chapter. However, the application of market segmentation to MOA does complicate these forecasts since segmentation can set boundaries at different market levels: specific product/market segments and branded product/market segments.

If market segmentation is only applied at the specific product/market level, segment potential is defined essentially the way market potential was in the previous chapter: *the total volume of end user purchases that*

---

[23] Cardozo, "Segmenting the Industrial Market," pp. 433–40; and Wilson, Mathews, and Sweeney, "Industrial Buyer Segmentation," pp. 327–31.

FIGURE 8–4

Variables Used to Form Consumer Profiles

Geography (region and residence)	Brand preferences
Demographic characteristics	Personality characteristics
Socioeconomic characteristics	Media habits
Cultural values	Product usage
Subcultural values	Product attribute preferences
Opinion leadership	Product/brand information sources
Social class ranking	Relative importance of information sources
Family member buying roles	Type of store shopped in
Family life cycle stage	Product purchase rates
Life style characteristics	Product purchase volume
Product attitudes	Brand purchase rates
Product preferences	Private/national brand preferences
Brand attitudes	Dealing preferences

is potentially available to all firms offering a specific product to the same specific product/market segment within a given geographical area and time period. If, in addition, market segmentation is carried to the branded product/market level, then segment potential must be further confined to that portion of the specific product/market that has been identified as a branded product segment. The reason for this is that several brands can compete for the same branded product segment. For example, Table 8–7 shows that McLeans, Plus White, and Ultra-Brite all compete for the Sociables segment which is defined in terms of the principal benefit sought from toothpaste—brightness of teeth. In this case, the segment potential definition is *the total volume of end user purchases that is potentially available to all firms offering a brand to the same branded product/market segment within a given geographical area and time period.* This definition can be visualized by using the following relationship (where g = geographic area and t = time):

(1) Brand Segment Potential $_{g,t}$ = (specific product segment potential $_{g,t}$) $\times$ (percent contained in branded product/market segment $_{g,t}$).

Analysis of Competitive Positions

Prior to selecting segments as market targets, management must assess the strengths and weaknesses of competitors that are or will be likely to serve each candidate segment. A firm should not fall into the trap of automatically assuming that those few segments having the largest

TABLE 8–7

Illustrative Consumer Profiles for Toothpaste Market Segments

Profile Variables	*The Sensory Segment*	*The Sociables*	*Segment Name* *The Worriers*	*The Independent* *Segment*
Principal benefit sought............	Flavor, product appearance	Brightness of teeth	Decay prevention	Price
Demographic strengths.............	Children	Teens, young people	Large families	Men
Special behavioral characteristics...........	Users of spearmint flavored toothpaste	Smokers	Heavy users	Heavy users
Brands disproportionately favored...........	Colgate, Stripe	McLeans, Plus White, Ultra-Brite	Crest	Brands on sale
Personality characteristics............	High self-involvement	High sociability	High hypochondriasis	High autonomy
Life style characteristics.........	Hedonistic	Active	Conservative	Value-oriented

Source: Haley, "Benefit Segmentation," p. 3.

FIGURE 8–5

Industrial Customer Segment Profile Variables

Organizational Characteristics:
Geography; end use of the product purchased, type of business engaged in by customer; type of supplier profiles developed by customer;
type of buying situation (new task, modified rebuy, straight rebuy);
type of market served by customer; value added by customer; basis for
competitive advantage (e.g., price, personal selling, etc.); customer
profit margin; customer innovativeness; purchasing profiles; corporate
name and address.

Organizational Buyers' Characteristics:
Purchasing strategies used by buyers; primary role of buyer; buyer
self-confidence; differences in buyer information processing; buyer risk
tolerance and preference; perception of risks and problems by buyers;
buyer evaluation style; buyer's working relationships with others;
buyer workloads; buyer decision-making style (normative and conservative); and buyer personality traits.

---

demand potential will provide the greatest opportunity for a firm. Sometimes called the "majority fallacy,"[24] this assumption overlooks the positions of competitors in serving market segments. Other firms will also be
attracted to the largest demand potential segments. While firms are competing fiercely for shares of the largest segments, smaller segments may
not be adequately served. Thus, greater opportunity could exist for a
firm in these smaller market segments, depending on the costs of serving
each segment.

Recall from the previous chapter that sales generated by a firm is
dependent on both market potential *and* the effectiveness of the firm's
marketing offer, relative to those of competitors, in establishing market
share. Applied to segmentation analysis, a sales forecast can be determined by using the following relationship:

(2)   Segment Sales Forecast = Segment Potential × Segment Share

To illustrate the majority fallacy, suppose an analysis of two segments
showed that segment A has a potential of $20 million and segment B
has a potential of only $10 million. On the surface, segment A may look
like the greater market opportunity than segment B since it has twice
the demand potential. However, suppose that two competitors are now
serving segment A and that two more will probably enter soon. So,

---

[24] Alfred A. Kuehn and Ralph L. Day, "Strategy of Product Quality," *Harvard
Business Review*, vol. 40 (November–December 1962), p. 102.

management estimates that a market share for the firm of greater than 15 percent is unlikely. Yet, only one competitor is serving segment B and no others are known to be contemplating entering this market, indicating that a 50 percent market share is obtainable. Using equation (2), the sales opportunity in the smaller segment B is more attractive than in segment A:

Segment A Sales Forecast = $20,000,000 × 15 percent = $3,000,000.

Segment B Sales Forecast = $10,000,000 × 50 percent = $5,000,000.

The majority fallacy is most likely to hold in an established market where there are several competitive firms serving market segments. Firms looking for new opportunities in established markets should carefully assess the opportunity in the smaller segments, particularly when existing firms are successfully positioned in the larger segments. However, for untapped specific product markets, such as may exist for radically new products, the greatest opportunity will undoubtedly be in the larger segments since competition will be minimal, if not nonexistent.

Developing Marketing Strategy and Tactics

The most important test of the managerial usefulness of a segmentation approach is whether or not understanding gained about customers can be used to design customer-satisfying marketing offers. If not, the demand response to offers will not justify the increased costs of identifying and serving segments. For example, returning to the toothpaste illustration in Table 8–7, consider how a toothpaste manufacturer might use the customer basis and profile information. If management wanted to enter the Worriers segment, the principal benefit sought (decay prevention) determines key product design features, suggests where R&D resources will be most productive, and helps pinpoint promotional themes; the demographic information can be used to aid in the selection of media; and the personality, life style, and special behavior characteristics provide insight into appropriate advertising layouts and promotional themes.

The development of a marketing strategy and set of tactics for each candidate target segment also allows management to estimate the cost of serving segments. Costs should include all resources required to satisfy customer demand in segments including the information needed to identify segments and to control corporate performance in segments. These costs represent the investment required to implement a market segmentation strategy, and provide a partial basis for comparing opportunities in different markets. Table 8–1 shows how costs of serving segments can be included in a profitability analysis.

Analysis of Potential Goal/Objective Achievement

The previous stages should prepare management for the analysis of the potential for corporate goal and objectives achievement in market segments. For segments already entered with existing brands, this kind of analysis is a periodic control task to identify changes in market conditions. For new segments, this analysis is essential for the growth and expansion decisions of an organization involving new/modified products or penetration of existing products into new markets.

Corporate and marketing goals and objectives vary considerably from corporation to corporation. Typically, there are both quantitative goals such as profits, market share, and return on investment and more qualitative goals concerning company and product reputation. The analysis of segment opportunity should involve an evaluation of the extent to which each of these goals and objectives can be achieved. The quantitative goals require a forecast of sales from each segment and an assessment of costs needed to maintain a desired market position. Assessment of the qualitative goals requires more judgmental analysis of customers' product and brand attitudes and preferences and the particular marketing strategy deemed necessary to effectively reach each segment.

Selection of Target Market Segments

The final task for management in the segmentation decision process is to use the information and analyses from the previous stages to select segments as target markets. When more than one segment offers a potential opportunity, alternative segmentation strategies are available to a firm's management.[25] These can be classified according to the number of segments entered, intensive versus extensive segmentation, and according to the number of marketing mix components used to cater to segment differences. These alternatives are shown in Table 8–8.

Extensive Market Segmentation. An extensive market segmentation strategy is implemented when management wants to enter all or at least most of the identified market segments. This is a high sales strategy since greater penetration into each segment is combined with broad coverage of a total market.[26] Yet, it also requires the most resources to implement of all segmentation strategies due to the economies of scale that must be given up. As a result, this strategy is most likely to be adopted by a large organization. For example, General Motors offers a wide line of auto-

---

[25] Alternative market segmentation strategies are discussed in Brandt, "Dissecting the Segmentation Syndrome," p. 26; Kotler, *Marketing Management,* pp. 182–87; and Wendell R. Smith, "Product Differentiation and Market Segmentation as Alternative Marketing Strategies," *Journal of Marketing,* vol. 21 (July 1956), pp. 3–8.

[26] Alan A. Roberts, "Applying the Strategy of Market Segmentation," *Business Horizons,* Fall 1961, p. 66.

TABLE 8–8

Alternative Segmentation Strategies

	Totally Unique Marketing Mix	*Partially Unique Marketing Mix*
Extensive	(1)	(2)
Intensive	(3)	(4)

mobile brands to reach several probable market segments, IBM offers computer hardware of varying size and capabilities, and Coca-Cola, Inc., offers a variety of soft drinks and bottle sizes for different household wants.

An extensive market segmentation strategy can be implemented by designing entirely unique marketing programs for every target segment (cell 1). General Motors uses this approach through its Chevrolet division, Pontiac-Oldsmobile-Buick divisions, and Cadillac divisions, since each of these brand strategies appeal to different segments with different products, prices, promotion, and channels. An extensive strategy can also be implemented by designing only partially unique marketing offers for different segments (cell 2). This is exemplified by the Coca-Cola Company's use of primarily package size and type variations and advertising messages to reach different segments with the same cola product. Significant cost savings can be achieved on the undifferentiated parts of the marketing offer by utilizing economies of scale. However, care must be exercised to ensure that offer similarities do not substantially lessen the ability of the firm to match the unique customer wants and needs that caused the existence of segments.

Intensive Market Segmentation. An intensive market segmentation strategy involves selecting only one or a few of the identified segments as market targets. Corporate resources are then used to serve the unique wants and needs of this portion of the total market. Since this strategy requires less resources than the extensive market segmentation strategy, it is often implemented by the smaller firms in an industry. For example, in the automobile market a new company has decided to enter only one segment, the sportscar segment, with its initial offer of the Bricklin.[27] Moreover, several small steel companies specialize in specific types of steel to appeal to selected industrial segments.

An intensive segmentation strategy offers several advantages for the smaller firm. It obviously does not require as great a resource commitment as the extensive strategy due to the fewer markets being served.

---

[27] "Safety Fast," *Playboy,* September 1974, pp. 158–59.

Yet, it is still a high sales approach, relative to the amount of resources expended, because the marketing offer is being tailored to the unique needs of selected segments leading to greater penetration and market share. Finally, the fewer the segments entered, the greater a firm's ability to take advantage of economies of scale since resources are being devoted to one or a few segments. When several segments are selected, management may decide to design a totally unique offer for each segment (cell 3), though economies may be increased by designing only partially unique offers (cell 4).

A major drawback to the intensive strategy is that a firm is dependent upon one or a few segments for its success. This means that the firm is highly susceptible to market segment changes such as shifts in customer preferences or the entry of additional competitors. Thus, an intensive strategy may lead to instability of sales and overall performance. However, a small firm has little choice since it doesn't have the resources to appeal to many segments or to a mass market.

Intensive and extensive market segmentation strategies represent the opposite ends of a strategy continuum. For example, a small firm may begin with a intensive strategy, and then as the firm grows, move into additional segments. Eventually, the firm may grow sufficiently to make a complete transition to the extensive strategy. Over time, then, a firm can gradually shift from one strategy to the other. Moreover, the shift can be in either direction. A firm having performance problems in multiple segments, as may happen when competiting in a mature market, can move toward the intensive strategy by withdrawing from less profitable segments and intensifying effort in one or a few more profitable segments. This appears to be characteristic of the American Motors Corporation strategy of increased emphasis on smaller, more economical cars.

ALTERNATIVE APPROACHES TO IMPLEMENTING SEGMENTATION STRATEGIES

The timing of a segmentation strategy can vary with respect to corporate introduction of new products. One approach is to conduct a segmentation decision process after a product has been introduced into an aggregate market to determine for which segments, if any, the product has greatest appeal. This has been termed the customer self-selection approach.[28] The other approach is to conduct the process in parallel with the new/modified product decision process. This can be called the customer participation approach.[29]

---

[28] Ronald E. Frank, William F. Massy, and Yoram Wind, *Market Segmentation* (Englewood Cliffs, N.J.: Prentice-Hall, 1972), pp. 9–11.

[29] Ibid.

Customer Self-Selection Approach

In pursuing the self-selection approach, management must believe that the mass market for a product has divided itself into segments. Segments are self-selected since customers, themselves, determine through buying decisions whether the brand is a sufficient match for their needs. Management uses the segmentation decision process to discover who comprises the most profitable segments as well as to determine underlying reasons for others not desiring the brand. The process ultimately leads to a fine tuning of the marketing strategy and tactics to improve further the match beween the corporation's offer and existing segments. This approach could also be helpful for reassessing segments periodically as a performance control procedure.

The customer self-selection approach can be illustrated by examining the marketing strategy and segmentation efforts of a manufacturer of a well-known condiment.[30] The company, given the fictitious name of the Flavorfest Company for proprietary reasons, introduced the new condiment into an aggregate consumer market. The overall brand image was built around the product's unusual taste and appropriateness for experimental cooking. Advertising was used to stress an exotic and exciting image. Flavorfest then used marketing research to identify and describe market segments. Since potential customers had already been exposed to the product and brand, volume of the product/brand regularly purchased (i.e., volume segmentation) was selected as the segmentation basis. Accordingly, sample respondents to a marketing research questionnaire were classified into one of three groups: heavy users, light users and nonusers. Then the analysis of questionnaire information focused on developing consumer profiles for each segment. These profiles are shown in Table 8–9 on page 276.

The most important market for the condiment was the heavy-user segment. This segment was rather large, comprising 39 percent of the aggregate market, and so it was important to continue appealing to these customers. Though the brand image strategy needed no major changes, Flavorfest can use the profile information to fine-tune their current marketing tactics. For example, the geographic-demographic-socioeconomic heavy user characteristics should facilitate selecting media. Also, their interest in expressing individuality, creativity, and experimental cooking can help advertisers design advertising themes and promotional materials to encourage expanded use of the condiment.

The light-user segment presents a challenge to Flavorfest. This seg-

---

[30] The source of this example is James F. Engel, Hugh G. Wales, and Martin R. Warshaw, *Promotional Strategy* (Homewood, Ill.: Richard D. Irwin, Inc., 1971), pp. 160–62.

ment is comprised of 20 percent of the aggregate market, but was not using the product very much. The profile information provides several clues to the reasons for limited use. First, these housewives were interested in experimental cooking but lacked confidence in their ability to do so. Therefore, Flavorfest might try to increase usage in this segment by demonstrating the ease of cooking with the condiment and by providing "foolproof" recipes. Second, light-user housewives were interested in pleasing their families more than themselves. Here, promotion could be used to show that using the condiment in cooking is compatible with pleasing other family members. Finally, promotion might be used to try to change light users' attitudes, since these housewives believe that Flavorfest's condiment is only appropriately served with one kind of food. This could be accomplished by designing advertising that shows how it might be used with a variety of foods. All of these adjustments in marketing tactics would more precisely match Flavorfest's product offer with the desires and unique characteristics of the light user segment which may lead to increased use of the product.

The nonuser group does not appear to be a viable market target. While comprising a large (41 percent) portion of the aggregate market, these housewives have little purchasing power. Moreover, the interests, attitudes, and personality traits characteristic of this group are inconsistent with the brand strategy already developed by Flavorfest. Thus, the only alternatives would involve drastic changes in this strategy which would quite likely alienate the heavy- and light-user segments.

Customer Participation Approach

The customer participation approach more closely ties segmentation to the new/modified product decision process by seeking untapped segments that can be selected as market targets. Knowledge of customers is used to design initial brand strategy and the introduction is made directly into preselected segments rather than into an aggregate market. In essence, customers, through their segment bases and profile information, "participate" in the design and implementation of marketing strategy.

The customer participation approach to segmentation is illustrated by a market segmentation analysis performed by Market Facts, Inc., a marketing research organization.[31] The analysis was conducted in the aggregate market for beer in Chicago using a sample of 500 male beer drinkers. To determine the key product attributes that the sample was

---

[31] The source of this example is Richard M. Johnson, "Market Segmentation: A Strategic Management Tool," *Journal of Marketing Research*, vol. 8 (February 1971), pp. 13–18.

TABLE 8–9

Segmentation Basis and Customer Profiles for the Flavorfest Company

Profile Variables	Heavy Users	Light Users	Nonusers
(1) Demographics	Housewives; aged 25–45; large families; children under 5.	Housewives; aged 35–54; large families; children under 12.	Housewives; older; large families.
(2) Socioeconomics	Well educated, higher income categories.	Middle income categories.	Lower income categories.
(3) Geography	Concentration in Northeast and Midwest regions; both suburban and farm areas.	Located mostly in Southeast, Pacific, and Southwest states.	Located mostly in Eastern states and some parts of the South.
(4) General interests and attitudes	Strong desire not to be old-fashioned; desire to express individuality through creative action and use of exciting new things; traditional role of the housewife is viewed with displeasure; experimentation with new foods is done to express her individuality.	Strong desire to express individuality through creative cookery, but this desire is constrained somewhat by a conflicting desire to maintain tradition and subvert herself to her family's desires; lacks confidence in the results of her experimental cooking.	Strong desire to maintain tradition and emotional ties with the past; identifies with her mother and her role in the home; has a conservative, nonventuresome personality; her role as a mother and housewife discourages experimental cookery.
(5) Brand attitudes	Image of Flavorfest suggests exciting and exotic taste; flavorable attitudes toward taste, appearance, and food value; Flavorfest is highly prized in experimental cooking.	Image of Flavorfest is favorable; positive attitudes toward taste, appearance, and food value; belief that Flavorfest is appropriate only with one kind of food; viewed as unacceptable with other foods.	Image of Flavorfest connotes exotic flavors and a degree of modernity which is unacceptable; no interest in new uses and experimentation with Flavorfest.

Source: Engel, Wales, and Warshaw, *Promotional Strategy*, pp. 160–62.

using to distinguish between competitive brands of beer, respondents were asked to rate seven brands on 35 different attributes (e.g., the degree to which respondents believed that each beer possessed such characteristics as lightness, pale golden color, mild flavor, high price, full body, etc.). Then discriminant analysis was used to determine how brands related to each other in the minds of these consumers. Moreover, by comparing this relationship to the way in which brands were rated on each of the 35 attributes, the most important attributes for differentiating one brand from another were identified. Figure 8–6 shows a "map" of the relationship between the brands on the two most important attribute dimensions, premium/quality and lightness.

The interpretation of this map is based on the relative positions of each beer brand on each attribute dimension. For example, Miller's is perceived as both a lighter and a more premium brand than Hamms, Schlitz, and the four unnamed brands; Budweiser is perceived to be heavier and more premium than all other brands; and so forth. When combined these relationships provide management with a picture of the differences and similarities between brand images. Moreover, the picture shows the relationship between brand images directly in terms of important determinants of beer brand choice.

Once the brand image map has been determined, the analysis moved to the estimation of beer drinker preferences for beers having various combinations of lightness/heaviness and premium/popular price. Information can be obtained in several ways to pinpoint the ideal combination of attributes that each drinker would prefer to have in a brand of beer. Each of these ideal beers can be plotted on the brand image map so that management can compare how close real brands are to these ideal brands. To simplify this task, another multivariate tool (cluster analysis) is used to group these ideal brands into segments. Each segment contains beer drinkers who have similar ideal beer preferences. This is an example of benefit segmentation since product characteristics desired by customers is the segmentation basis. Figure 8–7 shows the results of this analysis. The circles represent the segments identified by drinkers'

FIGURE 8–6

The Chicago Beer Market as Perceived by Beer Drinkers

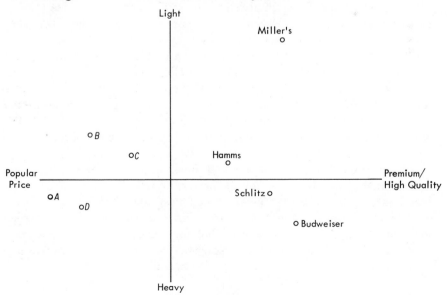

Source: Adapted from Johnson, "Market Segmentation," p. 14.

FIGURE 8–7

Beer Market Segments Based on Beer Attribute Preferences

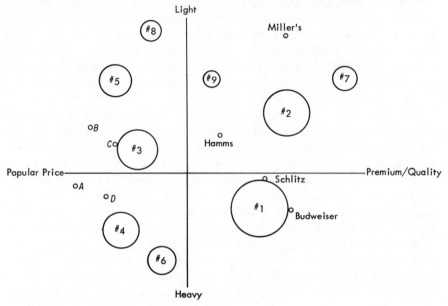

Source: Johnson, "Market Segmentation," p. 16.

ideal preferences and the number in each circle indicates its size relative to the other segments. Also shown is the relationship between each segment and the existing seven brands.

In addition to the information contained in Figures 8–6 and 8–7, the segmentation analysis must identify profile characteristics describing consumers in each of these segments. Also the relationship between consumer ideal brand preferences, existing brand images, and consumer brand choice must be determined (e.g., how "close" does a real brand have to be to an ideal brand before a consumer will purchase and consume the real brand?).

To demonstrate the managerial application of the beer market information, assume that consumers prefer brands closer to their ideal brands than those further away. Since preference determines choice of beer brands, management of a particular brand might increase market share by changing brand image so that the brand is "closer" to a large segment, more "distant" from competing brands, and perceived favorably on important attributes.[32] For example, brand A is more distant from

---

[32] Ibid., p. 18.

segments than any other brand. Management may elect to reposition A closer to segment #4 or #3 and #5 depending upon costs and competitive strengths of brands B, C, and D. Or, management may decide to introduce a new brand to appeal to segments not being adequately served such as #4 and #6.

FUTURE FOR SEGMENTATION APPLICATIONS

The major challenge in market segmentation applications is in operationalizing the concept. The requirements for a managerially useful application, particularly identifying customer variations and profiles and translating this information into marketing offers, have impeded the widespread use of market segmentation analysis results due to current level of sophistication of approaches and tools. However, this is not unusual given the relatively short period of time that concentrated effort has been devoted to research on alternative segmentation approaches and tools. Actually, the numerous reported successful applications provide support for an optimistic prediction that market segmentation will become increasingly operational as more research is done on tools and techniques.

Segmentation application improvements can be obtained by concentrating in three areas. Substantial effort is needed to develop and refine more appropriate bases for classifying customers into segments. These bases must more closely approximate customer response elasticities to marketing offer components than many currently available bases have done. Possibly too much attention has been concentrated on linking past behavior to customer profiles rather than in assessing whether profiles were linked to the most appropriate bases. Some progress is being made as illustrated by the current attention being given to product attribute preferences as bases. However, this approach is relatively new and has not overcome all difficulties to date. For example, appropriate models for relating preferences to brand choice are not widely available.

In addition, identifying segmentation bases and developing customer profiles involves analyzing information on a large number of variables. Consequently, there is a need for greater use of multivariate statistical techniques in market segmentation analyses. A variety of multivariate techniques are available for segmentation research, though there are difficulties in interpreting results in terms of managerial implications for marketing strategy. Greater experience with the techniques should help to resolve some of these difficulties.

Finally, in a developing area such as market segmentation there is usually a time lag between the introduction of more appropriate and useful tools and techniques and their widespread application by management. Segmentation analysis is not totally an analyst's activity, but requires considerable attention from management. For example, in the beer market segmentation illustration managerial experience can contribute to determining (1) the relevant brands to include, (2) the likelihood of particular attributes being true choice determinants, (3) appropriateness of assumptions underlying analyses; and (4) strategic implications of results for brand images. Therefore, management personnel will have to become more familiar and involved with segmentation decision processes.

EXERCISES FOR REVIEW AND DISCUSSION

1. Carefully show how market segmentation overlaps with market opportunity analysis. Are there any significant differences between these concepts?

2. Suppose you work for a manufacturer of an all-purpose household cleaner now using a mass marketing strategy. Explain how management should decide whether to change to a market segmentation strategy for this product.

3. "Market segmentation is the process of dividing people into segments where those in each group have similar product wants." Evaluate how well this statement captures the meaning and application of market segmentation.

4. "An appropriate, practical approach to segmentation begins with marketing research to identify the largest segment within a specific product market in terms of market potential. This largest segment is selected as a market target." Evaluate the appropriateness of this approach to market segmentation.

5. Suppose you are on the marketing staff of a leisure time products company now selling a line of sailboats. Explain life style segmentation and how this strategy might improve the marketing of this product.

6. As part of a MOA for a new snack food that your company is going to introduce, you have received the information in the table on the opposite page. Using this information, recommend some positive market target and marketing mix strategy actions you believe appropriate for this product.

7. Explain why General Motors has a broad product line apparently appealing to multiple segments while a competitor, American Motors, has a much more limited line of primarily small car models.

	Heavy Users	*Light Users*	*Nonusers*
Average volume purchased........	12–15 boxes per month	1–6 boxes per month	0 boxes per month
Demographics.......	Urban or rural residence Low-moderate income Blue-collar occupation Less than high school education Large family	Moderate income White-collar occupation High school graduate Suburban residence	High income Over 50 Suburban residence College educated
AIOs..............	Socially active Prefers informal "get-togethers" with friends Nontraveler Concerned with high inflation Politically inactive	Socially inactive Very concerned with increasing food prices Sports enthusiast	Entertains by having formal dinner parties Socially active Church goer Politically active Concerned with community affairs
Behavioral characteristics.....	Heavy beer drinkers Heavy TV watcher	Heavy TV watcher Heavy buyer of sporting equipment	Watches very little TV Wine drinker

9

Buyer Decision Processes

Market opportunity analysis and market segmentation demonstrate the need for marketing managers to understand and predict buyer behavior. This chapter focuses on managerial applications of buyer behavior information, and presents a framework for organizing the behavioral concepts and processes underlying this information. The first section discusses applications by different types of organizations to illustrate the widespread interest in understanding buyers. Then a comprehensive model of consumer behavior is presented to serve as a managerial framework. A study of consumer clothing buyers is discussed to show how the model is used to guide collection and analysis of buyer information for marketing decisions. Finally, industrial buying behavior is compared and contrasted with consumer behavior.

APPLICATIONS OF BUYER BEHAVIOR INFORMATION

Definition of Buyer Behavior

Predicting buyer response requires, at a minimum, identifying the most likely buyers for a product offer. In some cases, a description of the most likely buyer is all the information needed. A manufacturer of cameras, for example, may only need to know that high income consumers have been the primary purchasers of cameras to predict that these same types of individuals will comprise his market for the next operating period. However, being able to describe the characteristics of buyers in a market does not mean that a firm understands the *causes* of buying behavior. It is quite possible to predict the future without fully understanding why the predictions will be accurate.

To increase their confidence in predicting and influencing buyer decisions, managers try to uncover the causes of these decisions. For example, suppose the camera manufacturer wanted to evaluate the potential for selling cameras to lower income households. How can this market be evaluated or an offer designed when the manufacturer does not understand why low income households have not been buying cameras? To evaluate the low income market and to incorporate appropriate features into a camera offer requires uncovering the reasons why low income people have not been purchasing cameras. Low income may not be the cause. The underlying reason might be lack of education which, in turn, may cause low income households to have a psychological reluctance to cope with the complexity of cameras. Appropriate marketing strategy will differ depending on which of these reasons is the true cause.

The discipline to which managers can turn for assistance in determining how best to describe and understand buyers is buyer behavior. Buyer behavior is concerned with *the decision processes that buyers or groups of buyers go through to make a purchase decision including all those influences that explain the outcome of the decision.* This definition recognizes that buyer decision making is not a single act, but a series of sequential steps or stages that buyers may go through. Moreover, individuals may not be the true buying decision unit, but rather groups of individuals may be jointly going through the process (e.g., a corporate buying committee, a family, etc.). Finally, buyer behavior is not just concerned with describing buyers, but is also concerned with uncovering the reasons that explain why buyers will behave in a particular way.

Business Decision Making

Business firms have been the primary users of buyer behavior information. Successful business applications have demonstrated that understanding markets can have payoffs in: (1) analyzing opportunities available in markets, (2) designing marketing strategy, and (3) controlling marketing programs. The decision making activities that led to the introduction and monitoring of Ford's Mustang illustrates the use of buyer behavior information in each of these areas:

> For a number of years prior to 1962, Ford had been trying different strategies to counteract General Motor's substantial competitive advantage in selling and servicing cars. A major component of Ford's approach had been to broaden their product line, which led to the introduction of the Edsel, Fairlane, and Falcon lines. Moreover, they had been interested in the possibility of tapping an additional market for sports cars.
>
> To determine the probable size of a sports car market and to get a feel for the characteristics of the product that would best meet the needs of this market, two personal interview surveys were conducted. Included in the first study's sample were owners of sport-type cars (Thunderbird,

Corvair Monza, foreign imports) and their neighbors living in Dallas, Chicago, and Philadelphia. In addition to demographic and socio-economic characteristics, the survey measured consumer attitudes toward alternative sport-type car models such as a single seat, two passenger car, three sports models of current Falcons, and a fast-back Falcon. The second survey was more directly concerned with obtaining attitudes and opinions toward a model designed to compete with the Corvair Monza. The sample was comprised of owners of Monzas, Falcon sedans, foreign sports cars, and foreign economy cars. Results of both of these studies showed considerable interest in a five or six passenger modified sports car model with six- and eight-cylinder options. It was estimated that such a car would generate between 50,000 and 100,000 units, excluding any possible purchases from standard size car buyers.

The initial survey results were sufficiently encouraging to pursue this potential market opportunity further. Recognizing the geographical and type-of-respondent limitations of these studies, Ford researchers decided to carry out a national probability sample survey by personally interviewing 950 prospective new car buyers. "The questionnaires used in this survey generally followed the format of earlier studies. Pictures of a Ford fast-back Galaxie, the fast-back Falcon, and Fairlane hardtops were used along with a Corvair and other competitive sports cars. The properties used were side views of the test cars and three-quarter front and rear views of the various cars. Specification sheets covering the test cars and other cars currently available, along with diagrams to illustrate shoulder room and clearance, were also used." The results indicated a much larger market with a volume between 150,000 and 300,000, though two-thirds would be substitute sales for other Ford models. Demographic and attitude data relationships showed the importance of the young buyer under 25. Also, style was frequently given as a reason for preferring the proposed sports car over other models. "Although many sports-type features (bucket seats, four-speed transmission, and tachometers) were desired by a higher-than-average proportion of respondents, the majority still desired the conventional car accoutrements."

The product concept research studies were highly encouraging and provided substantial insight into the size and characteristics of the target market, as well as product design features wanted by these customers. Yet, there were still other important decisions that had to be made, particularly on brand name, price, and advertising strategy. Again, Ford turned to buyer behavior research to guide them during these critical decisions. The information on the characteristics of the market including attitudes and preferences generated from the previous studies was useful for designing advertising copy. However, the pricing and brand name decisions required new research.

To determine the most appropriate price, Ford's market research department conducted a thorough study of possible price levels using a sample of 1600 prospective buyers of hardtop-convertibles and sports cars from 12 cities. The crucial dimension was how much substitution for other Ford models would characterize sales of the proposed sports car, since the more substitution taking place, the higher the price would have to be. The final price selected based on this research was $2,368 f.o.b. Detroit which was quite low compared to other sports cars. This economy price was also used as an advertising theme, along with style uniqueness and versatility of the car.

The original, tentative choice of a brand name was Torino. Yet, it was felt that this name, in addition to other alternatives, should be tested before the final selection. An independent research agency was hired to conduct a two phase study. Phase I was a small sample, unstructured group interview study in which respondents gave their perceptions and opinions of car features and alternative brand names. Phase II followed with a larger, personal interview study asking 203 individuals to give their impressions of the brand names identified as alternative candidates from Phase I.

"Potential names were judged against a variety of criteria: (1) The name should be a word that was liked, that had pleasant associations independent of its suitability as a name for this particular car, (2) The connotations of the word should be suitable as a name for the car, (3) The name should be easy to pronounce, (4) The name should be easy to remember." As a result of this research, the decision was made to name the proposed sports car Mustang rather than Torino.

The Mustang was introduced in April of 1964, and Ford began to monitor results by gathering data on new car purchases of the Mustang and other models. This information on consumer buying decisions showed that the Mustang was an instant success with a year-end total sales volume of over 248,000 cars.[1]

The development and introduction of the Mustang illustrates a highly successful application of buyer behavior information. More importantly, it gives some indication of the variety of business decisions in which knowledge of buyers can be useful. For example, initial and follow-up studies were used to determine the size and key characteristics of the potential market. This data was essential for analyzing the potential profitability of entering the market as well as the amount of funds (for advertising, sales personnel, production, etc.) that was necessary to take advantage of the opportunity. Further, a variety of behavior information was collected to guide management through the critical marketing offer design decisions on product features, options, and styling, on price, and on selling activities. Finally, information on purchase decisions by customers allowed Ford's management to evaluate how well the sports car innovation was actually meeting the wants of the target market.

---

[1] Roger D. Blackwell, James F. Engel, and David T. Kollat, *Cases in Consumer Behavior* (New York: Holt, Rinehart and Winston, 1969), pp. 298–314.

Governmental Decision Making

Government can also benefit from knowledge of customer decision processes. Government has the responsibility of determining policy and enacting and enforcing laws that are in the "best interests" of society. Quite recently the three branches of government in general as well as selected agencies, notably the Federal Trade Commission and the Consumer Protection Agency, have become increasingly interested in the welfare of citizens in their role as consumers. The result has been enactments of laws intended to protect consumers from hazards inherent in using products, to provide information believed to be important for buying decisions, and to set standards for appropriate conduct by business decision makers in their everyday dealings with customers.

Governmental policy makers are recognizing that understanding buyer decision making is essential for their decisions affecting consumer welfare. For example, while a commissioner for the Federal Trade Commission, Mary Gardiner Jones made an eloquent plea to members of the Association for Consumer Research to keep in mind the FTC's need for behavioral information:

> I see two broad areas which continually confront the Commission where gaps may exist in our present approaches. The first is in the allocation of our resources to problem areas and the second is the development of effective remedies within problem areas.
>
> I strongly feel that our efforts in these two areas can be greatly enhanced by a systematic utilization of research on consumer behavior. The reasons for this should be obvious. Our past efforts have implicitly relied on models of the consumer, and to the extent that these models were lacking, our own efforts were less effective.[2]

The FTC has done more than express the need for buyer behavior information. In very recent years, the Commission held public hearings to gather information about the impact of advertising on consumers (including children). Experts from advertising agencies, corporations, and universities gave testimony on the role that advertising plays in consumer buying decisions. Important policy decisions on regulation of advertising to adults and to children are currently pending, but are being made with the benefit of a greater understanding of this complex process.

Other Nonbusiness Decision Making

In time, recognition of the usefulness of understanding "buyers" will spread beyond business firms and government. There is clearly a po-

---

[2] Mary Gardner Jones, "The FTC's Need for Social Science Research," *Proceedings of the 2d Annual Conference of the Association for Consumer Research* (College Park, Md.: Association for Consumer Research, 1971), p. 2.

tential for broadening applications to many types of nonbusiness organizations such as universities, hospitals, churches, and charities. These kinds of organizations do not have profit-oriented goals, but they do attempt to appeal to groups of people for financial and other kinds of support. Moreover, they are providing a service that must satisfy the needs of some groups in a society in order to maintain support from these groups. In this respect, nonbusiness organizations are faced with very similar decision tasks as are businesses: identifying "market" opportunities, designing service offers for those markets, and controlling performance.

Religious organizations represent one type of nonbusiness institution that is in need of "buyer" behavior information. To survive, churches must obtain several kinds of support from people, including monetary pledges, committee participation, and attendance at functions. To win this support, churches must identify the specific needs of these "buyers," must design an "offer" (comprised of such components as religious services, family counseling, social activities, religious training for children, and various community activities) to meet these needs, and must determine how well the offer is satisfying members.

Over the past few years, it has become apparent that many churches have not kept pace with changes in the markets being served. While church membership has remained rather stable, church attendance has been declining. Moreover, attitude surveys have shown widespread dissatisfaction with institutionalized religion. To counteract this loss of "market" acceptance, some churches have encouraged greater use of techniques borrowed from business practice. Included are various efforts to obtain information from members that will provide insight into the local market needs. Programs can then be designed more directly to respond to demands of the membership. Moreover, "buyer" information can also be used to assess the success of past decisions made by the church's administrative board.

Consumer Training

There is also a potential for the application of buyer research to help buyers themselves:

> . . . Some may argue that the locus of the consumer behavior field ought to center around the consumer—to help consumers better understand their behavior, in order to improve their functioning as consumers in the marketplace. Consumer behavior has not yet been studied from the point of view of the consumer, for the sake of the consumer, in order to benefit the consumer. Perhaps the consumerist sees this as his role, but until now, consumer protection proposals have been based largely on what is "good" for the consumer, from the point of view of his advocate, and not based on empirically-established needs.

Consumer decision processes have not been researched from the point of view of how they might be improved. This requires almost an anthropological point of view, in the sense that consumer behavior must be understood in terms of the needs it fulfills for its participants, much as a culture must be understood in terms of the totality of needs which it fulfills for its members.[3]

It should not be surprising that past research on consumer behavior has not been done solely for the benefit of consumers. Buyer behavior research is costly, and so, those that supply the funds required for such research can rightly expect to have results geared toward answering their questions and serving their needs. Since business and governmental agencies are the primary sources for research funds, buyer behavior studies have clearly reflected these sponsors' needs.

However, it probably is only a matter of time before a significant portion of buyer research activities is oriented toward achieving improvements in consumer decision making. This research would identify current decision making practices of specific consumer groups (e.g., the poor) in order to determine what kinds of improvements to incorporate into consumer training programs. Who should provide the necessary research funds and objectives is unclear, though conceivably business, government, and/or consumer groups could perform this function.

Potential for Applications

The potential for applying knowledge of buyer behavior is both great and diversified. Consequently, managers in a variety of types of organizations will be increasingly expected to incorporate behavioral information in their decision making activities. Moreover, much of the needed information will come from research and intelligence activities than from personal experience. This puts an additional burden on the manager to become familiar with the kinds of buyer behavior information that can be provided.

An important question for management concerns what skills are needed to develop and maintain their ability to effectively use buyer behavior information. Clearly, the typical manager cannot be expected to keep current on all the most recent developments in buyer behavior concepts, theory, or methodology. The constraints on the manager's time preclude his ability to read and comprehend the many buyer research reports continually appearing in the literature. This is a task for the researcher rather than for managers.

If managers cannot keep current in the field of buyer behavior, what

---

[3] Thomas S. Robertson and Scott Ward, "Toward the Development of Consumer Behavior Theory," *Marketing Education and the Real World* (Chicago: American Marketing Association, 1972), p. 59.

can they do to ensure that knowledge of customers will be used in decision making? Every manager can become familiar with an appropriate model of buyer behavior in order to better understand the variety of factors, relationships, and processes that may explain the behavior of customers. Moreover, a manager can develop and maintain at least a general awareness of the "state of the art" in the field of buyer behavior so that realistic expectations as to the benefits of applying behavioral information are developed.

A MODEL OF BUYER BEHAVIOR

Nature of a Behavioral Model

A model of buyer behavior is a representation (e.g., a diagram, a verbal description, a mathematical function) of the important factors (variables), relationships between factors, and processes that describe customer decision making. Currently, buyer behavior models are descriptive in nature,[4] but can be either quantitative or qualitative. Models of buyer behavior are not the same as a theory of buyer behavior:

> Theories consist of principles, postulates, hypothetical ideas and relationships among them, theorems and statements derived from them, and coordinating definitions relating theoretical terms to empirical statements and hypotheses. Models, on the other hand, provide representational, inferential, or interpretational functions for theories. Thus, models are related to—but not the same as—theories.[5]

Behavioral models are developed by utilizing one or more theories that attempt to explain a behavioral process such as buyer decision making. Models, then, are intended to represent and interpret theory. In the field of buyer behavior, comprehensive models incorporate multiple theories, each theory explaining only a part of the total. For example, theories of learning, attitude change, and perception underly all these models. The importance of the model-theory distinction is that any discussion of buyer behavior models should *not* be viewed as presenting "the" theory of buyer behavior. There is no single, comprehensive theory of buyer behavior, and there probably will not be one for many years to come. The field of buyer behavior is simply too young to have generated all the conceptualization and research necessary for building and testing a comprehensive theory of consumer buying.

---

[4] Future modeling efforts may turn to the development of normative models. Such models may be needed by those who undertake the design and implementation of a consumer training program. The normative model would serve as a standard for those consumers undergoing training.

[5] Robertson and Ward, "Toward the Development of Consumer Behavior Theory," pp. 60–61.

Managerial Use of Buyer Behavior Models

Underlying all uses of buyer behavior models is the fact that a model can serve as a *framework* for understanding and analyzing customer behavior. Over the years, business experience has shown that customer decision making is a very complex and dynamic activity. It simply is not always an easy task to explain or to predict how buyers will respond to the decisions of marketing management. A model serves as a framework to help managers cope with this complexity by pulling together those factors that theory and research indicate are important for understanding behavior into an integrated "picture" of buying.

The importance of having a framework cannot be overstated. All decisions that affect the offer of business or other organizations are at least implicitly based upon some beliefs about buyer behavior. For example, in 1971, Brown-Forman Distillers Corporation brought out a dry, white whiskey, Frost 8/80, to take advantage of a long term consumer trend away from bourbons and U.S.-made blended whiskies. This decision was based on the belief that those consumers leading this trend, mostly women and young adults, did not like the taste of liquor and wanted more bland whiskies. The introductory advertising campaign was based on the additional beliefs that potential buyers would use the new whiskey primarily with mixers, and had their own notions about which mixers to use. Consequently, the advertising emphasized product versatility with the slogan, "The color is white. The taste is dry. The possibilities are endless."[6]

Notions about customers depend as much upon whether they deal with variables that influence customer decisions as on the accuracy of the notions themselves. A buyer behavior model framework encourages a manager to determine whether or not his beliefs about buyers cover the most important variables that may influence market response. A failure to consider an important buyer decision influence can lead to unsuccessful decisions. Returning to the Brown-Forman example, management decided to withdraw Frost 8/80 two years after introduction because the product did not meet performance objectives. At least part of the reason for failure appears to have been due to management overlooking an important buyer influence—the lack of drinkers' previous experience with white whiskies. This was suggested by William Carroll who was responsible for the sales effort for Frost 8/80: "As it turned out, uniqueness was our biggest problem. The product looked like Vodka but tasted like whiskey. It upset people. They didn't know what to make of it."[7]

---

[6] "Putting a New Product on Market Is Costly, Complicated—and Risky," *The Wall Street Journal*, February 18, 1971, pp. 1–14.

[7] "How a New Product Was Brought to Market Only to Flop Miserably," *The Wall Street Journal*, January 5, 1973, p. 10.

By having a comprehensive buyer behavior model firmly in mind, a manager can tie together information from different sources. Beliefs about buyer behavior are frequently developed from a variety of sources over extended time periods. For example, in a new product decision, market information may come from salesmen, distributors and dealers, purchased research studies, and organizational research studies. Moreover, this information will deal with different aspects of potential buyers. The manager must integrate all this information into as complete a picture of the buyer as the information will allow, which can be done most effectively by "filling in" an already existing framework of variables and variable relationships.

Managers are constantly faced with the difficult task of identifying new information that is needed for a particular decision. A manager can use a model framework to assess what he does and does not already know about buyers. Determining which variables and/or relationships have not been measured at all, or recently enough, provides direction for setting objectives for information gathering activities. Moreover, in this way the manager will play an essential part in setting these objectives rather than simply reacting to proposals by marketing research personnel. In the Frost 8/80 decision, for example, having a model framework in mind might have encouraged managers to pay closer attention to potential buyer's past experience and familiarity with the white whiskey concept.

Finally, when several managers are jointly responsible for a decision and all have similar buyer behavior model frameworks, communication of premises and rationales for proposed strategy or tactics is greatly facilitated. Each manager has the same general understanding of those variables and relationships that may influence buyer decisions which will aid in articulating rationale for a marketing decision as well as in understanding the rationale of others. Moreover, model frameworks may help in justifying decisions to outside groups, particularly governmental groups such as the Federal Trade Commission. A comprehensive framework backed up by well-developed behavioral information can help a manager explain to outsiders exactly why an important decision affecting buyers was made. For example, a major drug company might have to explain to a congressional committee why an advertising campaign for a new drug will not encourage young people to develop permissive attitudes toward the taking of drugs.

One of the leading experts in the field of buyer decision making summarizes the managerial advantages of using a comprehensive model:

> This integrated, causal picture of the influences affecting the buyer will provide a powerful lever to the marketing manager's understanding of the market by giving him concepts which cut through the maze of complexity and which will encourage sharp diagnosis of marketing

failures and successes. These diagnoses will be adding to his comprehension of the market, enable the marketing manager to build a marketing philosophy which aids imaginative innovation and prevents him from being misled by minor aberrations of the market.[8]

The EKB Model

Only a few comprehensive models of buyer behavior have been developed and published to date. In fact, just three models have gained most of the attention in the field of consumer behavior: the Nicosia model,[9] the Howard and Sheth model,[10] and the Engel, Kollat, and Blackwell (EKB) model.[11] While all three offer particular advantages and limitations for use as a managerial framework, the EKB model has been selected for presentation here. This model is a more recent development than the Nicosia model, and is conceptually simpler than the Howard and Sheth model while still being adequately comprehensive.

FIGURE 9–1

The Black Box Model

A useful starting place for understanding this model is to examine a very simple stimulus–blackbox–response model of behavior that underlies all the more comprehensive models. As shown in Figure 9–1, this model identifies the three major classes of variables that form the basis for understanding buyer behavior: (1) stimuli from the external environment, (2) characteristics of a buyer (the black box), and (3) the responses to external stimuli made by the buyer.

Essentially, the black box model[12] suggests that to predict purchase decisions, a manager must know what stimuli (e.g., advertising, competitive offers, recommendations from friends, etc.) customers have seen, and understand how these stimuli interact with buyer characteristics. The difficulty of predicting behavior cannot be fully appreciated from a

---

[8] John A. Howard, "Buyer Behavior and Related Technological Advances," *Journal of Marketing*, January 1970, p. 19.

[9] Francesco M. Nicosia, *Consumer Decision Processes: Marketing and Advertising Implications*, (Englewood Cliffs, N.J.: Prentice-Hall, 1966), Chapter 4.

[10] John A. Howard and Jagdish N. Sheth, *The Theory of Buyer Behavior* (New York: Wiley, 1969).

[11] James F. Engel, David T. Kollat, and Roger D. Blackwell, *Consumer Behavior* (New York: Holt, Rinehart and Winston, 1973), pp. 49–62.

[12] The individual is frequently called a "black box" because it is physically impossible to see the processes of thinking and decision making occurring in a person's mind. The black box analogy, then, is based on the fact that one also cannot see into a closed black box.

cursory look at this simple model, however. Consequently, the more comprehensive models build on the basic characteristics of the black box model by identifying the variety of variables that are included in each of these three classes. Moreover, they hypothesize in much greater detail the possible relationships between variables.

The complete EKB "multimediation" model of consumer behavior is shown in Figure 9–2. Each of the boxes in the diagram represents a

FIGURE 9–2

The Engel, Kollat, and Blackwell Multimediation Model of Consumer Behavior

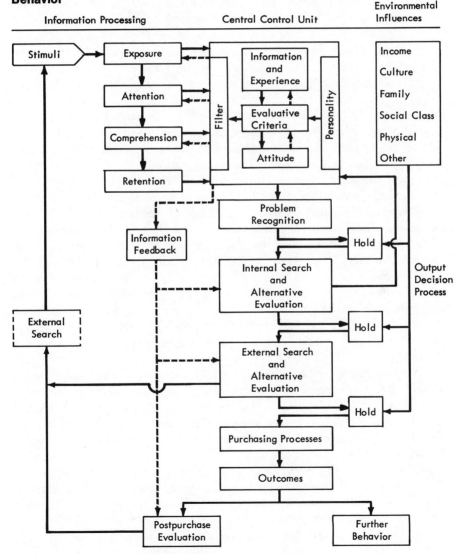

Source: Engel, Kollat, and Blackwell, *Consumer Behavior*, p. 58.

variable that may influence behavior. The arrows connecting boxes describe relationships between variables as well as emphasizing that buyer behavior is a dynamic ongoing process.

Environmental Stimuli and Perception

The EKB model shows that people are continually exposed to stimuli. A stimulus represents anything, generally inherent in the environment, that has the potential for triggering some kind of behavior. Managers are quite concerned with many of the stimuli to which potential customers are exposed, since the total offer designed to influence buyer behavior is really a set of stimuli. For example, the shape of a product is one kind of stimulus that may cause behavior if the buyer is exposed to it in a store, in an advertisement, or even in a neighbor's home. In general, marketing decision making can be viewed (at least in part) as putting together and controlling a set of stimuli intended to influence customer buying behavior. Of course, any marketing offer represents only a fraction of the total stimuli to which buyers are exposed. Many other stimuli, some controlled by competitors, some controlled by noncompetitive organizations, some originating from other people, are also competing for buyers' attention.

One of the most important processes identified by the EKB model is information processing. Stimuli provide information that consumers must process. This task includes the stages of exposure, attention, comprehension, and retention. *Exposure* refers to a stimulus reaching one of the senses (sight, hearing, smell, touch, and/or taste), while *attention* indicates on which of these stimuli the consumer will focus. For example, when a housewife walks down an aisle in a supermarket, she is being exposed to a variety of products; however, not all of these products will gain her attention since she will quickly pass over those in which she is not interested. If she should stop to inspect one particular brand, then that set of stimuli (package shape, size, weight, label, etc.) has won her attention.

Comprehension is the process by which consumers attach meaning to stimuli. Because a consumer is attentive toward a marketing offer does not mean that the offer will be comprehended as management intended it to be. For example, suppose that Cadillac division of General Motors decided to reduce price on all its models in order to pass on cost savings to buyers. If the price reduction was large, consumers might believe that Cadillac is sacrificing quality and prestige since price is tied so closely to these attributes. This particular meaning of the price reduction stimulus would not be the one intended by Cadillac's management. The ever present potential for consumer miscomprehension of marketing decisions strongly suggest that managers should consider testing important decisions on samples of consumers before putting them into full scale operation.

Retention refers to the memory process that determines which of the many stimuli that have gone through the initial three stages of consumer information processing will be remembered. Not all stimuli that have been comprehended will be retained in memory. In fact, the percentage of stimuli remaining in memory is generally quite small, particularly after a period of weeks has passed since exposure.[13] Unfortunately, it is not very well understood why some stimuli will be remembered while others are forgotten.

An important implication of the processing of stimuli is that consumers actively interact with some businesses while avoiding interaction with others. They are certainly not passively receiving information and being influenced accordingly. On the contrary, a very difficult and challenging task for management is to design marketing offers that target customers will be attentive toward, will comprehend in a way consistent with the intended meaning of the offer, and will be remembered through the time period required for purchase. An offer that is filtered out anywhere during this process by a significant number of customers will not achieve performance goals.

Consumer Characteristics. Since the consumer is an active participant in interaction between buyers and sellers, the characteristics that form an individual's psychological makeup have an important impact on the success of an offer. A set of stimuli comprising the marketing program must interact with one or more key individual characteristics before a consumer determines what response will be made. Consequently, an important part of a manager's buyer behavior framework ought to include a working knowledge of these key characteristics.

The EKB model depicts the individual as having a central control unit, which is the center for thinking, memory, and decision making—all of which guide behavior. Through considerable research on behavior, it is generally believed that the central control unit contains a relatively few key variables that describe the uniqueness or individuality of a person: (1) personality traits, (2) motives (included in the EKB model as a part of personality), (3) attitudes, (4) past information and experiences, and (5) evaluative criteria. The common thread running through all of these variables is the process of learning. People have the ability to learn from their experiences, and so, the behavior that people will adopt in the future is at least partially dependent on what they have experienced in the past. At a given point in time all these variables summarize and describe what a person has seen and done to

---

[13] For example, see Leo Bogart, *Strategy in Advertising* (New York: Harcourt, Brace, 1967), Chapter 5.

date, and more importantly, suggest the behavior that consumers will be likely to take in the future.

The concept of *personality trait* is difficult to define in a very precise manner since different definitions abound. However, there is at least one commonality of most definitions that provides sufficient insight into this variable for managerial purposes:

> Unfortunately, analysts do not agree on any general definition of the term "personality," except to somehow tie it to the concept of consistent responses to the world of stimuli surrounding the individual. Man does tend to be consistent in coping with his environment. This consistency of response allows us to type politicians as charismatic or obnoxious, students as aggressive or submissive, and colleagues as charming or "blah." Since individuals do react fairly consistently in a variety of environmental situations, these generalized patterns of response or modes of coping with the world can be called personality.[14]

On the surface, the potential for applications of customer personality trait information appears great. It is not hard to visualize the purchase of particular brands or products as being extensions of customer personalities. For example, consumers who have a tendency to be hypochondriacs may be much more likely to purchase Crest toothpaste which emphasizes a medicinal function as a tooth decay preventative, than Ultra Brite which emphasizes the more cosmetic function of whitening teeth. Moreover, since personality refers to consistent tendencies to behave in a particular way, understanding customer personality traits may greatly facilitate managerial prediction of future behavior.

While personality theories suggest that personality traits are at least one cause of buyer behavior, empirical research has not been particularly successful in demonstrating this relationship.[15] These discouraging research results appear to be primarily due to inappropriate methodologies (improper personality measurement instruments, lack of theoretical justification for specific relationships tested, and failure to account for other variables influencing behavior) rather than to inappropriate theories.[16] This is an issue that researchers must and will resolve.

The concept of *motive* refers to a tendency for people to behave in a general way in order to satisfy a need or drive. Commonly researched motives include affiliation, achievement, and esteem. The fact that people do have buying motives indicates that consumer behavior is generally purposive or goal-directed. Understanding the goals that customers are trying to achieve through buying is clearly important for marketing de-

---

[14] Harold H. Kassarjian, "Personality and Consumer Behavior: A Review," *Journal of Marketing Research,* November 1971, p. 409 published by the American Marketing Association.

[15] Kassarjian, "Personality and Consumer Behavior: A Review," p. 415.

[16] Kassarjian, "Personality and Consumer Behavior: A Review," pp. 415–16.

cision makers. However, managers should not make the mistake of believing that knowledge of customer motives is totally sufficient for understanding and predicting behavior, particularly highly specific behavior such as purchase of a brand. Motives are not the only cause of behavior. For example, suppose a marketing manager knew that one group of potential customers had a psychological need for recognition from others. The corresponding motive might be to achieve status or prestige. This motive would probably encourage these customers to engage in certain types of buying behavior such as buying conspicuous products, expensive products, and/or national brands, and would allow the manager to make these general kinds of predictions. However, knowledge of this motive would not allow him to predict which of several expensive or prestigious brands (e.g., Cadillac versus Continental versus Mercedes Benz) these customers will buy, or even what brands are "seen" as expensive and prestigious by them. Information on other variables (e.g., on attitudes, income, evaluative criteria, etc.) is also needed to make these more specific predictions.

Closely related to the concept of motives are consumers' *evaluative criteria* which refer to the dimensions or performance characteristics desired from a product or service. These criteria are used by consumers to compare alternative products and brands and include such dimensions as economy, durability, reputation, and convenience. The performance characteristics desired in a product or service determine what that product must do in order to satisfy a consumer's purchase motives. Evaluative criteria are developed from a consumer's past experiences, personality traits, and the influences of other people, and so, are more than just manifestations of consumer motives.

Products or services that will win customer acceptance must usually be consistent with consumers' existing evaluative criteria. Fortunately, these criteria typically correspond to parts of a marketing offer that can be controlled by managers. For example, if customers use convenience to judge which stores will be patronized, retailers can use several controllable parts of their offer—location, parking space, store layout, personnel—to influence how convenient their stores will be to customers as a way of generating partonage.

Past information and experience refer to all the accumulated results of previous actions and occurrences that a consumer stores in memory for future use in similar situations. This ability to retain information from experiences over time is the basis for consumers' learning. In turn, learning helps to explain the considerable amount of regularity of consumer behavior, which is very important to those trying to predict future behavior. For example, consumer loyalty to certain brands is one kind of behavioral regularity desired by marketing managers.

The information and experience variable has received comparatively little direct attention from researchers and practitioners. Measures of consumer awareness (of advertisements, messages, product/service features, etc.) in studies of promotional effectiveness are quite commonly used by business firms, but these studies cover only a fraction of the relevant past information that may influence purchase decisions. There is some evidence to suggest that this variable can be measured more completely than is typically done by concentrating on the degree of uncertainty felt by consumers in a purchase situation.[17] Consumer uncertainty has been shown to be related to information processing efforts of consumers.[18] Consequently, this variable may be of even greater interest to organizations in the future as measurement techniques improve and additional research sheds more light on the role played by past information and experience in consumer purchase decisions.

Of all the consumer characteristics shown in Figure 9–2, the greatest conceptual and empirical attention has been given to consumer *attitudes*. As is true for most behavioral variables, there is some controversy as to exactly what an attitude is. For manager purposes, though, an attitude is a learned tendency to respond to some object (e.g., a product, organization, person, product features, etc.) in a consistent way. Attitudes are developed from a person's past information and experiences (i.e., a learned tendency), and so are important for further explaining the regularity of consumer behavior.

The controversy over definition of an attitude concerns the meaning of "tendency to respond." Some view attitude as a unidimensional concept by classifying an attitudinal response as either a favorable or unfavorable feeling toward some object.[19] In this view, an attitude is an evaluative response showing like or dislike. Others consider attitudes as comprised of at least two different but related dimensions: (1) affective (like-dislike) dimension, and (2) cognitive dimension (the beliefs or knowledge that a person has about an object).[20] The affective dimension would be apparent in the statement, "I like Crest toothpaste," while the cognitive dimension would be reflected in the quite different statement, "Crest toothpaste has fluoride." The latter statement only expresses what a person believes about Crest but says nothing about how that person

---

[17] Robert B. Woodruff, "Measurement of Consumers' Prior Brand Information," *Journal of Marketing Research,* August 1972, pp. 258–64, published by the American Marketing Association.

[18] Robert B. Woodruff, "Brand Information Sources, Opinion Change, and Uncertainty," *Journal of Marketing Research,* vol. 9, November 1972, pp. 414–18, published by the American Marketing Association.

[19] Martin Fishbein, "A Behavior Theory Approach to the Relations between Beliefs about an Object and the Attitude toward the Object," in Martin Fishbein (ed.), *Readings in Attitude Theory and Measurement* (New York: John Wiley & Sons, 1967), p. 389.

[20] Daniel Katz, "The Functional Approach to the Study of Attitudes," ibid., p. 459–60.

evaluates the product (some like toothpastes with flouride, others do not.) Finally, some consider attitude as having, in addition to the affective and cognitive dimensions, a conative or a behavioral component referring to a person's tendency to act toward an object.[21] This would be reflected, for example, in the intentions statement, "I intend to buy Crest toothpaste on my next shopping trip."

Of what importance is this definitional issue to managers? The measurement of customers' attitudes in a research study is based upon the researcher's definition of an attitude. Therefore, to interpret and act upon attitudinal information, a manager should understand which attitude concept is reflected in the measures. Moreover, a manager's expectations as to the ability of attitudinal information to predict future consumer behavior should be tempered by which conceptualization was used. Having information only on the affective feelings of consumers (unidimensional concept) will most likely not predict customer purchases as well as information on affective, cognitive, and behavioral dimensions. For example, knowing that a consumer likes Mercedes-Benz automobiles will not help managers predict what brand of auto will be purchased nearly as much as if they also knew that the consumer had read extensively about Mercedes in car magazines and talked with friends (cognitive dimension), and has a very strong intention to buy Mercedes within the next three months (behavioral dimension).

For purposes of managerial application, how an attitude is defined is much less important than the availability of information on affective feelings, beliefs, and behavioral tendencies. Clearly, all three concepts are highly interrelated, whether they are viewed as combining to form an attitude or considered to be separate variables. Managers and researchers should heed the caution voiced by a leading proponent of the unidimensional (affective) view of attitudes:

> Taking a unidimensional view of attitude does not imply that one should ignore cognition and conation. Rather, it implies that beliefs and behavioral intentions must be studied in their own right, as independent phenomena that may be related to behavior. Thus, the problem is not simply to investigate relationships between attitude and behavior; rather, one must be concerned with at least four things: attitudes, beliefs, behavior intentions, and behavior. The problem, then, is to investigate the interrelationships among all four of these concepts.[22]

The combined buyer characteristics performs a very important function for individuals. Attitudes, personality traits and motives, past information and experience, and evaluative criteria act as a kind of *filter*

---

[21] Harry C. Triandis, "Exploratory Factor Analysis of the Behavioral Component of Social Attitudes," ibid, p. 208.

[22] Martin Fishbein, "Attitude and the Prediction of Behavior," in Fishbein (ed.), *Readings in Attitude Theory and Measurement*, p. 479.

through which people process information (stimuli) continually coming from their environment. For example, a consumer's needs and motives influence which stimuli will receive attention and which will not. Attitudes, traits, and past experience help consumers interpret and comprehend stimuli that have gained attention. These characteristics and their impact on consumer information processes help to explain why people can and do respond quite differently to the same offer. For example, some may feel that only American built, high priced cars (Cadillac, Continental, etc.) are prestigious, while others may believe that an auto must be of European origin (Mercedes, Jaguar, etc.) to be prestigious. The uniqueness of individual buyers evidenced by these buyers characteristics demonstrates that management needs to delineate the boundaries on target markets carefully in order to separate those people who will respond favorably to an offer from those who will not. Offers can then be tailored to fit more exactly the needs and characteristics of buyers comprising target markets.

Consumer Decision Processes.   One of the most important features of the EKB model is the depiction of consumer purchasing as a process comprised of several stages rather than a single act of buying or not buying. There is considerable variation in the processes consumers go through, but for conceptual purposes, these can be grouped into three basic types. An *extended decision process* is the most complete type of decision making. It begins when a consumer recognizes a problem which might be solved by the purchase of some product. This encourages a consumer to search for product and/or brand information to evaluate how well each of several alternatives will solve the problem. Product and brand evaluations lead to a purchase decision, and then the outcome of the decisions is evaluated.

Extended buying decision processes are most likely to occur when the product being considered has never been purchased before, is not repurchased very frequently, or is particularly important to the consumer (e.g., the product may be very expensive, a gift, highly visible to others, or used for a long time).[23] For less important or more routine purchases decisions, a consumer may only go through a *limited decision process* by evaluating only those product/brand alternatives already known with no attempt to search for new alternatives. Finally, *habitual decision making* is the least complicated type of process where a consumer, upon recognizing a problem, proceeds directly to making a purchase decision on a favorite brand.

As shown in the EKB model, consumer decision making is influenced by person characteristics as well as by the processing of information. For example, suppose RCA runs a year-end sale on color televisions.

---

[23] Blackwell, Engel, and Kollat, *Cases in Consumer Behavior,* pp. 60–61.

Some consumers will be exposed to and attentive toward RCA's advertisements of price reductions. Further, based on their past experience and knowledge of RCA prices as well as attitudes toward RCA quality, many of these consumers will comprehend the sale prices as a worthwhile savings for a high quality brand. This may, in turn, trigger problem recognition (a need for a new television), and since a color television is an important purchase, the consumer goes through an extended decision process. Memory may be searched further for past experiences and knowledge of RCA as well as other alternative brands. Evaluative criteria emerge to guide information search and processing. The consumer may seek information about the availability of other brands as well as about how well these brands will satisfy evaluative criteria. Sources of this information may include advertisements, sales brochures, dealer salesmen, family members and friends, and reports from product testing organizations.

The decision as to whether or not to buy a color television, and if so, which brand is partially the outcome of this evaluation process. However, the decision is also the result of such other situation factors as whether a satisfactory dealer can be found who handles the desired brand, whether this dealer has the desired model in stock, and whether financial resources are still sufficient at the time of purchase to pay for the model selected. Finally, the process does not stop with a purchase decision. The consumer will use the new color television, and will evaluate the ability of the chosen brand to satisfy needs. In fact, new problems may be recognized as a result of the purchase which would lead to a new decision process. For example, the consumer may recognize a need for accoutrements to decorate the top of the new television.

The EKB model's emphasis on consumer decision processes rather than on just the outcome of a purchase decision is important. Managers need to learn about consumers' activities during the stages *prior to* purchase in order to understand why particular choices were made. Information showing that consumers rated the firm's brand as inferior to new competitive brands on one or more important evaluative criteria may help to explain a declining sales trend, for instance. Or, survey results that uncover the fact that consumers in a test market are largely unaware of the firm's new brand may explain poor test market sales.

In addition, managers may set objectives for marketing mix decisions in terms of desired consumer behavior at decision process stages other than the purchase stage. For example, if a firm knew that a significant number of customers were evaluating its brand quite low on a key evaluative criterion dimension, an objective for advertising (upon determining that the brand does, in fact, perform well on this dimension) might be to provide information that will encourage these customers to change their evaluation. The rationale is, of course, that if advertising accomplished this objective, the likelihood of these customers now deciding to buy the firm's product would be increased.

Environmental Influences. A variety of environmental variables also help to explain consumer purchases. The EKB model appropriately shows such environmental factors as income, culture, social class, and family influencing consumers activities at each of the decision process stages. As an illustration, a family's social class ranking in a community may influence which magazines and television shows will be viewed, which, in turn, determine which advertisements will (and will not) be seen.

Environmental influences help to shape a consumer's life style. Life style refers to a characteristic way of living or an approach to life adopted by an individual or group. This is reflected in the way people allocate their time, energy, and money. For example, one person may desire a very active, socially involved life style by participating in sports, joining clubs, frequently entertaining friends, and working in political organizations. Another may adopt a more quiet, leisurely-paced life style by watching rather than playing sports, reading books, infrequently entertaining, and working crossword puzzles. While these life styles are quite different, each is influential in determining what these individuals want to do in life. Of particular importance for marketing managers is the fact that people buy products to enhance their life styles. The heavy buyer of sporting equipment, for instance, is probably trying to maintain the more active type of life style.

Household Decision Making. The EKB model is an *individual* decision process model since it views a single consumer as the basic decision making unit. The model does recognize influences from other people, but the central focus is still on the individual. For some firms households may be the more relevant unit of analysis. The household is generally the primary income earning unit, and therefore, income is more likely to be a household asset rather than an individual asset.

Moreover, for many consumer goods purchases there is some degree of joint effort between various household members during a decision process. This accounts for important differences from individual decision making. For example, there is clearly a potential for conflict to occur between those members involved in a buying decision process. Since conflict may result in a decision not to buy, it is an important factor for managers to consider. Some kinds of products and services are more likely to involve conflict than others. In these cases, managers should understand the reasons for conflict as well as how conflict is resolved to better predict future buying decisions.

Multiple household member involvement also may lead to allocation of the decision process tasks to the various members. Here a manager should know which members are performing what activities in each stage. For example, while husbands may be most likely to recognize a need for a particular product such as autos, the seeking of information may be shared by husbands, wives, and even children where each member gathers information about those evaluative criteria important to them. Marketing mix decisions intended to reach consumers at each stage should recognize the different roles played by household members during the decision process.

Application of the EKB Model: An Illustration[24]

A large department store in a southern city had a well-developed marketing strategy for its clothing departments that centered around maintaining an image of fashion leadership and quality merchandise. Store management was relatively pleased with the success of this strategy in their primary markets. However, management was interested in gaining access to a group of potential customers that they believed had not been reached. A large state university was located in the same city, and so it was felt that there was considerable potential for clothing sales to students. Yet, for unknown reasons, students did not seem to patronize the store very much. Consequently, management decided to gather survey information on student buying decision processes for clothing in order to discover the reasons for student reluctance to shop at their store. More specifically, the purpose of the project was to determine how the store's offer (merchandise, fashion guidance, advertising, etc.) might be tailored to better fit the needs of students in order to encourage greater student patronage.

Information about this potential market segment was provided by survey questionnaires completed by a sample of students attending classes at the University. Using the EKB model as a framework, the questionnaire was designed to identify important student characteristics and to provide insights into the decision process that students were using to decide upon stores in which to shop for clothing. Selected findings from this survey are presented.

Student Demographic Characteristics. In order to check on how well the sample represented the entire student population, data on demographic characteristics were collected (Table 9–1). This information also provided management with a better description of the target market. For example, over 30 percent of the sample students were over 22. While this is still quite young, management's belief that students were primarily under 22 caused the firm to overlook a significantly large percentage of students. In addition, the percentage of students who did not belong to fraternities or sororities was more than three times as large as the percentage that did belong. This suggested that the Greek organizations

---

[24] The research discussed in this section was undertaken as a graduate class project at the University of Tennessee.

TABLE 9–1

Student Demographic Characteristics

Characteristic	Percent
Age	
17–19	38.3
20–21	31.0
22–24	16.4
Over 24	14.3
Sex	
Male	44.5
Female	55.5
Marital status	
Married	16.8
Single	83.2
Sorority/fraternity membership	
Member	23.7
Nonmember	76.3

were not nearly as important as reference groups for fashion adoption as was previously believed by management.

Clothing Decision Process. Applying the decision process portion of the EKB model, the analysis concentrated on student store selection processes. Little insight into the reasons for *problem recognition* was provided by the study. However, the analysis showed that a particular situation, going back to school in the fall, was an important factor in causing students to recognize a need for clothing. This was largely uncontrollable by store management. The information was useful to management, though, because it helped to explain why a large percentage (over 50 percent) of students bought most of their clothes outside the city.

The study did provide considerable insight into the *search and alternative evaluation* part of student decision processes. Students were asked to rank the importance of several sources of clothing-fashion information according to how each one influenced their purchase decisions. As shown in Table 9–2, two information sources controllable by store management, advertising and store displays, were ranked only slightly less important than information provided by friends, classmates, and personal preference. However, sales personnel and fashion shows were rated significantly less important than the other sources. This was particularly enlightening to management because they had been depending almost entirely on fashion shows to draw students into the store, and then using sales personnel to help them select the most appropriate fashion. Almost no advertising was being aimed directly to students.

To examine student store choice decisions further, the study provided comprehensive attitude information toward the store and a major com-

TABLE 9–2

Importance Rankings of Buyer Information Sources

Fashion Information Source	Average Rank (1 = most important, 2 = next important, etc.)
Personal preference........................	1.88
Friends and classmates....................	2.26
Advertising..............................	2.75
Store displays...........................	2.81
Sales personnel..........................	4.26
Fashion shows...........................	4.59

petitor. This information was obtained by semantic differential scales, a commonly used quantitative measurement technique. Notice in Table 9–3 that the scales were designed to measure attitudes toward specific store dimensions. These were believed by management to correspond to students' evaluative criteria for store choice decisions.

The attitude information reflected how students evaluated each of the two stores. Upon analyzing and interpreting the data, management was able to improve its understanding of student behavior significantly at the search and evaluation stage of the store selection process. For example, management was very pleased with the favorableness of attitudes toward merchandise offerings. Their store was rated above the competitive store on the first three criteria in Table 9–3 (type, quality, and brands of clothing) in addition to having over 60 percent of the sample checking the two most favorable categories (extremely and slightly) for each one. Moreover, advertising to students appeared to be far more effective than management had expected. Over 50 percent of the sample were frequently being exposed to the store's advertising and almost 60 percent felt it was appealing and informative. Given that the advertising had not been designed (in message or media) to appeal directly to students, this finding was particularly encouraging.

Data on the remaining three evaluative criteria—comparative prices, value for dollars spent, and sales personnel—suggested possible reasons for lack of student patronage. Students believed the store was charging relatively high prices for its merchandise, while the value received for dollars spent was rated quite unfavorable. Since quality of merchandise was evaluated highly, the cause was narrowed to either past price decisions made by management or to the possibility that value for dollars spent was not being communicated effectively in their promotional strategy. In addition, sales personnel were not viewed as being particularly friendly or courteous by over 50 percent of the students. Since the sales force was considered by management to be a critical part of

TABLE 9-3

Students' Attitude Ratings of the Store under Study and a Competitor

Store Dimension	Extremely	Slightly	Neither One nor the Other	Slightly	Extremely	Store Dimension
Wide selection of different types of clothing	38.4 (23.1)*	38.4 (44.5)	11.6 (17.4)	7.8 (9.7)	3.8 (5.3)	Limited selection of different types of clothing
High quality of merchandise	31.7 (28.3)	47.9 (47.0)	14.6 (17.4)	4.2 (6.5)	1.6 (0.8)	Low quality of merchandise
Numerous brands	23.6 (18.4)	39.5 (41.6)	19.5 (22.9)	13.2 (13.9)	4.2 (3.2)	Few brands
Appealing, informative advertising	20.4 (18.6)	37.1 (30.9)	28.2 (30.5)	9.4 (15.0)	4.9 (5.0)	Unappealing, uninformative advertising
Advertisements frequently seen by you	23.7 (22.7)	28.0 (25.9)	24.6 (25.5)	16.1 (17.3)	7.6 (8.6)	Advertisements seldom seen by you
Low prices compared to other stores	1.3 (0.4)	8.9 (11.1)	24.2 (27.5)	34.7 (38.9)	30.9 (22.1)	High prices compared to other stores
High value for dollars spent	5.9 (8.2)	21.6 (23.0)	37.7 (34.2)	22.5 (21.4)	12.3 (13.2)	Low value for dollars spent
Friendly, courteous sales personnel	18.1 (11.3)	29.8 (33.5)	29.4 (25.8)	13.0 (18.1)	9.7 (11.3)	Cold, discourteous sales personnel

* The first number in each scale location is the percentage of respondents who checked that scale value for the store under study. The second number, in parentheses, is the percentage of respondents who checked that scale value for the competitive store.

TABLE 9–4

Preference for Type of Store for Clothing Purchases

Type of Store	Percent Most Preferring
Department store	51
Specialty shop	28
Discount store	21

its selling strategy, these results were very disturbing. Note also that the competitive store was having similar problems, though not quite to the same extent.

Several insights into student *purchasing processes* for clothing were gained from the study. Management was pleased to learn that about half of the students preferred to buy their clothing in a department store more than other types of stores, as shown in Table 9–4. However, about the same percentage, 52 percent, were not buying very much of their clothing in the city, as shown in Table 9–5. This suggested that students were arriving on campus in the fall or from vacation periods with most clothing purchase decisions already made.

Store Decisions Based on Results of the Study. Overall, the survey of student store selection processes was instrumental in guiding management's subsequent marketing decisions. Because of students' buying power coupled with the fact that student attitudes toward the store's merchandise were more favorable than had been expected, it was decided to allocate more resources to the student market segment. Beginning with advertising, a portion of the ad budget was aimed directly at increasing student patronage. Media having a high percentage of students in their audiences (e.g., the student newspaper, student radio station, and the local radio station appealing largely to young people) were included in the media schedule. Messages were designed to provide information on specific fashions available at the store and to emphasize the general theme of fashion leadership. This was the same message strategy used in all advertising since the survey had shown that

TABLE 9–5

Geographical Location of Clothing Purchases

Location of Purchases	Percentage
Outside the city	52
In the city—downtown	20
In the city—shopping centers	21
In the city—shops near campus	7

student attitudes toward previous advertising were basically favorable. Yet, the use of popular words, a generally irreverent tone, and the stressing of fashion as an expression of individuality were important differences from advertising messages aimed at other segments.

Sales promotion decisions responded to several weaknesses in previous tactics as shown by the study. The low rating given to fashion shows as a clothing information source caused management to discontinue their major fashion shows. These shows had been quite elaborate affairs with many models, varieties of fashions, considerable lighting and sound equipment, and correspondingly high costs. To justify this expense, audiences had to be large (which they had not been for several years). It was felt, based partly on informal discussions with students, as well as on the survey, that this format was inappropriate. But rather than give up completely on the fashion show, management decided to use a highly mobile and rather small unit to put on future shows. A van was outfitted with equipment for a mini-fashion show with only two or three fashion models that could easily travel from place to place, was very simple to set up and operate, and was comparatively inexpensive. Furthermore, the emphasis was on disseminating fashion knowledge rather than showing a wide variety of fashion items. This show could be given to both large and small groups and without much advance notice or preparation.

A second sales promotion decision concerned a store booth to be set up at fall student registration at the University. The booth provided refreshments for students and at the same time disseminated information on current fashions, location of the store, and available store merchandise. Management believed that this booth would demonstrate the store's interest in students as customers as well as their ability to serve students.

Finally, because student attitudes toward store personnel were not highly favorable, the personnel training program was reevaluated. The objectives of the program were modified to ensure that fashion knowledge as well as the appropriate interest in customers' needs were being taught. While this change in training emphasis was considered important for future dealings with all customers, management expected that it would improve student attitudes toward store personnel.

THE "STATE OF THE ART" IN BUYER BEHAVIOR

While having a model framework is essential for managers, there is an additional skill that will aid in applications of buyer behavior information. Marketing managers may have to interact with researchers (inside the organization or in other organizations) who are specialists in behavioral theory and concepts as well as research methodology. To be able to communicate with researchers, managers must have a general awareness of the "state of the art" in the field of buyer behavior. This awareness will allow managers to "speak the language" of the specialist. Moreover, managers will be in a better position to develop realistic expectations as to how helpful research information will be for a particular decision. Equally importantly, it will allow the manager to engage actively in setting objectives to guide the acquisition of information.

Buyer Behavior—A Youthful Discipline

Applications of research information concerning buyers are generally based on some theoretical or conceptual beliefs about the nature and causes of buyer behavior. For example, the use of attitude information by the department store's management was based on the theoretical belief that attitudes are an important cause of buying behavior. Naturally, management's success in using this information for marketing decisions depends on how well this belief describes student store selection decisions. Because of the unavoidable connection between theory and application, management should have a general awareness of how far the field has advanced in concept, theory, and measurement sophistication.

Theory of Buyer Behavior. The study of buyer behavior is a very young discipline when compared to the physical sciences and even other behavioral sicences. In fact, one has to go back no more than 15 to 20 years to account for most of the conceptual and empirical work that has contributed to an understanding of consumer decision making. Moreover, since the interest in this discipline is accelerating quite rapidly, the next 15 to 20 years will likely produce more advances than the entire history of consumer behavior research to date.

One particularly important consequence of the youth of this discipline is that buyer behavior analysts have not had sufficient time to develop and test a comprehensive, general theory of buyer behavior. The lack of a general theory, particularly one that has a solid empirical foundation, means that the various studies of behavior performed by organizations do not have a single, accepted theoretical basis for determining which variables and relationships must be measured, and what interpretations should be made from the resulting data. In fact, there are often competing theories, each with some empirical support, and each with a following among researchers.

Buyer Research Methods. Consistent with the early stage of theory development is the apparent diversity of opinion as to the most appropriate ways to gather some kinds of buyer information. Part of the reason for this is that there are differing conceptualizations of the same variables.[25] Unfortunately, when definitions of variables differ among re-searchers, so can the methods for measuring those variables, and, there-fore, the resulting information provided to management. Consequently, managers must be alert to the potential for varying definitions under-lying information in research reports in order to assess implications for use of the information. Of course, a manager may have to rely on the researcher to explain the conceptualization of variables included in a study, and to help determine how best to apply the results.

Management Implications

Because the discipline of buyer behavior is young, managers must develop realistic expectations as to the potential usefulness of buyer behavior information from research. Clearly, unquestioning reliance on behavioral studies is as undesirable as totally rejecting this source of market information. Managers must understand that there are theoreti-cal, definitional, and methodological limitations to buyer behavior as a discipline. This fact emphasizes the need for managers to interact with the research specialist during all of the design, analysis, and interpreta-tive stages of the research process, so that enlightened judgments on the appropriate extent of reliance on this source of information can be made.

Again, it is stressed that managers cannot (and need not) have the same level of expertise as the research specialist. But a manager must understand enough to be able to communicate with specialists about the objectives for behavioral research and interpretation of results. Since managers are much more aware of their information needs for particular decision tasks than are specialists, managers should be involved in setting specific research objectives. However, research objectives also must reflect what information can realistically be provided within technical (theory and method) and cost limitations which is the re-searcher's domain of expertise. Consequently, these objectives should be set jointly by managers and researchers and to effectively accomplish this requires that each have at least a general understanding of the other's problems and needs. Moreover, interpretation of results of a study will invariably reflect the researcher's theoretical underpinnings and so, the manager must be able to question and discuss these interpretations with the specialist. Management decision makers can develop and main-tain sufficient expertise in the field by starting with a model framework

---

[25] One explanation for differing variable definitions is that many buyer variables cannot be directly seen, but must be inferred from observing behavior (e.g., buying decisions, response to a questionnaire). For example, managers cannot directly see their customers' attitudes, but must infer them from their customers' behavior. This inference process can lead to different interpretations of the same variable.

firmly in mind, then periodically interacting with research specialists, and selectively reviewing the various literature (particularly summaries of basic research areas and discussions of major advancements or breakthroughs) available on buyer behavior. For example, research specialists may be asked to periodically review with management the most recent developments in the state of the art.

INDUSTRIAL BUYING BEHAVIOR

The discussion so far has primarily focused on the buying behavior of consumers. This should not obscure the fact that consumers represent only a portion of all buyers. Business firms and other types of organizations also buy goods and services, and so, for many sellers, industrial buying behavior is of paramount concern. Managers of these firms have no less a need to develop a framework for understanding their buyers as well as understand the "state of the art" in the field of industrial buying behavior. To help build these perspectives, consider the industrial buyer behavior model shown in Figure 9–3. This model sug-

FIGURE 9–3

An Integrative Model of Industrial Buying Behavior

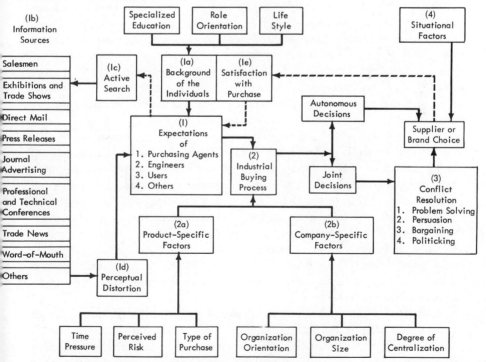

Source: Jagdish N. Sheth, "A Model of Industrial Buying Behavior," *Journal of Marketing*, vol. 37 (October 1973), p. 51, published by the American Marketing Association.

gests both similarities and important differences between industrial and consumer buying.

Differences in Industrial and Consumer Buying

The differences between industrial and consumer buying stem largely from the fact that industrial buyers are professional employees of a formal organization, while consumers are not. Such factors as organizational characteristics, expectations of buyers, buyer characteristics, and the nature of demand account for these important differences.

Since industrial buyers must purchase products and services within the context of an organization, the *characteristics of that organization* will influence buying decisions. These are the company-specific factors in the Sheth model. The size of the buying firm will dictate quantity needs, for instance. Moreover, the relative importance of different organizational functions and the degree of decision centralization determines who in the firm will make buying decisions. For example, a firm dominated by engineers and quality control specialists will have people from these functions influencing many purchase decisions.

Organizational factors significantly change the selling task from that faced by consumer-goods companies. Industrial sellers frequently can and must deal directly with at least the more important endusers. Each industrial buyer purchases in greater quantities and accounts for a larger portion of a seller's total sales. Correspondingly, there are fewer industrial buyers comprising a market. A large consumer-goods company such as Procter & Gamble must sell to millions of endusers, while a large packaging firm deals primarily with a few hundred firms. This allows industrial sellers to concentrate on individual customers by offering more personalized services than can a consumer-goods firm.

For many industrial buying decisions, a rather large number of people can be involved in the process including product users, engineers, top level management from financial control, purchasing agents, and research and development specialists. This complicates the task for industrial sellers trying to understand the decision process as well as causes misallocation of resources. For example, industrial salesmen may spend too much time with company purchasing agents because of their accessibility when other company personnel such as quality control engineers may have more influence on the decision. Identifying the key decision makers in buying organizations is essential so that marketing effort can be directed toward them.

Industrial *buyer's motives and related evaluative criteria* (i.e., the expectations of purchasing agents, engineers, users, and others in Sheth's model) are often dominated by economic and technical kinds of considerations. One study of determinants of vendor selection found such factors as delivery reliability, quality/price ratio, general vendor reputation, vendor location, reciprocity relationships, supply of information and marketing services, technical ability and knowledge, and technical innovativeness were important to buyers.[26] Compare these with common consumer evaluative criteria such as prestige, aestheticness, convenience, image, taste, and style. Thus, industrial sellers may have less difficulty understanding customer buying criteria except in situations where sellers' products are rather similar. Then industrial buyers may turn to less economic criteria such as personnel services offered by a seller's salesman (e.g., gifts, dinner entertaining, help in solving company problems related to use of a product, etc.) to choose between suppliers.

Since industrial purchase decisions are made by employees, the *background and characteristics of these individuals* are influencing variables. Industrial buyers are likely to have greater training and technical knowledge of needed products than do consumers. This is true particularly when technical people in addition to the purchasing agent (e.g., scientists, engineers, quality control specialists, production managers, etc.) are involved in a buying decision. Thus, industrial seller's marketing mix is likely to have a more technical orientation than a consumer-goods firm's offer. For example, industrial promotional efforts are likely to be much more concerned with the technical specifications of products offered for sale.

Finally, the *nature of demand* for industrial products has added dimensions beyond that faced by consumer goods sellers. Typically, demand for industrial products is derived from demand for the buying firm's products. This complicates the task of understanding and predicting industrial buying behavior. For instance, a demand analysis for a furniture manufacturer must assess consumer furniture purchase decisions. The same kind of analysis for a furniture parts fabricator selling preassembled furniture components (e.g., chair frames) to furniture manufacturers might have to assess both consumer furniture demand and the buying process of furniture manufacturers to predict sales. Moreover, industrial buyers typically choose a supplier rather than just a product which means that a company and its product are being evaluated simultaneously. Thus, evaluative criteria and motives are both company and product specific. Consumer evaluative criteria are more concerned with the product.

There is also likely to be a longer lead time between marketing effort of selling firms and an industrial buying decision than is typical of consumer buying.[27] An IBM salesman may work with a company for several

---

[26] Yoram Wind, Paul E. Green, and Patrick J. Robinson, "The Determinants of Vendor Selection: The Evaluation Function Approach," *Journal of Purchasing*, August 1968, p. 37.

[27] Frederick Webster, "Industrial Buying Behavior: A State-of-the-Art Appraisal," in B. A. Morin (ed.), *Marketing in a Changing World* (Chicago: American Marketing Association, 1969), p. 258.

years before a decision is made to buy computing equipment, for instance. This means that the industrial seller may often have a more difficult task of evaluating how effective marketing effort has been in influencing industrial demand.

Similarities between Industrial and Consumer Buying

Care should be taken not to overemphasize the differences between industrial and consumer buying. There are some striking similarities which are due primarily to the fact that in each case people are making buying decisions. The Sheth industrial buying model shown in Figure 9–3 has several components that compare closely with components included in the EKB model (see Figure 9–2). Of particular significance are the similarities in individual characteristics, description of decision making as a process, and the distinct types of decision processes.

The Sheth model recognizes the importance of individual characteristics as possible influences on industrial buying. Thus, to fully understand industrial buying behavior industrial sellers cannot be content with classifying and analyzing buying organizations. There is also a need to learn about the people in buying organizations who are involved in purchase decisions. Individual characteristics such as attitudes, life styles, personality traits, and past information and experience that are so important to understanding consumer behavior also contribute to understanding industrial buying behavior. Moreover, industrial and consumer buying decisions can be group decisions. The purchasing agent is often not the most influential person in an industrial buying process. This increases the potential for conflict between people in both kinds of buying decisions, and a corresponding need for sellers to understand how conflict is resolved.

Another similarity is apparent in the view of industrial and consumer buying as a process comprised of stages rather than a single act. Both types of decision making are designed to solve problems as perceived by those involved in the purchase decision. The marketing task is essentially the same since offers have to be developed that will provide solutions to customer problems. Moreover, customers must be convinced during alternative search and evaluation decision stages of the competitive effectiveness of the firm's offer. Thus, the decision process concept provides a conceptual framework for understanding industrial as well as consumer buying.

Consumer decision making processes differ in the extent to which a buyer goes through each of the process stages (e.g., extended, limited, and habitual decision processes). Industrial buying can be similarly classified depending on how new the purchasing task is to the buying organization. For example, an extended decision process is likely to be used in a major one-time-only purchase, such as for a plant or expensive equipment. In these cases, considerable time, information seeking, and supplier evaluation may be needed before a purchase decision is made. Some shortcutting of stages (limited and habitual decision making) will occur for rebuys which are more frequently purchased items such as some raw materials and cleaning supplies. These decision types require different marketing approaches by industrial sellers.[28]

Industrial Buyer Behavior Research State of the Art

Based on published research on buyer behavior, considerably more attention is being devoted to consumer behavior than to industrial buying behavior. For example, in the development of models, the consumer behavior field is more advanced, particularly in the empirical support underlying model variables and relationships. The importance of models as managerial frameworks has been acknowledged, yet only quite recently have comprehensive industrial buying behavior models been published for widespread usage.[29] Beyond the application of buyer models, there does not appear to be nearly as much research effort directed toward identifying and examining relationships between industrial buying and various influences on buying as in the field of consumer behavior.

There are a number of possible reasons for the lesser attention given to industrial buying behavior. Industrial sellers may depend heavily on the relationship between salesmen and individual customers for their understanding of market behavior. Salesmen and sales managers have more contact with fewer buyers, and consequently, have the opportunity to develop more permanent relationships. Moreover, buyer motives, dominated by economic/engineering considerations, are believed to be less difficult to understand. This may also account for a more product orientation among industrial sellers. The industrial goods firms have been slower to adopt the customer-oriented concept. Combined, these reasons suggest that industrial sellers feel less need for buyer behavior research and are more willing to rely on personal experience and judgment when dealing with buyers.[30]

There is a need for more work to develop a better understanding of industrial buying behavior. The usefulness of behavioral information has

---

[28] Frederick E. Webster, Jr., and Yoram Wind, *Organizational Buying Behavior* (Englewood Cliffs, N.J.: Prentice-Hall, 1972), pp. 5–6.

[29] See Frederick Webster, Jr., and Yoram Wind, "A General Model for Understanding Organizational Buying Behavior," *Journal of Marketing*, vol. 36 (April 1972), pp. 12–19; and Jagdish N. Sheth, "A Model of Industrial Buyer Behavior," *Journal of Marketing*, vol. 37 (October 1973), pp. 50–56.

[30] For a more in-depth assessment of the reasons for lack of industrial buying behavior research, see Webster, "Industrial Buying Behavior," pp. 257–59.

been demonstrated sufficiently by consumer marketers to suggest the potential payoffs from greater attention to industrial buying. Moreover, because of the important similarities between consumer and industrial buying, there may be considerable opportunity for transfer of knowledge between the two areas.

SUMMARY AND CONCLUSIONS

Understanding buyer behavior is clearly one of the most important kinds of expertise that a marketing manager must bring to organizational and business decision making. At the same time, marketing managers in middle and upper management levels are often prevented from having direct contact on a regular basis with customers. Consequently, they must frequently rely on behavioral information from marketing intelligence and research activities to have any chance of fulfilling this responsibility. To develop and maintain needed market expertise, a manager must have a comprehensive framework (model) representing the key variables, interrelationships, and processes that underly his customers' behavior. Moreover, familiarity must be developed and maintained with the usefulness and limitations of intelligence and research as a major source of information for "filling in" the framework.

While this chapter is a start toward developing the needed skills for applying buyer behavior information to decision making, maintaining this expertise is a career-long task. Advancements in models, concepts, methods, theories, and empirical support will continue to be rather rapid. So, a marketing manager must identify ways to maintain general awareness of the state of the art as it increases in sophistication. Fortunately, there are a variety of ways available: (1) attend annual meetings of major associations such as the American Marketing Association and the Association for Consumer Research; (2) read summary and overview articles in publications of these associations; (3) interact with research specialists inside and/or outside the organization; (4) read articles on the topic in such business publications as *Fortune, Business Week,* and *Advertising Age;* (5) attend executive development programs; and (6) review new textbooks on buyer behavior when they are first published. Most of these activities should be carried out, in any case, to keep abreast of developments in management practices, so it is merely a matter of adding buyer behavior to the list of topics in which a manager wants to keep current.

EXERCISES FOR REVIEW AND DISCUSSION

1. The Federal Trade Commission (FTC) is currently faced with regulation decisions that will affect both consumer buying and marketing decisions in business firms. As an example, the FTC is examining regulation proposals

that will place restrictions on advertising content. Explain the role that buyer behavior research can play in helping FTC commissioners with these kinds of decisions.

2. A national fast-food chain has been faced with a persistent decline in sales and market share. Marketing managers believe the problem has been caused by market changes that have not received adequate response by the firm. So, a major research program has been proposed to study fast-food buyers. Describe how the EKB model can be used to guide this research effort.

3. Compare and contrast the probable buyer decision processes for the purchase of a refrigerator by consumers and the purchase of an important machine to be used in a firm's production line.

4. Suppose you were elected to the administrative board of a church in your community. The church has experienced, at best, stable membership and declining attendance at functions. Adapt the EKB model of buyer behavior to the situation faced by the church (e.g., who are the churches' "buyers," what is the "buying" decision process, what are key "buyer" influences, etc.), as the basis for recommending corrective action to the board.

5. Explain how the buyer behavior concepts of life style and attitudes might be useful to the distributor of a line of wine.

6. Buyer behavior models are, currently, descriptive in nature since the focus for studying buyer behavior is on explaining how buyers actually decide on products and brands. Is there any need for normative models of buyer behavior (i.e., models that prescribe how buyers ought to decide)? Discuss.

7. A key feature of most comprehensive models of buyer behavior is the description of buying as a decision process comprised of multiple stages. What is the significance of the buying as a process concept to marketing decision making?

part four

Marketing Strategy and Decision Making

Formulation of marketing strategy should lead to an integrated marketing program for achieving the firm's objectives in the marketplace. Designing marketing strategy involves assembling the marketing mix into the marketing program which is comprised of the product or service, channels of distribution, price, advertising, and sales force. This part of the book presents certain basic concepts for use in strategy design; provides necessary guidelines for decision making and marketing information planning; and develops essential concepts and methods needed for planning the marketing program. The material discusses and illustrates important concepts, approaches to analysis, and planning tools for use in decision analysis of the various mix components which are considered in Part V. Additionally, Part IV examines the task of assembling the marketing mix components into an integrated marketing program.

In Chapter 10, "Corporate and Marketing Strategy," the relationship of marketing strategy is considered in the context of the firm's overall mission and purpose. A framework is developed for identifying and describing alternative marketing strategy situations that may be encountered by a given organization based on the chosen product-market areas of the firm. The implications of marketing strategy positioning are examined with regard to marketing program planning. Major factors influencing the design of the marketing organization are discussed.

Chapter 11, "Decision Making Concepts and Models," presents decision making as an analytical process comprised of problem analysis, selection of alternatives, and control of actions taken. Using this process model, decision making tasks are categorized by certainty, risk, and uncertainty. An overview is provided of the types of models which can be used by the marketing manager in his decision making activities.

319

In Chapter 12, "Marketing Information Planning," the key role of information in reducing the uncertainty surrounding decision making is examined. Information is linked to the decision making process and an integrated approach to planning for and acquiring needed information is developed. An essential part of the approach is the important task of assessing benefits and costs of information for decision making. The roles of the decision maker and the information specialist are considered in terms of the various stages in planning for needed information.

Chapter 13, "Planning the Marketing Program," building on the three previous chapters, considers various aspects of programming the marketing mix. Different levels of marketing program analysis are described and illustrated including market response, single variable analysis (e.g., advertising), and multiple variable decisions. The marketing plan is presented as a tool for guiding the development, implementation, and control of marketing strategy which, in turn, provides a basis for analyzing each marketing mix element.

10

Corporate and Marketing
Strategy

The strategic business planning concept adopted by the General Electric Company in 1970 illustrates the linkage between corporate and marketing strategy and the types of decisions that are involved in marketing strategy design.[1] The approach consists of detailed assessment of market share, growth estimates, profitability, and cash generating power of each existing and proposed business unit of the company. This type of comprehensive appraisal or situation analysis can identify opportunities and problem areas which provide a basis for strategic planning activities. For example, application of the strategic planning concept in GE's Housewares Business Division resulted in an interrelated sequence of corporate and marketing strategy decisions:

1. In November 1971, a new division manager was appointed. He reorganized the division's management team, including combining three previously separate businesses (food preparation products, personal appliances, and portable home products) into one with a single manager each for marketing, manufacturing, and other functional areas.

2. Production and marketing of blenders, fans, heaters, and vacuum cleaners were halted. These products were at the mature level of their "product life cycles" and were not expected to contribute to the division's growth goals.

3. Building on higher level divisional strategy decisions, resulting marketing program decisions included use of product managers (reporting to the marketing manager), thus enabling specialized market planning for various products; and a reduction of the sales force by

---

[1] For a detailed account of General Electric's strategic business planning from which this illustration is drawn, see "GE's New Strategy for Faster Growth," *Business Week*, July 8, 1972, pp. 52–58.

50 percent to 290 salesmen. Each salesman now sells the full house-wares line. Related marketing mix decisions included an increase in advertising expenditures by 25 percent to over $3 million in 1972 and scheduled reduction of field warehouses from 53 to 20 by 1974.

The marketing strategy pursued by the GE Housewares Business Division can be characterized as a "balancing strategy" in that management was seeking to achieve profitable results in an existing product-market situation. A variety of other strategy situations may occur in a given organization depending upon variations in the market, types and maturity of products, competition, and other factors.

The plan of the chapter is first to examine in greater detail the inter-relationships between corporate and marketing strategy followed by an identification and discussion of alternative strategy positions which can confront marketing management. These positions provide a classification scheme for guiding specific marketing strategy decisions. The implications of the various strategy positions are considered with regard to corporate interrelationships, environmental considerations, market targets, and marketing program design. Next, the influences of the product life cycle and competition upon marketing strategy are discussed. Finally, factors that influence design of the marketing organization are examined.

CORPORATE AND MARKETING STRATEGY

Because of the close interrelationship between corporate and marketing strategy, it is important to identify the nature and types of guidelines provided to marketing management as the result of organizational strategy decisions. Recall that in Chapter 7 it was pointed out that the analysis of market opportunities should be guided by determination of the kind of business the enterprise's top management chooses to pursue. While various corporate strategy options exist for a given firm, the focus of business purpose is guided by the particular product (or service) and market combinations selected by management. As one business strategy authority has observed:

> The end product of strategic decisions is deceptively simple; a combination of products and markets is selected for the firm. This combination is arrived at by additions of new product-markets; divestment from some old ones, and expansion of present position. The change from previous position requires a redistribution of the firm's resources—a pattern of divestments and investments in company acquisitions, product development, marketing outlets, advertising etc.[2]

---

[2] H. Igor Ansoff, *Corporate Strategy* (New York: McGraw-Hill Book Company, 1965), p. 12.

Marketing strategy design must function within the overall corporate strategy framework. Management's assessment of long range trends in technology and market needs and selection of specific product-market areas for the firm provide the basic definition of a business. Mission definition will yield broad business goals which provide guidelines for marketing management as well as all other areas of the business. For example, the corporate mission of the Wm. Wrigley, Jr., Co., world's largest maker of chewing gum, is product oriented in that the firm has concentrated on the manufacture and distribution of one primary product. Aggressive marketing of gum has been the basic thrust of marketing strategy; diversification or expansion into new markets and products have been avoided. Alternatively, Procter and Gamble has defined its business purpose much more broadly and has positioned its strategy in terms of consumer markets that the firm has product capabilities to serve. The overall corporate mission is best described as developing and marketing a wide range of products for consumer markets. P&G is one of about 25 firms that is characterized as a "consumer company." The logic underlying the emergence of this type of corporate mission is: ". . . a desire to feast upon splurging consumer affluence and to keep abreast of faster changing consumer tastes. The consumer's insatiable thirst for new products has speeded the group's growth."[3] As the result of using consumer markets as a focus for business purpose, P&G produces and markets a variety of products from toothpaste to potato chips (Pringles).

A brief examination of the corporate planning process will be helpful in positioning marketing strategy within the overall corporate strategy framework. An overview of the strategic planning process is shown in Figure 10–1. Note the various stages in the development of the strategic plan where marketing management is involved. Assessment of the external environment draws heavily from marketing's knowledge of markets and competition. Development of company objectives includes elements relating to marketing such as innovation and market standing.

The corporate planning process is clearly an organizational activity involving managers representing all areas of the business. In order to develop specific operational strategies in marketing, finance, production, personnel, research and engineering, and other relevant areas in a given firm, it is essential that the corporate plan be a team effort, guided by top management. The design of marketing strategy flows logically out of the overall corporate planning process.

The marketing management decision framework discussed in Chapter 1 is shown in Figure 10–2 to indicate the decision areas we have ex-

---

[3] "The Spectacular Rise of the Consumer Company," *Business Week*, July 21, 1973, p. 48.

FIGURE 10–1

Overview of the Strategic Planning Process

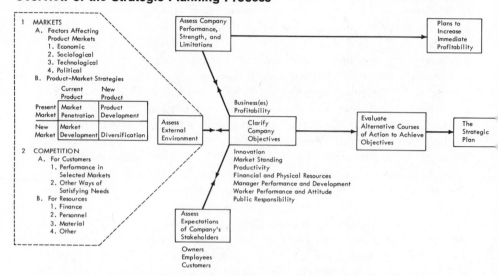

Source: Reproduced by permission from John W. Humble, *Management by Objectives*, Occasional Paper no. 2 (London: Industrial Educational and Research Foundation, 1967).

amined in prior chapters (shaded boxes), and to overview the decision areas that comprise the remainder of the book. As shown marketing strategy development consists of setting operational marketing objectives for each market target that are consistent with the organizational mission and goals; developing appropriate policies and plans regarding use of marketing resources to achieve objectives; design of the marketing organization needed to accomplish the marketing program; implementation of planned actions; and evaluation and control of actions taken to move toward desired performance targets. The marketing manager has available the various elements of the marketing mix for use in designing a marketing strategy. Decisions must be made concerning the allocation of available financial resources, executive talents, and technical capabilities in each of the marketing mix areas. The result of strategy design is the marketing program which serves as a plan of action, a guide to implementation, and a basis for evaluation and control of actions taken.

The importance of setting specific marketing objectives is so fundamental to marketing strategy design that it should be an obvious first step in the process. Yet in practice, there is a surprising number of firms that fail to formulate and quantify marketing objectives. Consider, for example, the experience of the marketing management group of a manufacturer of valves and other fluid control devices. After experienc-

FIGURE 10–2

Marketing Management Decision Framework

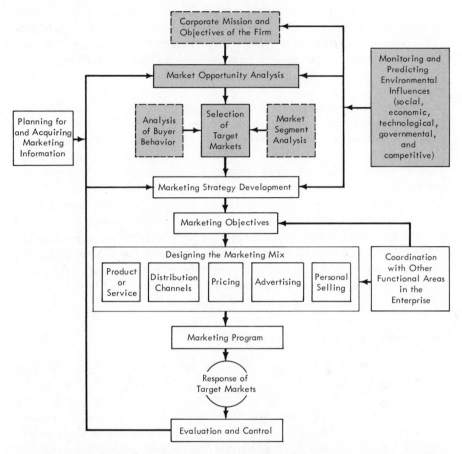

ing a long period of declining profits and actual losses in recent months, top management was appropriately concerned. When assessing markets currently served, it was determined that no priorities existed concerning market targets. For example, the firm was preparing quotations on essentially every customer inquiry that was received from field salesmen, many of which involved significant engineering man-hours and spanned a variety of industry applications. In attempting to be all things to all markets, the firm was not effectively serving any one customer group. Moreover, in the process of assessing markets served, existing capabilities, and product line profitability, marketing management discovered that one market target—oil and gas production controls—represented the firm's most profitable market opportunity. Yet, this market had been largely ignored by corporate and marketing management for several years. Specific objectives for serving this market target had not been formulated and an integrated marketing strategy for achieving objectives had not been developed. By finally recognizing this problem and thus assigning a top priority to the oil and gas production market target as well as specific priorities for other markets of interest, marketing management was able to set marketing objectives and to develop integrated marketing strategies. Through implementation and control of planned strategies, significant improvement was made in operating profits.

In order for marketing objectives to provide needed guidelines for strategy design, implementation, and control, they should be expressed in a manner that will enable determining whether or not they have been achieved. For example, an objective to "increase sales" is far too general. Targets should be expressed in quantifiable terms such as: "Our goal for market target B is to increase sales by 15 percent for the year ending December 31." An increasing number of firms and non-business organizations are using management by objectives (MBO) systems for goal setting and planning. This participative approach to management between superiors and subordinates seeks to develop specific result targets for all managers and a basis for measurement of each result. Objectives and the specified means of accomplishing desired results are used as a guide to planning and performance evaluation.[4]

MARKETING STRATEGY POSITIONS

A firm's *marketing strategy position* is determined by the market and product areas which top management chooses to pursue. The nature and extent of the opportunities present in a given strategy position are influenced by environmental and competitive forces as well as actions taken by the firm. Marketing strategy position is defined as the market-product situation faced by a particular firm. Based on variations in the market-product situation experienced by a firm which can range from new to existing products and markets, five alternative strategy positions can be identified as shown in Figure 10–3.[5]

---

[4] For a comprehensive discussion of the MBO approach see John W. Humble, *Management by Objectives in Action* (New York: McGraw-Hill Book Company, 1970); Stephen J. Carroll, Jr. and Henry L. Tosi, Jr., *Management by Objectives* (New York: The Macmillan Company, 1973); George S. Odiorne, *Management by Objectives* (New York: Pitman, 1964); and Michael J. Etzel and John M. Ivancevich, "Management by Objectives in Marketing: Philosophy, Process, and Problems," *Journal of Marketing*, vol. 38 (October 1974), pp. 47–55.

[5] Related uses of product-market variations to array strategy positions are discussed in Ansoff, *Corporate Strategy*, pp. 122–38; David T. Kollat, Roger D. Blackwell, and James F. Robeson, *Strategic Marketing* (Holt, Rinehart and Winston, Inc., 1972), pp. 21–23; and John W. Humble, *How to Manage by Objectives* (New York: AMACON, A Division of American Management Association, 1973), p. 75.

FIGURE 10–3

Alternative Marketing Strategy Positions

Balancing Strategy

In a balancing strategy an organization seeks to balance its use of marketing resources against a relatively stable, mature market to achieve corporate goals. Firms whose products have reached advanced stages of their life cycles frequently occupy a balancing strategy position. In this situation, the industry is mature and decision making uncertainties are at relatively low levels. In the organization, operating guidelines between functional areas are well established and there is a clear emphasis upon efficiency and control. For many years, commercial banks followed balancing strategies by functioning largely within existing product-market boundaries. In the last decade or so, several banks throughout the nation, particularly the large ones, shifted their strategies toward market retention, market development, and in some cases, growth.

Because top management of a firm may be unwilling (or unable) to occupy a balancing strategy position over a long period, there should be a continuous effort to monitor the environment for new opportunities and threats to existing products and markets. Environmental changes suggesting possible strategy realignments should be identified and evaluated. In this strategy position, the aggregate market should normally be well defined and competition well established in the market place. Market segmentation is frequently an essential strategy, and high priorities should be set for market targets where the firm has the greatest competitive advantage.

Adjustments to the marketing program are typically small unless operating results are unsatisfactory as, for example, in the General Electric Housewares Business division marketing strategy cited earlier in the chapter. There is normally a reasonably good base of past experience concerning the responsiveness of the market to various elements of the marketing mix. Marketing management decision activities are likely to be more concentrated upon control rather than planning. Product elimination decisions are more probable in this strategy position compared to the other four.

Market Retention Strategy

This strategy is a logical extension of a balancing situation. It is probably the most frequently occupied position of the five shown in Figure 10–3. It differs primarily from the balancing strategy in that the firm is seeking to expand its markets or modify product lines. A market retention strategy is pursued by many automobile, appliance, and other consumer durables manufacturers. Corporate relationships, environmental considerations, market opportunity analysis, and marketing program design are similar to those in a balancing strategy position. Although changes are necessary in strategy design, revisions are typically implemented within the existing marketing program framework.

Market Development Strategy

Management's desire to increase sales and profits by expanding opportunities or inability to achieve acceptable results with prevailing product-market combinations create a need for a market development strategy. This strategy extends from an existing base of product-market knowledge and experience. The market development situation is likely to occur more frequently than, for example, the growth or new venture strategies. Continuous assessment of market development opportunities should be a regular part of the marketing manager's responsibilities. Examples of product-market situations that position a firm for a market development strategy include:

1. Aluminum and plastic applications in automobiles.
2. Development of electronic gasoline pumps with computer tie-ins by a pump manufacturer to overcome drastic slowdown in conventional pump business due to the energy crisis in the mid 1970s.

Pursuit of a market development strategy may extend an organization beyond its present market or product capabilities and typically will require financial resources in excess of existing levels. A new product or market situation could require some realignment of organizational relationships and procedures. Because of these increased demands upon management and corporate resources, use of a market segmentation strategy is important in guiding the effective allocation of the organization's resources. Substantial changes in existing marketing capabilities may be involved such as different salesman qualifications or new channels of distribution for a new market. In most cases, a specific marketing program should be developed rather than to work within the existing marketing program. This is particularly appropriate for a new product or market situation.

Growth Strategy

While a growth strategy situation involves less product-market uncertainty than a new venture, it differs primarily in degree. The major difference is that the firm has some prior experience either with the product or the market. Yet, a new product or new market situation is involved. The growth strategy represents a higher level of uncertainty than a market development strategy because of the substantial variations in market and product. From a marketing strategy point of view, a growth position resulting from a modified product and a new market presents a major marketing program design task. New decisions on all elements of the marketing mix are frequently necessary. Consider, for example, the experience of a manufacturer of glass filament rocket motor cases in the early 1960s.

Management was optimistic as to the use of a modified rocket motor case (larger volume but lower tensile strength) for storage of chemicals, gasoline, foods, and other liquids. The firm possessed adequate engineering and production capabilities for modifying the product but it had limited experience in the possible markets which appeared to provide potential sales opportunities. After a preliminary feasibility analysis and market study, management decided to pursue the growth opportunity, recognizing that continued reliance upon government contracts for product sales was hazardous. They recognized that each type of application (e.g., food versus gasoline storage) was a separate market. It was necessary to develop a different marketing program for each product application area. Gasoline storage was selected as the first area to enter and a full-scale marketing program was developed including potential user product specifications, distribution systems (including use of manufacturers representatives for sales coverage), pricing strategy, and promotional programs.

In the case of a market expansion using a new product, marketing program design is less extensive than with a totally new market, and will typically involve modifications in existing marketing strategy. Nevertheless, with a new product and new customers, the demands upon the marketing management team are significant. Pricing and advertising changes will be necessary at a minimum plus provision of information on the product to those involved in customer contact. Market segment identification is likely to be particularly important in order to identify customer groups within the aggregate market that offer the most promising potential for the new product.

In growth strategy situations, there should be heavy emphasis upon planning. They should be recognized as major corporate undertakings in terms of resources and talents required. Moreover, a significant time period will typically elapse before acceptable revenue and cost levels can be achieved. In the rocket motor case example, over three years elapsed before acceptable sales levels were attained.

New Venture Strategy

Xerox's pioneering efforts in the copying field are illustrative of the new venture strategy position. Risks and uncertainties are at the highest possible level concerning both the product and market. Little or no historical information is available to aid market opportunity analysis and strategy design. Market segmentation may be difficult since the market is not well defined. Experience is limited regarding the relative effectiveness of various elements of the marketing mix. Primary marketing strategy emphasis is upon communicating the functions and features of the new product to likely prospects in the marketplace and developing channels to reach customers. Management attention is focused on planning the new venture rather than control. Some amount of experimentation will occur in seeking a proper balance of the marketing mix. Channels of distribution, pricing policies, advertising media, and sales force coverage must be developed.

Key considerations in marketing strategy design are to avoid making errors that will be difficult to correct in the future. For example, if a price level is established that will not provide satisfactory profit levels, it would be difficult to increase the price after consumers have experienced a lower price level. In consumer markets, firms sometimes use test markets to determine customer responsiveness to various marketing mix combinations (e.g., price, package sizes, and advertising program).[6]

For many firms, new venture and/or growth strategy positions do not occur very frequently. Because of the risks and associated resource commitments, major opportunities should be present. Before pursuing

---

[6] For an interesting discussion of several firms' experiences in test marketing, see *Market Testing Consumer Products* (New York: National Industrial Conference Board, Inc., 1967).

either strategy, the feasibility of the undertaking should be carefully analyzed and assessed. Various approaches are available for assessing new venture situations.[7]

Implications of Strategy Positions

A summary of descriptive characteristics of the five marketing strategy positions is shown in Table 10–1. The summary focuses upon corporate interrelationships, environmental analysis, market targets, and marketing program design. While these characteristics should be viewed as illustrative, there are certain general implications relative to marketing strategy contained in Table 10–1:

A particular firm may occupy several different strategy positions depending upon its market-product mix.

The marketing manager should assess and respond to the particular characteristics of applicable strategy positions in designing the marketing program.

Risk and uncertainty associated with a new venture strategy (as well as adjacent positions) place heavy demands upon the marketing decision maker.

A particular firm's marketing strategy position may not fall neatly into one of the five categories shown in Figure 10–3. Actually, a range or continuum of strategy positions can occur.

Marketing management in a firm that occupies a particular strategy position should recognize that environmental forces, competition, and other factors will cause the position to shift over time.

Our examination of marketing strategy positioning provides a general understanding of how variations in market and product situations place a firm in a particular strategy position. Consideration of the specific influences of the *product life cycle* and *competition* will provide additional insights into forces that tend to shape the design of marketing strategy in a given strategy position.

INFLUENCES ON MARKETING STRATEGY

Product Life Cycle

The concept of the *product life cycle* is a helpful frame of reference for viewing the need for changing marketing strategy over the life of a product. Study of a variety of products from introduction in the market-

---

[7] See, for example, Mack Hanan, "Corporate Growth through Venture Management," *Harvard Business Review,* January–February 1969, pp. 43–61.

TABLE 10–1

Summary of Characteristics Regarding Alternative Marketing Strategy Positions

Marketing Strategy Position	Corporate Interrelationships	Strategy Characteristics — Environmental Considerations	Market Targets	Marketing Program Design
A. Balancing Strategy	Well established operating guidelines between other functional areas. Mature industry. Emphasis on efficiency. Decision making uncertainties at relatively low levels.	Management should be monitoring environment for new opportunities and threats to existing products and markets; environmental changes suggesting possible strategy realignments should be identified and evaluated.	Market well defined. Segmentation is essential; priorities should be set for market targets. At the maturity stage of the product life cycle. Competition well established in the market place.	Adjustments are typically small unless operating results are unsatisfactory. Good base of history to guide decision making. More emphasis on control than planning, since strategy is well developed; regular marketing audits are essential. Elimination of certain products may be appropriate.
B. Market Retention Strategy	Logical extension from a balancing strategy position; triggered by management's desire to improve corporate performance and/or sustain historical growth patterns. Market shares relatively stable. Can be undertaken within existing organizational framework.	Knowledge of relevant environmental influences should be reasonably good. Assessment of rate and direction of changes (e.g., technology) important in avoiding future threats.	Refinement and/or extension of existing market targets. To concentrate efforts, certain low priority market targets may be dropped to provide for more comprehensive coverage of remaining targets.	Marketing strategy well established; good base of experience on market's responsiveness to marketing mix elements. Strategy typically implemented within existing marketing program.
C. Market Development Strategy	Strategy may extend the organization beyond existing market or product capabilities.	Comprehensive environmental change forecasting should be accomplished prior to pursuing market development opportunities.	Market opportunity analysis critical in establishing and/or revising market target priorities.	Substantial changes in existing marketing capabilities may be involved (e.g., different salesman qualifications, channels of

Strategy	Characteristics	Environmental Analysis	Market Knowledge	Segmentation	Marketing Program
	Needed financial resources in excess of existing levels. New product or market situation will require some realignment of organizational relationships and procedures.			Segmentation strategy is important in guiding effective allocation of the organization's resources.	distribution for a new market). Specific marketing program should be developed rather than to work through the existing program.
D. Growth Strategy	New corporate operating relationships need to be developed. Typically involves significant new resource commitments and management. Essential that corporate and marketing planning efforts be closely coordinated to select most promising growth opportunities.	Firms seeking growth opportunities should pursue active environmental analysis program. Factors affecting growth opportunities difficult to identify and evaluate.	Knowledge of market limited. Market opportunity analysis (including market research) critical in identifying most promising market targets. Segment identification more difficult than in strategies A, B, and C.		Presents a major marketing program design task. Involves extension of existing market-product base of experience as compared to a new venture. Planning horizon longer than for more established strategy positions. Control guidelines difficult to establish.
E. New Venture Strategy	Uncertainties and risks at highest level concerning product-market. Acquisition approach may be used to acquire product-market experience. More emphasis on planning than on efficiency. New venture team is used by some firms as an organizational approach.	Influence of specific environmental factors on new venture must be determined through analysis and experience. Competition difficult to identify or non-existent.	At the introductory stage of the product life cycle; limited historical market knowledge. Market not well defined. Segmentation may not be possible; efforts concentrated on identifying the aggregate market.		Effectiveness of marketing mix elements largely unknown—experimentation will be necessary. Test marketing may be desirable for consumer products-services. Significant shifts in strategy are more likely than for any of the other strategy positions.

FIGURE 10–4

Product Life Cycle

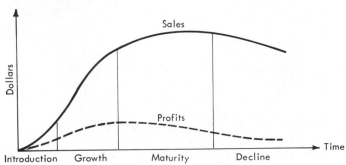

place until they reach maturity (and in some cases, death) suggests that sales and profits follow definite patterns as, for example, those shown in Figure 10–4. The sales pattern is frequently described in terms of four stages: *introduction, growth, maturity,* and/or *decline.*[8]

In the introduction stage the product is new in the market place. Sales begin to build as potential buyers become aware of the product, purchase it, and generally respond favorably. If favorable information diffuses throughout the market place and buyer interest expands (through product promotional efforts and informal communications among people) the product moves into its growth stage. More potential buyers want the product as its continues to gain market acceptance. Other firms, attracted by a potential market opportunity, may introduce similar products, thus expanding both product availability and marketing efforts aimed at building sales. As sales continue to expand, the product moves into the maturity stage. Competition is typically keen as the market reaches a saturation or leveling off point. Severe price competition often prevails, thus reducing profits. After reaching a maturity stage sales of some products actually decline from peak levels. (Some descriptions include a saturation stage of the product life cycle between maturity and decline.) New products may be introduced which provide substitutes to the existing product. Consider, for example, the impact of radial tires in the mid-1970s upon sales of conventional automobile tires. Due to intense competition and narrow profit margins certain firms may discontinue the product. As for example, General Electric's discontinuing vacuum cleaner production discussed earlier in the chapter.

---

[8] The product life cycle concept is discussed in greater detail in Theodore Levitt, "Exploit the Product Life Cycle," *Harvard Business Review,* vol. 43 (November–December 1965), pp. 81–94.

One might appropriately ask, "How valid is the product life cycle concept?" Certainly, it is not a theory. Moreover, the particular sales and profit patterns shown in Figure 10–4 are not necessarily typical for all products. Yet, there is empirical support to the effect that sales follow definite patterns over the life of a product. For example, in a study of 140 categories of nondurable consumer products (health and personal care, food, and tobacco) Polli and Cook commented as follows on their results of attempting to verify the life cycle model:

> While the overall performance of the model leaves some question as to its general applicability, it is clearly a good model of sales behavior in certain market situations—especially so in the case of different product forms competing for the same market segment within a general class of products.[9]

Polli and Cook used a hypothesized life cycle model with stages of introduction, growth, maturity, and decline and assigned boundaries to the theoretical distribution of the stages based on percentage changes in sales. For example, the introduction stage was defined as the period when annual sales were less than 5 percent of a peak level. Cox, in a study of 258 ethical-drug products introduced during 1955–59, found that 6 different sales patterns (curves) were needed to describe the products in the sample.[10] Yet only 28 percent of the products followed a simple parabola sales pattern similar to that shown in Figure 10–4. Nearly 40 percent followed a cyclical curve (first cycle similar to Figure 10–4 and the second cycle repeating the same general pattern at a point of sales decline in the first cycle). In part, these cyclical variations may have been caused by company actions to overcome declining sales.

Thus, there is empirical evidence that product life cycles exist at least for certain products. Perhaps most important, management judgment and experience tend also to support the logic of the product life cycle.[11] Acknowledging that the concept is not universally applicable to all products, and that predicting actual life cycle patterns for new products may be difficult, there are several implications of the concept regarding marketing strategy design.

The importance of various elements of the marketing mix will shift during different stages of the life cycle. For example, price may become much more important in countering competition during the maturity

---

[9] Rolando Polli and Victor Cook, "Validity of the Product Life Cycle," *The Journal of Business,* vol. 42 (October 1969), p. 400.

[10] William E. Cox, Jr., "Product Life Cycles as Marketing Models," *The Journal of Business,* vol. 40 (October 1967), p. 382.

[11] See, for example, Donald K. Clifford, Jr., "Leverage in the Product Life Cycle," *Dun's Review and Modern Industry,* 85 (May 1965), pp. 62–70; and Arch Patton, "Top Management's Stake in the Product Life Cycle," *The Management Review,* 48 (June 1959), pp. 9–14, 67–71, 76–79.

stage compared to the introduction stage. Communicating the availability and features of a new product through advertising and personal selling are essential in achieving buyer awareness during the early stages of the life cycle. The changing nature of the marketing program as a product advances through various life cycle stages is a key consideration in marketing strategy design.

Recognition of the life cycle emphasizes the need for a stream of new and improved products in order to stabilize and expand sales and profits over time. The high levels of research and development expenditures by many large corporations over the past decade are directed toward generating product and process improvements and innovations.

The exact pattern and timing of the life cycle for a particular product may be difficult to predict over a long future time horizon. For example, atomic power plants did not develop in the 1970s as rapidly as was predicted in the 1950s. Atomic power today contributes a much smaller portion of total power requirements than was estimated two decades ago. Thus, life cycle patterns should be monitored on a continuing basis, and projections revised as a result of new information and experience.

Environmental influences may over time drastically change a particular life cycle pattern. Recall, for example, the impact on the cigarette industry of publication of cancer research results regarding cigarette smoking. Changing life styles and affluence have accelerated wine sales in the 1970s compared to past periods. Giant increases in inflation rates in the early 1970s were responsible for major expansions in coin and postage stamp markets.

Analysis of life cycle patterns may be more successful if particular market segments are considered. For example, use of denim in work clothes in the mid-1970s had reached a stage of decline in the life cycle with many blue collar workers upgrading to more stylish and colorful polyester fabrics. Alternatively, cotton denim clothing for leisure wear moved into a growth phase. Shortages of production materials can also affect product life cycle patterns. During 1974, for example, several industries (e.g., paper, plastics) eliminated certain products from their lines in order to utilize scarce raw materials for more profitable products.

The product life cycle is not entirely independent of the marketing efforts of a firm (or industry), since sales response in the marketplace is, in part, the result of marketing effort expended. Thus, in using the life cycle concept as a guide for planning, marketing management should attempt to estimate the effect of the firm's and competitive marketing strategies upon life cycle patterns. The management challenge is to assess product performance in the marketplace over time; to determine the probable current phase of the cycle; and to attempt to predict future trends over the strategy planning horizon. This information forms a critical input to the marketing strategy process.

Competition

Traditional definitions of industry market structures (e.g., pure competition, oligopoly, monopoly, etc.) inadequately describe the nature and scope of contemporary competitive forces in the marketplace as they relate to the design of marketing strategy. Increasingly, firms are competing in nontraditional ways by concentrating their efforts in selected portions or segments of a particular market. By competing for certain market segments, small firms with specialized capabilities in one or more market segments can achieve competitive advantages over larger businesses. Moreover, large firms are increasingly recognizing that profits and growth can be improved by concentrating on certain parts of the market. Thus, the concept of market segmentation is an important basis for examining competitive behavior in the marketplace. Moreover, identification and selection of a basis for segmentation (as discussed in Chapter 8) can provide proprietary advantage to a firm. The relationship between market share and profits provides an important insight into competitive strategies in seeking to dominate particular segments of an aggregate market.

Market Share and Profits. While not conclusive, there is a reasonable amount of evidence in the form of research results and corporate experience that suggests the profitability of a particular firm is related to the size of the market share held by that firm for its various products in their particular target segments. Based on this relationship, the Boston Consulting Group has developed an approach to strategic planning using "experience curves" (developed from historical cost and price data) for determining the value of increasing market share of a particular product. By pursuing a strategy aimed at gaining market power through market share: ". . . a company should strive to dominate the market for a particular product, either by introducing the product, segmenting the market, or discouraging competitors by preemptive pricing."[12] An experience curve shows unit price and cost plotted against accumulated volume of a product produced over time.

In a study of 57 corporations with 620 diverse businesses, Schoeffler, Buzzell, and Heany investigated 37 potential determinants of profit performance (measured by return on investment).[13] They found the key influences on profit to be market share, product quality, marketing

---

[12] "Selling Business a Theory of Economics," *Business Week,* September 8, 1973, pp. 85 and 87. For additional details concerning experience curve planning, see also Patrick Conley, *Experience Curves as a Planning Tool: A Special Commentary* (Boston: The Boston Consulting Group, Inc., 1970); and C. Davis Fogg, "Planning Gains in Market Share," *Journal of Marketing,* vol. 38 (July 1974), pp. 30–38.

[13] Sidney Schoeffler, Robert D. Buzzell, and Donald F. Heany, "Impact of Strategic Planning on Profit Performance," *Harvard Business Review,* vol. 52 (March–April 1974), pp. 137–45.

TABLE 10–2

Illustrative Types of Competition

Illustrative Types of Competition	*Selected Characteristics*	*Examples*
Multiindustry Competition	Increasing breakdown of industry boundaries. Large, multiproduct, multimarket firms. May utilize conglomorate organizational structure.	Tenneco, Inc. (gas transmission, packaging, shipbuilding, farm equipment, etc.); Greyhound Corp. (buses, trucking, food and food services, etc.).
Within-Industry Competition		
Product competition	Product differentiation strategy frequently used or other elements of the marketing mix are varied.	Eastman Kodak versus Polaroid; Pizza Hut versus McDonalds.
Brand competition	Firms may pursue a product variety strategy (e.g., different toothpaste brands) or seek a certain segment of the market (e.g., McLeans toothpaste).	Crest versus Colgate toothpaste.
Dominant-Firm Competition	Industry frequently made up of a small number of large firms all tending to follow the industry leader.	General Motors Corporation; United States Steel Corp.; American Telephone and Telegraph Company.
Competing against Dominant Firm(s)		
Direct competition	Concentration on selected products and/or market segments, or regional areas (e.g., Coors Beer).	American Motors
Complementary competition	Smaller firms seek to complement the dominant firm's lines.	Various computer equipment firms providing complementary equipment for IBM computer systems (e.g., optical readers, plotters, data display, storage, and transmission).
Broad Market Competition	Corporate strategy focus on broad markets rather than products and/or industries (e.g., consumer markets).	Procter and Gamble

expenditures, research and development expenditures, investment intensity, and corporate diversity; in total the 37 factors explained over 80 percent of the variation in profitability. While these results reinforce the influence of market share on profitability, the contribution of other factors is also indicated.

Although, one might react that the linkage of market share dominance to profitability is logical (and perhaps obvious), corporate strategies have not widely reflected this goal, particularly within certain segments of a market. Moreover, achievement of the largest market share in an industry does not guarantee a profitable future as indicated by A&P's dominant market share in food retailing over a decade ago.

Types of Competition. Firms compete in various ways using alternative market-product strategies. Several of the more prevalent forms of competition are shown in Table 10–2. These examples are intended to be illustrative rather than exhaustive. Nevertheless, they suggest the various competitive strategies that can be developed by business firms.

Size, Resources, and Knowhow. The size of a firm, its available resources, and managerial and technical knowhow influence the strategy alternatives available to a firm. For example, a Canadian firm which ranked third place in consumer calculator sales in 1973 went into interim receivership in early 1974 because management chose to concentrate on marketing their product made from purchased components and assembled by outside contractors.[14] As a result of this strategy, the firm did not develop the internal technical knowhow necessary to keep their product competitive due to the extremely rapid technological change inherent in the electronic calculator market.

Competition is so pervasive in the marketplace that there may be a tendency to accept it without carefully attempting to analyze and predict competitive trends. Firms typically have certain alternatives in their strategic positioning with regard to competition as illustrated in Table 10–2. Nontraditional forms of competition are becoming increasingly prevalent in American business and industry. Monitoring of the competitive environment should be a key aspect of corporate and marketing planning.

THE MARKETING ORGANIZATION

Before concluding our examination of corporate and marketing strategy, certain aspects related to development of the organization should be considered. The marketing organization is the combination of managerial and technical capabilities that is responsible for planning, implementing, and controlling marketing strategy. The design of the marketing organization should be based upon the job to be accomplished—the activities to be performed.[15] Since organizational design

---

[14] "The Miscalculations at Rapid Data," *Business Week*, February 9, 1974, p. 26.

[15] Several types of marketing organizational structures used by various firms are described in Hector Lazo and Arnold Corbin, *Management in Marketing: Text and Cases* (New York: McGraw-Hill Book Company, 1961), pp. 79, 86–89 and 111–20.

concepts and principles are extensively covered elsewhere, our purpose is to briefly examine factors unique to the marketing area that should be considered in developing the organizational structure.[16]

Approaches to Organization Design

There are four general approaches to marketing organizational design: *functional, market, product,* and *combination.* The functional approach involves organizing marketing activities into different areas of specialization such as advertising, sales force, and marketing information. The market approach utilizes a concept of designing the marketing organization around the markets that are served such as consumer and industrial markets, or specific market segments within an aggregate market. The product type of design employs the grouping of marketing efforts for various product areas. Frequently combination approaches are used such as functional specialization within particular market or product groups. In assembling the marketing team the marketing manager should attempt to achieve the highest degree of integration of marketing efforts, and at the same time provide the necessary amount of specialization of technical tasks (e.g., advertising activities). Yet, these purposes tend to be in conflict. For example, a functional approach enables the grouping or specialization of marketing functions, but may make the integration of marketing program efforts more difficult. A comparison of alternative approaches to marketing organization design is shown in Table 10–3 on pages 342–43. Examples of the functional, market, product, and combination approaches are described below:

> *Functional Approach:*   Used by several large manufacturers of consumer products where mass marketing strategies are appropriate. Single uncomplicated product or line of products (e.g., cigarettes or beer) is sold. The various marketing activities are specialized to serve a single mass market with a particular product.

> *Market Approach:*   Used by large computer manufacturers where applications of the same basic line of equipment differ by type of user (e.g., retailers versus manufacturers). By concentrating on a similar group of users, a comprehensive marketing effort can be managed by each organizational unit set up to serve a particular market.

> *Product Approach:*   The product or brand management approach was pioneered by Procter and Gamble nearly a half a century ago is

---

[16] See, for example, Harold Koontz and Cyril O'Donnell, *Principles of Management,* 4th ed. (New York: McGraw-Hill Book Company, 1968); and Rocco Carzo, Jr., and John N. Yanouzas, *Formal Organization: A Systems Approach* (Homewood, Ill.: Richard D. Irwin, Inc., and the Dorsey Press, 1967).

illustrative of this organizational design. Marketing managers are assigned to various product groups.

Combination Approach: In some firms product managers have available corporate staff groups set up along functional lines, thus reflecting the combination approach to organization design. These groups provide the product manager with marketing research, advertising, packaging, and other specialized marketing assistance.

Illustrative organizational charts for the functional, market, and product approaches are shown in Figure 10–5. No one particular approach is better than another. Depending upon a firm's market-product situation,

FIGURE 10–5

Illustrations of Organizational Approaches

FUNCTIONAL APPROACH

MARKET APPROACH

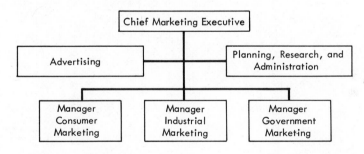

PRODUCT APPROACH

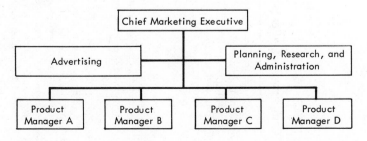

TABLE 10–3

Comparison of Alternative Approaches to Marketing Organization Design

Characteristics	Strengths	Limitations	When Appropriate
Functional Approach Grouping of marketing activities into various areas of specialization such as advertising, sales and information planning. May involve both line and staff functions (e.g., planning and sales force management). Widely used organizational approach.	Encourages development of managerial and technical skills in each individual marketing mix area. Marketing tasks can be clearly defined due to specialization of functions.	Places primary marketing program integrating responsibility upon chief marketing executives, since specialization by activity tends to inhibit integration by functional managers.	Large firms utilizing several marketing functions and personnel, thus facilitating specialization of efforts. Firm is concentrating on one primary market opportunity. Products do not require special knowledge and skills (e.g., single, uncomplex product line).
Market Approach Combining marketing mix activities to serve two or more market targets separately. An organization designed along geographical lines is a special case of the market approach providing customer needs and wants vary by location.	Organization design is focused on customer needs. Marketing resources are integrated to serve customer groups with similar characteristics. Marketing manager can concentrate upon managing markets rather than functions.	May involve duplication of functions and lead to inefficiencies unless scale of operations is sufficiently large. Requires more management levels (e.g., manager for each market area). Lack of coordination between groups when overlap or market commonalities exists.	Firm has more than one market target. Substantial differences exist between market targets such as industrial and consumer markets. Size of market opportunities sufficient to justify separate marketing approaches.

Product Approach

Specialization of marketing efforts by product line or product area. Sometimes used by multidivision firms where each division is responsible for a group of products.

Management attention can be directed to the particular characteristics, and requirements of different products.

Coordination of product decisions with other areas of firm (e.g., manufacturing, engineering, finance) is facilitated.

May tend to place too much emphasis upon products rather than markets, thus working against the philosophy of the marketing concept.

Tends to increase the number of management levels (e.g., corporate advertising, divisional advertising staffs).

Several products with distinct characteristics are marketed by the firm.

Significant technical/application differences exist between product groups.

Certain products require special knowledge/skills by personnel marketing them.

Combination Approach

Functional, market, and/or product approaches are combined to obtain multiple advantages and to overcome limitations of a single approach.

Frequently the market or product approaches are used in conjunction with the functional approach.

Enables combination of functional, market and/or product characteristics in organization design.

Encourages both integration and specialization of marketing efforts.

More flexible in responding to problems/opportunities than the other three approaches.

Delineation of responsibility for various marketing activities may be more difficult due to the combination of organization design approaches.

May lead to duplication and inefficiencies in the use of marketing resources if size of organizational units is not sufficiently large to provide economies.

Market/product breakdowns are sufficiently large to enable functional approaches within each grouping.

Large firms with multiple product groups and/or market targets.

FIGURE 10–6

Responsibilities of Marketing Heads in Nondivisionalized Companies

Percent of Chief Marketing Executives:

☐ Having Activity Directly under Their Control ☐ Giving Advice and Counsel ■ Having No Responsibility

Activity	Directly under Control	Advice and Counsel	No Responsibility
Marketing Planning	95%		5%
Merchandising	93%		5%
Marketing Research	91%		7%
Sales Promotions	88%		10%
Sales Research and Reporting	86%		12%
Corporate and Institutional Advertising	76%	24%	
Regular Product Planning	72%	26%	
Product Advertising	72%	25%	
Sales Training	68%	25%	
Field Sales Management	68%	22%	
New Product Planning	62%	38%	
Distributor/Dealer Relations	59%	34%	
National Accounts	57%	30%	
Customer Service	56%	37%	
Foreign Marketing Operations	52%	21%	
Public Relations	51%	37%	
Product Pricing	48%	48%	
Product Service	47%	47%	
Export Sales	46%	25%	
Physical Distribution, Warehousing	31%	45%	
Corporate Planning	22%	71%	
Mergers, Acquisitions, New Ventures	10%	68%	

Source: Reprinted by permission from David S. Hopkins and Earl L. Bailey, *The Chief Marketing Executive* (New York: The Conference Board, Inc., 1971), p. 16.

the design that best serves its needs should be utilized. The comparisons provided in Table 10–3 indicate certain of the strengths and limitations of each approach, and the conditions under which a given type of organization design may be appropriate.

An examination of the job description of the chief marketing executive provides a good indication of the marketing function in a particular organization.[17] Figure 10–6 shows an analysis of the responsibilities of the chief marketing executive in 45 manufacturing and service companies.[18] The variety of functions indicated provides a good description of the scope of responsibilities assigned to marketing management in many different types of firms.

Coordination with Other Decision Areas

The marketing manager and staff encounter a variety of situations which require coordination with other functional areas of the firm such as accounting and finance, engineering and production, personnel, and transportation. These relationships necessitate careful development and monitoring since many of the actions taken by marketing management to influence customers favorably in the marketplace are substantially influenced by individuals and groups outside the marketing organization. The success of the marketing effort can be greatly facilitated by a corporate team effort aimed at providing customer satisfaction.

Several illustrative types of coordination between marketing and other functional areas are shown in Figure 10–7. These are but a few of the many ways that the marketing organization interfaces with other activities in the firm. Regardless of the organizational mechanisms that are developed to aid and encourage coordination between functional areas, conflicts sometimes occur. The politics of marketing management may consume a substantial portion of the chief marketing executive's time unless relationships are carefully developed and strengthened over time. Various areas of conflict between functional areas can occur including competition for scarce resources (e.g., new machine for production versus an expanded advertising budget for marketing); differences in goal priorities such as manufacturing seeking to minimize inventory carrying costs versus marketing desiring to minimize sales losses and customer dissatisfaction; and power struggles between executives in functional areas competing for top management opportunities.[19] Functional area power tends to vary in different organizations. For example,

---

[17] Job descriptions for the chief marketing executive and other executives in the marketing organization for several companies are shown in Jo Ann Sperling, *Job Descriptions in Marketing Management* (New York: American Management Association, Inc., 1969); and David S. Hopkins and Earl L. Bailey, *The Chief Marketing Executive* (New York: The Conference Board, Inc., 1971).

[18] Hopkins and Bailey, *The Chief Marketing Executive*, p. 16.

[19] For a fascinating best-selling novel about executive power struggles and their impact upon a banking institution, read Arthur Hailey, *The Moneychangers* (New York: Doubleday & Company, Inc., 1975).

FIGURE 10–7

Illustrative Types of Coordination between Marketing and Other Functional Areas

Accounting and Finance
  Establishment of terms of the sale (credit, time of payment, consignment, etc.).
  Sales forecasting.
  Credits and collections.
  Accounting and financial information.
  Provision of financial resources.
Engineering
  Determination of new product needs.
  Development of product concepts.
  Product modification requirements.
  Market feasibility studies.
  Price determination.
Personnel
  Recruiting and selection of salesmen.
  Compensation and incentives.
  Administration of employee benefits.
  Personnel policies and procedures.
Production
  Product quality and performance.
  Packaging design.
  Handling of vendor warranties.
  Sales forecasting.
  Production/inventory scheduling and control.
  Price determination.
Transportation
  Scheduling of deliveries.
  Damaged and returned goods.
  Sales forecasting.
  Storage.
  Relationships with intermediaries.

in high technology firms the engineering function wields considerable influence upon overall organizational strategy.

SUMMARY AND CONCLUSIONS

In this chapter, the relationship between corporate and marketing strategy has been examined and a framework for examining alternative marketing strategy positions has been developed. Various marketing strategy positions associated with different market-product situations were defined and described. The influences upon marketing strategy of the product life cycle and competition were also considered. Marketing program design varies substantially between the various strategy positions that correspond to balancing, market retention, market development, growth, and new venture situations. Finally, factors which influence the design of the marketing organization were identified and examined. In the next two chapters, "Decision Making Concepts and Models" (Chapter 11), and "Marketing Information Planning" (Chapter 12), are examined and their use in providing concepts and approaches for marketing decision analysis is illustrated. In the last chapter of this part of the book guidelines for planning the marketing program are discussed and illustrated.

EXERCISES FOR REVIEW AND DISCUSSION

1. Select a firm that you are familiar with and define its business purpose or mission in terms of market-product focus.

2. As marketing manager you have been asked by the chief executive of your firm to develop a set of specific objectives for the marketing function. What information do you need before preparing these objectives and what is the rationale behind having a set of marketing objectives for the firm?

3. Recognizing that strategic planning draws from all functional areas, what specific inputs can marketing provide throughout the strategic planning process?

4. While markets and products are the primary determinants of marketing strategy, environmental forces influence both of these. Discuss the impact of environmental forces in the mid-1970s which necessitated changes in markets and/or products of various firms.

5. Faced with a product in the stage of its product life cycle where sales are increasing but profits are beginning to decline, what possible marketing strategy changes might you want to consider in seeking to improve profits? What information would you want before making a decision?

6. In the last quarter century Polaroid Corp. has coupled innovative product and process development with a strong and integrated marketing effort, resulting in over a $500 million dollar market for instant photography. Today, how would you describe the firm's marketing strategy position?

7. The Consumer Products Corporation markets various products which fall into different strategy positions. The firm's major line is cosmetic products (shampoo, soap, body lotion, etc.). Management is considering the introduction of another product entirely different from their existing product line: french fries which would provide the advantage of not being greasy. Discuss the strategy position that the greaseless french fries market-product combination would occupy. What are the implications of this strategy position concerning the firm's existing strategy position/s and associated marketing program?

8. In mid-1974 International Business Machines Corp. announced that the firm would acquire CML Satellite Corp.—the space age communications satellite firm. Discuss the implications of this move in terms of IBM's corporate mission and its market-product strategy positioning.

9. Assume that you have recently taken over as chief marketing executive for a firm serving multi-markets with a broad range of consumer and industrial electrical equipment and products. The firm's present marketing organizational approach and marketing program have been developed along functional lines (e.g., advertising, personal selling, marketing information, etc.). Discuss what changes in the firm's marketing strategy approach might be appropriate.

11

Decision-Making Concepts and Models

Management is essentially comprised of making, implementing, and controlling decisions. Every manager must develop and continually refine an approach to decision making that will serve as an effective guide through the more difficult decisions that will inevitably be faced. Moreover, there is an increasing number of new decision making concepts and tools that are becoming available to managers. To comprehend and use these concepts and tools depends upon an understanding of the process of decision making. In this chapter, a conceptual framework is developed to show the various tasks comprising analytical decision making. Building on this framework, decision making models are introduced. The focus is on identifying the kinds of decision making situations in which various types of models are most useful. Consequently, this section will be more concerned with classifying models than describing them in detail. Finally, one particular model is described to illustrate the importance of matching model features with decision situations.

ANALYTICAL DECISION MAKING

Decision Process versus Decision Outcome

With organization decision making increasing in complexity, the traditional focus on decision outcomes as the *sole* measure of managerial success probably should be reevaluated. Managers must frequently consider multiple factors affecting a decision, some of which are difficult to evaluate or predict. Consequently, due to this uncertainty, some decisions over a manager's career will not fully achieve objectives. Yet, this does not mean that such decisions are "bad" decisions. A decision that ultimately fails may still have been the best one that could have been made, given information and opinions available at that time. This suggests that evaluating managerial decisions should cover the *process* used to reach decisions as well as decision outcomes.

There is considerable emphasis in the fields of marketing and management on decision making as an *analytical* process. For example, educational institutions (particularly in colleges of Business, Education, and Engineering) are treating decision making as an analytical process that can be taught through classwork, cases, and real world projects. Executive development programs offer similar training in decision making concepts and tools to managers who have been away from school for a period of time. Finally, at the heart of this trend is the recognition by established and successful managers of the importance of developing and improving analytical decision making skills. Consider what W. G. Myers, Vice President of Marketing at Lockheed Aircraft Corporation, has to say about decision making:

> For decisions in business to come naturally we also need to do a number of things. We need to get the organization onto the same wave length so that everybody is prepared to participate in the decision. We have to educate our people so that they are capable of handling the ingredients of the decision. And we need to have our communications so well developed that people stay informed on the state of the art, the problems at hand, and the decision issues.
>
> What advice would I give marketers? . . . Do some hard thinking about your own organization's processes of decision making. This should include the consideration of ways of improving your approach; how decisions can be made instinctively and correctly; and whether the organization has the training and discipline necessary to provide information upon which to make a proper decision.[1]

The importance of the process through which managers go to reach a decision can be further illustrated by contrasting two particular managers' styles when faced with a difficult decision:

> A product group manager for a large consumer goods firm was given responsibility for deciding whether or not a new product just being developed should be introduced. Prior to this, he had been forced to drop several consecutive new product ideas because the test markets had demonstrated insufficient demand. This time, he unexpectedly decided to skip the test market stage and go directly into full scale marketing of the new product because he, personally, liked the product and believed that it would sell quite well. The product turned out to be a success.
>
> A management team for another large consumer goods firm was given information from R&D showing the development of a new cooking

---

[1] W. Gifford Myers, "The Decision-making Process," in *Decision Making in Marketing* (New York: The Conference Board, 1971), pp. 21, 24.

process for a potential snack food addition to their product mix. The team implemented a series of activities to help them decide whether or not to introduce this product, including (1) setting goals for financial and market performance, (2) obtaining market information on competitive products and market potential, (3) testing prototypes on samples of potential consumers to determine preferences; and (4) forecasting revenues and costs of introduction. Based on the results of these activities, the decision was to introduce the product, and it was a success.[2]

In both instances, these managers made "good" decisions purely from the standpoint of outcomes. Both new products were introduced and achieved corporate and marketing objectives. However, it is evident that the decision processes were entirely different. The first manager is characteristic of a "seat of the pants" decision maker who arrived at a difficult decision with apparently very little analysis or information. Moreover, he was willing to go against the odds by skipping the test market, even though five previous test markets had kept him from introducing products that would probably have failed (he must have liked these products, too, or he wouldn't have spent the resources for their test markets). On the other hand, the management team for the other firm clearly went through an analytical, decision process before making the introduction decision.

On the basis of the outcome of a single decision, each was as successful as the other. Yet, management makes many decisions over time, not just one decision. The success of an organization in the long run, then, is dependent on management's "batting averages" or the percentage of successful decisions out of all decisions made. The current focus on decision making training emphasizes that a well developed, analytical process approach to decision making can significantly contribute to improved managerial batting averages.

Decision-Making Process[3]

If asked to describe how they make decisions, managers might discuss some sort of process including steps such as: (1) gather all informa-

---

[2] From a talk given by Arthur Howard, Division Manager of Procter and Gamble, to a marketing strategy class at the University of Tennessee, 1972.

[3] The concepts of analytical decision making are widely discussed in the management literature. See, for example, Herbert A. Simon, *The New Science of Management Decision* (New York: Harper & Brothers, Publishers, 1960), p. 3; John Dewey, *How We Think* (New York: D. C. Heath & Company, 1910), chapter 8; William H. Newman and Charles E. Summer, *The Process of Management* (Englewood Cliffs, N.J.: Prentice-Hall, Inc., 1961), part III; Charles H. Kepner and Benjamin B. Tregoe, *The Rational Manager* (New York: McGraw-Hill Book Company, 1965); and Alfred R. Oxenfeldt, *Executive Action in Marketing* (Belmont, Calif.: Wadsworth Publishing Company, Inc.), pp. 11–12.

tion on a problem, (2) evaluate the strengths and weaknesses of alternatives, (3) choose the best alternative, and (4) carry out the decision. While the steps may differ from manager to manager, many are familiar with the *concept* of analytical decision making: *moving through an orderly, logical process from identifying a problem to making a decision intended to solve that problem, being sure to make use of available, relevant information.* Nevertheless, this conceptualization does not describe the *actual* decision making process of many managers when faced with difficult decisions under time pressure. Too often

FIGURE 11–1

Analytical Decision-Making Process

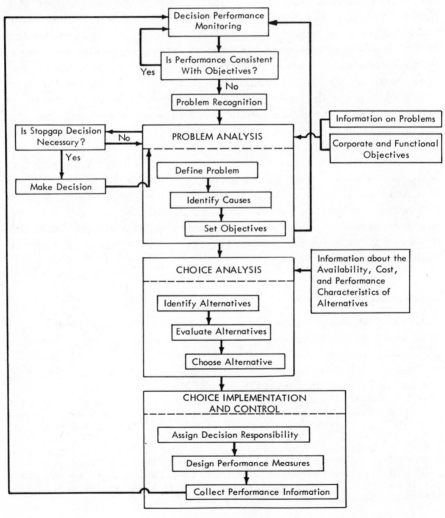

actual decision making is based on "hunch," out-of-date past experience, and some confusion in how best to proceed toward a decision. For example, one manager may see a "problem" as declining sales volume while another may see the same "problem" as what price to charge in the face of a declining sales volume. Intuitively, these two views of the problem are not at all alike. It is for these reasons that more attention is being given to how managers make decisions rather than only concern for the results achieved after the decisions are made. Analytical decision making must be learned and practiced by managers, since it is not necessarily a completely natural process.

Figure 11–1 presents a schematic diagram of analytical decision making showing steps in a complete process and types of information often needed to reach an effective decision. Certain general characteristics of analytical decision-making are evident from the diagram. First, the process is comprised of three major tasks: (1) problem analysis, (2) choice analysis, and (3) choice implementation and control (including performance monitoring). Second, decision making is a continual process of analyzing information on performance (which is the result of past decisions), identifying and solving problems uncovered by this information, and providing an information base (performance monitoring) for "seeing" new problems that will inevitably arise after current problems have been solved.

Problem Recognition and Analysis

Problem Definition. Decision making starts when a manager recognizes that a problem exists. Consequently, managers need to understand clearly how to define a problem and then, be set to "see" problems as quickly as possible after they arise. Yet, decision makers frequently spend too little time and thought in problem analysis and proceed to selecting an alternative without really knowing why a problem has developed or what the choice is supposed to accomplish. Consider the following illustrative decision situation:

> A marketing manager for a food manufacturer had responsibility for a new product under consideration as an addition to the product mix. Upon evaluating the results of the initial 5 months of test marketing, he noticed that sales were 20 percent lower than the sales volume objective set at the beginning of the test. He did not know why sales were off, though a check on distribution showed adequate supply on hand in retail stores. So he ordered a taste test from marketing research. In this test, a representative sample of consumers rated the new product and several major competitive products, once when the brands were unidentified, and again when they knew what brands they were testing. Results showed that the new product was rated quite favorably against

the competitive products when the brands were not identified, but rather unfavorably when the brands were known. The manager concluded from this that the advertising was at fault and proceeded to have the advertising themes and layouts changed. Unfortunately sales continued to be sluggish, and only later did he isolate the cause as a very unpopular brand name (not advertising) that apparently had very negative connotations to consumers.

Clearly, this manager jumped to an erroneous conclusion from the research, and as a result, made an inappropriate decision. In doing so, he incurred two costs. Considerable expense was involved in changing the advertising theme and layouts when, in fact, it was not necessary to do so. Moreover, the product continued in test market after the advertising change, and so additional losses were incurred during the time that the manager thought he had corrected the problem.

The manager in this example did, at least, recognize a problem and start the process of determining a cause. His concept of a problem is a very useful one: he recognized a problem when he noticed that sales were less than the volume that was expected to be sold during five months time. To him a problem was a *significant difference between what actually happened (performance) and what was expected to happen (objectives).*[4] Recognizing problems, then, is a process of analyzing performance information in order to make comparisons to predetermined expectations or objectives (see Figure 11–1). Furthermore, the manager described the problem in detail: sales were sluggish for a new brand in the only city in which it was being tested; the sales deviation was 20 percent (substantial) and occurred during the whole test period.

Identification of Causes. Recognizing a problem is only the beginning of a complete problem analysis. The manager proceeded correctly to the next phase by requesting some information that he felt would aid in identifying why sales were lower than he expected in the test market. However, upon receiving the information from marketing research the manager made a common error. He jumped to the erroneous conclusion that advertising was the cause (probably because advertising themes frequently play an important role in establishing brand images for consumer products and services).

Additional thought on the declining sales problem, given the research results, would indicate the information had narrowed the range of possible causes but the true cause had not been found. Consumers rating the product lower when they knew the brand than when they didn't indicated that the cause had something to do with the brand image being portrayed rather than with the physical characteristics (taste, color, etc.) of the product. However, there are several factors that to-

---

[4] Simon, *The New Science of Management Decision,* p. 27; and Kepner and Tregoe, *The Rational Manager,* p. 4.

gether establish an image. Advertising themes are one of these, yet, brand name, point of purchase displays, price, and type of appeals used by retail stores also add to a product's brand image. Therefore, the research established that the cause was very likely to be one of these factors, but did not establish which one was the true cause. Problem analysis had really not been completed before the manager proceeded to a choice of alternatives (changing the advertising). Unfortunately, his decision changed something that was not causing the problem, and so, the decision was not successful.

The manager would have increased his chances of making a good decision by completing problem analysis. He might have ordered some follow-up research to test the brand name and/or the effectiveness of the advertising and sales promotion devices, for instance. A decision that corrects a problem cannot be made (except by chance) unless it is aimed at correcting the cause of the problem. So the more certain a manager is that he knows a problem cause, the greater are his chances of making a decision that will solve the problem.

Frequently, a decision must be made even when the cause of a problem is not yet known. For example, the firm had a product in test market that was losing money. If the search for the problem cause takes time, then management must decide whether to continue losing money by keeping the product in test market or to do something to avoid incurring more losses. This decision will not really correct the problem, but will only deal temporarily with the *consequences* of the problem. This is the role of the stopgap decision as shown in Figure 11–1.[5] The stopgap decision is intended to *buy time* for the decision maker so that he can proceed through the entire decision process. It is highly unlikely to be corrective (again, except by chance), but tries to make the consequences of the problem more tolerable until the cause is isolated and the problem solved. In this case, the manager might temporarily withdraw the product from the test market to halt losses.

Setting Objectives. The final task for problem analysis, after a cause has been identified, is to set objectives for solving the problem. Often multiple objectives are set. In such cases, not only should the objectives be stated clearly and specifically, but also the decision maker must place priorities on them, since each alternative is not likely to achieve each objective equally well. Suppose the product manager established two objectives for the test marketed product with sluggish sales: (1) increase sales by 20 percent over current levels during the next three months, and (2) hold selling costs to their current level. While it is possible that a choice of an alternative could be made to simultaneously accomplish both these objectives, he must be prepared for the opposite possibility

---

[5] Kepner and Tregoe, *The Rational Manager,* p. 175.

(i.e., to achieve a 20 percent increase in sales might require additional selling costs beyond current levels). Determining the relative importance of the sales and cost objectives or combining them into a single criterion such as incremental profits guide the choice of an alternative when both objectives are impossible to fully achieve at the same time.

In some situations, decision making is necessary to respond to an opportunity rather than to a performance problem. An opportunity is a set of conditions present either in the organization or its environment that could lead, through appropriate decision making, to enhancement of the organization's goals. Examples of opportunities might be the discovery of an untapped market need/want, the internal development of new technology, or the identification of a cost-reducing production process improvement. While a problem and an opportunity are not identical the analysis of the latter parallels the former: (1) information must periodically be collected so that managers are set to "see" opportunities, (2) an opportunity must be described in detail to guide managers in determining why it exists and what is involved in taking advantage of it; and (3) finally, objectives must be set to provide standards for choice analysis and alternative implementation and control.

Choice Analysis

Choice analysis is probably the more familiar part of the process to decision makers. Moreover, this stage is usually a more straightforward and structured kind of analysis than is problem identification. This fact may, unfortunately, account for the tendency of decision makers to short-circuit the more difficult problem analysis and proceed to analyzing decision alternatives without a clear idea of what the decision should do.

Identification of Alternatives. Choice analysis involves several tasks necessary to complete the decision process (see Figure 11–1). Obviously, to make a decision, an alternative must be chosen and other alternatives must be rejected. Therefore, the first task in choice analysis is to identify a set of feasible alternative ways of solving a problem. Identifying alternatives is, in part, a creative process of reasoning from the problem causes to possible solutions and so, is dependent on the decision maker's creative abilities. Moreover, previous experience is often very useful since the solutions to similar past problems often suggest possible alternatives to current problems.

There are several guidelines for the selection process. First, simply knowing the causes of a problem should narrow the range of alternatives to those specially designed to cope with that problem. For example, if the brand name of a new food product is causing lower than expected sales, decision alternatives such as changes in distribution, price, and product features can be eliminated from consideration, and the decision maker can focus on changes in the brand name. There are still alternatives to be chosen (alternative brand names) but the range of feasible alternatives has been narrowed down considerably. Secondly, the objectives set for solving a problem guide the creative selection process. If one objective for solving the food product's sales deviation cause (poor brand name) is to have a name connoting "refreshing," only names that will do so will be identified. Finally, identifying alternatives may be facilitated by seeking information about the availability of feasible alternatives from others within the organization or from a variety of sources outside the organization.

Evaluation of Alternatives. Once alternatives have been identified, choice analysis turns to the evaluation of each one. This task is dependent on the objectives set for problem solutions. In fact, choice analysis is *a process of predicting how well each alternative will achieve each objective.* For quantitative objectives (e.g., sales, profits, market share, return on investment), prediction is in terms of expected payoffs; while for qualitative objectives (e.g., a specified reputation or image desired from the chosen alternative), prediction involves judgmental evaluations of the degree of consistency between the objective and the alternative.

Very often, particularly in marketing where decisions are intended to affect others (customers, competitors, channel members, etc.) there is considerable uncertainty about the ability of the alternatives to achieve objectives. Yet, the choice must still be made. Effective decision making must incorporate these uncertainties into the choice analysis so that the alternative chosen will have the best *chance* of achieving objectives. Decision making uncertainties refer to key factors that are largely uncontrolled by the organization and yet, will have a significant impact on the ability of the chosen alternative to achieve the objectives set for it. Key uncertainties include customer response, competitive reaction, acts of God, governmental regulation, technological developments, and states of the economy. Incorporating key uncertainties into choice analysis requires estimates of outcomes for each alternative under each possible reaction of each uncertainty, as well as opinions of how likely is it that each possible reaction will, in fact, occur.

Selection of an Alternative. Eventually, a decision must be made on the basis of a choice analysis. The choice should be the alternative that has the best choice or expectation of achieving the set of objectives (weighted by the priorities placed on them) determined during problem analysis. The choice should also have a degree of permanence to it. That is, the decision should prevent the same problem from recurring again and again. This can only be done by correcting the cause of the problem (if the cause is controllable) or at least adapting to the cause (if it is not controllable). Otherwise, all that will have been accomplished is a temporary postponing of the effects of a problem on performance. All too frequently, the postponement (or stopgap) type of decision is not recognized as such, and this leads to managerial "firefighting" (a series of decisions that only postpone a recurring problem) which continues to absorb a disproportionate amount of time and attention.

Implementation and Control

Effective decision making does not stop with the selection of an alternative. The tasks and responsibilities for implementing the decision must be planned and communicated to those involved in execution. For example, if the decision is to change brand name for a test marketed product, implementation may include: (1) notifying the firm's advertising agency to begin the search for and testing of a new brand name, (2) notifying packaging suppliers of the intention to change printing on new packages, (3) notifying salesmen to be ready to implement the name change in sales presentations to dealers, and (4) identifying and generating information that will convince dealers of the effectiveness of the new name.

In addition, procedures need to be determined for generating performance information so that effectiveness of the chosen alternative can be monitored. This information should be designed as closely as possible to measure performance directly in terms of the objectives used for choice analysis.

In marketing, the measurement of performance frequently is not a very easy or straightforward task. Consider, for example, trying to determine the effectiveness of a new advertising campaign in terms of a general performance goal such as the product's sales volume. Since there are so many variables affecting buyers' purchase decisions, simply noting sales changes will not provide a very good control measure. Yet, to filter out the effects of other variables on sales would require experimental manipulation and control that is difficult and expensive to do in real world settings.

Developing Decision-Making Skills

Upon taking a new job within any organization, managers should assess how well they are equipped to identify and respond to the problems and opportunities that will inevitably arise. In part this requires "rationalizing" the new position by identifying the performance responsibilities assigned to it, and evaluating the accessibility of needed information. Moreover, an effective way of dealing with problems and opportunities is required, and so managers must continually ensure that an analytical process approach to decision making is a well-developed skill.

A job description will help in delineating the areas of performance responsibility. However, much more is needed to truly be in command of a position. One must be set to see problems and opportunities very quickly after they begin to surface. This requires an assessment of the performance measurement information that is regularly flowing into the position. Answers to such questions as: (1) have objectives been set for performance?, (2) can performance information show achievement in terms of these objectives?, (3) are all objectives being monitored with performance information?, (4) is the form of the information input amenable to quick and efficient analysis?, and (5) how reliable are the information sources?—determine how quickly a decision maker can become aware of problems and opportunities. Clearly, these questions require considerable thought and anticipation of the problems and opportunities most likely to be faced by a decision maker in that particular position.

Effective decision making is also dependent upon being able to isolate problem causes or the dimensions of an opportunity. Thus, the decision maker should have a thorough understanding of how to use information services available to him. Chapter 12 provides considerable insight into several of these services. Familiarity with the various services upon which a decision maker can draw will enhance the smooth flow from one stage in a decision process to the next by providing key information inputs that may be needed but are not a part of the regular information inflow to a position.

The decision maker should have developed and be continually improving a style or approach to handling problems and opportunities. All styles should be built around an orderly, logical process including problem analysis, choice analysis, and choice implementation and control. However, while a text chapter can present a framework for developing a management style, it is clearly necessary to build experience by actually implementing these steps for real-world decision tasks. Such experience usually leads to development of very personal approaches to decision making that are still analytical in nature. For example, one manager may begin problem analysis by examining those possible causes on which information is readily available (e.g., check inventory stock in warehouses for a product with sagging sales), while another begins with those factors believed most important to product success.

DECISION-MAKING MODELS

Characteristics of Decision-Making Situations

While there is usually a period of time during which the transition to new ideas and concepts is slow and painful, decision making models are now, and will continue to be, an important part of the expertise required of the typical manager in the 1970s and 1980s:

The majority of today's top managers are struggling to grasp the jargon used by younger managers who are attempting to apply the new techniques in their companies . . . But just as size and complexity will not diminish, neither will the number of young managers conversant with these techniques. As they ascend to top decision making positions where the penalty for poor performance matches the stakes, they will call on new tools to help.[6]

To make effective use of the variety of decision-making models and tools, it is essential to understand not only their mechanical operations, but also the kinds of decision situations each one is most appropriately designed to handle. This section provides a classification scheme to aid the matching of specific decision models to situations most likely to benefit from each one. The scheme classifies models according to: (1) type of information required; (2) basic model purpose; (3) stage in the decision process; and (4) type of decision situation. Notice that (1) and (2) are model characteristics while (3) and (4) are situational characteristics affecting application. As an introduction to the classification, three types of decision-making situations are defined in terms of the quality and quantity of information available a decision maker: decisions under certainty, risk, and uncertainty.

Decisions under Certainty. Decisions under certainty represent the most complete or nearly perfect information-decision situation. Relating these decisions to the decision making process framework, a decision maker is able to: (1) identify a problem or opportunity, (2) determine problem causes or fully describe the opportunity, (3) identify choice alternatives, and (4) estimate payoffs for each alternative in terms of preset objectives. There are no key uncertainties, or if there are, the outcome of each key uncertainty is treated as if it is known with certainty. These characteristics approximate the perfect knowledge assumption so often made in microeconomics.

The primary difficulty facing a manager in this kind of situation is the processing of large quantities of information so that choice alternatives can be evaluated. If the information can be manipulated to highlight the relative payoffs of each alternative effectively, then the actual choice becomes automatic. The decision maker chooses the alternative with the highest certain payoff. The success of the decision, then, is totally dependent on the manager's ability to make use of the available information.

There are few organizational decisions, if any, that are truly decisions under certainty. However, the closest approximations are most likely to occur in the internal operations of an organization (e.g., production runs, materials handling, etc.). Organizations are often designed to insulate

---

[6] "Business Says It Can Handle Bigness," *Business Week*, October 17, 1970, p. 110.

internal operations from the uncertainties of dealing with the external environment. If environmental variables can be "eliminated" from influencing internal operations then generally greater efficiency can be achieved under such highly stable conditions.[7]

This insulation is generally achieved by having other functions in the organization (e.g., marketing, logistics) act as buffers between the uncertainties and fluctuations of dealing with an environment, and the desired certainty of internal operations. For example, to allow manufacturers the efficiency of spreading production of output rather evenly over an operating period, marketing and logistics will have to absorb the uncertainty inherent in the decision of how much output to produce. Marketing does this by forecasting sales and then using the selling functions to ensure that forecasts become reality. Logistics also may be needed to plan and implement inventory and transportation decisions so that the constant output flow can be matched to the uneven demands for output during the operating period.

Decisions under Risk. Decisions under risk introduce key uncertainties into the decision process. The decision maker recognizes that the success of any alternative depends upon what will happen with one or more key uncertainties, yet, he does not know, before making a decision, what these outcomes will be. For example, the success of introducing a new product is frequently dependent on both competitor and customer reactions, but management seldom knows with certainty what either reaction will be prior to the decision to go ahead. To make a decision under risk, it is still necessary to gather and use information in order to perform a problem analysis and identify alternatives. In addition, though, each possible reaction that each key uncertainty might take must be anticipated. If, for example, customer demand for a new product is uncertain, then management must determine what sales volumes are possible (from high to low) before a choice can be made. The same is true for possible competitor reactions and for other uncertainties that will determine the eventual success or failure of the product.

The distinguishing characteristic of a decision under risk, in addition to key uncertainties, is that the *likelihood* of each possible reaction of each key uncertainty is known. The decision maker cannot predict which one will occur with certainty, but he does know the *probability* that each reaction will occur. The decision maker must accept the risk of making the wrong choice, since that choice must be made prior to knowing what each key uncertainty will do. But, he does know the nature and extent of the risk he is taking.

An example of a decision under risk is represented by the pricing of life insurance policies. The major key uncertainty for this decision is

---

[7] James D. Thompson, *Organizations in Action* (New York: McGraw-Hill Book Company, 1967), pp. 11–12.

the death rates of people in different age groups. Death rates are highly predictable by using statistics on the actual life spans of people. Since death rates change very slowly (dependent on advancement in medical knowledge, nutrition, etc.) insurance companies have confidence in using them to estimate the probability of a person of a certain age dying within a given time period. Note that the company does not know for sure when each of its policyholders will die, but can only estimate the probability of a typical person in an age category dying within some designated number of years. Price, then, is based on the known risk of having to pay off on policies on persons within each age group. This risk is actually spread among all policyholders through lower prices since the insurance company can count on long-lived individuals to offset those that die unexpectedly soon.

Decisions under risk are most likely to be found in the "buffer" functional areas between an organization's internal operations and its environment, since the key uncertainties are generally environmental unknowns. However, this kind of decision is probably rather rare because decision makers do not often know for certain the probabilities of key uncertainty's reactions. Environmental variables are seldom so repetitious that sufficient experience can be built up to estimate these likelihoods accurately.

Decisions under Uncertainty. A decision under uncertainty is similar to a decision under risk except that the likelihoods of key uncertainties are not known for sure. Now, a decision maker does not even know the nature and the extent of the risk of making a poor decision. However, even though these likelihoods are not known for sure a manager will probably have some opinions as to what they are based on his judgment and experience.

Many of the decisions made by marketing managers are often of this type. For example, when deciding upon a price change, a key uncertainty might be the price elasticity of customers. However, customers' true price elasticity will probably not be known, nor will the likelihood of different price elasticities being the true one be known either (unless the firm makes many price changes in relatively short time periods and keeps accurate measures of resulting sales changes, or has done extensive marketing research).

In summary, all three types of decision situations require a manager to perform a problem analysis in order to prepare for evaluation of alternatives. The major difference between situations is: (1) whether or not there are key uncertainties that will affect the choice, and (2) if there are key uncertainties, how much information is available to predict the impact of each one. Since the availability and nature of information differs so greatly across decision situations, it is probably impossible to classify all decisions neatly into one of the three types. Rather, a more realistic appraisal of decisions suggests that there is a continuum between the types, as shown in Figure 11–2, with no well-defined cut-off points for each one. Moreover, this figure shows that the value of information to managers is largely determined by how much uncertainty is reduced with information. Value is determined by how far a decision situation is moved from the uncertainty side of the continuum toward a decision under certainty with the benefit of new information. For example, insurance companies move the pricing decision from a decision under uncertainty to a decision under risk by gathering death rate in-

FIGURE 11–2

Relationship between Decision under Uncertainty, Risk, and Certainty

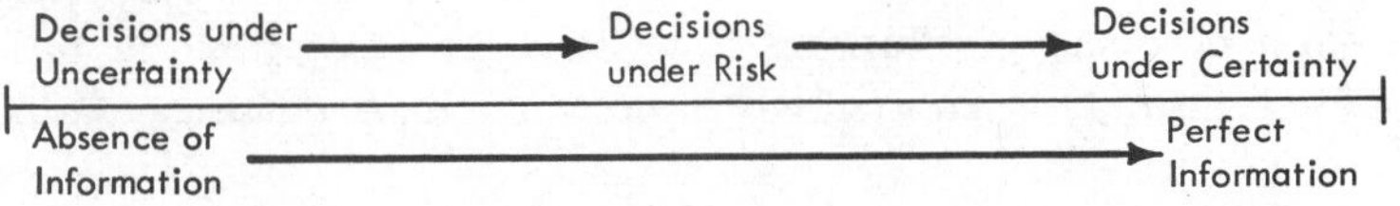

formation. The more accurate the death rate statistics are the more the pricing decision moves into the decisions-under-risk area of the continuum. Further movement toward a decision under certainty would require additional information to predict death of individual policyholders. The collection of medical histories and physical examination information on prospective policy holders help to increase the certainty of charging profitable prices, but does not move policy pricing all the way to the perfect information end of the continuum.

Classification of Decision Models

A model is an abstraction of a phenomenon of interest to the model builder and/or model user. This means that a model tries to show the key factors and relationships between factors that describe and explain the essential nature and workings of the phenomenon. Insignificant factors and relationships are typically purposely left out. As an example, customer demand for a grade of steel is a phenomenon of great interest to United States Steel and other steel companies. One possible model of steel demand is illustrated by a demand curve that shows the relationship between quantity of steel purchased and the price of steel. Use of a demand curve by steel company management would imply that price is believed to be the key determinant of steel purchases and that other possible factors (e.g., advertising) affecting demand are not sufficiently important to justify making the model more complex by including them.

The purpose of a model is to help the model builder and user better understanding and predict the phenomenon. Typically, models are built when the phenomenon is too complex to understand without separating out the key factors and relationships from those that are unimportant. For example, understanding the decision processes consumers go through when buying many products from toothpaste to houses is very difficult. So, consumer buying models (see Chapter 9) have been built to help researchers and managers understand and predict consumer buying. Model building, then, is a process of searching for those factors and relationships that are essential to describing and explaining the phenomenon of interest. How far this search goes is dependent upon the desired tradeoff between adding more factors and relationships to increase the explanatory or predictive power of the model and avoiding too much complexity and costs for the model to be useful to users.

Classification by Decision Characteristics. Models can be classified by the kind of decision situation that they are most directly designed to benefit. Figure 11–3 shows two important characteristics of decision

FIGURE 11–3

Decision Situational Characteristics Classification

	Problem Analysis and Control	*Choice Analysis*
Certainty	Multivariate statistical models Analysis of variance	Linear programming Marginal analysis-calculus Planning models General systems model
Risk	Buyer behavior flow models Planning models	Simulation Queing theory Planning models General systems model Expected value analysis
Uncertainty	General systems model Simulation	Bayesian decision theory Game theory Planning models General systems model

situations that help to explain differences in the use of decision making models: 1) the stage of the decision process and 2) the degree of uncertainty present in a situation. Notice that some models can be used for both problem analysis and control and choice analysis (e.g., systems models and simulation). In addition, models useful for problem analysis and control are *not* classified by certainty, risk, and uncertainty since all of these models can be applied in any of the three kinds of situations. It is primarily the choice analysis models that differ in application by certainty, risk, and uncertainty decision situations. Since the major distinctions between these situations lies in the presence or absence of key uncertainties, the corresponding distinctions between models in these cells are their ability and method for dealing with uncertainties. For example, the certainty models (particularly linear and related programming techniques and marginal analysis) are generally considered to be deterministic by requiring nonprobabilistic information inputs and providing nonprobabilistic outputs. The risk and uncertainty models (particularly simulation, queing theory, expected value analysis, Bayesian decision theory, and game theory) are designed to deal explicitly with uncertainties. All, except game theory and the general planning and systems models, can use probabilistic information inputs (i.e., likelihood of key uncertainty states occurring) and incorporate the notion of chance or likelihood into the assessment of choice alternatives. Game theory is designed to handle key uncertainties without having to rely on probabilistic information inputs.

Classification by Model Characteristics. Another useful way to classify decision making models is by selected characteristics of the models themselves. Figure 11–4 shows a classification by model purpose

FIGURE 11–4

Model Characteristics Classification

	Descriptive	*Normative*
Quantitative	Multivariate statistical models (multiple regression, discriminant analysis, factor analysis, etc.) Simulation Analysis of variance	Optimization models (linear programming, marginal analysis, etc.) Bayesian decision theory Game theory
Qualitative	Buyer behavior flow models	General decision framework models General system model Planning models (e.g., Pert)

(normative versus descriptive) and by type of information needed as inputs (quantitative versus qualitative). Turning first to model purpose, descriptive models are intended to *describe* some real world process. This kind of model identifies key variables and relationships underlying the process of interest. Often the descriptive model is used to facilitate the prediction of some future outcome of the process. For example, a frequently used descriptive model is multiple regression (multivariate statistical model). If a manager wanted to predict who would be most likely to purchase his product, multiple regression could be used to describe most important characteristics (demographics, attitudes, etc.) of previous purchasers.[8] Prediction is then possible by assuming that the same kinds of buyers as described by the model will also be future purchasers.

Normative models have quite a different purpose. These models are intended to *prescribe* how a real world process ought to be. Prescription is achieved by modeling how a decision maker *should* proceed through some part or all of a decision making/planning process. Moreover, such models will often prescribe what information inputs ought to be provided to accomplish the task. The general decision making framework presented in Figure 11–1 is an example of a normative model.

A second classification characteristic of decision models is type of information required as inputs. Quantitative models require that variables and information inputs be numerical. Moreover, the relationship between variables must be mathematical. Analysis of variance hypothesis testing models[9] as well as simulation[10] fall into this category. Qualitative models do not require numerical inputs or mathematical relationships. Instead, the variables and variable relationships are expressed verbally or by diagram. The general decision making framework shown in Figure 11–1 is a qualitative model.

Model Classification Relationships. There are some interesting relationships between the models in these classification schemes. For example, Figure 11–4 shows that buyer behavior models can be either qualitative or quantitative. Frequently, one hears the opinion that behavior cannot be quantified and therefore, models of buyer behavior must be essentially qualitative. However, many descriptive quantitative models are actually describing the way in which customers behave. As an example, regression analysis showing the relationship between sales and such buyer characteristics as income, age, education, and attitudes is really mathematically describing what buying decisions (sales) have been made by different classes of customers.

Also, there is a correspondence between the models classified by model purpose (Figure 11–4) and by stage in the decision process (Figure 11–3). Models that are descriptive are most likely to be applied in the earlier stages of a decision process. This is to be expected since

---

[8] As an example see Ronald E. Frank, "Correlates of Buying Behavior for Grocery Products," *Journal of Marketing*, vol. 31 (October 1967), pp. 48–53, published by the American Marketing Association.

[9] See, for example, Charles W. Holland and David W. Cravens, "Fractional Factorial Experimental Designs in Marketing Research," *Journal of Marketing Research* (August 1973), pp. 270–76.

[10] See, for example, Daniel J. Sweeney, "Improving the Profitability of Retail Merchandising Decision," *Journal of Marketing* (January 1973), pp. 60–68.

description of the characteristics of an opportunity or the discovery of problems and problem causes are the major tasks of problem analysis and control. On the contrary, the major task of choice analysis is to evaluate alternatives. Here the decision maker must relate alternative performance to decision objectives. The normative models, then, are useful to guide decision makers through the kind of analysis that will ensure that the alternative most likely to achieve objectives is identified.

Finally, the classification of models by certainty, risk, and uncertainty decision situations is most applicable for normative models which are primarily applied during choice analysis. This is reasonable since the distinction between these situations lies in the presence or absence of key uncertainties which are variables that the decision maker must assess during choice analysis.

An Example of a Decision Making Model

A model of growing importance to business decision makers is Bayesian decision theory. This model is normative and quantitative, and is intended to aid a decision maker during the choice analysis stage of a decision process under conditions of uncertainty. Recall that under uncertainty the decision maker is trying to choose between several alternatives to solve a known problem or take advantage of an opportunity. The task is complicated by one or more key uncertainties where it is not known for sure what reaction each uncertainty will take or with what likelihoods. In this kind of situation, Bayesian decision theory offers a procedure for the decision maker to follow by using the concepts of expected value and subjective probability.

To choose between several alternatives, the decision maker must have one or more objectives or criteria upon which to base a comparison. Bayesian decision theory uses the concept of expected value as an objective: *The decision maker should choose the alternative that maximizes the expected value of the decision.* "Value" can be expressed in a variety of ways (e.g., profits, ROI, market share, sales, etc.) as long as it is expressed quantitatively. The notion of "expected" is particularly appropriate for a decision under uncertainty because it recognizes that before making the final choice the decision maker does not know with certainty which reaction each key uncertainty will take. Consequently, it is impossible to know with certainty the value of each alternative. However, if a manager can estimate how likely each possible reaction is, then the value expected from each alternative can be calculated.

To illustrate the application of Bayesian decision theory suppose a decision maker was trying to decide whether or not to introduce a new product. The payoff to the firm from introducing the product depends upon how consumers will respond, and the decision maker is not certain what that market response will be. To conduct the analysis the decision maker estimates the possible responses (e.g., high, medium, low) the market will make as well as the value (e.g., profits) the firm will receive if the product is introduced and each response occurs. These estimates can be summarized in a payoff table:

	Market Response		
	High	*Medium*	*Low*
Introduce the product.........	$200,000	$40,000	−$160,000
Don't introduce..............	$ 0	$ 0	$ 0

Suppose that the manager believed (based on his judgment and experience) that a high response was twice as likely to occur as either a medium or low response and that a medium response was about equally likely to occur as a low response. These beliefs could be expressed in terms of probabilities by setting the probability of a high response equal to $\frac{1}{2}$, of a medium response equal to $\frac{1}{4}$, and of a low response equal to $\frac{1}{4}$. Given this information, the value that the decision maker "expects" to obtain from introducing the product can be calculated by weighting each possible payoff with the probability of the corresponding market response occurring:

$$\text{Expected Value} = \sum_{i=1}^{n} \text{Payoff}_i \times \text{Probability}_i$$

Where

i = the ith key uncertainty state
n = the number of key uncertainty states

The expected value of introducing the new product is $70,000 ($\frac{1}{2}(200,000) + \frac{1}{4}(40,000) + \frac{1}{4}(-160,000)$) and can be compared to the expected value of not introducing the product which is $0. Expected value, then, requires two kinds of information beyond identifying alternatives and key uncertainties—payoffs (value) from each alternative under each reaction of each key uncertainty, and likelihoods (expectations) of each reaction of each key uncertainty occurring.

While the concept of expected value is not difficult to grasp, the notion of likelihood is more complex. In a decision under uncertainty, the decision maker cannot use the traditional meaning of probability, objective probability,[11] to estimate the likelihoods required by expected

---

[11] Objective probability is defined as a ratio of the number of successes to the number of opportunities for success to occur, $p = \dfrac{\text{\# of successful events}}{\text{\# of total events}}$, where the denominator is large. For example, the probability of getting a head on the toss of a fair coin is $\frac{1}{2}$ because if the coin was tossed a large number of times, the ratio, $\dfrac{\text{\# of heads}}{\text{\# of tosses}}$ would be approximately $\frac{1}{2}$.

value. Objective probability is dependent on having considerable, repetitive "experience" (e.g., death rate statistics) with the event for which likelihoods are being estimated. This is seldom characteristic of marketing decisions and, by definition, not true for decisions under uncertainty.

In Bayesian decision theory, the concept of subjective probability is used in place of objective probability when calculating expected values. Subjective probabilities are quantifications or indexes representing a decision maker's judgment or opinion about the occurrence of key uncertainty states. Since managers may very well be able to express likelihood opinions even for rather unique decision situations (e.g., introduction of a new product), subjective probabilities are not dependent upon a history of repetitive experiences. But, since managers will often have different opinions about likelihood for the same key uncertainties in the same situation, subjective probabilities are clearly "personal" or unique only for each manager.

Application of Bayesian decision theory requires several inputs from managers as illustrated in the new product decision example above. Since the approach is a choice analysis model, the decision task must be structured to the point where choice alternatives are ready to be evaluated. Using Figure 11–1, this means that management must identify the problem or opportunity, determine causes, set objectives, identify alternatives, and determine the key uncertainties that will affect the decision outcome. A payoff table summarizes these inputs by listing alternatives down the side of the matrix and states of a key uncertainty across the top.

To complete the payoff table, management supplies estimates of payoffs conditioned on each key uncertainty state occurring for each decision alternative. For example, in Figure 11–5, P_{11} is the payoff that management expects to receive if alternative A_1 is selected and key uncertainty state S_1 happens. In addition, to calculate expected value for each alternative, management must assess the likelihood (P_r) of each key uncertainty state actually occurring by assigning subjective probabilities over all the states. Once the payoff table has been completely determined, the task becomes a mechanical one of computing expected values for the alternatives.

The central characteristic of Bayesian decision theory applications is the formal use of payoffs and subjective probabilities in decision making. Neither of these factors are scientifically obtained, but really represent the quantification of managerial judgment. Thus, Bayesian decision theory is intended to aid managers in making the best use of their experience and judgment when faced with a difficult decision under uncertainty. The model's value lies in its ability to show unambiguously the implications of the judgment expressed in the payoff table for select-

FIGURE 11–5

A Payoff Matrix

Decision Alternatives	States of Key Uncertainty				
	S_1	S_2	S_3	S_4	S_5
A_1	P_{11}	P_{12}	P_{13}	P_{14}	P_{15}
A_2	P_{21}	P_{22}	P_{23}	O_{24}	P_{25}
A_3	P_{31}	P_{32}	P_{33}	P_{34}	P_{35}
A_4	P_{41}	P_{42}	P_{43}	P_{44}	P_{45}
Likelihoods	P_{r1}	P_{r2}	P_{r3}	P_{r4}	P_{r5}

ing a choice alternative. Consequently, managers must develop the ability to supply numbers that accurately represent their beliefs.

The techniques for obtaining appropriate quantification of managerial judgment are still developing.[12] Clearly, the needed numerical estimates must come directly from managers since their judgment, rather than that of an analyst, is required. But, an analyst who is more familiar with the concepts of probability and distributions may be able to help a manager determine numbers that best represent judgment. At the present state of the art, this typically involves the analyst preparing a series of questions for the manager whose judgment is needed. The answers given by the manager will tell the analyst what numbers to use for the Bayesian decision theory application. Suppose, for example, that a single estimate of payoff was needed for a decision on whether to add a salesman in one of a firm's territories, given that competitors will not increase their sales force (a key uncertainty state). An analyst might assist the sales manager in quantifying this estimate with the following kinds of questions:

ANALYST: What do you think is the highest sales volume that the salesman will generate?

SALES EXECUTIVE: I'm not sure, but I believe it would be pretty high.

ANALYST: More than $1,000,000?

SALES EXECUTIVE: No, not that high. Probably only half that amount. No more than $500,000.

ANALYST: O.K., what's the worst the salesman could do?

---

[12] For an excellent discussion of techniques for quantifying judgment see Philip Kotler, "A Guide to Gathering Expert Estimates," *Business Horizons* (October 1970), pp. 79–87.

SALES EXECUTIVE: If he is as good as our other salesman, he would generate at least $75,000 in sales.

ANALYST: Do you believe the salesmen will sell closer to $75,000 than $500,000?

SALES EXECUTIVE: No, the territory is not fully developed. So, a new salesman ought to sell much closer to $500,000.

ANALYST: About $350,000?

SALES EXECUTIVE: No, that is a little high based on what our other salesmen are able to do.

ANALYST: How much too high?

SALES EXECUTIVE: About $50,000.

ANALYST: So you expect the new salesman will generate approximately $300,000 in sales.

SALES EXECUTIVE: Yes.[13]

Notice in the dialogue how the manager used his experience (e.g., knowledge of the territory, performance of existing salesmen) to arrive at an estimate of the payoff. The same process could be followed for sales volume expected under each of the other possible reactions of competitors (key uncertainty states). Moreover, the questioning could be changed slightly to estimate probabilities for each competitive reaction possibility. Rather than sales volume, the analyst would pose the questions in terms of how likely it is that a competitor will respond in a certain way if a new salesman is added. This would require that the sales executive understand the concept of probability. Other more complex procedures involving the estimating of entire payoff and likelihood distributions are also available, though the procedure is similar. The analyst must pose questions so that answers dictate the needed numerical estimate.

Several benefits are reaped by the use of Bayesian theory. First, the structuring of the choice analysis by building a decision tree forces the decision maker to be thorough and complete by ensuring that all ramifications of the choice have been considered. Moreover, the decision maker can focus entirely on identifying and providing the essential information and judgmental inputs, since the manipulation of the information (calculating expected values) can be turned over to a computer or even a clerk with a calculator.

Second, the quantification of managerial judgment through the use of subjective probabilities offers several advantages. As anyone who has had to assess subjective probabilities knows, supplying probabilities for analysis requires the decision maker rigorously to consider his own information and experiences that form the basis for his opinions: "What information do I have about this situation?" "What experiences

---

[13] This is illustrative of the approach discussed in Ibid. It is an accepted technique for obtaining subjective point estimates.

have I had with similar situations?" "How reliable are the sources of my information?" "Are there any inconsistencies in information from different sources?" These are all questions that may run through the decision maker's mind before he is willing to give a set of numbers reflecting his opinions. This can clear up the haziness that often accompanies the use of judgment. Of course, there is always the chance that a particular manager will state probabilities that hide true feelings or support a desired choice alternative regardless of true beliefs. However, this would be a misuse of Bayesian decision theory that will negate any help the manager might have gotten from the analysis for a decision. To use Bayesian decision theory as a tool for improving decisions, managers must recognize that it is in their best interests to state subjective probabilities reflecting true beliefs.

Marketing decisions often represent the result of joint efforts of several decision makers. For example, the development of an advertising campaign for a particular brand may be the responsibility of a brand manager, his assistants, and advertising agency account executives. Subjective probabilities represent an efficient language for individuals to use for group decision making. It would be clearly more efficient and concise to say, for instance, "I believe there is a .8 chance that our major competitor will spend more than $4,000,000 on their advertising campaign this year" than to provide the more vague expression of opinion, "I believe that our major competitor might very well spend more than $4,000,000 on their advertising campaign this year."

Finally, Bayesian decision theory can be effectively used as a tool for sensitivity analyses. Sensitivity analysis is the process of determining how sensitive the choice between alternatives is to the key estimates and judgments. This can be accomplished by seeing how much the subjective probabilities, payoffs, and/or key uncertainty states have to change before the selection of an alternative would change. If the choice is insensitive to a wide range of inputs, the decision maker knows that the accuracy of his estimates are not crucial to the choice. However, if the selection is sensitive to managerial inputs, then accuracy becomes much more critical and suggests the need for additional information before the choice is made (depending, of course, on how confident the decision maker is in the accuracy of his estimates).

The use of Bayesian decision theory is relatively new to business. However, there has been a clear trend toward greater application in the past ten years:

> Only a few U.S. companies appear to have used DTA (Decision Theory Analysis) in operations for any length of time. Two of these companies are DuPont, which got started with the approach in the late 1950s, and Pillsbury, which got started in the early 1960s. However, there has been a dramatic increase in DTA activity since about 1964.

That is when executive interest began to be stimulated, notably by articles in HBR (*Harvard Business Review*), executive orientation seminars, and reports of successful applications on the part of pioneering companies, and, perhaps most important of all, a steady stream of DTA-trained MBAs who began to enter managerial ranks in substantial numbers.[14]

Managerial Use of Models

Models can be used in an information system to replace the more routine decisions of management. For example, EOQ (Economic Ordering Quantity) models have been built into automatic inventory reordering systems where the decision to restock inventories of raw material, stock, or supplies is made mechanically based on computer manipulation of information. However, for many models, the applications are not designed to replace management decision making, but rather to provide tools to help managers improve their ability to successfully cope with complex, nonroutine decision tasks such as introducing new products, investing in plant and major equipment, and changing prices in highly competitive markets.

Since models are intended to aid and improve managerial decision making, it is essential for managers to be able and willing to use available models. Unfortunately, not all corporate experiences with various models have been positive, and so, there is skepticism among many managers concerning their practicality.[15] Part of the reason for this can be attributed to the lack of training possessed by the managers. This deficiency will eventually be remedied by the educational process.

A second and equally important reason for managerial skepticism lies in the model building process which is too often solely an operations research function. Without managerial involvement during the model design, managers may not understand the models developed and/or may not believe that they are appropriate for their needs because of faulty assumptions, requirements for unattainable information, or incompleteness. In either case, managers will not use the models that operations research groups develop unless they can be convinced of their utility in practical decision making situations. To remedy this, models must be designed to conform to a manager's analytical abilities and his view of important factors affecting his area of responsibility:

> If we want a manager to use a model, we should make it his, an extension of his ability to think about and analyze his operation. This

---

[14] Rex V. Brown, "Do Managers Find Decision Theory Useful?" *Harvard Business Review*, vol. 48 (May 1970), p. 81.

[15] For example, see Brown, "Do Managers Find Decision Theory Useful?" pp. 84–85.

puts special requirements on design and will often produce something rather different from what a management scientist might otherwise build. I propose a name to describe the result. A *decision calculus* will be defined as a model-based set of procedures for processing data and judgments to assist a manager in his decision making.

From experience gained so far, it is suggested that a decision calculus should be:

(1) *Simple.* Simplicity promotes ease of understanding. Important phenomena should be put in the model and unimportant ones left out. Strong pressure often builds up to put more and more detail into a model. This should be resisted, until the users demonstrate they are ready to assimilate it.

(2) *Robust.* Here I mean that a user should find it difficult to make the model give bad answers. This can be done by a structure that inherently constrains answers to a meaningful range of values.

(3) *Easy to control.* A user should be able to make the model behave the way he wants it to . . . I rather suspect that if the manager cannot control the model he will not use it for fear it will coerce him into actions he does not believe in. However, I do not expect the manager to abuse the capability because he is honestly looking for help.

(4) *Adaptive.* The model should be capable of being updated as new information becomes available. This is especially true of the parameters but to some extent of structure too.

(5) *Complete on important issues.* Completeness is in conflict with simplicity. Structures must be found that can handle many phenomena without bogging down. An important aid to completeness is the incorporation of subjective judgments. . . . One problem posed by the use of subjective inputs is that they personalize the model to the individual or group that makes the judgments. This makes the model, at least superficially, more fragile and less to be trusted by others than, say, a totally empirical model. However, the model with subjective estimates may often be a good deal tougher because it is more complete and conforms more realistically to the world.

(6) *Easy to communicate with.* The manager should be able to change inputs easily and obtain outputs quickly. On-line, conversational I/Q and time-shared computing make this possible.[16]

Models, when designed to meet these requirements, are highly practical and useful to managers. They require the manager to structure the decision task as much as is possible given the information available at the time. This can be clearly seen in the application of Bayesian decision theory. Structuring is necessary to ensure that all available and relevant information and judgments are incorporated into the analysis, and to enable the decision maker to identify information that is missing but obtainable. Thus, even models that are most useful at the problem analysis stage of a decision process require the decision maker to go as

---

[16] John D. C. Little, "Models and Managers: The Concept of a Decision Calculus," *Management Science,* vol. 16 (April 1970), B–469–70.

far as he can in structuring the problem so he can determine what he needs to know to complete the decision analysis.

In addition, models provide a tool for manager-model dialogues. To cope with uncertainty, managers often use models to probe the situation by asking "What if" questions: "What if there is a ⅚ chance of competition introducing a new product?" "What if the chance is only ½?" "What if consumers' response takes six months to show a trend?" "What if dealers don't push our new product?" In essence, management would like to have some indication of decision outcomes that would occur under different alternative choices, assumptions, estimates, and factors without having to actually try decisions in the real world. Decision models can be effectively used for this purpose by simply plugging in the implications of the "What if" questions and recalculating model outputs. With the aid of a remote terminal for the manager and the programming of the model on a computer, model-manager dialogues can be handled very quickly.

SUMMARY AND CONCLUSIONS

Management, whether it be in marketing, finance, production, or in any other function of an organization, is primarily decision making. Consequently, to be effective a manager must develop and continually refine a decision making style that will serve as a guide through even the most difficult and complex problem solving tasks. While management styles differ in subtle ways, effective decision making should be analytical in nature. That is, decision-making style should be built around an orderly, thorough process beginning with problem analysis and then moving into choice analysis and implementation and control. Certainly, each individual manager may develop unique and creative approaches to each of these stages but the process itself must form the foundation for the overall approach.

An inherent part of decision making processes is the use of appropriate information, estimates, and personal judgment to reach decisions in complex situations. It is becoming increasingly clear that the manager of the future will be equipped with decision making tools in the form of models to take over the routine decisions and to aid him in analyzing the more difficult, non-routine decisions. To be an effective applier of the many models becoming available, managers must not only understand the mechanics, but also the kinds of inputs required and the kinds of decisions situations in which these models are designed to be used.

EXERCISES FOR REVIEW AND DISCUSSION

1. A large food company charged a new product management team with the responsibility for deciding whether to introduce a new product. After a

careful analysis of market opportunity the team constructs the following payoff table summarizing the analysis conducted to date (where payoff is net profit). What decision should be made to maximize profits if no additional information is to be collected?

Payoff Matrix ($000)

	S_1 Very High Sales Response	S_2 High Sales Response	S_3 Moderate Sales Response	S_4 Low Sales Response
A_1: Do not introduce	0	0	0	0
A_2: Introduce Model 1	2,175	1,550	−505	−850
A_3: Introduce Model 2	1,050	790	480	−125
Subjective sales response probabilities	.12	.25	.40	.23

2. Suppose you were asked to review the decision made by the new product management team described in exercise 1. The team ultimately decided to introduce model 1. Unfortunately sales response was low to moderate and the company lost $240,000 on the venture. Did the management team make a bad decision? Discuss.

3. The Vice President of Sales for an industrial producer of packaging equipment analyzed the opportunity for adding additional salesmen to the company's sales force. The alternatives being considered ranged from maintaining the current size of the sales force by hiring no salesmen to hiring as many as five additional salesmen. The cost of hiring and training an additional salesman averaged $22,000 for the first year and then reduced to salary, commission, and expenses thereafter (the average compensation and expenses for current company salesmen is $19,000). To complete the analysis, the VP requested information from divisional sales managers on the expected additional sales that could be generated with the adding of a new salesman in their territories. This information would be used to estimate sales response that could be expected from each alternative. Should this decision be treated as a decision under certainty, risk, or uncertainty? Why?

4. Select one model from Figure 11–3 or 11–4 that you believe would help the Vice President of Sales in making the decision described in the previous exercise. Describe the purpose and nature of this model and then, show how it would be used in the salesman decision. (Hint: you will have to review outside literature to learn about the model).

5. Select a kind of marketing position or job (e.g., industrial salesman, sales manager, brand manager, etc.) within a company in which you might be

interested and then assume that you have just taken that job. Discuss how you would "rationalize" this new position by insuring that you will be able to be analytical in your approach to decisions you will have to make.

6. Suppose you overheard the following conversation between several corporate functional managers. Assess how well these managers appear to grasp the concepts of an analytical decision process.

DISTRICT SALES MANAGER: We have been receiving more complaints than usual from customers about our system controls. Our problem seems to be slow delivery.

TRAFFIC MANAGER: We are using the fastest mode of transportation now that we can afford. Perhaps our problem is that competitors are located closer to these customers than we are.

VICE PRESIDENT OF SALES: As I see it, we face the problem of lowering price to give our salesmen something more to talk about in their sales presentations. We will have to keep a tight rein on our costs to do this, though.

DISTRICT SALES MANAGER: I agree. My salesmen have been clamoring for more freedom to discuss price with clients.

TRAFFIC MANAGER: I believe we can keep shipping costs in line for the next six months. If we get into a bind we can use lower-rate modes without sacrificing very much service time.

DISTRICT SALES MANAGER: We can also reduce the cost per sales call, since my salesmen ought to have to spend less time with each customer with greater freedom over price.

VICE PRESIDENT OF SALES: Its agreed, then. We will recommend as much as a 15 percent reduction in price for these controls with salesmen having the authority to negotiate price with customers up to this maximum discount.

12

Marketing Information Planning

Relevant and timely information is essential to effective decision making. The importance of information to a given decision situation can be gauged by the amount of uncertainty which confronts the decision maker (the information gap). Montgomery Ward faced a severe "information gap" regarding new store location decision making in the mid 1950s. Confronted with the need for a major store expansion program the company had not opened a single new store since the beginning of World War II. Past store location decisions had been made by executive judgment with limited supporting information. Recognizing the need for careful analysis of location decisions, in 1957 Ward's top management hired a location specialist who established a store Research and Development Department.[1] This group collected and analyzed information and developed studies on population shifts, merchandise markets, transportation, competition-by-location, buyer preferences and habits, capital costs, breakeven points, and return on investment. Management, armed with detailed analyses and recommendations from the research group, was able to reduce the uncertainty surrounding their store location decisions and to assess more carefully the significance of the remaining information gaps. The location expertise developed by this group provided an important information resource when Robert Booker took over as chief executive in 1961. He initiated an expanded new store and existing store relocation program to deploy the firm into new markets as a central element of overall corporate strategy which is attributed to putting Wards "on the road to recovery."[2]

Marketing information should be viewed as a resource to be used by

---

[1] "Montgomery Ward: Prosperity Is Still Around the Corner," *Fortune* (November 1960), p. 142.

[2] "The Strategy that Saved Montgomery Ward," *Fortune* (May 1970), p. 226.

the marketing manager the same as the product or service, price, promotion, and distribution strategy components. Business executives frequently are faced with decisions associated with obtaining information, evaluating its quality, and determining its relevance in problem solving. Examples include: whether to conduct a market opportunity analysis study; assessment of product line performance; evaluation of the accuracy of intelligence on competitor activities; assessment of the feasibility of new product ideas; forecasting sales; and determination of the need for a marketing information system. Both the quantity and quality of information available to decision makers to aid them in making these decisions vary substantially. These variations necessitate that the marketing executive develop effective skills in using information.

This chapter provides the marketing decision maker with a set of integrated guidelines for information planning. The focus is upon the user of information as contrasted to the information technician or specialist. We first examine the nature and scope of the firm's marketing information activities and then develop a framework to aid the marketing executive in information planning. Each of the major phases of the information planning process is discussed and illustrated. These include: determining information needs; assessing the impact of additional information on marketing decisions; determining an information strategy; assembling information; and evaluation and interpretation of results. Finally, the basic structure and components of marketing information systems are examined.

THE ORGANIZATION'S MARKETING INFORMATION ACTIVITIES

Some writers have distinguished between information and data by indicating that information is "knowledge derived through the analysis of data."[3] Others characterize information as recorded experience which is relevant for decision making.[4] Our perspective toward marketing information is broad: *Marketing information is any communication or recorded experience (written, verbal, or visual) available to the marketing decision maker that is relevant or potentially useful to decision making activities.* Thus, information used by the marketing decision maker can range from formal research studies to intelligence on competitors' activities received from field salesmen. It can originate from various sources, both internal and external to the organization, and is used in many ways to aid the marketing decision maker in the management of his area of responsibility.

---

[3] James H. Myers and Richard R. Mead, *The Management of Marketing Research* (Scranton, Pennsylvania: International Textbook Company, 1969), p. 5.

[4] Paul E. Green and Donald S. Tull, *Research for Marketing Decisions*, 2d ed. (Englewood Cliffs, New Jersey: Prentice-Hall, 1970), p. 10.

TABLE 12–1

Examples of Marketing Information in Various Decision Areas

	Stage or Phase of Decision Making		
Decision Area	*Opportunity/Problem Information (where you are now and where you should be going)*	*Choice Information or Action (how to get there)*	*Control Information (how well you are doing)*
Managerial analysis of the marketing environment	Forecast of trends over the next decade in moving raw materials and finished goods by various transportation modes including air, water, rail, highway, and pipeline (developed by a large barge transportation firm)	Estimates of the potential market for industrial robots based on: (1) interviews with factory executives in manufacturing firms; (2) U.S. Government Census of Manufactures and Dun & Bradstreet listings of manufacturing establishments; and (3) detailed analysis of most promising user industries (conducted by a marketing research firm for a robot manufacturer) §	Audit of bank policies and practices relative to consumer affairs carried out by a team from the Ralph Nader (consumer crusader) organization at the request of a large, Southeastern bank, and aimed at providing the bank's management with an objective analysis and recommendations for improving customer services and overall corporate citizenship
Corporate and marketing strategy Market targets	National Menu Census conducted by Market Research Corp. and financed by General Mills, General Foods, Pillsbury, Campbell Soup, and several other food giants. These firms pay up to $125,000 each for the information obtained from a sample of 4,000 households concerning their food habits‡	Survey of a sample of 800 Interstate highway travelers by a fast-food franchise firm to determine: the consumers' socio-economic and demographic characteristics and their opinions and preferences toward the firm's food and services	Sales and profitability analysis of customers by a portable electric tool manufacturer which provided information for reducing the firm's active accounts by 40 percent which resulted in a 21 percent increase in sales, a 28 percent reduction in paperwork, and a 5 percent reduction in marketing costs‖
Product/service	General Electric's "consumer information system" (national probability sample of households that provides attitude and preference information on a continuing basis) used in the planning and evaluation of new products and product failures.*		

Distribution	Study conducted by a large retail food chain seeking to determine future potential for telephone purchase of food by consumers and delivery from a computer controlled warehouse system	Experimental development of point-of-sale (POS) automated checkout systems by supermarket chains and data processing firms. POS Systems are aimed at making check-stand operations more efficient and providing a variety of management reports#	Evaluation of effectiveness and efficiency of distribution via company-owned retail stores compared to use of franchised outlets
Price	Survey of potential industrial buyers concerning a probable acceptable price range for a proposed new quality control system for use in cotton mills	Use of a panel made up of husbands and wives to collect information concerning price perceptions for a new household security system	Study of sales/cost ratios of orders received versus orders lost to competitors by an industrial equipment manufacturer who sells by quoting to customer specifications and orders are awarded to the lowest qualified bidder
Advertising and sales force	Longitudinal (several waves of interviews) field studies conducted by a large automobile manufacturer to enable improved planning and control of advertising and measurement of effectiveness. Information collected includes brand preferences, product image, message registration, market behavior, product inventory, demographics, and media consumption†		Analysis of sales results of a pharmaceutical manufacturer's sales territories and various determinants of results including market potential, work load in territory, salesman experience and effort, and company experience and effort

* Robert W. Pratt, Jr., "Using Research to Reduce Risk Associated with Marketing New Products," in *Changing Marketing Systems*, Reed Moyer, ed. (Chicago: American Marketing Association, 1967), pp. 98–104.
† Gail Smith, "How G M Measures Ad Effectiveness," *Printers Ink* (May 14, 1965), pp. 19–29.
‡ "How Three Families Buy Their Food," *Business Week* (November 25, 1972), pp. 86–90.
§ Robert D. Buzzell, et al., *Marketing Research and Information Systems* (New York: McGraw-Hill Book Co., 1969), pp. 386–406.
‖ "Skill Finally Breaks the Profits Barrier," *Business Week* (November 25, 1972), p. 54.
"Supermarkets Seek Systems Solutions to Profit Squeeze," *Datamation* (November 1972), pp. 142–48.

How Marketing Information Is Used

In the last chapter three general phases of decision activities were identified. Moving through these stages essentially involves determining where you are now; where you should be going; how to get there; and after an appropriate course of action is selected and implemented, determining how well are you doing. The decision maker's information needs vary in each phase. Several examples of marketing information which illustrate the nature and scope of information used by the decision maker in the three phases of decision making as well as in the various decision making areas in marketing (e.g., decisions regarding market targets, distribution, advertising, etc.) are shown in Table 12–1. Several characteristics of marketing information are suggested by the examples provided in Table 12–1:

Marketing information may be collected by the organization or purchased from a marketing research firm.

Various types of information are used by the marketing decision maker including survey research data, internal operating data, and information resulting from judgment and experience.

A variety of sources contain information useful to the marketing decision maker including consumers, industrial customers, government agencies, trade associations, company files, competition, and experts in particular fields (e.g., Ralph Nader).

Information may be collected for the particular purpose at hand (primary data) or may already be available for a variety of uses (secondary data).

Information needs are more difficult for the decision maker to specify when the decision situation is poorly structured (e.g., opportunity/ problem monitoring) compared to clearly defined situations (e.g., control information).

Field collection of information may be at one point in time (cross sectional study) or periodically over some time period (longitudinal study).

Development of Information Activities

Development of marketing information activities in business firms has moved through two stages during the past fifty years. The first formal activities involved research aimed at collection and analysis of information concerning markets. The market research function has since expanded to encompass research on all aspects of marketing. Today, marketing research includes a wide variety of activities as illustrated in

TABLE 12–2

Marketing Research Activities

	Percent Doing	Done By Mkt. Res. Dept.	Done By Another Dept.	Done By Outside Firm
Advertising research				
A. Motivation research	33	18	2	16
B. Copy research	37	17	6	18
C. Media research	44	16	10	21
D. Studies of ad effectiveness	49	26	7	21
E. Other	7	5	—	2
Business economics and corporate research				
A. Short-Range forecasting (up to 1 year)	63	43	23	1
B. Long-Range forecasting (over 1 year)	61	42	22	2
C. Studies of business trends	61	46	16	3
D. Pricing studies	56	33	25	2
E. Plant and warehouse location studies	47	18	28	3
F. Product mix studies	51	36	16	2
G. Acquisition studies	53	25	30	3
H. Export and international studies	41	19	22	3
I. Internal company employees studies (attitudes, communication etc.)	45	13	29	6
J. Other	4	3	1	—
Corporate responsibility research				
A Consumers' "right to know" studies	18	9	7	4
B Ecological impact studies	27	8	16	5
C. Studies of legal constraints on advertising and promotion	38	7	28	5
D. Social values and policies studies	25	11	12	4
E. Other	2	1	1	—
Product research				
A. New product acceptance and potential	63	51	9	8
B. Competitive product studies	64	52	11	6
C. Testing of existing products	57	35	20	7
D. Packaging research: Design or physical characteristics	44	23	17	9
E. Other	3	2	1	1
Sales and market research				
A. Measurement of market potentials	68	60	8	6
B. Market share analysis	67	58	9	5
C. Determination of market characteristics	68	61	6	6
D. Sales analyses	65	46	23	2
E. Establishment of sales quotas, territories	57	23	35	1
F. Distribution channel studies	48	30	19	3
G. Test markets, store audits	38	28	6	9
H. Consumer panel operations	33	21	3	12
I. Sales compensation studies	45	11	33	2
J. Promotional studies of premiums, coupons, sampling, deals, etc.	39	25	13	6
K. Other	2	2	—	—

* Reprinted by permission from Dik Warren Twedt (ed.) *1973 Survey of Marketing Research* (Chicago: American Marketing Association, November 1973), p. 41.

Table 12–2. Moreover, marketing research forms an essential part of contemporary marketing information activities.

Since the first formalized effort by the Curtis Publishing Company in 1911, marketing research has expanded significantly from a data collection and analysis function to encompass today: "the systematic and objective search for and analysis of information relevant to the identification and solution of any problem in the field of marketing."[5]

During the past two decades marketing decision makers' perspective toward information has been significantly expanded beyond traditional marketing research. This broadened point of view of the marketing information function has been characterized as *marketing intelligence.* The key dimensions of the marketing intelligence concept are:

Information is viewed both as an essential input and an integral part of decision making in that decision making needs provide the focus for the design of information activities.

Marketing information of all types is processed by the intelligence function (e.g., research, internal operating, and judgment/experience information).

Information processing equipment and analytical methods (computers and management science techniques) are typically utilized.

The marketing information function is managed as an integrated system.

The information function, based on the intelligence concept, when fully implemented takes the form of a marketing information system (MIS) and has been defined as:

a structured, interacting complex of persons, machines and procedures designed to generate an orderly flow of pertinent information collected from both intra-and extra-firm sources, for use as the bases for decision making in specified responsibility areas of marketing management.[6]

While the marketing research function and the marketing information system clearly overlap and are interrelated, there are relevant distinctions in orientation, function, and perspective which should be recognized. Perhaps most important is the distinction in terms of the nature and scope of activities associated with the two functions as opposed to the organizational identity given to the information function. For example, an organization may designate its information function as marketing research while the nature and scope of the activities may have advanced to the marketing information system level. Moreover, simply changing the name of the traditional marketing research function to marketing intelligence or marketing information system does not achieve, in itself, a change in perspective.

In the remainder of this chapter the essential aspects of planning for

---

[5] Paul E. Green and Donald S. Tull, *Research for Marketing Decisions,* p. 2.

[6] Richard H. Brien and James E. Stafford, "Marketing Information Systems: A New Dimension for Marketing Research," *Journal of Marketing,* vol. 32 (July 1968), p. 21, published by the American Marketing Association.

marketing information are considered. These planning guidelines are important regardless of whether or not an organization is sufficiently large and complex to need an organized information activity which can range from the traditional marketing research function to an integrated marketing information system.

THE INFORMATION PLANNING PROCESS

Planning Framework

Information planning is a central aspect of any systematic approach to the marketing information function regardless of whether or not a firm has an information staff. Planning for marketing information is also relevant in any type of information activity ranging from traditional marketing research to a fully developed MIS. Information planning consists of an interrelated sequence of steps as shown in Figure 12–1.[7]

The first stage in the planning process is an identification of the purpose for which additional information will be used. The situation confronting the decision maker provides the basis for information use and can range from problem/opportunity monitoring to analysis and choice of alternatives (choice information) to evaluation and control of actions taken (control information).

The second stage in the process consists of determining the specific information needed to reduce the uncertainty surrounding the decision situation. For example, consider the owner of land adjacent to an Interstate highway interchange who is seeking to determine the potential profitability of constructing a motel on the site. The major area of uncertainty is obtaining realistic estimates of probable occupancy of the proposed facility since costs of operation can be estimated within an acceptable accuracy range. Thus, the primary information needs for this situation concern factors that will enable him to project probable occupancy rates on an annual basis over the useful life of the motel.

In the third stage of information planning an assessment should be made of the costs and probable benefits of needed information. In terms of the degree of uncertainty surrounding the decision situation, how much should the decision maker consider spending for additional information? For example, how much should the motel developer be willing to pay to obtain marketing research information for use in estimating occupancy rates? How much better off will he be with additional in-

---

[7] Related approaches to information planning are presented in: Keith K. Cox and Ben M. Enis, *The Marketing Research Process* (Pacific Palisades, California: Goodyear Publishing Company, Inc., 1972), pp. 54–55; and Robert D. Buzzell et al., *Marketing Research and Information Systems: Text and Cases* (New York: McGraw-Hill Book Company, 1969), chapter 2.

FIGURE 12–1

Information Planning Process

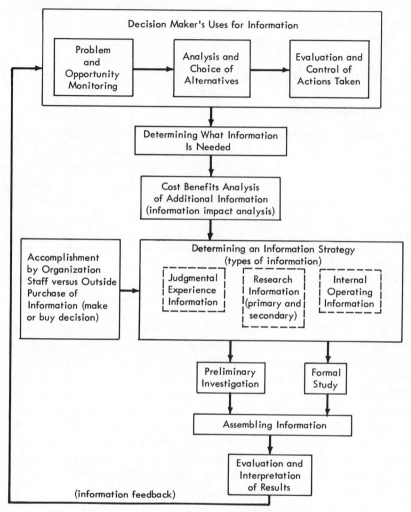

formation? Information impact analysis is one of the most difficult aspects of information planning yet clearly one of the most important.

Given some upper limit on the scope and magnitude (resulting from cost/benefit analysis) of a proposed information activity, the next step is the determination of an information strategy. What types of information will be utilized? Should the effort begin with a preliminary or exploratory investigation or should a formal study be launched? Closely related to the formulation of an information strategy is the "make" or "buy" decision which comprises the fifth stage in information planning.

Does the firm have internal capabilities for assembling information or should services be purchased from an outside specialist such as a marketing research consultant? In the case of the potential motel investor, he would probably not have the capabilities and experience necessary to conduct a motel feasibility study and would need to purchase the information.

The sixth stage involves assembling needed information and may include contacting a variety of sources; designing an appropriate sampling plan; information collection procedures (e.g., design of a questionnaire); and analysis of information collected. In the case of a formal research study, this step should typically be accomplished by individuals with special skills and experience in collecting and analyzing information.

Finally, the information which has been collected and analyzed must be evaluated and interpreted with respect to the decision situation which triggered the information planning process. This information feeds back to the decision maker and should contribute to reducing the uncertainty surrounding his decision. If the information effort was needed for problem or opportunity monitoring, then the results may help to define a particular problem or opportunity. This, in turn, could initiate a new information planning process.

The decision maker's role varies in the different stages of information planning since the information specialist also participates in the process. The specialist is an individual who is experienced in the technical aspects of information acquisition and analysis. For example, personnel assigned to a marketing research staff are information specialists. The relative importance of the decision maker and the specialist at different stages in information planning is illustrated in Table 12–3. Of course, these roles will vary somewhat from one information planning situation to another.

TABLE 12–3

Roles of the Decision Maker and the Information Specialist in Information Planning

		Role of	
	Stage in the Information Planning Process	*Decision Maker*	*Information Specialist*
I.	Identifying decision situation for which information is needed	Primary	Supporting
II.	Determining what information is needed	Primary	Supporting
III.	Cost/benefits analysis of additional information	Joint	Joint
IV.	Determining an information strategy	Joint	Joint
V.	Make or buy decision	Variable*	Variable*
VI.	Assembling information	Minor	Major
VII.	Evaluation and Interpretation	Joint	Joint

* Depends upon extent of internal capabilities for collecting and analyzing information.

The identification and production of relevant information for decision making necessitates careful inputs to the process by both the manager and the specialist. Without this cooperative approach to information planning there is a tendency "to remove research more and more from the decision-making process."[8]

Determining Information Needs

In order for the information planning effort to function effectively, information needs should be correctly determined. If this is not done, the resulting information is likely to be of limited value to the decision maker. Moreover, information not relevant to the decision situation can also be misleading.

Determination of information needs is guided by the decision situation confronting the decision maker. An approach for determining information needs is shown in Figure 12–2. This should be viewed as a general set of guidelines since the most effective process in a given situation will depend upon the problem at hand, the decision making style of the executive, and the nature and extent of interaction between decision maker and information specialist.

Decision Situation. Specification of information needs becomes more difficult in cases where the decision situation is not well defined such as problem/opportunity monitoring. For example, the fact that the marketing manager has determined that sales of his firm's major product line (portable power tools for home and professional use) have declined steadily for the past six months does not, in itself, provide a basis for identifying what possible causes underlie the sales decline. Possible causes must be identified and then information specified which will aid the manager in pinpointing the nature and extent of the cause of the sales decline. Possible causes might include:

Environmental changes such as economic conditions, technological advances, governmental requirements, etc., which might cause a decline in buyer preferences for the product.

Changes in the marketing strategies of competitors (such as introduction of an improved product, price reduction, increased advertising, etc.).

Weaknesses in the firm's marketing strategy (market targets, product, price, advertising, sales force, and distribution).

Seeking information in all of these areas would be prohibitive both in terms of time and cost. The task of the decision maker is to identify the

---

[8] James H. Myers and Richard R. Mead, *The Management of Marketing Research,* p. 6.

FIGURE 12–2

An Approach for Determining Information Needs

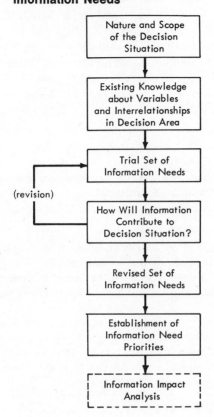

most probable causes of the sales decline and then to specify the information needed to further assess the reasons underlying the sales decline.

A more structured basis for specifying information needs exists in a decision situation involving analysis and choice of alternatives. The alternatives and possible outcomes for each provide a basis for formulating information needs. Information for use in the evaluation and control of actions taken can be specified within an even more structured decision framework. For example, information needed to monitor an ongoing sales effort in a sales region of a manufacturer of small electric motors would at a minimum include sales results (by customer, by product line, by salesman, etc.), expenditures, and profit margin compared to previous periods or established goals.

Illustrative characteristics of the process of determining information needs for each type of decision situation are shown in Figure 12–3.

Existing Knowledge.   The decision maker will normally have some knowledge about the decision situation confronting him. Suppose for example, that the marketing manager for the portable power tool firm is able to pinpoint the cause of the sales drop as a probable weakness in his firm's marketing strategy. Information he regularly receives from trade sources and market and competitive intelligence from his sales force has helped him to eliminate the other possible causes. By narrowing down the areas for information seeking, he is now in a position to identify aspects of his marketing strategy that may be responsible for

FIGURE 12–3

Characteristics of the Process of Determining Information Needs for Different Types of Decision Situations*

   I.   Problem and Opportunity Monitoring

      Decision situation is not clearly specified; heavy reliance upon knowledge and experience of the decision maker.

      Determination of needs facilitated by "what if" type of analysis (e.g., if this problem occurred, what information would help to detect it?)

      Various standardized information services (such as the Market Research Corporation of America and Nielsen food and drug information services) which have been designed to meet a variety of industry needs can be helpful for this type of decision situation.

  II.   Analysis and Choice of Alternatives

      Alternatives and possible effects or outcomes of each alternative provide the basis for determining information needs.

      Needs can be specified in a relatively straightforward manner although obtaining needed information may be difficult.

      Alternatives may be difficult to state in operational terms.

      Information typically used on an *ad hoc* rather than on-going basis.

      Indirect measures of factors of interest may be necessary.

 III.   Evaluation and Control of Actions Taken

      Information needs are determined by objectives and measures of performance for each area of evaluation and control.

      Information is typically needed on a continuing basis.

      Most easily determined information needs of any of the decision situations.

      Because of ease of determining information needs there may be a tendency to identify too much information.

---

* See Robert D. Buzzell, et al., *Marketing Research and Information Systems: Text and Cases* (New York: McGraw-Hill Book Company, 1969), pp. 24–32, for a more detailed discussion of information needs for different classes of decisions.

the sales decline. Moreover, he can then specify the information he needs to investigate particular elements of his strategy and to help determine which ones are faulty.

After pinpointing the problem in the area of the firm's marketing strategy, the marketing manager should consider possible indications of where problems might exist based on instances that may have occurred over the past several months. Suppose he decides to review customer sales (available by computer analysis on a month and year-to-date basis) over the past six months compared to the same period in the previous year. He finds that sales have fallen off to customers selling primarily to professional users of power tools, thus suggesting a shift in the preferences of professional users or possibly an overall decline in purchases in this target market. He also recalls that several complaints have been received from the field concerning delays in servicing power tools (serviced either by the factory or the dealer depending upon the type of servicing required). Additionally, he is aware that there have been some unusually long delays in shipping tools to dealers.

In assessing other elements of marketing strategy the marketing manager is reasonably certain that his products compare very favorably with those of his competition based on regular factory tests of competitive tools. He is confident that his pricing structure is competitive and that his advertising program is sound. Thus, he is able to focus his problem area in the professional market segment for power tools and has identified possible problems with servicing and distribution of the firm's products. Moreover, these possible problems could be of major significance to the professional user thus causing him to purchase competitive products. Trade association reports received each month indicate no over-all reduction in power tool purchases by professional users.

Specification of Information Needs. The decision maker is now in a position to specify a trial set of information needs and to assess how the information will contribute to the decision situation. Suppose he has identified the information needs listed below after consultation with his staff including his information specialist:

1. Attitudes and preferences of professional users toward the firm's products.
2. Brand preferences of professional users.
3. Factors most important to purchasers of power tools.
4. Types and frequency of service problems.
5. Needed improvements in service operations.
6. Service practices of competitors.
7. Possible product improvements which would reduce service problems.
8. Reasons for increased delivery time.

9. Particular products involved in slow delivery.
10. Distributors' opinions concerning service and delivery.

The marketing manager must now assess how the information will contribute to reducing the uncertainty surrounding his decision situation. During this process he will undoubtedly identify additional needs and eliminate some of the items listed initially. When this is completed he will need to establish priorities as to the importance of his revised set of information needs to guide information impact analysis and design of an information strategy.

ASSESSING THE IMPACT OF INFORMATION ON MARKETING DECISIONS

Information Impact Analysis

An essential aspect of the information planning process is establishment of guidelines to determine how much should be spent on the purchase of additional information for use by the marketing decision maker. Information costs money and should be expected to contribute benefits to the decision making situation.[9] Yet, information does not directly generate sales or profits. Rather, its potential contribution is to reduce the uncertainty surrounding a decision making situation, thus enabling the manager to make a better decision. For example, how much should a decision maker spend on information to:

Assess the feasibility of building a $500,000 motel?

Determine whether exclusive rights to a new product should be purchased from the inventor?

Determine consumer receptiveness to a proposed new package design?

Examine salesmens' attitudes and preferences concerning incentive compensation?

While limited information efforts such as an exploratory consumer attitude study may cost only a few thousand dollars, even a modest, full scale research study can cost $30,000.[10] The costs of test marketing (collecting information for determining if a new product will be successful, and if so, which marketing strategy is likely to be most effective) can range from under $100,000 to more than a million dollars depending

---

[9] We consider information provided by an organization's internal staff or obtained from outside suppliers (such as marketing research firms) as being purchased, since in either case resources are expended in acquiring the information.

[10] *Business Week,* "New Products: The Push Is On Marketing" (March 4, 1972), p. 74.

upon the scale and scope of the test effort. For example, before moving in the mid-1960s to the present three stage approach to test marketing, R. T. French Company "always had two or three products in classic market tests at all times, at an average cost of more than $300,000 per product."[11]

Because of the difficulty of measuring the size of the impact of information on a decision situation, three tendencies prevail in practice: (1) basing the information decision upon how much the firm can afford to spend, thus allowing cost to be the primary guide to the information decision (as opposed to both cost and benefit); (2) avoiding the collection of information altogether unless forced to do so for some reason (e.g., requirements stipulated by a source of capital such as a bank); or (3) specifying wanted information (not necessarily needed in a cost-benefit sense) and a minimal (and frequently unrealistic) cost of obtaining the information. While obtaining new information cannot guarantee improved decision making results, analysis of any decision making situation should include an assessment of the potential impact (benefit) that additional information can have. In some instances this information impact analysis will need to be made solely on the basis of judgment and experience. Alternatively, for certain classes of decisions formal methods of decision analysis can aid the decision maker in setting an upper limit on how much to spend for new information.

The key concept in information gap analysis is that for a given decision situation there is a limit to how much impact new information can have. This is illustrated in Figure 12–4. Assume there is an estimated level of decision results (such as gross profit contribution) determined by the marketing manager and his staff for a proposed new package design for a consumer product. This estimate is based on existing information

FIGURE 12–4

Maximum Impact of Information on a Decision Situation

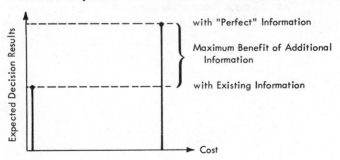

---

[11] Ibid., p. 74.

and acknowledges less than perfect understanding about what will happen if the package design is adopted. Now consider a state of perfect knowledge about the events that will occur in the future. By knowing which future events will affect the outcome of a particular decision situation, the most desirable alternative can be chosen. For example, an investor seeking to make a choice between the purchase of one of three stocks for short term gain could make the best possible selection if he knew with certainty how they would perform over the next 30 days. This is a state of "perfect" information. Given perfect information about future events that will influence the outcome of the decision, the expected decision results are likely to be greater than the expected payoff with some degree of uncertainty concerning the future. This gap between our existing knowledge and perfect knowledge provides a measure of the maximum impact that information can have upon the decision situation.

While the achievement of perfect information is typically not possible (unless the decision maker is so fortunate as to have a crystal ball), the concept is useful in illustrating the important principle that there is an upper limit to the impact of new information in any decision situation. Moreover, as we shall see later in the chapter, it is possible to obtain an objective estimate of the information gap for a decision situation involving choice among alternatives.

In addition to the information gap, the cost/benefit responsiveness of information in a decision situation is also important in assessing how much to spend on additional information. This is illustrated in Figure 12–5. Note that the rate of increase in benefits per unit of cost declines as additional information is obtained. While the relationship shown in Figure 12–5 is illustrative, it emphasizes that an attempt should be made to estimate how responsive new information will be to the decision

FIGURE 12–5

Cost/Benefit Responsiveness of Information for a Decision Situation

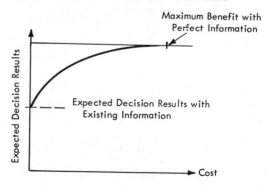

situation. Moreover, the incremental gain in benefits per unit of additional cost is likely to be smaller and smaller as the information level moves toward a state of perfect information.

Role of Judgment and Experience

There are decision situations where additional information will not be worth the cost of obtaining it, regardless of the cost. This can occur, for example, when there is a high likelihood that the most favored alternative in the decision situation will not change with additional information. In other instances the benefits to be derived from information may be estimated as a result of past experience in working with similar decision situations. For example, companies that have conducted test marketing for several years have developed a useful base of experience concerning both costs and benefits.[12] Also, firms with well developed marketing information functions have accumulated a wide range of information impact experience.

In decision situations where there is a clear recognition of a need for additional information coupled with uncertainty as to the probable magnitude of information benefits, it may be appropriate to approach information planning in two or more stages. The first stage consists of a preliminary investigation to define the problem better. An acceptable level of expenditure is determined based on the judgment of the decision maker and consideration of the importance of the decision and budgetary constraints. Then, based on information obtained in stage one, more precise estimates of costs and benefits for subsequent stages can be made.

In certain cases the benefits of additional information may be apparent and the costs modest compared to the significance of the decision. For example, reasonably comprehensive feasibility studies for proposed motels costing over a million dollars can be conducted in a range of $4,000 to $8,000. In these situations the information impact decision can be made without extensive analysis. Similarly, experience has substantiated the need for new product feasibility studies relatively early in the new product planning process.

Decision Analysis

When the decision maker can specify: (1) the alternatives that are relevant in a decision situation; (2) the possible outcomes for each alternative; (3) the likelihood (or probability) of occurrence of each

---

[12] The market testing experiences of several firms are discussed in *Market Testing Consumer Products* (New York: National Industrial Conference Board, Inc., 1967).

outcome, and (4) the payoffs (expected decision results) for each outcome, it is possible to analyze the problem using a decision model such as the payoff matrix.[13] An estimated value can be placed on the information gap between the present state of knowledge concerning the decision situation and complete elimination of uncertainty surrounding the decision. This approach to analysis is based on Bayesian decision theory in which the decision maker's subjective-judgmental estimates of the probability of outcomes of future events are essential information inputs to the analysis. Our objective is to present a simple example to illustrate the analysis recognizing that comprehensive treatment is beyond the scope of this text and is treated in detail in various other sources.[14]

There are three primary phases of decision analysis leading to estimates of the value of information:

1. Analyzing the decision situation using the existing knowledge of the decision maker.
2. Extending the analysis by assuming the decision maker knows what will occur in the future (a type of "what if" analysis) in order to determine an estimate of the maximum impact new information will have on the decision situation.
3. Examination of alternatives for obtaining additional information to determine which offers the most favorable cost-benefit contribution.[15]

We illustrate this approach with an example similar to an application used by the Pillsbury Company.[16] The first phase is shown in Table 12–4. The decision situation is a choice between the modification of a food package design and retention of the present design. The new design has a lower cost and management estimates that some consumers may react unfavorably to the change, thus some loss in sales will occur.

---

[13] Other, less comprehensive methods (simple savings, return on investment, and present-value) for assessing the value of marketing information are discussed in J. C. Myers and C. Samli, "Management Control of Marketing Research," *Journal of Marketing Research,* vol. 6 (August 1969), p. 267.

[14] The Bayesian approach is effectively covered in Robert Schlaifer, *Probability and Statistics for Business Decisions* (New York: McGraw-Hill Book Company, 1959). Green and Tull, *Research for Marketing Decisions,* include the approach as an essential part of their analytical treatment of marketing research. Similarly, Buzzell et al., *Marketing Research and Information Systems: Text and Cases,* provide discussion and cases on the formal analysis of decisions. Cox and Enis, *The Marketing Research Process,* include the Bayesian approach in their examination of the marketing process.

[15] See Ralph L. Day, "Optimizing Marketing Research Through Cost Benefit Analysis," *Business Horizons* (Fall 1966), pp. 45–54, for an excellent discussion of these phases including analysis of the potential contribution of additional information alternatives for narrowing the information gap in a decision situation.

[16] Guy-Robert Detlefsen, "Decision Theory in Marketing and Marketing Research," in *Decision Making in Marketing* (New York: The Conference Board, Inc., 1971), pp. 70–81.

TABLE 12–4

Analysis of a Decision Involving the Possible Modification of the Package Design for a Food Product

	Gross Profit Contribution (in $1,000s) if Sales Loss Is			
	0	10%	20%	30%
	Probability of Occurrence*			
Alternative	.10	.50	.30	.10
I. Modify package (lower cost)	1700	1600	1450	1300
II. Keep present design	1500	1500	1500	1500

Expected payoff for alternative with present state of information:
I = .10(1700) + .50(1600) + .30(1450) + .10(1300) = 1535 (best alternative)
II = .10(1500) + .50(1500) + .30(1500) + .10(1500) = 1500

* Based on management's assessment (judgment and experience) of the relative probability of occurrence of the different levels of possible lost sales.

Management has estimated, based on judgment and experience, that sales loss using the modified package will range between 0 and 30 percent. They have also indicated what they expect as to the probability of occurrence for each level of sales loss (e.g., 0.50 for a 10 percent sales loss). These estimates represent management's assessments based upon their existing state of knowledge about the decision situation.[17] The gross profit contribution for each level of sales payoffs for the present design is the same since if it is the alternative chosen an estimated profit contribution of $1.5 million will occur (e.g., no change in sales would be expected). Payoff is calculated by subtracting estimated costs from sales. This information should be readily available from the firm's manufacturing data base and experience. Using gross profit contribution as a decision criterion, the estimated expected (average) payoff of the modified package is $35,000 higher than if the present design is retained. On this basis the new design offers the most favorable alternative.

In phase two to estimate the impact of a state of certainty on the decision situation shown in Table 12–4, first *assume* that the decision maker knows a sales loss of zero will occur. If so, Alternative I, with a gross profit contribution of 1700, is the best decision. Similarly, for a 10 percent sales loss Alternative I is best; for both the 20 percent and

---

[17] More than four possible levels of sales loss between 0 and 30 percent could be considered. These have been used to simplify the analysis. We are assuming for convenience that one of four possible states of nature will occur if the decision to modify the package is made (e.g., 0, 10, 20, or 30 percent sales loss).

30 percent sales loss levels Alternative II is best. The decision maker cannot control which state of nature will occur. Rather, assuming the availability of perfect information (thus knowing what state of nature will occur), it would be possible to choose the best alternative for the state of nature. In order to calculate the maximum impact of information on the decision situation we are assuming that the decision maker knows what is going to happen which is a type of "what if" analysis. Next, using the probabilities of occurrence for each sales loss level and the payoffs associated with the best alternative for each sales loss level, the expected value of certainty can be estimated:

Expected Value under Conditions of Certainty
$$= .10 \ (1700) + .50 \ (1600) + .30 \ (1500) + .10 \ (1500) = \underline{\underline{1570}}$$

Since the decision maker actually does not know which state of nature will occur, the best choice (payoff) for each state of nature is weighted according to managements' estimate of its probability of occurrence. The value of perfect information or the maximum benefit of completely eliminating the information gap is 1570–1535 or $35,000. This is the maximum amount that the decision maker should pay for additional information relevant to the decision situation. While in many decision situations a level of perfect information exists in theory, it is typically not operationally achievable because of the high costs of eliminating all uncertainty and the difficulty of obtaining relevant information due to time and access constraints. Nevertheless, an estimate of the potential gain in decision results from eliminating the information gap (as illustrated in the above example) provides an important guideline to the decision maker:

1. A boundary is established for guiding information expenditures.
2. If the estimated maximum benefit is relatively small it may indicate that no additional information should be obtained.
3. It makes explicit the role of information as an active strategy instrument.

While this illustration is admittedly oversimplified, the approach provides a useful framework for estimating the impact of additional information on a decision situation. It should be noted that the output of the analysis is dependent upon the decision maker's ability (and willingness) to provide the information shown in the payoff matrix in Table 12–4. The most difficult estimates are the probabilities of occurrence for each sales loss level.[18]

---

[18] An excellent discussion of how these subjective-judgmental estimates can be made by the decision maker is provided in Donald H. Woods, "Improving Estimates that Involve Uncertainty," *Harvard Business Review*, vol. 44 (July–August 1966), pp. 91–98.

Provided with either a judgmentally determined or analytical estimate of the benefits to be gained by narrowing the information gap, the decision maker should next assess specific alternatives for obtaining additional information. Each should be evaluated in terms of cost and benefit (phase three of Bayesian analysis). Since this evaluation is beyond the scope of this text the interested reader is referred to the Bayesian references cited earlier.

DETERMINING AN INFORMATION STRATEGY

The decision maker is now faced with formulating a strategy for obtaining new information. The role of the information specialist becomes relatively more important in this and in subsequent stages of the information planning process. The essential aspects of formulating an information strategy include selection of the types of information to utilize; consideration of a preliminary investigation versus a formal research study (or a combination of the two); and determination of whether to accomplish the information effort with internal staff or purchase the service from an information supplier.

Types of Information

The types of information needed by the decision maker, in part, determine the appropriate strategy in a given situation. There are three broad types of information that can contribute to the decision maker: *Experience/Judgment Information; Research Information;* and *Internal Operating Information.*

Experience/Judgment Information. This type of information includes that resulting from the knowledge and experience of the decision maker and others in the organization, informal discussions with management of channel member firms, and discussions with key "experts" outside the firm. While much of the information in this category is "unscientific" or subjective in nature, procedural advances have been made to help managers collect such intelligence information more systematically and quantitatively.[19] Developmental work on such procedures coupled with a growing number of firms devoting resources to formal intelligence activities indicate the increasing utility of judgmental/experience information to marketing management.[20]

---

[19] Woods, "Improving Estimates that Involve Uncertainty"; Philip Kotler, "A Guide to Gathering Expert Estimates," *Business Horizons* (October 1970), pp. 79–87; and Marvin A. Jolson and Gerald L. Rossow, "The Delphi Process in Marketing Decision Making," *Journal of Marketing Research,* vol. 8 (November 1971), pp. 443–48, published by the American Marketing Association.

[20] William R. Fair, "The Corporate CIA—A Prediction of Things to Come," *Management Science* (June 1966), pp. B-489–503.

Research Information. This involves formal collection of information by a firm's own research personnel and/or outside research firms (primary data); or by standardized research information services who make the information available for a variety of purposes (secondary data). While research information has potential utility at all organizational levels of management, current uses by firms tend to be limited to isolated middle management decision problems.[21] Consequently, this source of managerial information has been underutilized by many firms. Nevertheless, on the technical side of marketing research, there have been major advances in data collection procedures, data analysis techniques, and model building efforts. Moreover, it is already apparent that larger firms are beginning to utilize marketing research more than ever before.[22]

Internal Operating Information. A variety of information is generated by the organization for use in planning and controlling operations.[23] Much of this information is the responsibility of the accounting area. Internal accounting systems provide information on a firm's cost and sales producing activities that aid in measuring performance. Accounting record keeping systems have had increasing demands upon them for more useful information for managerial decision-making. As Brien and Stafford point out, "the computer and more progressive accounting departments that see their role as the provision of management information rather than as simple 'scorekeeping' have been two of the most important contributors to the integration of such data, on a regular basis, into the marketing flow."[24]

Information Seeking Alternatives

An information strategy can take either the form of a preliminary investigation or a formal research study. Both may draw from all three types of information described above. An example of a preliminary investigation would be the assignment for a two week period of a member of an electric range manufacturer's marketing staff to collect and analyze

---

[21] Brien and Stafford, "Marketing Information Systems: A New Dimension for Marketing Research," p. 21.

[22] *Business Week*, "Business Says It Can Handle Bigness" (October 17, 1970), pp. 109–10; Pratt, "Using Research to Reduce Risk Associated with Marketing New Products," pp. 98–104; and Gail Smith, "How GM Measures Ad Effectiveness," *Printers Ink* (May 14, 1965), pp. 19–29.

[23] Detailed discussions of information originating within the firm are provided in Jerry E. Drake and Frank I. Millar, *Marketing Research: Intelligence and Management* (Scranton, Pennsylvania: International Textbook Company, 1969), chapter 9; and Kenneth P. Uhl and Bertram Schoner, *Marketing Research: Information Systems and Decision Making* (New York: John Wiley and Sons, Inc., 1969), chapter 9.

[24] Brien and Stafford, "Marketing Information Systems: A New Dimension for Marketing Research," p. 22.

published information on the microwave oven market and information from discussions with knowledgable individuals. The purpose of the investigation would be exploratory and would seek to develop guidelines and recommendations as to the need for a formal, more extensive study of the market.[25]

The preliminary investigation is a very important aspect of an information strategy since it alone may provide adequate information on the decision situation. Alternatively, an exploratory information effort will greatly facilitate the formulation and design of a formal research study, if needed. Specifically, the preliminary investigation can yield the following:

1. A more accurate basis for operationally defining the objectives and scope of a formal research study.
2. Identification of existing information thus possibly avoiding a duplicative effort.
3. Determination of whether overall project cost and time guidelines are realistic.
4. Establishment of a more accurate basis for estimating information impact.
5. Identification of potential problems to be avoided if a major information effort is undertaken.[26]

Thus, in many situations a multi-stage approach to information strategy is appropriate. The preliminary investigation provides the basis for planning a formal study (second stage).[27] An illustration of a three phase information strategy is shown in Figure 12–6 for obtaining information for use in evaluating market opportunities for a new type of industrial equipment. Phases 1 and 2 provide important guidelines for subsequent stages of information gathering and analysis.

Frequently, published information (secondary data) is available for use in a variety of decision making purposes. An essential aspect of any information strategy formulation should include consideration of this category of information because of the possibility of significant time and cost savings. Examples include: U.S. Census data, industry publications, *Statistical Abstract of the United States,* commercial services (e.g.,

---

[25] As a substitute (or supplement) to a preliminary investigation, market studies covering a variety of industries can be purchased for under $500 each from firms specializing in providing standardized information packages such as Frost & Sullivan, Inc., New York, New York, and Predicasts, Cleveland, Ohio.

[26] Myers and Mead, *The Management of Marketing Research,* p. 66.

[27] Guidelines for preliminary analysis and use of existing knowledge are provided in Lyndon O. Brown and Leland L. Beik, *Marketing Research and Analysis,* 4th ed. (New York: The Ronald Press Company, 1969), chapters 5 and 6.

FIGURE 12–6

Three Stage Approach for Obtaining Information for Use in Evaluating Market Opportunities for a New Type of Industrial Degreasing Equipment

---

Phase I

Describe the market in terms of applications, types of users, competitors, and related information. The effort would be exploratory in nature aimed at primarily providing specific guidelines for effectively moving into the next phase. The purpose would be to identify appropriate information sources and effective ways of gaining needed market data.

Phase II

Determine the approximate size of the market, competitor characteristics, methods of marketing and distribution, pricing, and related dimensions of the market.

Phase III

Interviews with a representative sample of users in selected locations to determine type of present degreasing equipment, purchase source, costs, satisfaction with present equipment, operating problems, and related user information.

Actions taken in Phases II and III will be based, in part, upon findings in the prior phase.

A. C. Nielsen Company, Market Research Corporation of America, Audits & Surveys Company), and libraries to name but a few.[28] The preliminary investigation should seek to identify relevant secondary data.

An example of a commercial information service is shown in Table 12–5. This type of information is available from Economic Information Systems, Inc., New York, New York. Firms can obtain market data on over 300 product groups such as that shown for corrugated boxes in Table 12–5. Included in these market analyses are consumption data by plant in all counties in all states.

A formal research study is typically conducted within the framework of established marketing research procedures. The work is carried out by the firm's marketing research staff, or alternatively can be purchased from an outside organization specializing in the service. A plan of accomplishment for the formal study should be developed and should include the following:

---

[28] For a detailed discussion of the use and sources of secondary information, see Harper W. Boyd, Jr. and Ralph Westfall, *Marketing Research*, 3d ed. (Homewood, Illinois: Richard D. Irwin, Inc., 1972), chapter 6; see also Drake and Millar, *Marketing Research: Intelligence and Management*, chapters 8, 9, and 10.

1. Purpose, scope, and specific objectives.
2. Study design or framework.
3. Information sources.
4. Data collection procedures.
5. Plan for analysis of information to be collected.
6. Form of final research report including probable usefulness (and limitations) to the decision maker.
7. Cost and time estimates.[29]

TABLE 12-5

Example of Estimated Annual Purchases of Corrugated Boxes by Industry, Company, and Location*

State and County Name	SIC	Number of Plants	Annual Purchase of Corrugated Boxes ($00)
Alabama			
Autauga	2256	1	109
	2631	1	258
	3559	1	150
County Total		3	517
Baldwin	2024	1	224
	2221	1	80
	2253	1	204
	2511	1	820
	3643	1	319
County Total		5	1,647
Barbour	2211	1	133
	3141	1	92
County Total		2	225
Bibb	2311	1	88
	3941	1	1,743
County Total		2	1,831
Etc.			

* Reproduced by permission of Economic Information Systems, Inc., New York.

Firms that do not have internal information staffs must rely upon outside suppliers of these services. Even those with the internal capability may choose to contract for certain phases of the information effort (such as interviewing of respondents). Regardless of how well developed the information capabilities of an organization are, purchase of outside services are typically used to some extent. Factors to be considered in determining the "make or buy" decision include internal professional know-how and experience, relative objectivity of inside and outside in-

[29] Myers and Mead, *The Management of Marketing Research,* pp. 68–69.

formation specialists, costs, influence on internal staff, and completion time.[30]

Assembling Information

Having determined an appropriate information strategy the decision maker is ready to develop and implement a plan for assembling needed information. The decisions regarding information planning up to this point provide important guidelines for assembling information. While the task of assembling needed information is largely the responsibility of the information specialist (either inside or outside the organization), the decision maker should have a general understanding of the assembly process. This knowledge is necessary in order to use the resulting information properly, including an appreciation of the strengths and weaknesses associated with the information. Moreover, although our discussion relates primarily to assembling information for a formal research study, an understanding of the general process can be helpful to the non-professional who is involved in assembling information for a preliminary investigation.

While the information assembly process will vary somewhat depending upon the particular information effort, the major aspects are: (1) selecting sources of information to draw upon; (2) sampling design; (3) information collection procedures; and (4) analysis of information collected. Our objective is to examine each of these phases briefly in order to identify the nature of each activity and those aspects relevant to the marketing decision maker.[31]

Various sources of marketing information exist as shown in Figure 12–7. An identification should be made of the relevant source of information as a first step in the information assembly process. In formal research studies, people are typically used as sources of information. In consumer markets, households are frequently surveyed to obtain needed information whereas in industrial markets, businesspeople are the object of interest. An example of information sources used to make marketing

---

[30] The make-or-buy decision is explored in greater detail in Cox and Enis, *The Marketing Research Process,* pp. 195–97; guidelines for evaluating suppliers of information services are provided in Charles S. Mayer, "Evaluating the Quality of Marketing Research Contractors," *Journal of Marketing Research,* vol. 4 (May 1967), pp. 134–41.

[31] Several excellent guides are available which present the basic methodology and procedures for information assembly such as Boyd and Westfall, *Marketing Research,* Brown and Beik, *Marketing Research and Analysis;* Drake and Millar, *Marketing Research: Intelligence and Management;* Uhl and Schoner, *Marketing Research: Information Systems and Decision Making;* Gerald Zaltman and Philip C. Burger, *Marketing Research: Fundamentals and Dynamics* (Hinsdale, Ill.: The Dryden Press, 1975); and Gilbert A. Churchill, Jr., *Marketing Research* (Hinsdale, Ill.: The Dryden Press, 1976).

FIGURE 12–7

Sources of Marketing Information

Personnel in the organization
Consultants and other outside experts
Households
Federal, state and local government agencies
Business firms
Other institutions
Trade and industry organizations
Commercial information services
Publications
    Directories and guides to reference sources
    Books, magazines, and newspapers
Libraries
Data and reports on internal operations

decisions by a European cigarette distributor is shown in Figure 12–8. Note the use of information from different levels in channels of distribution including consumers, retailers (from Nielsen surveys), and distributors (through sharing of sales information by competitors). It is interesting to note that libraries in European countries do not provide the information services that are available in the United States. Because of this, no direct library services can be utilized by the distributor. The firm does have access to independent marketing research institutes which provide a variety of research services.

Sampling. In cases where a population of interest is quite large (such as all households in the United States), it may be necessary both in terms of time and costs, to collect information from only a portion or sample of the total units which comprise the population. Use of a sampling approach, which yields information on the units that make up a total population, can provide good estimates of characteristics of interest (e.g., income, age, product preferences, etc.) in the overall population.

The essential idea underlying sampling is to use information obtained from a relatively small number of members of a population to estimate characteristics of the entire population. For example, a sample of 2,000 households might be used to estimate attitudes toward a firm's products or services for a population of 60 million households. Through proper design of the selection procedures reliable population estimates can be obtained from sample information. Since relatively small samples can be used even though the population of interest may be quite large, infor-

FIGURE 12–8

Sources of Information Used to Make Marketing Decisions in Belgium by a Large European Cigarette Distributor*

Monthly and Quarterly Market Surveys

Through cooperation of the firms comprising the industry, sales data are made available to all firms. Monthly tabulations include sales volumes and market share according to brand, blend (blond, black, menthol), and for filter and non-filter types. Quarterly tabulations additionally include sales and market share information according to price class and type of packaging.

Standardized Information Services

A. C. Nielsen's food index services are purchased by the firm. Food store channels of distribution account for about half of the firm's total cigarette sales. For example, a substantial sales volume is provided by newsstand outlets.

Primary Research Studies

Surveys of samples of 3000 people are conducted four or five times a year by an outside marketing research institute. Consumers are defined based on socio-demographic characteristics (age, sex, social class), smokers and non-smokers, and smoking habits.

Small sample studies (300 people) for a particular market segment, e.g., based on type of blend used, are conducted periodically to identify needed product changes such as packaging. Group discussions of one to two hours duration are held to obtain information. Two independent marketing research institutes are used by the tobacco firm to conduct these studies.

* Information provided by the firm's Marketing Research Director.

mation assembly costs can be kept at acceptable levels. The soundness of the sampling design provides a basis for determining how reliable the estimates obtained from the sample are as proxy estimates for the population.[32]

Information Collection Procedures. The data collection effort for a large scale field study should be carefully planned and detailed procedures developed to provide guidance and control of the work. Information can be collected in one of two ways: by observation; or by asking

---

[32] Most marketing research texts provide adequate introductory material on sampling. A good introductory technical treatment of the area is in William Mendenhall et al., *Elementary Survey Sampling* (Belmont, California: Wadsworth Publishing Company, 1971). More detailed coverage of the subject can be found in William G. Cochran, *Sampling Techniques* (New York: John Wiley and Sons, 1963); and M. H. Hansen et al., *Sample Survey Methods and Theory,* vol. I (New York: John Wiley and Sons, 1953).

questions (when people are the sources of information). Questioning is the most frequently used means of collecting information and can be accomplished through personal interviews, telephone interviews, or the mailing of questionnaires for completion by respondents. Each method of communication has certain advantages and limitations with respect to cost, speed, value of information needed, types of questions (e.g., sensitive questions such as those related to income, age, etc.), and percent of response. The design of data collection procedures should be guided by people experienced in this activity.[33]

An interesting indirect approach to obtaining information from consumers concerning beer brand images was used by Woodside.[34] Respondents were divided randomly into three groups. Those in each group were shown a shopping list of groceries to be used for a small informal party and asked to write a brief description of the personality and character of the person who they felt would be purchasing the items. The only variation between the three lists was the beer brand (for control purposes one of the three lists did not include beer). Significant differences were found between the respondents' image of the two brands of beer.

Approaches to Analysis. After information has been collected normally it is necessary to process it in some way to aid the user in interpreting its meaning. Alternative approaches to the analysis of information are shown in Table 12–6. Analysis in its most simple form consists of the review of the raw (unprocessed) information by the decision

Table 12–6

Approaches to the Analysis of Information

Type of Analysis	*Examples*
"Seat of the pants" or "eyeball" analysis	Review of a listing of customer sales arranged in alphabetical order.
Classification and comparison	Tabular breakdown of sales by product line for a firm's 18 sales regions.
Statistical analysis of relationships	Multiple linear regression/correlation analysis of the relationship between salesman performance and potential predictors of performance (e.g., age, education, experience, etc.).

[33] See Boyd and Westfall, *Marketing Research,* chapters 4, 7, and 11 for a detailed examination of the observation and questioning approaches, design of questionnaires, and related aspects of field data collection.

[34] Arch G. Woodside, "A Shopping List Experiment of Beer Brand Images," *Journal of Applied Psychology,* 56 (December 1972), pp. 512–13.

maker. If there is a limited quantity of information and the decision maker is a skillful information processer, "seat of the pants" type analysis may be adequate. Yet, if any quantity of data is involved then some form of systematic processing is typically needed to collapse the raw information into a form suitable for review by the decision maker.[35]

The most simple form of systematic analysis consists of the use of a table to combine information into various classifications. This is usually done by placing one basis of classification in column categories (e.g., different income groups) and a second basis of classification in row categories (e.g., different rates of purchase of a product). Classification and comparison tables are frequently used in analyzing information. They may also be used as a preliminary step to more sophisticated analysis. Their main limitation lies in the fact that analysis is restricted to a limited number of comparisons (e.g., row and column categories).

Beyond two-way analysis of information various statistical methods can be used to examine data for possible relationships between variables. Statistical methods include linear regression/correlation analysis, factor analysis, discriminant analysis, canonical correlation, and cluster analysis.[36] Applications of certain of these techniques will be discussed in later chapters to illustrate how use of the methods facilitates information analysis by the decision maker.

Evaluation and Interpretation of Results

The quality of the information planning process largely determines the usefulness of the results of the information effort. Evaluation and interpretation of the results should be a joint effort of the decision maker and the information specialist. It is essential that the decision maker understand the strengths (and limitations) of the information that has been assembled. Without this understanding he may over-react or under-react to the information collected. In the final analysis the decision maker must determine the usefulness of the information and the manner in which it will be used to facilitate decision making.

Each step in the information planning process offers potential opportunities for information contamination. Thus, the user of information must be alert to these problems and should work closely with the information specialist in assessing the overall quality of the effort. Areas

---

[35] Excellent guidelines for the decision maker are provided in Roger A. Golde, "Sharpen Your Number Sense," *Harvard Business Review*, vol. 44 (July–August 1966), pp. 73–83.

[36] A good introductory description of multivariate statistical analysis in marketing is in Jagdish N. Sheth, "Multivariate Analysis in Marketing," *Journal of Advertising Research*, vol. 10, no. 1 (February 1970), pp. 29–39; more detailed treatment of the techniques can be found in Green and Tull, *Research for Marketing Decisions*, chapters 10, 11, 12, and 13.

of possible contamination include inadequate identification of needs; faulty strategy determination; and incomplete or inaccurate information assembly. Specifically, in information assembly the representativeness of the sample must be assessed; the limitations of the collection process must be considered (e.g., possible inabilities of respondents in answering questions, amount of non-response, etc.); and the limitations of the methods used to analyze the information collected must be considered.

A classic example of the problems associated with the collection of information from people involved a survey in which respondents were asked their opinions on the Metallic Metals Act.[37] Although 30 percent of the respondents had no opinion, 70 percent indicated certain preferences concerning the Act. Yet, there is in fact no Metallic Metals Act. Thus, it is usually possible to get answers from respondents but the relevance of the resulting information may be questionable.

MARKETING INFORMATION SYSTEMS

Marketing information systems (MIS) represent firms' efforts to acquire and process information to serve the variety of regularly occurring decision needs which confront the marketing manager and staff. The speed and economy of computer processing of information have added

FIGURE 12–9

Basic Components of a Marketing Information System

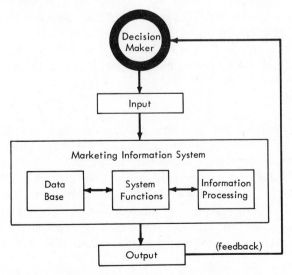

[37] See Boyd and Westfall, *Marketing Research*, p. 287.

substantial impetus to the development of integrated approaches to the management of the information function in many firms.

Although one particular marketing information system may vary from another, there are certain basic components that are present in any system. These components are shown in Figure 12–9. The decision maker must activate the system in some manner (input) such as a request for needed information. The marketing information system is comprised of three interrelated components: (1) a *data base* (accumulation of information); (2) various capabilities for *processing information;* and (3) *system functions* (e.g., file creation, report generation, etc.). The result of the functioning of the system (utilizing the data base and information processing capabilities) is an "output" which feeds back to the decision maker.

Decision Maker

The basic purpose of the MIS is to serve decision makers who have needs for information in their decision making activities. Thus, the particular functions and capabilities of a system must be guided by the information-decision needs of the marketing manager and his staff. "The manager's demands will depend upon the relevant problems he faces and the decision structure he uses in approaching the system."[38] A man-system interaction is inherent in the effective functioning of a MIS. The system cannot be properly developed until a clear understanding is gained as to what the marketing manager wants the system to provide.

Our examination of decision making and information planning provides helpful general guidelines as to the types of decision needs which can exist in any organization. In the remaining chapters of the book, specific information needs will be identified in the process of discussing the various marketing management decision areas.

Data Base

The most simple form of a data base is the conventional file system maintained by a business organization (e.g., customer files, order files, product information, etc.). Similarly, the data base for a MIS is the collection of information assembled to serve various purposes. Yet when the data base is developed for use in a computerized system, the task becomes much more complex because of the precise nature of file design. The computer age has generated a significant body of technical knowledge and experience related to data base design and utilization.

---

[38] David B. Montgomery and Glen L. Urban, *Management Science in Marketing* (Englewood Cliffs, N.J.: Prentice-Hall, Inc., 1969), p. 25.

In fact, the computerized data base is more than an ordinary collection of data:

> The data base must be viewed as a generalized, common, integrated collection of company or installation-owned data which fulfills the data requirements of all applications which access it. In addition, the data within the data base must be structured to model the natural data relationships which exist in a company.[39]

A typical marketing data base might include information on internal operations (salesmen's call reports, costs, etc.); customer information; channel information; competitive intelligence; and environmental information.[40]

Information Processing Capabilities

The information processing capabilities of the MIS refer to both the hardware (type of equipment such as size of computer) and software (programs for processing information). These capabilities generally fall into four categories: data retrieval; classification and comparison; statistical analysis; and modeling and simulation. Classification and comparison and statistical analysis were described in the last section so discussion here will be limited to data retrieval and modeling.

Data Retrieval. Information contained in the data base may be retrieved either to satisfy some specific request for information or to be used in one of the other information processing categories (for example, statistical analysis). While in concept, the retrieval of information from the data base appears quite simple, the development of effective program routines for efficiently achieving this has proven to be a formidable task for information scientists and computer programmers. The costs of retrieving information can exceed benefits gained from the information unless retrieval routines are carefully designed to take into account the size of the data base, type and frequency of user needs, and related factors. The design of information retrieval routines is closely related to the design and structure of the data base. When dealing with relatively large data bases, retrieval processing time and associated costs become important constraints upon MIS operating efficiency.[41]

---

[39] Richard F. Schubert, "Basic Concepts in Data Base Management Systems," *Datamation* (July 1972), p. 43.

[40] Relevant concepts and guidelines for building a data base are discussed in Shubert, "Basic Concepts in Data Base Management Systems," pp. 42–47; Albert C. Patterson, "Data Base Hazards," *Datamation* (July 1972), pp. 48–50; and Richard L. Nolan, "Computer Data Bases: The Future is Now", *Harvard Business Review,* 51 (September–October 1973), pp. 98–114.

[41] For a discussion of various aspects of information retrieval, see Lawrence Berul, *Information Storage and Retrieval—A State of the Art Report* (Philadelphia: Auerbach Corporation, 1964).

Optimization Models and Simulation. This group of information processing methods discussed in Chapter 11 represents the most powerful set of tools for aiding decision analysis. Examples include linear and non-linear programming, Markov analysis, calculus, and simulation techniques.[42] Standardized computer software is available for many of the more frequently used mathematical models such as linear programming. There are also computer simulation packages that can be applied to a variety of situations.[43] Use of models and simulation will be illustrated in subsequent chapters.

System Functions

Several types of activities can be performed by the MIS: (1) data base creation and maintenance; (2) processing of information; (3) generation of regular reports and responding to special requests; and (4) responding to "on-line" inquiries from remote computer consoles. Outputs of the MIS may include scheduled reports such as product line sales performance, district sales analyses, customer sales by size of account, etc. Since it would be difficult (and expensive) to design a series of reports and analyses to meet all of the marketing decision makers' needs, the system should have a capability to provide information on ad hoc requests. These might include an historical market share analysis in a particular sales territory or a detailed analysis of particular customers.

On line inquiry of a computerized MIS represents the highest level of capability using a remote terminal system such as those used by several airlines and stock brokers. This type of capability can provide the decision maker with a powerful aid in decision analysis. Of course, the benefits of such a system must be weighed against the costs. In particular, the importance of speed-of-response and convenience must be assessed. For example, the Federal Bureau of Investigation through their National Crime Information Center has placed an important file of information at the fingertips of law enforcement officers throughout the nation by using an on-line network of terminals in combination with radio communication.

The MIS components and functions we have been discussing are shown in Figure 12–10 and the important interrelationships between the

---

[42] An extensive examination of the use of management science methods in the analysis of various marketing management decisions is provided in David B. Montgomery and Glen L. Urban, *Management Science in Marketing* (Englewood Cliffs, New Jersey: Prentice-Hall, Inc., 1969); and Philip Kotler, *Marketing Decision Making: A Model Building Approach* (New York: Holt, Rinehart and Winston, Inc., 1971).

[43] Thomas H. Naylor et al., *Computer Simulation Techniques* (New York: John Wiley & Sons, Inc., 1966), pp. 37–39.

FIGURE 12–10

Overview of MIS Components and Functions

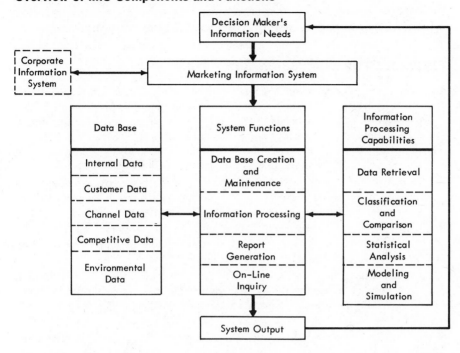

elements are indicated. The possible linkage of the MIS to the corporate or organizational information system is indicated. The MIS must depend upon the decision maker's marketing information needs to provide direction as to the system's range of capabilities. The system functions are supported by its data base and information processing capabilities. A given system may not contain all of the information categories, capabilities, and functions shown in Figure 12–10. Rather, these represent the various alternatives available.

SUMMARY AND CONCLUSIONS

Planning for marketing information is a key function performed by the marketing manager and staff. Information acquisition and use require resource expenditures and should be evaluated against the benefits the information promises to provide. A systematic, operational approach to planning for needed information has been developed in this chapter. The approach can be used in planning for, acquiring, and using information needed in environmental analysis, market opportunity analysis, and marketing strategy design, implementation and control. Recognizing the increasing trend of many firms toward the development of marketing information systems as a means of managing their information resources, the basic components that comprise most MISs were described and their interrelationships and functions in the total system were indicated.

EXERCISES FOR DISCUSSION AND REVIEW

1. A cigarette manufacturer is considering changing the design of one of the firm's cigarette packages. Use the information planning process to indicate probable information needs on this decision situation and then outline an information strategy for obtaining needed information. Make whatever assumptions that are necessary in developing your analysis of the situation and associated recommendations concerning an information strategy.

2. How would the task of determining information needs by a manager interested in assessing the performance of the sales force differ from that of a manager concerned by a long-run decline in sales by the firm?

3. Under what conditions might a firm with a very competent marketing research department decide to purchase the services of marketing research firm to aid in obtaining of additional information?

4. Assume a large bank is trying to identify potential locations for new branch bank sites. How might management determine how much should be spent on obtaining additional information to aid them in making location decisions?

5. If you were assigned the responsibility for describing the size, characteristics, and participants (e.g., suppliers, and distributors) of the microwave oven market, indicate how you would proceed with the task.

6. For the proposed motel venture discussed in the chapter, identify the types of information that would be helpful in estimating probable occupancy rates.

7. An industrial distributor is currently marketing ten different products (Product A, B, C, D, E, F, G, H, I, J). Overall company sales have gone down for the last year, although the sales of products B and C have increased. The company is selling in five different geographical territories. Outline an approach for planning for and acquiring information to aid in the analysis of this decision situation.

8. A brewer has been considering introducing a beer-based beverage which does not taste like beer, although it would have roughly the same alcoholic content as beer. Presumably the product would appeal to people who do not like the taste of standard beers but who are not turned on by soda pop, either. The company does not know exactly which taste (e.g., fruit) they should use for their new beverage. What information needs should be considered by management? Suggest an approach for establishing a priorities among the information needs. Indicate the probable impact that this information could have upon the decision whether or not to introduce the new beverage.

13

Planning the Marketing Program

Our examination of corporate and marketing strategy in Chapter 10 provides an overall perspective for considering the task of planning the marketing program. The factors that influence marketing strategy were assessed and the range of strategy positions that a firm can occupy due to variations in the market-product situation were described. After the marketing strategy position is determined, the various aspects of designing an appropriate marketing program can be undertaken. First, the marketing strategy process is described. Relevant concepts for use in guiding decisions on the allocation of marketing resources are discussed. Building on these concepts, approaches to the analysis of marketing program decisions are examined and illustrated. Finally, guidelines for developing the marketing plan are considered.

MARKETING STRATEGY PROCESS

Strategy Stages

The major stages in the marketing strategy process are shown in Figure 13–1. The general framework for the process is provided by the organization's purpose and goals. Within this corporate mission definition, market opportunities should be identified and specific market targets selected that are consistent with the corporate purpose. Determination of market targets and marketing objectives provide specific guidelines for planning the marketing program which consists of decisions concerning products, channels of distribution, price, advertising, and personal selling for each market target. During the planning process needed changes in objectives may be identified; thus, feedback from planning to marketing objectives is indicated. For example, detailed analysis of marketing program alternatives (different marketing mix combinations) may indicate that achievement of the sales objective for a particular market target may not be feasible at acceptable program cost levels. Thus, management would need to revise the sales objective. Implementation of the marketing program is the next stage in the strategy process. After marketing efforts are underway, management must monitor progress to keep the gap between actual and desired performance as small as possible. This is the control function. Implementation and control efforts consume a major portion of marketing management's time.

FIGURE 13–1

Marketing Strategy Process

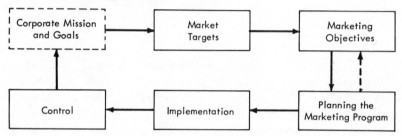

The various stages shown in Figure 13–1 are interrelated. Marketing strategy is a process; decsions made at each stage influence all other stages. Thus, the overall management job is to plan, organize, implement, and control the strategy process to achieve marketing objectives for chosen market targets within the framework provided by the organization's purpose and goals. In the remainder of this section, the nature and scope of the marketing mix decision are described.

Marketing Mix Decisions

Three groups of variables are relevant to the marketing programming decision:

1. Factors controlled by the firm.
2. Factors influenced but not controlled by the firm.
3. Factors neither influenced nor controlled by the firm.[1]

The controllable factors are the various actions which can be taken by the organization to influence market targets. These are the ingredi-

---

[1] Harry Allison, "Framework for Marketing Strategy," *California Management Review*, 4 (Fall 1961), pp. 75–95.

ents of the marketing mix.[2] Factors which the marketing manager can influence but not control include markets, competition and other organizations in the marketing system, and the non-marketing decision making areas in the firm. Uncontrollable factors include other external influences (e.g., technology, economic and social change, government and legal constraints) which were examined in Part II of the book.

Thus, the marketing mix decision is concerned with determining how those factors controlled by the firm can best be assembled in the form of the marketing program to achieve marketing objectives for each market target. Moreover, marketing program decisions must take into consideration relevant variables that cannot be controlled.

The fundamental concept underlying determination of the marketing mix is to assemble marketing resources in a manner that will yield the best possible results in terms of specified objectives. Contribution to profit over the relevant planning horizon is one criterion frequently used to guide these decisions. Objectives may also be specified for increases in market share and sales, mix of products sold, new customers, and other performance criteria for the firm's market targets. In a stable, mature business, the planning horizon is typically one to a few years with detailed budgeting accomplished on an annual basis. In a new venture or growth situation, there should be some attempt to project sufficiently far into the future feasible revenue-cost flows for guiding shorter range marketing mix programming. The end result of the marketing mix decision consists of three interrelated actions:

1. Determination of the total amount of dollars to spend on the marketing program during the relevant planning period. This represents the marketing budget to be used to accomplish marketing objectives.
2. Allocation of dollars to the various controllable factors that comprise the marketing mix. For example, what portion of resources is to be spent on advertising and personal selling?
3. Decisions on how to allocate dollars within each element of the marketing mix to achieve the best (highest quality) use of resources to achieve marketing objectives. For example, what advertising media should be selected? How shall salesmen be deployed among customers and prospects?

The process of making these decisions is interactive in nature. In some firms, the marketing manager is given a fixed annual budget which tends to set an upper limit on total expenditures. He must decide, utilizing recommendations from his staff (sales manager, advertising

---

[2] The channel of distribution may fall into the "influenced" category of factors unless the organization has complete control (e.g., through ownership or contractual arrangements). Variations in degree of control over the channel of distribution are considered in chapters 16 and 17.

manager, etc.), how to allocate available financial resources within the assigned budget. Initial recommendations may exceed available resources. If the marketing manager is unable to obtain additional dollars, then it is necessary to trim recommended amounts in one or more marketing mix areas. In situations where the total amount of dollars is not fixed, the marketing manager must compete with the other functional areas of the firm for scarce financial resources. In this case, he will have to justify why, for example, he wants to increase the marketing budget over last year's expenditures.

In practice, top management's frame of reference for total expenditures is frequently what has been done in the past. Determining a new marketing program is often accomplished by assessing how much to increase or decrease last period's resource allocations to achieve new objectives. Thus, even if the marketing manager is given an opportunity to adjust total expenditures substantially above (or below) historical levels, the request will typically be assessed in terms of past revenue-cost relationships plus future projections including the logic underlying the estimates.

In analyzing the marketing mixes used by two competitors serving the same markets, one may find that their use of marketing resources is not the same. For example, some insurance firms market life insurance by mail while others sell through a company sales force or independent agents. Similarly, term life insurance rates for various firms show a substantial range of variation in charges made for similar coverage. Thus, price does not play the same role in the marketing mix for different firms. Those that charge more may provide more extensive customer services. As will be illustrated in this and subsequent chapters there are many possible marketing mix combinations that may be used by a particular firm depending upon available resources, existing marketing expertise, and management's assessment of the relative effectiveness of various elements of the marketing mix.

The marketing manager must coordinate decisions concerning elements of the marketing mix with other functional areas of the organization. For example, product planning is a corporate activity that is shared by various members of the management team. Decisions on new products, product modification, and product elimination affect various areas including finance, personnel, and manufacturing. The channel of distribution decision, in addition to typically being a long-term decision, may like the product decision, require coordination within the firm. For example, it would be a rare situation in which the president or chief executive officer would not be involved in a decision to shift from a factory sales force to manufacturers representatives, or a decision to move toward corporate ownership of existing franchised retail outlets. Similarly, pricing decisions necessitate careful coordination within the firm. Advertising and sales force decisions are typically the exclusive responsibility of the marketing manager.

RESOURCE ALLOCATION PRINCIPLES

Central to the process of developing the marketing program is that the responses of buyers will vary depending upon the magnitude and composition of the marketing mix. Since there are many possible levels to the marketing mix, and a very large number of allocation alternatives at each level, choice of the "best" marketing mix in a given strategy situation is complex if not impossible. The difficulty of identifying all relevant marketing program alternatives, extensive time and costs associated with investigating these alternatives, and the uncertainties inherent in developing estimates of the effectiveness of various marketing mix combinations prevent the marketing manager from selecting the very best marketing program from all possible alternatives. Yet, good mix decisions can be made even though they may not be optimal in the sense of being the very best of all possible alternatives. There are certain concepts and allocation guidelines which can assist the marketing manager in this decision making task. First, the concept of market response is considered, followed by an examination of decision principles useful in determining how marketing resources should be allocated. Next, certain of the factors which affect the effectiveness of marketing variables are discussed. Finally, the concept of gaining a differential advantage over competition is presented.

Market Response

Determination of market response to marketing effort is a major aspect of programming marketing resources. Market response can be considered from a company or an industry point of view. Company market response is the change that occurs within a given target market due to the influence of a firm's marketing effort. The change resulting from the aggregate efforts of all firms serving a particular target market reflects industry market response. While market response (change) can be measured in various ways (e.g., customer brand preference, number of people exposed to a firm's marketing effort) sales is a frequently used basis for assessing market response. When sales projections are combined with information on the cost of marketing effort, profit contribution can be estimated. By examining alternative levels of marketing program expenditures, profit contributions can be estimated and the most promising program selected.

Estimation of market response presents marketing management with a major challenge. As shown in Figure 13–2, there are various influences,

FIGURE 13–2

Conceptual Model of Market Response

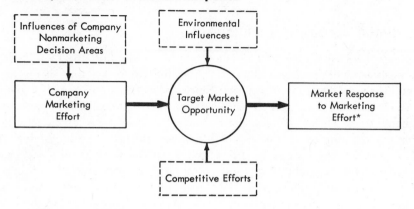

* Sales, preference levels, exposure, etc.

in addition to company marketing effort, upon the target market opportunities that are selected by a firm. Estimation of the individual effect of these factors is clearly difficult. Since there are several interrelated factors which must be considered, including variables that cannot be controlled by the firm, there are many uncertainties present when estimating sales response. For example, marketing actions taken by a particular firm (e.g., increase in the size of the sales force) may precipitate actions by competitors. A shift to unfavorable general economic conditions can slow down consumer purchases. Moreover, the specific impact of each influence upon a firm's market target is frequently difficult to estimate. Analysis of market response can be facilitated by assuming initially that the influences of all other factors (e.g., competition, environmental forces) remain at their present level. Then the possible effects of the other factors can be incorporated into the analysis.

To illustrate the concept of a sales response function, consider the relationship of sales to a single marketing mix variable, advertising effort, shown in Figure 13–3. The relationship shown in Figure 13–3 assumes all other marketing and non-marketing factors that influence sales are held constant at a given level while advertising effort is allowed to vary as indicated. At low levels of advertising, increases in effort might be expected to yield nominal increases in sales. In fact, in some situations initial advertising effort might not yield any sales response until a threshold level is reached. Consider, for example, the large expenditures necessary before a national television advertising campaign would have any impact upon the market place. After this initial buildup, advertising expenditures reach a level where sales increase at a faster rate than

FIGURE 13–3

Illustrative Sales Response Function

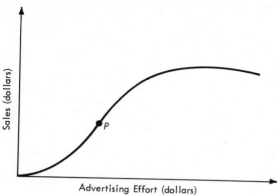

expenditures. Customers have become aware of the product and are responding favorably to the offer. Sales continue to increase at a faster rate than expenditures up to point P in Figure 13–3. Beyond point P, sales increase at a diminishing or declining rate for additional amounts of marketing expenditures. This portion of the curve represents the law of diminishing returns from economics which states that *"if the input of one resource is increased by equal increments per unit of time while the inputs of other resources are held constant, total product output will increase, but beyond some point the resulting output increases will become smaller and smaller."*[3] For example, in an area where a substantial portion of available business has been obtained, the addition of more advertising to the area may yield modest increases in sales compared to the additional expenses. Finally, a level of saturation might be reached beyond which more advertising effort would yield no increases in sales, and perhaps as shown in Figure 13–3, decreases would occur. For example, past experience has shown that too much advertising can have a negative effect upon sales.

The influence upon sales response of other factors can be incorporated as shown in Figure 13–4. The estimated sales response for three sizes of the sales force, including the present size of S_0, is shown in Figure 13–4A. This demonstrates the impact upon sales response when two marketing mix variables are varied together. Economies in marketing resources can frequently be achieved when marketing mix elements are used in combination. As shown on S_1 and S_2 of Figure 13–4A, advertising and personal selling working together accomplish greater

---

[3] Richard H. Leftwich, *The Price System and Resource Allocation*, 3d ed. (New York: Holt, Rinehart and Winston, 1966), pp. 99–100.

FIGURE 13–4

Sales Response Incorporating Factors in Addition to Advertising

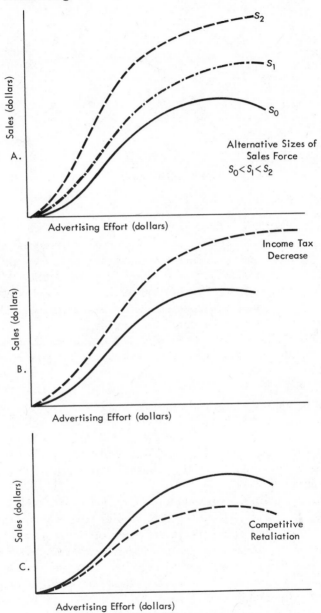

sales response than by holding sales force at a constant level. This is because additional advertising develops awareness and interest in the product, thus creating expanded personal selling opportunities. Of course, costs of marketing resources must be considered as well as sales response in determining the appropriate composition and magnitude of the marketing program.

In Figure 13–4B the influence of an environmental change is illustrated. For example, assume the product is a household appliance. A reduction in personal income tax is anticipated to increase sales response at all levels of advertising expenditures for the firm's target market. As shown in Figure 13–4C the assumption of aggressive retaliation by competitors to the firm's higher level advertising expenditures is expected to have an adverse effect upon the sales response experienced by the firm.

There are four major approaches to estimating probable response of sales to marketing effort: *judgmental, analytical, testing,* and *combination.* Judgmental approaches utilize management's experience and knowledge of market behavior as a basis for estimating probable responsiveness of sales to alternative levels of marketing expenditures. For example, the marketing manager could estimate sales for a 10 percent increase and a 10 percent decrease over last year's marketing budget. Such estimates are useful in determining whether to expand or contract marketing effort for a particular market target. In cases where uncontrolled factors remain relatively constant over the short-to-intermediate term, judgmental methods may be useful in developing sales response relationships to guide marketing resource allocation decisions.[4] While it may not be possible to determine the complete shape of the curve, a reasonable estimate may be feasible of the relationship between sales and marketing effort for the range around the current operating level.

If historical data are available or can be collected, analytical methods such as multiple linear regression analysis can be used to develop sales response relationships. This involves empirically developing a relationship between sales and possible determinants of sales including uncontrollable factors (e.g., market potential). These methods are often used to develop sales response relationships for particular elements of the marketing mix such as personal selling.[5] Analytical methods are also used

---

[4] See, for example, Leonard M. Lodish, " 'Vaguely Right' Approach to Sales Force Allocation," *Harvard Business Review,* 52 (January–February 1974), pp. 119–24.

[5] See, for example, David W. Cravens, Robert B. Woodruff, and Joe C. Stamper, "An Analytical Approach for Evaluating Sales Territory Performance," *Journal of Marketing,* 36 (January 1972), pp. 31–37; and Z. Lambert and F. Kniffin, "Response Functions and Their Application in Sales Force Management," *Southern Journal of Business,* 5 (January 1970), pp. 1–11.

to prepare sales forecasts for particular market targets as discussed in Chapter 7 and 8.

Market testing of new consumer products is sometimes used to determine the responsiveness of sales to variations in the marketing mix. It "is a research technique in which the product under study is placed in one or more selected localities or areas, and its reception by consumer and trade is observed, recorded, and analyzed."[6] The approach can be used to evaluate market response to new products, advertising programs, package designs and sizes, pricing, and other marketing program variations. The major aspects of test-market operations include: determining objectives, selecting test market locations or areas, time span of testing, identifing information to be collected for analysis, and projecting test results for a target market.[7]

Any use of analytical methods or testing typically involves considerable management judgment in combination with the methods. Thus, combination approaches to estimating market response are normally used. It is also possible that judgment and analytical methods will both be incorporated into the design and analysis of market testing programs.

Estimation of market response will be illustrated in subsequent chapters with respect to particular marketing effort variables. Management must develop the best possible estimates of sales response consistent with costs and benefits.

Decision Principles

Decisions involving the use of marketing resources should be guided by: (1) appropriate decision criteria (objectives); and (2) decision principles (rules) for choosing among alternative uses of resources. The marketing programming decision task is described as follows:

> The process of choosing among the relevant alternatives involves the marketing staff in an attempt to maximize long-run total revenue net of selling (marketing) costs at particular output levels, given the outside-imposed and firm-imposed restrictions on the marketing staff's actions.[8]

Recognizing that goals other than long-run profit maximization are relevant, they can be incorporated into the analysis by considering them as firm-imposed restrictions. Thus, the goal of the enterprise can be viewed as seeking long-run profits that are as large as possible,

---

[6] Jack A. Gold, as quoted in *Market Testing Consumer Products* (New York: National Industrial Conference Board, Inc., 1967), p. 11.

[7] David T. Kollat, Roger D. Blackwell, and James F. Robeson, *Strategic Marketing* (New York: Holt, Rinehart and Winston, Inc., 1972), p. 424. Chapter 18 contains a concise discussion of the purpose, strengths, weaknesses, and approaches used in test marketing.

[8] Allison, "Framework for Marketing Strategy," p. 75, parenthesis added.

within the constraints imposed by the firm's non-profit objectives.[9] Examples of constraints or restrictions include market share limits (due to governmental influences), budget limitations, environmental improvement, and other non-economic goals.

As an introduction to the allocation of marketing resources consider the illustration shown in Figure 13–5. Assume that management has

FIGURE 13–5

Comparison of Sales Response in Two Markets

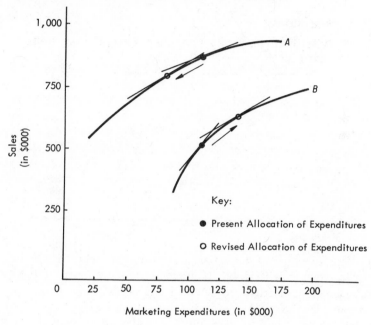

estimated (based on judgment, experience, and analysis of historical information) the sales response relationships for Markets A and B around the current range of expenditures. Only a portion of the sales response curve for each market is indicated and the relationship is shown as being nonlinear. Suppose you are asked (based on the information contained in Figure 13–5) if you can improve the use of marketing expenditures, but you cannot spend more than the current total amount expended in Market A plus Market B. It would be logical to reduce expenditures somewhat in A and increase a corresponding amount in B. A shifting of expenditures from A to B would result in a gain in sales at no additional cost. This reallocation is logical, given a long run profit

---

[9] Ibid., p. 76.

maximization goal, because the sales increase that can be obtained per dollar of additional marketing expenditure in B is higher than the corresponding loss of sales in A. As shown in Table 13–1 by decreasing marketing expenditures in Market A about $27,000 and increasing expenditures in Market B the same amount, sales would increase approximately $38,000.

It is important to recognize from the example in Figure 13–5 and Table 13–1 that shifts in the use of marketing resources should not be guided by average response information (total sales ÷ total expendi-

TABLE 13–1

Results of Reallocating Marketing Expenditures from Market A to B

Market	*Marketing Expenditures*	*Sales (in $1,000s)*
Present Allocation		
A..............................	113	875
B..............................	113	525
Total..........................	226	1,400
Revised Allocation		
A..............................	86	800
B..............................	140	638
Total..........................	226	1,438

tures). The average sales response in Market A is $875 \div 113 = 7.7$ whereas in Market B it is 4.6. If average sales response at the present allocation levels is used to guide the resource decision, then one might be prompted to shift more resources into A and away from B. Yet, as shown by the information in Table 13–1, allocation away from A and into B will result in higher sales at no increase in costs.

The example shown in Figure 13–5 illustrates one important principle for guiding decisions on the use of marketing resources. *Marginal returns for the last dollar spent on one marketing variable should be equal to the marginal returns from allocations to all other marketing variables.* In Figure 13–5 returns are represented by sales. Before resources were shifted from Market A into B, the marginal return (slope of the sales response curve) in B was greater than in A. By increasing expenditures in B to a point where the marginal returns are equal (revised allocation shown in Figure 13–5), revenues can be increased at no increase in marketing costs. As Allison points out:

> Unless the marginal revenues net of selling (marketing) costs are equal for the last dollars spent in advertising, location, personal selling, services, etc., at a particular level of output, the firm's total revenue net of

selling (marketing) costs—and, therefore, the firm's profits—for that output level can be increased by transferring marginal dollars from the controlled factors yielding the lower marginal return to the controlled factors yielding the higher marginal return.[10]

The marginal decision rule provides a key guideline for allocating resources to the various elements of the marketing mix. It is also useful in allocating resources within a particular mix area such as advertising or personal selling. In cases where a firm is serving more than one market target the same marginal equality should apply between different market targets, as illustrated for example in Figure 13–5. While the marginal rule is conceptually sound, certain implications should be recognized in adopting the principle to marketing practice:

Typically marketing expenditures are made in increments of dollars rather than a dollar at a time. Portions of a salesman or advertisement obviously cannot be considered; thus, allocations between mix variables cannot be perfectly balanced according to the decision rule.

Uncertainties in estimating revenue-cost relationships prevent the marketing manager from making precise allocation decisions. Yet, the decision rule can be quite useful in indicating the direction of resource shifts.

Use of the rule implies that the marketing manager can select the best use of resources for each marketing variable. For example, various possibilities exist for use of a given budget for advertising. Skill, experience, and creativity are essential in selecting the alternative uses of marketing mix dollars to be evaluated. The decision rule does not identify the appropriate alternatives which should be evaluated.

Effectiveness of Marketing Variables

In applying the marginal or incremental rule certain characteristics of marketing variables should be recognized. These include the time lag in market response, scale economies, substitution and combination effects and decay rate of marketing variables.[11]

Time Lag in Response. The time lag in market response to marketing effort has an important bearing on programming decisions. For example, increasing the sales force by ten percent does not immediately

[10] Ibid., p. 82 (parentheses added).

[11] Several guidelines that are helpful in making marketing programming decisions are discussed in R. P. Willett, "A Model for Marketing Programming," *Journal of Marketing*, 27 (January 1963), pp. 42–44. The following discussion is largely based on this source.

produce sales. Salespeople must be trained, accounts must be assigned and developed, and competitive efforts must be countered. In industrial sales, it is not unusual to find that a salesman must be on the job for one or two years before beginning to contribute more than he costs. Similarly, the effects of advertising may not all occur during the period of expenditures. The carry-over effect of advertising appears more probable for consumer products than for industrial products because of the heavy portion of marketing expenditures allocated to advertising for consumer markets. Tull has conducted empirical studies which tend to support the carry-over effect.[12] In programming resources the marketing manager must attempt to estimate the flow of revenues and costs over time resulting from marketing actions.

Scale Economies. There are certain economies (and diseconomies) of scale inherent in the use of marketing resources. In particular types of retailing such as fast foods, local advertising costs are typically too high to be absorbed by a single outlet. Accordingly, fast food firms tend to locate in metropolitan areas where a network of stores can be provided with management assistance, advertising, and other marketing and operational support. Cooperative marketing and distribution efforts are also common in certain lines of agricultural products where growers work together to overcome diseconomies of scale. Scale economies may vary for various elements of the marketing mix. For example, a small manufacturer selling through manufacturer's representatives may be unable due to costs to undertake an advertising program. We observed in Chapter 1 that A&P attempted to adopt a discount price structure via its "WEO" concept, while many of the firm's food stores were too small to generate the sales volume necessary to operate profitably under the discount price structure.[13] Diseconomies of scale due to management inefficiencies may result when operations become too large. For example, in firms with very large sales forces (several hundred or more) several management levels are needed. To overcome the inefficiencies inherent in multilevel operations companies may establish separate, independent divisions. Such approaches are used by certain large oil companies where marketing operations function independently within geographic regions. Thus, the marketing manager must carefully integrate the various elements of the marketing program. "Choice of inputs in the mix and their levels of operation should reflect the balance of economies and diseconomies of scale likely to appear in the marketing cost structure."[14]

---

[12] Donald S. Tull, "The Carry-over Effect of Advertising," *Journal of Marketing*, 29 (April 1961), pp. 46–53.

[13] Eleanor Johnson Tracy, "How A & P Got Creamed," *Fortune*, 88 (January 1973), pp. 103–14.

[14] Willett, "A Model for Marketing Programming," p. 43.

Substitution and Combination Effects. The interrelationships among marketing variables are important in planning the marketing program. Certain alternative marketing mix elements can be used for the same purpose. Advertising and personal selling perform many similar functions. Some firms use direct mail marketing approaches for their products or services rather than advertising and personal selling efforts. The combination effects of two or more marketing effects working together should also be assessed, since one mix element may be needed to complement another. For example, promotional efforts are typically used to launch and sustain a new product in the marketplace. The price charged for a product has an important bearing on a consumer's perception of the product. In addition to substitution and combination effects the sequence that marketing variables are introduced into the marketplace is an important determinant of marketing program effectiveness. Have you ever searched the shelves of a food or drug store for a heavily advertised new product only to learn that the distribution system has not yet moved the product into your retail trade area?

Decay Rate. The effectiveness of marketing program elements inevitably decay over time. Products are often modified after they have been in the market for a long time. New packaging designs are introduced on a regular basis for many consumer products. Similarly, business firms revise advertising programs on a continuing basis in attempting to improve the effectiveness of advertising expenditures. The marketing must continually be alert to needed changes in the use of marketing resources due to their possible loss of effectiveness over time.

Achieving an effective combination of marketing variables is a complex task. The use of marginal or incremental analysis in combination with the guidelines concerning the effectiveness of marketing variables discussed above can facilitate program design. One additional resource allocation guideline that is central to the marketing program decision is the concept of achieving a differential advantage over competition.

Concept of Differential Advantage

Nearly two decades ago, Alderson, building on concepts developed in economics, proposed that competition among firms be viewed as a process of *competition for differential advantage.*[15] This point of view of competition recognizes that a business firm possesses certain characteristics and capabilities that are unique in particular respects to all other firms. The logic of competition for differential advantage is significant with regard to marketing variables and is widely demonstrated by the

---

[15] Wroe Alderson, *Marketing Behavior and Executive Action* (Homewood, Ill.: Richard D. Irwin, Inc., 1957), chapter 4.

marketing strategies adopted by business firms. As Alderson has observed:

> Every business firm occupies a position which is in some respects unique. Its location, the product it sells, its operating methods, or the customers it serves tend to set it off in some degree from every other firm. Each firm competes by making the most of its individuality and its special character.[16]

Differential advantage can be gained in various ways including market segmentation, distribution channel design, advertising appeals, product and process improvement, and new products. Central to the marketing programming effort is an attempt to utilize marketing variables that are insulated from competitive duplication or counter action. For example, competition can duplicate a price change much more quickly than a new product. Some examples of firms that have achieved differential advantages over competition include:

The strong market position established by Coors' beer as a regional brand through an effective product differentiation effort, in a market dominated by a few national brands.

Xerox's revolutionary copying process which through patent protection enabled the firm in the time span of a decade to grow into a major corporation.

American Motors strategy of focusing on the small car segment of the market, recognizing that the firm could not effectively compete with the "big three" over the complete range of automobile sizes and style.

The Maytag Company's concentration upon home and commercial laundry equipment enabled the firm over the years to establish a strong product image and a good performance record in a highly competitive industry.

Acquisition of a savings and loan business by Fred Meyer, Inc., the leading one-stop shopping chain in the Northwest. The chain has located S&L branches in its retail stores, thus benefiting from the high customer traffic generated by its large stores.[17]

There is also some degree of risk inherent in seeking a differential advantage. Being different is not necessarily being better. Revolutionary differentiation may not bring about favorable response in the market place. For example, certain style changes in women's clothing are not successful. Various new food products do not gain sufficient sales to justify continuing to offer them. Because of the risks in being first in

---

[16] Ibid., p. 101

[17] "What a Time to Buy an S&L," *Business Week* (October 5, 1974), p. 48.

the marketplace, some firms pursue a strategy of attempting to duplicate marketing strategy actions that are successful. When a competitor offers a new product that is well received in the market place, a competitor will seek to develop a comparable product quickly. The strategy of following the firm that has achieved a differential advantage is feasible when duplication can be achieved sufficiently quickly to overcome the market acceptance gained by the initiating firm. A "following" strategy may be more appropriate for a small firm whose limited resources preclude extensive product and market development activities. A firm with a small market share may be able to improve its market position relatively quickly if it can successfully duplicate an innovating firm's strategy. Such as effort would have a limited effect upon the market position of the large firm.

DECISION ANALYSIS

Building upon the resource allocation principles discussed in the previous section, these concepts and guidelines are now applied to illustrate their usefulness in decision analysis. First, determination of resource allocation for a single marketing mix variable is considered. This is then extended to decision analysis where multiple factors are involved including two or more mix elements, and multiple market targets. Finally, use of analytical decision models to assist the marketing manager in programming resources is discussed.

Single Factor Analysis

Analysis of alternative resource levels for a single marketing variable is illustrative of the type of decision that occurs in the various areas of the marketing mix. These decisions include: what size of sales force is appropriate; what magnitude of advertising budget should be planned; or which type of distribution channel should be selected? As an illustration of single factor analysis, consideration of alternative sizes of sales force will be used. Consider a firm that produces and markets industrial equipment using technical sales representatives. Selling expenses comprise the major portion of the marketing budget. The present size of the sales force is 30 sales representatives plus sales management. The director of sales is interested in determining whether the sales force should be increased or decreased from the current level. Information which is helpful in assessing this decision is shown in Table 13–2:

Sales estimates for various sales force sizes above and below the present size have been developed considering the factors that influence sales response (e.g., market potential, competition, selling

TABLE 13-2

Illustrative Analysis of Sales Force Size

	Dollars (in 1,000s)			
Size of Sales Force	*Estimates Annual Sales*	*Gross Margin**	*Selling Expenses*	*Margin Less Selling Expenses*
10.................	3,750	563	275	288
20.................	7,000	1,400	575	825
30†................	9,000	2,700	875	1,825
40.................	10,600	3,710	1,200	2,510
50.................	11,750	3,525	1,535	1,990

* Sales less cost of goods sold.
† Present size of sales force.

effort). The sales director recognizes that sales per man above the current level would be somewhat less due to competition for available business and somewhat higher per man for smaller sales force sizes.

Gross margin estimates reflect the fact that some excess plant capacity exists, thus providing lower unit costs for increased sales up to a sales force size of 40. Beyond this unit costs are expected to increase. Moreover, below the present level of sales unit costs are estimated to be higher.

Costs (salary plus expense) per salesman are estimated to be constant at all levels although management costs are expected to increase more than proportionately at larger sizes of the sales force due to administrative, supervisory, and training costs.

The sales director, after analyzing the information shown in Table 13-2, has a basis for considering an increase in the sales force size since movement to a size of 40 is estimated to yield a substantial improvement in gross margin after deduction of selling expenses. Of course, such a proposed increase should also include consideration of possible increases in nonmarketing costs such as operating capital, management, and other general and administrative expenses.

The analysis shown in Table 13-2 is an illustration of how the marginal or incremental decision rule can be applied. By developing estimates of sales and costs incremental changes in the level of a marketing resource can be evaluated, and possible directions of change determined. A major shift of resources, such as increasing sales force size by one third, is likely to be accomplished in stages. Yet, the analysis can be quite useful in indicating the direction of change, or if a change is appropriate. The example also indicates that a complete sales response relationship often is not needed to guide shifts of resources around the current level.

Multiple Factor Analysis

Frequently it is necessary in programming marketing resources to consider multiple factors that affect market response. Such decisions include new ventures, additions to the product line, store location, and designing marketing programs for particular market targets. Normally, it is impossible to consider the various factors separately that may be relevant in a given decision situation. To illustrate the nature of multiple factor analysis, assesment of a proposed motel venture has been selected.

A decision regarding the building of a new motel involves a variety of factors that may influence the success of the venture including site location, quality of service, competition, price, size of facility, and environmental factors such as seasonal patronage patterns. To illustrate decision analysis for this type of venture assume that an investor can purchase a site at an interchange of a major Interstate highway, and that he is considering the construction of a 60-unit facility.[18] He is concerned with determining the feasibility of the business venture.

A motel involves a heavy proportion of fixed costs, thus offering substantial profit contributions above break-even level, and equally substantial losses at operating levels below break-even. Thus, a key factor in feasibility determination is estimating probable average annual occupancy of a particular facility. Determining possible occupancy involves consideration of various factors including:

1. Seasonal travel patterns.
2. Mix of possible pleasure versus commercial customers.
3. Traffic volume (by time of year).
4. Patronage patterns for non-competing adjacent facilities (e.g., service stations).
5. Occupancy experience of possible competing motels.
6. Quality and mix of services provided.

Because there are no historical data available, it is necessary to consider various indirect measures that may indicate probable patronage patterns. This information would include interviews with nearby motel operators concerning business prospects; discussion with service station operators to determine the magnitude and character (e.g., pleasure versus commercial travelers, local versus cross country travelers) of patronage; analysis of highway traffic data (from state highway depart-

---

[18] Assume this size is the most feasible for the site. The approach to analysis illustrated on the following pages can be expanded to consider alternative facility sizes (e.g., 40, 80, 100 units).

ment); and discussions with operators of interstate food and gift shops. Consumer surveys could also be conducted at service stations adjacent to the proposed site to assess possible patronage of the proposed motel. Assume that the investor has retained a motel location consultant who has collected and analyzed available information on the proposed site, and has forecasted occupancy rates for the proposed facility to range between 50 and 70 percent with 60 percent to be the most likely level of patronage.

Using these occupancy estimates the investor next prepares a revenue and expense analysis as shown in Table 13–3. This analysis for the range of feasible occupancy levels (50, 60, and 70 percent) provides a basis for making return on investment estimates. Assume that the investor

TABLE 13–3

Motel Revenue and Expense Analysis (60-unit facility)

	Average Annual Occupancy		
	50 Percent (30 units) $	60 Percent (36 units) $	70 Percent (42 units) $
Revenues*			
Room Rental @ 12.50/rm./dy	137,000	164,200	191,500
Other (telephone, misc.)	2,000	2,000	2,000
Total Revenues	139,000	166,200	193,500
Operating Expenses			
Salaries			
Manager	6,000	6,000	6,000
Maids	9,000	10,800	12,600
Repairman	3,600	3,600	3,600
Desk and PBX	18,000	18,000	18,000
Payroll taxes	2,231	2,306	2,411
Maintenance			
Cleaning supplies	3,420	4,105	4,780
Laundry and linens	8,230	9,852	11,500
Other	2,740	3,284	3,820
Repairs	5,480	6,568	7,650
Utilities			
Telephone	3,600	3,600	3,600
Heat, light, power	4,500	5,000	5,500
Other Overhead			
Insurance	5,040	5,040	5,040
Accounting	1,000	1,000	1,000
Office supplies	800	900	1,000
Property taxes	6,000	6,000	6,000
Franchise fee	2,000	2,000	2,000
Advertising and Promotion	6,000	6,000	6,000
Total Operating Expenses	87,641	94,055	100,501
Contribution to			
Debt service, taxes, and return on investment	51,359	72,145	92,999

* Coffee shop not included in the analysis. Assumed to be leased and to operate on a break-even basis.

TABLE 13–4

Return on Investment (ROI) Analysis (60-unit facility, initial year of operation)

			Average Annual Occupancy		
			50 percent $	60 percent $	70 percent $
1.	Contribution margin per				
	schedule (Table 13–3)................		51,359	72,145	92,999
	Interest deduction*....................		25,000	25,000	25,000
	Depreciation deduction†...............		38,800	38,800	38,800
	Taxable income (loss).................		(12,441)	8,345	29,199
2.	Income taxes‡........................		–0–	2,330	9,015
	After tax income........................		(12,441)	6,015	20,184
	Cash flow to service debt				
	1 – 2 1st year.....................		51,359	69,815	83,984
	Less debt service*				
	(4751 × 12)......................		57,012	57,012	57,012
	Contribution to ROI..................		(5,653)	12,803	26,972
	Investment				
	Land...................... 100,000				
	Cash invested in facility..... 100,000				
	Total................. 200,000				
	Return on investment.................		(loss)	6.4 percent	13.5 percent

			1st Year Depreciation D.D.B.†	
Cost of:				
Buildings...................	360,000		28,800	(25 yrs.)
Furniture and fixtures........	40,000		10,000	(8 yrs.)
	400,000		38,800	

* Assuming 300,000 loan @ 8½ percent for seven years; equal monthly payments.
 † Double Declining Balance method, 25 years on buildings—8 years, furniture and fixtures. Note that the tax shield effect of this depreciation method is greatest during the initial years. Therefore, income taxes will require increasing amounts of cash toward the end of the useful lives of the assets.
 ‡ 28 percent for first $25,000; 48 percent over $25,000.

buys the land for $100,000, uses $100,000 of his cash, and borrows $300,000 to build, equip, and operate the motel at a total cost of $500,000 including the land. His investment would be $200,000. Analysis for occupancy levels of 50, 60 and 70 percent is shown in Table 13–4. During the first year the estimated return on investment will be a loss at 50 percent occupancy, 6.4 percent at 60 percent occupancy, and 13.5 percent at 70 percent occupancy. Since 60 percent was estimated to be the most likely level of patronage, the investor might expect something in excess of 6 percent return on invested capital. This would increase in later years due to proportionately lower depreciation changes. If the investor through effective management of the facility could achieve patronage patterns at the 70 percent occupancy level substantial improvement in ROI would be achieved. Using this estimate of the feasibility of the proposed venture the investor must decide if it is sufficiently attractive to warrant use of his capital. Moreover, the estimates of occupancy are not certain, thus some degree of risk is present in the proposed investment.

To illustrate how the investor could incorporate an assessment of the risk inherent in the venture, suppose that the motel consultant, based on his analysis of the proposed site, has estimated the probabilities of occurence of different levels of occupancy as follows: 50, 60, and 70 percent occupancy at 0.2, 0.5, and 0.3 respectively. This information can be incorporated into a payoff matrix using the return on investment contribution estimates from Table 13–4 as indicated below:

	Contribution to ROI (in $1000s) at Occupancy Level of		
Alternative	*50 percent (.2)**	*60 percent (.5)**	*70 percent (.3)**
60 Unit Motel............	(5.7)	12.8	27.0
Do not Build.............	0	0	0

* Estimated probability of occurrence.

Using expected value as a decision criterion the expected value of the 60 unit motel (based on the first year of operation) is .2(−5.7) + .5(12.6) + .3(27.0) = 13.3. Thus, the expected return (weighted average of the outcomes) is a contribution to ROI of $13,300. The alternative of not building the motel would yield an expected return of 0. Building the motel would offer an expected return on the investment of $13,300 ÷ $200,000 or 6.7 percent.

Allocation to Market Targets

In cases where a firm is serving two or more market targets, it is necessary to design a marketing program for each market. Since sales and corresponding profit opportunities are likely to vary from one target market to another the marketing manager must also determine the appropriate level of resources to be used for each target market.

To illustrate the nature of decision analysis involving different marketing programs for separate market targets consider the following situation. A manufacturer of small appliances is serving three market targets. The characteristics of each market and the type of marketing mix used are outlined below:

Market Target A. Medium-income consumers who purchase through department and jewelry stores, and other speciality outlets. Products are handled by distributors and local cooperative advertising support is provided in major metropolitan markets. Products fall into a medium price range compared to competition.

Market Target B. This is an upper income prestige market comprised of holders of credit cards for major oil companies and other charge services, airline travelers, and other consumers than can be reached through direct mail programs. This product line is of higher quality than marketed to target Market A, and it commands a higher price. Direct mail programs are conducted in cooperation with the above firms.

Market Target C. This market is made of businesses and institutional users of small appliances such as hotels, motels and government agencies. The marketing program is personal selling intensive where direct selling efforts are focused on a relatively small number of customers who purchase large quantities of appliances.

In seeking to develop a plan for the most effective use of resources the marketing manager has prepared the analysis of costs and profit contribution shown in Table 13–5. The present allocation of marketing

TABLE 13–5

Analysis of Marketing Costs and Profit Contribution in Three Target Markets (in $1,000s)

| Level of Marketing Effort | Total Marketing Costs | Profit Contribution* | | | Total |
| | | Market Target | | | |
		A	B	C	
100	300	−230	205†	−45	−70
200	600	−45	385	430†	770
300	900	215	370	725	1,310
400	1,200	525	215	810	1,550
500	1,500	885†	65	795	1,745
600	1,800	1,095	−185	605	1,515
700	2,100	935	−370	315	1,150

* Net of marketing costs.
† Present allocation of marketing effort.

effort consists of $500,000, $100,000, and $200,000 in Markets A, B, and C respectively for a total level of marketing expenditures of $800,000 and profit contribution of $1,520,000 (net of marketing costs). By examining these allocations is it possible to improve profit contribution with no increase in marketing expenditures? Based on the Table 13–5 data, expenditures in Market B could be eliminated entirely and the $100,000 used to increase marketing effort in Market C. This reallocation would result in a $90,000 improvement in total profit contribution.

This, of course, assumes that there would be no adverse affects in discontinuing marketing efforts in target Market B. The improvement is possible because the incremental profit contribution of shifting an additional $100,000 into Market C is greater than taking the same amount away from Market B, or adding to Market A.

Suppose that the marketing manager has been given the go ahead to increase marketing expenditures by 25 percent in the coming year. By examining the incremental profit changes within and between the three markets the most profitable allocation would be to spend $600,000, $100,000, and $300,000 in markets A, B, and C respectively. This would yield an estimated $2,025,000 profit contribution. If no limit is placed on marketing expenditures the $1-million budget could be increased by $200,000 through movement of the marketing effort expenditures in Market B up to $200,000 and $400,000 in market C. This would yield an estimated profit contribution of $2,290,000.

Additional Considerations in Decision Analysis

In our discussion of decision analysis thus far, a time frame of one year has been utilized. Frequently the planning horizon is much longer than this, particularly when assessing new product feasibility, new ventures, changes in distribution channel design, and other longer term decisions. In such situations, revenue and cost estimates used in decision analysis should be extended over the relevant time horizon. Marketing decisions of this type are similar to expenditures for plant, equipment, and other investments that influence business operations over several years. Capital budgeting techniques can be used to facilitate analysis of these types of decisions. For example, the motel feasibility illustration discussed earlier in this section could be analyzed by estimating revenue and cost flows over a relevant planning period such as seven years (a typical time period for replacement of furniture and fixtures and other major maintenance expenditures).

Various capital budgeting techniques are used in practice including the payback (time required to pay back investment) and discounted cash flow methods.[19] The discounted cash flow approach is based on the time value of money, thus recognizing that a sales dollar received now is worth more than one to be received one, two, or several years in the future. The difference in the time value of money is reflected by the interest that could be earned on the money if it were currently available. Since capital budgeting techniques are extensively covered

---

[19] These methods are discussed in detail in Charles T. Horngren, *Accounting For Management Control: An Introduction* (Englewood Cliffs, N.J.: Prentice-Hall, 1965), chapter 14.

in various finance and managerial accounting textbooks, it is sufficient for our purposes to emphasize that these methods should be used when analyzing marketing resource decisions which may span over a long time horizon.

Another aspect of decision analysis concerns the variations in available information for ongoing situations versus new ventures. Incremental analysis methods can be used with a reasonable degree of precision when assessing modest changes in marketing program composition. Uncertainties present in developing totally new programs do not enable the same degree of precision. Historical sales response patterns are not available and the effectiveness of a new marketing program for a new market target is typically difficult to predict. Yet, the same decision concepts regarding resource allocation are applicable, recognizing that differencies exist in the quality and quantity of available information, particularly concerning sales response.

Decision Models

Modeling the total marketing program decision is difficult due to the number of variables involved, interactions that occur between variables, and the uncertainties about cause and effect relationships. Analytical decision models suited for use in assessing particular marketing mix areas such as advertising and personal selling will be discussed in the chapters that follow. Two models, decision tree analysis and simulation, will be considered here because of their potential usefulness in aiding marketing mix decisions.

Decision Tree Analysis. As an illustration of how Bayesian statistical decision theory can be used in examining alternative marketing programs consider the case of a manufacturer of industrial equipment seeking to choose between two program alternatives. Program A involves the use of manufacturers representatives (independent sales people paid on a commission basis) to perform the selling function. Representatives will provide all sales contact work supported by a small staff of factory product specialists. This approach would involve limited marketing program expenditures until orders are actually received, shipped, and invoiced. Program B consists of a company sales force and use of a direct mail product information program (to inform prospects about the product and solicit inquiries) in combination with trade journal advertising.

Program B is expected to generate much higher levels of sales than Program A, although marketing costs will also be higher. Yet program B provides the manufacturer with greater control over the selling function. Management estimates the following profit contribution after deduction of marketing program costs for the two programs:

	Profit Contribution (in $1,000s) if Sales Response Is:		
	Low	*Medium*	*High*
Program A...............	100	300	600
Program B..............	200	700	1,000

While the profit contribution associated with B appears better than A at all levels of sales response, management is concerned about possible aggressive competitive reaction, particularly in regard to program B. In seeking to analyze the possible effects of these uncertainties the marketing manager has developed the decision tree shown in Figure 13–6.[20] Based on consultation with his staff and his own judgment and experience, he has estimated the probability of occurrence of three different levels of competitive reaction (limited, moderate, active) for each program alternative. For example, a 70 percent chance (0.7) of limited competitive reaction to Program A is estimated. Correspondingly, if limited competitive reaction occurs for program A, the estimated probabilities of occurrence of high, medium, and low sales response are respectively 0.6, 0.3, and 0.1. In a similar manner the marketing manager has attempted to estimate probabilities of occurrence of the various events (alternative competitive reactions and levels of sales response associated with each) shown by the decision tree in Figure 13–6.

Having described the decision situation, including the possible outcome paths for each marketing program alternative, the marketing manager is prepared to determine which mix alternative promises to yield the best profit contribution. This is accomplished by working backward through the decision tree. For example, beginning with the three outcomes (consequences) at the top right of the of the tree, the expected value (average) for low, medium, and high sales response would be: $.1(100) + .3(300) + .6(600) = 460$. Results of similar computations for the other corresponding nodes or intersections are shown in the circles on Figure 13–6. By working backward to the next intersection the expected value of each decision alternative can be calculated. For example, for marketing program A the computation is: $.7(460) + .2(350) + .1(210) = 413$. This enables a comparison of the expected returns from the two programs. Program A at $413,000 is somewhat less than B's expected profit contribution of $539,000.

The decision tree illustrates how the marketing manager can incorporate his judgment and experience with a systematic method for

---

[20] For an extended discussion of the concepts and procedures associated with constructing and analyzing decision trees see Robert D. Buzzell, Donald F. Cox, and Rex V. Brown, *Marketing Research and Information Systems* (New York: McGraw-Hill Book Company, 1969), chapters 9, 10, and 11.

FIGURE 13-6

Decision Tree Analysis of Alternative Marketing Programs

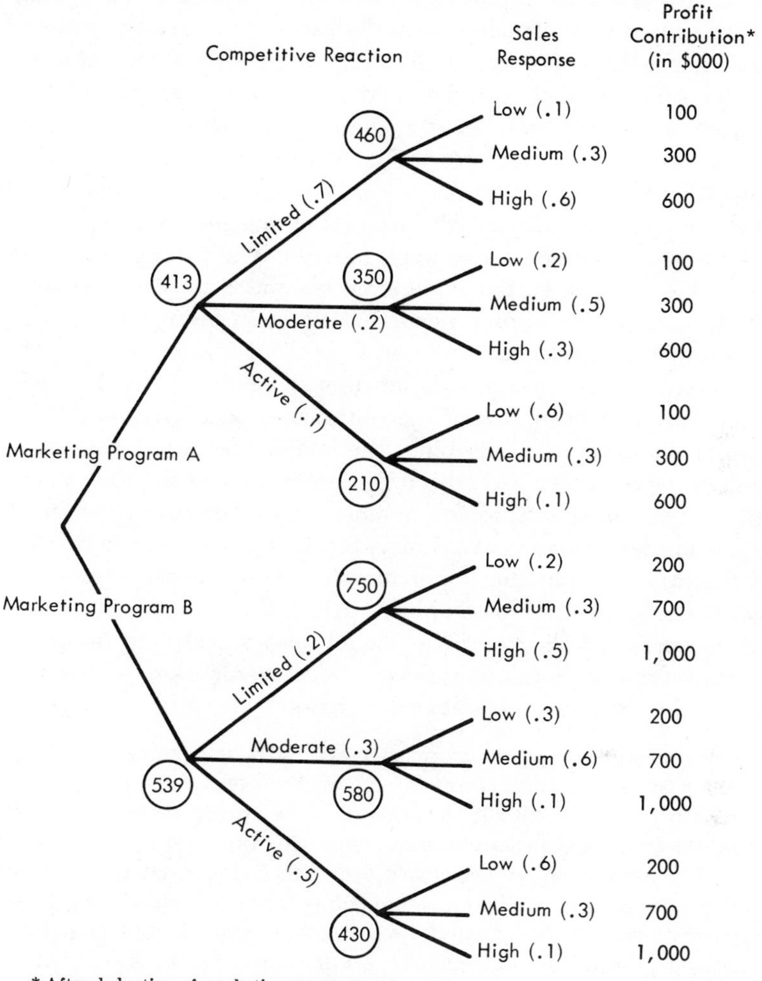

* After deduction of marketing program costs.

analyzing a decision situation. The analysis is, nevertheless, entirely dependent upon the information provided by the decision maker. As can be seen the relative magnitude of the different probabilities has a substantial impact upon the estimated profitability of the decision alternatives (program A vs. B). Yet, management in making decisions must at least implicitly assess these probabilities. The decision tree simply serves as a basis for making the estimates explicit and thus enabling the systematic examination of the possible consequences of decision alternatives.

Simulation. Use of simulation models incorporating several marketing variables has expanded substantially in the past decade due to the major advances speed, capabilities, and economics of electric computers and the rapidly increasing availability of marketing professionals trained in the concepts and skills of model development and application. Simulation models can be used in analyzing alternative decision strategies, or to help train existing and future managers in developing their decision making processes.[21] For example, Cerro de Pasco Corp. has designed a computer model for use in short-term planning using linear programming techniques which link marketing, production, and finance variables into an integrated strategy model.[22] The model, which contains 370 variables and over 150 equations, generates information on where products should be shipped, needed production adjustments, and other short-term planning decisions.

A promising computer simulation model has been developed for use in evaluating alternative retail merchandising decision rules.[23] Variables and interrelationships describing the major decision areas for retail managers were identified through interviews with the buyer and assistant buyer responsible for a merchandise classification in a large Midwestern department store. This information was used to develop flow diagrams repersenting the major merchandising decision routines. Historical data "were used to establish operating parameters for the model, to determine the validity of the model, and to provide initial starting conditions for the simulation runs."[24] A flow diagram of the model is shown in Figure 13–7 and is described below:

> The model is designed to operate within a time context of 13 months per year, each month consisting of two two-week review periods. The 13 months are divided into two seasons, the spring season comprising six months, and the autumn season comprising of seven months.
>
> The *season planning routine* establishes dollar sales, inventory, and markup plans as well as unit inventory assortment and depth plans for each season. It is executed three months prior to the beginning of a season. The *sales and reorder routine* determines the amount of inventory on hand, levels of demand, sales, and reorder quantities for each item in the classification. This routine is executed at the end of each re-

[21] Brief descriptions of over 50 simulation games are provided in Charles R. Goeldner and Laura M. Kirks, "The Games Marketing Students (& Trainees) Play," *Marketing News*, 8 (October 1, 1974), pp. 6–7.

[22] "A Computer Model to Upgrade Zinc Profits," *Business Week* (August 26, 1972), pp. 74–76.

[23] Daniel J. Sweeney, "The Application of Computer Simulation Techniques to Retail Merchandise Management: A Feasibility Study," in Fred C. Alvine (ed.) *Combined Proceedings 1971 Spring and Fall Conferences* (Chicago: American Marketing Association), pp. 498–503.

[24] Ibid., pp. 499–500.

FIGURE 13–7

Flow Diagram of Merchandising Model*

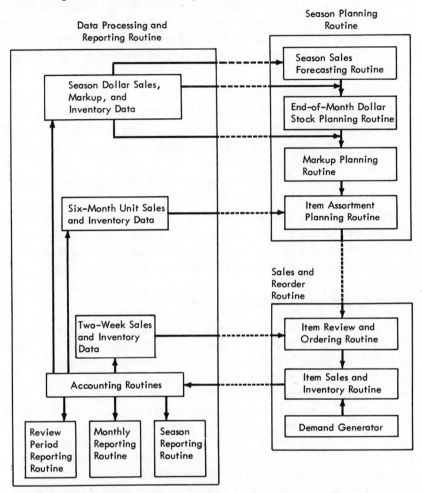

* Reproduced by permission of the American Marketing Association from Daniel J. Sweeney, "The Application of Computer Simulation Techniques to Retail Merchandise Management: A Feasibility Study," in Fred C. Alvine (ed.) *Combined Proceedings 1971 Spring and Fall Conferences* (Chicago: American Marketing Association), p. 500.

view period. The *data processing and reporting routine* provides the other operating routines with the historical information needed to operate in an adaptive manner. That is, decisions made in the model at one point in time are contingent upon data reflecting operating performance during preceding periods.[25]

---

[25] Ibid., p. 500.

Sweeney independently validated each of the major decision routines by comparing how well the model conformed to observed behavior of the real system under study. The results of the validation indicated a high degree of consistency between the model and the actual ordering behavior of the cooperating retail manager.[26] This type of simulation can be used in several ways to aid retail managers in the analysis of decision situations:

Alternative merchandising decisions can be analyzed and compared.

Various strategies can be pretested before actual implementation.

Alternative assumptions concerning customer behavior, supplier behavior, or internal operating conditions can be incorporated into the simulation and evaluated.

The interaction of various operating decisions and environmental assumptions can be analyzed.[27]

The Sweeney model illustrates the potential of simulation models in the analysis of marketing strategies for use in planning the marketing program.[28] Application of high-speed computers in combination with model building skills can yield useful tools for decision analysis.

DEVELOPING THE MARKETING PLAN

The various decisions involved in planning the marketing program should be incorporated into a marketing plan for use in implementing and controlling marketing activities. The marketing plan provides a basis for assembling and integrating the various components of the marketing strategy process over the relevant planning horizon. Usually in firms where formal planning is accomplished, detailed plans are developed on an annual basis within longer range planning guidelines. For example, a company with a five-year target of increasing its market share in a particular target market by 50 percent would develop its annual marketing plans to move toward this objective in stages.

The concept of planning is central to the effective use of marketing resources:

> Formal marketing planning is an integrative process which blends corporate goals and resources with information on opportunities external to the firm. The object of planning is to develop creative and innovative policies to guide corporate efforts in the market place.[29]

---

[26] Ibid., p. 500–501.

[27] Ibid., p. 502.

[28] Use of the model to analyze return on investment in individual retail departments and merchandise classifications is described in Daniel J. Sweeney, "Improving the Profitability of Retail Merchandising Decisions," *Journal of Marketing*, 37 (January 1973), pp. 60–68.

[29] Eugene J. Kelley, *Marketing Planning and Competitive Strategy* (Englewood Cliffs, New Jersey: Prentice-Hall, 1972), p. 52.

Planning Framework

The concepts and approaches discussed throughout this book provide an overall framework for developing the marketing plan. Planning must be accomplished in the three major marketing decision making areas: *environmental analysis; market target selection,* and *marketing strategy design.* Planning is an integrated process of decision making over a specified time horizon.[30] The marketing plan provides a mechanism for describing the various marketing decisions that have been made and how they are linked together into an overall strategy design. While formal planning procedures are not used by all firms, there is research evidence that those who utilize formal long-range planning have historically out-performed comparable firms that do not.[31] In some organizations, formal planning consists primarily of sales and cost projections for use in financial budgeting. While this information is part of the planning process, it falls far short of a complete planning effort.

There are several benefits to be gained from effective planning. The process of developing the plan is quite useful in focusing the chief marketing executive's attention on all relevant decision making areas. Coordination and communication within the marketing area, and among other functional areas of the enterprise, are facilitated. A sound marketing plan provides a basis for monitoring marketing program effectiveness and guiding needed changes in the use of marketing resources.

The need for a formal plan is probably more critical in the case of a new venture than for an established marketing effort since a variety of new activities must be implemented and coordinated in the new venture marketing program. Yet, the benefits of formally developing plans can be substantial regardless of the stage of maturity of the business venture. Of course, to be effective, the plan must be used as an operational guide to management action and control. If superficially prepared to satisfy a corporate staff planning group and subsequently forgotten, the plan is of little value to the marketing manager.

While the specific content of the marketing plans will vary among firms, there are certain basic components that should be included in all plans.[32] A complete plan of action should include an assessment of the corporate and external situation (including history and future trends); description of market targets; marketing objectives; marketing strategy

---

[30] The use of an integrated systematic approach for marketing planning developed from a study of marketing planning practices recognized as leaders in the area is described in Leon Winer, "Are You Really Planning Your Marketing?" *Journal of Marketing,* 29 (January 1965), pp. 1–8.

[31] Stanley S. Thune and Robert J. House, "Where Long-Range Planning Pays Off," *Business Horizons,* 13 (August 1970), pp. 81–87.

[32] The marketing planning approach used by the Hooker Chemical Corporation is discussed in William F. Christopher, "Marketing Planning That Gets Things Done," *Harvard Business Review,* 34 (September–October 1970), pp. 56–64.

FIGURE 13–8

Components of the Marketing Plan

Situation Assessment
    General assessment of past history and future trends regarding the business unit for which the marketing plan is being developed. This would include identification and evaluation of relevant environmental opportunities and constraints. Relationship of marketing to corporate mission and strategy. Appraisal of marketing strengths and weaknesses. Premises upon which marketing plan is based.

Market Targets
    Description of market targets including customer characteristics, priorities, future trends, and competitive situation.

Marketing Objectives
    Statement of specifically what (and why) the firm intends to accomplish for each market target including how results will be measured for use in monitoring performance. Objectives should be stated in quantitative terms (e.g., sales, market share, etc.) whenever possible.

Marketing Strategy
    Identification of how objectives will be achieved, when (time scheduling), and by whom. Description of the overall marketing program and specific actions regarding each element of the marketing mix.

Organizational Design
    Description of the organizational design to be used for implementing and managing the marketing program.

Revenue-Cost Projections
    Financial estimates for budgeting. Estimates of sales and costs by target market, geographical area, product, and other relevant revenue-cost groupings.

Corporate Interrelationships
    Identification of other decision making areas in the firm that will influence (and constrain) marketing program accomplishment. Assumptions made concerning projected accomplishments in these areas and planned coordination.

---

for achieving objectives; organizational design, revenue-cost projections, and relevant corporate interrelationships. These components are shown in Figure 13–8, along with a description of the general content of each area.

Planning Levels

Marketing planning occurs at three levels: *corporate, marketing program,* individual *program areas.* Various elements of the plan for corporate strategy are related to the marketing program. Recall the discussion of corporate-marketing strategy interrelationships in Chapter 10. Planning for the marketing program consolidates the various decisions associated with overall marketing operations as shown in Figure 13–8. Additionally, plans may be developed for specific marketing decision areas such as advertising and personal selling. Planning at the various levels is interrelated as indicated in Figure 13–9. The marketing program plan builds upon the specific plans in each of the marketing mix areas. Thus, its development represents a major integrating task for the marketing manager.

FIGURE 13–9

Marketing Planning Levels and Interrelationships

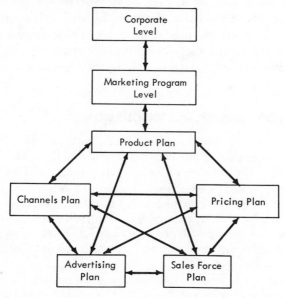

A key question is whether planning should flow upward or downward in the marketing organization. Actually information flows in both directions should occur since various interactions between levels are needed. General planning guidelines should be communicated to lower planning levels to serve as a basis for specific planning activities. These include objectives, resource constraints, and other relevant priorities and constraints. Based upon this information specific plans at each level can be formulated and transmitted upward for analysis, consolidation, and possible revision after discussion between management levels.

SUMMARY AND CONCLUSIONS

Building on the examination of corporate and marketing strategy in Chapter 10, in this chapter guidelines for planning the marketing program were developed. The major stages of strategy development were described and the nature and characteristics of marketing mix decisions were considered Principles useful in guiding marketing resource allocation decisions were identified and their use in decision analysis illustrated. The key role of market response estimates in resource allocation decisions was discussed. Marketing programming decision analysis was examined with respect to single and multiple factor analysis, allocation of resources to market targets, and the use of decision models. Finally, guidelines for developing the marketing plan were outlined.

The four chapters in this part of the book provide a framework and decision guidelines for developing an integrated marketing program as well as for decision making in each of the marketing mix areas. In the remaining chapters of the book, decisions for the various components of the marketing mix are examined with particular emphasis upon the concepts that are useful in guiding decision making and the task of designing, implementing, and controlling strategy in each area.

EXERCISES FOR REVIEW AND DISCUSSION

1. Why do marketing managers concentrate their efforts on those factors known as the marketing mix rather than other factors which may substantially influence the outcome of the marketing program? Discuss.

2. With respect to sales response relationships, how might management's assessment of the probable existence of a threshold level of marketing effort influence the decision by management to introduce a new product nationwide. Discuss not only in terms of its impact on the advertising budget, but other marketing factors as well (channels of distribution, price, test marketing, sales force, etc.)

3. Use an example to demonstrate why marginal returns for the last dollar spent on one marketing variable should be equal to the marginal returns from allocations to all other marketing variables. Develop your own figures or diagrams.

4. Assembling marketing resources into an integrated marketing program is clearly a major responsibility of the chief marketing executive in a firm. What are the essential aspects involved in this task? Develop a frame of reference for guiding decision making in this area and indicate what you consider to be the major problems confronting the decision maker in working toward more effective use of marketing resources.

5. It is budgeting time at the XYZ Corporation. $1.2 million has been scheduled to be spent in the current year on the marketing budget. This was allocated to the various marketing mix elements as indicated below:

```
Product ................. $300,000
Promotion ................ 700,000
Channels ................. 200,000
```

The executive vice-president has suggested to the marketing v.p. that since sales are projected at roughly 10 per cent higher next year, he probably should plan to increase product, promotion and channels expenditures also about 10 percent (thus, next year's budget would, on this basis, be $1.32 million). If you were called in as a consultant and were asked to assess the above action, to what questions would you want answers in seeking to develop a recommendation? Discuss.

6. The marketing vice president of a food products manufacturer has been asked by the president of the firm to prepare a feasibility study regarding the introduction of a freeze-dried soluble coffee into the market. Assume that this will be the first firm to introduce the new product. Prepare a detailed outline of the areas that should be assessed in the feasibility study.

part five

Marketing Decision Areas

Building on our examination of overall marketing strategy and decision making in Part IV, each marketing mix component is individually considered in Part V. Beginning with new product decisions, chapters are sequenced in order of decreasing decision dependence upon other corporate functional areas. Decisions concerning products and services involve, in addition to a key role played by marketing, a number of other members of the corporate management team such as top management, finance, production, personnel, and engineering executives. Product decisions are typically top management decisions with the marketing manager functioning as a member of the product decision making group. In contrast, sales force decisions fall largely within the scope of the marketing manager's responsibilities. In each chapter a decision process framework is developed to guide understanding of the marketing mix component, and to facilitate decision analysis and determination of the specific information needed by the marketing manager and staff. Key variables and interrelationships affecting each mix variable are identified.

The central role of new products in the marketing mix is examined in Chapter 14, "Managing New Products." The influence of new products upon corporate performance is illustrated and alternative organizational approaches to product management are indicated. In Chapter 15, "Evaluating New Product Opportunities," the evaluation of new product ideas are considered.

Chapters 16 and 17 are concerned with the design and management of the firm's channels of distribution. Similar to product decisions, the channel used by a firm serves as both a guide and constraint to marketing program decisions. Since the channel decision is typically long-term in nature and provides the means for a firm to reach selected market targets, it tends to focus and constrain decisions on price, advertising, and sales force. In Chapter 18 relevant concepts and factors for developing price policy guidelines are considered, a decision-making framework

451

is presented, and operational approaches to the price decision are outlined and discussed.

Communication of the marketing offer by an organization to its customers is accomplished through promotional activities. The management of promotional components is considered in Chapters 19 through 22. Advertising and personal selling together comprise a major portion of marketing management's annual operating budget. Annual expenditures in total are in excess of $50 billion in the United States. In Chapter 19 the major advertising management decisions are examined, followed in Chapter 20 with a comprehensive discussion of the elusive yet critical task of evaluation of advertising effectiveness. Chapter 21, "Sales Force Decisions" considers the various decision areas confronting the sales manager, and examines in depth sales force size and allocation decisions. Chapter 22 "Managing the Sales Force," presents the various activities that comprise the ongoing sales management activity of sales force staffing, personnel development, supervision, and evaluation and control of sales operations.

Finally, in Chapter 23, "Controlling the Marketing Program," the essential activity of management control is examined from the point of view of three levels of evaluation: strategy positioning analysis, marketing program effectiveness, and marketing mix component effectiveness. The product elimination or drop decision is presented as an illustration of marketing management control.

14

Managing New Products

This chapter begins a two-chapter discussion of new product decisions. The initial section defines a new product and examines the importance of new product decisions to corporate growth and viability. To put these decisions in proper perspective, reasons for the substantial risk inherent in new product introductions are offered. Then, two management decision tools for coping with this risk are discussed. One tool is the development of an organizational structure to facilitate new product decisions. The other is an analytical decision process designed to reduce new product risks. The chapter ends with a discussion of techniques for determining candidate new product ideas. Chapter 15 concentrates on the processes and techniques for evaluating these new product ideas in preparation for new product introduction decisions.

THE IMPORTANCE OF NEW PRODUCT DECISIONS

Definition of New Products

When is a proposed innovation considered to be a new product as opposed to a minor improvement in an existing product? This distinction is important because of the managerial assignment of responsibility. For a minor improvement, responsibility will very likely be given to managers of the existing product. For innovations classified as new products, managers specializing in new product decisions may be needed. Moreover, the amount of resources and special activities required to determine the desirability of introducing an innovation is typically greater for a new product than for a minor product improvement. Classifying a product proposal as a new product is obvious for innovations that are radically different from any existing product such as the Polaroid camera, Mustang, the process for removing salt from sea water, and MOS circuitry. Yet, the radically new product is not very common. Most innovations represent a change or variation in some existing product as illustrated by adding fluoride to toothpaste, changing automobile styling, adding ring pull tabs to cans, and development of improved aerosol valves. Here, management must decide whether a change to an existing product is sufficiently great to justify treatment as a new product decision.

A new product should be defined from the organization's point of view rather than that of an industry. An innovation that is new to a firm can be classified as a new product even though similar products are already being offered for sale by other firms. For example, General Motors considered Camaro to be a new product decision even though Ford already had the very similar Mustang in the marketplace at that time. Moreover, to qualify as a new product, an innovation ought to have a significant impact upon demand and consequently on the market target decision. If an innovation will cause redefinition of market targets, will attract new customers with which the firm does not have considerable experience, or will materially alter the purchase behavior of current customers (e.g., increase brand loyalty), then it should be considered a new product. Finally, if the introduction of an innovation significantly affects the functions of the firm such as requiring new sources of supply, separate managerial departments or divisions, and/or a considerable number of new personnel, there is justification for classifying it as a new product. Using these guidelines, a new product may be defined as *an innovation that is new to the firm and that is judged by management to require a redefinition of market targets and/or a significant change in managerial functions in order to introduce it into selected markets.*

The history of business in the United States provides overwhelming evidence that the life of existing products is limited. So, replacing existing products with new products is essential to the growth and viability of corporations. There are a number of reasons for this including (1) inevitable market changes; (2) periodic changes in competitors' strategies and/or tactics; and (3) the attractiveness of new product introductions as a growth strategy.

Market Changes and New Product Decisions

Markets will inevitably change in important ways. For example, major population structural changes (e.g., age, education, income, etc.) are occurring which will lead to changes in product demand through their impact on consumer life styles. An increase in the proportion of the population having a college education and higher paying jobs will open the door to life styles previously unattainable. New life styles, in turn lead to changes in wants and needs which are reflected in product and brand preferences as well as buying decision processes. Similarly, industrial buyers' needs and wants will undergo significant changes, since buying organizations also have "life styles" based on managerial hierarchies, goals and objectives, policies, product mix, and personnel. When market change occurs, organizations serving those markets must adapt by changing all or a part of their marketing mixes. New product offerings provide a primary vehicle for firms to use in adjusting and adapting to market change.

Competitors' Actions and New Product Decisions

Competitors' actions within the same industry as well as those of firms outside an industry create pressure for innovation. Consider the shifting in market shares between American and Japanese calculator manufacturers caused by innovation. In the 1960s the Japanese had expanded market share of calculator sales in the United States by competing on price which was made possible by much lower labor costs. The introduction of MOS circuitry by Texas Instruments allowed American firms to gain back market share and open new markets (consumers) for the calculator by drastically lowering costs and prices.[1]

This competitive threat is not confined only to a firm's industry. In fact, "it is almost automatic that major new technologies come from *outside* the industry they affect."[2] Once an industry becomes established, much of the R&D effort of firms is devoted to improving products and processes since the payoff from this kind of research is more certain and immediately profitable.[3] This means that established firms are also vulnerable to the radically new product developed and introduced by firms in other industries.

The impact of competition on corporate goal achievement throughout product life cycles emphasizes the essential part that new products must play. As one analysis of the life cycles of a large number of products in a cross section of firms indicates, ". . . sooner or later every product is preempted by another or else degenerates into profitless price competition."[4] Recognition of this fact should lead to pressure to innovate as protection against trying to compete with a superior new product.

New Products for Growth

The strategic alternatives available to firms seeking profitability and growth are more numerous with new products than with existing products. Consider the matrix of marketing strategy alternatives discussed in Chapter 10 and shown again in Figure 14–1. Six of the nine

---

[1] "Calculators Slim Down in Size and Price," *Business Week* (October 9, 1971), p. 50.

[2] Lawrence Lessing, "Why the U.S. Lags in Technology," *Fortune* (April 1972), p. 71.

[3] Ibid., p. 72.

[4] *Management of New Products* (New York: Booz-Allen and Hamilton, Management Consultants, 1968), p. 5.

FIGURE 14–1

Marketing Strategy Alternatives

Markets	Products		
	New	Modification	Existing
New	X	X	
Expansion	X	X	
Existing	X	X	

cells in this matrix involve the introduction of new products into selected market targets including both radically new products and significant existing-product modifications. Firms might use two quite different approaches to implement these strategies. New products can be developed internally which requires a firm's management to go through all decision process stages and activities necessary for introduction. Or, a firm can merge with an existing firm in order to add new products to its product mix. This latter approach is characteristic of the conglomerate strategies so prevalent in the 1960s.

Currently, there is strong indication that firms will lean more heavily on internal development than mergers to implement new product strategies. The experience of conglomerates indicates that performance achievement from this approach is difficult.[5] While there are undoubtedly numerous reasons for their relatively poor performance, one in particular may be the difficulty of managing products in markets unrelated to the buying firm's markets and technical capabilities. One of the significant advantages of internal development is that managerial expertise is developed throughout the new product decision process. By the time an introduction decision is made, management has gained considerable familiarity with the product and with market targets. In addition, there are increasing legal sanctions against mergers of all kinds. Federal government agencies are increasing their scrutiny of proposed mergers involving firms in the same and in different industries for possible violations of antitrust laws. This should cause firms to place more emphasis on internal development as the primary source of new products.

New Products and Shortages

The early 1970s began a period of materials and energy shortages that is likely to continue for a long time. Supply shortages will have a con-

---

[5] "Emergency Landing For a High-Flier," *Business Week* (April 13, 1974), p. 28.

siderable effect upon the new product decisions of corporations. For example, Glamorene Products Corporation was forced to delay for several months the introduction of a new product, *Drain Power,* due to shortages of chlorinated fluorocarbon used in the aerosol package.[6]

The impact of actual or possible material shortages on corporate new product decisions will be multifaceted. Anticipated shortages of key materials will cause firms to screen out new product ideas even though there is a high probability of substantial market acceptance. This will add considerable importance to the purchasing function's inputs into new product decisions. In addition, materials shortages may lead to fewer new product introductions due to the unwillingness of management to venture into areas where they are not as familiar or as experienced as with the company's existing products. Finally, the difficulty of forecasting supply of materials for totally new products, particularly when the materials differ from those used in existing products, may also lead to proportionally more emphasis on modifications of existing products.

While material shortages will alter new product decisions in corporations, new products will not necessarily become a less important part of long run strategy. Market change and the threat of competitor innovation will keep the pressure on firms to innovate. There will still be the lure of substantial rewards for those firms able to introduce successful product innovations. Moreover, materials shortages will affect supplies for existing products and so, new product decisions may be mandatory for survival when shortages impede the production and sale of products currently in a firm's mix. Finally, material shortages will increase the importance of each new product decision since new product failures will become even more costly in terms of wasted resources.

THE RISKS OF NEW PRODUCT DECISIONS

Sources of New Product Risks

Management decisions on new product introductions involve substantial risks. To understand these risks better, consider the factors that are characteristic of new product decisions including (1) decision process lead times, (2) length of forecasting time periods, (3) payback lead time, and (4) high cost of failure.[7]

Decision Process Lead Time. A rather long length of time can pass between the generation of a new product idea and introduction of the product into the marketplace. One study of new products introduced

---

[6] "The Two-Way Squeeze on New Products," *Business Week* (August 10, 1974), p. 130.

[7] For an excellent discussion of management risks in product decisions, see Thomas A. Staudt, "Higher Management Risks in Product Strategy," *Journal of Marketing,* vol. 37 (January 1973), pp. 4–9.

by a variety of firms found that the decision process lead time ranged from six months to fifty-five years with five to ten years being quite common.[8] Such long lead times influence the timing of a new product introduction which is an important determinant of success or failure.[9] Major changes in markets, competitive strategies, supply conditions, and/or economic conditions occurring during this time may adversely affect new product success.

Forecast Time Periods. New product success is based on the length of time that a market opportunity will last.[10] Consequently, long run forecasts of technology, sales, market share, costs, supply, and other factors affecting product performance are required by management. Yet, as the length of time over which forecasts must be made increases, the accuracy of forecasts generally declines.

Payback Lead Time. High initial costs are characteristic of new product activities. Beyond the costs of development and testing, introducing a new product requires setting up production processes, hiring and/or training salesmen, developing a promotional campaign, and so forth. These costs can easily run into millions of dollars for regional or national scale introductions. High costs coupled with the typically low sales returns in the initial life cycle stage almost guarantee that losses, or at best low profits, will result for some period of time varying from months (e.g., the hula hoop) to many years (e.g., microwave ovens). The longer this payback period, the greater risk management must be willing to take due to possibility of adverse, unpredicted events occurring.

Historical Failure Rates. The magnitude of new product decision risks are most apparent when historical failure rates are examined. Studies of new product failures vary significantly in the products covered and definitions of failure. Yet, estimates appear to show consistently that 50 percent or more of all products developed by American corporations fail.[11] Thus, the odds of achieving a successful new product introduction are not very great. Moreover, the waste of resources is often staggering. Table 14–1 shows several selected products that failed and estimates of resulting losses. Beyond dollar losses, new product failures can have more intangible, but still detrimental impact upon a company's image and reputation as well as upon employee morale.

---

[8] Lee Adler, "Time Lag in New Product Development," *Journal of Marketing,* vol. 30 (January 1966), p. 18.

[9] William J. Constandse, "How to Launch New Products," *Michigan State University Business Topics,* vol. 19 (Winter 1971), p. 33.

[10] Staudt, "Higher Management Risks in Product Strategy," p. 5.

[11] Failure rate estimates are included in Theodore L. Angelus, "Why Most New Products Fail," *Marketing Insights* (May 12, 1969), p. 14 (over 80 percent); and *Management of New Products,* p. 2 (over 60 percent).

TABLE 14–1

Selected Product Failures and Estimated Losses

New Product Failure	Estimated Dollar Loss
Ford's Edsel	$350,000,000*
DuPont's Corfam (synthetic leather)	100,000,000†
Scott Paper Company's Baby Scott (disposable diapers)	12,800,000‡
General Food's Freeze-Dried Fruit Cereals	5,000,000§
Hunt's Pizza and Hickory Flavored Ketchups	1,200,000§
American Home's Easy-Off Household Cleaner	850,000§

Sources: * Thomas L. Berg, *Mismarketing: Case Histories of Marketing Misfires*, Garden City, New York: Doubleday and Company, Inc., 1970, p. 2.
  † "Leather's shoes prove tough to fill," *Business Week*, Oct. 30, 1967, p. 28.
  ‡ "Scott shifts marketing execs to stave off P & G incursions, *Advertising Age*, July 6, 1971, p. 1.
  § Theodore L. Angelus, "Why most new products fail," *Marketing Insights*, May 12, 1969, p. 14, 16.

Why New Products Fail

Examining why new products fail illustrates many of the complexities faced by managers that account for high risks. In part, causes relate to management inefficiencies during the decision process. Other reasons can be traced to lack of market acceptance of the innovation.

Management Inefficiencies. A firm may have difficulty achieving new product successes due to inappropriate organizational structure. The bureaucratic hierarchy characteristic of large companies is highly efficient in controlling existing products. This often means that too little attention is devoted to the new product decision process.[12] A management structure focusing on today's business may even resist the disruption and change inherent in new product introductions:

> When dramatic new business possibilities do emerge internally, though, their most frequent immediate effect is to impinge on the status quo. Since the fundamental corporate thesis of most companies is squarely based on continuity, change appears as its antithesis. The more truly innovative a change seems to be, the greater the resistance to it that can be expected. . . As a result, the history of innovation is a history of overlooked potential and demeaned ideas.
>
> Xerox saw the novel promise of Chester Carlson's copying machine; IBM and Eastman Kodak did not see it at all. RCA was able to envision the innovative opportunity of radio; the Victor Talking Machine Company could not. . . Marshall Field understood the unique market development possibilities of installment buying; Endicot Johnson did not, call-

---

[12] Russell W. Peterson, "New Venture Management in a Large Company," *Harvard Business Review*, vol. 45 (May–June 1967), p. 68.

ing it "the vilest system yet devised to create trouble." And so it has gone.[13]

Beyond organizational weaknesses, managerial inefficiencies may surface in a broad range of activities affecting new product performance. For example, managements may underestimate the budget required to produce a successful new product.[14] There may be poor market support planning (e.g., inadequate training of salesmen, lack of salesman incentive to push new products, wrong pricing or distribution channels, insufficient promotion),[15] development of new products that do not capitalize on corporate purpose or strengths,[16] or lack of a new product performance monitoring system.[17]

Finally, a strong argument can be made that a firm without any failures is either not innovating or not accepting sufficient risk in seeking successful replacements for today's products. When failures occur, management should use this unfavorable experience to best advantage by conducting "post-mortems" to learn what went wrong. Such studies should provide information to management that will allow refinement of their approach to new product decisions so that the same mistakes are not repeated. Yet, the practice of post-mortem analysis of failures does not appear to be as widespread an activity as might be expected.[18]

Technical Flaws in the New Product. New product failures may occur in spite of the best efforts of a management team. For instance, a technical flaw in the product may go undetected until customers use it over a period of time. One of the reasons for the failure of DuPont's Corfam was a technical flaw that, ironically, was initially felt by management to be a product strength. Corfam was primarily used as a leather substitute in the manufacture of shoes. DuPont's management believed that Corfam's ability to return to its original shape would keep shoes looking like new. Yet, consumers complained that Corfam shoes could not be broken in like leather shoes which meant that if a perfect fit was not obtained, the shoes would always be uncomfortable.[19] It appeared that comfort was more important to customers than appearance in shoes, since demand for Corfam did not meet DuPont's performance expectations.

---

[13] Mack Hanan, "Corporate Growth Through Venture Management," *Harvard Business Review*, vol. 47 (January–February 1969), p. 44.

[14] Constandse, "How to Launch New Products," p. 32.

[15] Ibid., p. 33.

[16] Fred L. Lemont, "New Products: How They Differ; Why They Fail; How to Help Them Do Better," *Advertising Age* (April 5, 1971), p. 44.

[17] Constandse, "How to Launch New Products," pp. 33–34.

[18] Lemont, "New Products: How They Differ; Why They Fail; How to Help Them Do Better," p. 44.

[19] "Leather's Shoes Prove Tough to Fill," p. 28.

Lack of a Competitive Point of Difference.[20]   A new product is undertaking considerable risk of market failure when there are no important differences from competitors' products to encourage customers to switch brands. Of course, in the early stages of a product life cycle there is likely to be room for a "me too" product when a market has not been fully developed. In other life cycle stages, however, competing with established brands can be extremely difficult unless the new product has something unique and important to offer customers. For example, Kaiser Aluminum Company had to withdraw its aluminum sheet foil because of lack of competitive advantage over Alcoa or Reynolds Wrap in a market that was not big enough to support all three brands.[21] The established brand has already developed an image among customers. A new product lacks this image and performance reputation. So, a new product strategy must be built around important differential advantages over competitive offerings to attract customers.

It is essential that a new product's point of difference be important to the customer rather than just to management. New product managers may believe there is a point of difference, yet the real test occurs when customers compare the new product with existing brands. For example, Easy-Off household cleaner's point of difference was an aerosol foam application introduced into a market dominated by such liquid cleaners as Formula 409 and Fantastic. Yet, consumers did not see any advantage to Easy-Off and so, the product failed.[22] Contrast this failure with the success of Procter & Gambles' Head & Shoulders shampoo. Head & Shoulders has an important point of difference as a medicated shampoo designed to alleviate dandruff.

Inadequate Communication of a Point of Difference.   Even when a point of difference does exist, customers must understand the product's advantages. The old adage, "if you build a better mousetrap people will beat a path to your door," will not hold unless customers are aware of the "better mousetrap" and understand why it is better for their needs. Thus, a new product's supporting strategy is a key to market success or failure. For example, Head & Shoulders successfully communicated its point of difference as an effective "dandruff fighter." Other products have not done as well in explaining product uniqueness. Brown and Foremans' supporting strategy for its new light whiskey did not help consumers identify how best to use the product. Consumers were confused

---

[20] The discussion of market reasons for new product failures in this and the following subsections is based on a study of consumer product failures reported in Angelus, "Why Most New Products Fail," pp. 14–16. No doubt the same reasons account for industrial product failures, too.

[21] Ibid., p. 15.

[22] Ibid., p. 14. Other reasons given for failure were inadequate marketing support and proliferation of brands.

as to whether it competed with whiskey or should be used in place of gin or vodka, and consequently, did not buy enough to make the product a success.[23]

Mismatch between Point of Difference and Market Targets. A new product should have one or more features or dimensions that can be used as primary appeals to reach potential customers. In fact, different features may appeal to different market segments. Thus, a new product may not perform well if the most effective combination of appeals and market targets have not been found. For example, Right Guard was introduced as a man's deodorant, emphasizing its neutral scent as a primary selling feature. However, when a change was made in marketing strategy to a "family deodorant" by emphasizing both scent and the spray application, sales increased by $20 million a year.[24]

The New Product Decision Dilemma

The need for new products when contrasted with the high risks of failure present management with a serious dilemma. This is clearly illustrated by the market situation facing Gerber Products Co. Gerber's primary product line has been baby foods with which it has dominated the market. Currently, there is a major change going on in the baby food market due largely to the declining U.S. birthrate and greater price competition. These changes have caused Gerber's management to recognize that baby products can no longer be the source of all future sales growth. This is reflected by the fact that their advertising slogan, "Babies are our business . . . our *only* business," was changed to "Babies are our business," and then was completely dropped from advertising.[25] To adapt to these market changes, Gerber is relying heavily on product development. However, recent new products have not been completely successful, particularly the children's day care centers and life insurance division. Several other products intended to appeal to adults face stiff competition from long established brands. With its new peanut spread, Gerber faces Best Foods' Skippy, Swift's Peter Pan, and P&G's Jif peanut butter; and competing with its new catsup are Heinz, Hunt-Wesson, and Del Monte.[26] None of these products have been declared failures, but they all face considerable risk in gaining market acceptance.

Complete elimination of new product failures is an unrealistic, unattainable goal. There are too many factors that affect new product

---

[23] "How A New Product Was Brought to Market Only to Flop Miserably," *The Wall Street Journal*, January 5, 1973, p. 10.

[24] Theodore L. Angelus, "Why Most New Products Fail," p. 15.

[25] "The Lower Birthrate Crimps the Baby Food Market," *Business Week* (July 13, 1974), pp. 44–50.

[26] Ibid.

performance over which management has little or no control including market behavior, competition, technological advances, government regulations, supply availability, and the state of the economy. For example, due to the threat of competitive retaliation management can seldom take all the time necessary to collect sufficient information to be sure of market acceptance of each new product candidate. Consequently, management must determine an acceptable level of risk of new product failure in reaching decisions concerning introductions. This means that some failures will occur over the long run.

Management can and should strive to improve their new product "batting average," which is the percent of new product successes out of all new product decisions made. There are at least two areas upon which management can concentrate to achieve needed improvement. First, more effective use of organization structure can be made to facilitate new product decision making. In addition, management can ensure that a formal, analytical decision process is understood and utilized by those involved in new product decisions. Each of these areas are discussed in the next sections of the chapter.

ORGANIZING FOR NEW PRODUCT DECISIONS

Nowhere is the need for coordination and cooperation among managers more pressing than in the new product decision process. To determine the opportunity represented by a new product idea usually requires a variety of expertises. For example, estimating the level of resource commitment will most likely depend upon the judgment and analyses of personnel in production, purchasing, finance, and marketing. In fact, the introduction of a new product can be compared to the establishment of a new enterprise, since all the functions of a business are required to implement strategy and tactics.

A number of organizational structure alternatives have been used by firms to facilitate new product decisions. These include (1) product or brand managers, (2) new product managers, (3) new product committees, (4) new product departments, and (5) venture teams. Each of these alternatives has certain advantages and drawbacks which suggest that none are clearly superior to all others for every firm.

Product Managers

Product managers are typically part of a company's middle management who are assigned performance responsibility for a single product or a group of related products. These managers coordinate the design and implementation of strategies and tactics for their products by working with specialists in a wide range of functional areas including sales, advertising, production, and finance. Moreover, a considerable amount of time is spent analyzing market performance to identify problems that must be corrected.

In some companies, product managers are also given responsibility for product innovations. While the final authority for the new product introduction decision is most likely placed at top management levels, product managers may be expected to take an active part in determining potential market opportunity. This ensures that the experience developed with similar existing products is utilized during the new product decision process. Moreover, the product manager has already developed a working relationship with other functional specialists who will be needed during the analysis of new product feasibility.

Offsetting these advantages are several serious drawbacks. First, product managers must divide time between the management of existing products and developing new products. Managing existing products is the product manager's primary responsibility. So, day-to-day control activities and pressures may mean that new product decisions will not be given the time or attention needed to ensure a flow of new products over the long run. In addition, a product manager is not necessarily a highly competent new product decision maker. Again, their training and experience is primarily concerned with existing products rather than in coping with new products. Development and analysis of new products require quite different skills from the managing of existing products.

Finally, a product manager's new product responsibility typically extends only to innovations that are related to current products. This is quite likely to lead to emphasis on product modifications rather than on totally new product opportunities. Moreover, the product manager is seldom given authority over the various functional areas that are required to design, test, and implement a new product strategy. Thus, persuasion and bargaining must be used to achieve needed cooperation, increasing the difficulty of coordinating all activities.

New Product Managers

Some of the disadvantages inherent in using product managers to develop new products can be overcome by using new product managers. Still a part of the product manager organization, these managers are assigned the responsibility for developing new products. Yet, because new product managers are attached to product groups, there is still the potential for using experience developed with similar products. Moreover, new product managers should bring the necessary expertise to the new product decision task since their primary responsibility is new products rather than managing existing products.

Other disadvantages are not overcome. The new product manager is still tied to a particular corporate product group, and so, the emphasis may be placed too heavily on product modifications and on products for existing markets, rather than discovery and development of totally new products. Also, new product managers typically have the same authority limitations as product managers. So, new product managers must also rely on persuasion to coordinate necessary activities.

New Product Committees

A new product committee is comprised of top level corporate executives from several key functional areas who meet periodically to assess new product candidates. For example, Gerber Products Co. has a planning committee comprised of the board chairman and chief executive officer, president, executive vice president, and four top operating officers who meet once a month to consider new product proposals.[27] This ensures that those who have sufficient authority to make new product introduction decisions are involved in the decision process. Moreover, having executives from various functions means that the evaluation of new product proposals will be done by personnel who have expertise in areas that are required to implement a new product strategy. For these reasons, new product committees are commonly used by business firms.

New product committees have several disadvantages when they are used for more than screening of proposals such as coordinating the development and testing activities. Since committee membership is comprised of top executives the new product decision task is not a full-time activity. There is the danger that committee members will not give the task the full attention is deserves. Moreover, committee members are not necessarily new product decision specialists. Their interest and abilities may be more in managing the existing business rather than in managing new product evaluation activities. Finally, committees meet only periodically with members returning to their primary responsibilities after each session. Thus, the new product decision may lack continuity in leadership and supervision.

New Product Departments

New product departments are separate organizational functions concentrating on new product decisions. A department will usually have a top level executive directing activities and providing a position of authority for decisions on new products. In addition, a new product department can be staffed with new product decision specialists including technicians, researchers, and functional managers. Because the sole func-

---

[27] Ibid., p. 47.

tion of a department is the discovery and development of innovations, its staff will have the necessary expertise and time to deal with the unique aspects of identifying, developing, and testing ideas. Finally, the new product department should have a wider perspective for new product opportunities since it is not necessarily tied to an existing product group in the firm.

Care must be taken in establishing performance objectives for new product departments. Absolute certainty of a new product's success is a luxury that can seldom be afforded, so some level of risk must be accepted. Yet, if departmental objectives are stated in terms of expected new product introduction successes, too much conservatism may result. Conservatism usually leads to too much testing and too much time spent in the whole process. In addition, competitors may be given extra time needed for their own development activities, actually reducing the chances for new product success.

New product departments are unlikely to be completely independent of all other functional areas of a firm. When the department requires outside assistance, there is no authority to command the needed cooperation, so persuasion must be used. Thus, new product departments are often dependent upon the quality of interdepartmental working relationships.

Venture Teams

The venture team concept appears to be gaining popularity as an organizational approach to facilitating the discovery and development of innovations. A venture team is a separate organizational entity established to develop and implement a new product strategy and relies heavily on an entrepreneurial spirit and flexibility characteristic of small firms to achieve new product successes. Moreover, the venture team is free from the constraints of existing operations to pursue ideas that may not be similar to existing products. At the same time, the venture team benefits from the personnel specialities and resources made available by the firm.[28] Based on a study of existing venture teams, several characteristics are common to corporate applications: (1) venture teams are separate from the operating organization in terms of organizational structure and physical locations; (2) venture teams are comprised of personnel with varying expertise including engineering, production, marketing research, finance and others. Also, personnel with needed specialities are phased in and out at different stages of new product decision processes; (3) while venture teams do have managers, there is much

---

[28] Richard M. Hill and James D. Hlavacek, "The Venture Team: A New Concept in Marketing Organization," *Journal of Marketing*, vol. 36 (July 1972), pp. 49–50, published by the American Marketing Association.

less of a hierarchy evident in the organizational structure; (4) an entre-preneurial spirit is often developed by financial agreements that allow venture team members to share any profits resulting from a new product success; (5) a venture team manager usually reports to a high level executive which assures top management support; (6) the missions (goals) of a venture are typically market oriented rather than product or process oriented, and are broad enough to allow considerable discretion to managers in achieving them; and (7) venture teams do not usually operate under strict time constraints, though periodic checkpoints are built into the operating plan.[29]

The venture team approach requires support from top management as well as cooperation from functional managers. For example, personnel must be encouraged to develop new product ideas worth evaluating. Also, specialists throughout a firm must be allowed to join the venture team when needed for some activity. Finally, the balance of specialists from various functional areas must be controlled since too many of one kind of specialist (e.g., engineering) may lead to lack of sufficient expertise in other areas.[30]

In general, due to the importance and difficulties of making successful new product decisions, the organizational structure adopted should ensure that sufficient managerial time and expertise is devoted to this decision area. The structures most likely to meet this requirement are the new product department and the venture team approaches. Thus, the more essential new product decisions are to achieving corporate goals and objectives, the more these two structure alternatives have to offer a firm.

ANALYTICAL NEW PRODUCT DECISION PROCESS

Regardless of which new product organization is used management must implement an analytical decision process to ensure that important new product decision dimensions are considered. Figure 14–2 presents a flow diagram of an analytical approach to new product decisions. The starting point for the process is the direction provided by the corporate mission and overall product policy decisions made by top management. These broad policy areas recognize that an ongoing firm has established a basic purpose by identifying particular market needs to serve and has an existing product, product line, and/or product mix within which new products must fit. Even a new firm should set such policy when planning for future growth. For example, a product policy might concern the number of products desired within a company's line. General Motors offers automobile models in a very wide variety of price

---

[29] Ibid., pp. 46–47.
[30] Ibid., p. 51.

FIGURE 14–2

Analytical New Product Decision Process

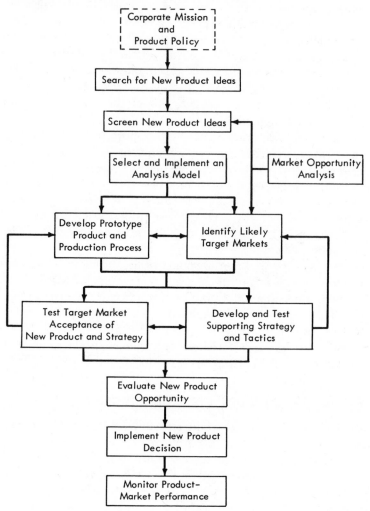

ranges from the relatively inexpensive Chevrolet to the more high priced Cadillac. This suggests that GM has a product policy of being a full-line manufacturer. The full-line policy, in turn, has guided the more recent new car introductions of Vega at the lower end of the line and the Cadillac Seville at the higher end of the line. Other product policy decisions affecting new product decisions include:

Family versus individual brands Procter & Gamble develops a separate brand name and position for each product (e.g., Crest, Tide, Head & Shoulders, Bold, and others are all P&G brands); other companies such as RCA use the company name to cover most, if not all new products.

Private versus national brands Companies often establish a policy concerning whether other firms may add their name to a product and thereby give up brand recognition among customers. In order to ensure that Sears is part of the channel, many suppliers allow Sears to put its name on their products, for instance.

Competitive product position A company may set a policy dictating the relationship of a new product to existing competitor products. A manufacturer might require that product quality superiority over competitors be established prior to considering it for introduction.

Within the context of corporate mission and product policy, new product decisions are dependent upon the discovery of ideas that offer potential opportunity. A firm may choose to wait for ideas to appear without any directed effort to seek them out. However, a central characteristic of this process is that new product decisions are too important to depend upon the chance appearance of ideas. Rather, a firm should actively search for new product ideas to ensure an ongoing supply of potentially attractive ideas for evaluation. For example, a firm might conduct small group, indepth personal interviews with consumers to help identify new product ideas.

The result of the search process is a pool of new product ideas for evaluation. The next step is for management to screen these ideas to find those that have the best potential opportunity for the firm. Screening at an early stage can only be preliminary. Management really wants to know which ideas are sufficiently promising to warrant more extensive evaluation. Information is likely to be scarce, and considerable reliance on judgment may be needed. However, since the decision is whether to continue evaluating an idea, management typically does not need highly precise and accurate estimates. For example, highly favorable growth in the volume of tourist travel through a southern city was sufficient information for a firm to launch an extensive feasibility study for a restaurant even though the estimates of the level of travel were not considered precise.

Ideas passing the initial opportunity screen are then evaluated in greater depth to determine whether to go to a full-scale market introduction. To guide an extensive evaluation management must select an analysis approach or model. These vary from a simple break-even analysis to much more complicated simulations. The key to selection is the help provided for management in determining factors and information that should be assessed. Most formal models are primarily concerned with quantifiable factors such as cost and revenue flows. So, new product evaluations are likely to extend beyond a model to more qualitative factors. For instance, a firm may need to consider a new product's potential for enhancing corporate image, avoiding government scrutiny, avoiding harm to the physical environment, and so forth.

A product idea, which may be no more than a verbal description, must be made operational through development of a physical product having attributes dictated by the idea concept. Then a production process must be designed to meet desired output capacity. While these are largely technical tasks, there can be considerable interaction between technicians and marketing personnel. For example, if an idea is for a consumer food product, marketing research may be needed to discover consumer taste preferences to determine the best combination of ingredients. Similarly, development of an industrial product such as a new package design may require questioning customers about alternative designs, materials specifications, and tolerances.

Prior to any assessment of market preferences and acceptance of new product ideas, management must identify the most likely target markets. MOA information can contribute to new product evaluations by describing likely markets and analyzing how well these markets are already being served through industry, competitor, and channel analyses. For example, suppose a group of entrepreneurs were evaluating an idea for a new food franchising operation. A logical starting point to screen this idea would be to conduct an aggregate market analysis at the generic and specific product/market level by assessing the opportunity in all food services and in food franchising. An MOA may contribute further by analyzing opportunity in the proposed specific product/market segment (e.g., steakhouse franchising). From this more detailed analysis would come descriptions of consumers representing market potential.

Upon selection of likely market targets, the decision process turns to the testing of market acceptance of the new product concept and to the development and testing of supporting selling and distribution strategies and tactics. Both of these activities can and should be conducted simultaneously since they are highly interrelated. Tests of target market acceptance involves obtaining information concerning the reaction of potential customers (opinions, attitudes, preferences, purchase decisions) to the product itself or the total offer. These tests may be formal marketing research projects (most likely for consumer products) or more informal interchange with selected customers (most likely for industrial products). At the same time, managers in the supporting functional areas (advertising, personal selling, pricing, etc.) should be developing and testing strategy and tactics needed to convert the potential opportunity into a reality.

The next stage in a new product decision process is the focal point for all preceding activities—the decision on whether to introduce the new product and accompanying supporting strategies into target markets. If management decided to go ahead with the introduction, a plan or schedule of activities must be formulated and implemented. Typically, the introduction must be phased into full-scale operation due to the many different activities that must be coordinated. For example, to introduce a new calculator for consumer markets, an electronics manufacturer would have to plan for building production capacity, contract with suppliers of materials, possibly hire personnel, develop distribution capability, implement advertising, train salesmen, set up repair facilities, print price lists, and determine sequencing of geographic market introductions.

Upon introduction of a new product into target markets, the task for management switches to managing and controlling product performance through each of the product life cycle stages. This involves setting product performance objectives, monitering actual product-market performance, and altering product-marketing strategy to improve performance when necessary. While much of the decision making affecting product-market performance for an ongoing product involves manipulating supporting strategy, there are key product decisions made during this process. A product may be modified in response to market, competitor, or other changes that have caused the existing product's performance to become unacceptable. If considered a significant modification, this triggers the new product decision process again.

The other major product decision that inevitably must be faced is the product-drop decision. The discussion of this decision is postponed until Chapter 23 which covers the managerial control process. Dropping a product is the result of control activities which uncover those products that are no longer capable of making a sufficient contribution to corporate performance. So, this decision is used to illustrate the control process in action. More importantly, the decision to drop a product often significantly affects the other marketing mix decision areas. For example, channel relationships between a supplier and a distributor may have to be changed if a supplier eliminates a product from its line. Thus, the product drop decision can be more meaningfully treated after discussion of these supporting marketing mix areas.

DETERMINING CANDIDATE NEW PRODUCT IDEAS

Marketing can play a vital role in the management of a firm's new product effort by ensuring that a steady stream of new product ideas is continually becoming available for in-depth analyses. This requires both searching for new product opportunities and subsequently conducting preliminary screenings.

Managing New Product Ideas

Management must have potentially opportune new product ideas available for analysis to *plan* for introductions rather than to simply re-

FIGURE 14–3

Sources for New Product Ideas

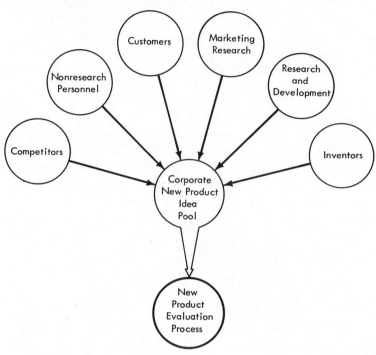

act to the random or chance recognition of a new product opportunity. Planned introductions may be necessary, for example, to replace existing products being phased out of a firm's product mix. Moreover, the proportion of all new ideas actually converted into successful new products is amazingly small. Based on studies of a large number of corporate new product decisions, Booz, Allen and Hamilton, Management Consultants, estimated that about 58 new product ideas are required to yield a commercially successful new product.[31] While this ratio varies from firm to firm, a contining flow of ideas is necessary to increase the chances of identifying the relatively few commercial successes.

Sources for new product ideas are quite numerous and diverse as indicated by Figure 14–3. Not all sources of new product ideas are under the control of management. Unsolicited ideas from independent investors, competitive new product activities, and customers may not become known unless appropriate information channels are established. For example, customer complaint letters may contain product modifica-

---

[31] *Management of New Products*, p. 9.

tion ideas that could go unrecognized unless the letters are scanned by personnel. Also, salesmen should be trained to pass on information about competitive activities and customer suggestions to designated corporate personnel. The remaining sources—marketing research, research and development, and non-research personnel—are clearly under greater control of management, and can be more easily directed. Yet, even with these sources, there is still the need for *managing* the flow of ideas. Non-research personnel must be given the training and incentives (e.g., bonuses for ideas adopted) necessary to ensure that their ideas are submitted. Research personnel also need training in technical skills and techniques for seeking ideas as well as incentives to allocate a desired portion of their time and efforts to the search task. At a minimum, the organization structure installed to facilitate new product decision making should provide for a central "idea pool" into which ideas can be funneled. Moreover, personnel should be familiar with the channels for reaching this pool easily and efficiently.

Active Search for New Product Ideas

Some quite successful products have resulted from ideas that were not actively sought. For example, the development of Corning Ware cooking products was the outcome of the accidental discovery of a glass material that could withstand extreme heat and cold. An experimental piece of glass had been overheated and when a worker dropped it on the floor the glass did not break. From this incident the idea for Corning Ware products was developed.[32]

While a firm should recognize and be receptive to the possibility for chance discoveries of new product opportunities, there are also a variety of approaches that might be used to actively seek ideas. These approaches rely on research and development, non-technical personnel, or marketing research to identify new product ideas.

Research and Development. An important search activity stems from the research and development functions of firms. For example, in Sunbeam's fiscal year 1973, $8 million was spent on R&D resulting in the identification of 120 new product ideas from one of the two plants alone.[33] Many well-known products such as nylon, polyethylene, DDT, the transistor, and long-playing records were also the result of corporate R&D efforts.

A question worth considering is whether the use of R&D to search for new product ideas is consistent with the marketing concept. Strictly interpreted, the marketing concept cautions firms to first determine

---

[32] James Berry, *Exploring Crystals* (London: Crowell-Collier Press, 1969), p. 68.

[33] "Why Sunbeam Succeeds in Small Appliances," *Business Week* (January 20, 1973), pp. 64 and 68.

market needs and then to design marketing programs, including new products, to meet these needs. This would suggest that R&D only work on developing new products for known market needs. For example, Sunbeam Corporation salesmen are asked to report back from the field any consumer complaints or needs. This information is used by R&D personnel to devise new or improved products.[34] Yet, to expect R&D to get all its direction from knowledge of market needs is not realistic. Consumers do not or cannot always communicate their specific needs, particularly when there is no existing product to suggest that a particular need can be satisfied. Who could have verbalized a need or want for television before such a product was invented? Thus, R&D may have to determine what products are technologically possible in order to identify innovative new product ideas. Of course, such ideas should be assessed to determine if there really is a market need for the innovation. As long as a market need is established during the new product decision process, the marketing concept is not being violated.

Nonresearch Personnel. Employees of a firm who are not primarily involved in the search for new ideas may still be a source worth tapping. These personnel must understand how to make their ideas known and be encouraged to do so. One way to do this is to offer some kind of incentive or reward for ideas later deemed marketable. Another approach is to use "brainstorming."

Brainstorming attempts to capitalize on the backgrounds and creative abilities of selected employees. People are brought together in a group and encouraged to interchange ideas about products. Often some direction is given to the group such as a product category or particular customer problem within which to focus their attention. Then individuals are asked to "throw out" ideas. No evaluation or criticism of ideas is allowed, since this might discourage involvement. However, participants are encouraged to expand on, modify, or add to ideas that are suggested. Brainstorming sessions are largely unstructured and freewheeling, though some leadership is needed to keep the interchange moving and to keep the discussion on the desired track.[35] The output of brainstorming sessions is a list of new product ideas that can be added to the corporate idea pool.

Marketing Research. Marketing research search techniques range from observation of customers in product use situations to group discussion sessions to customer surveys. For example, *direct observation* might be used when a firm is searching for new product ideas to solve a particular customer problem or need. Suppose an appliance manufacturer wanted to determine whether preparing a meal in the home could

---

[34] "Why Sunbeam Succeeds in Small Appliances," p. 64.

[35] H. Ronald Hamilton, "Screening Business Development Opportunities," *Business Horizons* (August 1974), p. 15.

be made easier or more efficient through new or modified products. One approach might be to set up a fully equipped kitchen so that housewives can be brought in to actually cook a meal. Movement and activities of each housewife would be observed for clues to new product ideas. If these housewives seemed to be having trouble, for instance, in finding foods in the refrigerator, this may suggest that redesigning the refrigerator interior is a needed product modification.

Another marketing research technique called *focus group interviewing* is similar to brainstorming except that the participants are potential customers. Respondents are led in a discussion of a product category for which they are potential users. For example, Beckman Instruments Company, an industrial manufacturer of precision instruments, has used focus group interviewing to generate ideas and designs for a new line of process control equipment that was subsequently introduced. Previously, new product efforts had been typically directed at a few users for each new product. Yet, to achieve cost economies, Beckman's management wanted to identify and design products with a much broader based appeal. So Beckman Instruments brought together 46 engineers from process control equipment user companies at a per capita cost of cocktails and $40 for expenses. Sessions were held after work hours to ensure a three-hour uninterrupted participation by the engineers. Participants began by filling out a 30 to 45 minute questionnaire on the process control equipment field. The remainder of each session was spent in open discussion of process control equipment which was recorded on tape. The anonymity of Beckman as the originator of the sessions was maintained to allow more openness among the engineers. Out of the session tapings came several important new product ideas including the need for a different type of process printing device, the need to make process control equipment more convertible to computer control, and the need for a larger viewing window for viewing measurement scales than was typical on competitive equipment.[36]

An Illustrative Analytical New Product Search Process.[37] A currently developing methodology that illustrates the use of marketing research to analyze customer wants and satisfaction with existing competitive products uses data collected from multiple samples of potential customers. The process is comprised of four stages: (1) determine the relevant product-market within which to conduct search; (2) represent these products in a configuration meaningful to both customers and the firm;

---

[36] "Beckman Gets Customers to Design Its Product," *Business Week* (August 17, 1974), pp. 52 and 54.

[37] The discussion in this section is based on the analytical search process presented in Allan D. Shocker and V. Srinivasan, "An Analytical Methodology for the Generation of Product Ideas," in Fred C. Allvine (ed.), *1971 Combined Proceedings* (Chicago: American Marketing Association, 1972), pp. 158–62.

(3) develop a model relating customer preferences to choice behavior; and (4) develop a method for searching the product configuration for new product ideas.

Determination of the relevant product-market should identify which products are perceived by customers as competitive for the same need. For example, to identify headache remedies, customers might be surveyed to find out which products from a predeveloped list are appropriate for relieving headache pain. Results may indicate that such products as aspirin, cold remedies, and digestive ailment remedies (e.g., Alka Seltzer) are believed to be useful for relieving headache pain. This stage is essential, since customers are likely to view a different set of products as competitive for the same need than would the manufacturer. For example, an aspirin manufacturer might be likely to restrict the relevant product-market to all aspirins and aspirin substitutes since these are the most obvious headache remedies.

The second stage, determination of a product configuration, requires additional customer data describing how competitive products are related to each other in terms of various attributes. These attributes must be those that are used by customers to choose which product to purchase and use. Moreover, the attributes should be "actionable" for management so that some part of the controllable marketing mix can be used to influence customer perceptions of each attribute.[38] For example, sweetness of a food product is an actionable attribute because consumer perceptions of product sweetness can be influenced by the amount of sugar

FIGURE 14–4

Illustrative Attributes and Product Relationships

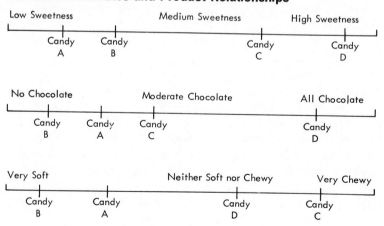

[38] Ibid., p. 160.

or sugar substitute added to the product. However, sportiness of an automobile is probably less actionable due to the greater difficulty of determining what design alternatives are viewed as sporty by customers. The result of this stage is a set of attributes that determine customer choice and the relative position of competitive products on each attribute. Figure 14–4 provides an illustrative example of the positioning of four candy products along three attribute scales based on perceptions of a sample of customers. Assuming these attributes are those that customers consider important when buying candy, the scales show how existing products relate to each other on determinants of customer choice.

Probably the most difficult, yet important, stage in the process is to develop a model that will predict customer product choice based on the actionable product attributes. One approach is based on analyses of customers' stated preferences for existing products within the relevant product market. The resulting model must show how preference is related to the actionable product attributes uncovered in the previous stage. An example of such a model is a preference-attribute relationship of the form shown below:[39]

(1)
$$P_{jk} = f\left[\sum_{i=1}^{n}(A_{ijk})w_{ij}\right]$$

where:

P_{jk} = the jth customer's preference for product k.

A_{ijk} = the level of attribute i perceived by customer j to be possessed by product k.

w_{ij} = the salience of attribute i to customer j for choice in the product-market.

n = the number of salient attributes for choice in the product-market.

In addition to preference for existing products, an ideal combination of actionable attribute levels must be determined for each customer. This is a key step since it allows the subsequent search for new product ideas to explicitly consider customer wants as reflected by this ideal product. To continue the illustration consider the intuitively reasonable assumption that a customer's ideal product has a combination of attribute levels more similar to those characteristic of more preferred products than less preferred ones. Figure 14–5 shows the relationship between the four existing candy products in terms of two attributes. These

---

[39] Allan D. Shocker and V. Srinivasan, "Consumer-Based Methodology for Identification of New Products," *Management Science*, vol. 20, no. 6 (February 1974), p. 927.

FIGURE 14–5

Location of Consumer J's Ideal Point

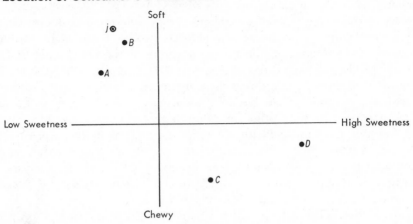

relationships were determined by plotting the scale locations for the products on the sweetness and softness attributes from Figure 14–4. Now, suppose that customer j had ranked the four candy products from most preferred to least preferred; $B > A > C > D$. Using this preference assumption, point j in Figure 14–5 represents an ideal product for customer j since the point is located closer to B than A, closer to A than to C, and closer to C than to D. Moreover, by simultaneously conducting the analysis for all customers in the sample, Figure 14–5 can be expanded to show the relationship between the four existing candy products and all ideal points.

Using the familiar distance function from geometry (i.e., Pythagoras' theorem), a model of the following form can be used to predict preference for each of the real products or any other combination of the attributes in this space:[40]

$$(2) \qquad P_{jk} = f\left[\frac{1}{\left(\sum_{i=1}^{n} (A^{(I)}{}_{ij} - A_{ijk})^2 w_{ij} \right)^{\frac{1}{2}}} \right]$$

where:

P_{jk} = customer j's preference for a combination of attributes forming product k.

$A^{(I)}{}_{ij}$ = level of attribute i possessed by consumer j's ideal brand I.

---

[40] Ibid., p. 932.

$$A_{ijk} = \text{the level of attribute } i \text{ perceived}$$
by customer j to be possessed
by product k.

$$w_{ij} = \text{the salience of attribute } i \text{ to}$$
customer j.

$$n = \text{the number of attributes that}$$
are salient to customer j.

In essence, the model quantifies the behavioral assumption stated above. P_{jk} will be greater, indicating greater preference, for those attribute combinations close to more preferred existing candy products and lower for those combinations located a greater distance away.

These three stages provide the basis for seeking new product ideas by identifying and relating actionable product attributes to customer preference. The search for new product ideas can be visualized by examining Figure 14–6 which shows an illustrative result of the analysis of a representative sample of customer candy perceptions and preferences. The circles represent segments in which ideal products are sufficiently similar and where relative circle size indicates relative segment size. The points labeled A, B, C, and D are the four existing candy products. All other points in the product space represent non-existent, but potentially new combinations of attributes that might be possible new products. For example, point NE represents a unique combination of sweetness and softness that might be developed into a new candy product.

The search for new ideas involves examining these new attribute combinations. Since there is an infinite number of such combinations included in the product space, some criteria for selecting ideas must be established. These might include (1) the technical ability to pro-

FIGURE 14–6

Product Space for New Product Idea Search

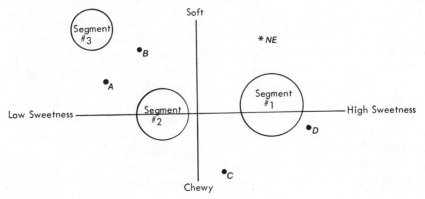

duce a product with that combination of attribute levels; (2) the closeness of new attribute combinations to large segments of customer ideal points; (3) the degree of differentiation or distance from existing competitive products; and (4) the complementary or substitute relationship of the new combination to existing products in the firm's mix. New attribute combinations that pass these criteria would be added to the corporate new product idea pool for further evaluation.

This new product search process, as well as focus group interviewing, is more likely to generate product modification ideas than totally new product possibilities. This appears to be true, at the present state of the art, for marketing research approaches in general. The reason is that to obtain information from customers, particularly consumers, requires establishing a frame of reference for answering questions by having them think of existing products. This necessarily restricts their attention to products or attributes of products that already exist. Moreover, the ability to foresee products that are totally unlike any that already exist is a rather rare ability possessed by a relatively few people. For these reasons, marketing research may not be the best approach for generating radically new ideas. Rather, these ideas may have to come from non-customer sources such as inventors and R&D personnel.

Screening New Product Ideas

If the new idea generation process has been successful, there will be more ideas than can be handled by a firm due to limited resources. The task now is to screen ideas from the corporate new product idea pool to identify those most worthy of continued development and evaluation. Because new product ideas lack development and are rather new to management, the screening task is only a preliminary evaluation relying heavily on managerial judgment and experience. Nevertheless, screening must cull out ideas that cannot justify commitment of additional resources, and identify those ideas that are most likely to be real opportunities for the firm.

Effective screening must avoid making two potential errors. First, there is the possibility of screening out ideas that, in fact, would have resulted in very successful new product introductions. This risk is very difficult to assess since there is so little experience developed in analyzing when and why these errors are made. Obviously, ideas that are screened out are not likely to receive any additional management attention. Second, there is the error of passing ideas through the screening process that eventually turn out to lack sufficient opportunity to justify resources expended. Experience concerning this error can be accumulated through post-mortem analyses of new product ideas rejected during subsequent development and evaluation and of new product failures. In addition, the screening process should be accomplished without large resource commitments. Resources for new product decisions must be conserved for development and evaluation of those ideas that pass the screening process. Moreover, there may simply be too many ideas subjected to screening to make heavy resource commitment to each one very practical.

A new product screening process, as shown in Figure 14–7, is essentially comprised of evaluating ideas against some set of criteria. These criteria represent standards that management believes must be surpassed by new product opportunity to be sufficiently attractive for further development and more extensive evaluation. So, the initial step in the screening process is to determine screening criteria. The task is then to gather information dictated by these criteria so that management can evaluate the extent to which each idea meets or exceeds each one. Those ideas that satisfy enough criteria to indicate potential opportunity are then passed on to subsequent stages in a new product decision process.

While specific criteria vary from firm to firm, two categories of screening criteria are commonly used. These are illustrated in Figure 14–8. New product ideas are screened against corporate goals and objectives to determine consistency with the basic purposes and expected performance of a firm. A corporate mission directed toward serving the packaging needs of customers will cause a company such as American Can Co. to cull out ideas that would require entry into substantially different markets (e.g., steel production). Or, a firm that is building a reputation of being a full-line manufacturer of electrical motors will be

FIGURE 14–7

New Product Idea Screening Process

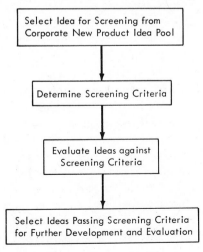

FIGURE 14–8

Types of New Product Screening Criteria

Corporate Goal and Objective Criteria
  Consistence with corporate mission
    Satisfying similar customer needs
    Similarity to existing products
  Consistence with corporate image and reputation
    Product quality
    Completeness of product offering
    Superiority over competitors' products
    Degree of newness
  Consistence with desired financial performance
    Sales level (market size, existing and potential
      competition)
    Payback period
    Return on investment
  Market opportunity potential
    Ability to market to existing vs. new customers
    Market potential size
    International market potential
    Seasonal fluctuations

Corporate Resource Capabilities
  Investment commitment
  Market development required
  Product life span
  Technical skills required
    Research and development
    Engineering
    Production
    Quality control
  Marketing program requirements
    Advertising
    Personal selling
    Distribution
    Customer service
    Probable price
  Patent protection

---

attracted to new motor ideas that complement their existing line. Moreover, firms have well-established financial and market performance objectives that also serve as screening criteria.

The other type of screening criteria require management to evaluate new product ideas in terms of the firm's ability to take advantage of an opportunity. These criteria should reflect the key skills and capabilities on which a firm has built its success. Skills may lie in specific personnel or in functional specialties such as production, marketing, financial control, or quality control. For example, Procter & Gamble has tremendous distribution and selling capability through supermarket channels. The most attractive new products for P&G would be those that can be sold through these channels as evidenced by their more recent new product introductions: Pampers, Pringles New Fangled Potatoe Chips, and Bounty paper towels.

Multistage Approach to Screening. With criteria selected, management can turn to the task of gathering needed information and evaluating how well a new product idea meets these criteria. Columbus Laboratories, Battelle Institute uses a multistage approach to screening new product ideas that illustrates the use of corporate goals and resources criteria in an evaluation process.[41] Stages of screening are established according to the information requirements needed to evaluate an idea against criteria in that stage. Some stages may involve a single criterion that must be satisfied to avoid being rejected. Other stages include several related criteria where a decision rule is used to indicate how many of the criteria must be met for the idea to pass. Once stages have been sequenced for the screening process, an idea must successfully pass through all stages before being judged worthy of subsequent product development and more intensive evaluation. Actual sequencing of stages might be based upon the difficulty and expense of obtaining needed information for screening in each stage (e.g., stages sequenced from low to high expense stages) or in terms of the ability of various stages to predict overall product success (i.e., passing some stages may be a better indication of eventual success than others).

For one approach to a multistage process, a firm screens an idea first against culling criteria, then against rating criteria, and finally against scoring criteria (see Table 14–2). Culling criteria consist of qualitative new product guidelines that are applied dichotomously—either a new product idea meets each criterion or it doesn't. For example, a culling criterion for Procter & Gamble might be whether a new product can be sold through supermarkets. Such criteria are considered first because they require the least expensive information to assess. Rating criteria are not absolutely dichotomous but can be evaluated by using a dichotomous approach. However, management must establish boundaries that will guide the determination of whether an idea meets a criterion or doesn't. As an illustration, evaluating whether an idea fits the corporate image may require only a yes or no judgment as long as management has determined what is required for a product to meet the image objective (e.g., a specific materials quality level, design configuration, price, etc.). Finally, scoring criteria include those that are not dichotomous and cannot be treated as if they were. A new product idea scores within some range of values characteristic of each scoring criterion. These criteria

---

[41] H. Ronald Hamilton, "Screening Business Development Opportunities," *Business Horizons*, vol. 17 (August 1974), pp. 13–24.

TABLE 14-2

Culling, Rating, and Scoring Criteria

	Yes	*No*
Illustrative Culling Criteria:		
1. Can the product be marketed through supermarkets?	____	____
2. Does any one competitor have over 50% market share?	____	____
3. Is this product a high technology product?	____	____
4. Can the product be marketed internationally?	____	____
Illustrative Rating Criteria:		
1. Is the product hard for competitors to duplicate?	____	____
2. Does the product offer a considerable market for after-sale parts and service?		
3. Does the product fit the desired corporate image?	____	____

Illustrative Scoring Criteria:

	Low	*Medium*	*High*
1. What is the annual market growth rate?	1	2	3
	Short	*Medium*	*Long*
2. What is the length of the life cycle?	1	2	3
	Not Likely	*Quite Likely*	*Very Likely*
3. How likely is it that competition will enter?	1	2	3

Source: Adapted from H. Ronald Hamilton, "Screening Business Development Opportunities," *Business Horizons*, vol. 17 (August 1974), pp. 20–21.

are usually the most expensive to evaluate due to the more precise judgment requested.[42] Estimating growth in sales, for example, may have to be based on a generic and specific product/market demand analysis to be sufficiently accurate.

When a screening stage contains more than one criterion, management must select a decision rule that shows what an idea must achieve to pass that particular stage. For culling and rating criteria, this decision rule can be stated in terms of the number of criteria that must be met before an idea is passed out of that stage. For example, if a stage has five related rating criteria, a new product idea may have to pass three in order to pass the entire stage. For scoring criteria, the decision rule is more complicated. Each criterion in a stage must have a predetermined set of values within which an idea is to be evaluated. In Table 14–2, a range of three values was selected for each of the illustrative scoring criteria. Also, a weight should be attached to each criterion to indicate the relative importance of that criterion relative to the others. This allows the determination of a total score for the idea on all criteria in that stage by applying the model:[43]

---

[42] Ibid., pp. 19–22.

[43] A similar model is discussed in Marshall Freimer and Leonard S. Simon, "Screening New Product Ideas," in Robert L. King (ed.), *Marketing and The New Science of Planning* (Chicago: American Marketing Association, 1968), pp. 99–104.

(3)
$$S_I = \sum_{i=1}^{n} C_i w_i$$

where:

S_I = Total score for the new product idea in Stage I.

C_i = Score for the new product idea on the ith criterion in Stage I

w_i = Relative importance weight for the ith criterion in Stage I

n = Number of criteria in Stage I

Once a total score for an idea has been determined, a comparison can be made to a preselected cutoff score for that screening stage. If the idea's score is above the cutoff, the idea is passed onto the next stage; if the score is below the cutoff, the idea is screened out.

A key to effective idea screening is obtaining information needed to compare ideas against criteria. Since the resources available for screening are usually restricted, heavy reliance must be placed on less expensive information sources—secondary sources, expert opinion, and managerial judgment. Primary data collection through marketing research may require more resources than are available unless limited to smaller scale studies. For example, to screen an idea against market related criteria (e.g., sales, need satisfaction) a firm may collect information by conducting a market opportunity analysis. Yet the MOA should be limited to analyses at the generic and specific product/market levels since these levels are least dependent on primary data collection. Fortunately, many of the typical criteria imposed by companies can be evaluated by use of relatively inexpensive information. In Figure 14–8, for example, the culling and rating criteria would probably require only expert opinion (e.g., salesmen, managers of channel organizations) and managerial judgment for evaluation.

Other Approaches. Because the criteria evaluation approaches are the most commonly used screening tools does not mean that they are completely satisfactory. One problem arises when the screening process is performed by a management team rather than a single individual. For those criterion evaluations over which team members disagree, some method for reconciliation must be used such as the Delphi process. Moreover, members may have differing degrees of confidence in their evaluations which current methods do not reflect.[44] In addition, there is

---

[44] Allan D. Shocker, Dennis Gensch, and Leonard S. Simon, "Toward the Improvement of New Product Search and Screening" in Philip R. McDonald (ed.), *Marketing Involvement is Society and the Economy* (Chicago: American Marketing Association, 1969), p. 169

the difficulty of determining appropriate decision rules, criteria weights, and cutoff scores for screening stages in which there are multiple criteria to evaluate. Often there is little experience available to management to predetermine these rules, weights, and scores that will discriminate between successful and nonsuccessful new product ideas.[45] Finally, the quantitative scoring approaches illustrated by model (3) are not particularly sensitive to changes in criteria weights or to criteria score evaluations.[46] This suggests that these approaches are more valuable for identifying extremely good or very poor new product opportunities rather than differentiating ideas with more similar potential. Difficulties have led to the search for improved screening tools. However, current proposals are still in a formulative stage of development.[47]

SUMMARY AND CONCLUSIONS

Identification and development of new products has been presented as an important management task. The risk of making new product introductions is substantial, and so management must strive to improve new product "batting averages" by making use of available decision tools. Two particularly important tools are corporate organizational structure and analytical decision processes. Both require a directed effort on the part of management to implement. Finally, new product decisions stem from having potentially opportune new product ideas available for analysis. Thus, an important part of managing new products is insuring that a steady flow of ideas is encouraged. This requires search for and screening potential new product candidates.

The next chapter continues the discussion of new product decision processes. The focus is on the post-screening stages leading to a new product introduction decision. Particular attention is devoted to the tools and techniques for developing and testing market acceptance of new product strategies and tactics.

EXERCISES FOR REVIEW AND DISCUSSION

1. An industrial producer of product quality monitoring systems is rapidly expanding its new product effort. One outcome of this effort has been the establishment of a new product department to complement the product manager organization handling existing products. This department is given responsibility for handling all new product decisions. However, a con-

---

[45] Ibid., p. 169.

[46] Marshall Freuner and Leonard S. Simon, "Screening New Product Ideas," pp. 103–4.

[47] For an overview and evaluation of alternative screening tools, see Allan D. Shocker, Dennis Gensch, and Leonard S. Simon, "Toward the Improvement of New Product Search and Screening," pp. 168–75.

troversy has arisen between the new product managers and existing product managers over who has responsibility for modifications to existing products. Each side wants authority for making modification decisions. Develop guidelines for the company that will overcome this controversy by showing which management group should handle each modification decision as they arise.

2. "Raw material and energy shortages will substantially reduce the ability and the need for firms to maintain an active ongoing new product development program." Do you agree with this statement? Why or why not?

3. Choose any of the following new product failures and analyze the reasons for that product's lack of success by using published information sources: Ford's Edsel, DuPont's Corfam, Scott's Baby Diapers, or RCA's computer systems. (Hint: Start with the Business Periodicals Index.)

4. Suppose a firm has comprehensively analyzed the market opportunities for its existing line of products. Top management has concluded that the firm must expand into new products and new markets to improve upon more recent growth rates. It is expected that this strategy will be accomplished through internal new product development rather than mergers. Recommend a new product organizational structure that will best facilitate this strategy including a comprehensive rationale for your choice.

5. A marketing vice president of a large chemical producer has made a radical proposal for the role of marketing research and development (R&D) functions in generating new product ideas. Her proposal essentially says that R&D personnel should curtail all (or at least most) of its basic research that cannot be tied to known market needs. Rather, marketing research should be given the major responsibility for identifying new product ideas based on analyses of customers and markets. Then, R&D should direct its efforts toward determining the technical feasibility of these new product ideas. This would bring the company's new product development function in line with the marketing concept. Do you agree with this proposal and its rationale? Why or why not?

6. "Screening criteria should be developed for each individual new product idea proposal. New product ideas should not be subjected to the same criteria since each idea will be different from other ideas." Discuss.

7. For the screening criteria in Table 14–2, show how a market opportunity analysis might contribute to management's evaluation of new product ideas against these illustrative criteria.

Evaluating New Product
Opportunities

Identifying and screening new product ideas trigger the evaluation stages in a new product decision process. The central focus for these stages is to evaluate the relative efficiency of using corporate resources for a new product introduction when compared to using these resources for other purposes. This chapter discusses the evaluation stages that management should follow to determine these key estimates analytically and the marketing strategy and tactics upon which they are based. The first section presents alternative new product evaluation models to guide the evaluation process. This is followed by an examination of product development and designing and testing of supporting strategies for market introduction. Then, marketing research approaches to determining market acceptance of product designs and of a total marketing strategy are presented. The process of actually introducing a product into target markets is also discussed. Finally, the chapter ends by examining the key characteristics of the entire evaluation process that allow management to reduce new product decision risks.

NEW PRODUCT EVALUATION MODELS

Firms are increasingly turning to decision models that serve as a framework for guiding new product evaluation activities. These models are quantitative and are directed toward assessing the profitability of a new product opportunity. To put these models in proper perspective, keep in mind that profitability may not be the only basis for evaluation. For example, the 1960s and 1970s have seen increased concern for corporate social responsibility. A firm wishing to recognize such responsibility in new product decisions may have to go beyond profitability analysis to also consider the new product's impact on such environmental and societal factors as pollution, destruction of the natural environment, potential danger to customer health and safety, and the usage of scarce national resources.[1] Some of these factors may have already been assessed during the screening process (e.g., use of scarce resources) while others may have to await further product development before evaluations can be made (e.g., danger to customer health). These more qualitative factors can be assessed in addition to, but separate from profitability analysis. Or, management may attempt to incorporate environmental and societal factors directly into the profitability analysis by quantifying them as costs. For example, costs of pollution may be directly included in a total cost analysis for a proposed soap product.

Several of the more popular new product evaluation models include breakeven analysis, discounted cash flow analysis, Bayesian decision analysis, and simulation.[2] These models are all intended to serve as a framework for helping management decide whether to (1) introduce the new product; (2) continue the development and evaluation process; or (3) drop the new product idea from further consideration.

Breakeven Analysis

The least complicated model for guiding new product evaluations is the breakeven model. Application requires management to determine a volume of sales that will provide just enough revenue to cover costs of producing, distributing and selling a new product. Notice that this sales volume is not a forecast of actual sales that can be achieved; rather it is the volume that must be achieved to cover costs. The model can be stated in the following functional form:

(1)
$$S_{BE} = \frac{TFC}{P_u - VC_u}$$

where:

S_{BE} = Sales volume needed to break even.
TFC = Total fixed costs incurred by the new product.
P_u = New product price per unit.
VC_u = Per unit variable cost incurred by the new product.

---

[1] This point of view is discussed more fully in Dale L. Varble, "Social and Environmental Considerations in New Product Development," *Journal of Marketing*, vol. 36, no. 4 (October 1972), pp. 11–15.

[2] For an excellent discussion of new product evaluation models, see Philip Kotler, "Computer Simulation in the Analysis of New-Product Decisions," in Frank M. Bass, Charles W. King, and Edgar A. Pessemier (eds.), *Application of the Sciences in Marketing Management* (New York: John Wiley & Sons, 1968), pp. 283–325.

The denominator, $P_u - VC_u$, is the gross margin generated by each unit sold. So, dividing this quantity into total fixed costs will determine how many units must be sold to generate sufficient total gross margin to cover all fixed costs. Breakeven volume provides management with a minimum volume that can be compared to estimates of demand. Rather than trying to pinpoint actual sales of the new product, a very difficult task, management can focus on whether sales will at least equal, if not exceed, the breakeven volume. Moreover, if management estimates by how much actual sales (S_a) are expected (if at all) to exceed breakeven volume, then profitability can also be assessed by using the profit (P) relationship:

$$(2) \qquad\qquad P = (S_a - S_{BE}) (P_u - VC_u).$$

The breakeven analysis model appears deceptively simple. In fact, there is a considerable amount of information (including managerial judgment) required. First, a time period must be selected over which the breakeven analysis will be conducted. One option is to view cost and price inputs as average period estimates over some stated number of periods (usually years). The interpretation of the breakeven volume would then be the number of units that must be sold each period, on the average, to cover fixed and variable costs incurred during that period. This option is only appropriate when price and costs are not expected to change dramatically during the periods included in the analysis. Another option is to use the analysis in a payback period model. Here, management would have to estimate total fixed cost over the entire time included in the analysis as well as an average price and variable cost per unit. Also, an estimate of expected sales per time period is needed. These estimates encourage management to consider the timing or pattern of sales and costs expected over the total time. Using these estimates, the total time required for new product sales to be sufficient to recover all costs can be determined:

$$(3) \qquad\qquad S_{BE} = S_1 + S_2 \ldots + S_n$$

where:

S_n = Sales expected in the nth time period.

In addition, breakeven analysis requires the design of a production, distribution, and selling strategy since this strategy will determine costs to be incurred. Of course, the model may be used to assess alternative strategies by comparing breakeven volumes, expected sales, and strategy costs. Yet, the value of a breakeven analysis is clearly dependent upon management's ability to estimate the costs of each strategy being considered. Moreover, the complexities of cost analyses, such as classifying costs as fixed, variable, semivariable, direct, or overhead, adds to the difficulty of applying breakeven models.

Finally, a breakeven model does not explicitly incorporate several key factors that should be included in a new product evaluation. There is no consideration given to the impact of the product on the company's existing product mix. This is a serious omission when there are complementary or competitive relationships between a new product and existing products in the mix. In addition, the confidence or uncertainty inherent in the estimates is not considered. The results of a breakeven analysis conducted early in the evaluation process are likely to be more uncertain than later analyses having the benefit of more information. Yet, the model does not show these uncertainty differences, nor will it aid in the assessment of whether more information is needed before making a decision on the new product. Lastly, it is difficult to use breakeven analysis to assess the time pattern of sales and strategy expenditures even though such patterns may be critical to the new product decision.

The weaknesses of the breakeven model suggest that it is at best a crude approximation of the new product decision. Dissatisfaction with the model has been a factor in encouraging the development of more complex and complete new product decision models. Each of the following models overcomes one or more weaknesses of the breakeven model.

Discounted Cash Flow Model

The discounted cash flow model recognizes the fact that both revenue inflows and cost outflows are likely to change over time. Also, the model incorporates the time value of money by discounting future revenue and costs by a company's opportunity cost of capital.[3] Both of these features represent improvements over the breakeven analysis and are shown in the following model.[4]

$$(4) \qquad PV = \sum_{i=1}^{n} \frac{(R_i - C_i)}{(1 + k)^i}$$

where:

PV = Present value of the new product decision
R_i = Expected new product revenue in the ith period.
C_i = Expected new product cost in the ith period.
k = Company's opportunity cost of capital.
n = Number of time periods over which the new product cost and revenue forecasts are made.

---

[3] A firm's opportunity cost of capital is a percentage or rate measure of the average cost of obtaining resources through all sources. The rate reflects out-of-pocket costs of funds such as the interest rate on bond indebtedness, and also less tangible costs such as increase in risk of business operation caused by greater debt.

[4] The concept of present value is discussed in Eugene M. Lerner and William T. Carleton, *A Theory of Financial Analysis* (New York: Harcourt, Brace & World, 1966), pp. 37–41.

While a discounted cash flow model improves upon breakeven analyses by explicitly evaluating the time pattern of new product costs and revenue, needed information and estimates are more difficult to obtain. Management must begin by deciding how many time periods into the future over which to evaluate a new product opportunity. The benefits of explicitly considering additional product life cycle stages must be weighed against the increasing difficulty of accurately forecasting future events as the time horizon is extended further and further. Management must design strategy for each of the time periods, determine costs of strategies, and forecast demand in each period. With these estimates and the company's opportunity cost of capital, the present value of the profits expected from the new product can be calculated. Then, present value of expected future profits is compared with the required investment to decide whether or not to introduce a new product into market targets. A present value greater than the required investment would support introducing the new product, while a present value less than the investment would support dropping the new product from further consideration.

There is no explicit treatment in model (4) of managerial uncertainty as to the accuracy of revenue and cost estimates. This could be formally incorporated by requiring management to supply a subjective probability estimate, p_s, of the likelihood of obtaining the calculated present value. This uncertainty estimate is then used to weight the present value of the profit expected (EPV) from a new product before a comparison is made with the required investment. In equation form, the weighted discounted cash flow is:

$$(5) \qquad EPV = p_s \left(\sum_{i=1}^{n} \frac{R_i - C_i}{(1 + k)^i} \right)$$

Another method for incorporating uncertainty asks management to supply a subjective probability estimate (S_{pi}) of achieving each time period's profit flow. This explicitly recognizes that management's uncertainty may change as estimates are made for time periods further and further into the future. The model would then be:

$$(6) \qquad EPV = \sum_{i=1}^{n} S_{pi} \left(\frac{R_i - C_i}{(1 + k)^i} \right)$$

None of the discounted cash flow models simultaneously consider alternative strategies and tactics for a new product. Of course, models (4), (5) or (6) could be reused for each strategy management wishes to consider in order to compare their relative attractiveness. Yet, management must decide to evaluate alternative strategies independent from any guidance provided by the model.

Bayesian Decision Model

A more detailed and flexible framework for evaluating new product opportunities is provided by application of a Bayesian decision model. This model allows management to explicitly evaluate alternative new product strategies by requiring management to provide payoff estimates for each of several decision combinations that might be employed. In addition, uncertainty felt by management about future payoffs is incorporated into the evaluation through subjective probability estimates of various events occurring that will affect payoffs (e.g., competition entering with a similar new product). Finally, the advantages of the discounted cash flow model can be retained by requiring that payoffs be estimated as discounted profits over a predetermined number of time periods.

An illustrative application of a Bayesian decision model is shown in Figure 15–1. Suppose a firm is evaluating the opportunity presented by a radically new automated aerosol filling machine to be sold to both

FIGURE 15–1

Illustrative Bayesian Decision Model Application to a New Product Evaluation

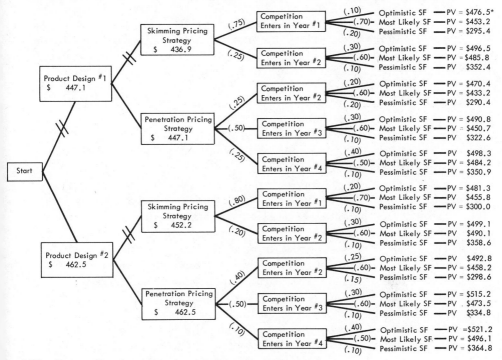

* PV = Present value of net income for 4 year forecast period in $000.

contract packagers and large consumer goods firms. While target markets have been identified and a distribution and promotional strategy decided upon, management is still considering the best product design (two alternatives are possible) and price. Also, management is uncertain about how quickly its major competitors will introduce a competitive machine, and about the level of sales that can be achieved in each of the four years following introduction. To evaluate these decision alternatives, management elects to assess the present value of future profits expected over this four year period. Specification of these factors affecting the new product decision allows the construction of the decision tree in Figure 15–1. For each branch of the tree management must supply estimates (based on information accumulated at the time of the analysis and judgment) of the likelihood of each competitive response and each (optimistic, most likely, and pessimistic) sales forecast in terms of subjective probability, and the present value payoff. With these inputs, the relative attractiveness of each new product strategy alternative can be assessed. Based on the inputs given, the best set of decisions is to introduce product design 2 with a penetration pricing strategy which has an expected net income of $462,500.

Simulation Models

The Bayesian model yields a single expected value for each of the strategy alternatives specified by management. This value is really the mean of a distribution of values that might be achieved with a particular strategy. In some cases, management may want to know the entire distribution for each strategy alternative since the dispersions and ranges of the distributions may be helpful in selecting the best strategy for the firm. For example, Figure 15–2 shows a new product strategy decision where the highest expected value strategy might not be best for the firm. Strategy 2 has the higher expected rate of return (the mean of distribution 2 is greater than the mean of distribution 1), but also has a much wider range of values that might possibly occur. On the other hand, Strategy 1 has a much narrower range of possible rates of return with higher probabilities of achieving a rate of return close to the expected rate of return. A conservative management might select Strategy 1 even though the expected rate of return is lower than Strategy 2 in order to avoid the chances of obtaining returns much lower than the expected return. A more risk-oriented management may find strategy 2 more attractive because of the higher expected value and the higher probabilities of achieving even greater rates of return.

Including entire probability distributions for possible decision payoffs from alternative new product strategies requires the use of a simulation

FIGURE 15–2

Estimated Probability Distributions of Rate of Return for Two Alternative New Product Strategies

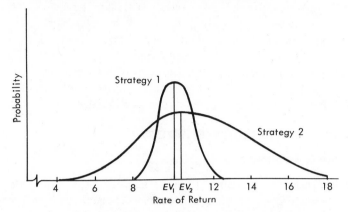

Source: Reprinted with permission from Kotler, "Computer Simulation in the Analysis of New-Product Decisions," p. 298.

model.[5] For example, if management can supply possible payoffs and corresponding probabilities for each of the uncontrolled variables in the model shown in Figure 15–1 (e.g., the mean, .25, and .75 quartile values of sales forecasts and competitive responses), then distributions for each variable can be developed. Simulation would then be used to extend the expected value outputs to entire probability distributions enabling a more complete evaluation of the strategy alternatives.

In general, simulation models are used to enable management to consider more of the many complexities of real world new product decisions. For example, simulation may be needed when there is a very large number of decision alternatives to consider, when the interrelationships between a new product and existing company products must be included in the evaluation, and when the model structure is too complicated to solve for an optimal strategy.[6] Simulation approaches are a rather recent development and are clearly still evolving for use in new product evaluations.

Selection of a model should be based on the relative ability of various

[5] A model developed by Edgar Pessemier for generating such distributions is presented and discussed in Kotler, "Computer Simulation in the Analysis of New-Product Decisions," pp. 297–303.

[6] For examples see Kotler, "Computer Simulation in the Analysis of New-Product Decisions," pp. 303–12 for presentation and discussion of the DEMON and SPRINTER Simulation Models.

models to incorporate management's desired decision objectives as well as on management's ability to understand and use model outputs. Once a model has been selected, the application should not be viewed as a single, separate stage in a new product decision process. Rather, the model is a framework providing direction for the entire evaluation process. A model should be applied several times during the process as more and more information is accumulated. At each application point, the model is used to assess the decision implications of the progress to date, then guide the activities needed to improve subsequent evaluations until management is satisfied that an action decision can be made.

DEVELOPING NEW PRODUCT STRATEGY

New Product Development

Ideas that pass the screening stage are usually insufficiently developed for extensive testing of customer acceptance. Consequently, a potentially attractive idea must be developed into a functioning product actually possessing the attributes and performance characteristics that are described in the idea statement. New product development is largely a scientific and engineering task requiring the design and building of working models of the product as well as manufacturing steps and activities.

Marketing management, and particularly marketing research, can play a valuable role in the development of new products. Typically, there are several alternative designs that are technically possible. To determine which one is best, information showing preferences of customers may be needed in addition to comparative costs. Customer preferences can be obtained informally through direct contact between management of the producing firm and customers as may happen when the product is being developed for a few industrial customers. Or, preferences may be obtained through marketing research which is necessary when there are many, widely dispersed customers. For example, a marketing research technique called preference testing can be used to help choose between alternative product features to build into a particular product.[7] Suppose a firm has screened a new food product idea and is now developing the specific composition of ingredients. Management believes that a key attribute is the sweetness of the taste which can be controlled primarily by the amount of sugar added. However, development personnel are unsure about the degree of sweetness to build into the product. Preference testing is quite suited to provide needed information in this kind of situation. A sample of prospective consumers would be asked to taste

---

[7] For a discussion of preference testing, see Ralph L. Day, "Preference Tests and the Management of Product Features," *Journal of Marketing*, vol. 32, no. 3 (July 1968), pp. 24–29.

various formulations of the food product differing only in the level of sugar added. In one procedure, consumers would choose the more preferred formulation from each of several pairs of formulations (a paired-comparison preference test), after tasting both products in each pairing. These data would then be analyzed to determine the distribution of preferences over the various levels of sweetness being tested. Figure 15–3 shows an illustrative distribution of preferences for varying levels of sweetness. Sweetness level A, which corresponds to a particular sugar content, is the level preferred by the greatest number of customers. Yet, there are consumers preferring both higher and lower sweetness levels. If the new food product has no competitors, designing in the sweetness level preferred by the largest number of potential customers has obvious merit. However, if there were competitive products with sweetness at or near A, then the best strategy might be to build in a lower or higher level of sweetness to differentiate the new product and capture a larger share of a smaller consumer market.

While new product development is a technical task, this stage should be considered to be a major part of the total evaluation of a new product idea. New product development will often uncover alternative designs that will achieve performance objectives. The interaction between marketing and technical personnel in determining which of the alternatives can best meet objectives will aid in the evaluation of market response or demand for the new product idea. Moreover, this evaluation can provide information for the design and testing of various components of the entire new product strategy beyond the physical product including advertising appeals, personal selling presentations, and point of purchase themes.

New product development also provides essential information for

FIGURE 15–3

An Illustrative Sweetness Preference Distribution

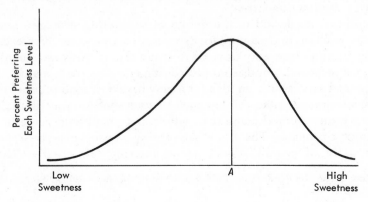

estimating costs of manufacturing, packaging, and distributing the new product. Such costs are required in all new product evaluation models discussed in the previous section. Finally, the development stage can be a rejection point in the new product decision process when: (1) the idea is not technically feasible to build, (2) the product can only be built with substantial, undesirable modifications, or (3) costs of development or production are prohibitive. As an example, a Minnesota Mining and Manufacturing Co. (3M) new product idea involving the commercial farming of oysters in a controlled situation was rejected because a small farming venture showed that it was not possible to cultivate enough oysters to make the idea financially attractive to 3M.[8]

Design and Tests of Supporting Strategies

Immediately after an idea has passed screening, work can also begin on the design and testing of supporting strategies. These strategies consist of all those marketing mix components that are required to support the introduction of a new product including advertising appeals, layouts, and media; personal selling time allocations and presentations; brand name and image; packaging; pricing; channel configuration and organizations; customer service; and sales promotion appeals, layouts, and media. Of particular importance is the design of a coordinated set of supporting strategies to complement and enhance the selling strengths of the new product idea.

Chapters 16 through 21 discuss in depth the design and implementation of these supporting strategies, so a comprehensive coverage of this topic is not presented here. However, several characteristics of this stage in the new product decision process are important. Design of supporting strategies can take place simultaneously with the development of the idea into a functioning product. An idea description should provide enough direction for this task and so the total lead time between screening and an introduction decision can be significantly cut by performing the two activities concurrently.

In addition, as an aid to the design of supporting strategies, tests of customer reaction to design alternatives can be conducted. For example, word association tests may be used to study the meaning or connotation of various proposed brand names to consumers. Suppose a manufacturer has screened successfully an idea for a new breakfast food product that is high in nutritional value. To enhance this key nutrition attribute, management wants a brand name that will connote high food value to market target customers. The firm's advertising agency may be asked to submit a list of possible brand names meeting this criteria. Then, a

---

[8] "How Ideas Are Made Into Products At 3M", *Business Week*, September 15, 1973, p. 227.

sample of consumers would be asked to listen to each one and to say the first thing that comes to their mind. From this data brand names that consistently elicited responses having nothing to do with food value or nutrition or suggesting lack of food value can be weeded out. Similarly, package tests may involve asking a small sample of customers to examine and evaluate alternative package designs. In one such test, management learned that customers wanted to see the product before making a buying decision. So the package was designed with a clear plastic "window" so that customers could see the package contents without actually opening the package. Supporting strategy tests frequently utilize small sample size in order to hold down the total costs of this stage while permitting a number of such tests to be conducted.

Finally, tests of supporting strategies differ significantly from marketing research intended to estimate demand. The results of the small scale tests are too limited in scope to provide much aid in demand forecasting since they usually cover only one or at best a few of the supporting strategy components and are restricted in sample size. However, it is possible for the tests to provide inputs into the product development and/or target market decision. For example, a package test may provide product design constraints for product development if a new product is to be compatible with a particular package design most preferred by customers.

TESTS OF MARKET ACCEPTANCE

A critical part of the new product evaluation process is to estimate and assess market target response to a new product strategy. The task is to determine whether demand will be sufficiently great *for the proposed product* to warrant introducing it into selected target markets. Hopefully, the existence of an unfulfilled need has already been established by the time management reaches this stage.

New product decisions often require forecasts over extended time periods of two, five, or even ten or more years depending upon the degree of commitment and cost structure required, in order to adequately evaluate the opportunity. Forecasting over such long periods is by nature a hazardous task due to the difficulty of foreseeing future events that will affect product performance (economic condition changes, supporting strategy effectiveness, competitive actions, customer want changes, etc.). Moreover, there is the complex task of identifying the underlying determinants of buyer decisions that may be needed to improve forecasts. While demand analysis and sales forecasting for proposed new products is a risky art rather than an unerring science, there are several marketing research techniques to aid management. Three such techniques are concept testing, product use tests and test marketing.

Concept Testing

Concept testing is capable of obtaining customer reaction to a proposed new product quite early in the new product decision process. As suggested by the name, the technique involves asking customers to evaluate the *product concept* rather than the actual product. Customers are given a description (usually pictorial and verbal) of the concept described by the new product idea statement. Then, by visualizing the attributes, performance characteristics, and actual use of the product from this concept description, customers are asked to give their reactions and probable intentions to purchase the product if introduced.

As an example, concept testing was used to aid management of a land development firm in assessing the feasibility of constructing a planned unit development on a large tract of land. In preparation for the concept test, an advertising agency was asked to draw layouts of the proposed development showing the key characteristics that were to be incorporated into the total project. Figure 15–4 shows one drawing that was intended

FIGURE 15–4

Concept Test Layout of Multiunit Housing Design and Spacing

to show customers the design of the units, the amount of space between all units, and some of the recreation amenities that were planned. Management believed these were important features to potential customers. Figure 15–5 is an aerial-view drawing of the development intended to give customers a more encompassing perspective of the entire development. This drawing emphasized the amount of "green space" between units, the easy access to units, and a more complete picture of recreational alternatives. Together the drawings gave customers a visual aid in imagining what the planned development would offer, particularly emphasizing the features that were thought to be key determinants of their housing decision.

After a sample was selected from the target market, personal interviews were used to gather information. An interviewer explained the purpose of the visit to respondents, then showed the drawings to them. Respondents studied the layouts carefully and asked questions about the concept. The interviewer was trained to provide details about the de-

FIGURE 15–5

Concept Test Layout of Total Planned Housing Development

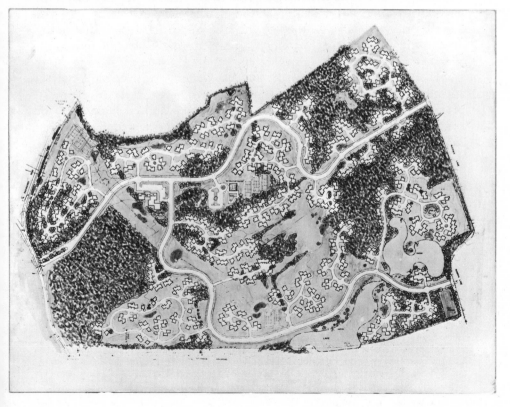

velopment. Thus, respondents had both a pictorial and verbal description of the housing concept. After the interviewer was satisfied that the respondent understood the concept, questions were asked to obtain reactions to the proposed development. These questions concerned (1) current housing usage; (2) attitudes toward the key characteristics of the development; (3) preferences for alternative design options; (4) intentions to purchase given certain prices; and (5) classificatory characteristics of respondents. This information was then analyzed to determine the extent of interest and buying intentions. For example, it is common for a management to feel that a very high percentage (between 80 and 90 percent) of respondents must show a positive buying intention to indicate that the new product idea being tested is sufficiently attractive to warrant either further evaluation or introduction.[9]

Concept testing should not be viewed as a highly accurate sales forecasting technique. Clearly, potential customers are reacting to the concept and not the product itself. The accuracy of the resulting data is dependent upon respondents ability to actually visualize the product and imagine how it would be used to satisfy their needs. Some individuals are more capable of doing this than others. Moreover, since a respondent's ability to visualize a product is partially dependent on the pictorial layouts and verbal description, the accuracy of results also depends on the quality of the devices used to aid the respondent in understanding the concept. In a sense, concept testing is actually testing the layouts and descriptions as well as the product concept.

Offsetting the weaknesses of concept testing are several important advantages. Concept testing does not require the existence of an actual product to collect demand information. Thus, this approach may provide key information needed by management to decide whether to commit considerable resources to product development. Or, concept testing may be used when an introduction decision must be made before product development can be completed. For example, in the land development firm's decision to introduce a new planned unit development, no units could be developed on a small scale for testing. So, concept testing was the only feasible marketing research test of demand.

Also, concept testing is inexpensive relative to other marketing research alternatives. The land development concept test was conducted for less than $10,000. Yet, a product use test or market test can cost from $20,000 to $500,000 or more depending upon the sample size and other research design considerations. Reasons for the lower cost include (1) a less complex and costly procedure for collecting information; (2) no

---

[9] James W. Taylor, John J. Houlahan, and Alan C. Gabriel, "The Purchase Intention Question in New Product Development: A Field Test," *Journal of Marketing*, vol. 39, no. 1 (January 1975), p. 90, published by the American Marketing Association.

costs of producing product prototypes since none are required, and (3) often a smaller sample size is used due to managements' greater tolerance for forecasting error at earlier stages in a new product decision process.

Finally, concept testing can uncover important problems with a new product idea that may or may not be able to be overcome through product development or design of selling strategy. For example, Brown & Williamson Tobacco Company used concept tests to obtain consumer reaction to a new cigarette paper design intended to cause cigarettes to even out tar delivery throughout a smoke. Typically, cigarettes increase tar delivery considerably from first to last puff. Concept testing indicated a serious problem when potential consumers in the sample said that they believed that the new cigarette would burn faster than cigarettes already on the market even though lab tests had shown that the burning time was not faster.[10]

Product Use Tests

Similar to concept testing, product use tests are usually designed to provide information only about the performance characteristics and attributes (including price) of the product rather than about both the product and its supporting selling strategy. Yet, the procedure gives potential customers the chance to examine and use the actual new product prior to providing information through a questionnaire. Respondents in the sample do not have to visualize or imagine using a product, but can actually try the product in a situation similar to that in which the product would be used if it had been purchased.

As an illustrative example of a product use test, consider a package-goods firm evaluating the probable demand for a proposed new deodorant. To set up the test, a representative sample of potential consumers is asked to participate in a research study. Respondents fill out a questionnaire to provide information about their current use of deodorant products including frequency of use, brand preferences, preferred application method, and deodorant attribute preferences, as well as classificatory characteristics. Upon completing this questionnaire respondents are given a supply of several deodorants to try for a period of time (say, two weeks). The new product being tested is not labeled and is to be used along with one other unlabeled product. Instructions are to use one product the first week and then switch to the second product the next week. The other product may be an existing brand (though the respondents would not know this) and/or an alternative new product

---

[10] Cornelius S. Muije, "How Decisions Are Made to Stop Developing or Testing New Products," *1973 Combined Proceedings* (Chicago: American Marketing Association, 1974), p. 161.

formulation that is under consideration. After the use period is over, respondents are asked to describe their reactions to the products and intentions to purchase each one. The questions asked would be quite similar, though in greater detail, to the questions asked for a concept test, since the research objective is essentially the same. Of course, when more than one product has been used by respondents, then comparison type questions can be asked (e.g., which of the products do you most prefer and why?). If an existing deodorant brand has been used, the analysis of the data can relate respondents' reaction to the new product to their reaction to a brand having known market acceptance. For example, suppose the distribution of responses to a five point intentions question for the new deodorant were more positively skewed than for a popular existing brand, such as is shown in Table 15–1. Management could then compare responses both to a predetermined decision rule (e.g., 70 percent of respondents must have a positive intention to buy to continue developing the product and supporting strategy) and to the intentions generated by a brand with known sales and/or market share (e.g., positive intentions must at least equal the intentions level for the competitive brand).

TABLE 15–1

Illustrative Intentions Response Distributions

Intentions Response Categories	New Deodorant Formulation	Popular Deodorant Brand
Definitely would buy	30%	25%
Probably would buy	45%	40%
May or may not buy	8%	10%
Probably would not buy	12%	15%
Definitely would not buy	5%	10%
Total respondents	100%	100%

A product use test is generally more expensive than a concept test. The product development activity must be sufficiently far along to allow actual manufacture of enough units to conduct the test. The cost of this small supply would be part of the total cost of the research. Moreover, the task presented to respondents is more complex and time consuming. To encourage respondents to participate, a product test may require some form of respondent payment such as a gift, which must also be included in the cost of the research. These two costs alone would push the total cost of a product use test beyond that of a concept test even for comparable sample sizes.

In return for higher costs, management usually has more confidence in the accuracy of the data than for a concept test. This is achieved because of the elimination of reliance upon customer imaginations. In most other respects the kinds of questions asked and data analyses performed in concept and product use tests are quite similar.

Market Testing

While product use tests obtain customer reaction to the actual use of the product, forecasts of demand must be based on opinions and intentions to purchase. This kind of information does not directly show what will happen when the product is offered for sale. Moreover, product use tests do not test reaction to the entire marketing strategy, but are limited to information concerning the product itself. For these reasons, a management having insufficient certainty about a new product opportunity even after product use tests may decide to implement a test market.

Market testing is a marketing research technique intended to duplicate a real market situation for the new product on a much smaller scale. Since the product is offered for sale in a restricted market, there is the opportunity to test the product and the supporting strategy at much less cost than would be needed for a full scale introduction. For example, in a market test a manufacturer of a new consumer packaged product may use salesmen to obtain shelf space in retail stores; employ a "normal" advertising budget, media, and appeals; charge the intended price; set up customer service procedures; and so forth. Thus, customer decisions to buy (or not buy) the product are really market reactions to the entire strategy.

In establishing a test market, decisions must be made on at least three design features: (1) the number and selection of geographic test areas (usually cities), (2) the strategy alternatives to be tested, and (3) the data to be collected. Since each of these features affects the usefulness of the test market to management as well as cost, design decisions should be made jointly by management and research experts.

Test Cities. Choosing test cities for the research is actually a sampling decision. Management wants to project results from test markets to entire target markets. Selection of candidate cities should be based on an analysis of population characteristics within various cities in order to identify those that have concentrations of potential customers. Then, an appropriate number of cities is determined by weighing cost against management's information needs and accuracy requirements. Finally, cities should be randomly selected from a list of candidate cities to meet the predetermined sample size. In past practice, particularly for large firms expecting to introduce a new product into national markets, this procedure has been implemented by using a few, large "favorite" cities that were believed to be representative of the nation based on analysis of demographic and socioeconomic characteristics (e.g., Rochester, New York; Hartford, Connecticut; and Columbus, Ohio).[11] However, this selection procedure has a number of drawbacks including (1) possible reduction of market representativeness due to continual use as test market cities and due to multiple tests being conducted at the same time; (2) the ease with which competition can discover that a new product introduction is being evaluated; and (3) the questionable ability of a few cities to be representative of the entire U.S.[12] Some firms are selecting a greater number of smaller, more widely dispersed cities to overcome these difficulties.

Strategies to Be Tested. Cost aside, test marketing is quite flexible in providing strategy performance information. In some situations, management may wish to use test marketing as a kind of "dress rehearsal" for a single strategy that is already believed to be best. Here, management's uncertainty is less concerned with which strategy will perform best, but with the extent of opportunity that can be achieved. In other situations, test marketing may be used to help management evaluate the relative performance of two or more strategic alternatives. Each alternative is tried in a different set of test cities. For example, a firm may want to test the effectiveness of different levels of advertising expenditures to support a new product introduction. Cities would have to be selected that are not only representative of target markets, but are also quite similar to each other so that any differences in strategy performance could be attributed to the different advertising budgets rather than to any test city differences.

Data Collected. Finally, the kinds of data collected must be determined based on an information cost-benefit analysis. Options include collecting product-movements, sales, and/or customer panel data. Product-movement data measures the physical movement of products through intermediaries (e.g., wholesalers, warehouses). By auditing or counting the number of units flowing through intermediaries, management can estimate the sales of the new product in test markets. Typically, this is the least costly data from which customer reaction can be estimated. Yet, it is also a crude measure since there is little indication of how many of these units are being purchased by end-user customers and how many are being inventoried by other firms in the channel. To improve the data, actual sales of the product can be audited, though this is likely to be more expensive. Records have to be kept of beginning and ending inventories and purchases of test market intermediaries sell-

---

[11] "Test Marketing: The Most Dangerous Game in Marketing," *Marketing Insights* (October 9, 1967), p. 17.

[12] Ibid.

ing directly to end-user customers. Sales can then be calculated for each time period (e.g., weekly, bi-weekly, monthly) by using the following relationship:

Sales = Beginning inventory + Purchases − Ending inventory

For products that are sold through certain kinds of retailers (super markets and discount drug stores) there are standardized information services such as A. C. Nielsen Company and Audits & Survey & Company, Inc. that can be used for this purpose.

In addition to audit data, management may require information that will aid in the analysis of sales. For example, management may want to know how much of sales is accounted for by customers buying for the first time vs. customers buying the product again (repeat buying). Or, management may need to know why some potential customers did not buy the first time or have decided not to repurchase the product again. These kinds of questions can best be answered from data generated from a customer panel established at the beginning of the test period. In each test market city, a sample of customers representative of target markets would be selected for a panel. Of course, respondents would not be aware of the reason for the panel, since a research objective is to measure how quickly panel participants become sufficiently aware of the new product to make a purchase decision. Then, the panel would periodically provide diary or questionnaire data on their product and brand purchases within selected product categories. Moreover, panel members can be asked to give opinions of products/brands purchased and not purchased.

Of particular importance is the data showing first time and repeat purchases of the new product. An important advantage of the panel research design is that it allows data to be collected from the same respondent at several different points in time so that subsequent analyses can actually follow the purchasing activity of customers over time. Data can be analyzed by using transition matrices. Figure 15–6 shows an illustrative transition matrix. The column and row totals show the num-

FIGURE 15–6

Illustrative New Product Purchase Decision Transition Matrix

		No. in Time $(t + 1)$ Who		
		Bought	Did Not Buy	
No. in Time (t) Who	Bought	63	22	85
	Did Not Buy	154	169	323
		217	191	408

FIGURE 15–7

Illustrative Prediction of Long Run Cumulative Trial Rate

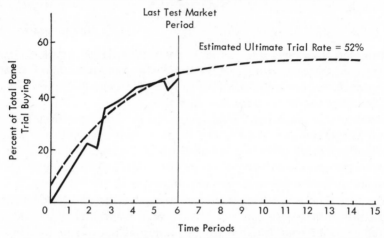

Source: Adapted with permission from David H. Ahl, "New Product Forecasting Using Consumer Panels," *Journal of Marketing Research,* 7 (May 1970), pp. 160–62. Published by the American Marketing Association.

ber of respondents in the total sample of 408 that purchased the new product in each time period (e.g., in time t, 85 bought the new product and 323 did not, while in time $(t + 1)$ 217 bought and 191 did not). The cell figures show the number of respondents who bought (did not buy) in $t + 1$ out of those who bought (did not buy) in time t. For example, of the 85 respondents who bought the new product in time t, 63 bought in time $t + 1$ while 22 did not buy in $t + 1$. Such information analyzed over several time periods can be used to aid management in estimating long run trial (first time) sales and repeat sales. The key forecast for infrequently purchased products (e.g., large appliances) would be first-time sales, while a frequently purchased new product (e.g., food products) would require forecasts of repeat sales to adequately evaluate the opportunity.

Customer panel data allows management to employ forecasting models to estimate long-run sales and market share. Essentially, currently developed models attempt to project trial and repeat purchases in the early stages of the test market to future time periods.[13] Customer panel data is used to estimate the parameters of a known distribution that is assumed to characterize buying of new products. This is illustrated in Figures

[13] For examples, see J. H. Parfitt and B. J. K. Collins, "The Use of Consumer Panels for Brand Share Predictions," *Journal of Marketing Research,* 5 (May 1968), pp. 131–46; W. F. Massy, "Forecasting the Demand for New Convenience Products," *Journal of Marketing Research,* 6 (November 1969), pp. 405–13; and Gerald J. Eskin, "Dynamic Forecasts of New Product Demand Using a Depth of Repeat Model," *Journal of Marketing Research,* 10 (May 1973), pp. 115–29.

15–7 and 15–8 where the solid lines are plotted from test market consumer panel data and the dotted lines are the fitted distributions projected into time periods beyond the test market. Of course, as new data is accumulated during the test market, the model can be updated to correct previous projections.

Using the projected cumulative trial rate and repeat purchase rate curves (models), target market sales can be forecasted for individual time periods and accumulated over time periods by using the following relationships:

(7)   Market Share = Estimated Trial rate × Estimated repeat rate

(8)   Sales in Test Market = Market Share × Market Population
$$\times \text{ Consumption per Family}$$

(9)   Sales in Total Market

$$= \text{Sales in Test Market} \times \frac{\text{Total Market Population}}{\text{Test Market Population}}$$
$$\times \text{ Correction Factors}[14]$$

Information for equation 7 is obtained from fitted distributions such as shown in Figures 15–7 and 15–8. Trial and repeat rate estimates may be for a specific future time period or expected ultimate rates that will

FIGURE 15–8

Illustrative Prediction of Long Run Repeat Purchase Rate

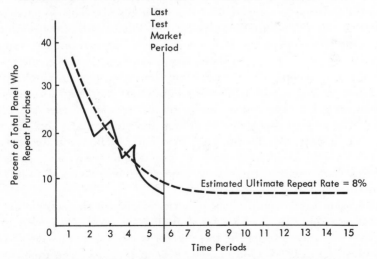

Source: Adapted with permission from David H. Ahl, "New Product Forecasting Using Consumer Panels," *Journal of Marketing Research*, 7 (May 1970), pp. 162–63. Published by the American Marketing Association.

---

[14] These relationships and required data are discussed in David H. Ahl, "New Product Forecasting Using Consumer Panels," *Journal of Marketing Research*, 7 (May 1970), pp. 160–67.

be achieved. The output of equation 7 is a market share of the panel consumers obtained by the new product. Equation 8 projects the panel market share to expected sales in the entire test market. Assuming the panel is representative of the test market, panel market share should be a good estimate of test city's market share for the new product. So, market share multiplied by test market population will yield number of purchasers in the test market. To obtain test market new product sales, number of purchasers must be multiplied by the average usage or consumption per family. This estimate is made from panel data on frequency and quantity of purchases by respondents. Finally, test market sales are projected to total target markets by equation 9. Assuming the test market is representative of target markets, test market sales is multiplied by the relative size of target markets to test market and then adjusted by correction factors, if necessary. These correction factors represent managements judgment about possible differences between test and target markets. For instance, management may feel that distribution has been better in the test market area than can be expected for national distribution. A correction factor would be included to adjust sales downward (i.e., the correction factor would be a number less than 1.0) to account for this difference.

Test marketing is not without several problems that must be weighed by management in deciding whether to use the technique. One of the most serious concerns the actions of competitors. A competitor with a well-functioning marketing intelligence system may discover the existence of a test market and begin to monitor results. This is particularly dangerous when there are no barriers to duplicating the new product by competitors. A competitor willing to take more risk can quickly duplicate the product and be ready to enter target markets before or along with the innovating company while avoiding the expense of conducting their own research. For example, General Foods test marketed an innovative snack product later introduced under the brand name *Toast'em Popups*. Kellogg Co. was able to go into national distribution at about the same time with a very similar product, *Pop-Tarts*, without a test market. General Food's management believes that Kellogg was able to accomplish this feat because they were able to "read" General Food's test market results.[15]

In addition, some competitors may try to disrupt the conducting of a test market. This can be done by changing the selling situation in any one of several ways so that the test market is less representative of target markets than intended. One maneuver is to buy up large quantities of the new product. This is particularly devastating since it can overstate test market sales forecasts while being very difficult to catch by the test marketing firm. It may also mean that the new product ends up being

---

[15] "Test Marketing: The Most Dangerous Game in Marketing," p. 16.

introduced with flaws that might otherwise have been caught during the test. Another tactic is to create an unrealistic competitive situation by overspending on advertising or by significant reductions in price. For example, when Procter & Gamble test marketed Crisco Oil, a smaller competitor cut the price of its own product in the test market. P&G was aware of the tactic and retaliated by cutting the price on Crisco Oil, but could not force the competitor to return to a realistic price.[16] In this case, even though P&G knew about the action there was little that could be done to correct the market test. The price cutting by both companies simply made the test market more and more unrealistic, since these were not prices that would be maintained in all target markets. Disruption of test markets is not illegal, but ethically it is very questionable. Often, the customer pays the price for this practice in terms of buying flawed products introduced too soon, higher prices on products that must absorb the costs of product failures, and unavailability of potentially useful and successful products erroneously withdrawn based on test market results. Yet, in spite of the questionable ethics, disruption appears to be a reality that must be considered when deciding to test market.

An equally serious problem can be created by company personnel who are responsible for the conducting of the test market and who are emotionally committed to the success of a particular new product. Intentionally or unintentionally, personnel may rig the test market to obtain results that will ensure that the hoped-for introduction decision will be made. Rigging may show up as unusually aggressive selling to retailers, larger than usual advertising expenditures, overuse of promotional tactics (e.g., coupons), and unusual display conditions. In all of these tactics, the fact that the supporting strategy or tactics are in some way unusual means that the test market is not really an accurate indication of the kind of support the new product is likely to receive in target markets after introduction. For example, a food manufacturer decided to introduce a meat product that had very favorable test market results. The product failed nationally because a technical flaw had not been caught by the test market. Personnel implementing the test market had set up ideal display conditions for the product, but in the more normal situation found in retail stores nationally, fluorescent glare in display cases turned the meat blue.[17] A less enthusiastic and more normal display set-up during test market would have probably caught the flaw and led to more product development. Test market results can be adjusted downward for this "overenthusiasm bias," but it is difficult to know when and to what extent the bias is represented in the data.

Finally, there is a risk of selecting the wrong cities for testing a particular product. The difficulty of anticipating all conditions under which

---

[16] Ibid., p. 17.
[17] Ibid., p. 18.

a product should be tested means that this risk is impossible to eliminate. For example, Dow Chemical Co. chose to test market a new lubricant for use in outboard motors in Florida. The rationale was sound since the lubricant would be in greater use during the year and so, provide a more demanding test of product performance. However, in Florida motors are not stored for the winter. It so happened that under cold weather conditions, the lubricant congealed allowing stored outboard motors to rust. The Florida test markets never uncovered this product flaw. (Fortunately, Dow also test marketed the product in Michigan where the flaw was discovered).[18]

Alternative Techniques to Test Marketing. Recently, modified test market techniques have been developed that are intended to overcome some of these problems. An example is the Simulated Store Technique.[19] Sample groups of respondents (representative of target markets) are brought to a predesignated location where they are exposed to advertising commercials in the context of program material and other commercials. Then, respondents are given money and asked to shop in a simulated store (a store set up to duplicate an actual retail store with shelving, product assortments, point-of-purchase displays, aisle, and so forth). They may use the money to buy products or can keep all or part of it. After shopping, respondents participate in a group interview to discuss reasons for their purchase decisions. Finally, respondents are contacted two or three weeks later to determine their usage of a new product, satisfaction with it, and intentions to buy it again.[20] The advantage of this technique is that it maintains competitive secrecy of the test while still obtaining information concerning actual customer purchase decisions. Yet, the technique differs from test marketing in that the data are primarily on trial purchases, since measuring repeat purchase experience is not possible. Moreover, there is no opportunity to fully test the distribution, after-sale customer service, and personal selling components of supporting strategy.

Overview of Demand Analysis

An appropriate perspective on marketing research techniques for demand analysis should include several factors. First, at least a tentative selection of target markets must take place prior to conducting these tests. Analysis of market opportunities during the idea generation and/or the

---

[18] Ibid.

[19] Pieter P. deKadt, "New Techniques in Evaluating Test Markets," in Fred C. Allvine (ed.), *1971 Combined Proceedings* (Chicago: American Marketing Association, 1972), pp. 154–57. This article contains a more detailed discussion of four alternatives to test marketing and their advantages and disadvantages.

[20] Ibid., p. 155.

screening stage will provide the basis for the initial target market identification. This is essential since demand analysis tests require the drawing of representative samples of potential customers so that projections can be made from test results to target markets. Such projections are clearly evident in equations 7, 8, and 9. The analysis of demand test data may, in turn, enable management to adjust and refine their understanding and selection of target markets by providing additional information on customer characteristics, opinions, and preferences.

To some extent, one test may be substituted for another. For example, more extensive product-use tests may be used instead of a market test when management believes a market test will alert competitors to the new product decision being made. Alternatively firms may decide to use some combination of the tests at different stages of product development. A concept test may help management decide whether to commit resources to product development. Then, product-use tests may be conducted to determine whether a particular product design will generate consumer response. This may be followed by a market test to estimate long term sales and to test an entire strategy.

Finally, while all of the techniques generate information for demand analysis, there are important differences. Each technique collects inherently different information on customer response ranging from the concept test's measurement of reaction to an idea to the market test's measurement of purchase decisions (sales). Balancing these information differences are substantial cost differences. Thus, cost-benefit information analysis are crucial to deciding if and when to use these techniques for demand analyses.

NEW PRODUCT INTRODUCTIONS

At some point, the evaluation of a proposed new product must end, and a decision on whether to introduce the product into selected target markets is made. This decision is based on management's assessment of the degree to which the product and supporting strategy can be expected to achieve objectives, and the degree of confidence management has in the assessments. While decision models and research information greatly help management, the ultimate decision on whether to introduce a new product is dependent on managerial judgment.

Introduction Timing Alternatives

The decision to introduce a new product begins a series of resource commitments required to operationalize a total new product strategy. Raw material and component contracts must be made with suppliers;

specific channel of distribution organizations must be lined up; manufacturing facilities, equipment, and processes must be built, bought, and set into operation; salesmen may need hiring and/or training, and so forth. Generally, such commitments involve very large amounts of company resources. For example, when Rapid Data Systems and Equipment Ltd. decided to introduce the Rapidman 800 handheld calculator into mass consumer markets, suppliers of components for 100,000 calculators (an initial order only) had to be found; major retail stores such as Montgomery Ward, the May Company stores, and Alexander's were signed by contract as outlets in the U.S.; and a production process eventually capable of producing 2,500 units per day had to be established.[21] Such major commitments must be planned and coordinated to ensure a smooth introduction process. Moreover, management must determine a time horizon over which the introduction will take place. Options include a "crash" introduction or some variation of a "rollout" introduction.

Crash Introduction. A crash introduction involves a decision to reach full-scale commercialization of a new product as quickly as possible. This requires a rather immediate commitment of all resources required to move into target markets, but allows the least amount of time for competitors to prepare their responses to the new product. Thus, if a firm has sufficient resources available, a crash program would be most likely selected when competition can counter rather quickly, and maximum lead time to establish market position is needed. Of course, a crash introduction tends to also maximize risk since all resources are committed very quickly.

Rollout Introduction. The alternative to crashing is to introduce a new product on a rollout basis. Target markets must be divided into several geographic areas into which the company will sequentially introduce the new product. The general procedure is to select one or more, but not all, geographic areas for initial introduction, and then sufficient resources are committed to establish a supply capability for these areas. If the new product is successful, the process continues until all target geographic markets are being served.

Rollout offers several advantages over crashing. By moving more slowly into target markets, management has more time to monitor the degree of success achieved by a new product before all resources are committed. Thus, management can control risk to some degree by holding down resource commitments while additional information is gathered. This is not the same as continuing the test market stage since an introduction decision has been made, much larger market areas are

---

[21] Christopher S. Redabock, "From Office Equipment to Mass Merchandising: Getting New Products to New Markets," in Blair Little (ed.), *New Products, New Markets* (London, Canada: Research and Publications Division, School of Business Administration, The University of Western Ontario, 1973), pp. 47–48.

entered, and a less elaborate monitoring of performance is conducted. Yet, management does get more time to assess the wisdom of the decision to introduce. In addition, the rollout procedure is the only one feasible for the firm with insufficient resources available for the crash program.

At least partially offsetting these advantages is the fact that competitors gain valuable time to determine and implement a response to the new product. Moreover, revenues are being foregone in all markets not initially entered which should be viewed as an opportunity cost. Thus, the decision on whether to rollout, as well as the speed of rolling out, should be based on four factors: (1) management's confidence in the decision to introduce; (2) the time needed for competitors to respond; (3) availability of resources for the new product introduction; and (4) the level of resources required for full scale introduction.

Management of New Products after Introduction

After introducing a new product into target markets, management's task changes from development and evaluation to control of performance. In fact, a major post-introduction decision is the timing of the transfer of responsibility from new product management to existing product management. The nature of the transfer depends on the new product's relationship to products in the firm's product mix as well as on the type of marketing organization being used. For example, if new product management was organized as a venture team, then the transfer may involve a new corporate division being established with the venture team personnel becoming divisional managers. Or, if the new product is related to one or more existing products and the new product management is part of a separate new product function in the firm, profit responsibility may be transferred to a brand or product manager handling a related product.

As the time lengthens since market introduction, the control task for new products becomes more and more identical to control of existing products (which is the focus for Chapter 23). However, during the early periods after introduction, management should be particularly attuned to the nature and rate of the customer adoption process occurring in the target markets. Research on new products has established the fact that individual customers go through a decision process leading toward a decision to adopt (use the product regularly) or not to adopt a new product. This process is comprised of various stages as shown in Figure 15–19. Moreover, it is known that not all individuals who ultimately decide to adopt a product, will begin this process at the same time nor will take the same amount of time to go through the process to the decision stage. This is shown in Figure 15–10.

The objectives for much of new product supporting strategy and

FIGURE 15–9

An Individual Adoption Decision Process

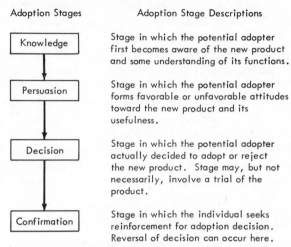

Adoption Stages   Adoption Stage Descriptions

Knowledge — Stage in which the potential adopter first becomes aware of the new product and some understanding of its functions.

Persuasion — Stage in which the potential adopter forms favorable or unfavorable attitudes toward the new product and its usefulness.

Decision — Stage in which the potential adopter actually decided to adopt or reject the new product. Stage may, but not necessarily, involve a trial of the product.

Confirmation — Stage in which the individual seeks reinforcement for adoption decision. Reversal of decision can occur here.

Source: Adapted with permission from James F. Engel, David T. Kollat, and Roger D. Blackwell, *Consumer Behavior* (New York: Holt, Rinehart and Winston, 1973, pp. 586–88.

tactics is to influence potential customers to move through the adoption stages. Thus, control is directed toward evaluating how quickly target market customers are moving through the knowledge, persuasion, and decision stages as well as watching for unusually high decision reversals. In addition, management may want to monitor how much time is being taken by innovators, early adopters, and early majority to make the

FIGURE 15–10

Distribution of New Product Adopters

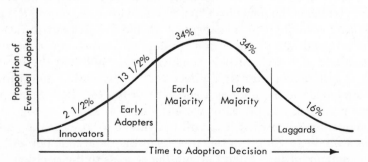

Source: Reprinted with permission from Everett M. Rogers, *Diffusion of Innovations* (New York: Free Press, 1962), p. 162.

adoption decision. Information for this control task would require customer panel information identical to that collected during a test market.

SUMMARY AND CONCLUSIONS

An analytical decision process has been presented and discussed in detail to provide an understanding of the complexity and degree of marketing managerial involvement required for new product decisions. This process is comprised of a sequence of interrelated stages beginning with idea generation and ending with the introduction and control of new products. Note how the entire analytical process helps to reduce the risk of making new product decisions. First, the process sets up a number of different decision points where management must choose to either (1) drop the product, (2) introduce the product, or (3) delay the action decision to collect more information. Thus, there are several points within the process at which management can weed out the potential new product failures.

Second, as a management team moves through the process, generally more and more resources are committed to new products that pass each decision point. This means that the process encourages the gradual commitment of resources throughout the process which tends to spread the risk of new product decisions over time. Finally, this spreading of resource commitment coincides with the collection of decision information. As a new product passes through each decision point, more information is accumulated until the decision to introduce or drop is made. This means that as more resources are required for each subsequent stage, more information is available to plug into management's evaluation model to aid in the next decision.

EXERCISES FOR REVIEW AND DISCUSSION

1. A new product development team has made the revenue and cost estimates shown in the table below for a new snack food that is being eval-

Proposed Snack Food Revenue/Cost Analysis

	Years After Introduction				
	1	*2*	*3*	*4*	*5*
Most likely sales volume (000's of units)...	275	290	500	875	1,450
Selling prices per unit..................	1.49	1.49	1.30	1.25	1.25
Annual fixed costs ($000s).............	38	38	50	50	77
Annual variable costs per unit					
Factory..........................	.25	.25	.30	.30	.35
Distribution.......................	.03	.03	.04	.04	.06
Selling............................	.40	.40	.25	.25	.20
R&D development cost...............	$100,000				
Company cost of capital..............	.12	.12	.10	.10	.10

uated. Use the breakeven model and discounted cash flow model to assess the decision alternatives (introduce vs. not introduce this product). Then compare and contrast the usefulness of these two models for helping management make new product decisions.

2. A consumer goods manufacturer recently experienced a declining "batting average" on new product decisions. You have been asked to review and evaluate the firms new product decision process to determine whether weaknesses in this process could be a cause of the problem. After extensive interviews with key personnel, you are able to describe the process as follows: R&D is given the primary responsibility for initiating new product ideas, though, on occasion, ideas have been suggested by company salesmen based on contact with retailers. A management committee is then formed to evaluate the proposed idea and consists of vice presidents from finance, manufacturing, advertising, and purchasing. If approved, the idea is passed back to R&D for prototype development. If this effort shows that the idea is technically sound, advertising is asked to develop an introduction strategy covering advertising, personal selling, and distribution. Cooperation is requested from personal in all these areas. Also, a survey of retailer reaction to the new product is conducted. At the conclusion of these activities, the management committee meets again to make a decision on whether to introduce the new product.

Evaluate both the strengths and weaknesses of this new product decision process. Make recommendations where appropriate to improve the process. (Hint: you should use both Chapters 14 and 15 to do this exercise.)

3. A test market for a new women's deodorant is currently being conducted in three cities. In each city, a consumer panel has been formed to provide needed information. Management has requested a sales forecast for the new product for the first year after introduction. Use the data in the table below to provide this sales forecast. The data summarizes the results of the three month period over which the test markets have been run to date.

	Test Market Populations	Projected Annual Trial Rate	Projected Annual Repeat Rate	Average Annual Usage Rate per Woman (number of units)	Correction Factors*
Test City 1........	1,200,000	.43	.76	5.1	.84
Test City 2........	378,000	.36	.54	4.3	.87
Test City 3........	185,000	.39	.57	4.8	.91

Note: Total target market population size = 15,000,000 females.
* Correction factors are subjective estimates by management reflecting their judgement of the representativeness of each test market.

4. "When conducting tests of market acceptance of a new product it is essential that all market opportunity analyses be completed and final deci-

sions on selection of market targets be made prior to these tests." Do you agree with this statement? Discuss.

5. New product development may be just as important for nonbusiness organizations as for business organizations. Choose one of the following kinds of organizations and adopt the analytical new product decision process presented in Chapters 14 and 15 to that organization: a church, a charity, a political candidate election organization, a hospital, or a governmental agency.

16

Channel of Distribution Strategy

Channel of distribution decisions are of vital importance to all types of firms involved in marketing activities including producers, wholesalers, and retailers. Each member of the channel system is but one link in the distribution network that spans from the producer of products or services to end users that consume them. A substantial portion of the price paid by end users for products and services is frequently accounted for by the distribution process. For example, nearly two-thirds of each dollar spent for food is used to pay for distribution and processing activities.[1] Although some firms perform all channel functions, typically, organizations are linked together in a distribution channel to perform various distribution functions such as storage, transportation, sales contact, service, and sorting and re-packaging. These middlemen or intermediaries serve as "re-marketers" (or re-sellers) in that they perform the marketing function for buyers at the next stage in the distribution channel (e.g., the wholesaler re-markets to the retailer).

The marketing system was examined in Chapter 2 to provide a perspective toward the total distribution system that links products and services with customers. The rationale for middlemen was discussed and the structure and various types of marketing institutions were described. You should review this material, since a clear understanding of middlemen and their functions is assumed in the following discussion of channel decisions from the point of view of the firm. In this and the next chapter, a perspective toward the channel system is presented followed by a discussion of channel strategy development. Decisions concerning selection of proper channels to meet a firm's needs are examined, illustrated, and approaches to analysis indicated. Next, the continuing activity of man-

---

[1] "Who Profits When Food Bills Rise," *U.S. News & World Report* (March 19, 1973), p. 21.

aging channel relationships is considered. Finally, guidelines for appraisal of channel performance are indicated.

CHANNEL SYSTEM IN PERSPECTIVE

In order to develop a general understanding of the nature and scope of the channel system, the characteristics of channels are described and illustrated, interrelationships between channel decisions and the marketing mix are discussed, and the relationship between channels and the physical distribution function is considered.

Characteristics of Channel Systems

The channel of distribution is the means by which products and services are made available to customers in the market place. It is "an organized network [system] of agencies and institutions which, in combination, perform all the activities required to link producers with users, and users with producers in order to accomplish the marketing task."[2] The channel is an integrated system made up of participants that accomplish different marketing functions through specialization of tasks and allocation of various responsibilities. Consider the various firms, functions, physical and information flows, and inter-firm relationships that are involved in transforming a steer on a ranch in Texas into a beef roast on the dinner table of a family in Washington, D.C. The animal may be sold by the rancher to a feedlot operator for fattening; purchased by a meatpacker for processing; the hind-quarter of the carcass sold to a large retail food chain; the quarter transported from the retailer's regional warehouse to a supermarket in Washington, D.C.; processed by the butcher into steaks, roasts, and ground beef; and finally packaged and arranged in the meat display case for purchase. The relative economies, technical knowledge, and experience inherent in specialization of functions that must be performed in linking products with markets bring about the need for different types of channel institutions such as processers, retailers, and other intermediaries.

An understanding of several general characteristics of distribution channels is helpful in developing a perspective toward their nature, scope, and function. These include consideration of the basic nature of the channel system, types of flows that occur in the channel, and the concept of the channel as a basic unit of competition.[3] Viewing the chan-

---

[2] Reavis Cox and Thomas F. Schutte, "A Look at Channel Management," in Philip R. McDonald (ed.), *Marketing Involvement in Society and the Economy* (Chicago: American Marketing Association, 1969), p. 100.

[3] Several channel characteristics are discussed in an excellent and comprehensive analysis of channel systems by Bert C. McCammon, Jr. and Robert W. Little, "Marketing Channels: Analytical Systems and Approaches," in George Schwartz (ed.), *Science in Marketing* (New York: John Wiley & Sons, 1965), pp. 321–85.

nel as an organized system that pursues goals that are mutually acceptable to participants, yet displays conflict as well as cooperation, is fundamental to understanding its behavior. Moreover, since end-user market targets are the final link in the channel, they should be considered a part of the overall system. The producer often exercises control of the channel organization, and there is a prevailing tendency to view the system from the manufacturer's perspective. Yet, the channel network can be examined with a focus on any level in the system (e.g., wholesaler, retailer, consumer).

While there is an inclination to focus on the flow of the actual product or service through the channel system, certain other flows are involved including transfer of ownership, information (e.g., new price list sent to distributors by a manufacturer), financial transactions, and transfer of risk (e.g., insurance on warehouse inventory).[4] Product and ownership flows are typically the most important in many channels. Yet, an understanding of all the flows is important in making effective channel decisions. For example, distortion, delays, and loss of information can seriously affect channel performance.

The channel should be viewed as a competitive unit, where firms comprising a particular vertical channel of distribution compete as a system with other channels. The channel provides the structure within which a firm's marketing mix must function. In designing marketing strategy for target markets a firm should consider the complete channel system. Focusing only on the firms that are adjacent in the distribution channel provides an incomplete perspective of markets, competitive processes, and the tasks the marketing program should be designed to perform.

Several illustrative channel systems are shown in Table 16–1 to provide an indication of how firms function within their particular distribution channels. Note for example, the relatively large and complex channel of which the grocery wholesaler is a member compared to the short, direct channel used by the computer systems manufacturer. Frequently, channel systems for industrial products are shorter and more direct than those for consumer products. Remarketers tend to be used rather than direct marketing to end users when: the number of sellers and buyers and distance of movement of products are relatively large; buyers' purchase frequency is higher; lot sizes needed by end users are smaller; and markets are more decentralized.[5]

A diagram of the channels of distribution for an importer/distributor

---

[4] These flows are examined in greater detail by George Fisk, *Marketing Systems* (New York: Harper & Row, Publishers, 1967), chapters 9–13.

[5] Louis P. Bucklin, *Competition and Evolution in the Distributive Trades* (Englewood Cliffs, N.J.: Prentice-Hall, 1972), p. 40.

TABLE 16–1

Illustrations of Channel Systems

Company	Product/Service	End-User Market Served	Participating Firms	Facilitating Firms
Burrough's Corp. (manufacturer)	Computer systems, business machines, and supplies	Business firms, government, and other institutions	Markets direct to end-users using company sales force (no participating firms are involved)	Burroughs Finance Corp.; advertising agency; transportation firms
Garcia Corp. (distributor)	Recreational equipment for fishing, hunting, camping, tennis, and skiing	Primarily ultimate consumers	Wholesalers, retailers, and manufacturers of equipment (both corporate owned and independent firms)	Advertising, transportation, financial institutions
Holiday Inns of America, Inc. (motel and hotel chain)	Motel and hotel facilities; motel equipment and services; bus and water transportation	Business and pleasure consumers of hotel and transportation services	Franchised motel operations (some owned by Holiday Inns); suppliers of services and equipment for motels (some corporate owned)	Insurance, finance, and construction firms (some corporate owned); advertising services
Royal Crown Cola Company (producer)	Carbonated beverages	Consumers	Independent and owned bottlers, brokers, food and beverage retailers	Advertising services; transportation firms
Scrivner Inc. (wholesaler)	Foods (also handles line of general merchandise)	Consumers and institutional end-users (e.g., hospitals)	Suppliers of food products (including company owned bakery, ice-cream suppliers); brokers; retailers (independent, franchised, and corporate-owned); institutional customers	Banks; transportation firms; insurance firms

FIGURE 16–1

Channels of Distribution Used by an Importer/ Distributor of Recreational Equipment (major lines include fishing tackle, sporting arms, tennis equipment, and winter sports equipment)

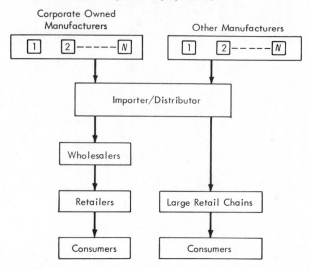

of recreational equipment is shown in Figure 16–1.[6] In this illustration we are viewing the channel system from the perspective of an intermediary rather than a manufacturer. Note the distributor's backward integration within the channel by acquisition of manufacturing firms, thus providing the distributor with greater management control over the suppliers. Similar efforts aimed at backward integration of suppliers have been accomplished by large retail chains such as Sears Roebuck and Company.

Channel Decisions and the Marketing Mix

In many firms, the channel system receives substantially less marketing management attention than personal selling, advertising, pricing, and product management.[7] This occurs, in part, because distribution functions are often carried out by several departments in a firm and because the channel is not viewed as an active variable in marketing strategy. There is also a tendency in loosely aligned systems to not consider rela-

---

[6] This discussion is based on the *1974 Annual Report* of the Garcia Corporation.

[7] Examples of management problems raised by channels are discussed in Cox and Schutte, "A Look at Channel Management", pp. 99–105.

tionships with channel intermediaries as a management responsibility since other firms are involved. The channel is perhaps the least well understood element of the marketing mix. Taking a narrow intra-firm perspective of the distribution function fails to recognize the central role of channel strategy in the marketing program. It is the marketing system within which the marketing mix must function. An example of the distribution of dietary liquid foods illustrates the role of the channel system in marketing performance:

> Mead Johnson and Company introduced Metrecal in powder form in 1959 through pharmaceutical distribution channels. Because of its Pablum line the firm could have used available food distribution channels. The product was a rapid success, attracting many competitors (primarily dairy companies). A relative late arrival in the market, the Pet Milk Company with its Sego Liquid Diet Food, near the end of 1964 had gained an estimated 51 percent of the liquid diet food market compared to 46 percent for Metrecal. By this time, Metrecal was marketed substantially through food brokers while Sego was sold by Pet's sales force to chains and grocery wholesalers. In combination with a well-developed channel system Pet had developed a somewhat different product and a highly effective advertising program, thus utilizing an integrated marketing strategy.[8]

While the distribution channel decision was not the only factor contributing to Sego's rapid and substantial penetration into the dietary food market, the channel system was an essential element in the marketing mix that was used. Pet's well-developed channel system enabled the firm to quickly reach mass markets with its product. The availability of a company sales force made possible aggressive promotion of the new product to wholesalers and large retailers. Moreover, the example indicates the key role of an integrated marketing mix. Decisions on product, price, advertising, and sales force are highly interrelated with channel system decisions.

Channel decisions represent longer commitments than other marketing decisions due to the time, costs, and intermediary relationships involved in developing a new channel or gaining access to an established channel. The channel, once selected, imposes certain constraints upon other marketing mix elements. For example, a manufacturer interested in producing private label brands for a large retail chain will likely have to comply with certain product specifications and probably will have to accept lower purchase prices than if an alternative channel is used. This type of channel commitment places the manufacturer highly

---

[8] For further details see "The Rise of 'Instant Skinny,'" *Sales Management* (November 4, 1960), pp. 52–54; "Tying Up a Market by Tying in Fashion," *Printers Ink,* 287 (May 8, 1964), pp. 39, 41; and "The Race Is to the Smart," *Forbes,* 94 (October 1, 1964), p. 24.

dependent upon the retailer, if all or a substantial portion of output is produced for the retailer. Yet, certain benefits are gained along with the constraints that are imposed such as the strength of the retailer in the market place and reduced marketing costs (e.g., no advertising expenses or sales force expenses).

The length (number of remarketer levels) of the channel system influences the methods used to promote the product or service. For example, in a large channel system for a consumer product a producer may find it appropriate to advertise direct to consumers, thus stimulating interest in the product at the end user level. This is characterized as a "pull" strategy where promotional efforts seek to pull the product through the channel system. Alternatively, a "push" strategy seeks to promote the product through channel intermediaries. Thus, the type of promotional strategy used, in part, depends upon the particular channel system selected by the firm.

Channels and Physical Distribution

The physical distribution function in channel systems has received increased attention in the past several years due to huge costs involved in moving goods and services and the associated opportunities for achieving better balance between customer service and distribution costs. Consider, for example in 1973, "the top 500 industrial companies spent an estimated $69 billion moving their products to market. This compares with $40 billion for the same function ten years ago, and this upward trend will almost certainly continue and may even accelerate."[9]

The contemporary concept of the physical distribution function is that it should be managed as an integrated system of activities including order processing, inventory control, warehousing, transportation, customer service, and related tasks leading to the effective and efficient flow of products through the channel system. Thus, the function is an essential part of the distribution channel yet is broader in scope than marketing alone because manufacturing, transportation, and other organizational activities are involved.

Physical distribution management involves achieving the most effective trade-off between alternative levels of customer service and the costs of providing services. In general, costs increase as higher service levels are pursued. For example, if a potential buyer of automobiles is to obtain exactly the style, color, and accessories that are most preferred it will normally be necessary for the dealer to order from the manufacturer, thus causing the customer some degree of dissatisfaction in waiting for delivery. Yet, to attempt to carry a sufficiently wide inventory

---

[9] Steven B. Oresman and Charles D. Scudder, "A Remedy for Maldistribution," *Business Horizons,* 17 (June 1974), p. 61.

to meet all possible customer preferences would be prohibitive in terms of costs. Thus, a decision must be made as to the proper balance between customer service and costs.

Marketing can contribute important decision making guidelines regarding the probable influence on customer demands of alternative service levels. Manufacturing and transportation can provide information on physical distribution costs. Depending upon the organization, responsibility for managing the overall physical distribution function may be assigned to marketing, manufacturing, or some other group in the firm. The important point is that in cases where physical distribution costs are substantial, the various activities that comprise the function should be coordinated and managed as an integrated system.

The concepts and activities involved in physical distribution or logistics management, in addition to marketing, represent a number of specialized areas including raw materials management, inventory control, transportation, and warehouse and plant location. Thus, an adequate examination of the area is not possible in this book.[10] Nevertheless, the close relationship of the function to marketing in general and to channel system management in particular should be recognized. Regardless of the organizational approach used in managing physical distribution it should be carefully integrated with channel system decisions.

CHANNEL STRATEGY DEVELOPMENT

Channel strategy should be based upon the firm's market targets and marketing objectives. The channel system provides access to the firm's selected market targets. The role of the channel of distribution should be carefully integrated with the various components of the marketing program to achieve an effective marketing strategy. As a guide to channel strategy development the major decisions which must be made are shown in Figure 16–2. Based upon the firm's market targets and marketing objectives, the role that the channel is to play in the marketing program should be determined. The result of this strategy development consists of channel system objectives and determination of the actions necessary to accomplish the objectives.

Channel strategy guidelines must be formulated; channel system alternatives must be identified; the alternatives must be evaluated; and one or more distribution channels selected. Next, the participants in the channel system must be chosen. Modifications in channel strategy may

---

[10] Several texts examine in depth the management of physical distribution as an integrated system. See, for example Donald J. Bowersox, *Logistical Management* (New York: The MacMillan Company, 1974); James L. Heskett, Nicholas A. Glaskowsky, Jr., and Robert M. Ivie, *Business Logistics*, 2nd ed. (New York: The Ronald Press Company, 1973), and Ronald H. Ballou, *Business Logistics Management* (Englewood Cliffs, N.J.: Prentice Hall, 1973).

FIGURE 16–2

Channel of Distribution Decision Process

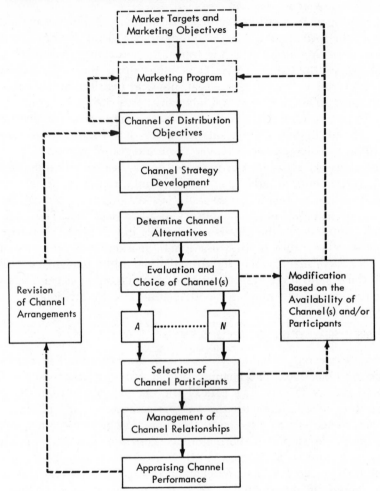

be necessary based on the availability of channels and/or particular intermediaries. After channel of distribution relationships are established with specific firms they must be managed or coordinated. The extent of management is based substantially upon the degree of control that is developed by the firm. Regular appraisal of the performance of a firm's channel/s should be accomplished, which may lead, over time, to revision of channel arrangements.

Channel objectives that guide determination of channel strategy and the specific channel strategy decisions that must be made are discussed in this section. Selection of types of channels and participating firms; management of channel relationships and appraisal of channel performance are considered in the following chapter. We shall assume the point of view of a manufacturer in our discussion, although the same general approach may be used by a firm at any level in the distribution system.

Channel Objectives

Channel objectives should specify what the firm's channel/s are expected to accomplish with regard to market targets and support of the marketing program. Objectives should be indicated regarding *channel performance, extent of control, financial support* to be provided in channel development, and other *operational* objectives. Channel performance factors include sales, market share, and profit contribution targets. A firm should indicate the desired role it seeks to play in coordination and control of channel operations. Financial support objectives are concerned with the magnitude of dollar commitment management is willing to make in building the channel of distribution. For example, is the firm interested and capable of owning intermediaries such as retail stores? Various operational objectives may be established such as support to be provided to remarketers, product servicing arrangements, and related activities to help develop market opportunities.

An illustrative set of channel objectives for an industrial firm with a new product is shown in Figure 16–3. Performance, financial commitment, and operational objectives are indicated. Quantitative targets are specified where possible as well as the time horizon for accomplishment.

Channel Strategy Decisions

Have you ever considered why certain brands of golf equipment can only be purchased in pro-shops; why Fuller Brush Co. products are not located on the shelves of drug stores; or why certain manufacturers sell a substantial portion of their output to large retail chains such as Sears and Montgomery Ward? These actions are the result of distribution strategy decisions based upon assessment of factors beyond control of management and based on management's preferences in selecting a method of distribution.

Certain strategy decisions should be made early in the channel decision process. These include: (1) determining whether the firm intends to sell direct to end users or to utilize one or more levels of intermediaries; (2) deciding upon the appropriate intensity of distribution; and (3) selecting the type of channel system (conventional or vertically coordinated). These decisions are closely related to channel objectives and

FIGURE 16–3

Illustrative Channel of Distribution Objectives (industrial firm with a new line of liquid and gas flow meters for use in the petrochemical and natural gas industries)

Channel Objectives

Performance
  Achieve an annual rate of sales of $0.5 million and $1.0 million respectively for natural gas and petrochemical target markets within two years, and an annual rate of increase of 20 percent for the subsequent 5 years.
  Maintain a profit contribution margin net of marketing expenditures of 15 percent of sales during the first two years and 20 percent thereafter.

Control
  Play leadership role in channel operations by coordinating management activities.

Financial Commitment
  Hold channel development expenditures to $75,000 or less during the first two years.
  Avoid investment in additional field facilities and/or personnel.

Operational
  Provide product technical assistance to intermediaries/end-users by factory product specialist group.
  Maintain calibration and service facilities at manufacturing facility.
  Provide advertising and product information support to remarketers.

may be incorporated into the process of selecting appropriate objectives. They have been separated here to emphasize their importance in establishing key guidelines for use in selecting specific channels of distribution. There are four key determinants that influence the three channel strategy decisions: market targets, marketing program, product or service characteristics, and corporate capabilities and resources. Their influences will be considered as each strategy decision is examined.

Direct Distribution versus Intermediaries. In direct distribution the manufacturer performs the channel functions by making direct contact with consumer and/or industrial and institutional end users through a sales force or by mail. This approach considerably simplifies the distribution network and offers certain advantages as well as limitations. Direct distribution provides the manufacturer with relatively complete control over marketing activities and facilitates buyer-seller communications. Profit margins do not have to be shared with remarketers. Yet, direct distribution does not eliminate necessary channel functions, and the approach requires substantial resources if personal selling contact is made with end users. In certain cases a firm may be in a position to pursue either a direct or remarketer distribution channel as illustrated by the use of a direct channel to the household by Avon Products compared to prevailing use of marketing intermediaries by most other cosmetic firms. In general, direct distribution is more prevalent in industrial markets than in consumer markets. In either type of market certain characteristics should exist with regard to market targets, marketing program, products/services, and/or corporate capabilities that facilitate or make feasible a direct marketing approach. Several illustrative characteristics favorable to a direct marketing approach are shown in Table 16–2.

The channel decision is simplified through use of a direct marketing approach in that the firm is not faced with evaluating specific channel alternatives and selection of particular remarketer firms. The focus is upon designing a marketing organization to accomplish the direct marketing task.

If the characteristics of the market and/or other factors do not favor a direct marketing approach then use of intermediaries is necessary. Alternatively, the firm may want to evaluate both types of approaches before making a decision. A distribution approach involving intermediaries necessitates decisions regarding desired intensity of distribution and the type of channel system to be utilized.

Desired Intensity of Distribution. Distribution alternatives include use of exclusive remarketers, selective approaches, and widespread or intensive use of resellers. In an exclusive distribution arrangement the wholesaler or retailer does not market competing brands of other producers. In contrast, an intensive distribution approach seeks to accomplish a wide remarketer network (e.g., department stores, discounters, specialty stores, and other appropriate outlets). For example, Kodak film is distributed through an intensive retail network. Selective distribution falls between the two extremes. There are two major influences to be considered in making the intensity of distribution decision: market response relationships for different distribution intensities, and product-service characteristics.

Consider the sales response relationships shown in Figure 16–4.[11] In examining the relationship between number of retailers and producer sales there are distinct differences between response curves A, B, and C. Moreover, these differences suggest alternative distribution intensity

---

[11] From Frederick D. Sturdivant, et. al., *Managerial Analysis in Marketing* (Glenview, Ill.: Scott, Foresman and Company, 1970), p. 595.

TABLE 16–2

Illustrative Characteristics Favorable to Use of a Direct Distribution Approach

Type of Factor	*Illustrative Characteristics*
Market Targets	Relatively few customers comprise the market target.
	Size of purchase in terms of quantity or unit price is large.
	Customers tend to be concentrated geographically.
	Sufficient margin exists to support personal selling or mail contact efforts.
	Purchase decision represents a major, long-term commitment by the buyer.
Marketing Program	Personal selling is a major component of the marketing program.
	Intermediary functions are not needed (e.g., storage, local credit, inventory, packaging, etc.) or can be efficiently performed by the manufacturer.
	Marketing strategy favors a direct marketing approach (e.g., qualified intermediaries are not available).
Product/Service Characteristics	Product complexity requires use of manufacturer's personnel in selling and service (e.g., computer sales and service).
	Width of product line sufficient to support direct marketing approach (e.g., Avon Products, Fuller Brush).
	Product application assistance is required (e.g., steam turbines).
	Product technology changing rapidly.
Corporate Capabilities	Resources are available to support a direct marketing approach (e.g., establishment of a sales force).
	Firm has experience in marketing similar products to comparable market targets (e.g., direct channels exist.).
	Sufficient time is available to develop needed direct marketing channels before potential competition becomes a threat (e.g., patent protection).

decisions depending upon which sales response relationship applies to a given producer. In the case of response curve A, an intense distribution approach would be appropriate since sales increase in direct proportion to the number of retailers. Alternatively, when the relationship is of the type reflected by response curve C, an exclusive or possibly selective approach would be more appropriate since a substantial proportion of total sales would be achieved with relatively few retailers. Response relationship B suggests a selective approach. Thus, a key input to the distribution intensity decision is estimating the probable response of sales to number of intermediaries.

FIGURE 16–4

Functions of Producer Sales Response to Number of Retailers in a System, Other Factors Held Constant

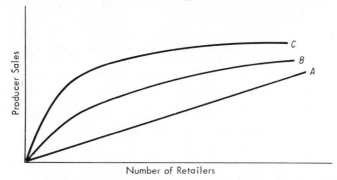

From *Managerial Analysis in Marketing* by Frederick D. Sturdivant, Louis W. Stern, John R. Grabner, Jr. et al. Copyright 1970 by Scott, Foresman and Company. Reprinted by permission of the publisher.

A policy of exclusive or selective distribution may not be appropriate for certain types of products:

> At retail, selective distribution is probably effective for most specialty lines and shopping lines, but it is not satisfactory for convenience goods which, by definition, must be available at many locations within easy reach of consumers.[12]

Thus, products such as cigarettes, chewing gum, and candy have sales response curves similar to A in Figure 16–4. Alternatively, various industrial products are marketed using exclusive or selective approaches. Factors in addition to type of product which suggest more selective approaches include strength of product-brand image to attract sufficient customers, adequate margins to support necessary remarketer efforts, and availability of qualified intermediaries.

Although market and product characteristics influence to some extent which distribution approach is appropriate, a reasonable degree of flexibility exists regarding the intensity of distribution selected by the firm. The distribution concept utilized by Ethan Allen Industries illustrates how a furniture manufacturer has moved away from department store distribution to a relatively small number of exclusive resellers at the retail level. The firm has successfully developed an exclusive distribution channel, in an industry where typically more intense distribution approaches prevail.

---

[12] Edwin H. Lewis, *Marketing Channels: Structure and Strategy* (New York: McGraw-Hill Book Company, 1968), p. 86; see pp. 85–88 for a discussion of general versus limited distribution.

Ethan Allen Industries has over 200 franchise outlets frequently located in suburban shopping centers. They provide these exclusive retailers various types of assistance at no charge (site selection, merchandising, etc.). While the firm's Early American furniture line is relatively high priced, a variety of high quality, exclusive designs is offered to customers. Ethan Allen has expanded the lines offered to dealers to include furnishings such as floor and wall covering and draperies. Household customers are offered a variety of services as a part of the firm's overall marketing strategy, including decorating advice, an expensive 400-page catalog which contains decorating suggestions, and other assistance.[13]

Recognizing the importance of developing strong relationships at all levels in the channel of distribution, the firm offers an interior decorating course package for use at the high school level.[14] The kit includes filmstrips, booklets, and copies of the *Ethan Allen Treasury* catalog and decorating guide.

Type of Channel System. The arrangements between channel participants which serve to bond the system together vary from ownership of all participants by a single firm to loosely organized groupings of firms. There are two major types of channel systems: (1) the conventional channel where members have joined together on the basis of consensus or mutual agreement but are not coordinated on any formal basis (members are loosely aligned and relatively autonomous); and (2) vertically organized marketing systems where coordination is achieved through *ownership* of all members by a single firm, *contractual arrangements* (e.g., franchising retail outlets by the producer), or an *administered* relationship among channel members for a line or classification of merchandise (e.g., Magnavox Company home entertainment products).[15] Thus, the vertically organized channel is distinguished from the conventional channel by the coordination throughout the channel that is achieved via a contractual arrangement or by exercise of power (e.g., by Kraftco Corp. among food retailers). In the conventional channel, participants are linked together through consensus or joint agreement. Yet they tend to function on an independent basis; there is a lack of overall channel coordination; and sub-optimization typically occurs. Davidson indicates that vertically organized channel systems are rapidly emerging as the dominant type of system in the economy. Illustrative characteristics and examples of the major types of channel systems are shown in Table 16–3.

A firm must first decide upon the type of channel system to be utilized,

---

[13] See "Ethan Allen Breaks with Tradition," *Business Week* (June 10, 1972), pp. 22, 24.

[14] "Marketing Observer", *Business Week* (February 24, 1975), p. 78.

[15] William R. Davidson, "Changes in Distributive Institutions," *Journal of Marketing*, 34 (January 1970), pp. 7–8.

TABLE 16–3

Illustrative Characteristics and Examples of Different Types of Channel Systems*

Type of Channel	Characteristics	Examples
Vertically Coordinated Channel Systems		
Ownership	Ownership may occur at manufacturer, wholesaler, or retailer levels. Firms may also utilize contractual systems (e.g., certain franchisers own a portion of retail outlets). Substantial financial resources and levels of investment are required.	Evans Products Company (Building Products) Sears Roebuck & Company Singer Co. (retail sewing centers) Sherwin-Williams (paint) Genesco, Inc. (shoes, apparel)
Contractual	Consist of wholesaler sponsored voluntary chains, retailer-cooperative organizations, and franchise systems. Normally involves a written agreement in which responsibilities of channel participants are specified.	McDonalds' Corp. Holiday Inns of America, Inc. Ethan Allen Industries Buick Division of General Motors, Corporation
Administered	Coordination achieved through power and influence of dominant firm in the channel. Normally involves a line or classification of products.	Magnavox Company Kraftco Corp. (dairy products)
Conventional Channel Systems		
	Absence of dominant power in the channel. Decision making focus is within each firm rather than from a channel perspective. Entry and exit to and from channel easier to accomplish than in vertically coordinated systems. Integrated programmed approach to channel management does not exist.	Channels used by independent supermarkets, shoe stores, and various other retail outlets. Use of agent-broker intermediary channels by small manufacturers to access industrial end-users.

* Vertically coordinated systems are discussed in greater detail in William R. Davidson, "Changes in Distributive Institutions," *Journal of Marketing*, 34 (January 1970), pp. 7–10.

and then determine if access to the channel system is feasible. Vertically coordinated channel systems are the most predominate forms found for consumer products, and direct or coordinated systems are used by many industrial firms. Yet, there are also many types of conventional channels of distribution functioning within the marketing system.

Channel Strategy Alternatives

Through development of channel objectives management should be in a position to determine first if an intermediary system is to be used; and, if so, the desired intensity of distribution and the type of channel system to be utilized. Using this overall channel strategy, specific channel alternatives can be identified, evaluated, and one or more selected. The various channel strategy alternatives are shown in Table 16–4. As indicated there are 12 major strategy alternatives recognizing that certain of them would probably not be utilized in particular product market situations. Examples of firms utilizing each type of strategy are also indicated in Table 16–4. Note that firms may utilize more than one channel strategy. For example, certain motel and fast-food chains own a portion of their retail outlets in addition to those that are franchised.

Selection of one or more channel strategy alternatives provides a basis for identifying particular distribution channel alternatives. For example, a large manufacturer seeking intensive distribution through conventional channel systems will need to identify the specific channels of distribution that provide intensive access to end-user markets. It is also possible that more than 1 of the 12 strategy approaches might be considered by a particular firm.

TABLE 16–4

Channel Strategy Development Alternatives and Examples of Firms Using Each

	Intensity of Distribution		
Type of Channel	*Intensive*	*Selective*	*Exclusive*
I. Conventional	National brands of cigarettes	Cross writing instruments Bulova Accutron watches	Certain prestige brands of watches, stereo equipment, and clothing Certain industrial products
II. Vertically Coordinated A. Ownership	Sears Roebuck & Company retail and catalog stores	Singer Co., retail sewing centers Sherwin-Williams paint stores	Prestige clothing chains such as Garfinckel-Brooks Brothers mens stores
B. Contractual	McDonald's Corporation Various major brands of gasoline	Certain hotel-motel chains	Ethan Allen furniture Cadillac Division of General Motors Corporation
C. Administered	Kraftco Corp. dairy products General Electric household appliances	Magnavox home entertainment products	Prestige products where manufacturers administer channel policy—Schwinn bicycles

SUMMARY AND CONCLUSIONS

In this chapter we have developed a perspective toward the purpose of the channel of distribution in the firm's overall marketing efforts. The channel system links together the producer, various types of remarketers, and consumer and industrial end users. The specific influences of channel decisions upon the different elements of the marketing mix were examined and illustrated. A decision process to guide channel of distribution decisions was developed to guide marketing management in identifying, analyzing, and choosing various alternatives associated with channel design and management of channel relationships. Building upon this discussion of the nature and scope of channel of distribution decisions, the important task of channel strategy development was considered in terms of determining how to best access the firm's selected market targets. A firm may choose to go direct to its end user markets or to work through one or more types of marketing intermediaries.

In pursuing a channel strategy involving the use of intermediaries 12 channel strategy alternatives were identified and their characteristics described and illustrated. These different strategy alternatives occur as a result of a firm choosing a conventional channel or one of the alternative vertically coordinated channel types in combination with a desired intensity (intensive, selective, or exclusive) of distribution.

Building on the channel strategy guidelines developed in this chapter, we continue our examination of channel of distribution decisions in the following chapter. The evaluation and selection of one or more specific distribution channels are considered, and an approach to selecting channel participants is outlined and illustrated. Attention is also given to the on-going tasks of managing channel relationships and appraising channel performance.

EXERCISES FOR DISCUSSION AND REVIEW

1. In order to understand the concept of a channel of distribution system, it is very useful to examine the different steps a raw material goes through in its transformation into a consumer product. Discuss an example of the distribution process, explaining the different stages in the distribution process. Include in your discussion consideration of the functions performed by different channel intermediaries.

2. A medium-size manufacturer of small household appliances has experienced various problems in its channels of distribution. Assume you have been called in as a consultant to assess the firm's channel operations and to make recommendations for improving operations. Develop a framework for use in identifying problems and information needs and for guiding development of appropriate recommendations.

3. A chemical manufacturer has developed a new chemical for use in swimming pools. Identify the channel strategy alternatives that might be used by the firm to reach end users of the product. Discuss the appropriateness and feasibility of the use of a vertically coordinated channel of distribution by this firm. In the past all of the firm's chemicals have been marketed to industrial end users.

4. An electronics manufacturer with a full line of home entertainment products (TV, radio, stereo, etc.) has developed a TV electronic game which easily attaches to any black-and-white or color television set. Several different games are available including sports games, arithmetic games, and geography games. The product is designed to appeal to both children and adults. Currently the firm is distributing its products through selected department stores and exclusive dealers (selective distribution strategy in a vertically coordinated type of channel). Identify and evaluate alternative distribution strategies for the electronic game.

5. Many of the large companies serving consumer markets distribute through vertically coordinated channel systems; often these firm's control their channels of distribution. Select a large consumer-goods firm (e.g., Sears, P&G, Genesco). Analyze the channel strategy used by the firm indicating the logic, strengths, and possible weaknesses in the firm's approach.

17

Channel Design, Implementation, and Control

Chapter 16 examined the role and purpose of the channel of distribution in the marketing program. A framework for guiding channel decisions was developed, and the important first step in the channel decision process—selecting a channel strategy—was considered. In this chapter the three remaining stages in the channel decision process are discussed: channel of distribution design; management of channel relationships; and appraising channel performance.

CHANNEL OF DISTRIBUTION DESIGN

The major stages involved in designing channels of distribution are shown in Figure 17–1. Based on the guidelines established as a result of channel strategy development, specific channel alternatives that correspond to a given strategy (Table 16–4) must be identified and screened to select those to be evaluated on a comprehensive basis. In-depth analysis of these alternatives should include projected cost-revenue flows, control considerations, legal constraints, and determination of channel availability. Based on these criteria, one or more channels must be selected. The last step in the selection process is the determination of specific channel participants.

Identification of Channel Alternatives

While determination of a particular channel strategy to be used eliminates various channel alternatives, there are often several possible channels that might be utilized for a particular channel strategy (for

FIGURE 17–1

Channel of Distribution Design Process and Decision Criteria for Each Design Stage

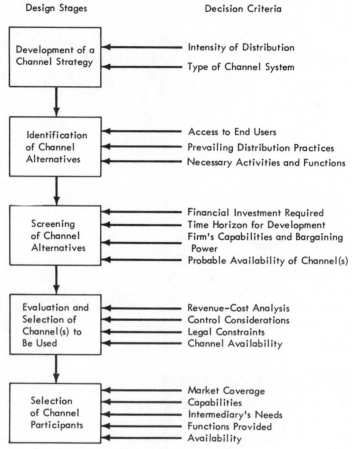

example, a conventional channel with a selective intensity of distribution). Moreover, a firm may be interested in using and/or evaluating one or more channel strategies. Three major criteria that are useful in identifying channel alternatives are consideration of a potential channel's access to end users, prevailing distribution practices, and the necessary activities and functions that channel participants are expected to perform.

Access to End Users. The access that a potential channel of distribution provides to end users in the firm's target market/s is a key criterion in identifying a channel alternative. By working back from an end user target market, the possible intermediaries that may be used to reach the

FIGURE 17–2

Alternative Distribution Channel Configurations

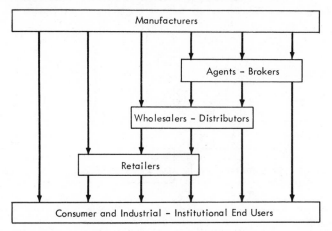

market can be identified. Several alternative distribution channel configurations are shown in Figure 17–2. The channel strategy to be utilized provides the first step in identifying alternatives. For example, consider what channels might provide access to consumer end users of a hair curling iron for use by women in the 16 to 35 age group assuming a conventional type of channel design and an intensive distribution approach. At retail certainly department, drug, and discount chains would provide access to the target market. Similarly, drug and other small electrical appliance wholesalers and distributors would be involved. Direct sales to large chains should be considered. Private branding for a firm such as J. C. Penney is another alternative. Attention should also be given to geographic coverage of various channel configurations and the approximate sales potential provided by each.

Prevailing Distribution Practices. An analysis of prevailing channel practices for similar products or services can be useful in identifying the types and functions of various intermediaries.[1] Study of competitors' channel systems and their market performance may also yield useful insights. For example, illustrative channels of distribution for a food products firm are shown in Figure 17–3. A firm considering movement into food products would normally use one or more of the channels in Figure 17–3. If an intensive distribution strategy is used, then the various types of retailers would need to be reached through the manufacturer's channels.

---

[1] For a discussion of certain dominant channels by product type see E. Jerome McCarthy, *Basic Marketing*, 4th ed. (Homewood, Ill.: Richard D. Irwin, Inc., 1971), pp. 501–5.

FIGURE 17–3

Illustrative Channels of Distribution for Food Products

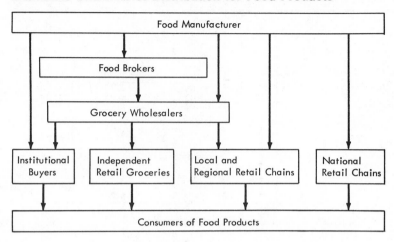

Necessary Activities and Functions. The manufacturer should identify what functions (e.g., storage, transportation, customer contact) are required in making the product available to end users in the market place. Those functions which can best be performed by the firm should be separated from those which are appropriate for intermediaries. For example, if a manufacturer of consumer products cannot directly make contact with prospective customers at the retail level, then resellers must be obtained. Need for inventories in various geographic locations indicates a function that wholesalers could perform. Assessment of the various types of channel flows (ownership, risk, financial, physical distribution, and information) needed to serve target markets provides useful insights as to necessary activities and functions in a given product market situation. Analysis should be made of the functions and capabilities of different types of intermediaries that are feasible in a proposed channel system. Factors to be considered include services provided by middlemen, their availability, attitudes of middlemen toward the producer, sales opportunities, and costs.[2]

Consider the channel design situation faced by a manufacturer of industrial chemicals.[3] The firm has developed a new swimming pool chemical for use by swimming pool owners although the company has no prior experience in consumer markets. Based on consideration of

---

[2] These factors are examined in William J. Stanton, *Fundamentals of Marketing,* 3d ed. (New York: McGraw-Hill Book Company, 1971), pp. 362–63.

[3] This example is drawn from the Commodity Chemical Company Case in Edward C. Bursk and Steven A. Greyser, *Advanced Cases in Marketing Management* (Englewood Cliffs, N.J.: Prentice-Hall, 1968), pp. 156–65.

FIGURE 17–4

Channel of Distribution Alternatives for New Swimming Pool Germicide (product end users: swimming pool owners)

Channel Alternatives:

1. Use of the firm's existing industrial chemical distributors which would involve relatively low promotion costs.

2. Access to end users through specialized pool supply distributors.

3. Acquire a small firm that has established distribution channels to target market end users.

4. Test market for one year using a variety of promotional approaches to reach pool owners directly.

5. Sell the product in bulk to firms already in the business.

Source: This example is drawn from the Commodity Chemical Company Case in Edward C. Bursk and Steven A. Greyser, *Advanced Cases in Marketing Management* (Englewood Cliffs, N.J.: Prentice-Hall, 1968), p. 165.

access to end users, prevailing distribution practices, and necessary activities and functions management has identified the five channel alternatives shown in Figure 17–4. Based on these alternatives, the firm is in a position to move forward in the channel design process.

Screening of Channel Alternatives

The purpose of the screening stage in channel design is to reduce the number of alternatives to be evaluated on a comprehensive basis due to costs of information collection and analysis for this purpose. Thus, after various channel alternatives have been identified, they should be screened to determine whether comprehensive evaluation is appropriate assuming there are several alternatives available. If only a few alternatives exist, then screening and comprehensive analysis may be combined. Factors which may be used to screen alternatives include financial investment required for channel development, time horizon for development of channel relationships, the firm's capabilities and bargaining power, and probable availability of the channel alternatives.

Certain types of channels require substantial financial investment by a manufacturer. Costs may include promotional support at the retail level, inventory, credit, training, and various other activities needed to accomplish the marketing task. Also, to what extent will price concessions, financial assistance, and risk protection be necessary to secure cooperation and support of intermediaries? For example, the normal commission paid to manufacturer's representatives for a particular type of product may be inadequate in stimulating necessary sales development for a new product. Certain of these costs may be absorbed by intermediaries in return for margins received on the products they handle.

Speed of development of a channel system may be important in cases where competition may emerge rapidly for certain types of new products. Thus, the time necessary for a given channel alternative to reach an acceptable level of performance should be assessed. Time for development also affects cost and revenue flows and the resulting returns from a new channel activity.

A firm seeking to enter a particular channel system should make a careful analysis of its strengths and limitations. Since the various distribution channels that comprise the marketing system are already functioning, a prospective entrant must take a realistic appraisal of channels into which entry is feasible. Large firms with well-developed channel systems are able to launch a variety of new products into the market place using their existing channels. Development of channel systems typically requires several years and substantial resource commitments. The lack of strong dealer networks at the retail level was a significant contributing factor to the failure of several automobile manufacturers in the 1950s when competitive markets developed after the accumulated demand generated by World War II began to level off.

It is not always possible for a firm to enter a particular channel system and if resources and experience are limited, it may not be feasible to develop a totally new channel of distribution. A company's bargaining power is an important determinant in gaining access to a channel system in terms of whether it will be able to select and control intermediaries, participate on an equal basis, or be controlled by another member of the channel system. This essentially involves determining what the firm has to offer channel members in return for an opportunity to participate in the channel system. A major factor of interest to resellers is the chance to improve their current profit contributions.[4] Such an incentive may result from the sales potential offered by the product, customer brand preference developed by the manufacturer (e.g., through advertising) and profit margins available to resellers. These factors should be assessed in terms of their potential attractiveness to channel intermediaries.

As an example of how a firm might determine channel of distribution alternatives consider a manufacturer of industrial equipment with a new product:

> The firm has developed a new process for heating liquids used in various industrial processes. The line of equipment is custom designed

---

[4] Alfred R. Oxenfeldt, *Executive Action in Marketing* (Belmont, Calif.: Wadsworth Publishing Company, 1966), p. 414.

and requires technical application, installation, and servicing assistance. Market opportunities exist in a number of process industries (e.g., utilities, chemical processors, etc.), but limited company resources, market inexperience, and time required for market penetration preclude the use of a company sales force. Management has identified two channel of distribution alternatives: (1) utilize manufacturer's representatives currently serving target markets with non-competitive products; or (2) establish a distribution arrangement with a manufacturer serving the markets of interest with a complementary line of products. Technical assistance will be provided by factory applications engineering and technical specialists to assist manufacturer's representatives or another firm's sales force in developing sales and assisting customers in applications, installation, and service.

In this situation, the manufacturer, through consideration of relevant factors, has arrived at two feasible channel system alternatives that can be evaluated to determine which should be selected.

Evaluation of Alternatives

The end result of the screening process should be one or more channel alternatives to be subjected to comprehensive analysis and evaluation. The evaluation process includes comparison of alternatives on the basis of relevant criteria, determining whether a single or multiple channels are to be utilized, and selecting the particular channel system to be used.

Evaluation of alternative channel systems should include consideration of estimated revenue and costs, the extent to which control over channel relationships can be accomplished, legal constraints, and channel availability.

Revenue-Cost Estimates. A basic criterion for use in evaluating alternative channel systems is estimated economic performance—an assessment of probable revenue and cost flows over the planning horizon. For example, intensive distribution through a variety of retail outlets may be more costly but will probably generate larger sales volume. The logic of specialization of functions by remarketers within the channel system is that distribution cost efficiencies can be achieved—recognizing that, in part, costs are the result of performing the functions necessary to meet market needs (e.g., width and depth of product selection in a retail shoe store). Evaluation of alternatives is complicated by the interrelationships between the channel decision and other elements of the marketing mix since selection of a particular channel system influences costs associated with other marketing mix elements. Moreover, because of the participation of other firms in many channel systems, total system revenue and cost analysis is more difficult than in any of the other marketing mix areas. Consider the following situation:

A food products manufacturer is evaluating whether to use food brokers to move the firm's products through the channel system or to develop a company sales force. Costs of a sales force are estimated to be in excess of broker costs, but would enable the manufacturer to have direct contact with marketers at the wholesale level. Management and control of selling efforts would be more effective with a company sales force. Use of brokers would, of course, substantially eliminate personal selling costs, thus shifting a higher proportion of the marketing budget to channel expenditures and away from personal selling. Similarly, with brokers the manufacturer might determine that heavier advertising and sales promotion would be needed at the consumer level to pull the product through the channel.

Thus, economic evaluation of alternative channel systems must include all relevant cost trade-offs among mix elements and estimates of probable sales for each alternative. Distribution cost analysis is central to the selection of channel systems.

A channel-decision model for use by a manufacturer is shown in Figure 17–5. It provides a useful basis for identifying relevant information needed for evaluating channel alternatives. Various intermediary routes to end user markets are shown including information which should be obtained about markets for use in the evaluation process. In particular the model provides a good framework for sales and cost analysis of channels which are being considered.

To illustrate the types of financial information needed to evaluate

FIGURE 17–5

Channel-Decision Model for a Manufacturer's Product Line

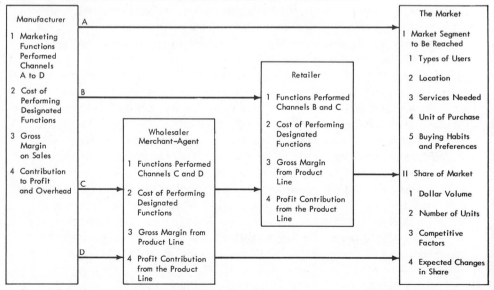

Source: Reproduced by permission from Edwin H. Lewis, *Marketing Channels: Structure and Strategy* (New York: McGraw-Hill Book Company, 1968), p. 132.

TABLE 17-1

Comparison of Two Distribution Channels for a Cosmetic Company

	Percent of Net Sales	
	Drug Stores	*Department Stores*
Cost of goods, freight, commission, insurance..............................	56	53
Co-op advertising........................	3	10
Salesgirl salary support....................	0	21
Commissions in outlets....................	12	11
Total...............................	71	95
Contribution to profit and overhead..........	29	5

Source: Reprinted by permission. Copyright 1971 by the American Institute of Certified Public Accountants, Inc., Neil Doppelt, "Down-to-Earth Marketing Information Systems," *Management Advisor* (September–October 1971), p. 23.

channel alternatives a comparison of two distribution channels for a cosmetic company is shown in Table 17–1. All estimates are expressed in percent of net sales. Various channel costs are included in the analysis in obtaining an overall picture of financial performance. Note the substantial differences in contribution to profit and overhead between the two distribution channels. Providing estimated sales results in drug outlets would be at least as good as through department stores, the drug channel offers the higher profit potential. This is primarily due to high salesgirl salary support in the department store channel.

Analyzing costs and prices at different channel levels provides a basis for observing differences in functions performed by channel intermediaries. Consider, for example, illustrative prices and margins for phonograph records. Based on an average retail list price of $5.98, the manufacturer's cost is $1.83, the price to distributor $2.51, and the distributor's price to the retailer is $2.92.[5] The margins at various levels are used to provide adequate compensation for functions performed by remarketers. In comparing costs and revenues for various channel alternatives estimates of these costs and probable sales response must be made.

Control of Channel Relationships. Qualitative factors in addition to sales and profit contribution are also important in selecting a channel of distribution. "Marketing channels are complex economic, political and social entities, and the analyst must incorporate all these factors into his channel model."[6] For example, given two channel alternatives that are similar in estimated economic performance, the basis of selection

---

[5] "A Prosperous Turnaround for Records," *Business Week* (July 27, 1974), p. 72.

[6] Bert C. McCammon, Jr., and Robert W. Little, "Marketing Channels: Analytical Systems and Approaches," in George Schwartz (ed.), *Science in Marketing* (New York: John Wiley & Sons, 1965), p. 336.

might rest upon assessment of the extent of management control the firm could exercise in the two channel systems. Factors such as the degree of possible management control, bargaining processes, potential coalitions of participants, flexibility in responding to changing conditions, communications flows, and avoidance of possible conflict, are illustrative of the variety of qualitative considerations that may be relevant in the channel choice process. Typically, the channel decision reflects the influence of several of these factors.[7] Moreover, the long term nature of the channel decision should be recognized by management. The cost of changes, possible adverse influences on trade and customer relationships, and sales losses during the period when a shift is made to another channel (or intermediary) tend to exercise constraints upon major modifications in channel participation by both manufacturers and intermediaries.

Power and control in the channel system vary both by type and level of channel.[8] In certain cases such as the automobile and gasoline industries, manufacturers tend to dominate channel relationships. In other product areas, middlemen may exercise greater control over the distribution channel. Sears Roebuck & Co. clearly controls the channel system of which it is a part. The degree of domination in a channel may range from control by a single firm, joint control, to situations where no firm has any influence over other firms.[9] Generally, the rationale for seeking control is based on a logic of improving efficiency in the channel system, although this may be viewed from the perspective of the particular firm seeking control. Bucklin suggests that "a more cautious attitude is warranted toward the conclusion that authoritarian relationships within the channel will invariantly improve performance."[10] Although considerable attention has been focused upon the issue of channel control, it remains a complex management area due to the influence of behavioral as well as economic factors.[11]

The extent to which a member of a channel system can exercise control over other participants is an important management issue, since the premise is that greater control will enable the firm to better achieve its

---

[7] See Ibid., pp. 336–54 for a comprehensive discussion of various determinants of channel behavior.

[8] Several examples of channel control are discussed in Louis W. Stern, "Channel Control and Interorganization Management," in Peter D. Bennett (ed.), *Marketing and Economic Development* (Chicago: American Marketing Association, 1965), pp. 655–65.

[9] Louis P. Bucklin, "The Locus of Channel Control," in Robert L. King (ed.), *Marketing and the New Science of Planning* (Chicago: American Marketing Association 1968), p. 142.

[10] Ibid., p. 145.

[11] A conceptual model for analyzing supplier-middlemen control relationships is discussed in Adel I. El-Ansary and Robert A. Robicheaux, "A Theory of Channel Control: Revisited," *Journal of Marketing*, 38 (January 1974), pp. 2–7.

objectives. The corporate-owned vertically organized system displays the greatest degree of management control that can be achieved in terms of market coverage, price determination, inventory, customer service, promotion, and related aspects of marketing strategy and tactics. Since the channel is competing as a unit, all parts of the unit can be managed and coordinated as an integrated marketing system linking the producer to end users. While management of channel relationships is facilitated through ownership of all participants, administration of the system is nevertheless a formidable challenge. Various interactions and conflicts occur between organizational units as well as between firms even when they are linked together for a common purpose.[12]

Since vertical integration provides a basis for achieving control over a channel, a relevant question is "What internal and external factors tend to be associated with moves toward integration?" Sturdivant, in a study of determinants of vertical integration, developed the analysis shown in Table 17–2.[13] As indicated by Sturdivant's evaluation there was no single determinant that tended to dominate, although internal conditions were rated as more dominant than were external conditions.

The achievement of control over a channel system is significantly dependent upon the extent to which the producer is willing (and able) to commit financial resources to support the channel.[14] Moreover, because of the long term nature of the channel decision, financial resources for use in developing a proposed channel system should be evaluated against other marketing expenditures as well as alternative investment opportunities available to the firm.

Legal Constraints. As has been indicated in other parts of the book laws and government regulations impose constraints upon marketing actions. The anti-trust laws are of primary importance for channel selection decisions. Several aspects of channel decisions may be affected by existing legislation including the following: extent of product or brand exclusiveness that can be granted to resellers; geographical restrictions on remarketer coverage (and possible penalties); other allowable restrictions and requirements upon marketers and consistency of terms

---

[12] The interactions and conflicts that occur in channel systems are examined in Larry J. Rosenberg and Louis W. Stern, "Toward the Analysis of Conflict in Distribution Channels: A Descriptive Model," *Journal of Marketing*, 34 (October 1970), pp. 40–46; Frederick S. Sturdivant and Donald L. Granbois, "Channel Interaction: An Institutional-Behavioral View," *The Quarterly Review of Economics and Business* (Summer 1968), pp. 61–68; and Louis P. Bucklin, "The Locus of Channel Control," pp. 142–47.

[13] Frederick D. Sturdivant, "Determinants of Vertical Integration in Channel Systems," in Raymond M. Haas (ed.), *Science, Technology, and Marketing* (Chicago: American Marketing Association, 1966), pp. 472–79.

[14] An excellent analysis of the channel selection decision from a financial point of view is contained in Eugene W. Lambert, Jr. "Financial Considerations in Choosing a Marketing Channel," *MSU Business Topics* (Winter 1966), pp. 17–26.

TABLE 17–2

Assessed Influence of Various Factors upon Vertical Integration Moves of Selected Firms

	External Conditions			Internal Conditions			
	Threat Posed by Competing System	Change in Market Conditions	Favorable Legal Environment	Broad Horizontal Base	Channel Conflict	Entrepreneurial Drive	Duplication of Functions
Hospital Supply Industry*	1.9	1	2.1	1.5	1.6	1.1	1.3
American Hospital Supply	0.5†	1	1.9	1.9	1.8	2.4	1.3
Keystone Co.	0	0	2	3	2	4	0
Don Baxter, Inc.	2	1	2	0	4	3	2
Pharmaseal.	0	2	2	0	3	2	0
Campbell Labs.	0	0	3	3	0	0	3
Dade Reagents, Inc.	0	3	2	4	1	3	4
American Wheel Chair.	0	0	2	3	3	1	3
Parenteral Div. M-J.	2	1	2	0	3	2	0
Massillon Rubber.	2	2	2	3	4	2	3
Hartman-Leddon.	0	2	2	3	1	2	3
Arnar Stone.	0	1	2	0	0	3	0
Bruck's, Inc.	0	0	2	0	0	3	0
Midwest Dental.	0	0	2	0	0	3	0
Convertors, Inc.	0	3	1	3	2	2	0
Storch Pharm. Co.	0	0	2	2	0	3	0
McGaw Laboratories.	2	1	1	4	4	3	1
Institutional Industries.	0	0	2	3	1	3	2

* The difference in mean scores for the hospital supply industry and American Hospital Supply Corporation is because of values assigned other companies not shown in this abbreviated matrix.

† This low score is because of American Hospital Supply's role as an innovator. The industry average is much higher because other companies in the industry were adapting to these innovative moves. (0 = no measurable or known influence, 4 = a dominant influence)

Source: Frederick D. Sturdivant, "Determinants of Vertical Integration in Channel Systems," in Raymond M. Haas (ed.) *Science, Technology, and Marketing* (Chicago: American Marketing Association, 1966), p. 474.

and arrangements between resellers.[15] These are illustrative areas that may be affected by existing federal legislation (see Chapter 6). State and local laws and regulations may impose additional constraints.

An example will illustrate the impact that anti-trust laws can have upon channel strategy. A large grocery wholesaler pursuing a policy of expanding its channel network arranged an acquisition of a smaller wholesaler that served a different but adjacent geographical market area. The acquisition was viewed as quite favorable to both firms, and could result in increased efficiencies for both due to combining certain functions (e.g., warehousing). A request for approval of the merger was sent to the federal government. A decision was not reached for several months. During this period each firm developed plans to facilitate the transition, since management and their legal advisors believed the approval would be forthcoming. The request was denied over six months after the request was filed. The government's decision indicated that the merger would place the acquired firm in a dominant position in the markets it served even though there was no market overlap in the previous coverage of the two firms. The decision was essentially based upon definition of trade areas and analysis of the firms serving these areas. In this situation expansion of the wholesaler's channel network was prevented by the federal government.

Channel Availability. In the selection of channel alternatives a firm should determine that there is a reasonable possibility of being able to enter the distribution network. As discussed earlier the process of screening channel alternatives should give consideration to the firm's strengths and limitations, including the feasibility of entering particular channel systems. At this final stage in the channel selection process it may be appropriate to contact members of the channel systems of interest to make a more comprehensive evaluation of channel availability. Alternatively this may be done as a part of the process of selection of channel participants.

Single versus Multiple Channels. A firm may utilize two or more channels of distribution to reach its target markets. For example, large food manufacturers sell direct to large institutional buyers (e.g., federal government), distribute through grocery wholesalers to reach independent groceries and regional chains, and sell direct to large retail chains such as A&P and Krogers. American Garden Products, Inc., in the nursery industry, uses three distribution channels to reach its target markets: company owned regional suppliers of retail outlets; direct mail

---

[15] A detailed discussion of government control of restrictive distribution policies is provided in Theodore N. Beckman and William R. Davidson, *Marketing*, 8th ed. (New York: The Ronald Press Company, 1967), pp. 405–12; see also Richard W. McLaren, "Marketing Limitations on Independent Distributors and Dealers—Prices, Territories, Customers, and Handling of Competitive Products," *The Antitrust Bulletin* (Spring 1968), pp. 161–75.

(e.g., seed catalogs) to consumers; and direct distribution to institutional markets (e.g., city agencies).[16]

When a firm utilizes more than one distribution channel to reach its selected market targets, it is important to consider the interrelationships between two or more channel systems. Will conflicts result between different intermediaries? How will end-users respond if they can gain access to more than one channel system and buy at different price levels? The experience of a large men's clothing manufacturer is illustrative of the problems that can develop through multiple channels. The firm sold through several clothing retailers in a large metropolitan area where one of its plants was located. Additionally, it sold "seconds" through company owned mill outlet stores in the same area, at substantially lower prices and generated very large annual sales volumes. Considerable adverse reaction to the practice was developed by local retailers who were losing business to the factory store.

Selection of Channels

The various criteria for channel alternative evaluation that have been examined on the preceding pages must be consolidated to form a basis for the channel selection decision. This can be accomplished judgmentally or through the use of some type of systematic evaluation procedure. Conventional methods of sales and cost analysis and breakeven analysis provide important guidelines for comparison of channel alternatives. Additionally, it may be appropriate to utilize the weighted factor score method, the hierarchical preference ordering method, or the method of strategy simulation.[17] The first method consists of identifying relevant evaluation factors, weighting each as to relative importance, scoring each factor as to its contribution, multiplying each factor weight by its score, and summing the results to obtain a weighted factor score for each channel alternative. This method is subject to certain limitations.[18]

An example of the hierarchical preference ordering method is shown in Table 17–3 where five alternative distribution channels are analyzed. The information used in the analysis and the evaluations of each factor must be provided by management based on judgment, experience, and available information. Use of the method provides a basis for ranking the channel alternatives that are being considered.

Simulation of proposed distribution strategies offers definite advan-

---

[16] "Creating the Chiquita of Azaleas", *Business Week* (May 25, 1974), p. 155.

[17] Each of these methods is explained and illustrated in Philip Kotler, *Marketing Decision Making: A Model Building Approach* (New York: Holt, Rinehart, and Winston, Inc., 1971), pp. 293–98.

[18] See Ibid., pp. 293–94 for an example of the method and a discussion of its limitations.

TABLE 17–3

Hierarchical Preference Ordering Method Applied to Five Distribution Methods

Factors in Order of Importance	Minimum Pass Level	Strategy Number				
		One	Two	Three	Four	Five
1. Amount of investment involved...............	.3	.8 = P	.6 = P	.2 = F	.9 = P	.9 = P
2. Amount of profit if this alternative works well..................	.5	.5 = P	.8 = P	.6 = —	.5 = P	.4 = F
3. Ability of company to cut short its losses.......	.5	.7 = P	.6 = P	.1 = —	.8 = P	.8 = —
4. Effectiveness in reaching swimming pool owners................	.3	.3 = P	.7 = P	.8 = —	.6 = P	.3 = —
5. Experience company will gain in consumer marketing.............	.4	.2 = F	.5 = P	.6 = —	.2 = F	.4 = —
Ranking....................		3d	1st	5th	2d	4th

Note: P = Pass
F = Fail
Source: From *Marketing Decision Making: A Model Building Approach* by Philip Kotler. Copyright (c) 1971 by Holt, Rinehart and Winston, Publishers. Reprinted by permission of The Dryden Press.

tages over the previous two methods, although it requires more specific information and analysis. This method provides more quantitative guidelines for evaluating distribution alternatives than do the other methods.[19] Examples of input data and simulation results for evaluating four distribution alternatives are shown in Tables 17–4A and 17–4B.

In situations where choice between two channels of distribution is difficult due to a new product, lack of experience of the firm, and other uncertainties it may be appropriate to test alternative channel designs using different geographical areas. This type of approach would be undertaken on a smaller scale than if a clear cut decision was made to utilize a particular channel. Moreover, management should be reasonably certain that the alternative/s tested offer a reasonable promise of being successful. Such an approach might be appropriate for an industrial firm seeking to market a new consumer product.

Selection of Channel Participants

The final step in the channel design process is selection of channel participants. Selection of remarketers is essentially a matching process.

---

[19] Ibid., pp. 296–98.

TABLE 17–4

A. Example of Data Input for Simulation of Alternative Distribution Strategies

	Distribution Strategies			
Variables	*(1)* *Present* *distributors* *alternative*	*(2)* *New* *distributors* *alternative*	*(3)* *Acquisition* *alternative*	*(4)* *Private* *brand* *alternative*
Investment.....................	$300,000	$500,000	$2,500,000	$100,000
Price per bag....................	$2.7	$2.5	$2.7	$2.2
Contribution margin per bag......	$1.2	$1.0	$1.2	$0.7
Mean monthly advertising budget......................	$ 5,000	$ 50,000	$ 10,000	$ 5,000
Advertising effectiveness co-efficient......................	1/2	1/1.8	1/1.9	1/2
Initial number of distributors.....	80	20	60	60
Growth rate per month in number of distributors.........	.02	.04	.01	.02
Maximum number of distributors permitted............	150	150	150	150
Distribution effectiveness co-efficient......................	1/2.5	1/2.0	1/2.2	1/2.2

B. Results of Simulation of Alternative Distribution Strategies

	(1) *Present* *distributors* *alternative*		*(2)* *New* *distributors* *alternative*		*(3)* *Acquisition* *alternative*		*(4)* *Private* *brand* *alternative*	
Criterion	*Value*	*Rank*	*Value*	*Rank*	*Value*	*Rank*	*Value*	*Rank*
Pay-back period (months).............	14	3	8	1	25	4	9	2
Share of potential........	44%	4	100%	1	62%	2	43%	2
Accumulated dis-counted profit (millions)............	3.25	3	6.10	1	5.60	2	1.99	4

Source: From *Marketing Decision Making: A Model Building Approach* by Philip Kotler. Copyright (c) 1971 by Holt, Rinehart and Winston, Publishers. Reprinted by permission of the Dryden Press.

The producer must identify specific firms that can perform the channel functions needed, and convince them that the relationship can be mutually beneficial. Thus, it is important to examine the selection decision from both points of view. The bargaining power at the disposal of the producer is an important determinant in the selection process, as is the availability of suitable intermediaries. Several of the factors that may be important in a given selection decision are shown in Figure 17–6.

FIGURE 17–6

Producer and Reseller Selection Criteria

Factors Important to the Producer in Selecting Resellers

Contacts and relationships with customers in target markets.

Capabilities, reputation, and past performance as a reseller.

Match of functions provided by reseller with producer's needs.

Potential contribution of producer's product or service to middleman's needs (e.g., profit contribution, gaps in line, etc.).

Probability of effective long-term working relationships between producer and reseller personnel.

Factors Important to Resellers in Establishing Relationship with Producer

Producer's product or brand image.

Support and assistance provided by producer.

Compatability of product with existing lines.

Trade reputation of producer.

Potential profit contribution if product is handled by reseller.

Anticipated reaction of other producers and resellers to the addition of the producer to the channel system.

Estimated start-up costs in moving the product through the distribution channel.

While many of these criteria are frequently relevant in linking the producer with a reseller system, they should be viewed as illustrative rather than exhaustive. A particular situation may involve other factors that should be considered.

The experience of the manufacturer of custom-fabricated industrial process heating equipment discussed earlier demonstrates the impact that proper selection of channel intermediaries can have upon sales. The firm decided to use agents to reach its market targets. In establishing a channel system for the new line of equipment the firm retained a consultant who specialized in bringing together manufacturers and representatives to handle their products. In 30 days after a sales agent in the northeast was selected and approved by the manufacturer, the representative obtained an order totaling nearly a quarter of a million dollars! The reason for this rapid success was due to the customer relationships already established by the agent, his experience and capabilities, the effective support provided by the manufacturer, as well as the quality of the new product offered by the firm.

Establishment of a *new* channel system is often a long and time-consuming process. It requires a careful understanding of the distribution channel of interest in terms of participants, their capabilities and needs, and related factors. In a multi-level channel, the producer must look beyond the first level of contact. Although the firm may only be involved in selecting resellers at one level in the system, careful appraisal of the entire network is important. Entering an existing channel system with a new product or service requires various changes in the channel network. These changes must be anticipated and properly implemented. Finally, it should be recognized that final choice of channel participants will normally involve compromises. Reseller candidates may simply not exist; or if available, they may be unwilling to handle the producer's product.

MANAGEMENT OF CHANNEL RELATIONSHIPS

Failure to recognize the ongoing responsibilities of channel management is one of the most critical gaps in marketing practice today, particularly by those firms that are not members of vertically integrated systems. Design of new channel systems is important but such decisions occur on an infrequent basis. Yet, concentration up to this point in the chapter upon channel system design was deliberate since an understanding of the determinants of channel design and methods of evaluation and selection of channels and participants provide an important framework for accomplishing the continuing channel management task.

Channel Management

The various characteristics of channel systems discussed earlier in the chapter make the channel difficult to manage compared to the management task in a single organization. These factors include differing (and sometimes conflicting) objectives of channel members, complexity of channel networks, geographical dispersion of participating firms, and lack of direct control. Yet, management theory, concepts, and practice "have concentrated upon the administration of single organizations and have not specifically recognized that a system of separate organizations requires administration also."[20]

Responsibility for channel management should be assigned within a given organization, with appropriate consideration given to the nature and extent of management activities that should be undertaken in line with ethical and legal factors. Several areas related to the management of channel relationships include operating policies and procedures, motivation of channel members, and information and communication flows.

Various operating policies and procedures must be developed regardless of the type of channel system that is used. Guidelines for territory

---

[20] Valentine F. Ridgeway, "Administration of Manufacturer-Dealer Systems," *Administrative Science Quarterly*, 1 (March 1957), p. 466.

responsibilities, financial support, pricing, promotion, training, and servicing are illustrative of the many areas that must be worked out between channel intermediaries.[21] The less explicit these policies and procedures are, the more likely it is that conflicts and problems will result. In certain channel relationships written contracts are used to indicate responsibilities of both parties. In such cases criteria for terminating a channel arrangement are normally indicated. Contracts are typically used, for example, in franchise systems, automobile dealerships, and with manufacturer's representatives. In loosely aligned systems there may be no formal agreement between the parties involved. An example of a statement of policy concerning manufacturer and distributor relationships is shown in Figure 17–7. Note that what the manufacturer views as obligations and those of its distributors are indicated. Thus, the policy statement provides a basic framework for channel relationships.

Maintaining a continuing high level of motivation among channel members is essential to achieving the producer's channel system objectives. Regular contact is essential, and various other activities can be helpful in maintaining channel effectiveness. Contests and incentives are often used to encourage resellers. For example, automobile manufacturers utilize dealer rebates on automobiles sold in slow sales periods when increased selling effort is desired or as a reward when sales quotas are exceeded. Various other manufacturers incorporate incentives into their channel tactics to gain greater emphasis on various aspects of channel activities. Polaroid Corp. offered retail dealers special rebates on sales of their SX-70 camera and film when they were first introduced in the market. Meetings and conferences for resellers are often used for motivation and to enable them to better perform various intermediary functions. These meetings can be useful in communicating information about new products, policy changes, and other matters. Meetings provide an opportunity for obtaining feedback from channel members concerning problems, market conditions, and competitive activity.

The development of effective communications and information flows in both directions in the channel system are necessary for all parties involved if the channel is to function properly. A producer aligned in a long channel system is quite distant from the end users of his product. Recognition of this problem, in combination with the pressures generated by consumerism, has prompted manufacturing firms in various industries such as appliances, automobiles, and insurance to establish direct communications channels with consumers to handle complaints, requests for information, and other questions concerning products and services. The provision of unit pricing information to consumers to enable them to

---

[21] A detailed examination of the administration of a distribution system is contained in Oxenfeldt, *Executive Action in Marketing*, pp. 426–36.

FIGURE 17-7

An Illustrative Channel Policy Statement

It is our firm belief that Black & Decker and its duly Authorized Distributors have fundamental obligations to each other.
We believe that mutually profitable operations depend upon mutual acceptance of those obligations as outlined.

WHAT DISTRIBUTORS CAN EXPECT FROM BLACK & DECKER

1. Selective Distribution:

- Appointed on the basis of power tool potential in each marketing area.
- Adequate to insure penetration of all markets for our products.
- Selected in accordance with the terms of this "Statement of Policy."

2. Specialized Field Sales Assistance Through:

- The largest, best-trained field sales organization in the industry.
- Product and market training (for Distributor's sales organization by means of effective sales meetings, power tool clinic sessions and joint sales calls in the field.
- Availability of market potential information to assist Distributor's sales planning.
- Assistance in the maintenance of a well balanced and current power tool and accessory inventory.

3. Healthy Profit Opportunities Through:

- Equitable profit margins on power tools and accessories.
- Assured inventory turnover.
- Maintaining an orderly market.
- Refusal to deal with Distributors who do not feel that the sales policies we suggest are based upon sound business judgment.

4. Aggressive Advertising and Sales Promotion Through:

- The best-known brand name in the industry.
- The largest and best program of national advertising, direct mail assistance and display materials in the power tool field.

5. Leadership in Research and Development Through:

- The broadest, most complete line in the industry.
- Continued leadership in product performance, value, styling and innovation.

6. Leadership in Manufacturing From:

- The largest, most modern plants in the industry.
- Unparalleled quality control standards.
- Thorough testing of all products before shipment.

7. Nation-wide Network of Factory-operated Service Facilities Which:

- Offer prompt, expert repair service at reasonable cost.
- Stock genuine Black & Decker replacement parts.

8. The Famous Black & Decker Guarantee Which:

- Protects the purchaser against defective material or workmanship for the life of the product.

WHAT BLACK & DECKER EXPECTS FROM DISTRIBUTORS

1. Effective Sales Results Through:

- An aggressive sales organization, knowledgeable in the application and selling of Black & Decker products.
- Effective sales management focus on our line.
- Adequate penetration of the potential market for our products in the Distributor's normal trading area.
- Cooperation with Black & Decker's field sales personnel in developing sales programs, meetings and work schedules designed to build sales performance.

2. Vigorous Promotional Activity Through:

- Imaginative advertising, direct mail activity, displays and catalog coverage of the Black & Decker line.

3. Protection of Black & Decker's Brand Name and Reputation By:

- Following the sales policies recommended by the company.
- Restricting sales to the Distributor's normal trading area.
- Discouraging the sale of Black & Decker products through non-authorized sales organizations, so that the customer will receive maximum service after purchase.
- Abstaining from marketing practices that, in any way, damage the reputation of the company or its products.

4. Maintenance of an Adequate Inventory By:

- Stocking tools and accessories of a variety and quantity commensurate with markets served and the highest standards of customer service. ("Adequate Inventory" shall be a matter of agreement between each Distributor and the appropriate Black & Decker sales representative.)

5. Provision of Those Other Services and Functions Which Characterize a Good Distributor, Such As:

- Extending credit to the user.
- Following up customer inquiries.
- Rendering prompt delivery from local stocks.
- Making available prompt technical services to customers.
- Keeping informed on market conditions.

With this STATEMENT OF POLICY, we reaffirm our belief in the economic soundness of the Distributor, our resolve continually to improve and diversify the products we offer and, through Distributor channels, to cultivate an ever-widening market for Black & Decker products.

THE BLACK & DECKER MANUFACTURING COMPANY

President

Chairman of the Board

Source: Roger Pegram, "Selecting and Evaluating Distributors Studies in Business Policy No. 116," New York: National Industrial Conference Board, 1965.

make cost comparisons between package sizes and brands is an illustrative area that has presented a real communications challenge to members of channel systems because of the variety of package sizes used by producers, costs of providing the information (usually borne by the remarketers), and the potential impact of the better informed consumer upon marketing strategy.[22] Channel management should give careful consideration to the types of information that are needed to help the channel system function properly, appropriate media for transmitting information, and the factors that may contribute to ineffective information flows.[23]

Evaluation of Existing Channels

Approaches to analysis of operating efficiency in a channel system from the point of view of a firm are of three general types: (1) use of checklists or market audit forms; (2) development of measures of channel system efficiency; (3) use of distribution cost analysis.[24] The last two approaches are really elements in an integrated management control process and can be consolidated. Appraising channel performance along with other marketing program elements should be a continuing management function. The major stages in the process consist of the following:

1. Defining the channel system in terms of participants, interrelationships, functions, and flows.
2. Specification of quantitative and qualitative objectives (e.g., sales, market share, costs, levels of end user satisfaction, etc.).
3. Based on objectives establishing relevant criteria and measures of performance.
4. Collection and analysis of sales, cost, and marketing research information.
5. Identification of performance gaps.
6. Formulation and implementation of needed corrective action.

Our examination of channel strategy development provides guidelines for defining the system. Within this framework operational objec-

---

[22] For an interesting analysis of unit pricing see Lawrence M. Lamont and James T. Rothe, "The Impact of Unit Pricing on Channel Systems," in Fred C. Allvine (ed.), *Relevance in Marketing: Problems, Research, Action* (Chicago: American Marketing Association, 1972), pp. 653–58.

[23] An approach to information management in the channel is outlined in Walter Gross, "Profitable Listening for Manufacturers and Dealers: How to Use a Communication System," *Business Horizons*, 11 (December 1968), pp. 35–44.

[24] McCammon and Little, "Marketing Channels: Analytical Systems and Approaches", p. 360.

tives should be specified. These serve as benchmarks for monitoring channel performance. Development of models and tools for guiding analysis and evaluation of channel results has been quite limited. This is understandable considering the difficulty of describing channel systems in terms of various economic, political, and social interactions. Thus, channel analysis has largely been concerned with assessments of sales and cost performance in combination with various types of attitude, preference, and opinion surveys obtained from channel system participants.

In selecting appropriate criteria and measures for evaluating channel system performance, management must recognize the flows, delays, and feedbacks that occur in the system. Evaluating performance should be linked to end user markets, as well as intermediaries. If market penetration is a performance criterion, then comparative measures of market share over time are needed. This requires an operational definition of the market, and assembly of information that corresponds to the market. For example, in the carbonated beverage market measures of market share obtained from consumers may not be consistent with retail dealer surveys, particularly if all types of outlets are not surveyed.[25] Similarly, analysis of retail or distributor stocks can be misleading because of leads and lags in channel flows.

When gaps in channel performance are identified the nature and extent of the corrective action will vary depending upon the seriousness of the problem. This can range from revisions in policies and procedures, increased motivational efforts, and other modifications such as replacing channel participants. In extreme cases, it may be necessary to change the entire channel system.

An illustrative analysis of the financial performance of four channels of distribution is shown in Table 17–5.[26] In Table 17–5A sales and cost data are shown for a manufacturer's four channels of distribution. The analysis indicated several unprofitable accounts which were contributing to the poor performance of channels C and D. In Table 17–5B, estimates are indicated for proposed changes including: elimination of channel D, dropping unprofitable small customers in Channel C; and increasing sales pressure on the remaining, profitable customers. The results for the year after the above changes were made are shown in Table 17–5C. Profits were nearly double in the year after the changes were made.

---

[25] An excellent illustration of the difficulty of measuring market share for a carbonated beverage in a large metropolitan market is provided in "The Southport Coca-Cola Bottling Company" case in Robert D. Buzzell, Donald F. Cox, and Rex V. Brown, *Marketing Research and Information Systems* (New York: McGraw-Hill Book Company, 1969), pp. 333–59.

[26] This example is drawn from Charles H. Sevin, *Marketing Productivity Analysis* (New York: McGraw-Hill Book Company, 1965), pp. 76–77.

TABLE 17–5

Illustrative Channel Productivity Analysis

A. Before Changes in Channels

Channels of Distribution	$ Sales	$ Variable Costs*	$ Profit Margin	% Sales
A...............	750,000	400,000	350,000	47
B...............	250,000	100,000	150,000	60
C...............	300,000	300,000		
D...............	200,000	250,000	−50,000†	−25†
Total.....................	1,500,000	1,050,000	450,000	30
Less: Nonvariable expense.........................			300,000	
Net profit..			150,000	10

B. Estimated Effect of Changes in Channels

Channels of Distribution	$ Sales	$ Variable Costs*	Net Profit
C..............	−150,000‡	−205,000	55,000
D..............	−200,000‡	−250,000	50,000
A and B..........	100,000§	85,000	15,000
Total....................	−250,000	−370,000	120,000

C. After Changes in Channels

Channels of Distribution	$ Sales	$ Variable Costs*	$ Profit Margin	% Sales
A................	825,000	415,000	410,000	50
B................	315,000	130,000	185,000	59
C................	120,000	110,000	10,000	8
Total.....................	1,260,000	655,000	605,000	48
Less: Nonvariable expense...........................			310,000	
Net profit..			295,000	23

* Production plus distribution costs.
† Loss.
‡ Eliminated.
§ Added.
Source: Reproduced from Charles H. Sevin, *Marketing Productivity Analysis* (New York: McGraw-Hill Book Company, 1965), p. 77.

Revising Channel Arrangements

Channel systems become obsolete in both consumer and industrial markets. Also over time improvements are made in their design. Distribution channels must be responsive to changing needs and wants of customers and to the innovative actions of competitors in developing new channel systems. Channel change in general tends to be more prevalent for consumer markets than for industrial markets. This may be due to greater attention placed by management on channel decisions in the consumer sector. Also, the greater complexity of many consumer product channel systems provides a greater opportunity for possible improvement. Changes can occur throughout an entire vertical distribution channel or at a particular point in the system such as at the wholesale or retail level.[27] For example, the catalog showroom warehouse, during the time span of a few years had developed by 1973 into a $4 billion retail discount business and was estimated to reach $5 billion by 1975.[28] Concentrating on jewelry, china, and small appliances and using price as a major instrument of competition, this retail innovation has had a major impact on conventional discount stores.

Marketing management must continuously monitor channel system effectiveness and seek improved distribution networks to meet changing conditions and potential market opportunities. While shifts in distribution channels usually occur over a period of several years, assuming that they will remain fixed indefinitely can be hazardous. "Institutions, like products, may be regarded as having life cycles which consist of stages such as inception, rapid early growth, maturity and decline."[29] The time span of these life cycles is growing increasingly short as evidenced, for example, by the fast food industry reaching maturity in less than a decade.

Various types of revisions in the channel system may be necessary including replacement of intermediaries that have removed themselves, or due to poor performance need to be eliminated; changes at a particular level in the system (e.g., addition of services to food convenience stores by a grocery wholesaler); or re-design of the entire channel system. A major change in a distribution channel has far reaching implications. Management typically does not undertake frequent modifications in channel design or shifts from one type of channel to another, since "every change involves a moderately long-term commitment (economically and ethically, if not legally), costs and benefits become vague, and the task of assigning magnitudes to each of them also becomes extremely difficult."[30]

When the decision to change a channel system is made it requires extensive planning and careful implementation. Unlike entering a new channel, a transition must take into account the need to maintain continuing service to existing end users and possible effects on remaining parts of the system. For example, shifting to a factory sales force from brokers or agents necessitates rapid development of customer contacts by salesmen who presumably can be effective in a very short time span.

---

[27] For several illustrations of emerging trends in marketing channels see Louis E. Boone and James C. Johnson (eds.), *Marketing Channels* (Morristown, N.J.: General Learning Press, 1973), pp. 431–500.

[28] "Catalog Discounting Is A Small Man's Game," *Business Week* (October 13, 1973), p. 70.

[29] William R. Davidson, "Changes in Distributive Institutions," *Journal Of Marketing*, 34 (January 1970), p. 9, published by the American Marketing Association.

[30] Oxenfeldt, *Executive Action in Marketing*, p. 444–45.

In many situations such quick response is not feasible. When faced with this type of change, a gradual transition on an area-by-area basis may be the only feasible alternative.

SUMMARY AND CONCLUSIONS

Unlike other elements of the marketing mix the channel system frequently cannot be completely controlled by a particular firm. Moreover, the central role of the channel system in the marketing program should be recognized. The channel is the process through which the marketing program must function. It can be viewed as a delivery system comprised of not only the physical product but also the various other elements of the marketing offer. Much like product or service decisions, the distribution channel after it is established tends to remain relatively fixed over a long time period; indeed, it may outlast many products. Yet, changes in distribution patterns are necessary in responding to changing environmental influences and customer needs and wants. Thus, the channel design should incorporate as much flexibility as possible to enable modifications as they become necessary.

While firms do not frequently develop new channel systems or seek entry into existing systems, a sound understanding of channel strategy development is an essential foundation to managing the existing channel system. A framework for designing distribution channels has been developed with three purposes in mind: (1) to provide an understanding of the purpose, structure, and interrelationships of channel systems as a basis for more effective management of channel relationships; (2) to outline an approach for designing a new channel system when this decision situation is encountered; and (3) to present a framework within which the appraisal of channel system performance can be more effectively accomplished.

EXERCISES FOR REVIEW AND DISCUSSION

1. A manufacturer is presently using five channels of Distribution: A, B, C, D and E. The sales and cost data for the five channels of distribution are:

Channel	$ Sales	$ Variable Costs	$ Profit Margin	Percent of Sales
A	350,000	350,000	—	13
B	600,000	400,000	200,000	22
C	200,000	300,000	−100,000	7
D	700,000	600,000	100,000	25
E	900,000	400,000	500,000	33
Total	2,750,000	2,050,000	700,000	100
Less Fixed Expenses			300,000	
Net Profit			400,000	

Based on the above information what changes in the channels of distribution would you propose in order to improve profits? What additional information would be useful in making a more complete evaluation of the five channels?

2. The National Music Corporation is a small manufacturer of musical instruments. Management is considering two different alternatives in selecting a distribution system: (*a*) use of brokers who could sell the musical instruments to different wholesalers and retailers, and (*b*) direct sales to three or four different wholesalers. What are the advantages and disadvantages of each method? On what criteria would you base your decision?

3. A firm has developed a new swimming pool chemical to be used by swimming pool owners, but the company has no prior experience in consumer markets. Evaluate the channel of distribution alternatives listed in Figure 17–4. Use the different criteria introduced in the text and discuss the advantages and disadvantages of each alternative. Select the best alternative.

4. The channel of distribution decision may be a part of the marketing mix and, at the same time, an uncontrollable factor by management of a firm (unlike advertising or personal selling). Discuss.

5. Suppose you have been asked by the marketing manager of a firm to develop a plan for changing from use of manufacturer's representatives to a factory sales force. Outline an approach to this task, identifying the major components of your plan. Make whatever assumptions that are necessary.

18

Price Decisions

Price can be one of the most visible elements of the firm's marketing mix. Potential buyers of some products scrutinize prices more closely than they do promotional messages, product quality, or other product features. Companies marketing such products view price as an active and critical decision variable. For other products, potential buyers pay relatively little attention to prices. Managers within these firms consider price to be a passive or inactive variable in their marketing mix. Regardless of the specific role played by price in a particular firm's marketing program, the impact of pricing decisions on sales and profits requires that decision makers understand pricing concepts and approaches. Illustrative of pricing decisions made by managements are:

In March, 1975, major can producers reduced the list prices of soft drink and beer cans in response to the increasing competition from glass container manufacturers.[1]

In 1975, manufacturers and marketers of electronic calculators were selling for under $30 models which a decade earlier had sold for up to $1000. Continuing technological breakthroughs and growing competition among calculator marketers had led to these tremendous price reductions.[2]

In the midst of declining demand for air travel services, National Airlines in April, 1975, appealed to the Civil Aeronautics Board (CAB) and was allowed to offer consumers a "No Frills" discount of 35 percent of its standard coachfare on selected flights. Passengers were allowed to pay less for fewer luxuries.[3]

[1] Gene G. Marcial, "Container Price Pressures Make Some Analysts Trim '75 Profit Estimates for Major Can Firms," *The Wall Street Journal* (April 14, 1975), p. 29.

[2] "The Semiconductor Becomes a New Marketing Force," *Business Week* (August 24, 1974), p. 35.

[3] Todd E. Fandell, "Fare Warfare: Plenty of Bargains Lure Air Travelers, But for How Long?" *The Wall Street Journal* (April 15, 1975), pp. 1, 21.

In the fall of 1974, when coal was in short supply, electric utility companies were paying $55 per ton for coal which sold for $5 to $15 per ton in 1970. Many utility companies were forced to request electric rate hikes in response to their rapidly rising fuel costs.[4]

This chapter initially provides an overview of the multiple roles of *price* in the U.S. economy. The major factors, both within and without the firm, which influence product pricing decisions are highlighted. Illustrations of price decision analyses are also presented. The major focus of the chapter, however, is the development of a framework for making price decisions.

AN APPROACH TO PRICING PRODUCTS

When Are Price Decisions Made?

When planning new product introductions, managers should anticipate possible changes in competitive, supply and demand markets and select appropriate initial strategies and tactics. These decisions must be accompanied by plans to make changes as they are needed. Price changes are planned by many firms before their products are introduced in the marketplace. However, even these firms find that additional decisions are usually required after introduction as products move through the various stages of their life cycles. Managers must make initial price decisions or evaluate and modify their past decisions whenever:

New products are added to their product mix;

Important environmental conditions change after pricing plans have been made;

Consumers and/or industrial users fail to respond as expected to the firm's price or offer;

It becomes appropriate to implement preplanned price changes; and

They bargain with potential buyers under variable price conditions.

Since price is a vital element of the marketing mix of most firms, management should develop an approach to setting prices that increases its probability of achieving corporate and marketing objectives. The importance of various types of price decisions and the appropriateness of utilizing specific pricing techniques varies among companies depending upon each firm's unique market, channel and organization characteristics. A general framework for the pricing process is presented below and the important factors which influence price decisions at each stage of the process are discussed.

---

[4] "Pocketing Those Millions: Wagner Calls Coal Producers 'Culprits,'" *Knoxville News Sentinel* (April 16, 1975), p. C-7.

A Price Decision Framework

An analytical framework for guiding management in making price decisions is shown in Figure 18–1. The process must begin with the major corporate decisions on *mission, target markets,* and *marketing objectives.* These decisions serve as very broad, general guidelines for subsequent price decisions. For example, a marketing objective of only offering superior quality products relative to competitors' products would be useful for narrowing the range of price alternatives to those that are at or above competitor prices. Typically, high product quality and product differentiation allows a firm to charge premium prices.

Consistent with these guidelines, *pricing objectives* must be established. These objectives not only serve as additional guidelines for subsequent pricing decisions, but also insure that prices set are consistent with the other components in the firm's marketing program. As an illustration, a firm that is trying to achieve an increased market share for a product may establish a pricing objective such as "price must be 10 percent lower than the average of competitors' prices for the same

FIGURE 18–1

A Framework for Making Price Decisions

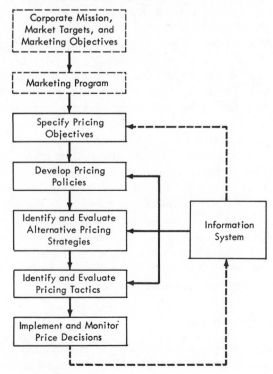

product." This objective integrates price with other decision areas also intended to achieve the market share objective.

Price objectives typically allow considerable flexibility in the way in which price is used by management to achieve marketing objectives. So, to assist management further in selecting appropriate prices, firms establish *pricing policies* that must be followed. These policies are also guidelines, but are designed to deal with foreseeable future situations that generally reoccur. An industrial products manufacturer may set a price policy that determines how much buyer-salesman negotiation will be allowed to vary actual price from the company's list price. Such a policy would be set because management knows that buyers will try to bargain for a discount off list price when interacting with company salesmen.

The feasible range of price alternatives can be narrowed even further by deciding upon *price strategies* for each product. A price strategy is a plan that management devises to achieve price objectives within a specific time period (that is consistent with present policies). A price strategy may be needed to react to some special circumstance that management had not anticipated. Suppose a competitor has just brought out a significantly modified product that will change the competitive situation. Management must devise a price strategy to react to this new situation that will achieve pricing objectives such as gradually lowering price over a designated time period.

The decisions made to this point in the analytical pricing process are designed substantially to reduce the number of price alternatives that must be considered for a product by establishing a range of prices that can be evaluated. These decisions ensure that the price selected will be consistent with the entire marketing program. The task now is to choose a *specific price* for the product to quote to customers.

The price decision making process is not completed once specific prices are determined. After prices are determined, they must be *implemented*. This requires coordination with other departmental activities within the firm (especially the advertising and production activities) as well as with the activities of resellers of the firm's products. Finally, a system must be developed and operated to *monitor* the impact of each price decision on company and reseller operations and upon consumer demand. Based upon information provided by the monitoring system, managers should continually reexamine their past price decisions and, when appropriate, make new decisions.

Basic Determinants of Prices

Price decisions, like other marketing decisions, are affected by a myriad of factors external to the firm. Each manager must identify and

FIGURE 18–2

Downward and Upward Sloping Demand Curves

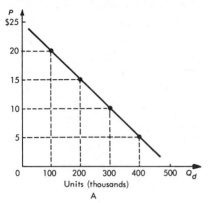
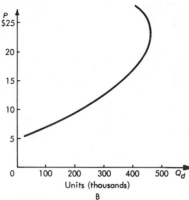

assess the major factors which constrain or define the boundaries of pricing decisions. Basic factors which influence most managers' decisions include: *market demand, competition, costs, economic climate, laws and ethics, organizational interrelationships, marketing mix interdependencies and channel relationships.*

Impact of Buyer Demand. The traditional "law of demand" states that price reductions generate demand increases and price increases generate demand reductions (if all other things are equal). This law prescribes the general character of the market "demand curve," a curve which depicts the quantity of market demand for a product at each possible price. According to this law, the demand curve slopes downward and to the right when plotted on a vertical price and horizontal quantity axis as in Figure 18–2A. Not all products exhibit the traditional inverse relationship between price and quantity demanded. Instead, some products have a price-quantity relationship that is described by a positively sloped demand curve as shown in Figure 18–2B. Demand may be greater at higher prices whenever consumers perceive:

1. Product prices to accurately reflect product quality;
2. The negative consequences associated with purchasing an unsatisfactory brand to be great;
3. The variation in product quality among competing brands to be great;
4. The social importance of brand selection to be significant; and,
5. The task of assessing product quality to be very difficult.[5]

---

[5] See Zarrel V. Lambert, "Product Perception: An Important Variable in Price Strategy," *Journal of Marketing,* vol. 34 (October 1970), pp. 68–76; Benson P. Shapiro, "The Psychology of Pricing," *Harvard Business Review,* vol. 46 (July–August

The marketing strategist is concerned not only with the absolute level of demand at each price level but also with the direction and the rate at which demand changes as price changes. If a 10 percent increase in price yields only a 5 percent decrease in unit sales and no perceptable change in average unit costs, then the increase results in higher profits. Conversely, if a 10 percent price hike cuts sales by 20 percent, then total revenues fall. If average unit costs are unaffected by the volume cutback, profits will decline. A measure of the responsiveness of demand to price changes is the *price elasticity of demand coefficient* (E_p). It is the ratio of the percentage change in units demanded to the percentage change in a product's price.

$$E_p = \frac{\text{Percent change in quantity demanded}}{\text{Percent change in price}}$$

Or

$$E_p = \frac{\dfrac{\text{Absolute change in demand at new price}}{\text{Demand at old price}}}{\dfrac{\text{Absolute change in price}}{\text{Old price}}}$$

For the hypothetical product whose demand curve is shown in Figure 18–2A, for example, a reduction in price from $20 to $15 (a 25 percent cut) increases demand from 100,000 to 200,000 units (a 100 percent jump). The price elasticity of demand for reductions from $20 to $15 for this product is 4.0.

$$E_p = \frac{\dfrac{100,000}{100,000}}{\dfrac{\$5}{\$20}} = 4.0$$

When the coefficient is greater than 1.0, a product is *price elastic*. Since price changes yield greater than proportional changes in demand, price hikes decrease and price cuts increase total revenues (price times quantity demanded). When the coefficient is less than 1.0, a product is *price inelastic* or not very responsive to price changes. Price hikes on price inelastic products increase revenues and price cuts decrease revenues. When demand changes exactly in proportion to changes in price, a product is *unitary elastic* and the elasticity coefficient is 1.0.

Price elasticity of demand varies throughout the entire range of feasi-

1968), p. 20; D. S. Tull, R. A. Boring and M. H. Gonsior, "A Note on the Relationship of Price and Imputed Quality," *Journal of Business,* vol. 37 (April 1964), pp. 186–91; Kent Monroe, "Buyers' Subjective Perceptions of Price," *Journal of Marketing Research,* vol. 10 (February 1973), pp. 70–80; and Robert A. Peterson, "The Price-Perceived Quality Relationship: Experimental Evidence," *Journal of Marketing Research,* vol. 7 (November 1970), pp. 525–28.

ble prices for most products.[6] For example, raising the price of a marketing textbook 20 percent, from $12.50 to $15.00 may have an insignificant impact upon sales. (In fact, if price is believed by buyers to be positively correlated with quality, sales may increase.) Demand may become very elastic at prices above $17, however. Thus, if price was raised another 20 percent above $15 to $18, demand may decline substantially. If unit average costs serve as "price floors," price elasticity coefficients can identify "ceilings" or price levels which are perceived by the majority of the potential buyers to be "too high."

Demand elasticity also varies by product type. National Airlines in 1975 believed that consumer demand for air travel was price *elastic* and that demand could be stimulated and total revenue increased by cutting fares. Initial sales response to selected 35 percent fare reductions indicated that demand was more *inelastic* than expected, however. Too few new passenger miles were generated to offset the unit revenue reductions and total revenues fell.[7] Most oil industry executives for years believed that demand for gasoline in the U.S. was highly inelastic; i.e., not very responsive to price changes. One Chase Manhattan Bank economist in 1975 estimated that 50 percent price increases (from 38 to 57 cents) would reduce demand by 7.5 percent.[8] The elasticity of demand coefficient of 0.15 ($.075 \div .50$) suggests that demand for gasoline was estimated to be very price inelastic. Large gasoline price increases were expected to reduce demand only slightly, so, total revenues were expected to increase with price hikes.

Influence of Competition. Implicit in the law of demand is that buyers and sellers interact in a free market environment and the prices at which goods are exchanged are determined by that interaction. The extent to which free market forces determine prices depends greatly upon the structure of markets. Under conditions of pure competition (i.e., many buyers and sellers with perfect information, homogeneous products, easy industry exit and entry, and rational decision making), economic price theory predicts that the interaction of buyers and sellers will result in prices which will, in the long run, cover all costs and allow only a "fair" return on investment. The structure of many markets in the United States precludes this kind of buyer-seller interaction, however. Most markets exhibit some degree of monopoly power. Monopoly power allows sellers to have greater freedom to set prices by ad-

---

[6] Research which reports on the phenomenon of price ceilings or thresholds is reported in Kent B. Monroe, "Measuring Price Thresholds by Psychophysics and Latitudes of Acceptance," *Journal of Marketing Research,* vol. 8 (November 1971), pp. 460–64.

[7] "National Airlines' 'Frill' May Be Gone but So Is Its Business," *The Wall Street Journal* (May 2, 1975), p. 24.

[8] Sharon Sabin, "Don't Fill'er Up: With Gasoline Higher, Motorists Buy Less, Surprising Experts," *The Wall Street Journal* (August 1, 1974), p. 1, 13.

ministrative fiat rather than to have prices completely determined by supply and demand forces. Such pricing has been termed "administered pricing."[9] The ability of firms to administer prices depends upon the number of competitors in the industry, the degree of differentiation among competing products and consumer brand preferences, and the ease of industry entry by potential competitors.

Costs. The costs of producing and marketing products are usually major determinants of product prices. Many manufacturers and most wholesalers and retailers establish their selling prices by adding fixed percentage markups to their costs. While consumer prices do change, sometimes suddenly and dramatically, these prices are generally more stable in the short term than the prices that manufacturers and resellers pay for materials and finished goods supplies. Manufacturers' costs vary not only with their supply costs but also with their cumulative production experience. One common relationship between costs and production experience, discovered long ago in the aircraft industry, is that as the *cumulative* number of units produced increases, total production costs decline by a fixed percentage (an experience or "learning curve" effect).[10] The characteristic relationship between changes in production costs and product prices is shown in Figure 18–3. When a new product is introduced, price is sometimes set slightly below initial total costs. (See Point A in Figure 18–3). As cumulative production and sales volume grow over time, costs typically decline. If price is maintained and does not reflect these declining costs, then high profits usually attract competition that drives price down to a more "reasonable" level above costs.[11] Between A and B, perhaps year 1 and year 3, costs decline at a rate much greater than the decline in price.

Economic Climate. The general economic climate, which reflects supply, demand, cost and competitive factors, always influences price decisions. Raw materials and finished goods shortages create special problems for marketers. Some sellers find that the sellers' market conditions allow them to demand higher prices and provide fewer services to their customers. Pricing during periods of rampant *inflation* also requires special attention.[12] With static prices and steadily rising materials, labor,

---

[9] Gardiner C. Means, "The Administered-Price Thesis Reconfirmed," *American Economic Review* vol. 62 (June 1972), pp. 292–306. For another view see Gilbert Burck, "The Myths and Realities of Corporate Pricing," *Fortune Magazine*, vol. 85 (April 1972), pp. 84–89, 125–26.

[10] Patrick Conley, "Experience Curves as a Planning Tool," *IEEE Spectrum*, vol. 7 no. 6 (June 1970), pp. 63–68; and W. B. Hirshmann, "Profit from the Learning Curve," *Harvard Business Review*, vol. 42 (January–February 1964), pp. 125–39.

[11] Conley, "Experience Curves as a Planning Tool."

[12] "Staying Loose: More Suppliers Shun Fixed Price Contracts to Outwit Inflation: Price at Time of Delivery Becomes Popular Tactic: Consumers Feel Impact," *Wall Street Journal* (April 15, 1974), p. 1.

FIGURE 18–3

Costs and Prices: The Characteristic Pattern

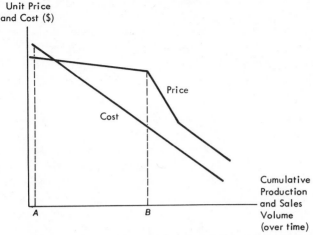

Source: Adapted from Patrick Conley, "Experience Curves as a Planning Tool," *IEEE Spectrum*, vol. 7, no. 6 (June 1970), pp. 63–68.

occupancy and other costs, many marketers find that selling prices must be adjusted upward to protect required profits. This condition makes necessary a system to provide managers with timely and relevant information regarding short and long-run supply conditions, operating costs and competitive prices.[13] Pricing formulae (e.g., standard markup systems) must incorporate an "inflation factor" to protect future profits. Finally, since competitors typically face similar rising costs and respond by raising prices in apparent concert, corporate executives must be especially careful *not* to exchange price information, meet informally or engage in any practices that may lead to charges of illegal collusion and price fixing during periods of rising prices.[14]

Legal and Ethical Constraints. Legal and ethical considerations limit decision-makers' price alternatives.[15] The principal body of law which governs price decisions is *antitrust legislation.* The Sherman (1890), Clayton (1914) and Federal Trade Commission (1914) Acts and subsequent amending legislation (Robinson-Patman, 1936; Miller-Tydings, 1937; and, McGuire, 1952) provide the basis for tests of the legality of pricing decisions.

---

[13] Nessim Hanna, "10 Ways Inflation-Recession Challenge Marketers with Pricing Responsibilities," *Marketing News* (February 28, 1975), p. 4.

[14] Alan B. Hobbes, "Antitrust in an Inflationary Economy," *The Conference Board Record* (August 1969), pp. 22–23.

[15] These issues were previously treated in Chapter 6.

Ethical considerations which extend beyond the boundary of legal and illegal activities also influence price decisions. When do prices generate too much profit? Is a firm justified in setting prices equal to buyers' perceptions of value even if such prices are far above actual costs? These types of questions must be answered by the decision maker and he must always be cognizant of the social and political environments.

The growing probability of increased direct government influence in corporate price decision making is best summarized by the following statements:

". . . inflation will drive all the Western countries into a planned economy via price controls."[16]

> Friedrich A. von Hayek,
> 1974 Nobel Prizewinner in Economics

". . . our economic system is steadily shifting from a private enterprise, free market economy to one that is centrally directed and under public control."[17]

> C. Jackson Grayson, Jr.,
> Former Head of the Price Commission

Direct control of corporate pricing activities by the U.S. government is not a unique phenomenon of the seventies. Rather, since the early days of this nation the government has intermittently controlled prices to protect domestic industries threatened by foreign competition, to restrain rising prices on items in short supply during wartime, and to promote general economic stability. Both monetarists and Keynesians have repeatedly failed to provide complete economic stability since the end of the second world war. Also, citizen demands for egalitarian policies and international interdependencies have increased while domestic faith in the free market system has been eroded. Although it is only a remote possibility, if these trends continue, marketers may face even higher levels of federal control of their pricing decisions.

Organizational Influences. Price decisions are most appropriately made by marketing executives after they receive cost, market demand and competitive information. Yet, because of conflicting personal and departmental goals and attitudes, prices do not always change in tempo with fluctuating costs and market conditions. For example, a market research study may suggest that unit sales of a product could be increased by 10 percent if price is reduced by 5 percent. Cost accounting figures may indicate that unit costs would be reduced if output was expanded. However, a key executive with pricing authority and something other than a market orientation may veto such a suggestion. Table 18–1 in-

---

[16] Tibor R. Machan, "Economics, Politics and Freedom," *Reason,* vol. 6 no. 10 (February 1975), p. 12.

[17] C. Jackson Grayson, Jr., "Let's Get Back to the Competitive Market System," *Harvard Business Review,* vol. 51 (November–December 1973), p. 103.

TABLE 18–1

Executive Participation in New Product Pricing Decisions

Title or Function	Participates in Pricing Process	Has Primary Responsibility for Setting Prices	
		Shared	Alone
General executives			
Chairman of the board........................	3	3	
President....................................	36	29	1
Other general executives......................	26	23	1
Division head...............................	47	34	6
Marketing or sales			
Chief marketing or sales executive..............	121	96	14
Other marketing or sales executives.............	26	19	
Product managers............................	27	23	1
Marketing research...........................	10	4	
Marketing services...........................	8	4	
Market or commercial development.............	4	3	
Merchandising...............................	3	3	
Advertising..................................	2	1	
Distribution.................................	1	1	
Finance			
Financial vice-president or treasurer............	24	18	2
Controller or accounting head..................	43	17	
Cost department.............................	9	3	
Estimating department........................	4	3	
Manufacturing................................	31	18	
Technical			
Engineering..................................	10	6	
Industrial engineering........................	6	4	
Product development..........................	6	6	
Research and development.....................	9	6	
Other			
Pricing department...........................	3		2
Program department..........................	1		
Economist...................................	1		
Pricing committee*...........................	18	13	5

* Where committee members were identified by respondents, they have been included above in the list of specific titles or functions.

Note: In a number of divisionalized companies, titles or functions mentioned above are at the divisional level. For example, in forty-three reporting companies, the chief marketing or sales executive of each division is involved in new-product pricing (sharing primary responsibility in thirty-two companies and holding this responsibility alone in five others).

Source: N.I.C.B., *The Conference Board Record*, 1, no. 4 (January 1964), p. 11.

dicates that in most firms, many executives participate in new product pricing decisions.

Marketing Interrelationships. Price decisions are interrelated with other marketing decisions and the failure to recognize this can lead to suboptimization. The decision to set a price on one item in a product line should not be made without considering the impact that price might have upon other items in the line. Many firms carry substitutable products (e.g., Procter and Gamble's Tide and All detergents) and/or complementary products (e.g., golf balls and gloves). Pricing of all items in a product line should enhance overall profitability by stimulating sales of high margin items at the expense of less profitable items.[18] Pricing decisions are also interrelated with the firm's promotional decisions. A price change may require price list, label, advertising copy, and other changes. The costs associated with these changes could be greater than the additional revenue generated by a price change. It is also true that additional advertising and other promotional expenditures in some cases allow the firm to enjoy production, marketing and administrative economies of scale and, thus, reduce average unit costs. Significant reductions in retail prices (in constant dollars) of children's toys, for example, have been attributed to promotion. It has been argued that lower wholesale and retail margins have been made possible by more rapid inventory turnover.[19]

Channel Implications. Since market success for manufacturers, wholesalers and retailers depends ultimately upon consumer or user purchases, pricing decisions must be made in light of supplier and reseller interests and decisions. Some suppliers believe it is in their best interest for resellers to maintain suggested resale prices. Reseller cooperation is often cultivated with high suggested margins, promotional support and other attractive services.[20] Cultivation alone doesn't always generate the desired level of voluntary cooperation, however. Some resellers demand that they be allowed to set their own resale prices with no supplier influence. Suppliers on occasion have taken coercive actions to force compliance. The Sony and Matsushita Corporations, for example, have been strong advocates of price maintenance at the retail level. (Matsushita markets Panasonic brand appliances.) These two firms have taken a dim view of discounting from their suggested retail prices. Both have employed comparison shoppers to shop their resellers to identify discounters. Discounting retailers who were identified in states which allowed vertical price fixing received letters from the manufacturers warning that legal action would be taken unless suggested prices were maintained. If

---

[18] Alfred R. Oxenfelt, "Product Line Pricing," *Harvard Business Review,* vol. 44 no. 4 (July–August 1966), pp. 137–44.

[19] Robert L. Steiner, "Does Advertising Lower Consumer Prices?" *Journal of Marketing,* vol. 37 (October 1973), pp. 19–26, published by the American Marketing Association.

[20] See for example Martin R. Warshaw, "Pricing to Gain Wholesalers' Selling Support," *Journal of Marketing,* vol. 27 (July 1962), pp. 50–54 and Louis W. Stern, "Approaches to Achieving Retail Price Stability," *Business Horizons,* vol. 5 (Fall 1964), pp. 75–86.

discounting continued, the violators were subpoenaed and compliance was enforced.[21]

Texas Instruments, Inc., the successful calculator marketer, made frequent and aggressive price decisions without regard to the impact of those decisions upon resellers which led to a loss of channel support and cooperation. Texas Instruments intermittently slashed its suggested retail prices without warning dealers who were maintaining suggested prices. Some dealers were caught with insufficient inventories to meet customer demand at the new lower prices advertised by TI and others were forced to sell items which they purchased at high prices at unprofitable margins.[22] These examples demonstrate how some firms make pricing decisions without regard for the probable impact they will have upon either suppliers or resellers.

MAKING PRICE DECISIONS

Managers make a series of interrelated decisions to develop a comprehensive pricing program. A framework for making price decisions, as shown in Figure 18–1, must incorporate many significant influences on managers' decisions at each stage of the process. Each stage of the decision process is discussed in order below.

Price Objectives

As important as objectives are to the process of management, too many firms fail to establish specific objectives for their pricing programs. Just as corporate objectives are prerequisites to corporate strategy formulation, pricing objectives must precede strategic and tactical pricing decisions. Like objectives in every area of business operations, pricing objectives should be clear, concise and understood by all involved in making pricing decisions. Further, they should be stated in a manner that will enable those charged with evaluating pricing effectiveness to compare subsequent performance to objectives.

A study of corporate pricing has identified the diversity of pricing objectives of some of the largest U.S. corporations.[23] Few of the firms

---

[21] Jonathan Kwitny, "Fair Trade Fight: Discounters Campaign Against Laws that Let Retail Prices Be Fixed," *The Wall Street Journal* (May 13, 1974), pp. 1, 19.

[22] "Texas Instruments: Pushing Hard into the Consumer Markets," *Business Week* (August 1974), pp. 39–42.

[23] A. D. H. Kaplan, Joel B. Dirham and Robert F. Lanzillotti, *Pricing in Big Business* (The Brookings Institution: Washington, D.C., 1958). A concise presentation of the findings related to pricing objectives is found in: Robert F. Lanzillotti, "Pricing Objectives in Large Companies," *American Economic Review*, vol. 48 (December 1958), pp. 921–40. The survey was limited to those companies whose managements permitted extensive interviews with top executives to allow the researchers to determine pricing objectives and practices. Thus, the findings are not generalizable to all U.S. corporations.

surveyed actually stated pricing objectives in terms of maximizing profits. Rather, most tried to attain a "satisfactory" or target level of profits or return on investment. Moreover, almost all firms surveyed had some pricing objectives that were not directly related to profits. Examples of such objectives include:[24]

1. "to meet the prices of competitors," Goodyear;
2. "to follow the price of the most important marketer in each area," Gulf;
3. "to maintain existing market share," Kroger.

Even companies whose primary pricing objectives were stated in terms of profit margin or return on investment had collateral pricing objectives such as the following:[25]

1. "to promote new products," Alcoa and General Electric;
2. "to stabilize industry prices," Esso (Exxon) and Johns-Mansville;
3. "to maintain a full-line of food products and novelties," General Foods.

A partial list of illustrative areas for pricing objectives, presented in Table 18–2, demonstrates the diversity of corporate pricing objectives.

Price Policies

Price policies are the guidelines or rules which decision makers follow when making strategic and tactical price decisions. Almost all firms adhere to specific price policies even in the absence of formal price policy statements. Particularly important policy areas include variability of prices, relation to competitors and relation to resellers.

Variability of Prices. Before price strategies can be adopted, management must decide whether it will adhere to a *single* or *variable* price policy. In other words, will the selling price for each product be the same for all buyers or will it be different for different buyers? A variable pricing policy enables the firm to achieve higher profits because it allows sellers to negotiate with potential buyers and set selling prices approximately equal to each buyer's perception of product value. Automobile salesmen, for example, strive to assess each potential buyer's desire to own a new automobile and to make the sale at the highest price that is acceptable to the buyer. The dentist whose time is perceived by him to be very valuable may not wish to "haggle" over a couple of hundred dollars when shopping for a second car. The high school teacher with a family to support and a very tight budget may make several shopping trips and bargain for days for additional discounts totaling $200.

---

[24] Lanzillotti, "Pricing Objectives in Large Companies," pp. 924–27.
[25] Ibid.

TABLE 18–2

Potential Pricing Objectives Areas

1. Maximum long-run profits
2. Maximum short-run profits
3. Growth (sales and/or profits)
4. Stabilize market prices
5. Desensitize customers to price
6. Maintain price-leadership arrangements
7. Discourage entrants
8. Speed exit of marginal firms
9. Avoid government investigation and control
10. Maintain loyalty of middlemen and get their sales support
11. Avoid demands for "more" from suppliers—labor in particular.
12. Enhance image of firm
13. Be regarded as "fair" by customers (ultimate)
14. Create interest and excitement about the item
15. Be considered trustworthy and reliable by rivals
16. Help in the sale of weak items in the line
17. Discourage others from cutting prices
18. Make a product "visible"
19. "Spoil market" to obtain high price for sale of business
20. Build traffic
21. Recover development and introductory costs rapidly
22. Establish market position rapidly
23. Provide a promotional theme
24. Contribute to the development of a product's image
25. Fill out the firm's product line

Source: Adapted from Alfred R. Oxenfelt, "A Decision-making Structure for Price Decisions," *Journal of Marketing*, vol. 37 (January 1973), pp. 48–53, published by The American Marketing Association.

Each buyer may eventually pay what he perceives to be a fair price for the same model. Had a single price been set for both buyers, however, the seller would have likely lost the teacher's purchase because the price would have been too high or sold the car to the dentist at a price below what he would have willingly paid.

Because of the limitations imposed upon sellers by the Robinson-Patman Act, most firms selling to industrial users or resellers avoid a completely variable pricing policy. In many companies, however, explicit or implicit variable price policies allow the granting of trade (or functional), quantity, cash and/or geographical discounts to buyers. Some firms also use minor product variations or label some output as "seconds" to justify setting different prices to different customers.[26]

Relation to Competition. Managers must determine the role of price in competitive activities designed to give the firm a differential advantage. How will the firm respond to price changes by competitors? Will price decisions be made to inflict serious competitive injury or even drive

[26] E. Raymond Corey, *Industrial Marketing* (Englewood Cliffs, N.J.: Prentice-Hall, 1962), pp. 219–20.

selected competitors out of business?[27] Antitrust legislation prohibits firms from engaging in "predatory" pricing practices designed to destroy competitors if the effect is to substantially impair subsequent competition in the marketplace. However, the FTC and the courts have repeatedly upheld the legality of competition which weakens or even destroys individual competitors but does not substantially destroy "competition." Between the extremes of competitive price collusion and predatory price coercion is a range of possible pricing activities so diverse that price policies are needed to guide managers.

Relation to Suppliers and Resellers. Marketers of goods supplied by other firms must adopt a policy either to passively abide by the repricing suggestions of suppliers or to attempt to influence suppliers' policies regarding reseller pricing. Further, firms selling through resellers must have policies to govern its reseller related price decisions. Two major reseller-related price policy areas are: the structure of trade discounts and substitutes (e.g., display materials, sales "spiffs" or bonuses paid to retail salespeople who sell certain "hard to move" merchandise, promotional allowances, etc.) and price protection policies.[28] In the late 1950s Schick attempted to change the structure of its distribution system by eliminating its independent wholesalers and selling directly to retailers. Schick reduced its suggested retail prices sharply (by 29 percent) but held the line on its prices to retailers. To compensate the retailers for having to operate on lower margins, advertising and promotional funds were offered to those retailers who adhered to the new suggested prices.[29] These programs were designed to increase retail turnover which was needed to maintain retail profits when unit margins were reduced.

Price Strategies

Price strategies are the long range plans devised by management to accomplish the objectives of the pricing program. Managers making strategic price decisions are guided and/or constrained by the price policies adopted by the firm. For example, if a firm does not allow price variability, then its salesmen are not allowed to discriminate in selling to different buyers. Price strategies are plans for pricing a specific product, a line of products or the entire mix of products offered by a company. Price strategies do not specify product prices; those are tactical pricing decisions (see Figure 18–1). Six common price strategies are:

[27] Alfred R. Oxenfelt, "A Decision-making Structure for Price Decisions," *Journal of Marketing,* vol. 37 (January 1973), p. 50, published by the American Marketing Association.

[28] Bert C. McCammon, Jr., "Perspectives for Distribution Programming," in Louis P. Bucklin, ed., *Vertical Marketing Systems* (Glenview, Ill: Scott, Foresman and Co., 1970), pp. 32–51.

[29] Stern, "Approaches to Achieving Retail Price Stability."

pricing level, life cycle pricing, product line pricing, psychological pricing, stability pricing, and discriminatory pricing.

Price Level. The relationship between the price of a product and unit costs and competitors' prices can affect sales and can attract or discourage potential competitors. Whenever a new product is added to a firm's product mix, a general price level must be determined before a final price can be set. For truly unique products which face no immediate competition, the extremes of the strategic price level continuum are "skim" and "penetration" pricing. A "skim" strategy sets introductory prices at relatively high levels in relation to average unit costs. "Skimming" may be appropriate if the firm expects to engage in extensive generic demand promotion activities which require large advertising and personal selling expenditures and high reseller margins. Many firms choose to "skim" when they are unsure of the elasticity of consumer demand. In the absence of immediate competition, they feel it is safe to set initial new product prices very high in relation to costs and gradually lower price as dictated by market conditions. Skimming may allow a seller to recover his investment very rapidly but the high margins often attract competition. If a firm wishes to be a long-term competitor in the industry *and* if it believes that it could retain an acceptable share of the market if faced with competition, then it would be appropriate to skim.

The extreme opposite of a skim strategy is a penetration strategy. It is a plan to set new product prices relatively low in relation to costs. This strategy is employed primarily to acquire a large share of a potential market. The relatively low margins also often discourage rapid competitive entry. If a market is large enough, however, competitors may be attracted even if margins are relatively low. Then, the appropriateness of a penetration strategy depends upon the ability of the firm to retain its desired market share once competition develops.

DuPont, for example, was the first company to produce cyclohexane, a product which is directly integrated with oil refining. Knowing that oil refiners with an inherent cost advantage would soon develop competitive products, the company realized that it had only a short period of time to recover its high developmental expenses. DuPont set the initial price on cyclohexane at a very high level (a skim strategy) and planned to get out of the market once the U.S. oil refiners developed competitive products. DuPont discontinued production of cyclohexane when the number of competing producers increased to a certain level, and left the oil refiners in a state of severe price competition.[30]

Strategic price level decisions must also be made by firms when they introduce new products in the face of existing competition and when

---

[30] Robert Stobaugh and Phillip L. Townsend, "Price Forecasting and Strategic Planning: The Case of Petrochemicals," *Journal of Marketing Research,* vol. 12 (February 1975), pp. 26–27.

they consider adapting their marketing program to a changing environment. In such cases, firms decide to price above, at, or below competitors' prices. Decision makers must consider among other things their firm's current and desired image, product line objectives, competitive strengths and weaknesses, competitors' prices and the state of the economy.

Sears' decision to alter its marketing strategy in general and its pricing strategy in particular in the mid-seventies was influenced by several of these factors.[31] Before World War II, Sears appealed to the price conscious shoppers and priced its products below competitors' prices. After the war, however, Sears capitalized on rising American affluence and "traded-up" their shoppers to more expensive merchandise. While profits grew steadily, Sears lost the price-conscious shopper to J. C. Penney, Co., S. S. Kresge Co. and Montgomery Ward and Co. Between 1964 and 1974, Sears' share of the total sales of retailing's Big Four (i.e., Sears, Penney, Kresge and Montgomery Ward) fell from 56 to 47 percent with Kresge's K-Mart stores picking up the majority of the price sensitive customers who were forfeited by Sears.[32] With profits falling during the recession of 1974–1975, Sears sought to return to its basic low price strategy. The company began to exert its influence upon its suppliers to cut costs and it increased the number of "budget shops" to appeal to price-conscious shoppers. At the same time, Sears began to slash prices throughout its mix of 100,000 plus items. Because Sears' competitors also reduced prices in response to the unfavorable economic climate, the impact of Sears' change in strategy was minor.

Life Cycle Pricing. Preplanning price changes as products move through the stages of the life cycle is a major price strategy of some companies. In general, average prices (in constant dollars) decline and the number of competing firms increase over most products' life cycles. Each company must assess its ability to compete effectively and to develop a differential competitive advantage at each stage of a product's life cycle. Average prices and the number of competing firms for eight petrochemical products during distinct life cycle stages are shown in Table 18–3. These figures show that prices generally fell and the number of competitors rose over time.

Semiconductor component manufacturers, such as Rockwell International, Texas Instruments and National Semiconductor Corporation, have used a life cycle pricing strategy which has squeezed the nonintegrated firms out of the consumer calculator industry.[33] About 70 percent of the manufacturing cost of calculators is accounted for by semiconductor components. The main weapon of the semiconductor manufacturers has been

---

[31] David M. Elsner, "Back to Basics: Recession Spurs Sears to Cut Prices, Return to Past Sales Strategy," *The Wall Street Journal* (February 10, 1975), pp. 1, 14.

[32] Ibid., p. 1.

[33] "The Semiconductor Becomes a New Marketing Force," p. 34.

TABLE 18–3

Number of Competitors and Average Prices for Eight Petrochemicals by Stage of the Product Life Cycle*

| | Stage of Product Life Cycle† | | | | | |
| | Stage I | | Stage II | | Stage III | |
Product	Average Number of Competitors	Average Price	Average Number of Competitors	Average Price	Average Number of Competitors	Average Price
Acrylonitride	2	30.8	6‡	14.5‡	N.A.	N.A.
Cyclahexane	2	4.9	5	5.3	10‡	3.4‡
Methanol	3	19.0	5	7.5	9‡	3.6‡
Orthoxylene	5‡	3.6‡	N.A.	N.A.	N.A.	N.A.
Paraxylene	1	18.8	5‡	10.0‡	N.A.	N.A.
Phenol	3	37.7	4	18.6	9‡	13.7‡
Styrene	2	24.2	5	14.5	9‡	8.1‡
Vinyl chloride	3	30.1	10‡	8.4‡	9‡	N.A.

* Average prices are expressed in 1958 cents/pound by using the GNP deflator to correct actual prices to real prices.
† Stages of the Product Life Cycle are defined as follows:

| | Growth Rate of Consumption in U.S. Market (normalized by GNP measured |
Stage Number	in constant dollars)
I............................	20 percent or more
II............................	7 percent to 20 percent
III............................	0 percent to 7 percent

‡ Product had not left this stage of the product life cycle as of 1966.
Source: Adapted from Robert B. Stobaugh and Phillip L. Townsend, "Price Forecasting and Strategic Planning: The Case of Petrochemicals," *Journal of Marketing Research*, vol. 12 (February 1975), p. 20, published by the American Marketing Association.

"learning curve pricing." They have been able to anticipate manufacturing cost reductions which follow production and sales increases and, therefore, slash prices to build volume. Texas Instruments' prices, for example, *fell* by an annual average of 8 percent while average prices in the U.S. private sector rose 4.4 percent per year between 1968 and 1973. The result was that simple four-function calculators which sold for up to $400 in 1970 were selling for $20 to $30 by 1975.[34]

Price Lining. Price lining is the strategy of offering a product at each price level of competitive products in a particular category. The Chevrolet Division of General Motors, for example, offers a product to appeal to specific segments of the total auto market at each price level with models ranging from a "stripped-down" Vega to a "loaded" Caprice Classic. The ultimate in retailer price lining is "inverted pricing." The traditional approach to setting prices is to "build up" a selling price by adding required markups to costs at each level of the marketing channel. "Inverted pricing" begins with a target retail price for a product from which normal

[34] "Texas Instruments: Pushing Hard into the Consumer Markets," p. 40.

markups are deducted to identify a necessary manufacturing cost. Thus, it is an inversion of the traditional approach. Inverted pricing is used by many manufacturers to fill "gaps" in their line of goods offered at retail. The first step in the process is to subtract distributor margins and costs from a retail price goal to get manufacturer prices. Based upon these figures, products are designed to fit into the line strategically and yield the needed manufacturer and reseller margins. With prices of men's suits polarized at the $175 to $225 and $65 and $85 levels, one clothing manufacturer identified a target market for average quality, conservative, yet stylish suits selling for approximately $130. Recognizing the required 40 percent retail, 30 percent wholesale and his own 25 percent markups, the manufacturer determined that he had to manufacture the suits for $57.00 or less (see Table 18–4).

TABLE 18–4
Inverted Pricing of Suit of Clothing

Desired Retail Price..........................	$130.00
Required Cost to Retailer (Allowing a 40 percent retail markup on cost)...........................	93.00
Required Cost to Wholesaler (Allowing a 30 percent wholesale markup on cost)...................	71.50
Required Manufacturing Cost (Allowing a 25 percent manu- facturer markup on cost)...................	57.00

Psychological Pricing. As was indicated in the earlier discussion of upward-sloping demand curves, the law of demand is invalid for some buyers of some goods. Psychological pricing strategies include pricing just below round numbers (e.g., $9.99), adhering to customary price levels (e.g., the once common five cent candy bar), and pricing to benefit from "snob appeal" (the "if you ask the price you can't afford it" psychology) as well as setting price to imply quality.[35] The appropriateness of psychological pricing strategies is dependent upon consumer price consciousness more than any other factor. Before final prices are set, management should determine if consumers' purchases are significantly influenced by their perception of product "quality" and if those consumers use price as an indicator of quality.

Consumers Union is a nonprofit organization which monthly publishes *Consumer Reports.* In that magazine CU publishes its evaluations of the

---

[35] An excellent integrative summary and critical analysis of psychological pricing research is presented in Benson P. Shapiro, "The Psychology of Pricing," pp. 14–25 and 160.

TABLE 18–5

The Relationship between Price and Consumers Union Quality Ratings of 23 Slide Projectors

Product	List Price Rounded to Nearest Dollar*	Consumers Union Overall Rating Score†	Rank Order of List Prices	Rank Order of Ratings
A	$190	90	3	1
B	85	87	22	2.5
C	160	87	6.5	2.5
D	90‡	64	19.5	4
E	49‡	57	23	5
F	90	56	19.5	6.5
G	119‡	56	16	6.5
H	165	54	5	8
I	100	53	18	9.5
J	150	53	9	9.5
K	89‡	52	21	11.5
L	159	52	8	11.5
M	135	51	13	13.5
N	140	51	10.5	13.5
O	290	49	1	15
P	200	44	2	16
Q	120‡	42	15	17.5
R	140	42	10.5	17.5
S	109‡	41	17	19
T	139‡	40	12	20
U	130	39	14	21
V	175	30	4	22
W	160	29	6.5	23

* While prices shown are list prices, discounts are generally available.

† All quality ratings were based mainly on image sharpness. Other factors considered were ease of focusing, accuracy of automatic focusing (where offered), convenience of slide trays, image brightness and uniformity, and slide and housing temperatures.

‡ Catalog prices excluding shipping charges.

Source: "Slide Projectors," *Consumer Reports*, vol. 40 no. 5 (May 1975), pp. 316–23.

estimated overall quality of products. The products tested are purchased by CU shoppers and the quality ratings are based upon laboratory tests, controlled use tests, and/or expert judgments.[36] In one study, product list prices were compared to CU evaluations of overall quality for 48 product categories and a positive and statistically significant price-quality correlation was found in only 12 categories.[37] A summary of a 1975 CU study of 23 slide projectors is presented in Table 18–5. There is no statistically significant relationship between the slide projector prices and CU quality ratings. This led Consumers Union to the conclusion that

[36] *Consumer Reports*, vol. 40, no. 5 (May 1975), p. 275.

[37] Ruby Turner Morris and Claire Sebulski Bronson, "The Chaos of Competition Indicated by Consumer Reports," *Journal of Marketing*, vol. 33 (July 1969), pp. 26–34, published by the American Marketing Association.

". . . the expensive models didn't project or handle slides better than the cheap ones—in some instances they didn't even do as well in those tasks."[38] The implication of this finding is that buyers who desire quality and who use price as a measure of product quality are sometimes making "inappropriate" purchase decisions (assuming brand prestige is unimportant to the buyer). It is recognized, of course, that the CU evaluations do not consider all dimensions of product quality (e.g., consistency of product performance). Based upon the CU studies, however, it appears that some sellers perceive consumers' purchase decisions to be positively correlated with prices and set prices high to imply a level of quality which does not exist.

Price Stability.[39] If a marketer adopts a resale price stability objective, any of several strategies might be employed to accomplish that objective. The once most effective strategy, resale price maintenance agreements with resellers, promises little stability today. Fair trade laws have been weakened or eliminated in most states and are under attack in almost all others (Chapter 6). Further, the U.S. courts have shown great reluctance in this age of consumerism to punish fair trade violators.[40] A manufacturer has a better chance of controlling resale prices if the number of resellers who market his products is small.

If a firm cannot refuse to sell to distributors unless they agree to maintain prices, it *may* choose to limit its resellers to those who provide a high level of service and who traditionally adhere to manufacturers' suggested prices. Some firms sell almost all of their items to their distributors but limit sales of special high margin, quality items to exclusive outlets. Other manufacturers shorten their distribution channel and market direct to retailers or consumers to increase their influence on resale price decisions. Resale price stability might also be achieved through contractual agreements with independent distributors. In the presence of interbrand competition, manufacturers may include price floors in retailer franchise agreements and refuse to sell to violators. Finally, consignment selling will contribute to retail price stability. When a distributor acts as an agent for a manufacturer and the manufacturer retains title to goods throughout the channel, the manufacturer is free to dictate all terms of resale, including prices.

Promotional program policies can also be used to encourage resale price stability. It is common for a manufacturer to share advertising ex-

---

[38] "Slide Projectors," *Consumer Reports,* vol. 40, no. 5 (May 1975), p. 316. The Spearman rank order coefficient (which measures the relationship between two sets of rank-ordered data) is −.2735 for the projector prices and CU quality ratings. This relationship is not significant at the .10 level, however.

[39] Much of this section is based upon Louis W. Stern, "Approaches to Achieving Retail Price Stability."

[40] Kwitny, "Fair Trade Fight: Discounters Campaign Against Laws that Let Retail Prices Be Fixed," p. 1, 19.

penses with retailers only if the retailers advertise manufacturer suggested prices. A typical policy of one photographic equipment manufacturer indicates how cooperative advertising policies can be used to promote price stability:

> 1) when a dealer advertises the price of a (company) product, such price must be at the dealer's actual selling price; 2) no advertisement will be approved which advertises a price which is more than 15 percent lower than the (company's) suggested list price; and 3) no advertisement will be approved which makes a comparison between the dealer's advertised selling price and the (company's) suggested list price.[41]

Manufacturer national advertising, preticketing, and price lists also tend to stabilize prices.

Increasingly throughout the last two decades, discount retailers have sold below manufacturer suggested prices and antagonized full service, non-discounting retailers. In the presence of growing pressure from these non-discounters, some manufacturers who desire consistent and stable retail prices have revamped their price discount structures and eliminated attractive quantity, cash and other discounts. Thus, discounters willing to buy in quantity and pay cash are forced to incur the same product costs as the full service retailers.

Price Discrimination. If the firm seeks to maximize profits and adopts a variable price policy, then it may choose to employ a strategy of price discrimination; i.e., selling the same products at different prices where the difference is not due to variations in costs. Discrimination is appropriate when the market is comprised of different segments with different price elasticities. The objective of employing this strategy is to charge higher prices in the segments with inelastic demand and lower prices in markets with very elastic demand. Illustrative of discrimination strategies are:

1. Offering identical products to different consumers at different prices (e.g., sales of automobiles).
2. Charging different prices for goods offered for sale at different places (e.g., lower prices for warehouse sales);
3. Charging significantly different prices for only marginally different products (e.g., higher prices for white side wall tires);
4. Charging different prices at different times (e.g., charging $1.00 for a martini at lunch and $1.75 at dinner).

Price Tactics

Tactical pricing decisions are those made by managers to set specific prices at which products are offered for sale. As is indicated in the deci-

---

[41] Louis W. Stern, "Approaches to Achieving Retail Price Stability," p. 81.

sion framework in Figure 18–1, tactical decisions are appropriately made after pricing objectives policies and strategies (which are consistent with company and marketing objectives) have been formulated. Table 18–6 summarizes the findings of a study to determine the relative importance to managers of several approaches to setting prices. Nearly 500 U.S. manufacturing corporations participated in the study which was conducted in the late 1960s. Each respondent allocated 100 points among the five approaches according to his perception of their importance in pricing products. Results were very similar across industrial, consumer durable and consumer nondurable manufacturing companies with pricing in relation to competition receiving the greatest average value in all three groups. Cost-plus pricing ranked second throughout.

TABLE 18–6

The Perceived Relative Importance of Various Approaches to Setting Prices*

	Type of Product		
Approaches to Setting Prices	Industrial	Consumer Durable	Consumer Nondurable
Competitive level.....................	46.7	45.0	46.0
Certain percent above or below competitive level.............	6.7	8.1	11.1
Cost-plus.........................	25.1	28.2	27.1
What the market will bear............	13.4	15.8	14.2
According to government rules and regulations...............	8.0	2.7	1.6
Other approaches....................	0.1	0.1	—
Total........................	100.0	99.9†	100.0

* These approaches were referred to as "pricing strategies" in the study. However, they are more similar to pricing tactics as presented in this chapter.
† Does not add to 100% due to rounding.
Source: Jon G. Udell, *Successful Marketing Strategies in American Industries* (Madison, Wisconsin : Mimir Publishers, 1972), p. 152.

A sound approach to pricing products incorporates cost, competition and demand considerations. Based upon their primary focus, several price setting methods are discussed as cost, competition or demand oriented below. It should be recognized, however, that it is seldom appropriate for a manager to set a price on a product by considering only cost, competition or demand factors in isolation from the others (see earlier cited determinants).

Cost-Oriented Approach. The simplest approach to setting price is to build it up from costs. Cost-plus or markup pricing is the cost-oriented method most frequently used by manufacturers, wholesalers and retailers. Markups are traditionally calculated on the basis of selling price and not costs. Since only unit cost and the desired percentage markup on selling price are known to the manager developing a selling price, the following simple formula is used to determine price.

$$\text{Selling price} = \frac{\text{Average unit cost}}{1 - \text{Desired markup percentage}}$$

For example, if an item costs $7.00 and the desired markup on selling price is 30 percent, then price is set as $10 [$7 ÷ (1 − .3)].

Manufacturers generally add an allowance for fixed overhead costs to unit variable costs and then calculate a percentage markup (on price) which covers selling, administrative and general expenses as well as a desired profit percentage. To estimate unit costs, however, manufacturers must assume some level of production, such as normal operating capacity. Prices for a particular receiver, speaker and amplifier sold by a stereo component manufacturer are calculated using markup pricing in Table 18–7. A standard percentage is used to allocate overhead to each

TABLE 18–7

Markup Pricing by a Stereo Component Manufacturer

	Product Items		
	Receiver 101	*Speaker 201*	*Amplifier 301*
Unit Variable Costs.....................	$120.00	$ 68.00	$ 90.00
Percentage Allowance for Overhead.......	12	15	10
Dollar Overhead Allowance..............	14.40	10.20	9.00
Percentage Markup on Price			
(covers expenses plus profit)...........	40	50	30
Selling Price.........................	$224.00	$156.40	$141.42

product. For the receiver, the average unit cost is $134.40 ($120.00 + $14.40). Using the 40 percent markup for receivers, selling price is calculated as $224.00. ($134.40 ÷ 0.6). The overhead allowance and markup differs for speakers and amplifiers.

Wholesalers and retailers typically markup each class of products by a different fixed percentage over the prices they pay. Unlike manufacturers, trading organizations seldom attempt to allocate fixed and operating expenses to each product. The percentage markups for each product category are most frequently determined by industry tradition, company strategy (e.g., price level strategy), individual operating expenses (e.g., rent, insurance, pilferage, etc.), expected turnover and a myriad of other factors.[42] Using the markup on price formula, prices for five different items sold in a retail department store are calculated in Table 18–8.

---

[42] Mark I. Alpert, *Pricing Decisions* (Glenview, Ill: Scott, Foresman, and Company, 1971), pp. 25–26.

TABLE 18–8

Markup Pricing for a Retail Department Store

	Product Category				
	Cameras	*Books*	*Dresses*	*Tobacco*	*Costume Jewelry*
Price to Retailer..........	$135.00	$ 7.50	$44.25	$.68	$4.30
Traditional Markups (in percent)............	28	34	41	20	46
Selling Prices.............	$187.50	$11.35	$74.99	$.85	$7.99

The practice of markup pricing accentuates or magnifies price hikes or reductions that occur at one level of the distribution channel. When farmers demand price increases from food processors, for example, the processors' selling prices are calculated on the basis of their higher costs. Then, food brokers calculate their commissions and wholesalers calculate their fixed markups on the higher prices paid to the processors. Finally, prices rise at the retail level by an amount much larger than the original increase to farmers because each middleman's prices were set by a fixed percentage markup. Of course, when prices fall at one level, that effect is also magnified by the fixed markup practice.

Breakeven pricing is a second cost-oriented method. Breakeven analysis determines the level of sales needed to cover all relevant fixed and variable costs (see Chapter 15). If fixed costs are $100,000, unit variable costs are $2.00 and price is $4.00, then the firm must sell 50,000 units to break even [$100,000 ÷ ($4.00 − $2.00)]. This relationship is graphically depicted in Figure 18–4A.

Target return pricing, popular among manufacturers, is based upon breakeven analysis. Managers first identify their standard or normal output level (e.g., 80 percent of capacity). Total costs of producing and offering the goods for sale at that level of output are then determined. A desired percentage return, a target, is then added to total costs at the standard output level. The sum of total costs and the target return identifies the total revenue that must be generated by the firm if it is to achieve its target return on total costs at normal operating capacity. Selling price is determined by dividing the target total revenue level by the standard output level.

Suppose that the firm has a standard output level of 80,000 units and management wishes to achieve a 20 percent return on total costs at that level of output ($260,000). Then $52,000 (20 percent times $260,000) is added to $260,000 to obtain a target total revenue of $312,000. Price must be set at $3.90 ($312,000 ÷ 80,000) to achieve the target return on costs. This relationship is shown in Figure 18–4B. The obvious weak-

FIGURE 18–4

Using Breakeven Analysis to Determine Price

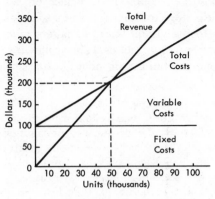
A. Traditional Break-Even Analysis

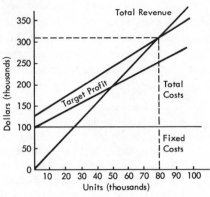
B. Target Return Pricing

ness of this and other cost-oriented pricing methods is that the quantity to be sold at the determined price could easily be greater or less than actual market demand. Prices determined according to these methods are derived from costs without regard for market demand.

Competition-Oriented Approach. In many firms, prices are set primarily in relation to existing competitive prices and in anticipation of competitors' price changes. When employing an approach which focuses on pricing in relation to competition, managers do not totally disregard cost and demand factors; but, they devote primary attention to the relationship of their firms' products to competitors' products. One simple competition-oriented method is to set product prices at a percentage above or a percentage below all or selected competitors' prices. The appropriateness of each depends ultimately upon the firm's corporate, marketing and pricing objectives, the structure of the competitive market, relative production, selling and administrative costs, and consumers' preferences for the firm's brand among other factors. Many managers simplify their cost setting problem by pricing their products in relation to competitors' prices when:

They believe competitors are better able to select appropriate prices so they "follow the leader;"

Price changes by competitors can reasonably be expected to have a substantial effect on company sales and responsive price changes are demanded; and/or

Costs, demand, competition and other factors which affect sales and profits are stable and the company believes that it is safe to rely upon following general industry pricing trends.

Many retailers employ simplified competition-oriented pricing methods in conjunction with the more traditional markup method. Comparison shoppers are frequently employed to survey competitors' prices on selected items. It is also common for chain store top managements to delegate some price adjustment authority to individual store managers who are more aware of local competitors' pricing tactics. The following describes some of the mechanics of one discount drug chain's competition-oriented pricing program.

> . . . headquarters distributes three lists—designated as AAA, A, and B —to its store managers every four weeks. For the items appearing on the lists, managers report prices and those of the closest (in proximity) competitors. For the AAA list, on which the 20 to 24 most highly identifiable nonprescription drugs and cosmetic items appear (e.g., Crest toothpaste, family-size; Right Guard aerosol deodorant, large; Bayer aspirin, 100's), the manager has almost blanket authority to alter his store's prices in order to meet the competition's. . . . For A- and B-listed items, (drug chain) must approach, but not necessarily meet, competitors' prices.[43]

Increasingly, managers have incorporated Bayesian probability analysis into their pricing procedures. A decision-tree approach to pricing allows the decision-maker to estimate expected payoffs for each of several prices under alternative conditions (e.g., economic climates, anticipated competitive reactions, etc.). The value of this method is related directly to the ability of managers to identify all relevant conditions and to apply reasonable subjective probabilities of occurrence to each condition.[44] When the primary focus of a manager is on setting his product's prices in relation to competitors' prices and anticipating their reactions to his prices, Bayesian analysis can be a helpful tool.

For example, a manufacturer of components for electronic digital watches wanted to enter the consumer digital watch market with a model carrying its own brand. Controlled experiments were conducted which measured consumers' preferences for digital watches at various price levels. This preliminary consumer research suggested that the total demand for electronic digital watches was price inelastic. However, among the segment of the total watch market that preferred digital watches, there was some price elasticity. In other words, lower prices on digital watches would not substantially increase the total volume of digital watch sales. However, one competitor's lower prices could garner for him a larger share of the digital watch market.

---

[43] Leonard J. Parsons and W. Bailey Price, "Adaptive Pricing by a Retailer," *Journal of Marketing Research*, vol. 9 (May 1972), p. 128, published by the American Marketing Association.

[44] For an example of a computer application of decision-tree analysis refer to: Paul E. Green, "Bayesian Decision Theory in Pricing Strategy," *Journal of Marketing*, vol. 27 (January 1963), pp. 5–14.

Management knew that it possessed an inherent cost advantage over nonintegrated digital watch competitors. The company's major problem was consumer unfamiliarity with its brand. Because its production capacity was quite large, capable of producing nearly a third of the annual sales of digital watches, a pricing objective was adopted to achieve a 25 percent initial year market share for the first model. Penetration pricing was identified as a strategy which would help achieve that objective and would allow the firm to enjoy its potential economies of scale.

Recognizing their brand's competitive disadvantage as well as their inability to accurately forecast anything other than "ballpark" unit costs, management decided to set its retail selling price below the prices of substitute watches on the market. One competitor dominated the market for low price yet accurate digital watches with a 55 percent market share. That firm's best selling item was priced at $59.95. The marketing vice-president of the component manufacturer carefully studied the consumer research report on digital watch price elasticity and concluded that a price of $39.95 would guarantee his firm a 25 percent market share. The vice-president for finance, however, strongly urged that a $45.95 price be set on the new watch. Based upon his analysis of the same consumer research report, he believed that the firm would break even on its investment sooner at the higher price. The two vice-presidents agreed that the total market potential would remain about the same if the watch was priced anywhere between $59.95 and $39.95. Also, they felt that their entry would appeal to the same segment of the digital watch market if price was set within that range.

The company president of this fledgling watch manufacturer was responsible for setting the price of his firm's first consumer product. He was quite concerned that his major competitor's reaction to his initial price decision might prevent the accomplishment of the 25 percent first year market share objective. The president asked his marketing and finance executives to assess the major competitor's probable response to potential initial prices of $45.95 and $39.95. The executives agreed upon the probabilities of the competitor's reaction to each price. The president then asked for an assessment of the probabilities of their company achieving various market shares for each reaction that the competitor might take. Estimates were made by the vice-presidents based upon their experience in the watch market and their interpretation of the study of consumer price sensitivity. From their responses the president developed the decision-tree shown in Figure 18–5. If price was set at $45.95, the executives believed that there was a 70 percent chance that the competitor would stand pat. If that occurred, there was a 35 percent probability of achieving 15 percent of the market, a 50 percent chance of getting 25 percent and a 15 percent chance of getting 35 percent. At an introductory price of $39.95, the executives expected a dif-

FIGURE 18–5

A Pricing Decision Tree

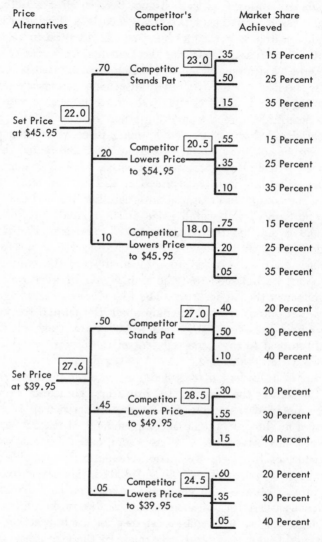

Note: Numbers in boxes provide intermediate and final calculations.

ferent set of possible competitive reactions and probable market shares. From the decision tree, the president calculated the market share that the firm could expect to achieve with prices of $45.95 and $39.95. The expected market share at a price of $39.95 was 27.6 percent and only 22 percent at a $45.95 price.

Many firms engaged in competitive bidding on potential purchases or sales contracts use bidding models, a third competition oriented pricing tool. The appropriateness of a particular competitive bidding model depends upon whether the bidder has a chance to modify his bid (as in auction situations) or is limited to a single sealed bid. Some firms engaged in competitive bidding use mathematical models developed for their specific situations to guide their price decisions.[45] Experience based probabilistic bidding models can be developed to suggest the bid amount expected to yield the greatest profit. The general notation for a probabilistic model which identifies the most profitable bid is:

$$E(X) = P(X)Z(X)$$

where:

X = amount of the bid;
$E(X)$ = expected profit of a bid of X;
$P(X)$ = probability of a bid of X being accepted;
$Z(X)$ = profit if a bid of X is accepted.[46]

The amount of profit made if a bid of X is accepted [$Z(X)$] equals the difference between the bid price (X) and the expected costs associated with the project for which the bid is submitted. This data should be obtained from the financial and accounting analysis of the project. The probability of a bid of a certain amount above project costs being accepted can be determined by an analysis of historical patterns. For example, one firm might discover that a bid of 30 percent above its direct costs on certain types of products has been lower than competitor A's bid 95 percent of the time, below B's bid 85 percent of the time and under C's bid 90 percent of the time. Since these events are independent of each other, the probability of underbidding all three major competitors with a bid of 130 percent of direct costs is 72.7 percent ($.95 \times .85 \times .90$). A bid price of 130 percent of direct costs yields a contribution margin of 23 percent. Therefore, the expected contribution margin for bids 130 percent above direct costs is 16.7 percent. ($.727 \times .23$) Expected contribution margins for other bid prices as a percent of direct costs are shown in Table 18–9. Bids of 130 percent of direct costs are expected to yield the highest value to the bidder.

---

[45] Several general models can be used to direct the formulation of situation specific competitive bidding models. The reader is referred to Franz Edelman "Art and Science of Competitive Bidding," *Harvard Business Review*, vol. 43 (July–August 1965), pp. 53–66; I. H. Lavalle, "A Bayesian Approach to an Individual Player's Choice of Bid in Competitive Sealed Auctions," *Management Science*, vol. 13 (March 1967), pp. 584–97; Wayne J. Morse, "Probabilistic Bidding Models: A Synthesis," *Business Horizons*, vol. 16 (April 1975), pp. 67–74; and R. Stark "Competitive Bidding: A Comprehensive Bibliography," *Operations Research* (March–April 1971), pp. 484–90.

[46] Morse, Probabilistic Bidding Models: A Synthesis," p. 68.

TABLE 18–9

Expected Contribution Margin When Bidding against Three Competitors

Bid as a Percent of Estimated Direct Cost	Z (X) Contribution Margin (Percent)	Probability of Underbidding			P (X) Overall Probability of Having the Lowest Bid	E (X) Expected Contribution Margin (Percent)
		Firm A	Firm B	Firm C		
110..............	9	1.00	.98	1.00	.980	0.9
120..............	17	.98	.90	.95	.838	13.8
130..............	23	.95	.85	.90	.727	16.7
140..............	29	.80	.50	.55	.220	4.8
150..............	33	.40	.25	.30	.030	0.9
160..............	38	.20	.05	.10	.001	0.0
170..............	41	.05	.00	.00	.000	0.0

Source: Wayne J. Morse, "Probabilistic Bidding Models: A Synthesis," *Business Horizons*, vol. 16 (April 1975), pp. 67–74.

Demand-Oriented Approach. Marketers view price as a demand generating mechanism and the potential benefits to the firm of pricing products in relation to demand to be great. Firms that set price in relation to costs or competition alone implicitly assume that there is a very close relationship between traditional markups of competitors' prices and actual market demand schedules.

Demand considerations can be explicitly incorporated in some simple pricing methods, however. Estimates of market demand can be used in conjunction with traditional breakeven analysis to approximate profit maximizing decisions. This method requires estimates of market demand at each feasible price. With these estimates, breakeven points and expected levels of total sales revenue can be calculated easily. To obtain the highest level of profits, price should be set at the level which is expected to produce the greatest positive difference between expected total revenue and total costs. A graphic and tabular example is presented in Figure 18–6 where fixed costs are $200,000, unit variable costs are $2.50 and demand forecasts are for prices of $5, $10, $15, and 20. Of the four prices considered, the $15 price yields the highest profits ($360,000).

Obtaining valid and reliable estimates of price-quantity relationships is a complex task. For established products, some firms employ a time series analysis of historical price (in constant dollars) and sales volume levels to infer a price-quantity demand schedule. To use a schedule derived from historical data to plan future prices, however, the firm must be willing to assume that the numerous exogenous factors which affected sales in the past will affect sales in the same way in the future.

Price-quantity demand data have been generated in controlled in-store experiments. This method promises greater validity than the time

FIGURE 18–6

An Application of Breakeven Analysis Modified with a Market Demand Schedule

Unit Price ($)	Market Demand (Units)	Total Revenue ($)		Total Costs ($)	Breakeven Points (Units)		Expected Profits ($)
$ 5...........	65,000	(d')	$325,000	$362,500	(d)	80,000	($ 37,500)
10...........	55,000	(c')	550,000	337,500	(c)	26,667	212,500
15...........	45,000	(b')	675,000	314,500	(b)	16,000	360,500
20...........	30,000	(a')	600,000	275,000	(a)	11,429	325,000

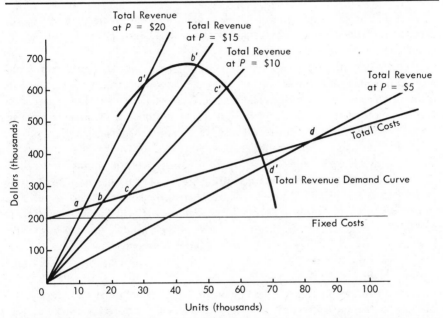

series approach because buyers make actual purchase decisions within a relatively short time period and a greater number of the exogenous variables can be controlled. The Quaker Oats Company, for example, identified two items in one of its product lines which were not adequately contributing to the line's profitability. The company considered raising the unit price for each item by four cents. To determine the impact of the higher prices on demand (sales) and, more importantly, line profits, the company conducted an in-store controlled experiment.

Within 120 grocery stores, a randomized block design was used to test four treatments:

1. Raise price of A by 4¢; no change in price of B.
2. No change in price of A; raise price of B by 4¢.
3. Raise price of A by 4¢; raise price of B by 4¢.
4. No change in price of A; no change in price of B.

Three monthly audits were conducted in the 120 stores to measure the effect of each treatment upon sales. Analysis of the sales results produced the following findings:

There was evidence to suggest that increasing the price of A alone would reduce total line profits.

There was no evidence to suggest that increasing the price of B alone would significantly change total line profits.

There was no evidence to suggest that changes in the price of A and B together would have any impact on line profits.

As a result of the experiment, Quaker Oats' management decided to increase the price of item B by an amount less than four cents, but, to make no change in the price of A.[47]

If properly planned and executed, controlled experiments can yield valuable information for setting prices. However, many firms find it difficult to execute a carefully controlled experiment. Further, some feel that the frequent price alterations in stores which are usually associated with experiments, create reseller and consumer dissatisfaction. Coca Cola U.S.A. has used "trailer simulations" to estimate the impact of price changes upon sales. That company has presented major product groups to invited consumers in a motorized van which simulates a portion of a retail outlet. Housewives are carefully selected and invited to "shop" in this simulated supermarket. Although the shopping situation is artificial, a demand estimating method which simulates the buying situation offers an advantage of research efficiency because many treatments (e.g., price changes on 16 ounce 8-packs of Coke) can be tested quite easily.[48]

Determining the price that would encourage potential industrial buyers to purchase a product or service from an industrial marketer differs only slightly from the task of determining prices for consumer products. Often the price of an industrial product is determined as much or more by the potential benefit (e.g., cost savings) which the product offers the buyer as by the seller's cost of providing the product. This is especially true when the industrial marketer faces no direct competition. For example, the price that a manufacturer would be willing to pay to purchase the services of an independent plant security team would be directly related to the manufacturer's perception of the losses he would incur without the services, the number of firms willing and able to pro-

---

[47] For a more detailed description of the Quaker Oats experiment and the data analysis, see: William D. Barclay, "Factorial Design in a Pricing Experiment," *Journal of Marketing Research*, vol. 6 (November 1969), pp. 427–29.

[48] Roy G. Stout, "Developing Data to Estimate Price-quantity Relationships," *Journal of Marketing*, vol. 33 (April 1969), pp. 34–36, published by the American Marketing Association.

vide the service and the financial and managerial capability of the manufacturer to hire, train and maintain his own security force.

Implementing and Controlling Price Decisions

Once prices are determined, plans to implement and control those decisions must be executed. Company salesmen, channel resellers and ultimate consumers or users are groups most immediately affected by price decisions. Consumers' and users' responses to price decisions are often anticipated with demand estimation market research activities. The reactions of salesmen and distributors also deserve to be estimated since these two groups are responsible for performing the distribution marketing tasks.

Successful implementation of new product price decisions and product price changes is dependent upon coordination of the activities of salesmen and resellers as well as other company marketing, accounting, manufacturing, and purchasing personnel. Since final price decisions affect and are affected by decisions of each of these groups, their inputs to the decision process should be solicited and plans developed to guide their implementation. From the perspective of company salesmen and distributors, optimal prices are those which generate a desired level of sales and effectively satisfy consumer needs. Salesmen and distributors interact most frequently with each other and with consumers. Since they are the voice of the company and must explain all prices to buyers, they must be aware of the rationale for all price decisions. Since prices communicate something about corporate goals, policies, and philosophies, it is imperative that steps be taken to minimize the difference between the messages intended by corporate and marketing executives and the messages received by resellers and consumers.

The publication of new price lists and suggested markups, the premarking of prices on product labels and the advertising of price changes are techniques usually used to communicate initial or modified prices. Messages communicated through these media should never be totally unexpected and perceived as unjustified by salesmen and distributors.

To control its price decisions, the firm must assess their impact upon corporate and marketing performance, reseller performance, competitive marketing reactions and customer satisfaction. The firm's information system should be programmed to collect data and present information to those responsible for making price objectives, policies, strategies and tactics decisions. A price decision warning system is highlighted in Figure 18–7. The figure suggests that several problems identified through analysis of data collected by a price monitoring system may allow the firm to avoid probable failure to achieve its objectives. For example, a price monitoring system might detect the emergence of strong negative

FIGURE 18–7

A Price Decision Warning System

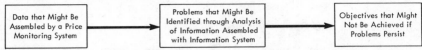

Data that Might Be Assembled by a Price Monitoring System	Problems that Might Be Identified through Analysis of Information Assembled with Information System	Objectives that Might Not Be Achieved if Problems Persist

1. Sales—in units and in dollars:
  a. Previous year comparisons.
  b. Different markets/channels comparisons.
2. Rivals' prices.
3. Inquiries from potential customers about the line.
4. Company's sales at "off list" price:
  a. Measured as percent of total sales.
  b. Revenue as percent of sales at full price.
5. Types of customers getting the most and largest price reductions.
6. Market shares—in individual markets.
7. Marketing costs; production costs; production costs at nearly output.
8. Price complaints:
  a. from customers.
  b. from salesmen.
9. Inventories of finished goods at different levels.
10. Customers' attitudes toward firm, prices, etc.
11. Number of lost customers (brand-switching).
12. Inquiries—and subsequent purchases.
13. Marketing costs.
14. Entry and exit of competitors from industry.
15. Consumer and reseller responses to competitors' price reductions.
	1. A decline in sales.
	2. Prices are too high—relative to those charged by rivals, relative to the benefits of the product. (Prices might be too high in a few regional markets and very appropriate elsewhere.)
	3. Price is too low, again in certain markets and not in others.
	4. The company is regarded as exploitative of customers and not to be trusted.
	5. The firm places excessive financial burdens on its resellers.
	6. The price differentials among items in the line are objectionable or unintelligible.
	7. Its price changes are too frequent—or do not take account of major changes in market circumstances.
	8. The firm's price reflects negatively on itself and on its products.
	9. The price is unstabilizing the market which had finally become stabilized after great difficulty.
	10. The firm is offering its customers too many price choices and is confusing its customers and resellers.
	11. The firm's prices seem higher to customers than they really are.
	12. The firm's price policy attracts undesirable kinds of customers who have no loyalty to any seller.
	13. The firm's pricing behavior makes customers unduly price sensitive and unappreciative of quality differences.
	14. The company has fostered a decline in market discipline among sellers in the industry.
		1. Maximum long-run profits.
		2. Maximum short-run profits.
		3. Growth.
		4. Stabilize market.
		5. Desensitize customers to price.
		6. Maintain price-leadership arrangement.
		7. Discourage entrants.
		8. Speed exit of marginal firms.
		9. Avoid government investigation and control.
		10. Maintain loyalty of middlemen and get their sales support.
		11. Avoid demands for "more" from suppliers—labor, in particular.
		12. Enhance image of firm and its offerings.
		13. Be regarded as "fair" by customers (ultimate).
		14. Create interest and excitement about the item.
		15. Be considered trustworthy and reliable by rivals.
		16. Help in the sale of weak items in the line.
		17. Discourage others from cutting prices.
		18. Make a product "visible."
		19. "Spoil market" to obtain high price for sale of business.
		20. Build traffic.

Source: Adapted from Alfred R. Oxenfelt, "A Decision-Making Structure for Price Decision," *Journal of Marketing,* vol. 37 (January 1973), pp. 48–53, published by the American Marketing Association.

attitudes of resellers toward a policy of not allowing end-of-season price discounting (which would help retailers to clear out their inventories). With this data, the firm could take remedial actions and, hopefully, eliminate the feelings among the resellers that the firm is exploitative and not to be trusted. Otherwise, the firm may find it very difficult to maintain the loyalty of its distributors and may lose their sales support altogether.

SUMMARY AND CONCLUSIONS

As part of the effort throughout this text to provide guidelines for planning effective marketing programs, a framework for making price decisions was developed in this chapter. From the viewpoint of the marketing manager, prices do much more than serve as passive images of consumer and user perceptions of product value. Prices are major determinants of corporate profits because they affect both demand and average costs. As markets throughout the world become increasingly characterized by insufficient supplies of raw materials and finished goods, buyers and sellers are once again regarding price as one of the most important elements of each firm's marketing program.

Making appropriate price decisions is a difficult task because of the many and varied factors which affect and are affected by those decisions. Factors which are always changing and which greatly affect the appropriateness of specific price decisions include: buyer demand, competition, costs, economic climate, laws and ethics, intraorganizational dependencies, marketing mix interrelationships and channel relations. Because of the dynamic nature of the environment of most firms, few managers can afford the luxury of static or permanent price decisions.

Since companies must frequently make new price decisions and evaluate past price decisions, marketing managers should have a sound understanding of the role of price in their total marketing program and a logical approach to setting prices. The general framework developed in this chapter specifies an approach to setting prices. The suggested sequence is to set pricing program objectives, policies, strategies, and tactics. Overcoming the problems associated with implementing price decisions throughout the firm and, where applicable, the distribution channel, is critical to achieving pricing objectives.

EXERCISES FOR REVIEW AND DISCUSSION

1. Discuss the role that price might play (in a consumer's decision process) in reducing uncertainty surrounding the purchase of a component sound system (e.g., speakers, tape deck, receiver).

2. Identify and discuss factors worthy of consideration in pricing a new snack food product. The product will be distributed through a conventional channel of distribution from the manufacturer through wholesalers via food brokers, to retailers and to consumer end-users.

3. Taking the point of view of an industrial buyer for a large consumer goods manufacturer, identify several factors that could be used to evaluate alternative suppliers for a container (e.g., glass jar, metal can or cardboard box). Discuss how information on these factors could be used to determine the price which you should offer to pay for the product your company needs.

4. Discuss possible variations in the role of price in the marketing mix of a nationally advertised brand of aspirin versus a much lower-priced privately labeled brand.

5. A critical element in determining the commercial potential of a new consumer product is obtaining information on the probable response of potential buyers to different price levels. Discuss several types of marketing

research studies which might be developed to obtain this type of information.

6. In an era of double digit inflation, reinstatement of wage and price controls by the federal government is a continuing possibility. If this occurs, some argue the need for price decisions in business firms would be eliminated. Discuss.

7. Cite and discuss the implications for the retail prices of food and gasoline if certain "middlemen" were to be eliminated from the respective channel of distribution.

19

Advertising Decisions

Attention in the next four chapters turns to the promotional component of an organization's marketing mix. This chapter introduces the various decision areas comprising a promotional program, and then concentrates on the advertising decision process. The following chapter considers the challenging task of evaluating the effectiveness of advertising decisions. The remaining two chapters focus on the personal selling component by discussing the management of personal selling resources (Chapter 21) and managing the sales force (Chapter 22).

THE PROMOTIONAL MIX

Communication and Promotion

An important tool for influencing customer purchase decisions is the communication of information concerning the firm and/or its offer to customers. This information may be either facts, opinions, or persuasive arguments for (or against) a particular action that customers might take. Consequently, the basic purpose of promotion is to *inform* and/or *persuade* customers.

To accomplish these purposes, managers must make decisions in five areas that combine to determine a promotional mix: audiences, desired audience behavior, messages, source, and vehicles. These decisions areas and their relationships are shown in Figure 19–1.

Audience. An organization uses promotional resources to accomplish objectives that are typically stated in terms of the desired behavior of some group. So, a starting point for promotion decisions is to determine the particular group of individuals (consumers or those in other organizations) that should comprise the intended audience. Frequently, the audience coincides with one or more market targets selected by the firm. In these cases, the market target decisions become an input into the pro-

FIGURE 19-1

Areas of Decision Making for Promotion

motional processes. However, promotion may be used to inform or persuade other kinds of audiences including channel organizations, the general public, governmental officials, and suppliers. Firms such as United States Steel, Burlington Industries, and others that do not sell products directly to ultimate consumers engage in institutional advertising to develop and maintain an awareness and image of the firm by the general public.

Desired Audience Behavior. Upon selecting a target audience, management must identify the particular behavior that promotion is intended to influence. This is the task of selecting objectives. Since promotion's purpose is to inform and persuade audiences, objectives are most appropriately stated in terms of the desired or expected impact of communication on target audiences. Audience impact may take a wide variety of forms but usually can be classified as one of two types. Desired audience behavior may be either a specific mental state of audience members (e.g., awareness of product or brands, development or change of attitudes, or intentions to buy) or an overt behavior (e.g., purchase of a product or brand, political support of proposed legislation, or granting of needed financing). When promotional objectives are set in terms of desired mental states, management usually expects that the particular state will influence an overt behavior at some future time. For example, when the American Cancer Society uses promotion to inform the public of the seven danger signals for detecting cancer, there is the expectation that the awareness of these symptoms will influence people to see a doctor upon noting one or more of them.

Promotional Message. Audience behavior is influenced by communicating a message containing opinions, facts and/or persuasive arguments. Thus, an essential promotion decision is to determine what information must be provided for selected audiences in order to achieve desired behavior. This requires an understanding of the characteristics and information needs of audience members. Moreover, the information must be communicated in a way that will ensure that audience members see, comprehend, and remember the intended content.

Message Source. Messages originate from some source. In a behavioral context, a source can be best viewed as the communicator (e.g., a person or an organization) that is perceived by audience members as originating the message. A well accepted behavioral research finding is that the source of information does influence the use of information by audiences.[1] At least one reason for this phenomenon is that audiences attach differing levels of credibility (e.g., trustworthiness and/or expertise in the topic of the message) to different information sources. For example, a study showed that a presumably highly credible source, *Consumer Reports*, had greater effect upon consumers in the evaluation of brands of shirts than did salespeople when the information content disagreed with consumers' preconceptions of the brands.[2]

An organization does have some control over the source of promotional messages and so, message source should be considered to be a promotional decision area. A firm may influence the audience's perception of the origin of a message through different parts of a total promotional program. For instance, by using publicity a firm may disassociate itself from the message. A firm can also control the source of promotional messages by influencing audiences' perceptions of source credibility. A firm may engage in institutional advertising to build a favorable corporate image which will carry over into the perception of the trustworthiness or expertise of promotion. Or, a firm might increase the expertise of its salesmen by putting them through a training program.

Promotional Vehicles. Promotional messages must be carried to individual members of selected audiences. This is the function of promotional vehicles which are the media through which information is disseminated to audiences. A firm has a very large number of alternative vehicles from which to choose including other organizations in the business of transmitting information (e.g., newspapers, magazines, radio, television, etc.), company personnel (e.g., salesmen, managers, other employees), shows and exhibitions, point-of-purchase displays, packages, and so forth. Generally, a firm must select a combination of media that will reach intended audiences since no one medium will be likely to achieve the promotional objectives set by the firm.

Promotion in the Marketing Mix

The communications view of promotion suggests the many uses of promotional resources. Yet, the bulk of promotion is directed toward facilitating and enhancing the sales of specific products and brands.

---

[1] For example, see Donald J. Hempel, "An Experimental Study of the Effects of Information on Consumer Product Evaluations," in Raymond H. Haas, ed., *Science Technology and Marketing* (Chicago: American Marketing Association, 1966), pp. 589–97; Theodore Levitt, "Persuasibility of Purchasing Agents and Chemists: Effects of Source, Presentation, Risk, Audience Competence, and Time," in Donald F. Cox, (ed.), *Risk Taking and Information Handling in Consumer Behavior* (Boston: Division of Research, Graduate School of Business Administration, Harvard University, 1967), pp. 541–58; and Robert B. Woodruff, "Brand Information Sources, Opinion Change, and Uncertainty," *Journal of Marketing Research*, vol. 9 (November 1972), pp. 414–18.

[2] Hempel, "An Experimental Study of the Effects of Information on Consumer Product Evaluations."

Thus, promotion is most often intended to be a supporting component in a marketing mix. This does not mean that it is any less important than product or other marketing decision areas. Rather, promotion decisions must be integrated and coordinated with the rest of the marketing mix, particularly product/brand decisions, so that it can effectively support an entire marketing mix strategy. Promotion is comprised of a mix of decision areas including:

Advertising is the dissemination of information by nonpersonal means through paid media where the source is clearly identified as the sponsoring organization.

Personal selling is the dissemination of information by personal, usually face-to-face, contact between audience members and one or more employees of the sponsoring organization. The source of the information is identified as the sponsoring organization.

Sales promotion is the dissemination of information in a very broad sense through a wide variety of activities including free samples, gifts, coupons, point-of-purchase signs and displays, stamp programs, cents-off sales, contests, and the like. The sponsor is identified.

Publicity is the dissemination of information by personal or nonpersonal means which is not directly paid for by the organization and for which the organization is not clearly identified as the source.

In practice, many firms are organized so that components of the promotional mix are managed by different functional areas or departments. Typically, sales promotion is included within the advertising function. Publicity is more likely to be an informal activity with no departmental recognition in the smaller firms, but is treated as a separate function (public relations) in many larger firms. Responsibility for advertising and personal selling is almost always assigned to different departments. The result is that promotional components generally are rather independent functions competing for corporate resources. Attention now turns to the advertising function.

AN ADVERTISING DECISION PROCESS

Advertising's Use of Resources

In 1972 all expenditures on advertising in the United States amounted to $23.1 billion, and this total is expected to grow to $37 billion by 1980.[3] For individual firms the amount allocated to advertising varies substantially. Yet, a glance at Table 19–1 illustrates how much

---

[3] "U.S. Advertising Hits $23.1 Billion; Expect Rise to $37 Billion by 1980," *Advertising Age* (November 21, 1973), p. 6.

TABLE 19–1

1972 Ad Expenditures for the Top Ten Advertisers

Company	1972 Ad Expenditures
Procter & Gamble	$275,000,000
Sears, Roebuck	215,000,000
General Foods	170,000,000
General Motors	146,000,000
Warner-Lambert	134,000,000
Ford Motor Company	132,000,000
American Home Products	116,000,000
Bristol-Myers	115,000,000
Colgate-Palmolive	105,000,000
Chrysler Corporation	95,415,400

Source: Adapted with permission from *Advertising Age* (November 21, 1973), p. 22.

some of the larger firms put into their advertising effort. What do firms get in return for all this advertising? The answer to this question depends upon who is asked, for advertising is one of the most controversial of business decision areas. Critics of advertising often paint a picture of advertising as a very powerful tool that has the ability to manipulate consumers into buying products whether they want or can afford them. Others, including those involved in the advertising and business system are more skeptical about the effectiveness of advertising. For example, Professor John Howard of Columbia University has said that his research provides little evidence that advertising plays a very strong part in consumer buying.[4] Much of this controversy is a result of the unfortunate fact that it is very difficult to determine precisely what effect advertising, in general, has upon consumer decisions on products and services.

In spite of this controversy management has definite expectations about what advertising is supposed to do for a firm.[5] Since the sponsor is identified with an advertisement, an ad represents the point of view of the company. It is not supposed to be totally unbiased or objective, but rather to represent the company's position concerning the product, service, or whatever is being advertised. The identification of the sponsor is very important so that the audience understands that an advertisement represents the company's point of view.

Advertising is presented by nonpersonal means through the use of paid media. Nonpersonal, of course, indicates the lack of face-to-face contact between the advertiser and the intended audience. In this

---

[4] Stanley E. Cohen, "Ads a 'Weak Signal' in Most Buying Decisions: Howard," *Advertising Age* (June 12, 1972), p. 3.

[5] This idea is discussed in "What Is Advertising? What Does It Do?," *Advertising Age* (November 21, 1973), p. 8.

way, advertising can be thought of as a substitute for personal selling. Without face-to-face interaction, advertising is undoubtedly less effective than a salesperson who can tailor the appeal to each individual customer being served as well as respond to questions, explain, and refute objections that may be raised. Yet, advertising has an important advantage over salespeople by being able to reach much larger audiences for a given level of resources expended. Thus, advertising is intended to inform and persuade *in mass,* and is used more extensively by those firms that must reach mass markets (national firms, consumer goods firms, etc.).[6]

The extensive resource allocation often made to advertising by firms as well as the performance expectations of management argue strongly for advertisers to adopt an analytical approach to advertising decisions. Figure 19–2 presents a flow diagram of such a process showing the essential advertising decision areas and activities. The remainder of this section will briefly overview the process before examining in more depth key steps in the diagram in the remainder of this and the following chapter.

Advertising Decision Areas

Figure 19–2 serves as a useful framework by identifying the advertising areas requiring managerial decisions. These include (1) determining the role that advertising should play in the total marketing mix for a product, (2) setting an advertising budget, (3) selecting target audiences, (4) designing a creative strategy and tactics, and (5) determining a media mix and media schedule.

Role of Advertising. The advertising decision process begins by determining the role that advertising should play in the total marketing mix. Actually, this involves two different, but related decisions. First, management must decide whether there should be any advertising at all for each product. This amounts to determining whether there is a profitable opportunity for advertising and requires management to examine what advertising can do for the firm. Few companies have decided that advertising should not be a part of their promotional mix. Yet, for some firms the rationale for including advertising is based less on an analysis of the role of advertising and more on a fear of the consequences of not advertising.[7] This unfortunate situation appears to stem from the inability of top managements, particularly of industrial firms, to determine how effective advertising really is. In any case, the decision on whether to advertise is almost always made in favor of advertising despite uncertainty about exactly what contribution advertising makes to the total performance of firms.

---

[6] Ibid.

[7] "Industrial Ads: A Debate Heats Up," *Business Week* (July 17, 1971), p. 68.

FIGURE 19–2

An Analytical Advertising Decision Process

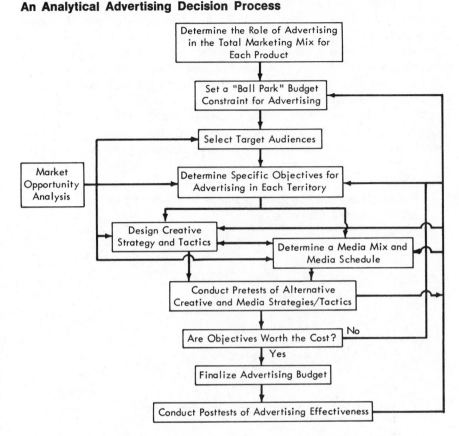

Deciding to advertise leads to the second consideration of what role advertising should play in the promotional mix. This decision requires assessing the relative ability of advertising, as opposed to the other promotional tools, in accomplishing promotional objectives. The starting point should be determining what management expects from the promotional component in a marketing mix. There are numerous promotional objectives that might be set; however, typically they fall into a relatively few categories including communication (generating awareness of products, features, company reputation, etc.), sales, and profitability.

By necessity, determining the role of advertising is a decision made by top management since it involves resource allocations to several different corporate functions. Firms handle this allocation task in different ways. Yet, to achieve the needed coordination between the various parts of the promotional mix requires participation of managers from all areas. For example, top management at Bellows-Valvair Co. has established a "communications group" including managers from sales, marketing, advertising, the advertising agency, and corporate staff. Periodically, this group discusses problems for which promotion can be at least a partial solution as well as the directions being taken.[8]

Setting Advertising Budgets. Once the role of advertising in the marketing mix has been determined, allocation of resources to advertising for each product and corresponding market target can be done through the development of budgets. An advertising budget is a financial document showing the total dollar resources and the way in which those dollars are to be spent. The budget may also show comparisons of the current period's allocation with one or more previous periods. Table 19–2

TABLE 19–2

An Advertising Budget for a Single Product of a Multidivisional Company

Budget Number	Item	Amount
.13	Trade and technical publications	$ 12,735
.14	Telephone directory advertising	30,000
.15	Catalogue advertising	2,100
.18	Preparation of ads	3,300
.21	Printing	32,700
.35	Merchandising	2,000
.42	Display materials	16,000
.51	Special campaigns	17,000
.61	Motion pictures (special training film)	6,000
Total for product #3		$121,835

Source: Adapted with permission from *Some Guidelines For Advertising Budgeting* (New York: The Conference Board, Inc., 1972), p. 49.

shows an advertising budget for one product of a large multidivision firm. Budgets for individual products would then be accumulated into total advertising budgets for divisions and/or the entire company. A division's advertising budget is shown in Table 19–3 for the same company.

Advertising budgeting in many firms is an iterative process involving both advertising personnel and financial control managers. The advertising decision process in Figure 19–2 illustrates this by showing the budgeting process beginning with a "ball park" budget constraint which would be established during the division or company-wide budgeting process for all functions. In some firms this is a fixed constraint within which advertising management must operate. In other companies, this amount is more flexible since advertising managers can negotiate for a larger budget by demonstrating (through budgets for individual prod-

---

[8] Ibid., p. 69.

TABLE 19–3

A Division's Advertising Budget for a Division of a Multidivision Company

	Budget Year	Preceding Year	+ or −
Product No. 1	$ 47,500	$ 23,760	+$ 23,740
Product No. 2	39,200	40,200	− 1,000
Product No. 3	121,835	74,450	+ 47,385
· · ·	·	·	·
Division's portion of the company's ad budget	824,022	819,747	+ 4,275
Subtotal	$2,185,000	$1,886,000	+$299,000
District or local advertising	15,000	15,000	−0−
Total	$2,200,000	$1,901,000	+$299,000

Source: Adapted with permission from *Some Guidelines for Advertising Budgeting* (New York: The Conference Board, Inc., 1972), p. 50.

ucts, supporting data, and rationale) the opportunity that can be tapped with more resources.

Selecting Target Audiences. Advertising is directed toward groups outside the firm which have some impact upon corporate performance. As is true for promotion in general, advertising may be used to inform and/or advocate a point of view to a wide variety of audiences in addition to customers. For example, to win governmental support for badly needed subsidies, a major railroad recently ran advertisements showing the deplorable condition of track and equipment. However, since the majority of advertising is used by companies to sell products and services, there is typically considerable overlap between target audiences and target markets. This means that selecting target audiences is heavily dependent upon the identification and description of company markets through the analysis of market opportunities. Figure 19–2 illustrates this dependence by linking MOA to the target audience selection decision.

Advertising Creative Strategy/Tactics. At the heart of advertising is the message or messages that a company wants to deliver to target audiences. Decisions here must cover two different but related aspects First, management must determine what to communicate to target audience members. This is the content portion of creative strategy. Content must be coordinated with other components of the marketing mix by communicating the strengths and uniqueness of company offers. For example, when Procter and Gamble began to market the disposable diaper, Pampers, advertising was given the task of demonstrating the ease and convenience of using Pampers rather than conventional cloth diapers. Advertising may also be used to communicate other marketing offer strengths such as low price, convenient product availability, prestige, and so forth.

Determining appropriate advertising content will not guarantee advertising effectiveness. Creative strategy also includes deciding how to best communicate messages to target audiences. Customers are exposed to more messages from all sources than they can possibly use. Consequently, each organization's advertising competes with other information sources for the limited attention of audience members. Successfully getting an audience to listen and understand advertising may be as much, if not more dependent on how messages are communicated as on content. For this reason creative advertising personnel spend considerable effort inventing new and different ways to attract attention as illustrated by the use of magical beings (e.g., the soap companies' white knight and Mr. Clean), humor (Alka Seltzer's "I can't believe I ate the whole thing."), and unusual symbols

("FÓRD has a better idea").

The design of creative advertising involves both strategic and tactical decisions. Strategic decisions must be made on the general themes and ideas that should be communicated to each particular audience. These themes largely determine how a product is to be positioned against its competitors in target markets and so, must be coordinated with the entire marketing mix strategy. An example of strategy advertising creative themes, *Wheaties* is positioned as a cereal for the sports-minded person by advertising as the "Breakfast of Champions," while *Special K* is positioned toward those concerned with health by concentrating on a nutritional theme. Tactical decisions determine how a particular advertising creative strategy will be implemented. For any particular strategy there are typically several tactical alternatives from which to choose. Wheaties, for instance, can be shown as the breakfast for the sports enthusiast by having actual champions from various sports give testimonials, by having a single person (such as Reverend Bob Richards) discuss the use of Wheaties as part of an athlete's training table, or by showing "typical" Wheaties eaters participating in, and winning at, various sports.

Media Mix and Media Schedules. The final advertising decision area shown in Figure 19–2 is concerned with the vehicles for carrying advertising messages to target audiences. These vehicles are primarily organizations that are in the business of transmitting information to their own audiences such as magazines, newspapers, billboard companies, television stations, and radio stations. As shown in Table 19–4, hiring these organizations to carry advertisements account for the bulk of advertising expenditures. However, there are a variety of other media used by firms (included in the "other" category in Table 19–4) including direct mail, transit advertising, in-store signs, displays, and on packaging.

Advertising management must make two highly related media decisions. First, the mix of specific media must be determined. In most

TABLE 19-4

1972 Advertising Expenses on Media

Medium	Expenses (in $ millions)	Percent of Total
Newspapers	$ 6,960	30.2
Magazines	1,480	6.4
Television	4,110	17.9
Radio	1,530	6.6
Regional farm publications	29	0.1
Outdoor	290	1.3
Other	8,661	37.5
Total	$23,060	100.0%

Source: Adapted with permission from *Advertising Age* (November 21, 1973), p. 7.

situations, a single medium will not reach the entire target audience for a product because no medium's audience is likely to be identical to the target audience for advertising. Thus, management must select a combination of different media to provide the desired coverage of target audiences. This decision is dependent on the cost of alternative media as well as the degree of overlap between media and target audiences. Moreover, media mix decisions must consider coverage in terms of national, regional, and local advertising.

The second media decision is the determination of a schedule showing the frequency and timing of advertisements in each medium. Frequency refers to the amount of repetition of individual ads over a given time period. Both buyer behavior and advertising research have shown that repeating ads increases awareness, comprehension, and remembering of messages by audiences.[9] Consequently, management must determine the number of times each ad is to be shown over the advertising planning/budgeting period in each medium. Media timing determines the spacing or amount of time that is allowed to elapse in between each repetition of an ad.

Setting Advertising Objectives

One of the key features of the advertising decision process shown in Figure 19-2 is the use of objectives to guide the budgeting, creative design, media mix, and media schedule decisions. As surprising as it may seem, the advertising function in business firms, particularly industrial firms, does not have a strong tradition of setting meaningful objectives for advertising. A study conducted for Marketing Communications Re-

---

[9] For a review and discussion of this research, see James F. Engel, David T. Kollat, and Roger D. Blackwell, *Consumer Behavior* (New York: Holt, Rinehart and Winston, Inc., 1973), pp. 338-42.

search Center (a nonprofit, industry-supported organization) showed that only 25 percent of the 30 industrial companies in the sample set objectives and most of these were quite vague.[10] Of course, advertising is not viewed by top management of industrial firms to be a very important part of the marketing mix. Yet, the lack of advertising objectives and resulting uncertainty concerning what advertising is accomplishing for industrial firms may well account for this top management viewpoint.

Setting meaningful objectives should be the starting point for advertising decisions. Objectives should cause advertisers to narrow their focus to only those advertising alternatives that are likely to accomplish objectives. For example, consider the goal statement in Figure 19–3 which was set for a particular model car (the name "Watusi" is used to

FIGURE 19–3

An Advertising Goal Statement for General Motors

DIVISION: _____ Series or Product: Watusi
Advertising Objective: to increase rating of Watusi regarding "Trade-in
        Value"
Target Market: all male heads of new car-owning households
Size of Target: 19,100,000
Dates Goal is to be in Effect: October 1963 to September 1964

Source: Reprinted from Gail Smith, "How GM Measures Ad Effectiveness," *Printer's Ink* (May 14, 1965), p. 26.

disguise the information) in the General Motor's line. The objective of increasing the rating of Watusi's trade-in value provides considerable guidance for creative people in determining appropriate creative tactics. Moreover, the description of the target audience whose trade-in value rating is important to GM will help in the selection of appropriate media. Also, the combination of creative and media tactics needed to achieve the objective will allow management to estimate the budget allocation required.

Equally important is the use of advertising objectives to control advertising performance. Evaluating advertising performance only becomes meaningful when there is a standard against which to compare actual advertising accomplishments. This standard is provided by objectives which determine what management wanted advertising to achieve (i.e., defines performance in terms of specific tasks to be done) and by how much (i.e., the magnitude of the task) within a time period. Figure 19–3

[10] "Industrial Ads: The View From the Top," *Business Week* (May 30, 1970), p. 92.

illustrates these characteristics of objectives. Note that the goal statement defines a specific task—increase consumer ratings of Watusi trade-in value—so that GM can actually measure whether the goal has been accomplished. Consumer rating information can be obtained both before and after the advertising has been conducted to assess the amount of change in ratings. Also, the magnitude of the task has been partially determined by stating the size of the target audiences, though it would have been even better to specify how much the ratings should increase. Finally, the time period allowed for advertising to accomplish this objective is given.

Role of Research

An important characteristic of the advertising decision process in Figure 19–2 is the use of advertising research to aid advertising managers. Research can help advertising management choose between alternative advertising strategies and/or tactics through pretests of the relative effectiveness of alternatives. Pretests are conducted prior to the finalizing or implementation of an ad or ad campaign, and are intended to provide managers with information on the reaction of target audience members to alternatives being considered. The importance of conducting pretest research is illustrated by a decision to drop a creative advertising idea for Schick Super Chromium razor blades. The idea consisted of a human face living independently from its body. With this premise, an ad was created showing a head floating around a bedroom while talking about how it could control the headless body standing nearby. The last part of the ad has the head saying that the body had better buy Schick Super Chromium blades or else the head wouldn't eat. Before airing this television ad, a pretest was conducted to determine if people would be repulsed by the separation of the head and body. The ad passed this test since only 2 percent of the sample said they were repulsed. Then the ad was pretested to measure how well people would remember the ad. Here, the ad failed badly—it was not an ad that stayed with its audience—and was dropped from further consideration.[11]

Advertising research is also an essential part of the post-testing of the effectiveness of advertising. For most kinds of advertising, it is nearly impossible to determine how well an advertisement is doing without research. (The exceptions are those advertising techniques that advocate some immediate response from the target audience, such as mailing in a coupon, that is highly visible or measurable without research). Overall corporate performance measures such as changes in sales, market share, or profitability are clearly inadequate unless advertising is the only factor

---

[11] This example is discussed in James MacGregor, "How a 'Creative' Type Struggles to Create a Pitch for Blades," *The Wall Street Journal* (April 3, 1972), p. 14.

determining performance which is highly unlikely for most organizations. So, post-testing is conducted after advertising has been run long enough for expected results to occur in order to determine how well advertising is achieving its performance objectives.

The Role of Advertising Agencies

In no other corporate functional area is the use of outside help so prevalent as in advertising. Particularly for national and regional consumer goods manufacturers, there is a heavy dependence on advertising agencies during the advertising decision process. Perhaps because of the acknowledged difficulty of developing advertising that will communicate with target audiences rather than being ignored, advertising agencies have specialized in the service of creating and preparing advertising. Agencies employ both creative and advertising production (e.g., artists, TV producers, print production manager, etc.) personnel to do this kind of work for client firms, and can spread their cost among all clients. Clearly, individual advertisers could not justify the very high costs of having such a wide range of talent on their payrolls.

Beyond the creative task, advertising agencies provide a variety of other services. One of the more important is media planning. Agencies employ media specialists to help clients in determining media mixes and schedules. Much of the significant advancement in the development of models for media planning has been the result of work and financial support of agencies. Moreover, media specialists also perform the more routine task of obtaining space in all media categories (print, television, radio, billboards, etc.). Additional services may include helping clients make decisions on product pricing, package design, and distribution; conducting marketing research; making presentations of advertising strategy to client personnel such as salespersons; and performing public relation tasks.[12]

Advertising agencies can be characterized as either full service firms or boutiques. Full-service agencies are capable of performing all of the above services for clients. These are the larger agencies employing personnel with a wide range of talents. More recently, there have been a number of agencies, usually smaller firms, appear in the industry that specialize in one or a few advertising functions. These are the boutiques. For example, a boutique may specialize only in buying media space for clients, or only in doing the creative design work. For a fee, clients can purchase the kind of service needed without having to pay for other unwanted services as may be the case if a full service agency is hired. In

---

[12] For an excellent discussion of advertising agencies, see "The Advertising Agency —What It Is and What It Does for Advertising," *Advertising Age* (November 21, 1973), pp. 34–42.

response to the boutiques, though, some full service agencies have been changing their relationship with clients by allowing them to purchase only the specific service or services needed.

One of the major changes occurring in the advertising industry, partly due to the fee structure used by boutiques, has been the pricing system used by agencies. It has been customary for full-service agencies to charge a commission of 15 percent of total billings for their service plus reimbursement for advertising production costs. Yet, the 15 percent commission comes from the media in which a client firm's advertising is placed rather than from the firm. An advertiser is billed by its agency for the full cost of advertising space used in the media. Then, media bill the agency for full cost of its space less a 15 percent commission (any early payment discount is passed back to the client). The agency's revenue, then, is primarily the difference between what it bills clients and what it pays to media. In effect, the media are paying the agency a 15 percent commission through a reduction in its billing to the agency. Moreover, this 15 percent commission must cover most expenses of operating the agency, so that a client is actually paying for the full service offering. Boutiques, on the other hand, charge a fee, rather than commission, for services performed. Movement toward a fee system will change the agency-client relationship to the advantage of the client since advertisers will be better able to buy only services needed from agencies.

Overall, Figure 19–2 provides a framework for identifying and integrating the key components of advertising management in organizations. The discussion now turns to a closer examination of the major advertising decision areas.

BUDGETING FOR ADVERTISING

Allocation of Resources to Advertising

Budgeting for advertising involves allocation of a portion of total marketing resources to the advertising function in a firm. In principle, the size of the budget allocation should be based on the potential contribution that advertising can make to achieving company operating objectives. Thus, advertising budgeting should be based on a careful analysis of the opportunity for using advertising. The marginal analysis approach to the allocation of resources provides a useful framework. Accordingly, the size of the advertising budget should be large enough to maximize the profit contribution of advertising to the firm. Both sales that can be generated from various size advertising budgets as well as the corresponding costs of sales and of the advertising must be estimated to assess the profit implications of each budget.

Table 19–5 shows an illustrative marginal analysis of advertising expenditures for a small company. This analysis assumes that management desires to maximize the profit contribution from advertising for their product, that the firm has sufficient resources to achieve this objective, and that it is not feasible to spend in less than $5,000 increments on advertising. Net revenue refers to sales less all non-advertising costs which are based on a predetermined non-advertising marketing mix (i.e., all other marketing mix components have been set for the budget period).

As indicated by the data in Table 19–5, advertising has the potential for making a significant contribution to company profits. At lower levels of advertising (less than $50,000) the company cannot generate sufficient sales to cover all costs. So $50,000 represents an absolute minimum advertising budget for the company to make any profit at all. At the upper end of the budget alternatives, advertising is unable to generate enough net revenue to more than cover its own budget at $95,000, so this sets the upper limit on the advertising budget.

Column 3 of the table shows that net revenue is increasing at every level from $50,000 to $95,000. Thus, examining net revenue alone is of little help in deciding upon an optimal advertising budget within this

TABLE 19–5

An Illustrative Marginal Analysis for Advertising Budgeting (in $1,000)

(1) Alternative Advertising Expenditures	(2) Marginal Advertising Costs	(3) Net Revenue	(4) Marginal Revenue	(5) Total Profit	(6) Marginal Profit
30		20		−10	
35	5	24	+4	−11	−1
40	5	30	+6	−10	+1
45	5	40	+10	−5	+5
50	5	55	+15	+5	+10
55	5	77	+22	+22	+17
60	5	88	+11	+28	+6
65*	5	95	+7	+30	+2
70	5	98	+3	28	−2
75	5	99	+1	+24	−4
80	5	99	0	+19	−5
85	5	97	−2	+12	−7
90	5	95	−2	+5	−7
95	5	90	−5	−5	−10
100	5	83	−7	−12	−7

* Optimal size advertising allocation.

range. The key to the decision evaluation is the analysis of both marginal revenue (column 4) and marginal cost (column 2). By subtracting column 2 estimates from column 4 estimates, management can assess advertising's contribution to total profits, shown in column 6. Clearly, advertising continues to add to total profits until a budget level of $70,000 is reached where profits actually decline by $2,000 from the profits achieved at an advertising expenditure of $65,000. Consequently, the optimal advertising expenditure is $65,000 where profits are maximized at $30,000.[13] Any more or less spent on advertising will generate a smaller profit.

Marginal analysis provides a very useful framework for guiding management towards the appropriate information, estimates, and analysis required for advertising budgeting. According to the framework, management must select performance objectives for advertising to assess potential contribution from various advertising expenditures. Marginal analysis relies on sales and profitability which are important performance objective areas for business, though the framework will work just as well with any quantifiable performance objective that a firm may set. In addition, the budget decision should be based on the analysis of change in marginal revenue and marginal cost by examining different budget levels. A practical procedure consistent with the marginal analysis framework is to begin with the previous period's advertising budget and analyze the change in performance contribution resulting from budget levels both lower and greater than this starting point. For advertising decisions with no previous history (such as for a new product introduction), management may determine a minimum budget level and then assess different levels above this minimum.

The marginal analysis framework also provides a basis for evaluating advertising allocation procedures used in practice. In actual advertising budgeting decisions, implementing the marginal analysis framework is usually a difficult and complex task. Advertising is seldom the only factor affecting corporate or product performance. So, a major difficulty is encountered when management tries to determine the contribution of just advertising, separate from other factors, to performance objectives such as net revenue. Moreover, it is often difficult to predict the time pattern of contribution during the budget period since it cannot be assumed that advertising will have an immediate impact on target audiences. Management also must face the task of trying to understand how advertising will affect target audiences and how this effect will translate into the area of performance expected of advertising. All of these difficulties make net sales, marginal revenue, or other performance contributions estimates hard to make very precisely. On the cost side, estimates are generally easier to develop, though complications arising from short term cost changes, unanticipated costs, and the difficulty of separating joint advertising costs add to the complexity of marginal cost estimates.

---

[13] This increment restriction keeps the firm from truly maximizing profits since at $65,000 marginal revenue is greater than marginal cost. However, marginal revenue will equal marginal cost at some level between $65,000 and $70,000 which is not a feasible level.

To cope with these realities of advertising budgeting, a variety of procedures have been adopted which vary considerably in appropriateness when compared with the marginal analysis framework.

Ad Budget Allocations by "Rules of Thumb"

One approach to the advertising appropriation task is to apply various "rules of thumb" to determine the total amount of resources to be allocated to advertising. The decisions on how to spend this amount are then made by advertising managers typically in cooperation with advertising agency personnel. Three such rules of thumb are percent of sales, competitive parity, and resources available for advertising.[14]

Percent of Sales. The percent-of-sales allocation procedure involves the multiplying of a predetermined percentage times a forecast of sales for the budget period:

$$\text{Advertising allocation} = \text{X\%} \times \text{\$sales}$$

This procedure can be applied by territory, by product, by market target, or by other breakdowns depending upon the way in which sales forecasts are broken down.

As a budgeting allocation procedure, how well percent of sales compares to the marginal analysis framework depends upon how the percentage is determined and how sales forecasts are developed. The most inappropriate use of this procedure occurs when a firm uses historical percentages and forecasts sales prior to determining the advertising budget. Here, management is doing little or no assessment of the contribution that advertising can make to company performance. Using historical percentages, at least implicitly, makes the unlikely assumption that opportunities for advertising in the budget period are identical to the opportunities in past periods. Moreover, forecasting sales prior to determining an advertising budget does not recognize the purpose of advertising. After all, if advertising does not make a contribution to generating sales, there can be little justification for spending *any* resources on product advertising.

A more appropriate use of percent of sales is as a ratio, $\dfrac{\text{Advertising}}{\text{Sales}}$ to aid in the analysis of alternative advertising expenditures.[15] Here, advertising expenditures and a resulting sales forecast are determined and combined into a ratio that can be quickly compared to other ratios (e.g., ratios for different budgets, territories, etc.). However, in this

---

[14] For a discussion of these procedures see *Some Guidelines for Advertising Budgeting* (New York: The Conference Board, Inc., 1972), pp. 5–13.

[15] Ibid., p. 6–7.

usage percent of sales is less of a budget setting procedure and more of an analysis tool.

Competitive Parity. It is common for companies to monitor the marketing programs (as well as other activities) of competitors. As a part of this activity, firms assess the advertising effort of major competitors and the industry as a whole. This practice can lead to setting company advertising budgets by *matching* competitive spending in some way. Called "competitive parity," budgets can be determined in several different ways:

Spend the same dollar amount on advertising as a major competitor.

Spend the same percentage of sales on advertising as a major competitor.

Spend the same percentage of sales on advertising as the average for the entire industry.

Use one of these "rules of thumb" in a particular market.[16]

All of these alternatives have one characteristic in common—the actions of competitors are allowed to dictate company advertising budget determination. Yet, when competitive parity reasoning dominates the advertising appropriation decision, a company faces several risks. Sufficient information may not be readily available to estimate competitors' advertising budgets. Such information is more completely reported in secondary sources for some products (primarily certain consumer products) than others.[17] When only partial information can be obtained, such as expenditures on media, competitive parity may be misleading by not indicating total effort (e.g., advertising not using paid media would be left out).

Even more serious is the implied assumption underlying competitive parity approaches that all firms in an industry have the same opportunities for profitable advertising. While this may hold for companies of the same size offering similar products through the same channels to the same markets, not many companies fall into this category. More typically company advertising opportunities are not entirely the same as competitors. If, for example, a company were to introduce a new product to compete with a competitor's already established brand, the opportunity for advertising for these two brands would be entirely different. The new product probably needs heavier promotional effort just to generate awareness among customers that it exists and compares favorably with the established brand.

Comparison of company versus competitor advertising expenditures can be a useful analysis tool for advertising managers. For example, the

---

[16] Ibid., p. 11.

[17] Ibid.

following ratio has been used by companies in planning advertising budgets:

$$\frac{\text{Company share of industry advertising}}{\text{Company share of market}}$$

By using historical data, a company can develop guidelines for the size of advertising budgets needed for both existing and new products. One such guideline was developed from the analysis of 34 new brands of non-durable consumer products by a market research/sales audit firm: to compete with existing brands, a company's advertising/market share ratio should by 1.5 to 1.6 times the market-share objective established for a new product.[18]

Resources Available for Advertising. A final "rule of thumb" for advertising appropriations is to allocate all funds that are "available" after the other functions have been budgeted and a satisfactory profit or return has been planned. In this approach, advertising is treated as a residual activity of a firm that is funded only after resources have been given to other corporate functions presumably deemed more important. If resources available for advertising are rather automatically spent, a firm can experience two potential dangers. It is possible that the allocation is too small to allow advertising to be very effective. At the other extreme, a firm might spend more than it needs on advertising by using all resources available. For example, running three ads in a local newspaper may do little more in making potential customers aware of a department store's sale than would two ads.

On balance, the available funds approach does ensure that advertising expenditures are assessed in light of profit objectives of the firm. Moreover, it does put advertising in perspective with other corporate functions as contributors to corporate objectives achievement. Difficulty arises only when funds are allocated to advertising without carefully evaluating the likely contribution that advertising at different budget levels can make to the firm.

"Rule of Thumb" Summary. In practice few firms actually allocate funds to advertising in the purely mechanistic way evident in these rules of thumb. Rather, percent-of-sales, competitive parity, and available funds rules are more likely to be guidelines used by management to evaluate varying size advertising budgets. The key to determining how appropriate the rules of thumb are for the advertising budget decision is how much they are allowed to dominate the final selection of an appropriation. In their place along with advertising opportunity assessments, the rules may be useful as additional guidelines. The real danger occurs with all such rules when there is the ". . . temptation in some

---

[18] Ibid., p. 9.

companies to let arbitrary guidelines loom a bit too large in the equation, with perhaps not quite enough attention paid to the analysis and research that provide the factual underpinning for a rationally defensible budget."[19]

Building the Budget by Objective and Task

A more analytical approach to setting an advertising budget begins with an assessment of the company's need for advertising. Typically called the objective and task approach, management must determine specific objectives for advertising before a budget is determined. These objectives determine what tasks advertising must perform. Advertising personnel then design advertising that will be likely to accomplish these tasks and by doing so, achieve the desired objectives. In this way, the budget is build up by accumulating the costs of the advertising necessary to accomplish each task and objective. Management, thus, bases the budget allocation on the opportunity for advertising as reflected in the preselected advertising objectives.

When using this approach, the objectives must be sufficiently detailed and specific to guide the design of advertising appeals and media. Such ill-defined objectives as "to increase sales of product x" or "to make customers aware of product x" are practically useless to managers trying to establish tasks for advertising. Contrast these general objectives with the much more specific advertising objective stated earlier in Figure 19–3. By specifying what attitude (trade-in value) toward which product (Watusi) should be changed in what direction (upward movement on an attitude scale) for which market target (19,000,000 new car buyers), advertising personnel are given considerable direction in designing an advertising campaign.

Advertising objectives must also be based on a sound understanding of target audiences for advertising. Setting objectives has little meaning unless management has confidence that achieving these objectives will contribute to overall corporate performance. This requires determining what responses by target audiences are desired and understanding how advertising can help influence these responses. Returning to Figure 19–3, GM did not pull this goal statement out of the air, but based it on the results of market research on the behavior of potential auto buyers. Attitudes toward various features of the "Watusi" were measured for those consumers who indicated that this model was competitive for their business (i.e., generally had the features desired). Then, attitudes were compared between one subgroup indicating that favorable consideration would not be given to the "Watusi" and another subgroup in which

---

[19] Ibid., p. 6.

favorable consideration would be given. By this comparison, GM determined which attitudes could account for the differences between the subgroups. A glance at Table 19–6 shows why attitudes toward trade-in value were selected as the focus for an advertising objective (higher numbers indicate more positive attitudes). Since Watusi did have a very high trade-in value for cars in its class, advertising's task was to change this attitude to be more in line with reality.[20]

Management should not overlook the difficult task of determining the worth of achieving objectives. This involves assessing whether specific objectives justify the costs required. Undeniably, it is hard to estimate the dollar payoff from an advertising campaign since this would require

TABLE 19–6

Attitude Rating of "WATUSI" by Feature

Auto Feature	Those Who Will Not Give Favorable Consideration	Those Who Will Give Favorable Consideration	Difference
Smooth riding	86	91	3
Styling	76	89	13
Overall comfort	81	87	6
Handling	83	86	3
Spacious interior	85	85	0
Luxurious interior	79	85	6
Quality of workmanship	80	83	3
Balanced engineering	77	83	6
Prestige	73	82	9
Value for the money	76	79	3
Trade-in value	59	77	18
Cost of upkeep and maintenance	63	67	4
Gas economy	58	58	0

Source: Adapted from Gail Smith, "How GM Measures Ad Effectiveness," p. 25.

an indepth understanding of the degree to which advertising will influence buying decisions. Yet, it is quite possible to develop methods for estimating advertising benefits through careful analysis of target audiences. Returning to the GM example, management assessed the benefits of advertising by using marketing research. For example, the change in probability of purchasing a "Watusi" caused by the trade-in value attitude change was measured using panel data.[21] Suppose that this probability, based on an analysis of past buying decision, could be expected to increase from P_1 to P_2 for those that advertising successfully influenced to become more favorably impressed with "Watusi's" trade-in value. Then, by forecasting the number of people whose attitude will change,

---

[20] Smith, "How GM Measures Ad Effectiveness," pp. 25–26.

[21] Ibid., p. 24.

an estimate of advertising benefit could be obtained from the following relationship:

$$\text{Advertising payoff} = \text{APM} \times (P_2 - P_1)n$$

where

$$
\begin{aligned}
\text{APM} &= \text{average profit margin to GM for} \\
&\quad \text{each Watusi sold} \\
(P_2 - P_1) &= \text{change in purchase probability} \\
n &= \text{number of target audience members} \\
&\quad \text{expected to change attitude}
\end{aligned}
$$

Advertising Budgeting Models

Statistical Advertising Budget Models. One modeling approach concentrates on determining an optimal total advertising budget without specifically considering creative design or media decisions. These models are based on developing a functional relationship between advertising expenditures and some measure of desired market response, usually sales. Data is collected on both sales and advertising expenditures for some previous time period in order to estimate the relationship between the two. Models are usually of the form:

$$S = a + b_1X_1 + b_2X_2 + \cdots + b_nX_n + U$$

where

$$
\begin{aligned}
S &= \text{sales of a product or brand} \\
X_1 &= \text{advertising expenditures} \\
X_2 - X_n &= \text{other variables thought to in-} \\
&\quad \text{fluence sales such as competitors'} \\
&\quad \text{advertising, disposable personal} \\
&\quad \text{income, etc.} \\
b_1 - b_n &= \text{parameters estimated from the data} \\
&\quad \text{showing the relationship of the} \\
&\quad \text{corresponding variables to sales} \\
U &= \text{random error}
\end{aligned}
$$

If the analysis of data shows that a model sufficiently explains sales variations and that advertising is significantly related to sales, it can aid in the budgeting decision. By plugging in the sales objective for the brand being advertised and estimates for each of the X_2 to X_n variables, the size of the advertising budget needed to achieve the sales goal can be computed.

More recent work on statistical advertising-sales models has increased their complexity and descriptiveness by considering several factors central to the budget decision. First, econometric techniques have been used to incorporate the cumulative effects of advertising on sales.[22] This recognizes that current sales are dependent on current advertising and a carryover effect from previous periods' advertising. In addition, the interrelationship between advertising budget and creative decisions can be assessed by including variables representing copy design.

Data for statistical advertising budget models can be generated in several different ways.[23] *Time series data* can be used when a firm has kept records of sales, advertising expenditures, and other variables included in the model over enough past periods to provide a sufficient number of data points. Costs are modest since the data are already available from company records. Nevertheless, the resulting model must be used with some caution. Management must assess whether future operating periods will be sufficiently like past periods from which the data were collected. Any significant changes in influences on sales will decrease the descriptiveness and predictive power of the model. Moreover, since the statistical model building technique (usually regression) measures association rather than cause and effect, there is the possibility that this kind of model is not descriptive of the way in which advertising affects or influences sales. This would happen, for instance, when advertising budgets in the past have been set as a percentage of anticipated sales volume rather than based on the opportunities for advertising. Here, the model relationship may reflect the budgeting method rather than the ability of advertising to generate sales.

Cross sectional data may be used, when available, to counter the difficulty of relying on historical advertising-sales relationships. This kind of data is comprised of a single time period's sales and advertising expenditures from various geographic territories. Again, with the data already available the procedure is relatively inexpensive. Yet, there must be sufficient variation in advertising budgets across territories so that advertising will be capable of showing a relationship with sales. Finally, using cross sectional data does not eliminate the difficulty of determining a cause and effect relationship between advertising and sales.

To explicitly identify the effect of advertising on sales volume, management can turn to *marketing research*. Through a controlled field experiment, (e.g., test marketing), advertising expenditures can be sys-

---

[22] For discussions of these models, see Frank M. Bass, "A Simultaneous Equation Regression Study of Advertising and Sales of Cigarettes," *Journal of Marketing Research*, vol. 6 (August 1969), pp. 291–300; and Darral G. Clarke and John M. McCann, "Measuring the Cumulative Effects of Advertising: A Reappraisal," in Thomas V. Greer, ed., *1973 Combined Proceedings* (Chicago: American Marketing Association, 1974), pp. 135–39.

[23] The data generation alternatives are discussed in Peter Doyle and Ian Fenwick, "Planning and Estimation in Advertising," *Journal of Marketing Research*, vol. 12 (February 1975), pp. 1–6.

tematically varied in comparable geographic areas. Actual measures of sales in these areas during the experimental period are used to estimate the influence that advertising expenditures has on product sales.

Comprehensive Advertising Decision Models. A very recent development is the building of more comprehensive advertising decision models. Using simulation or programming techniques, these models explicitly recognize the interrelationships between the size of an advertising budget and the allocation of the budget to both media and creative message design. As an example, consider the objective function of a recently developed model called ADMOD:[24]

$$V = \sum \frac{N_s}{n_s} \sum_{i \in s} W_s \sum_{Z_i=0}^{\infty} A_{ci}(Z_i) f_{ci}(Z_i) - \sum_j k_j X_{cj}$$

where

V = the value of an insertion schedule
c = index referring the copy alternative
i = index referring the individual in the sample population
j = index referring the vehicles (medium)
s = index referring the market segment
N_s = the size of segments
n_s = the size of the sample from segment S
W_s = the value to the firm of the consumer action (i.e., a trial purchase) by a member of market segments
Z_i = the number of exposures received by the individual i, given the insertion schedule
$A_{ci}(Z_i)$ = the probability that the desired consumer action (i.e., a trial purchase) will occur, given the fact that Z_i exposures occurred
$f_{ci}(Z_i)$ = the probability that individual i will receive exactly Z_i exposures, given the insertion schedule
k_j = the cost of an insertion in vehicle j
X_{cj} = the insertion of copy alternative c into vehicle j ($X_{cj} = 0,1$)

Several interesting characteristics of this model are apparent. First, the advertising budget is determined by the opportunity for advertising as reflected in the objective function. The budget recommendation of the model is the cost of the insertion schedule (the list of times that a par-

---

[24] David A. Aaker, "ADMOD: An Advertising Decision Model," *Journal of Marketing Research,* vol. 12 (February 1975), p. 42.

ticular copy design is to be inserted in selected media) that maximizes V, the value of advertising to the firm. This cost is shown in the objective function as $\sum_j k_j X_{cj}$.

The model also requires an explicit evaluation of the contribution of alternative copy designs and media combinations to the firm. This is expressed as $\sum W_s \sum A_{ci}(Z_i) f_{ci}(Z_i)$. The $f_{ei}(Z_i)$ is a probability showing the likelihood that a consumer will be exposed to a copy design Z_i number of times and is estimated based on analysis of respondent samples from the segments, s, included in the model. The other probability, $A_{ci}(Z_i)$, links exposure to consumer behavior by showing the likelihood of a particular desired action given that consumers in each segment were exposed to a particular copy design (c) and media schedule (Z_i). These probabilities are multipled by the value of a particular consumer action to the firm, W_s, which determines an expected value or payoff from a combination of copy design and media schedule. In this manner, the model can be used to evaluate alternative copy designs, media schedules, and budget sizes simultaneously to help management identify the best combination of advertising decisions.

CREATING ADVERTISING APPEALS

Creative Design Decisions

A portion of an advertising budget is devoted to the creative design of advertising appeals. Essentially, the creative task is to determine *what to say* in advertising and *how to say it*. Message content determines what information will be disseminated to audiences in order to influence behavior, while message form contributes to the likelihood that audience members will see and comprehend messages.

Figure 19–4 shows the various activities that are typically part of the creative design process. Given a set of objectives to accomplish, creative design people prepare for the design task by examining information on the product offer of which the advertising is to be a part. This allows advertising messages to be integrated with the other components of the marketing mix. Usually, this kind of information can be gathered in meetings between creative personnel and marketing managers for the product. For example, to prepare for the design of advertising for Schick razor blades, creative designers from the New York ad agency, Doyle Dane Bernbach, met with Schick managers to learn about the company, the product and its marketing, and product comparisons with competitors.[25] These meetings can be quite useful for both ruling out untrue or otherwise unacceptable advertising themes and identifying those themes that will be likely to achieve objectives and approval by management.

---

[25] MacGregor, "How a 'Creative' Type Struggles to Create a Pitch for Blades."

FIGURE 19–4

**Activities Comprising the
Creative Design Task in
Advertising**

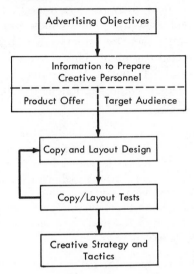

In addition, any information available that describes the target audience will also be helpful. Of patricular interest would be information that describes who is in the audience (demographics) and buying and consumption behavior with respect to the product. Either the advertising agency or the firm itself may gather this kind of information. As an example, the advertising agency of Batten, Barton, Durstine and Osborn gathered information about beer drinkers to assist in the design of an advertising theme for Schaefer Beer. This information not only identified some demographic characteristics of heavy beer drinkers, but also uncovered the fact that these drinkers felt the flavor of their beer tended to fade as more was consumed. Armed with some knowledge of the Schaefer's brewing process, ad agency personnel decided to base the advertising messages on the concept of Schaefer's advertising theme: "Schaefer is the one beer to have when you're having more than one."[26] This kind of insight into target audience behavior can lead to the design of very successful advertising appeals. Schaefer's ad campaign is over ten years old and has helped the company achieve substantial increases in market share.[27]

---

[26] Jonathan Kivitny, "Why Is Schaefer Beer the One Beer to Have When Having More. . . . ?" *The Wall Street Journal* (December 13, 1972), p. 1.

[27] Ibid.

Having become familiar with the product offer and target audience characteristics, advertising personnel can turn to the heart of the creative task which is the design of copy and layout. Creative types including artists, art directors, and copywriters must design an approach to communicating messages indicated by predetermined advertising objectives. Part of the process involves writing copy which is the verbal text of the advertisement. Copy must then be integrated with illustrations into an over-all design for the advertisement. This is the advertisement's layout.[28]

The design of copy and layout is an art that requires special skills. William Bernbach of Doyle Dane Bernbach, Inc., has put the creative task in proper perspective:

> Truth is essential in advertising today. You're not going to make it without it. But I must tell you that, while it may make you feel virtuous, it isn't its own reward. As far as your advertising budget is concerned, the truth isn't the truth until people believe you; and they can't believe you if they don't know what you're saying, and they can't know what you're saying if they don't listen to you, and they won't listen to you if you're not interesting. And you won't be interesting unless you say things freshly, originally, imaginatively.[29]

While a detailed discussion of the art of creativity is beyond the scope of this chapter, the contribution of creativity to the success of advertising should not be underestimated. Consider the difficult task set for advertising of Bic's fine line marker, a soft-tipped pen. When this product was introduced there were already dozens of markers in the marketplace. Yet, Bic's management wanted their new market entry to stand out among competitors so that potential customers would seek Bic's marker in retail stores. The creative strategy and tactics had to generate awareness and interest in Bic's marker as well as communicate product features. The copy and layout approach was a rather zany campaign centered around the theme of writing with a "Bic Banana." Humor was imaginatively used to make the message interesting and entertaining. With Mel Brooks as the narrator, one copy design said: "For thousands of years, civilization has searched for a different way to write. First we wrote with rocks. No good. Just writing 'Dear Sir,' you could hurt yourself. Then we tried sticks. But you couldn't make a lovely W with a stick. You could make a bump or a lump, but not a lovely W. It was a very bad time for man. Now we're modern and we're lucky. We can write with a Banana . . ."[30] This approach is much more likely to get

---

[28] Otto Kleppner, *Advertising Procedure* (Englewood Cliffs, N.J.: Prentice Hall, 1966), p. 127.

[29] William Bernbach, "Bill Bernbach Defines the Four Disciplines of Creativity," *Advertising Age* (July 5, 1971), p. 22.

[30] "A Zany Campaign to Sell the Bic Banana," *Business Week* (May 27, 1972), p. 77.

target audiences to listen to what Bic has to offer than a matter-of-fact statement about the availability of another soft-tipped pen.[31]

As shown in Figure 19–4, an important aid to the creative design task is the use of copy/layout tests to assess and compare alternatives. Samples drawn from target audiences are exposed to particular advertisements. Then, respondents are asked to give opinions on various aspects of an ad including how well it can be seen (or heard or read, etc.) under specific conditions, how quickly and easily the message can be understood, how interesting or liked an ad is, how believable it is, or how will it influence audience behavior.[32] There may be several iterations between the design and testing stages in the creative process. This is likely to occur when copy and layout alternatives are created sequentially and testing shows the inappropriateness of earlier alternatives.

One advertising budgeting decision is to determine what part of the total budget should be allocated to the creative task. Since there is little in the way of modeling effort available to help in this decision, the allocation task is usually done judgmentally. Yet, at least one writer believes that not enough has been spent in the past on the creative design of advertising in proportion to the amount spent on media. Irwin Gross has estimated that only 3 to 5 percent of media budgets are allocated to the creative task. Based on research using relatively conservative assumptions, he believes that closer to 15 percent should go to creative design.[33]

MEDIA STRATEGY AND TACTICS

Media Mix Decisions

Media Mix decisions involve the selection of a particular combination of media vehicles to carry messages to target audiences. This task is comprised of several interrelated decisions that result in a particular media mix. Management must choose the most appropriate combination of media types. The major alternatives at this level are shown in Table 19–4. Within each media type are numerous media vehicle alternatives. For instance, magazines are a media type that is comprised of hundreds of different publications such as *Playboy, Newsweek, Golf Digest, TV Guide*, and so forth. So, an additional decision is to select a particular combination of vehicles within each media type. Finally, most vehicles have multiple issues of differing frequencies. Newspapers are usually

---

[31] For an account of the development of the Bic Banana Campaign, see "A Zany Campaign to Sell the Bic Banana" pp. 76–78.

[32] Eugene E. Pomerance, "How Agencies Evaluate Advertising," in John J. Wheatley, *Measuring Advertising Effectiveness: Selected Readings* (Homewood, Ill.: Richard D. Irwin, Inc., 1969), p. 90.

[33] Irwin Gross, "A Condensation of An Analytical Approach to the Creative Aspects of Advertising Operations," Unpublished Ph.D. thesis (Boston: Case Institute of Technology, 1967).

issued daily or weekly; magazines are published on a weekly, monthly, or less frequent basis; television programs may be daily, weekly, or even one-time specials; and so forth. Thus, the number of times an advertisement is to be run in each vehicle must be determined. The result of the media mix decision is a list of media vehicles within the selected types showing the number of insertions of advertisements in each one.

Media mix criteria differ across firms and advertising situations. However, three criteria are commonly used among others. Media selections should be guided by the extent which the readers, listeners, or viewers (the vehicle's audience) overlaps with the firm's target audiences for advertising. Moreover, media capabilities must be matched to the special requirements for communicating specific messages. Finally, the cost of running an advertisement in a vehicle must be considered. Each of these criteria is briefly discussed.

Vehicle Audiences. The value of any particular media mix is dependent upon how well the vehicle combination reaches the firm's target audience. So, the selection of specific vehicles should be based, in part, on an analysis of the characteristics of vehicle audiences to determine how close the match with characteristics of target audiences is.

The audience matching task is complicated by the fact that firms' target markets and vehicle audiences are concentrated within certain segments or groups within a general population (e.g., all U.S. households). The phenomenon of the heavy buyer so familiar to marketers is also characteristic of media audiences. For example, "37 percent of all magazine households account for 75 percent of all magazine issue exposures, and 40 percent of all families account for 75 percent of all evening telecast exposures."[34] When an advertiser wishes to reach heavy user market segments, the analysis of media audiences involves a search for those vehicles that have the greatest numbers of heavy product (or brand) users in their audiences which, in turn, are concentrated among certain groups within the population.

Fortunately, media organizations assist in the media mix decisions of firms by conducting research on media audiences. In fact, results of audience research is an important tool used by media to sell their services to prospective clients. If the advertiser has already uncovered the key characteristics of target markets, vehicles can be evaluated by how well their audience characteristics match with target market characteristics. To be useful, though, vehicle audiences and target market audiences must be measured in terms of the *same* characteristics. This puts the extra burden on both advertisers and vehicles to coordinate the way in which audiences are described.

Media vehicles have been making progress over the past few years in

---

[34] Curtis C. Rogers, "Measuring Market Values of Media," in John J. Wheatley, *Measuring Advertising Effectiveness: Selected Readings,* p. 152.

the kind and amount of detail with which their audiences are described. The traditional measures of circulation (the number of readers, viewers, or listeners) proved to be inadequate as firms increasingly used market opportunity analyses to pinpoint specific market targets. Media have expanded descriptions, particularly in the 1960s, of audiences to include a variety of demographic characteristics and product purchasing behavior. Demographics were being heavily used during this period to segment markets by consumer goods firms.[35] As firms broaden their descriptions of target markets to non-demographic characteristics, media will no doubt do the same with their audiences. Such newer segmentation approaches including benefit and life style segmentation will guide the kinds of descriptions of vehicle audiences provided to advertisers. For example, Table 19–7 shows selected life styles characteristics of *Playboy* magazine readers that might be useful in matching its audience to target markets for a firm.

TABLE 19–7

The Playboy Profile: Percentage of Non-, Occasional, Light, and Heavy Readers Who Generally or Definitely Agree with Each AIO Question

Life Style Question	*Don't Read*	*Read Occasionally*	*Read One or Two of Last Four Issues*	*Read Three or Four of Last Four Issues*
I like sports cars	16	33	48	55
I would like to take a trip around the world	50	69	75	80
A woman should not smoke in public	53	32	32	26
I often wish for the good old days	31	24	20	16
There is too much emphasis on sex today	57	31	30	14
There is too much violence on TV today	54	28	25	19
I think I have a lot of personal ability	55	66	76	78
I often can talk others into doing something	39	47	45	60
I like to feel attractive to women	39	47	62	64
I like science fiction	27	41	43	52
Once I find a brand, I like to stick to it	74	71	67	57
I often try new brands before my friends and neighbors do	36	48	46	54
We will probably move once in the next five years	18	25	23	42

Source: Adapted by permission from Douglas J. Tigert, "Life Style Analysis as a Basis for Media Selection," in William D. Wells, ed., *Life Style and Psychographics* (Chicago: American Marketing Association, 1974), pp. 180–84.

---

[35] Since consumer goods firms use advertising so much more heavily in their marketing mixes than do industrial goods sellers, it is logical for media to focus their attention on consumer audience descriptions. However, vehicles with primarily businessmen in their audiences (e.g., trade journals, scientific journals, *Business Week*, etc.) perform the same audience description service.

Standardized information services also provide media audience information. By subscribing to a service, an advertiser periodically receives a report showing selected audience characteristics for specific vehicles. Typically, these services concentrate on audience size and demographic characteristics. For example, Arbitron conducts surveys of both television and radio station audiences in a large number of metropolitan areas. Figure 19–5 shows the kind of information that is available in one Arbitron Radio Service Report for selected radio stations in the Cleveland, Ohio area.

Media Communication Capabilities. Each of the major kinds of advertising media—newspapers, radio, television, magazines, and billboards—has special capabilities as well as limitations for delivering advertising messages. So, advertising managers must match the requirements for effectively communicating particular messages with alternative media's technical characteristics. For example, newspapers provide considerable selectivity in reaching audiences in local geographic areas due to the fact that newspaper circulation typically is concentrated in a single urban community. Thus, this medium is particularly appropriate for delivering messages concerning local buying conditions for a product such as sale prices, location of dealers, model availability and so forth. Yet, newspapers offer limited use of color in advertisements, and must use the written word for communication. This means that newspapers may not be the most effective medium for delivering messages centered on the aesthetic appeal of such products as food, clothing or furniture, or for product messages requiring personal demonstration such as for a new appliance. In these cases, television may be a more appropriate medium.

Media decisions rely heavily on managerial experience and judgment when matching media communication capabilities with message requirements. Advertisers, particularly advertising agency personnel, are very familiar with the unique capabilities and limitations of each medium through extensive past usage. Consequently, this experience is pivotal for selecting those candidate media that are most suited to delivering specific advertising messages. Moreover, advertisers may also judgmentally use this criterion to weight the relative importance of media within a candidate list for each advertising message comprising a campaign.

Cost per Thousand. Media planners are also concerned with the costs of alternative vehicles. Typically, a budget constraint is set for the media mix decision so that the sum of the costs of all media vehicles in the mix must not exceed a given amount. Within this constraint, though, a comparison of vehicle costs is meaningless unless costs are related to some measure of value. One criterion for making this kind of evaluation that is widely used by advertisers is the cost-per-thousand measure:

$$\text{Cost per thousand} = \frac{\text{Price of a single insertion (time unit)}}{\text{Audience size (in thousands) of a vehicle}}$$

FIGURE 19–5. Arbitron Radio Service—Audience Estimates in the Arbitron Market of Cleveland

Types of Estimates Reported
  Average Market Share Trends by Radio Station in the Metro Survey Area
  Average Quarter-Hour and Cumulative Listening Estimates by Radio Station in the Metro and Total Survey Areas
  Away-from-Home Listening Estimates by Radio Station in the Metro and Total Survey Areas
  Cumulative Listening Estimates for Day-Part Combinations by Radio Station in the Metro Survey Area
  Metro Ratings
  Metro Share

Time Periods for Which Estimates Are Reported*
  Monday–Sunday   6:00 AM–Midnight
  Monday–Friday   6:00 AM–10:00 AM
  Monday–Friday   10:00 AM–3:00 PM
  Monday–Friday   3:00 AM–7:00 PM
  Monday–Friday   7:00 PM–Midnight
  Saturday   6:00 AM–10:00 AM
  Saturday   10:00 AM–3:00 PM
  Saturday   3:00 PM–7:00 PM
  Saturday   7:00 PM–Midnight
  Sunday   6:00 AM–10:00 AM
  Sunday   10:00 AM–3:00 PM
  Sunday   3:00 PM–7:00 PM
  Sunday   7:00 PM–Midnight
  Weekend   6:00 AM–Midnight
  Monday–Friday   5:00 AM–1:00 AM
                   (hour-by-hour)
  Day-Part Combinations

Sex Groups for Which Estimates Are Reported†
  Men
  Women
  Total Adults

Age Groups for Which Estimates Are Reported‡

12–17	12–17
18+	18–24
18–34	25–34
18–49	35–49
25–49	50–64
25–64	Total Persons 18+
35–64	Total Persons 12+

* Day-Part Time Periods are typically cross-classified with age and/or sex group.
† Sex groups are typically cross-classified with age-groups.
‡ Age groups are typically cross-classified with sex group.
Source: Adapted with permission from Arbitron Radio—Cleveland, April/May 1975.

Cost per thousand shows the dollar cost of reaching each thousand persons in a media's audience with a single insertion of an advertisement. Since costs and audience size are typically available for vehicles within each media, this criterion provides a convenient index for comparing alternative vehicles. Table 19–8 shows cost and audience size data for five magazines that can be used for a cost per thousand analysis.

The apparent simplicity of the cost-per-thousand criterion should not cause advertisers to use it carelessly. The usefulness of the criterion is dependent in part on the way in which audience size is measured. If audience size is the total audience of the media, the index can be misleading, particularly when many in the audience are not in the firm's target market. It is only the overlap portion of a vehicle's audience with

TABLE 19–8

1974 Cost and Circulation Data for Selected Magazines

Magazine	Cost of a Black and White Full Page Ad	Cost of a 4-Color Full Page Ad	Circulation Size
The New Yorker	$ 5,900	$ 9,400	486,816
Time	$29,975	$46,460	4,294,562
Playboy	$32,340	$45,250	6,149,682
Ladies Home Journal	$29,400	$38,490	7,101,148
Forbes	$ 8,050	$12,220	631,318

Source: Reprinted with permission from Standard Rates and Data Service, Inc. (April 24, 1975), p. 150, 196, 220, and 364.

the firm's target audience that is of concern to the advertiser. Thus, the closer the audience size comes to measuring the number of the firm's target market members in the vehicle's audience the more meaningful the cost-per-thousand criterion is to the media planner.

There is also the question of potential vs. actual audiences. Planners would like to use cost-per-thousand target market members *actually* reached by a vehicle in a given time period. Yet, it is obviously much easier to determine the number in an audience that *potentially* can be reached even though not all of these people will be exposed to the vehicle or to the advertisement. To the extent that vehicles have differing ability to achieve exposure, the criterion can be misleading.

Cost per thousand is also difficult to use when deciding on the number of insertions to use per vehicle. The value of insertions after the first one are not likely to be the same. If audience composition and/or the exposure of audiences to the vehicle or to the advertisement change for each insertion, then a single cost-per-thousand criterion for each vehicle will not adequately compare the cost/value of alternative vehicles. Yet, suitable measures of these changes are typically not available.

Finally, the cost-per-thousand criterion does not include the more qualitative dimensions that are characteristic of vehicles. Such factors as the editorial content, reputation, audience overlap with other vehicles, special abilities to transmit messages (sound, color, movement, etc.), and the social environment when viewed by the audience contribute to the relative effectiveness of different vehicles to deliver a firm's advertising message.[36] Such qualitative factors must be used to adjust the quantitative cost-per-thousand indicies.

In general, the cost-per-thousand criterion, at best, should be used as one of several criteria for comparing vehicles. Moreover, it is likely to be a crude, rather than highly precise indication of the relative efficiency of alternative vehicles due to the above difficulties. In fact, since the comparability of audience measures across media types (e.g., print vs. broadcast media) is likely to be quite different, the criterion should be restricted to use in comparing vehicles within the same media type.[37]

Media Scheduling Decisions

The media mix decision will largely determine the reach (number of different target market members exposed to an advertisement) and the portion of media "impact" due to the special qualities of each vehicle. In addition, the media planner is concerned with the frequency and continuity of advertising exposures.[38] Frequency or number of insertions per vehicle is a part of the media mix decision, but is highly related to the continuity achieved with a media combination. Continuity refers to the timing of insertions throughout predetermined planning periods. Management must determine the amount of time that should elapse between each advertising insertion for each medium given a fixed number of total insertions. Or, if the number of insertions is not fixed, then the number of insertions necessary to achieve a desired frequency of exposure throughout each planning period can be assessed.

Determining the timing or schedule of advertising insertions in the media mix is a complex decision for advertisers. There appears to be little in the way of quantitative models to aid media planners. Moreover, there are a large number of schedule alternatives from which to choose. Figure 19–6 shows some of the media schedules that might be used by a firm.

While the media scheduling decision is largely based on the subjective

---

[36] Dennis H. Gensch, "Media Factors: A Review Article," *Journal of Marketing Research*, vol. 7 (May 1970), p. 216, published by the American Marketing Association.

[37] Albert Wesley Frey and Jean C. Halterman, *Advertising* (New York: The Ronald Press Company, 1970), p. 355.

[38] Advertising reach, frequency, impact and continuity are discussed in Frey and Halterman, *Advertising*, pp. 344–47.

judgment of advertisers, there are a number of factors to consider. Clearly, specific advertising objectives should be used as guides. For example, automobile manufacturers in the United States introduce new models in the late summer and early fall of each year. So, if advertising is to generate awareness and interest among prospective buyers, the media schedule should be heaviest immediately preceding and during this introduction period. Then, advertising frequency might taper off at other times of the year. This schedule would be similar to diagram B in Figure 19–6. A frequently purchased product such as a food item might need a more evenly spaced schedule (e.g., diagrams A or C) in order to maintain a constant level of awareness of the product over time.

Another factor concerns the nature of the target market. Research has shown that repetition of an advertisement affects both learning and remembering of messages. Thus, for any given time period, the advertiser must assess how many insertions/exposures are necessary to achieve a desired level of learning and remembering. Beyond this number, further insertions might be wasted. Clearly, audiences differ in their ability to be exposed to and remember advertising. So, the schedule would depend on the audience characteristics. For particular audiences, an advertiser may have to use intermittent (or bursts of advertising) schedules in order to increase the number of exposures for a given time period (dia-

FIGURE 19–6

Some Advertising Scheduling Alternatives

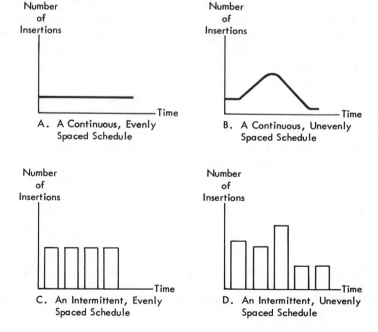

gram C and D). Given a fixed media budget, the greater the number of insertions in each "burst" the more time that must elapse between bursts. Thus, intermittent scheduling involves assessing the trade-off between the positive effects of more concentrated, larger number of insertions and the negative effects of low or no advertising frequency in-between bursts.

Media Selection Models

There has been considerable attention given to the development of models specifically intended to aid advertisers in making media selection decisions. This is probably due to the tremendous complexity of choosing from so many different vehicle alternatives. Given appropriate data, computer models can more quickly and efficiently compare and evaluate larger numbers of media candidates than can media planners. The output of models, a list of recommended media, can then be assessed by advertisers relying on experience and judgment. Available models generally fall into one of two categories—(1) optimization approaches (e.g., linear programming) and (2) nonoptimizing approaches (e.g., simulation).[39]

Linear Programming Model. Early modeling attempts involved the application of linear programming to the media selection decision. Linear programming (LP) is a mathematical model for maximizing the value obtained from the use of scarce resources. Moreover, LP allows the user to prespecify certain constraints on the way in which resources can be spent. One constraint, for instance, would be the amount of resources that are available. The value to be achieved (i.e., the objective function) and the constraints must be stated as linear equations. A linear programming computational technique is then used to determine states of the decision variables in the objective function required to maximize value.

The objective for the media selection decision is to choose the combination of vehicles and number of exposures in each vehicle that will maximize the contribution of advertising to the firm. So, to use LP a unit of contribution (profit, number of weighted exposures, etc.) must be determined. This unit is expressed as p_i in the following objective function characteristic of linear programming:

$$\text{Objective Function} = p_1 V_1 + p_2 V_2 + \cdots + p_n V_n$$

where

$$V_i = \text{the number of insertions or units to use in medium vehicle } i$$

[39] Dennis H. Gensch, "Computer Models in Advertising Media Selection," *Journal of Marketing Research,* vol. 5 (November 1968), pp. 414–42, published by the American Marketing Association.

p_i = the contribution of an insertion in medium vehicle i to the firm.

n = number of media vehicles

There are usually certain constraints imposed upon media planners. Some constraints are the result of vehicle factors. For example, if a monthly magazine is to be considered with no more than one ad per issue, then the model must be constrained to consider no more than 12 insertions in this vehicle. Other constraints are management imposed which may include restrictions on the size of the media budget, a minimum level of spending on certain media believed to be especially important to the firm, maximum levels of spending on selected media, and so forth. Combining each constraint equation with the objective function formulates the complete linear programming model:[40]

Maximize:

$$p_1 V_1 + p_2 V_2 + \cdots + p_n V_n$$

Subject to:

$$c_1 V_1 + c_2 V_2 + \cdots + c_n V_n \leq C_b \quad \text{(budget constraint)}$$
$$V_1,\ V_3,\ V_5 \leq 12 \quad \text{(monthly magazines)}$$
$$V_{12} \geq C_1 \quad \text{(minimum allocations)}$$

$$V_1,\ V_2,\ \cdots,\ V_n \geq 0 \quad \text{(no negative insertions)}$$

Once media planners specify the values of the constants in all equations (p_i, C_i, C_B, etc.), the task of determining the best number of insertions for each vehicle, V_i, is a purely computational routine that can be quickly done by a computer. The output is the optimal solution to the set of simultaneous linear equations forming the model. In this case, the optimal solution is the one media mix that maximizes the contribution of advertising to the firm as expressed in the objective function and that falls within all constraints imposed.

Linear programming media selection models have been widely explored. This experience has shown that, at best, LP models can only provide an approximate guide to the media selection decision. In part, difficulties arise because the linear programming requirements do not adequately describe the complexity of the media decision. The assumption of linear relationships between variables imposed by the model's objective function and constraints is particularly limiting. For example, no provision is made for any differences in the value of additional in-

---

[40] For a nontechnical discussion of formulating the media selection decision in a LP format see Ralph L. Day, "Linear Programming in Media Selection," *Journal of Advertising Research,* vol. 11 (June 1962), pp. 40–44.

sertions in the same vehicle. Advertisers are aware of the fact that the value of an insertion in a vehicle is likely to be a nonlinear function of the number of insertions in that vehicle such as is shown in Figure 19–7.

Another difficulty is apparent in the objective function. It is very hard to accurately determine the contribution that insertions in alternative vehicles will make. This requires data on the effectiveness of advertising to particular groups through different media which is either

FIGURE 19–7

A Nonlinear Relationship between the Number of Insertions in a Vehicle and the Value to the Firm of Each Insertion

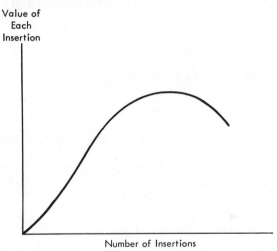

Value of
Each
Insertion

Number of Insertions

not available or not very precise. For these reasons, the linear programming media selection model has generally not been as useful as had been hoped.[41] However, this has had a positive impact by encouraging exploration of other models including more complicated programming approaches.

Interaction Models. Another optimization approach that is being used by some advertising agencies has been termed interaction models.[42] This kind of model involves an iterative search from a list of vehicles to select individual insertions, one vehicle and insertion at a time, until some constraint has been reached (generally a budget constraint). More-

[41] For a discussion of LP media selection model limitations see Frank M. Bass and Ronald T. Lonsdale, "An Exploration of Linear Programming in Media Selection," *Journal of Marketing Research*, vol. 3 (May 1966), pp. 179–88.

[42] Gensch, "Computer Models in Advertising Media Selection," p. 417–18.

over, after each vehicle insertion has been selected based on its contribution, the contribution from all other vehicles insertions not yet selected can be recomputed. This allows the model to consider such factors as audience duplication between and within vehicles. A diagram of an iteration media selection model is shown in Figure 19–8.

Simulation Model. A nonoptimizing approach to the media selection decision is to build a simulation model describing the impact of advertising through selected media or target markets. In essence, this approach is based on simulating the process by which vehicles reach individuals in target audiences. This requires research on the viewing habits of individuals as well as on the way in which advertising affects individual behavior. Once the simulation model has been built, alternative media mixes can be submitted to the model for evaluation. Unlike the optimiza-

FIGURE 19–8

Flow Diagram for Iteration Model

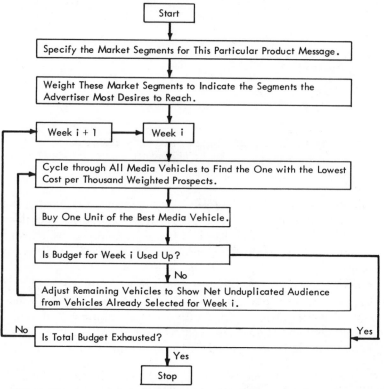

Source: Reprinted with permission from Gensch, "Computer Models in Advertising Media Selection," p. 416.

tion models, an optimal solution is not determined since the simulation model does not generally consider all alternatives. Yet, simulation models are typically more descriptive of the real world media selection decision situation. Optimizing models must make simplifying assumptions (e.g., the linearity assumption) in order to use the power of mathematics to find a single "best" media mix. Simulation is more concerned with describing the actual advertising process' impact on target population members. This provides a tool for testing the value of alternative proposed media mixes to aid managerial judgment.[43]

Evaluation of Media Selection Models. The variety of models in use today attest to the fact that the best or most useful media model has probably not been developed yet. Existing models and approaches all have advantages and disadvantages over others. Moreover, the models have not eliminated the need for managerial experience and judgment in the media selection decision. Rather, these models should be viewed as tools for aiding management in analyzing the factors influencing the media selection decision and to improve the use of judgment.

In addition, media models can be an important guide to the kinds of research needed to improve future model applications. Russell I. Haley, Senior Executive Vice President of Appel Haley Fouriezos, Inc., argues that the ultimate potential of computerized media models will not be realized without significant improvements in the data available for the models. He identifies eight kinds of needed data by most media selection models: (1) a list of candidate vehicles; (2) data on target audience size and composition; (3) a list of candidate media size and color units; (4) cost of each unit in each vehicle; (5) special restrictions on vehicle use; (6) weights indicating the relative importance of those in target audiences; (7) weights showing the relative impact of each unit in each vehicle; and (8) weight indicating the cumulative impact of multiple insertions.[44] Haley believes that data on (7) and (8) are very difficult to obtain, and that judgment of media planners is heavily relied on for these inputs. Moreover, these inputs are very important in determining model outputs. Thus, the usefulness of the models are heavily dependent on the accuracy of these key judgments concerning the impact of advertising on target audiences. The conclusion is that research is needed to improve understanding of how advertising influences individuals and to develop methods for gathering better data on advertising impact.[45]

---

[43] For a discussion of simulation models for media selection see Gensch, "Computer Models in Advertising Media Selection," pp. 421–24.

[44] Russell I. Haley, "Do We Really Know What We are Doing?" in Fred C. Allvine (ed.), *1971 Combined Proceedings* (Chicago: American Marketing Association, 1972), p. 217.

[45] Ibid., p. 219.

SUMMARY

This chapter has been primarily concerned with the design of effective advertising strategy and tactics. An analytical decision process was presented as a guide for advertising management in designing advertising to achieve specific objectives. In addition, the key design activities in this process—determining advertising budgets, creative appeals, and media mixes and schedules—were discussed in greater depth. Yet, designing advertising campaigns is only a part of the advertising decision process. It is also necessary to control advertising decisions.

Control of advertising is heavily dependent on having adequate understanding of the effectiveness of advertising. However, measuring advertising effectiveness is a controversial topic. For example, it is not clear what kinds of measures are most appropriate. The next chapter examines this topic by discussing the need for advertising effectiveness measures and alternative techniques for providing the essential information for control of advertising.

EXERCISES FOR REVIEW AND DISCUSSION

1. The advertising manager for National Control Systems, Inc., a producer of quality control monitoring systems, has developed a rationale for greater corporate allocation to advertising. In the past, most promotional resources were allocated to personal selling. His argument essentially is that advertising is capable of reaching buyers more economically than salesmen since the average cost per sales call is $50 and the advertising cost per audience member is typically well below this amount. The advertising manager believes that advertising can substitute for salesmen's calls on customers, and save the company money if resources are switched from personal selling to advertising for a given promotional budget. Do you agree with the advertising manager? Why or why not?

2. After consultation with the account executive of the company's advertising agency, the advertising manager for Southern Foods, Inc. established objectives for the current year's advertising campaign. This campaign will promote the company's line of snack foods. The objectives are:

    1. To reverse the decline in sales experienced over the past two years.
    2. To build awareness among teenagers of the variety of snack foods in the company's line.
    3. To establish Southern Foods as the leading snack food brand in the Southwestern United States.

    Carefully evaluate the usefulness of these objectives for Southern Foods' advertising decisions.

3. The advertising vice-president for a large manufacturer of skiing equipment sold in U.S. markets estimated the probable sales response to different size advertising budgets being evaluated. Last year's advertising budget

was $387,500 which was 6.7 percent of sales. For each sales volume, all costs exclusive of advertising were also estimated. These data are shown in the table below. If maximizing profits is the major advertising objective, what advertising budget should be recommended?

Analysis of Advertising Budgets ($000)

Advertising Budget	Probable Sales Volume	Estimated Total Costs of Sales Except Advertising	Advertising as Percent of Sales
$387.5	$5,768.7	$4,902.4	6.7
397.5	6,100.5	5,240.3	6.5
407.5	6,250.6	5,380.8	6.5
417.5	6,290.4	5,415.3	6.6
427.5	7,000.0	6,220.0	6.1
437.5	7,006.4	6,223.0	6.2
447.5	7,010.3	6,225.6	6.4

4. A manufacturer of high priced men's suits is developing an advertising budget as an imput to the marketing planning process for the current operating period. A media planner at the company's advertising agency is developing a media schedule. Using only the data in Table 19–8, evaluate the relative desirability of running a color advertisement in each of the magazine media listed in that table. Are these data sufficient for an appropriate media evaluation? Discuss.

5. Full-service advertising agencies are typically paid for their service to a client firm by receiving a 15 percent commission of total billings from the media in which the firm's advertising is run. Is this an appropriate method for advertising agencies to charge for their services? Why or why not?

6. Explain why target audiences for advertising may differ from the firm's target markets. Illustrate your answer by selecting one of the following kinds of business firms and discuss possible target audiences that might be selected by that firm: a bus line, a laundry detergent producer, a wine distributer, a can manufacturer, or an automobile manufacturer.

7. Critics of advertising often assail the fact that creative advertising copy does not present an unbiased description of product characteristics and weaknesses. Rather, advertising makes heavy use of such copy techniques as humor, gimmicks, imagery, and boasting. Why do advertisers use these techniques? Should advertising copy present an unbiased view of the product? Discuss.

Evaluating Advertising Effectiveness

This chapter continues the discussion of advertising decisions by considering one of the more controversial areas in all of marketing management: How much control should be exercised over the advertising decision process? Controlling advertising requires setting performance standards (goals, objectives) to determine what advertising should accomplish and then evaluating how well advertising meets these standards. The controversy extends into each of these aspects of the control process. In the first section, the control controversy is examined in more depth. A conceptual framework for understanding the role of advertising in buyer decisions is presented to help in understanding the complexities of the advertising control task. Alternative objectives for advertising are discussed within the context of this framework. Finally, advertising effectiveness procedures for each kind of objective are presented.

ADVERTISING EFFECTIVENESS CONTROVERSY

An Advertising Control Process

Few managers would contend that *no* control should be exercised over advertising decisions. Rather, the controversy is more concerned with the kind and extent of control that should take place. The issue can be seen more clearly by examining the advertising control process shown in Figure 20–1. Little can be said about the effectiveness of advertising decisions unless management has determined what advertising should do for the firm. Therefore, the control process must begin by setting performance standards for advertising decisions. These standards determine the tasks for advertising to accomplish such as expanding sales or

FIGURE 20–1

An Advertising Control Process

generating a higher level of brand awareness among target audience members.

The performance criteria that are used to state managerial objectives for advertising should also be used to guide the selection of appropriate measures of advertising performance. For example, if an advertising manager expects advertising to increase sales for a brand by 10 percent over last year, the most appropriate performance measure would be the amount of actual sales increases generated by advertising. This relationship between performance measures and statements of advertising objectives should encourage management to establish objectives for which performance can be measured. Expecting advertising to increase sales in a market target is not useful for control purposes if management cannot determine what contribution advertising made to generating sales.

Having selected appropriate measures of advertising performance, management must then decide what data are needed to implement these measures. For example, if percent sales increase is the measure of advertising effectiveness, data might include changes in gross sales, net sales, unit sales, or dollar sales figures obtained from corporate accounting records; warehouse or retailer product movement data obtained from a standardized research service such as Nielsen Audit Services; or marketing research sales data from a test market. The key decision here is to determine how much managerial judgment must be supplemented by more formal data collection, and given cost considerations, what data is best suited to help management evaluate advertising effectiveness.

If a research design is employed, the task is to collect data so that actual advertising performance can be compared to expected performance. Normally, control involves the collection of performance data after the full scale running of ads. This is called *post-testing* of advertising effectiveness since it follows the decision to use a particular campaign. Advertisers often collect effectiveness data prior to this decision to *pretest* the probable performance of one or more proposed alternatives. Pretesting advertising effectiveness can include collecting data on the performance of expenditure levels, creative designs, media mixes and schedules, or some combination of these. This data provide an input into managerial decisions by aiding in the prediction of target audience responses to proposed advertising. In general, the issue of how much resources to allocate to the formal measurement of advertising effectiveness includes both pre- and post-tests since each kind of data allows management to evaluate either probable or actual performance.

Should Advertising Effectiveness Be Measured?

There is a rather large number of firms that do not even attempt to measure the effectiveness of their advertising.[1] For these firms, advertising decisions are based primarily on managerial judgment. Perhaps this accounts for the fact that advertising tends to be the most subjective, nebulous decision area within many firms' marketing mixes. Given the generally acknowledged difficulty of understanding how advertising is used during customer decision processes, managerial judgment alone is not typically sufficient to maximize performance from advertising resources.

Reasons for the reluctance to measure the effectiveness of advertising are quite complex. Lawrence Gibson, Director of Marketing Research for General Mills, Inc., has suggested that arguments against measuring advertising effectiveness usually fall into three broad categories: (1) technical reasons, (2) philosophic reasons, and (3) economic reasons.[2] *Technical arguments* are concerned with the technical feasibility of using existing research techniques to measure advertising performance. Some advertisers and marketing managers express doubts about the availability

---

[1] David A. Schwartz, "Measuring the Effectiveness of Your Company's Advertising," *Journal of Marketing*, vol. 33 (April 1969), pp. 20–21, published by the American Marketing Association; and Donald C. Marschner, "DAGMAR Revisited—Eight Years Later," *Journal of Advertising Research*, vol. 11 (April 1971), pp. 27–28.

[2] Lawrence D. Gibson, "If I Don't Want to Loan You the Plow . . ." *Proceedings of the 14th Annual Conference of the Advertising Research Foundation* (New York: Advertising Research Foundation, 1968), pp. 37–43.

of appropriate measurement techniques, the validity of performance data, and the degree of accuracy of assumptions underlying techniques that are used. Yet, most of these reasons for not measuring advertising effectiveness have very little basis in fact. Measurement techniques are available and validation evidence for various techniques does exist.[3] There are unproven assumptions underlying some techniques, but these are not so unrealistic as to justify no confidence in all measurement techniques. Moreover, they may pale in significance to the unproven assumptions underlying advertising decisions made purely on subjective judgment. Unproven technique assumptions should provide direction for future research toward determining their accuracy rather than used as a reason for not doing any advertising effectiveness research.

Philosophic arguments center on the belief that designing advertising is a creative process that may be seriously hindered by control. Yet, creativity has no value for the advertiser unless it is effective and efficient in helping advertising to contribute to corporate goal achievement. Winning a "Cleo" award for excellence in creativity does not guarantee that an advertisement is contributing enough to company or product performance to justify its existence. Moreover, there is little reason to believe that increased advertising effectiveness measurement will inhibit creativity.

Finally, some managers suggest that while measuring the effectiveness of advertising may be technically feasible there is doubt as to whether the necessary research is worth the cost. Such *economic reasons* recognize the fact that advertising effectiveness data requires an allocation of resources just as does any other corporate function. Any fallacy in this argument arises only when management completely dismisses the economic worth of advertising effectiveness data without weighing the potential value of such data against costs.

The value of advertising performance research lies in helping management to uncover and weed out ineffective and detrimental advertising. Reported experiences in some companies show that unexpected results from advertising can and do occur. For example, an advertisement for a General Mills' product which involved a comparison with a major competitor caused sales of the product to decline in test market. For some reason the comparison as perceived by audiences favored the competitive product.[4] Thus, advertisers are continually faced with the risk of unanticipated effects when making advertising decision.

The economic kind of argument has more rationale when based on an evaluation of the opportunity for improving advertising decision results. Blaine Cooke, Vice President of Marketing for United Airlines, has put

---

[3] Ibid., p. 37.
[4] Ibid., p. 39.

this reason into proper perspective by saying that ". . . we must ask—is there something unique or particular about advertising that would warrant a unique or particular allocation of corporate resources to the effort to measure its effectiveness?"[5] Measurement of advertising performance should be subjected to a cost/benefit analysis to determine the amount of effort and corporate resources to allocate to this activity. However, this is far different from simply dismissing advertising effectiveness information as uneconomical.

The fact that many firms do not try to measure advertising effectiveness is not a rationale for other firms to also avoid collecting this kind of data. For some firms, advertising is a marginal or insignificant part of the marketing mix, such as is the case for some industrial sellers. In these cases, lack of advertising effectiveness measures may be economically justified. When management expects advertising to make an important contribution to corporate performance with a significant resource allocation, the need for performance information cannot be dismissed so easily. Even given the imperfectness of existing techniques (and there certainly are measurement problems and difficulties to be overcome) these firms should justify the use of research to aid management in controlling advertising performance. Here, the technical and creative art arguments against measuring advertising effectiveness do a disservice to firms needing to make the best use of advertising resources.

SETTING ADVERTISING OBJECTIVES

Advertising and Customer Decision Making

Advertising objectives must also consider the decision processes of buyers. Advertising must influence buyer decision processes to be effective, at least in the majority of cases where advertising is used to support the sale of company products or services. Yet, understanding the role of advertising in customer decisions is a difficult and challenging task. Figure 20–2 shows the relationship between advertising, customer decision making, and company sales. Note that advertising does not directly cause sales. Instead, advertising must have an influence on people, whether they be consumers or industrial buyers, in order to generate sales. As discussed in Chapter 9, *Buyer Decision Processes*, customers' state of mind (determined by such factors as customer perceptions and awareness, attitudes, intentions, etc.) will influence buying decisions. So, advertising must have an impact on target audiences members states of mind to be effective. This can occur when advertising creates a favorable state of mind, reinforces an already existing favorable state of mind, or

---

[5] Blaine Cooke, "Is Advertising Important Enough in the Corporate Budget to Justify the Cost of Extensive Research?" *Advertising Age* (July 18, 1966), p. 110.

FIGURE 20–2

Advertising and Nonadvertising Influences on Customer Decisions

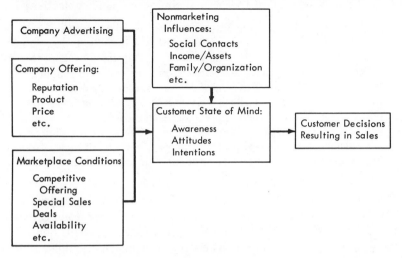

changes a previously unfavorable state of mind, all of which should increase the likelihood of purchasing the company's product or service.

Determining the relationship between advertising and customer buying decisions is further complicated by the many other possible influences on customers. Other components of a firm's marketing mix such as product functions, price, company or product reputation, service, and so forth will also influence customer decisions. This makes it difficult to determine the impact of advertising on customer decisions separate from the remainder of the firm's marketing mix. Moreover, there are a large number of marketplace conditions that will also influence buyer decisions. Competitive marketing practices and the marketing activity of channel organizations such as special sales and deals partially explain customer reaction to a firm's advertising and marketing offer.

Recognizing the many influences on buyers in addition to advertising, two quite different philosophies concerning the most appropriate kind of advertising objective have been adopted by advertisers. Some advertising managers believe that advertising should be expected to achieve communication objectives, while others argue for setting sales objectives. Essentially, these positions differ in the amount of consideration given to nonadvertising influences on sales during the control process.

Communication Objectives

The proponents of setting communication objectives believe that advertising cannot be expected to do the whole task of generating sales.

They point to the many nonadvertising influences on buyer's decisions as justification for not using sales as an indication of advertising effectiveness. Gail Smith has stated the case against using sales objectives:

> No one denies that the ultimate objective of advertising is to raise the level of performance for a product and, hopefully, to reap a benefit in terms of increased sales, but it does not necessarily follow that sales figures constitute a measure of advertising. To say so is roughly equivalent to saying that the measure of Mickey Mantle's prowess as a baseball player is whether the Yankees win or lose. As talented as he may be, I doubt if Mr. Mantle would appreciate being measured in those terms. He contributes, but he is not the only factor. The same principle holds of advertising; it is a marketing force, it contributes to the sale, it does not insure it—ever. Therefore, we prefer not to be saddled with that particular concept.[6]

The use of communication objectives is the result of a search for an alternative measure of performance for advertising. Reasoning that advertising must contribute to generating product sales, if not do the whole job, many advertisers focus on the way in which advertising can influence sales. Advertising can contribute to corporate profit and sales performance by directly trying to influence customer states of mind. The way to do this is to communicate with customers. Thus, the objectives for advertising, according to the communications philosophy, should specify the expected impact that advertising should have on target audience's states of mind in order to contribute to the total product sales effort. This is considerably different than expecting advertising to achieve sales objectives.

Implementing the communications philosophy requires an understanding of the process through which buyers move to reach a buying decision. So, several models of the steps which people go through during a buying process have been developed to better identify the communication tasks that advertising might accomplish.[7] These models were developed to describe consumer, rather than industrial buying, probably due to the much greater use of advertising by consumer goods firms. Nevertheless, the same approach can be applied to industrial buying. One such model, shown in Figure 20–3, was developed for use by Elrick and Lavidge, Inc., a marketing research and consulting firm.

Such models can be very helpful to management in setting advertising objectives. A communications model can guide research into target

---

[6] Gail Smith, "How GM Measures Ad Effectiveness," *Printers Ink* (May 14, 1965), pp. 19–20.

[7] Two of the better known models are discussed in Robert J. Lavidge and Gary A. Stiener, "A Model for Predicting Measurement of Advertising Effectiveness," *Journal of Marketing*, October 1961, pp. 59–62; and Russell H. Colley, *Defining Advertising Goals for Measured Advertising Results* (New York: Association of National Advertising, 1961).

FIGURE 20–3

A Communications Model for Advertising

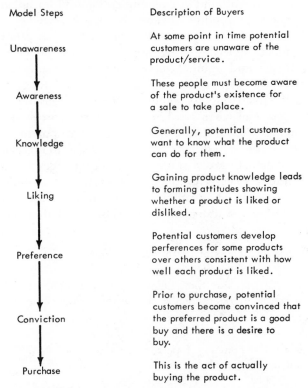

Model Steps	Description of Buyers
Unawareness	At some point in time potential customers are unaware of the product/service.
Awareness	These people must become aware of the product's existence for a sale to take place.
Knowledge	Generally, potential customers want to know what the product can do for them.
Liking	Gaining product knowledge leads to forming attitudes showing whether a product is liked or disliked.
Preference	Potential customers develop perferences for some products over others consistent with how well each product is liked.
Conviction	Prior to purchase, potential customers become convinced that the preferred product is a good buy and there is a desire to buy.
Purchase	This is the act of actually buying the product.

Source: Robert J. Lavidge and Gary A. Steiner, "A Model for Predictive Measurements of Advertising Effectiveness," *Journal of Marketing*, (October 1961), pp. 59–62, published by the American Marketing Association.

audiences that will aid management in determining advertising tasks. Advertising managers need to know the number of target market members at each stage in the process. Then, for those who are aware and have some knowledge of the product, research should show how many have favorable vs. unfavorable liking, preferences, and convictions toward the product. Finally, research can also help management assess the value to the company (in terms of sales, profits, market share, etc.) in having people move from one stage to another. This value is based on assessments of the increase in probability of an eventual purchase given that a target audience member advances one step closer to purchase. Panel data on the frequency of subsequently buying a product for those in each stage of the process illustrates the kind of data that is useful for this task.

Movement between each pair of stages in Figure 20–3 (e.g., unawareness to awareness, awareness to knowledge, knowledge to liking, etc.) requires a different kind of communication task for advertising. For example, to generate product awareness and knowledge, advertising may have to describe the features and functions of a product. To influence movement between liking and preference advertising should present arguments and opinions about the relative superiority of the product compared to competitors; while movement through the last two stages requires advertising to communicate the desirability of buying now. Thus, the model when combined with research can help pinpoint specific communication tasks for advertising. Corresponding advertising objectives would be stated in terms of state of mind characteristics crucial to movement between stages including changes in awareness of products, attitudes toward product attributes, and intentions to buy products. An example of communication objectives for advertising is shown in the objectives statement for a Marathon Oil advertising campaign:

> To increase awareness of the Marathon brand oil and instill confidence in it.
>
> To introduce the Marathon guarantee and convince motorists that it was a legitimate offer, completely backed by the company.
>
> To increase the number of persons who regarded Marathon as a major oil company.
>
> To increase the number of persons who regarded Marathon's gasoline and oil products as being of the highest quality.[8]

Sales Objectives

Some advertisers believe strongly that advertising should be expected to influence customers to buy a company's products and so, sales objectives are most appropriate. Sales-related objectives can be stated in terms of expected sales volume, market share, or profits to be generated by advertising. For example, when Wesson Oil found that it was losing market share to Procter & Gamble's Crisco Oil, it established as advertising objective, to stop the loss first, and then to increase market share at the expense of P&G.[9]

Advocates of sales objectives argue that their approach relates advertising responsibility to the overall performance objectives of the firm. Moreover, they point to the fact that the relationship between achieving

---

[8] Stuart Henderson Britt, "Are So-Called Successful Advertising Campaigns Really Successful," in Stuart Henderson Britt and Harper W. Boyd, (eds.), *Marketing Management and Administrative Action* (New York: McGraw-Hill Book Company, 1973), p. 556.

[9] Ibid., p. 554.

communication objectives and subsequent sales is not clear. The controversy over which type of objective to use would be far less significant if advertisers could accurately predict the impact on product sales of changes in the communications variables describing potential customers. However, research has not been able to fully establish such a relationship.[10]

Sales versus Communications Objectives[11]

While no attempt is made here to end the controversy over which kind of objective is most appropriate, the needs of advertising decision makers should weigh heavily on the choice. The fact that advertising managers should be accountable for the contribution advertising makes to corporate performance argues for sales objectives being the more relevant decision criterion. Yet, sales objectives provide little, if any, guidance to creative personnel in the firm or in advertising agencies since such objectives do not state *how* advertising should generate sales. Moreover, sales data used to measure advertising effectiveness does not explain *why* an ad on a campaign was or was not successful:

> Even if agencies could test using sales measurements, it probably would not be done . . . They want to know *why* a tested advertisement performed as it did, how it is strong, where it is weak, how to carry the strong elements over to the next ad, and how to correct the weak ones.[12]

Communication objectives are more useful for advertising decision making during the design and control stages of an advertising decision process. Moreover, it is generally considered to be easier, less expensive, and more reliable to measure advertising effectiveness in terms of communication objectives rather than sales objectives.[13] It is only advertising managers uncertainty about whether and to what extent achieving communication objectives leads to sales that keeps the issue alive. Yet, regardless of the direction in which the controversy will eventually be resolved, sales objectives, alone, will be unlikely to ever be entirely useful to management without an understanding of the process by which advertising influences buyers to purchase.

---

[10] For example, see Kristian S. Palda, "The Hypothesis of a Hierarchy of Effects: A Partial Evaluation," *Journal of Marketing Research* (February 1966), pp. 13–24.

[11] This controversy is far less significant for advertising by industrial sellers since advertising is typically not assigned a very significant role in generating sales. Advertising is used to aid salespersons who are given the major responsibility for selling. Thus, communication objectives are more appropriate.

[12] Eugene C. Pomerance, "How Agencies Evaluate Advertising," in John J. Wheatley (ed.), *Measuring Advertising Effectiveness: Selected Readings* (Homewood, Ill.: Richard D. Irwin, Inc., 1969), p. 90.

[13] Patrick J. Robinson, Homer M. Dalbey, Irwin Gross, and Yoram Wind, *Advertising Measurement and Decision Making* (Boston: Allyn & Bacon, Inc., 1968), p. 69.

COMMUNICATION EFFECTIVENESS MEASUREMENT

A large number of techniques may be used to measure the communications ability of its advertising. Several organizations such as Nielson, Sherwin, Starch, and Gallup & Robinson also provide standardized advertising effectiveness measurement services. Consequently, no attempt can be made to cover all these alternatives comprehensively. Rather, typical measurement techniques for more commonly used communication objectives are presented to demonstrate the variety of approaches in practice today. The objectives for which measurement is examined are awareness, attitude change, and predisposition change. Achieving these objectives correspond to using advertising to influence customers to move from non-awareness to the preference stages in the communications model shown in Figure 20–3.

Measuring Awareness

Awareness objectives can be operationalized in several different ways, including whether and how many members of the target audience have seen the ad, have read or listened to the ad, can remember the content of the ad, have heard of the product or brand, and/or can remember specific aspects of the product or brand. Typically, measurement procedures focus on awareness of the ad or ad campaign rather than of the product or brand. Awareness of advertising content should indicate awareness of the product or brand, though this relationship is not perfect since it is possible for people to remember an advertisement and its content without remembering the product or brand being advertised, or worse, to associate the ad with the wrong product or brand. Commonly applied measurement techniques for evaluating advertising's performance in achieving awareness objectives are recognition tests, recall tests, and physiological tests, all of which generally focus on awareness of the tested advertisements.

Recognition Tests. Recognition tests are intended to measure the percentage of sample target audience members who remember seeing an advertisement in a particular medium. People in the sample are asked if they remember seeing each advertisement being tested. For those who have seen an ad, the degree of attention given the ad is then examined. The number seeing each ad as well as the number reading or listening to some portion of the ad can be divided by the total size of the sample to determine recognition indexes or percentages. For example, if 220 out of a total sample of 500 said they saw a particular advertisement, then the ads recognition index is $\frac{220}{500}$ or .44. These indexes provide a quantitative measure of how effective the ad was in getting attention from target audience members. Moreover, indexes for alternative ads can be compared to assess the relative effectiveness of each one to help advertising management choose between them.

For recognition tests of magazine advertisements, Starch Readership Service provides an alternative to marketing research for recognition information.[14] Starch conducts personal interviews with an equal number of men and women from various areas who have read the magazine and issues covered by the service. An interviewer goes through the magazine page-by-page with each respondent and ask questions about each ad of interest. Respondents state whether they saw the ad and if so, to what extent the ad was read. Based on this research, clients of the Starch Readership Service receive statistics for each test ad showing the percent of respondents who said they saw the ad (noted score), the percent that said they saw or read any part of the ad which included the name of the product or advertiser (associated score), and the percent that said they read more than half the ad's copy (read most score). These percentages measure an ad's recognition effectiveness.

TABLE 20–1

Starch Readership Service Scores for Two Fleischmann's Margarine Ads

Tested Advertisements	*Noted*	*Associated*	*Read Most*
Ad (b) traditional appetite appeal.......	53%	38%	14%
Ad (a) factual approach...............	34%	25%	8%

Source: "Which Ad Attracted More Readers?" *Advertising Age* (June 2, 1975), p. 40.

As an illustration of the use of the Starch Readership Service, consider the readership scores in Table 20–1. These data were obtained from a test of the relative effectiveness of two advertisements for Fleischmann's margarine. The ads had essentially the same message to communicate but the copy differed substantially. One ad explained that Fleischmann's margarine was requested as the table spread for meals served to cardiologists attending a convention. These doctors wanted meals that were low in saturated fat and cholesterol, so their request demonstrated that Fleischmann's had these attributes.

The second ad used a more traditional approach to food advertising by showing Fleischmann's margarine with a variety of other foods. This is an appeal to peoples' appetite. The results showed that the traditional appetite appeal was more effective than the factual approach based on all three recognition scores.

---

[14] Description of the Starch Readership Service is in Robinson et al., *Advertising Measurement and Decision Making*, pp. 33–34.

Recall Tests. Recognition tests can be extended by having respondents *prove* that they actually saw and read an ad. Respondents who say they saw an ad are asked to try to recall the ad's content. Those respondents who can correctly recall all or part of an advertisement must have seen, read or listened to it. Recall tests may require that respondents remember messages with no help from the interviewer (unaided recall tests) or may have the interviewer prompt the respondent with cues such as a product name or a key word or phrase (aided recall tests). Aided recall attempts to correct for the possibility that a respondent who has seen an ad cannot remember what the ad communicated under the pressure of the interviewing situation. As an example of an aided recall test, an interviewer might ask the following questions of a respondent:

1. One of the commercials in this show was for a ——————— ———————
   (product category). Would you describe that commercial for me? Tell me what went on and what was said.
2. What did the commercial make you think of? That is, what thoughts came to your mind as you watched it?[15]

The recall ability of respondents is used to adjust recognition scores by showing the percentage of the sample who actually proved that they saw and read or listened to the ad by recalling message content.

Gallup and Robinson, Inc. provides an aided recall measurement service covering magazine and television media.[16] Recall studies are conducted periodically during the year. Respondents are asked to pick products from a list for which they remember seeing advertisements in a magazine (or a prime time television program). Then, for those products recalled, respondents are asked a series of questions concerning ad content and attitudes toward the product. Clients receive indexes of audience recognition, proved recall, remembrance of ideas communicated, and attitudes toward the product. Moreover, norms for these indexes for various product categories are also provided so that an advertiser can evaluate their ads against the recall effectiveness for the product category as a whole.

Physiological Tests. Recognition and recall tests have the common characteristic of depending upon what people say about advertisements. Some advertisers are concerned with the validity and reliability of this kind of data. People do not always say what they feel, believe, or have done. To counteract this source of bias in advertising effectiveness data, physiological measures of the impact of advertising have been tried.

---

[15] Clark Leavitt, Charles Waddell, and William Wells, "Improving Day-After Recall Techniques," *Journal of Advertising Research,* vol. 10 (June 1970), p. 13.

[16] Description of the Gallup and Robinson, Inc. service is in Robinson, et al., *Advertising Measurement and Decision Making,* p. 29–30.

The rationale for using physiological data rather than verbal reports is that people have much less ability to control various bodily functions than verbal responses to interview questions. Therefore, changes in these bodily functions may be a more accurate indicator of advertising impact. As an example, the measurement of pupil dilation as respondents scan an advertisement has been used to test effectiveness. A sample of target audience members are asked to sit in front of a camera while looking at slides of advertising layouts. While a respondent scans each slide, the camera takes photographs of one eye at very frequent intervals (e.g., every two seconds). One slide is used as a control since it has the same illumination characters as the other slides but shows a neutral stimulus such as a number. The photographs, matched with each advertisement, are then analyzed to determine the amount of opening and closing of each respondent's pupil. The measure of advertising effectiveness is the average increase or decrease in the pupil while viewing that ad as compared with the average pupil diameter while viewing the control slide. Presumably, an increase in the pupil diameter indicates greater awareness and interest in the ad while a decrease indicates lesser interest.[17]

Other techniques, such as the measurement of galvanic skin responses of respondents,[18] focus on different bodily functions but are based on essentially the same rationale. The question that remains to be answered for all physiological tests is what psychological activity is indicated by changes in bodily functions.[19] There are a number of possibilities including awareness, liking, disliking, interest, and thinking. Moreover, the predictiveness of these measures of subsequent behavior is also uncertain though there is some evidence of a positive relationship.[20]

The key assumption underlying use of all awareness measures of advertising effectiveness is that exposure and attention to advertising increases the probability of a future purchase. This assumption can be challenged on an intuitive basis. People may remember ads that were in some way unpleasant or obnoxious to them. Yet, advertisers counter with the persuasive argument that if an ad has not been seen by or communicated with people, then there is no chance for the ad to influence later buying decision making.[21] Thus, awareness techniques can

---

[17] This methodology description was based on a discussion of pupil measurement in Herbert E. Krugman, "Some Applications of Pupil Measurement," *Journal of Marketing Research* (November 1964), pp. 15–19.

[18] Xavier Kohan, "A Physiological Measure of Commercial Effectiveness," *Journal of Advertising Research,* vol. 8 (December 1968), pp. 46–48.

[19] For a discussion of this issue see Roger D. Blackwell, James S. Hensel, and Brian Sternthal, "Pupil Dilation: What Does It Measure," *Journal of Advertising Research,* vol. 10 (August 1970), pp. 15–18.

[20] For a test of the sales predictiveness of pupil measurement see Krugman, "Some Applications of Pupil Measurement."

[21] Pomerance, "How Agencies Evaluate Advertising," p. 91.

be justified as measuring whether an advertisement meets necessary conditions for effectiveness—exposure and attention.

Measuring Attitude Change

To influence potential customers to move from knowledge to liking or from liking to preference stages in the communications model shown in Figure 20–3, advertising objectives are set in terms of changing specific attitudes of target audience members. Advertising effectiveness is then evaluated in terms of the degree of attitude change that occurs after target audience members are exposed to a firm's advertising. These attitudes might be toward a product or service, a brand, some product or brand attribute, or the firm itself.

Measuring attitude change is more difficult than measuring recognition or recall. Attitude is a more complex variable than awareness and requires more sophisticated measurement techniques (open-ended questions, attitude scales, etc.). Moreover, since the attitude of interest is toward the product, brand, or firm, rather than toward the advertisement, target audiences members will already have some attitude before the ad is run (the exception being the introduction of a new product). Thus, the research design must allow for a comparison of attitudes of customers *before and after* seeing the ad or ad campaign. Awareness tests only have to measure ad recognition or recall after the ad has been run since there can be no awareness of the ad by audience members before it has been run.

Longitudinal Design. One approach to measuring attitude change associated with advertising is to use a longitudinal research design. A panel of respondents representative of target audiences is recruited who agree to be interviewed at several different times (called interview waves) during the length of the study. This allows data to be collected from the same people over time. Attitude scores are obtained before and after the panel is exposed to an ad or ad campaign. Comparison of attitude scores for each respondent from a pre-advertising wave and a post-advertising wave becomes the measure of how effectively advertising was able to achieve a positive change in key panel member attitudes.

An important advantage of using a longitudinal design is the guidance provided by the data from the pre-advertising wave(s) for setting advertising objectives. Analysis of this data can uncover attitudes that are not favorable and that reflect, in some way, target audience members' lack of understanding of the firm's product, brand, or brand characteristics. These attitudes become the focus for advertising. For example, General Motors, using a longitudinal approach, discovered that a particular group of consumers erroneously believed that a model in the GM line had low trade-in value. Advertising was designed to show that this automobile model had a high trade-in value for cars in its class. After running these ads, data from the panel showed that a substantial increase in trade-in value attitude scores was achieved, and so, the advertising was deemed effective by management.[22]

Experimental Design.   Another approach to measuring attitude change is an experimental research design. Rather than a before-after measure of ad effectiveness, groups of respondents who have been exposed to test advertising are compared with a matched control group known to have not seen the advertising. The difference in attitude scores between the exposed (i.e., experimental groups) and nonexposed groups is the measure of advertising's ability to *cause* a positive attitude change. In essence, the control group's attitudes correspond to pre-advertising attitudes of target audiences. This means that the control group must be carefully selected to represent target audiences. Equally important is the matching of control groups with experimental groups. Ideally, these groups should be identical in every way important to the product or brand purchase decision except for exposure to the advertising. The more perfectly these groups are matched, the better able management is to attribute any differences in attitudes to the advertising being evaluated.

Eric Marder Associates, Inc., a standardized information service, has used the experimental control approach to measuring the effectiveness of clients' advertising.[23] To conduct a test for a client, two experimental and one control group of 800 people each are formed from the readership of a magazine in New York, Chicago, and Philadelphia. A different test ad is inserted in the issues read by the two experimental groups while neither ad is exposed to the control group. Several days after respondents received the magazine issues, telephone interviews are conducted to measure both awareness and attitudes toward the product. The interviews are identical for each respondent and no mention is made of which ads are being tested. Any differences in respondents product awareness or attitudes between experimental and control groups or between the two experimental groups are viewed as having been caused by the test ads.

A more complicated approach is to test the effectiveness of multiple rather than a single exposure of an ad or advertising campaign. This allows an ad to have more time to work before the measure of effectiveness is conducted. For example, Ogilvy and Mather, Inc. has developed

---

[22] For more detail on GM's use of longitudinal research design for measuring ad effectiveness, see Gail Smith, "How GM Measures Ad Effectiveness," *Printers Ink* (May 14, 1965), pp. 19–29.

[23] This description of the Marder Ad Evaluation Program was adapted from Robinson et al., "Advertising Measurement and Decision Making," pp. 30–31, and David A. Aaker and John G. Myers, *Advertising Management* (Englewood Cliffs, New Jersey: Prentice-Hall, 1975), p. 461.

a multiple exposure testing system for its clients. A sample of 200 people who fit target market descriptions, subscribe to a TV cable system, and who agree to watch selected movie previews at specified times is drawn. An advertisement to be tested is included in four different 15-minute movie previews along with two control advertisements. The previews are run four times during a four day period. Attitude and other questions are asked of respondents by telephone interviews and then repeated after the multiple exposures have been run. The pre- to post-attitude measure change provides the data for evaluating advertising effectiveness.[24]

Attitude change measures of advertising effectiveness assume that there is a strong causal relationship between changing customers attitudes toward a product and their likelihood of subsequently purchasing that product. Certainly, there is more intuitive justification for such a relationship than there is for the relationship between advertising awareness and probability of purchase. Attitudes are measured toward the product or brand rather than toward the ad. Moreover, attitudes measure customers' evaluations of these products and brands, so it is reasonable to assume that people typically buy what they like. Research evidence of the attitude change-subsequent behavior relationship is available, but is not overwhelming:

> A great deal of evidence exists showing a positive correlation between attitude *level* and later purchased action. Less good evidence exists to demonstrate such a correlation between short-term attitude change and action, although there is some evidence, even if it cannot be found in the learned journals.[25]

While the attitude-buying behavior relationship requires further research, advertising agencies give strong support to the use of attitude data in measuring advertising effectiveness.[26] This is consistent with many advertisers' belief in the communications approach to setting advertising objectives. Yet, attitude measures of effectiveness are even more widely supported than other communications measures.[27]

Measuring Predispositions

A final communications objective requires advertising to change customer predispositions toward a product or brand. The concept of predisposition is usually operationalized by measuring customer preferences for products or intentions to buy a product. Such measures aid advertisers

---

[24] This description was adapted from "Ogilvy & Mather Finds M.E.T.S. expensive but Appropriate, Useful," *Marketing News* (May 23, 1975), p. 8.

[25] Pomerance, "How Agencies Evaluate Advertising," p. 93.

[26] Robinson, et al., *Advertising Measurement and Decision Making*, p. 59.

[27] Ibid.

in evaluating how well advertising was able to influence customers to move between the preference and conviction stages of the model in Figure 20–3.

Measuring advertising effectiveness in terms of changing customer predispositions is very similar to the task of measuring attitude change. Both involve measurement before and after advertising exposure, so that the degree of change determines how effective the advertising has been. Measurement of customer predispositions is more difficult than measuring attitudes, though, since the measurement techniques are less well developed.

As an example of predisposition measures of advertising effectiveness, the theater technique is quite common. The Schwerin Research Corporation has used this approach in the Schwerin Standard Testing Service.[28] For each test, a sample of approximately 350 respondents is invited to view a "new" television program in a theater. Each respondent is asked to state a brand preference in several different product categories. Respondents are told that a drawing will be held later for a free supply of the winner's prefered brand of one of the products. This is intended to make the preference statement more realistic. The theater audience is then shown the television program with advertising interspersed at appropriate times during the showing. The test advertisement is included in this advertising. After the showing, respondents are again asked to note their brand preference for each product category for the drawing. Any change in predispositions from before to after the watching of the television program and commercials is a measure of the effectiveness of advertising in changing customer brand predispositions.

The theater technique can be designed as a true experiment by having a control group go through the same procedure, but not exposed to the test advertisements. Any change in control group predispositions could be used to adjust the change in experimental group predispositions downward to account for extraneous influences. While this would allow more confidence in saying that the advertising *caused* whatever predisposition change occurred above and beyond the control group change, the additional expense would be substantial.

The use of predisposition measures of advertising effectiveness is also dependent on an assumed strong relationship between product or brand predispositions and customer buying decisions. Intuitively, this relationship should be even stronger than the corresponding relationships for either awareness or attitude change. Predispositions measure action tendencies of customers and so, the data should predict subsequent buying decisions. Predispositions are frequently considered to be a kind of

---

[28] Description of this service was adapted from Robinson et al., *Advertising Measurement and Decision Making*, pp. 32–33, and Aaker and Myers, *Advertising Management*, p. 73.

attitude[29] by researchers so that the empirical evidence for the predisposition-behavior relationship is similar to that discussed for attitudes. In general, there is evidence of a predictive relationship between predispositions and behavior, but whether predispositions cause subsequent behavior is less well established.[30]

SALES EFFECTIVENESS MEASUREMENT

For those advertising managers who firmly believe that advertising must be evaluated by determining advertising's impact on sales, some measures of sales response to advertising must be devised. Because of the many influences on sales in addition to advertising, total sales of a product from the period in which the ad was run is not a valid measure of advertising effectiveness. The only exception would be in those rare cases where management believes that advertising is the sole or at least clearly the most important influence on sales.

Historical Sales. Some insights into the effectiveness of past advertising can be obtained by measuring the relationship between advertising and product (or brand or company) sales over *several* time periods. For example, a multiple regression analysis of advertising expenditures and sales can show how sales changes have corresponded to changes in advertising expenditures.[31] This technique estimates the contribution advertising has made to "explaining," in a correlational rather than causal sense, the variations in sales over the time periods covered in the study. The data needed for this approach are period advertising expenditures which can be obtained from company budgeting records, and product sales measured by such techniques as store audits, warehouse shipments, or other sales records maintained by a company. Of course, historical sales analysis is only a post-test measure of advertising effectiveness and is not applicable to pretesting.

Experimental Control. To establish more clearly a causal relationship between advertising and sales requires experimental control. While considered to be quite expensive relative to other advertising effectiveness measures, it is possible to isolate advertising's contribution to sales. Moreover, this can be done as a pretest to aid advertising in choosing between alternative creative designs, media schedules expenditure levels, or some combination of these advertising decision areas.

---

[29] The reason for this can be better understood by reviewing the definition of an attitude as discussed in Chapter 9. *Buyer Decision Processes.*

[30] As an example, see Jan Staple, "Sales Effects of Print Ads," *Journal of Advertising Research,* vol. 11 (June 1971), pp. 32–36.

[31] For a discussion and example of this approach see Kristian S. Palda, *The Measurement of Cumulative Advertising Effects* (Englewood Cliffs, N.J.: Prentice-Hall, 1964).

One experimental approach to measuring the sales effectiveness of advertising is test marketing.[32] For example DuPont used test markets to measure the sales effectiveness of proposed advertising intended to reverse a declining sales trend for "Teflon" coated cookware.[33] Of primary interest to management was the level of advertising expenditures needed to sell the product in sufficient quantities to meet performance objectives. A complicated crossover experimental design, shown in Figure 20–4, was used to test the sales effect of five different levels

FIGURE 20–4

Experimental Design for Testing Sales Effectiveness of "Teflon" Advertising

Winter 1963 Product Advertising	*Fall 1962 Product Advertising*		
	10 Daytime Ads per Week	*5 Daytime Ads per Week*	*No Ads*
7 daytime ads per week	Detroit Springfield	Dayton	Wichita
3 daytime ads per week	Columbus	St. Louis Bangor Youngstown	Rochester
No ads	Omaha	Pittsburgh	Philadelphia Grand Rapids

Source: James C. Bucknell, Jr. and Robert W. McIsaac, "Test Marketing Cookware Coated with 'Teflon'," *Journal of Advertising Research*, vol. 3 (September 1963), p. 3.

of advertising (10, 7, 5, 3 and 0 daytime TV commercial minutes per week) in 13 test cities. The cities in which no ads were run served as control cities. To measure sales, a telephone survey of female heads of households in each city was conducted in the winter, and again in the spring to determine purchases of all cookware and "Teflon" coated cookware in particular. The data from this test marketing study provided considerable insight into the effect of advertising on sales. For example, to achieve significant increases in sales, DuPont had to advertise at the higher levels.

Firms not wanting to go through the considerable cost and effort of running a test marketing study may decide to use a standardized informa-

[32] See Chapter 15 for a more detailed discussion of test marketing techniques and applications.

[33] For more detail on this example, see James C. Becknell, Jr. and Robert W. McIsaac, "Test Marketing Cookware Coated with 'Teflon,'" *Journal of Advertising Research*, vol. 3 (September 1963), pp. 2–8.

tion service instead. One such service was developed by the Milwaukee *Journal* (a major newspaper in Milwaukee) and called the Milwaukee Ad Lab.[34] In essence, the Ad Lab partitioned the city of Milwaukee into matched groups by carefully allocating areas as small as city blocks into each group so that all groups are matched demographically and by purchasing behavior. This means that each group has almost exactly the same percentage of households in all income categories, age categories, and so forth. Moreover, the percent of families in each group buying various products such as instant coffee, regular coffee, and headache remedies is also closely matched. From each group the Ad Lab has drawn a representative sample of 750 respondents to serve on a continuing panel.

Each household on the panel agreed to have muters placed on their TV sets so that ads can be muted out to prevent viewers from seeing them. The muters are activated at the sending station, so local television stations cooperated in the effort. Participating magazines and the local newspaper (The *Journal*) can also control the reading of print advertising by using split runs. A split run is a publication technique allowing different (or no) advertisements to be printed in copies sent to different groups. Printing of the issues is split by advertisement under test.

The Ad Lab has essentially established groups that can become experimental or control groups for an advertising effectiveness test. The test is limited to Milwaukee rather than being conducted in multiple cities as was described for a test marketing study, but does provide the same kind of experimental control. Advertisers can conduct tests of media, messages, and/or expenditure alternatives for a fee, following the same procedures as for a test market. Moreover, the cost of operating the Milwaukee Ad Lab is spread over all clients using the service, rather than being absorbed by any single firm.

A PERSPECTIVE ON COMMUNICATION VERSUS SALES EFFECTIVENESS MEASURES

Deciding on an Approach

The choice of an approach to measuring advertising effectiveness can be put into perspective by examining major advertising control dimensions. There is an important difference in the *relevance* of each of the measures for advertising decisions. Management would ideally like to evaluate advertising in terms of its contribution to overall organizational performance. For business, this means using profit and return-on-

---

[34] This description was based on "The Lab That Could Make Milwaukee Famous," *Media Decisions* (May 1967), pp. 40–44, 67.

investment criteria. As actual measures of advertising effectiveness become less related to these criteria, they become less relevant for management. Decision relevance of communication objectives and measures is highly dependent on the link between sales and each objective (awareness, attitude change, and predispositions). For sales, the link is much more obvious. Overall, the decision relevance of each of the measures of advertising effectiveness discussed in this chapter can be ranked from high to low as shown in Column (A) of Figure 20–5.

Another important dimension is the *difficulty and cost* of obtaining the data needed to evaluate advertising effectiveness. Again, there are significant differences in the ease of measuring advertising effectiveness depending on the type of objective used. Column (B) of Figure 20–5 summarizes these differences by ranking each objective from easy to most difficult data collection requirements.

FIGURE 20–5

Major Dimensions of the Choice of Advertising Objectives and Corresponding Effectiveness Measures

Advertising Objective	(A) Decision Relevance	(B) Ease of Measurement
Sales	↑ High	↑ Difficult
Predisposition change		
Attitude change		
Awareness change	↓ Low	↓ Easy

Source: Adapted from David B. Montgomery and Glen L. Urban, *Management Science in Marketing* (Englewood Cliffs, N.J.: Prentice-Hall, 1968), p. 96.

A comparison of columns (A) and (B) shows that the choice of which measurement procedure to use should be based on a trade-off between decision relevance and ease of measurement.[35] The more relevant kinds of effectiveness data are also the more difficult and costly to collect. When marketing research resources are scarce, an advertiser may settle for a measurement somewhat lower in relevance in order to keep costs in line with available resources. Thus, there is no one right advertising effectiveness measure for all firms.

Combining Advertising Effectiveness Measures

An advertiser is not limited to selecting just one of the above measures of advertising effectiveness. Some combination of these measures may be needed. For example, those advertisers using the communications ap-

---

[35] This idea is also discussed in Robinson, et al., *Advertising Measurement and Decision Making*, p. 69; and David B. Montgomery and Glen L. Urban, *Management Science in Marketing* (Englewood Cliffs, N.J.: Prentice-Hall, 1969), pp. 95–96.

proach may set advertising objectives to influence movement between several of the stages simultaneously. For example, General Motors measures the effectiveness of advertising in terms of awareness, attitude change, and preference level.[36] Awareness data allows management to assess how well their advertising is reaching intended audience members. Attitude and preference change data aid managers in determining the contribution of advertising to corporate performance.

As another example, an advertiser may collect awareness and attitude data during a test marketing study. This data could then be used for analyzing why advertising alternatives are or are not effective in generating desired sales levels. Moreover, the relationship between sales and achieving communications objectives could be explored. Thus, the choice between advertising objectives and corresponding effectiveness measures does not have to force an advertiser into the sales versus communications controversy.

SUMMARY AND CONCLUSIONS

Measuring advertising effectiveness has generated considerable disagreement among managers as to the need to use research as well as the best approach to use. This chapter has demonstrated the technical feasibility of collecting data to evaluate advertising by discussing alternative procedures used by firms. Moreover, the nature of the task in choosing between procedures has been examined. Thus, the lack of advertising effectiveness evaluation cannot be justified by not having access to appropriate data. The real reason for many firms not measuring ad effectiveness is more likely due to a lack of willingness to commit resources to this task. This can substantially increase the risk of wasting resources when advertising is an important part of the marketing mix.

Attention turns now to another important component in a firm's promotional mix—personal selling. The next chapter discusses the decisions required to design and implement personal selling strategy and tactics. This is followed by a chapter on managing the primary resource in personal selling—people.

EXERCISES FOR REVIEW AND DISCUSSION

1. "Advertising must compete for corporate resources against other corporate functions by demonstrating its ability to contribute to performance. Since the most important operating objectives of our corporation are to achieve stated sales volumes and profit levels, the most appropriate objectives for advertising are also sales and profitability." Discuss.
2. A brand manager for a line of tennis racquets produced by a large manufacturer of sports equipment received the advertising effectiveness infor-

[36] Smith, "How GM Measures Ad Effectiveness," p. 21.

mation shown in the table below. For this information to be an appropriate advertising effectiveness measure, what kind of advertising objective must have been set? Which advertisement is most effective and why?

	Number of Useable Respondents	Number of Respondents Who Recalled the Ad	Number of Respondents Who Recalled the Brand Name in the Ad
Advertisement 1	405	221	115
Advertisement 2	395	218	153
Advertisement 3	415	209	165

3.   The marketing manager for a beer producer has just received data from the initial four interview waves of a longitudinal study of the effectiveness of advertising for her beer brand. The data shows average attitude scores of respondents toward selected beer attributes possessed by the brand. The advertising campaign began after wave 1 data was collected and is still running. Evaluate the effectiveness of the advertising campaign using this data. Then, assess the usefulness of this information for setting future advertising objectives.

Beer Brand Attribute	Average Respondent Attitude Score*			
	Wave 1	Wave 2	Wave 3	Wave 4
Lightness of taste†	2.43	2.67	3.34	4.28
Bitterness of taste	3.78	3.72	3.23	3.01
Premiumness†	2.12	2.26	2.34	2.29
Competitive price	4.05	4.09	3.98	4.02
Thirst quenching†	3.42	3.38	3.96	4.29
Filling†	1.94	1.87	2.01	2.50
Golden color	4.06	4.01	4.14	4.09
Alcoholic content	4.34	4.22	4.18	4.28

* Attitude score based on a 1 to 5 scale where 1 = very negative and 5 = very positive attitude.
† Beer brand attributes featured or emphasized in the advertising campaign.

4.   Suppose the brand manager in Exercise 2 decided to supplement the recall data with sales data. The level of sales of the tennis racquet brand was measured for the year period immediately preceding the advertising campaign (advertisements 1, 2 and 3 combined) and then measured again for the year in which the advertising was run. The difference between these two sales totals is the measure of the effectiveness of the advertising. Since this difference showed a sales increase of five times the cost of the advertising, the brand manager believed that the campaign was very effective. Carefully assess this use of sales data to measure advertising effectiveness.

5.   In the chapter, advertising campaign objectives were given for Marathon Oil Company. Design an advertising effectiveness program that will allow management to control advertising designed to achieve these objectives.

21

Sales Force Decisions

In June of 1973, Kim Kelley, a Honeywell, Inc., salesman, obtained an order for an $8.1 million computer system on which he would receive an $80,000 commission.[1] The development work had spanned three years including an intensive full-time effort during the last three months. His closing of the sale resulted in a lost sales opportunity for salesmen from four competing companies. While personal selling results are not always as significant as in this example, they account for a substantial and, in some firms, a dominant share of the marketing mix. For example, Avon Products has 2,300 U.S. district managers, each responsible for 100–150 part-time sales representatives whose average sales are $3500 (the Avon lady receives a 40 percent commission on retail sales).[2] Thus with annual advertising expenditures of $13 million, total commission payments are nearly forty times total advertising expenditures. Although national estimates of total annual expenditures for personal selling are difficult to obtain, the amount exceeds advertising expenditures by a substantial margin. Typically, the personal selling function accounts for the major share of personnel assigned to the marketing department.

The nature and scope of the sales management function is first examined to provide a background on the role of personal selling in the marketing mix. The major sales force decision areas are described and a decision framework developed to show the sequences and interrelationships among the decisions. Building on this overview of the selling function each decision area is examined in this and the following chapter in terms of relevant concepts and approaches to analysis. First, determining the size of the sales force is considered, followed by sales force allocation

---

[1] For an interesting account of Kim Kelley's experience, see "To Computer Salesmen, the 'Big-Ticker' Deal Is the One to Look For," *The Wall Street Journal* (January 22, 1974), pp. 1 and 35.

[2] "Troubled Avon Tries a Face-Lifting," *Business Week* (May 11, 1974), pp. 98–106.

decisions. Next, in Chapter 22 the continuing task of managing the sales force is discussed including sales planning, recruiting and selecting salesmen, training, and supervision and motivation. Finally, evaluation and control of selling operations are examined.[3]

SELLING FUNCTION IN PERSPECTIVE

Sales people comprise a substantial portion of the work force in the United States. Published estimates indicate that in 1972 there were some 5.4 million sales workers with a median annual income of $6,300.[4] Compensation of field sales personnel (e.g., salesmen assigned to geographic territories) is substantially higher than this. Based on the American Management Association's Executive Compensation Service 1973 annual survey, average compensation for a field sales trainee was $9,495 and $17,052 for a senior salesman (highest level of selling responsibility).[5] Moreover, a small number of professional salesman achieve impressive earnings. For example, according to industry estimates, the top 100 life insurance salesmen out of an industry total of over 200,000 are earning in excess of $100,000 a year, and one makes about a million a year.[6]

The selling function varies significantly throughout U.S. business and industry. For example, the health and beauty aids salesman for a wholesaler spends a major portion of his time delivering and arranging products such as aspirin, toothpaste, and razor blades on the shelves of grocery stores and other retail outlets. His function is largely service; very little actual selling effort is involved in the job. In contrast, generation of sales is the primary function of the life insurance salesman and it represents a very creative selling task due to the intangible nature of the product.

In general the sales job consists of three main activity areas: generating sales; providing market information; and customer service.[7] Selling activity includes locating prospective customers, making sales presentations, interacting with customers (e.g., overcoming objections), and closing sales. The focus is upon obtaining business. Salesmen also collect various types of information such as competitive intelligence, price in-

---

[3] There are several basic texts on sales force management that consider the area in considerably greater depth than is possible in these chapters. See for example, Kenneth R. Davis and Frederick E. Webster, Jr., *Sales Force Management* (New York: The Ronald Press Company, 1968); and William J. Stanton and Richard H. Buskirk, *Management of the Sales Force* (Homewood, Ill.: Richard D. Irwin, Inc., 1974).

[4] *U.S. Statistical Abstract* (Washington, D.C.: U.S. Government Printing Office, 1973), pp. 233–34.

[5] As reported in *Sales Management* (January 7, 1974), p. 60.

[6] Arthur M. Louis, "How One Man Makes $120,000 a Year Selling Insurance," *Fortune* 90 (July 1974), pp. 131–33.

[7] Davis and Webster, *Sales Force Management,* p. 44.

formation, customer reactions to product use, stock levels, and service and delivery problems. Customer service activity can span a variety of responsibilities including delivery, marketing assistance (e.g., promotional and display advice), credit evaluation, product application assistance, and repair of products. The relative importance of these job components varies between different sales positions. For example, the automobile salesman's major responsibility is generating sales, whereas detail men in the pharmaceutical field are more heavily oriented toward providing physicians with information, samples, and assistance in seeking to encourage them to prescribe drugs.[8]

The complexity of a sales position can be associated with the creative and technical skills required to perform effectively in the job. Contrast, for example, the relatively routine tasks of health and beauty aids salesmen described above to an insurance salesman who is a Certified Life Underwriter selling to business executives and professional people. Based on the extent of creative skills involved in a sales position McMurray has described different jobs in order of increasing difficulty or complexity including delivery, order taking, missionary selling, technical selling, and creative selling of tangible and intangible products.[9] Examples of each type of sales job are shown below:

Delivery	Various kinds of driver sales people whose products include milk, soft drinks, beer, potato chips, etc.
Order Taking	Includes both inside (e.g., retail sales people) and field sales positions where the salesman essentially records and processes the customer's order. Wholesale grocery salesmen typically perform an order taking function; selling the account such as a local chain is handled by top executives.
Missionary Selling	Sales people assist customers and undertake various promotional and goodwill activities. They do not actually sell in terms of soliciting orders. Examples include salesmen for pharmaceutical firms and brewers.
Technical Selling	Many firms in the industrial field utilize sales engineers where product and application knowledge is a central part of the selling function.

---

[8] An interesting analysis of research on commercial and non-commercial information sources used by doctors is discussed in Raymond A. Bauer and Lawrence H. Wortzel, "Doctor's Choice: The Physician and His Sources of Information About Drugs," *Journal of Marketing Research*, 3 (February 1966), pp. 40–47.

[9] Robert N. McMurray, "The Mystique of Super-Salesmanship, "*Harvard Business Review* (March–April 1961), p. 114.

Creative Selling   This type of selling involving both tangible and intangible products and services, offers the greatest sales challenge, and requires highly creative salesmanship. Typically, in these positions the need for the product or service is not clearly established from the customer's point of view (e.g., life insurance, encyclopedias, ocean cruisers, advertising, investment advice).

Sales positions may not fall distinctly into one of the above categories. Rather, a continuum of positions exists ranging from relatively simple, routine sales functions to highly complex sales situations that demand the highest level of salesmanship.

There are indications that, in general, selling is becoming more professional, particularly at the technical and creative levels. The historical image of the salesman as a "huckster" is changing. "The new-era salesman is involved with the whole distribution pipeline, beginning with the tailoring of products to the customer's desire and extending through their promotion and advertising to final delivery to the ultimate consumer."[10] Salesmen are increasingly being viewed as managers of their assigned market areas.[11] They are involved in coordination and management of various territory activities such as market analysis, local advertising, and providing home office support.

SALES FORCE DECISIONS

The decisions that comprise the sales management task are shown in Figure 21–1. The nature and scope of the personal selling function must be defined by top management in its selection of the role that the sales force is to play in the marketing program. The sales management decision process begins by developing personal selling goals within the guidelines provided by market targets, marketing objectives, and the marketing program. Estimates of sales response guide the determination of sales force size and allocation of salesmen to appropriate work units (e.g., territories, customers). The sales organization must be managed to move toward assigned objectives. Finally, evaluation and control of selling operations are accomplished to identify performance gaps and to focus corrective actions.

---

[10] Carl Rieser, "The Salesman Isn't Dead—He's Different," *Fortune,* 66 (November 1962), p. 124.

[11] For a detailed examination of the salesman's role as a manager, see Gerald J. Carney, *Managing a Sales Territory* (New York: American Management Association, Inc., 1971).

FIGURE 21–1

Sales Force Management Decision Process

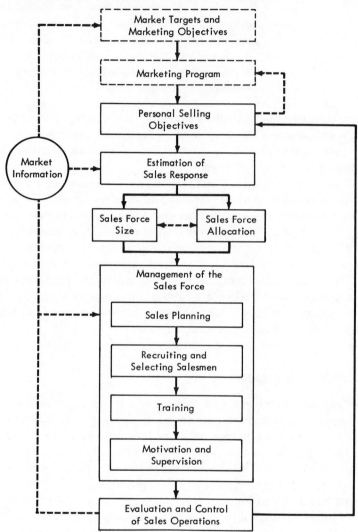

Influences on Sales Force Decisions

Market targets that are selected by the firm and the marketing program that is developed to achieve objectives for each target represent major influences on sales force decisions.

Market Targets. The size and characteristics of each market target provide important guidelines for determining how and to what extent personal selling will be used in the firm's marketing mix. For example, when the number of customers is very large such as in mass markets and the size (in dollars) of the purchase is relatively small, personal selling costs become prohibitive. The cost of a salesman's call may range from $20 to $50 and more depending upon the salesman's qualifications, degree of customer concentration, territory size, waiting time, and contact time with the customer. The average cost of an industrial sales call was $58 in 1972 (almost twice the 1962 cost), and was nearly $67 in 1974.[12] In contrast, a minute of national television advertising during prime viewing time costs about $5.00 per thousand viewing homes.[13] While customer exposures to personal selling and television advertising are not equivalent, these comparisons suggest how the characteristics of the market influence the extent to which personal selling is used in a firm's marketing program.

The sales force tends to be used as a major part of the marketing mix when certain customer needs can best be met through personal selling efforts and, when there are sufficient margins between purchase price and costs to cover sales force expenses. Personal selling is often used in industrial markets since the number of customers and prospects is relatively small (compared to consumer markets), and dollar amounts of purchase are sufficient to support salesmen. Of course, these same characteristics may exist in consumer markets, as for example in encyclopedia sales. Also, consumer markets may involve an emphasis on personal selling to channel intermediaries, and heavy use of advertising at the consumer level. Salesmen may be needed when potential customers cannot be identified sufficiently to utilize advertising effectively. Also, personal selling may be required to help develop a market for a new product or service.

Marketing Program. Sales force decisions must be carefully integrated with the other elements of the marketing mix. The characteristics and market influencing capabilities of the mix are major influences on how and to what extent personal selling will be used by a particular firm. Several illustrative characteristics of marketing program components which may indicate a relatively important role for personal selling are shown in Table 21–1. Marketing management's task is to select the most effective means of obtaining desired responses from selected market targets using the best combination of marketing program elements. In this process the intended contribution of the sales force must be defined. Management has some degree of flexibility in determining the role and importance of the personal selling function in the firm's total marketing effort. For example, one firm may choose to sell its products by mail while another may use local sales agents. Advertising and other

---

[12] See "Cheaper Ways to Reach the Customer, *Business Week* (September 9, 1972), p. 120; and "Marketing Observer," *Business Week* (August 3, 1974), p. 61.

[13] "TV Sales Slow From Rapid 1973 Pace, But Networks Still See Record Year," *The Wall Street Journal* (June 14, 1974), p. 30.

TABLE 21–1

Illustrative Marketing Program Characteristics Leading to Use of Personal Selling as a Major Element of the Marketing Mix

Mix Area	*Characteristics*
Product or Service	Product relatively complex and may require customer application assistance (e.g., computers, pollution control systems, steam turbines).
	Purchase decision represents a major commitment such as food items purchased by supermarket chains. The buyer may be concerned with the type and extent of supplier support (e.g., promotion at the consumer level).
	Features and performance of the product require personal demonstration and trial by the customer (e.g., private aircraft).
Distribution Channels	Channel system relatively short and direct to end users.
	Channel intermediaries require product and service training and assistance.
	Personal selling is viewed by management as essential in "pushing" the product or service through the channel.
	Channel intermediaries are available to perform the personal selling function for supplier with limited resources and experience (e.g., brokers or manufacturer's agents).
Price	Final price is negotiated between buyer and seller (e.g., appliances, automobiles, real estate), thus requiring a salesman to represent the seller.
	Selling price and/or quantity purchased enable an adequate margin to support selling expenses (traditional department store compared to discount house).
Advertising	Advertising media do not provide an effective link with market targets.
	Information needed by the buyer cannot be provided entirely through advertising and sales promotion (e.g., life insurance).
	Number and dispersion of customers will not enable acceptable advertising economies.

forms of sales promotion can be used to accomplish certain of the same tasks that sales people can perform (e.g., product awareness and product information). Alternatively, the salesman is unique in the marketing mix in that he can interact with the buyer, such as responding to customer objections or questions. Also an experienced and capable sales force with strong customer relationships is more difficult for new competitors to duplicate than, for example, is price or advertising. Management's challenge is to select the proper role for personal selling to perform in a given organization.

Sales Force Objectives

Determination of operational objectives to guide and evaluate sales force activities is a critical sales management task. Objectives provide a basis for planning the sales program. Based on an assessment of market and marketing program influences on sales force decisions, objectives for the personal selling function can be formulated. As shown in Figure 21–1 establishment of sales force objectives should be interactive with marketing program development. Formulation of sales force objectives should be part of the overall marketing programming task, and accomplished concurrently with decisions on other elements of the marketing mix.

Sales force objectives indicate what the sales organization is expected to accomplish in making its contribution to the overall marketing program. Thus it is essential that close coordination be achieved between the chief marketing executive and the manager responsible for the personal selling function. A simple statement of sales volume targets is an incomplete guide to managing the selling function. While the sales management task varies substantially from one firm to another, major areas for setting objectives include: market performance, contribution to profits, customer relations and service, sales manpower development, and marketing program support. These areas and illustrative objectives within each area are shown in Figure 21–2.

FIGURE 21–2

Illustrative Areas for Setting Sales Force Objectives

Market Performance
    Sales volume targets (by market target)
    Product mix emphasis
    Market share
    New business emphasis

Contribution to Profits
    Expected profit contribution (by market target)
    Cash flow (e.g., accounts receivable)
    Cost of operations
    Field inventory targets

Customer Relations and Service
    Guidelines for customer relations
    Post-sale emphasis

Sales Manpower Development
    Recruiting targets
    Training and manpower development targets
    Employee relations
    Reduction of turnover

Marketing Program Support
    Key results areas necessary in support of marketing program (e.g., market intelligence)

Estimating Sales Response

In Chapter 13 the importance of knowledge of sales response was discussed because of its usefulness in facilitating decisions on appropriate levels of marketing program expenditures. Determination of the responsiveness of sales to personal selling effort is a key factor in guiding sales force management decision making. The sales manager is faced with two interrelated decisions: (1) determining the total selling effort necessary to reach desired sales targets; and (2) allocating selling effort to the various levels within the sales organization such as districts, branches, and salesman territories. While making an optimal set of decisions in these two areas is normally not possible, estimates of probable sales response to different levels of selling effort can greatly improve the results of sales management decision making. A sales target selected by the firm should be based upon determination of the most favorable combination of estimated revenues and marketing mix expenditures considering market opportunities and relevant constraints (e.g., available financial resources). Since the overall marketing programming task was discussed in Chapter 13 emphasis in this chapter is placed on determining the total level of sales effort for a given sales target and the allocation of selling effort at different sales organization levels. Nevertheless, it should be recognized that the size and allocation of selling effort, in part, will determine the sales response resulting from the marketing program.

Sales Force Size and Allocation

Because of the close linkage of size and allocation decisions they should not be determined independently. Two basic approaches have been used: (1) determination of the size of the sales force followed by an allocation of needed salesmen to work units (e.g., territories); (2) estimation of the sales effort that should be assigned to each work unit, then aggregating this effort to provide an estimate of sales force size. Sales force size and allocation decisions span the range of possible strategy positions from a new venture situation to a balancing situation. In a new venture, initial levels of the sales force must be determined and salesmen deployed in order to develop potential sales opportunities. Because of lack of historical information and experience, management judgment plays a key role in the new venture. Frequently these decisions are made in stages. For example, management of a firm may have the ultimate objective of national sales coverage, but will decide to concentrate sales effort in selected metropolitan areas during the first few years. Expansion beyond these geographic markets may occur over several years and will involve continuing decisions on sales force size and allocation. Decisions in balancing strategy positions involve adjustment in size and sales force allocation, and are the result of sales management's regular monitoring of opportunities and problems and assessment of actual results compared to performance targets. Because of variations by customer, geographical area, products, and competition it is typically necessary to determine needed sales effort for relatively small management control units such as trade areas within territories. In cases where the number of customers served is relatively small, individual accounts may be analyzed.

Use of models and analytical approaches to aid decision making regarding sales force management has lagged behind other areas of marketing. Yet the potential is significant for applying analytical methods to aid decisions on sales force size and allocation.[14] One major analytical hurdle to modeling these decision processes has been the development of measures of sales response to personal selling effort. Of equal importance is gaining management acceptance of these important tools to help decision makers improve operating results. As will be illustrated in the subsequent two sections some promising progress has been made in overcoming these problems in the development and use of sales force decision models.

Management of the Sales Force

Once sales management has determined the size and allocation of the sales force, a major portion of the management task is the continuing process of planning, organizing, implementing, and controlling selling activities. Management of the sales force, as shown in Figure 21–1, consists of the following major activities:

Sales planning including, for example, revenue and cost budgeting, salesman time planning, and coordination with other marketing activities.

Recruiting and selecting salesmen. The composition of the sales force is rarely constant. Expansion, turnover, promotion, and retirement require a continuing effort to locate, screen, and hire sales people.

Most sales organizations have some type of training activity for the purpose of orienting new people to the job and to provide ongoing training (e.g., new product information) for the entire sales force.

Motivation and supervision of the sales force is a central management activity. Compensation (including incentives), counseling and assisting salesmen in planning and executing their work, and other supervisory tasks are important determinants of sales force results.

---

[14] For an excellent analysis of sales force decision models developed to 1969 see David B. Montgomery and Glen L. Urban, *Management Science in Marketing* (Englewood Cliffs, N.J.: Prentice-Hall, 1969), Chapter 6.

Evaluation and control of selling operations require a substantial portion of management effort. Monitoring of results with respect to goals, and determining the corrective action necessary to reduce the performance gap are continuing sales management functions.

This provides a brief overview of the sales force management decision process shown in Figure 21–1. As indicated the various decisions are closely interrelated and thus should be viewed as an ongoing management process. While major shifts in the size and allocation of the sales force do not occur frequently in a mature sales organization, decisions on size and allocation should not be considered fixed over time. An understanding of the factors that influence these decisions provides an important frame of reference for managing selling operations. Moreover, as a part of sales management's evaluation and control efforts, regular assessment of the number and deployment of sales personnel should be made.

DETERMINING SALES FORCE SIZE

Decision Analysis Concepts

In order to place the sales force size decision in perspective, consider a hypothetical situation faced by National Instruments Inc. With a sales force of 75 the firm obtained sales of $29.5 million last year. Gross profit contribution after deduction of $2.9-million selling expenses was $1.4 million. After allowing for advertising, engineering, and general administrative expenses, net profit before taxes was $200,000 or less than 1 percent of sales. Top management does not consider this level of profitability acceptable and has asked managers to examine their operations and to present plans for improving sales and cost relationships. The sales manager working with the marketing vice president and executives in accounting, engineering, finance, manufacturing, and personnel, developed the sales and cost analysis shown in Figure 21–3. The dominant portion of National Instruments' marketing budget was accounted for by personnel selling expenses. In developing their estimates the management group found it necessary to make certain assumptions about sales and cost behavior at alternative levels of sales force size:

Products to be sold above the current level would be produced in existing plant facilities using added shifts and overtime thus accounting for proportionately higher manufacturing costs at expanded sales levels. This causes gross profit contribution to increase at a decreasing rate at higher sales levels up to a point where a decline occurs (at a level of about 108 salesmen as shown in Figure 21–3).

FIGURE 21-3

Estimated Sales, Gross Profit Contribution, and Selling Expenses for Different Sizes of National Instruments' Sales Force

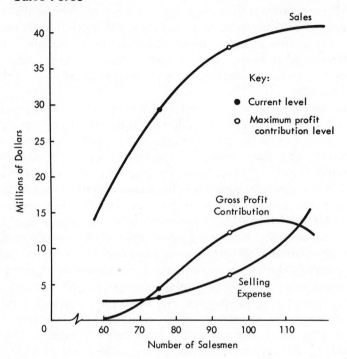

Marketing management, based on available market information and executive judgment, believe the sales response relationship shown is reasonable in terms of competitive assessment, projected marketing program expenditures, and estimates of market potential. National Instruments currently has less than a 15 percent share of the market. (Sales curve shown in Figure 21-3.)

Personal selling expenses for larger sizes of the sales force are estimated to be proportionately higher due to substantial increases in recruiting and training costs; difficulties in obtaining salesmen of comparable capabilities to the present group; and the additional sales management executives and product specialists required. (Selling Expenses curve in Figure 21-3.)

The analysis indicates that expanding the sales force to a size of about 94 people will yield the maximum gross profit contribution *net* of selling costs. Recalling the concept of marginal contribution discussed in Chapter 13, at a sales force of 94 incremental selling expenses are equal to incremental gross profit contribution (the slopes of the two curves are equal). A sales force expansion of this magnitude would require planning and implementation over a time period of at least one to three years. Also recognizing that the projections are management's best estimates (based on judgment and available historical information), and thus subject to future uncertainties, sales and cost estimates should be reassessed during the process of expanding the sales force. Nevertheless, the analysis provides a clear indication that additions to the sales force should be made.

While the estimates should be viewed as approximate, they illustrate the three main types of inputs needed to guide sales force size decisions: (1) decision criteria (in this example, gross profit contribution net of selling cost); (2) sales response projections; and (3) cost estimates. Any attempt to adjust sales force size, or to evaluate performance at current levels, should incorporate these three types of information into the decision making process. Management normally must synthesize the influences of available market opportunities, environmental factors, competition, and company marketing effort upon market response, since explicitly incorporating all possible determinants in a given analysis is virtually impossible. The sales response curve shown in Figure 21–3 represents management's best assessment of these factors utilizing internal operating information, judgmental experience, and research information.

Management also needs a unit of analysis for assessment of sales activities. Often, this management control unit is related to the market. For example, the control unit may be individual customers, groups of customers (e.g., trade areas), geographic territories, or customer-product groups (e.g., customers buying certain products). Similarly, it is necessary to define the salesman's work unit such as a geographic territory, specific customers, a customer-product group, or some other unit of sales responsibility assigned to the salesman. In some cases, a management control unit and salesman work unit may be the same.

Decision Models

There are two major types of decision approaches that are used in sales force size determination: (1) those that focus on one or more determinants of market response (e.g., market potential); and (2) those where an estimate of required selling effort is based on an assessment of the salesman workload necessary to serve the firm's market targets (e.g., number of calls needed per planning period). The two approaches are to some degree interrelated since the workload approach involves an attempt to distinguish between different types of customers in terms of workload. For example, the analysis of National Instruments, Inc. discussed above is illustrative of the market response approach. Three other decision models will be examined to indicate available methods for sales force size determination: (1) a single determinant (market potential) approach to estimating sales response; (2) a workload approach; and (3) a multi-stage model (size and allocation) incorporating various determinants of market response.

Market Potential Approach. This method developed by Semlow consists of: (1) development of an average sales response relationship for a firm using market potential and historical sales information obtained for existing salesman work units; (2) estimating sales, costs, and profits for various sizes of the sales force above and below the current level; and (3) using some type of profit performance criteria (e.g., profit contribution, return on investment) for selecting the level of personal selling effort.[15] Data similar to those shown in Table 21–2 must be assembled for each salesman work unit. Values from Table 21–2 on sales volume per 1 percent of potential and percentage of potential per territory are then plotted and a curve of best fit drawn for the points as shown in Figure 21–4. The resulting curve in Figure 21–4 is a type of sales response relationship which indicates historical sales as a function of market potential. It is an average relationship in that no allowances are made for variations in salesman experience and effort and other possible determinants of sales response. The influences of factors other than potential upon sales response are suggested by the resulting non-linear curve of best fit, and by the fact that the points representing the 25 territories do not fall perfectly along the curve. These variations may be due to differences between territories in salesman capabilities, competitive strengths, workload (e.g., geographical dispersion of accounts) and other factors. If a reasonably good curve cannot be drawn to represent the various salesman work unit data points then the market potential approach should not be used.

In stage two of the Semlow market potential approach estimates of sales, costs, and profits are developed for alternative sizes of the sales force. In examining different sizes of the sales force it is assumed that all salesman will be assigned territories of equal potential. For example, using the response curve shown in Figure 21–4 to determine estimated sales for a sales force of size 30, each of the 30 territories will have market potential equal to all others, or 3.33 percent of total market potential (100 ÷ 30). Then using the sales response curve, a sales value for 1 percent of potential is obtained that corresponds to 3.33 percent of potential per territory (See Figure 21–4). This value is $60,000 for one percent of potential or an estimated total sales volume of $6-million

---

[15] See Walter J. Semlow, "How Many Salesmen Do You Need," *Harvard Business Review,* 38 (May–June 1959), pp. 126–32. The following discussion is based on this source.

TABLE 21–2

Basic Factual Data Pertaining to 25 Salesmen's Territories (in $1,000s)

Territory Designation	Size of Territory in Percent of Total Potential	Total Sales per Territory	Sales per 1% of Potential
1.............	11.89%	$351	$ 29
2.............	9.53	300	31
3.............	7.68	244	32
4.............	6.36	179	28
5.............	6.07	393	65
6.............	4.78	200	42
7.............	4.75	192	40
8.............	4.64	312	67
9.............	4.58	169	37
10.............	4.10	187	45
11.............	3.75	218	58
12.............	3.42	210	61
13.............	3.33	151	45
14.............	3.08	186	60
15.............	2.65	234	89
16.............	2.61	235	90
17.............	2.56	194	76
18.............	2.50	398	160
19.............	2.16	208	97
20.............	1.86	344	185
21.............	1.83	288	158
22.............	1.80	140	78
23.............	1.43	252	177
24.............	1.39	346	250
25.............	1.25	257	206
	100.00%		

Source: Walter J. Semlow, "How Many Salesmen Do You Need," *Harvard Business Review*, 38 (May–June 1959), p. 128.

(100 × 60,000).[16] Based on this level of projected sales, estimates are then developed for selling costs, operating profits, total investment, operating profit on sales volume, and operating profit on investment. Finally, using an appropriate decision criterion such as operating profit on investment, the most profitable level of sales operations can be determined.

Since the market potential approach utilizes historical sales information it is primarily suited to analysis of sales force size in an existing organization. While market potential information may be useful in guiding sales force size decisions for a new organization, it would not be possible to develop a sales response function like that shown in Figure 21–4. Recognizing the possible uncertainties involved in estimating both sales and costs, the method should provide acceptable decision making

---

[16] Ibid., p. 129 (Exhibit II).

FIGURE 21–4

Relationship between Sales Potential per Territory and Sales Volume per 1 Percent of Potential

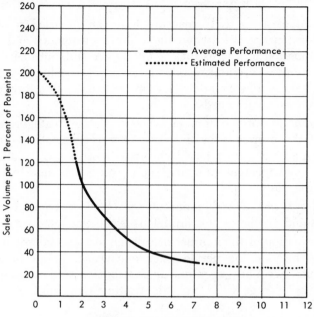

Source: Redrawn from Walter J. Semlow, "How Many Salesmen Do You Need," *Harvard Business Review*, 38 (May–June 1959), p. 129.

information concerning the most appropriate direction of changes in sales force size (e.g., increases or decreases). Since such changes are usually made in steps, management will have the opportunity to examine results before making further changes. Nevertheless, certain premises underlying the approach should be recognized. The firm using the method should not already have a major share of industry sales (if so, the opportunity for sales increases would be limited); possible company sales increases should not be expected to generate adverse competitive actions (e.g., price war); personal selling should be a major element of the marketing mix and thus capable of generating sales changes; and market potential information should be available or obtainable.[17]

Workload Approach. Talley has developed an approach to sales force size determination which is based upon the workload associated

---

[17] Ibid., p. 127.

with serving a firm's existing and/or prospective customers.[18] The method is also applicable for use in salesman work unit design (allocation decisions) using the principle of equal work load to develop work units. The major steps are as follows:

1. Selection of an activity measure that can be used to distinguish variations in work load among a firm's customers and prospects. Determination of a basis for classifying accounts into customer categories to achieve equal workload (activity) within groups. Possible activity measures include sales or potential sales, profitability of sales, and customer needs.

2. Determination of the number accounts in each category and selection of the proper level of selling effort (e.g., call frequency) for each type of customer based on analysis of past call patterns, sales results, management judgment and experience, and recommendations from salesmen.

3. Calculation of the total amount of selling effort required for the customers and prospects of a firm. This is the estimated total workload.

4. Determination of the number of calls an average salesman can make during the planning period (e.g., one year). This estimate should take into account geographical distribution and concentration of accounts, average time per call, waiting time, and other relevant factors.

5. Estimation of the number of salesmen needed to accomplish the projected work load. Sales force size is calculated by dividing the total number of calls required (3 above) by the number of calls an average salesman can make (4 above).

A brief illustration of the workload approach is shown in Table 21–3. Various factors, in addition to those indicated, can be incorporated into the analysis to account for other variations. For example, due to travel time differences rural and urban accounts can be separately analyzed. Similarly, differences in workload due to products applicable to each customer can be included by using a classification by customer-product type. Variations in call duration that might be necessary due to particular needs of accounts can also be included by increasing the required number of calls of a given duration.

Implicit in the approach is that call patterns can be determined which will generate desired sales response. While, precise selection of call frequency is probably not possible in most selling situations, it should be feasible to determine reasonable estimates for customers with different characteristics. Yet the approach depends substantially upon the judg-

---

[18] Walter J. Talley, Jr., "How to Design Sales Territories," *Journal of Marketing*, 25 (January 1961), pp. 7–13. The following discussion is based on this source.

TABLE 21–3

Illustration of the Workload Approach to Sales Force Size Determination

Customer Category	Number of Customers	Desired Call Frequency (per year)	Total Calls Needed
A	300	52	15,600
B	700	30	21,000
C	1,000	12	12,000
D	2,000	6	12,000
	4,000		60,600

Calls per year that can be made by an average salesman: 900
Number of salesmen needed: 60600 ÷ 900 = 67

ment of management and salesmen. The method can also be used to design salesman work units such that workload is approximately equal in each. The approach can be used to analyze an existing sales organization, or to approximate the size of sales force needed in a new venture, expansion to new market targets, or extension of sales coverage for new products.

Composite Factors Approach. The potential and workload approaches do not specifically consider the multiple factors that may influence sales response. A promising model that has been recently developed utilizes a multi-stage approach to account for the interaction between sales force size and allocation decisions and incorporates various determinants of sales response in the response function that is developed.[19] The major stages in the model are shown in Figure 21–5 and outlined below:

Development of a control unit response function based upon managerial judgment and historical data and estimates. Data on selling effort, market potential, workload, company effort and experience, salesman ability and experience, and prior sales history are used to determine the sales response function.

Allocation of selling effort to control units (in this case, trade areas) based on the response function, and considering relevant budget and resource constraints. This process also includes determination of sales force size.

Aggregation of control units to form salesman work units (in this case, geographic territories). Adjustment can be made for territory level variables (e.g., experience of the salesman).

---

[19] Charles A. Beswick, III., "An Aggregate Multistage Model for Sales Force Management" (Unpublished Ph.D. dissertation, The University of Tennessee, 1973).

FIGURE 21–5

An Aggregate Multistage Decision Model for Sales Force Management

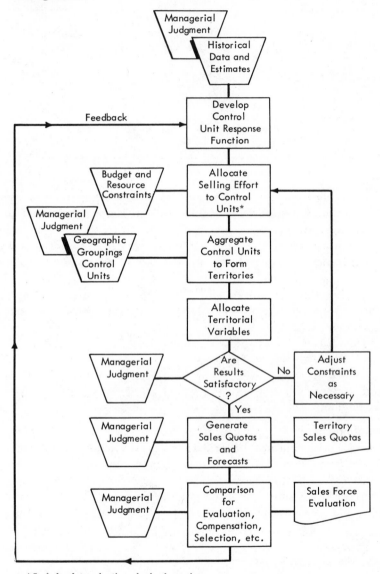

* Includes determination of sales force size.

Source: Charles A. Beswick, III., "An Aggregate Multistage Model for Sales Force Management (Unpublished Ph.D. dissertation, The University of Tennessee, 1973), p. 33.

Assessment of the results by management and adjustment where necessary. For example if management believes the response function is too conservative (or optimistic) it can be adjusted based on judgment and experience.

Generation of sales quotas and forecasts for use in evaluation, compensation, selection, etc.

The response function was developed (using an appliance manufacturer as a test firm) through nonlinear least squares analysis.[20] Selling time was optimally allocated to control units using a dynamic programming algorithm with profit contribution as a decision criterion. An example of the trading area allocation is shown in Table 21–4. Results of the analysis are shown for five territories of the organization used in study. Column 1 represents the percent of current effort allocated to each trade area (e.g., A1 is a trade area in Territory A). Column 2 indicates the desired allocation of selling effort to each trade area based on the model. Current sales response (Column 3) is the sales level predicted by the model for current effort (Column 1). Desired sales response (Column 4) indicates predicted sales response by the model at desired effort (Column 2) levels. Column 5 indicates actual sales results for the current period. For example, analysis of the results in Territory B suggests that 2.37 salesmen are needed rather than the one man currently assigned. Similarly, only .36 salesmen are needed in Territory C. A comparison of actual sales response (Column 5) to response predicted by the response relationship (Column 3) provides an indication of salesman performance. For example, in Territory D the salesman is performing at 0.77 (231 ÷ 302) of predicted performance; whereas, in E the salesman is performing at 1.43 of predicted performance.

The results of optimal allocation of selling effort for alternative sales force levels are shown in Table 21–5. With the current sales force size of 38, an increase in sales of $831,000 was predicted by the model using an optimal allocation.[21] Model predictions for larger sales force sizes are shown in Table 21–5. One interesting finding of the study was that reallocation of the existing sales force had a greater predicted influence upon profit contributions than did additions to the sales force. This suggests that in an existing organization, allocation of selling effort should be investigated before considering changes the size of the sales force. It also points up a possible weakness in the market potential approach

---

[20] This multiplicative factor model resulted in a response function of the form: Sales response $= a_1 x_1{}^{b_1} \cdot a_2 x_2{}^{b_2} \ldots \ldots a_n x_n{}^{b_n}$, where the x_i were response determinants (e.g., potential, salesman effort, workload, company experience, etc.). There were 232 control units (geographic trade areas, e.g., counties) used to develop the function. These comprised 38 salesman work units (territories).

[21] $831,000 is the difference between desired and current sales response for 38 salesmen.

TABLE 21–4

Trading Area Analysis of Selling Effort

Terr/Ta	Effort (%)*		Sales Response ($1000s)		
	(1) Current	*(2)* Desired	*(3)* Current	*(4)* Desired	*(5)* Actual
A1	40.	50.	308.	323.	223.
A2	10.	19.	105.	121.	104.
A3	10.	12.	70.	73.	54.
A4	5.	1.	3.	1.	2.
A5	5.	2.	9.	6.	17.
A6	10.	5.	31.	25.	22.
A7	10.	5.	33.	28.	25.
A8	10.	6.	40.	35.	67.
Total A	100.	99.	597.	612.	514.
B1	10.	61.	266.	396.	302.
B2	8.	20.	102.	126.	74.
B3	7.	21.	103.	131.	115.
B4	5.	11.	55.	65.	42.
B5	35.	35.	225.	225.	279.
B6	5.	11.	58.	70.	50.
B7	25.	70.	361.	452.	474.
B8	5.	8.	44.	49.	47.
Total B	100.	237.	1213.	1515.	1383.
C1	5.	2.	8.	5.	7.
C2	5.	2.	11.	8.	10.
C3	60.	19.	153.	118.	117.
C4	15.	8.	57.	50.	46.
C5	5.	2.	10.	7.	8.
C6	5.	3.	16.	14.	24.
C7	5.	1.	5.	2.	7.
Total C	100.	36.	261.	204.	219.
D1	10.	5.	31.	26.	24.
D2	70.	30.	231.	191.	181.
D3	15.	3.	26.	18.	18.
D4	5.	2.	13.	11.	8.
Total D	100.	40.	302.	246.	231.
E1	20.	20.	128.	129.	192.
E2	10.	3.	21.	15.	32.
E3	5.	6.	33.	34.	31.
E4	30.	15.	110.	94.	136.
E5	35.	31.	204.	199.	320.
Total E	100.	76.	496.	471.	711.

* 100% = 1 salesman

Source: Beswick, *An Aggregate Multistage Model for Sales Force Management*, p. 82. Column figures may not equal totals due to rounding.

since data are obtained from existing salesman work units where allocations are typically not optimal.

To illustrate the value of the model, in two adjacent territories the results indicated that slightly less than one person should be allocated in total to both areas. In discussions with the firm's management it was

TABLE 21–5

Sales Response for Varying Sales Force Levels

	Effort (percent)*		Sales Response†		
	Current	*Desired*	*Current*	*Desired*	*Actual*
38 Salesmen...........	3,800.	3,800.	23,019.	23,850.	22,986.
39 Salesmen...........	3,800.	3,900.	23,019.	23,990.	22,986.
40 Salesmen...........	3,800.	4,000.	23,019.	24,127.	22,986.
41 Salesmen...........	3,800.	4,100.	23,019.	24,261.	22,986.
42 Salesmen...........	3,800.	4,200.	23,019.	24,393.	22,986.

* 1 salesman = 100%
† In $1000's
Source: Charles A. Beswick, III., "An Aggregate Multistage Model for Sales Force Management (Unpublished Ph.D. dissertation, The University of Tennessee, 1973), p. 86.

learned that nearly two years prior to the analysis a territory had been split into two existing work units. Based on actual sales results management indicated an incorrect decision had been made and that had the information provided by the model been available at the time, the decision to split the territory could have been avoided.

SALES FORCE ALLOCATION

Work Unit Design Guidelines

The allocation of selling effort and the resulting sales organization design may be based on several factors including customers, geographic areas, products, or combinations of two or more factors. While analysis of allocation can be performed at various levels, typically the salesman's work unit or some smaller unit of management control is used. The crux of the allocation decision is to select the amount of selling effort (e.g., proportion of the salesman's time) that should be assigned to each management control unit (e.g., customers, trade areas). An optimal assignment of effort exists when additional shifts of selling effort between control units will produce no improvement in sales response.

Management and salesmen are faced with several types of allocation decisions. These include:

Decisions as to how much sales effort to devote to individual customers. How should the salesman divide his time among assigned customers and prospects? Should available effort be increased for some customers and decreased for others?

Allocation of selling effort to geographic areas such as trade areas, zip codes, cities, and other geographic units. When a large number of customers is involved, analysis at the customer level may not be possible due to lack of information on individual customers.

Determination of how effort should be allocated to various products in the line. Because many firms have several products the allocation of selling effort to products is an additional type of allocation decision beyond customer and/or geographic allocation.

Allocation of salesmen to territories, customers, products, or other bases of determining work assignment. The task of deciding how salesmen should be assigned sales coverage responsibility is important in terms of achieving sales results and in providing equitable distribution of opportunities among salesmen.

Work unit design largely determines a salesman's opportunity for achievement. Consequently, decisions concerning initial territorial assignments, splitting or combining territories, and other changes are important sales management activities. The objectives of work unit design are to pinpoint responsibility for market coverage and avoid duplication of selling effort. Frequently, in field selling organizations a geographic territory serves as the work unit.[22] There are, of course, certain types of selling situations where territories may not be appropriate such as in automobile and retail appliance sales. Yet, size of sales force must be determined and selling effort allocated even though actual territories do not exist. In principle, work units should be designed to provide equal workload and market opportunities for all salesmen. While this goal can be approached, typically it is not possible to achieve a complete balance of both opportunities and workload. Inequities can be allowed for by establishing performance standards (e.g., sales quotas) that are adjusted for inter-work unit variations that are beyond the control of the sales force.

Consider, the data from four actual sales territories of an appliance manufacturer shown in Table 21–6. There are definite variations in both market potential and workload. Compare Brown's territory with Cook's in terms of market potential, actual sales, number of accounts, workload per account, and rating of salesman. Cook's actual sales are substantially lower than Brown's, accounted for in part by Cook's lower potential and higher workload per account, and in part by the fact that Brown is apparently a better salesman (based on the rating by management). This example illustrates the kinds of variations that can exist in work units assigned to salesmen.

Determination of the salesman's work unit is based on two major considerations: (1) the time required to serve customers and prospects (based on their importance to the firm); and (2) the qualitative char-

---

[22] Davis and Webster, *Sales Force Management*, p. 345. This reference contains a good overall discussion of territory design on pp. 344–58. See also *Allocating Field Sales Resources, Experiences in Marketing Management* No. 23 (New York: National Industrial Conference Board, 1970).

TABLE 21–6

Comparison of Market Potential and Salesman Workload for Four Territories of a Consumer Appliance Manufacturer

Territory Salesman	Market Potential (units)	Actual Sales (units)	Number of Accounts	Workload/ Account*	Rating of Salesmen†
Adams...............	35,600	3,367	127	20	2.3
Brown..............	36,270	4,587	120	15	5.5
Cook...............	23,730	1,578	76	21	2.7
Davis...............	21,410	2,408	89	19	4.3

* Index ranging between 1 and 25 determined by consideration of dispersion and clustering of accounts.
† By sales management on 1–7 scale.

acteristics of customer and prospects. The more time required per customer, the smaller the number of accounts that can be assigned to a salesman. In selected instances the buying potential of an account and the time needed to perform the sales function may require assignment of a salesman full-time to a single customer. Beyond time requirements the qualitative needs of particular types of customers (e.g., in terms of product use) may require specialization of the sales force. In the case of complex products two salesmen might call on the same customer regarding different product lines.

Time Requirements. The time needed to serve customers and prospects is influenced by the number and location of active accounts, appropriate call duration and frequency, and the buying potential of each account. A group of geographically dispersed accounts requires more travel time than an equal number that is highly concentrated in a location. For example, substantially more time would be required to serve customers located throughout Montana than the same number located in metropolitan Atlanta. The length of time required per call is affected by the information that must be provided to the customers (e.g., applications assistance); the number of individuals influencing and participating in the buying decision (e.g., purchasing agent, manufacturing manager, etc.); the importance of the purchase; and other special requirements of the account. Call frequency is normally based upon customer buying practices and the customer's buying potential. While a customer that buys twice the amount of another does not necessarily require double call intensity and frequency, definite increases in time allocation are normally appropriate. Similarly, development of prospects may require more time than established customers even when buying potential is equivalent.

Qualitative Characteristics. When the personal selling variations between customers and prospects are largely due to time requirements and accounts are geographically dispersed, salesman work units are frequently established by geographical boundaries (sales territories). Yet, in various markets the qualitative characteristics of customers impose additional influences upon the design of salesman work units. A firm with more than one line of complex products may require specialization of salesmen in order that proper product knowledge can be developed. Differences in customer application or use of products may also necessitate assignment of salesmen to certain customer groups whose product use characteristics are similar. For example, certain business equipment manufacturers assign salesmen of a particular branch or district to different industry groups (e.g., retailing, manufacturing, service industries, etc.). The salesman's relationship with his customers is also important. Firms are hesitant to move a salesman from a work unit after strong buyer-seller relationships have been developed over several years. Also, different customers may respond more favorably to salesmen with certain personality characteristics.

Changing conditions necessitate regular assessment of assigned work units by sales management, and may lead to dividing or combining existing work unit responsibility. Unfair realignment of work assignments as perceived by salesmen can lead to serious morale problems and loss of good salesmen.[23] The basic guidelines used in initial work unit design can be used in revising geographic boundaries and/or customers responsibility.

Allocation Models

Various analytical models have been developed to assist management and salesmen in sales force allocation decisions.[24] These approaches incorporate certain of the time and qualitative factors discussed above that are relevant in a particular personal selling situation. Most analytical approaches to sales force size and allocation determination do not establish actual salesman work units, although valuable information is provided such as estimates of how many people are needed and sales effort required in various control units. Selected models for use in geographic, customer, and product allocation will be examined to illustrate their usefulness in guiding allocation decisions.

Geographic Allocation. The models discussed earlier relative to sales force size determination may also be used for geographic allocation according to workload (Talley), market potential (Semlow), and multiple factors (Beswick). Another promising computerized sales territory as-

[23] For a discussion of problems and guidelines for changing territories see M. A. Brice, "The Art of Dividing Sales Territories," *Dun's Review,* 85 (May 1967), pp. 47, 93–98.

[24] David W. Cravens and Charles A. Beswick, "Applications of Management Science to Sales Force Decisions," in E. Earl Burch and William R. Henry, eds., *Proceedings* (Ninth Annual Meeting, Southeastern Chapter, The Institute of Management Science, October, 1973), pp. 323–31.

signment model called GEOLINE has been developed.[25] The model seeks to minimize the geographic dispersion of a territory activity measure (e.g., number of calls) around territory centers. The major stages in the application of the model are as follows:

Selection by sales management of a territory activity measure (some measure of the salesman's time) such as number of calls, market potential, number of customers, sales results, or a weighted combination of two or more functions.

Selection of "trial" territory centers, which can be changed based on the results of initial analysis. For example, homes or offices of existing territory salesman might be used. The centers can also be selected randomly, but will cause computer processing time to increase since several trials may be necessary to close in on a solution.

Solution by computer of a transportation linear programming computation with the objective of minimizing the sums of: the squared distance between a territory center and each geographic unit times the activity for the geographic unit (e.g., county, zip code area, census tract). The program is constrained to hold total activity per territory nearly equal.

Split geographic units are recombined so that none is assigned to more than one territory.

Next, territory centroids (in effect, centers of gravity) are calculated and the computation is repeated until no improvement can be achieved regarding the compactness of territories.

The computational procedure "does not compact geography, but rather it achieves maximum compactness with respect to the activity measure employed."[26] This results in a higher concentration of activity (number of calls, potential, etc.) around the territory center. Thus, territories are established with approximately equal total activity and minimum dispersion of the activity around territory centers.

Hess and Samuels point out that the major problem encountered in several company applications of GEOLINE has been agreement on the part of management of a suitable activity measure. They indicate:

We have found unanimous difficulty on the part of sales management in expressing clear-cut goals for constructing sales areas. Only after protracted discussions have sales territory objectives, i.e., activity measures, emerged.[27]

---

[25] Sidney W. Hess and Stuart A. Samuels, "Experiences with a Sales Districting Model: Criteria and Implementation," *Management Science,* 18, Part II (December 1971), pp. 41–54. The following discussion is based on this source.

[26] Ibid., p. 47.

[27] Ibid., p. 41. The problem is that managers cannot isolate one or two activity measures that they consider appropriate in all cases (e.g., across all territories).

In situations where acceptable activity measures can be determined the model should prove very useful in improving existing territory design, or in making shifts due to addition or deletion of salesman. Some work has been done regarding use of two or more weighted activity factors. Unless combinations of criteria are feasible, computational problems will exist in dealing with multiple factors because of required solutions for separate factors.

Customer Allocation. Selection of appropriate call patterns for individual customers represents a continuing challenge for both sales management and individual salesmen. CALLPLAN is an interactive model that utilizes judgmental estimates of sales response obtained from salesmen.[28] The model is illustrative of the "decision calculus" approach to model building wherein the decision maker forms an essential part of the analytical process.[29] The resulting model is, in a sense, designed by the decision maker and can be modified to better express his judgment and experience about the situation under study (e.g., allocation of selling effort). The decision situation concerns determining the estimated contribution of all possible call policies (frequencies) for each customer and prospect; and based on these estimates in combination with available salesmen call time, selecting the best time allocation. Sales are assumed to be the result of calls made during a given response period (e.g., one year). A response curve is developed for each account by asking the assigned salesman to provide five estimates for the response period: expected sales for zero calls, one half present number of calls, present call level, 50 percent over present level, and expected sales with a saturation sales call effort. A computer program is used to generate a smooth "S" shaped curve based on the salesman's estimates. The resulting sales response relationship can be modified by the salesman if it does not reflect his assessment of customer response to calls. Then, using an incremental analysis computer routine, call frequency for a salesman's accounts and prospects is determined to maximize contribution considering travel time and costs, time required per call, account profitability, and maximum and minimum call frequency limitations. Several applications of the model have been made including firms selling dental products, industrial plastics, chemicals, and refrigerants. By using information supplied by the salesman (in effect, making him part of the modeling process) the likelihood of salesman and manager acceptance is greatly improved. Moreover, the difficulties of developing sales response using

---

[28] This example is based on Leonard M. Lodish, "Callplan: An Interactive Salesman's Call Planning System," *Management Science*, 18, Part II (December 1971), pp. 25–40.

[29] J. D. C. Little, "Models and Managers: The Concept of a Decision Calculus," *Management Science*, 16 (April 1970), pp. 466–85.

historical information are eliminated by allowing the salesman to build the function based on judgment and experience.

The success of analytical and testing approaches to estimating sales response has been somewhat limited due, in part, to necessary simplifying assumptions (e.g., sales response is a function of sales potential and selling effort).[30] Decision calculus methods as illustrated by the Lodish model appear to offer promising alternatives and have been receiving considerable attention during the past few years. A similar model for use in product allocation is discussed later in the chapter.[31] Thus, the use of subjective-judgmental information in combination with analytical models and computer processing may substantially advance the application of decision models for sales force allocation in the decade ahead. Considering the benefits (lower costs and/or increased sales) of even a modest improvement of 10 percent in allocation of a 100 man sales force, the returns from the use of these models can be substantial.

Product Allocation. In a firm with several products, allocation of product effort adds an additional factor beyond customer and/or geographic allocation. Decisions must be made as to how much time a salesman should devote to the various products in the line, or to different groups of products. Product allocation is clearly interrelated to customer geographic allocation, and can change desired levels of effort allocation to customers or geographic areas. While in concept, all factors relevant to allocation should be approached simultaneously, the complexity of the task normally precludes composite analysis.[32] In many firms product allocation is left to the judgment and experience of the salesmen. In others compensation arrangements are linked to product sales and/or profitability in seeking to influence salesmen in their use of available time on various products.

For a given work unit involving several customers and multiple products the allocation decision consists of determining how much time

---

[30] Early applications of the analytical and testing approaches are illustrated, for example, by Semlow, "How Many Salesmen Do You Need?"; Clark Waid, Donald F. Clark, and Russell L. Ackoff, "Allocation of Sales Effort in the Lamp Division of General Electric Company," *Operations Research*, 4 (December 1956), pp. 629–47; and Arthur A. Brown, Frank T. Hulswit, and John D. Kettelle, "A Study of Sales Operations," *Operations Research*, 4 (June 1956), pp. 296–308.

[31] See David B. Montgomery, Alvin J. Silk, and Carlos E. Zaragonza, "A Multiple-Product Sales Force Allocation Model," *Management Science*, 18, Part II (December 1971), pp. 3–24.

[32] One suggested approach to incorporating both customer and product in the allocation decision involves the use of commissions and quotas determined using an interactive procedure between salesmen. Quotas and commissions are revised until both management and the sales force are satisfied with the result. See Otto A. Davis and John U. Farley, "Allocating Sales Force Effort with Commissions and Quotas," *Management Science*, 18, Part II (December 1971), pp. 55–63.

should be devoted to each customer-product combination as shown below:

Customer	Product			
	P_1	P_2	. . . . .	P_m
C_1	e_{11}	e_{12}	. . . . .	e_{1m}
C_2	e_{21}	e_{22}	. . . . .	e_{2m}
.	.	.		.
.	.	.		.
.	.	.		.
.	.	.		.
C_n	e_{n1}	e_{n2}	. . . . .	e_{nm}

The decision criterion regarding effort allocation is to maximize the contribution resulting (e.g., profit, sales) from allocation of the salesman's effort (e_{ij}) over n customers and m products. The sales responsiveness of various customer-product elements to selling effort is a key factor in the allocation decision. If a given amount of effort is designated to each customer (e.g., call frequency) then the task is to determine how much effort should be devoted to each product.

Analytical approaches have been developed to aid management and salesmen in improving allocation of selling effort to products. One model developed by Montgomery, Silk, and Zaragonza, incorporates the decision calculus approach to allocate selling effort across a product line during a planning period.[33] A sales response function was developed to account for the effects of four alternative call policies for use in allocating selling effort across a product line during a planning period. These included complete, half, quarter, and no coverage. The function was based on management's judgmental estimates of the long run and short run effect (response of different call policies for each product). A computational procedure based on incremental profit contribution is then used to allocate effort in each of the periods within the planning horizon. The computer model can handle up to 50 products, planning horizons up to 10 periods, and up to 10 discrete levels of sales effort. Results of use of the model in a pharmaceutical industry application have been favorable based on user acceptance and apparent profit improvement.

SUMMARY AND CONCLUSIONS

In this chapter the major decision making areas related to determining the role of the sales force, its size, and the allocation of salespeople to

---

[33] See Montgomery, "A Multiple-Product Sales Force Allocation Model," pp. 3–24.

appropriate work units were considered. These decisions, once made, are typically not changed substantially on a frequent basis. While the size of the sales force will be modified over time shifts of as much as 25 percent or more do not normally occur on an annual basis. Yet changes are necessary due to shifting opportunities, workload (e.g., addition of new products), and competitive influences. Similarly, as sales people gain familiarity with their assigned work units it is not logical to frequently allocate their efforts. As with sales force size, some reallocations become necessary as conditions and opportunities change. The decision framework, concepts, and approaches to analysis developed in this chapter provide sales management with a systematic basis for considering these changes when they occur. Additionally, the material in the chapter provides important guidelines for designing new sales organizations.

We now turn in Chapter 22 to an examination of the ongoing task of managing the sales force. The sales force decision framework developed in Chapter 21 provides an important foundation for considering the sales manager's continuing management responsibilities of sales planning, recruiting and selecting sales people, training, motivation and supervision, and evaluation and control of sales operations.

EXERCISES FOR DISCUSSION AND REVIEW

1. A metal products manufacturer is selling to customers in five different industries. The number of customers in each industry category is as follows: A = 500, B = 1,000, C = 2,000, D = 5,000 and E = 7,000. The desired call frequency per customer per month in each of the categories is: A: 5, B: 6, C: 1, D: 2, E: 3. For categories A and B, an average salesman can make three calls per day, while working with categories C, D and E, an average salesman can make seven calls per day. What should be the approximate size of the sales force based upon the above information? How should the company allocate its salesmen to the different customer categories? What additional information would be useful in making a more complete assessment of sales force size?

2. In order to determine the size of a sales force, three important inputs should be used: (1) decision criteria; (2) sales response projections; and (3) cost estimates. Use these three inputs in a hypothetical example in order to determine the best size of the sales force. You are free to select appropriate decision criteria. Use your own figures and explain why a particular sales force size would be most appropriate.

3. A salesman has been assigned to sell a product in three different areas: trading area X, trading area Y and trading area Z. There are different types of customers and some require a greater call frequency than others. The number of accounts and the number of calls per month for each trading area are as follows:

Trading Area X

   20 accounts where two calls per month are necessary

   10 accounts where one call per month is necessary

   10 accounts where one call every two months is necessary

Trading Area Y

   5 accounts where two calls per month are necessary

   15 accounts where one call per month is necessary

   5 accounts where one call is necessary every two months

Trading Area Z

   10 accounts where two calls per month are necessary

   5 accounts where one call per month is necessary

   10 accounts where one call is necessary every two months

Based on this information, if our salesman averages a call frequency of five calls per day, would he be able to handle the three trade areas? Would he have some extra time left to work in another territory or would there be a need for an extra salesman?

4. A food products wholesaler is currently selling in six different districts. Based on a market potential analysis, a percentage of total sales has been allocated to each district. Two salesmen are assigned to each district. Sales figures for 1975 are as follow:

District	Market Potential (percent of total)	Sales Goals	Actual Sales
A	15	$ 450,000	$ 825,000
B	20	600,000	225,000
C	17	510,000	330,000
D	13	390,000	370,000
E	25	750,000	740,000
F	10	300,000	520,000
Total	100.0	$3,000,000	$3,000,000

What observations can you make concerning the performance of salesmen in the above districts? Should there be a readjustment of the sales force in some districts? Is there additional information that would be helpful in making an assessment of the six districts?

5. One of the difficult problems faced by sales management is determining the proportion of selling effort to be allocated between customers (those currently buying from the firm) and prospects (those that are not buying from the firm). Making whatever assumptions are necessary outline an approach for making this decision in a particular firm. How might the nature of this decision vary between a firm pursuing a new venture marketing strategy compared to a firm occupying a balancing strategy position?

6. Determination of the shape of geographical sales territories is subject to several different factors including for example account location, concentration, travel patterns, and method of travel. Illustrate different shape configurations assuming possible variations in the above factors that would favor different shapes.

Managing the Sales Force

In the last chapter a perspective toward the selling function was developed and the major sales force decision making areas were described and interrelated. The reader may find it helpful to refer back to Figure 21–1 in Chapter 21 where the "Sales Force Management Decision Process" was presented. We are now ready to consider the important tasks of staffing, development, and supervision of the sales force and evaluation and control of sales operations. They comprise the final two decision areas included in Figure 21–1. In an existing sales organization these activities represent the major portion of time devoted to management of the personal selling function.

SALES FORCE STAFFING, DEVELOPMENT, AND SUPERVISION

A substantial portion of the on-going sales force management function involves various aspects of staffing, development of people, and supervision. The task is complicated by the fact that in field sales organizations (as compared to a retail store sales force) close, day-to-day supervision is not possible. Similarly evaluation of sales personnel performance is frequently difficult due to the various factors beyond control of the salesman that must be taken into account such as available opportunities, workload, experience, company support, and competition. The methods and tools available for assisting in managing and evaluating sales people are largely qualitative in nature.

After determination of sales force objectives and sales force size and allocation, sales management must plan sales operations, recruit and select salesmen, train sales people, supervise and motivate the sales force, and evaluate and control sales force activities. Staffing, development, and supervision are considered in this section followed by an examination of evaluation and control in the next section.

Sales Planning

It will be helpful at this point to examine in greater detail the nature and scope of the sales manager's function, responsibilities, and relationships. An illustrative job description for the sales manager of a large pharmaceutical company is shown in Figure 22–1. The position includes responsibilities for developing and managing the sales program within the framework of the total marketing program and for coordination of sales plans and activities with other functional areas within the firm. Sales force size and allocation must be determined to reach specified market segments. Sales planning and control processes must be developed to provide a basis for managing the sales organization to achieve assigned performance targets. The management team reporting directly to the sales manager includes field (regional) managers and a management staff for services, sales training, sales analysis, and selected markets (government and hospital sales). While this job description is not necessarily typical of all sales management functions, it provides a realistic example of the types of activities that occur in a large sales organization.

The development of plans and control guidelines are important tools for use in managing the sales force. They set the stage for more detailed planning in the field including development of objectives for individual salesmen (e.g., sales quotas, number of calls, time with accounts, information collection, etc.). The first step in the planning process is the formulation of operational objectives against which the performance of the sales organization can be monitored. This involves translating corporate and marketing goals into overall performance targets for the sales force. An example of such a statement of objectives is shown in Figure 22–2.

Building on objectives, plans can be developed for achieving them.[1] Plans should specify strategies and tactics for reaching desired performance levels. They should include result targets, proposed changes in sales force size and allocation, sales forecasts and budgets, recruiting and training plans, compensation, and other management and supervisory guidelines. Our examination of planning concepts, methods, and guidelines in Chapter 13 provides a framework for sales force planning and control. The discussion that follows on various aspects of management of the sales force is also relevant to developing planning and control guidelines.

Recruiting and Selecting Salesmen

In a study of turnover rates for salesmen in over 500 companies, The Conference Board, Inc., found that "by the end of the fifth year of em-

---

[1] Sales planning and control using a company example to illustrate the approach are discussed in Jon R. Katzenbach and R. R. Champion, "Linking Top-Level Planning to Salesman Performance," *Business Horizons,* 9 (Fall 1966), pp. 91–100.

FIGURE 22–1

Illustrative Job Description for a Sales Manager

SALES MANAGER
Schering Corporation

REPORTS TO: Vice President, Schering Laboratories

FUNCTION: To manage and plan the field staff activities in support of domestic products and sales policies. Administer Government/Hospital Sales, Sales Services, Sales Training, and Sales Administration.

SCOPE OF RESPONSIBILITIES

- Participate with Rx and O.T.C. Marketing Managers in the preparation of marketing plans, budgets, and schedules as preliminarily approved by the Vice President for Marketing.
- In conjunction with the Advertising Manager, assist in the planning and timing of promotional efforts and on the relative emphasis to be placed on personal versus impersonal selling.
- Participate with O.T.C. and Rx Marketing in the planning of the field sales program and relative emphasis required for trade and professional selling.
- Direct the organization of field selling activity, the number and type of representatives to be employed, their distribution geographically, and their assignments by market segments (hospital, government, industrial, professional, trade, etc.).
- Set standards of field selling and supervisory performance and check actual operations against standards.
- Recommend methods of compensation and other conditions of employment, including incentive systems.
- Direct the sales training program.
- Review and approve all general communications between home office marketing personnel and the field organization.
- Cooperate closely with marketing product managers, contributing information on field marketing conditions, prices, competition, new product forms, unfilled needs, criticisms of Schering products, etc. Receive current information on marketing plans, including schedules, budgets, product changes, etc.
- Advise the Medical Services Director of supporting activity needed from that department for field operations.
- Supply information to the Vice President for Marketing, Vice President, O.T.C. and Distribution, and Product Managers on factors influencing the success or failure of programs as executed in the field.

FIGURE 22–1 (continued)

SUPERVISES

Directly   (8)   4 Regional Managers, Sales Services Manager, Sales Training Manager, Government and Hospital Sales Manager, Sales Analysis Manager.

Indirectly (444)   Sales Communications Manager, Field Sales Operations Manager, Assistant Sales Training Manager, Assistant Government and Hospital Sales Manager, 34 Division Managers, approximately 405 representatives.

RELATIONSHIPS

Within the Company

Advise the Vice President, Schering Laboratories, Vice President, O.T.C. and Distribution, and the Marketing Managers regarding the sales implementation of proposed marketing plans.

Advise the Medical Services Director regarding supportive activity from that department relative to the field staff effort.

Participate in the formulation of decisions relating to marketing objectives and policies and marketing programs.

Outside the Company

Attend various professional and trade association meetings.

Call on various distribution outlets (wholesalers, large chain distributors, etc.) as required.

POSITION REQUIREMENTS

Bachelor's degree, plus 12–15 years of related marketing experience, with thorough knowledge of pharmaceutical industry, distribution, and trade. Broad knowledge of sales and merchandising techniques. Knowledge of personnel and management techniques.

Source: Reprinted by permission of the publisher from AMA Research Study No. 94, *Job Descriptions in Marketing Management* (© 1969 by the American Management Association, Inc.,) pp. 194–96.

ployment, typically half of a given year's new sales recruits have terminated employment."[2] While certain factors influencing turnover cannot be adjusted or modified by sales management (e.g., economic conditions, family problems, etc.), other highly significant influences cited in the Conference Board study (compensation, job content, and career patterns) can be controlled, at least to some extent through sound management practices. Costs of recruiting and training a salesman can range from

---

[2] *Salesmen's Turnover in Early Employment* (New York: The Conference Board, Inc., 1972), p. 1. This report contains a detailed analysis of turnover in a broad cross section of industries.

FIGURE 22–2

Example of Sales Organization's Objectives

Oceanic Industries, Inc.
Retail Sales Manager

Primary Sales Objectives

1. Develop and achieve account gross profit potentials so that composite gross profit will increase 50 percent by 1971
2. Achieve annual gross profit potentials in all key accounts
3. Increase industrial accounts gross profits by $4 million by 1971
4. Increase consumer accounts gross profits by $8 million by 1971

Secondary Sales Objectives

1. Reduce controllable expenses from 24 percent to 20 percent of sales by 1971
2. Reduce the proportion of under-$20 orders from 20 percent to 15 percent of total business by 1971
3. Achieve and maintain target volume relationships among product groups, as indicated below:

Product Group	Present Percentage of Total Volume	1971 Target Percentage
A	21	21
B	27	27
C	12	12
D	12	12
E	18	8
F	10	20

Manpower Objectives

1. Reduce turnover rate of salesmen from 28 percent to 20 percent by 1971
2. Recruit an average of 15 new salesmen per year for the next five years
3. Qualify at least four salesmen for promotion annually through 1971

Source: Reprinted by permission from Jon R. Katzenbach and R. R. Champion, "Linking Top-Level Planning to Salesman Performance," *Business Horizons*, 9 (Fall 1966), p. 93.

$5,000 to $20,000, and even higher in certain highly technical sales jobs.[3] Annual costs of salary and support of a field salesman can exceed $20,000 annually. The development of good recruiting and selection policies

---

[3] Richard C. Smyth and Matthew J. Murphy, *Compensating and Motivating Salesmen* (New York: American Management Association, Inc., 1969), p. 13.

and procedures can contribute substantially to reducing turnover, recognizing that employment of the right people for the selling job is only one step in a sound sales manpower development program.

The major components of the recruiting and selection process include: (1) defining the selling job in a given organization; (2) development of selection procedures; (3) recruiting candidates; and (4) selection of suitable people. The process begins with a clear definition of the required skills, knowledge, and experience appropriate for a particular selling position. Defining the job to be done provides a basis for developing selection procedures, locating suitable applicants, and choosing people that appear to meet job requirements.

Defining the Selling Job. The characteristics of a good salesman have been a subject of widespread discussion for decades. Perhaps the most significant result of the continuing stream of research and analysis of experience is that sales positions are not homogeneous.[4] For example, a successful life insurance salesman may very well perform poorly in another selling environment. The first step in defining the sales job is to determine what is expected of the salesman. The personal selling function can consist of several activities which will vary in both importance and time demands from one firm to another. A salesman's duties may include, for example, soliciting and servicing orders, prospecting (developing new customers), missionary work (helping channel of distribution intermediaries), accumulating information, management responsibilities (e.g., supervision of service personnel), and non-sales work.[5] Sales management's first task is to identify the relevant components of the sales job and determine the relative importance of each part of the job. The job description is a useful means of defining the sales position.

Of equal importance is identifying the characteristics of salesmen that will serve as potential indicators of good sales performance. This task is far more complex than defining the job to be performed. In fact, it is one of the most difficult challenges that face the sales manager. Study of the job description, analysis of personal histories of salesmen, failure analysis, study of exit interviews, and sources outside the firm are useful ways of developing appropriate selection criteria for salesmen.[6] Various salesman characteristics fall into the following categories: mental, physical, experience, environmental (e.g., family status, membership in organiza-

---

[4] James C. Cotham, III, "Selecting Salesmen: Approaches and Problems," *MSU Business Topics,* 18 (Winter 1970), pp. 64–72. This article provides an excellent analysis of the "state of the art" of salesman selection.

[5] Robert E. Sibson, *Wages and Salaries: A Handbook for Line Managers,* rev. ed. (New York: American Management Association, Inc., 1967), pp. 161–62.

[6] William J. Stanton and Richard H. Buskirk, *Management of the Sales Force* (Homewood, Ill.: Richard D. Irwin, Inc., 1974), pp. 163–69. Chapter 6 contains a detailed discussion of job definition and determining the characteristics of people for performing the job.

tions, etc.), and personality. Selection criteria should be made explicit, but care should be taken to avoid arbitrary use of criteria to screen candidates. Predicting sales performance is an elusive task and requires careful use of management judgment and experience.

Selection Procedures. Selection procedures for salesmen vary in business and industry from formal systems to little or nothing in the way of organized approaches to the selection process. In firms where the personnel function is formalized, selection procedures are more likely to exist. Also responsibility for salesman recruiting and selection may range from highly centralized systems to situations where primary responsibility is assigned at the field level (e.g., district, branch) managers. Since there are advantages to participation in the process by personnel specialists, sales management, and field managers a selection procedure that includes all is recommended. For example, the new salesman will be assigned to a field unit; its manager should have a voice in the selection decision. A logical approach is to develop selection procedures centrally (with inputs from the field) for use by all field units.

Building on the job to be accomplished and specified selection criteria, several tools can be utilized to design a selection procedure including application forms, personal interviews, references and credit reports, physical examinations, evaluation forms, and intelligence, aptitude, and psychological tests.[7] Applications can be useful in screening people and for focusing the attention of interviewers on particular areas. Rarely are sales people hired without an interview. Exceptions include sales arrangements where straight commissions are paid for sales functions such as selling magazine subscriptions and greeting cards. Reference checks are also frequently included in the selection procedure. These, as well as physical examinations normally occur during the later stages of the selection process. Rating or evaluation sheets are sometimes used to provide systematic measures of interviewers' reactions to sales candidates. Use of tests in salesman selection procedures varies considerably. Their use is one of the most controversial aspects of the selection process because of the questioned validity of test results for predicting salesman performance. Some firms use tests to screen applicants. When tests are used they should be selected, administered, and interpreted by professionally qualified personnel.

Recruiting Candidates. In other than very small sales organizations locating suitable candidates to be considered for sales positions is a continuing activity due to salesman turnover, promotions, retirement, and growth. For example, a firm with a sales force of 100 and an annual turnover rate of 15 percent would need to hire 15 new people every year. To

---

[7] See Stanton and Buskirk, *Management of the Sales Force,* Chapters 8 and 9 for an extensive discussion of these selection tools.

obtain 15 salesmen many inquiries and applications would have to be processed; as many as 30 to 50 or more people interviewed and included in other selection procedures; decisions made on which candidates to extend offers to; and based on the acceptance rate, continuation of recruiting activities until the desired number of new salesmen is on the payroll. Thus a firm with other than a very small sales force should develop a continuing recruiting program. For example, several firms that seek college graduates for sales positions conduct regular recruiting visits to college campuses in order to identify interested and qualified candidates for sales positions. Various other methods for locating people include advertising in newspapers and magazines, employee referrals and transfers, and employment agencies.[8] The salesman recruiting program should be based on planning of manpower needs projected at least a year in advance.

Selection of Salesmen. The selection decision seeks to match the qualifications of available candidates against criteria for a particular sales position. In many cases all job offers extended will not be accepted so it will be necessary to make more offers than the number of salesmen needed. Decisions on selection may be made by the sales manager, field managers, personnel, or in some cases on a joint basis, depending upon company practices.

Training

There is general agreement among sales management authorities that both new salesmen and the existing sales force should receive training. Training needs will vary by organization. Efforts to meet these needs can range from on-the-job programs to formal courses and workshops, as well as combinations of formal and on-the-job training. Major considerations in developing a continuing program of sales training consist of the following:

1. *Determination of what the training effort should accomplish.* Training objectives should be based on what the sales force is expected to accomplish and the areas where training can contribute to improving sales force results (e.g., reduced turnover, improved morale, increased sales, and lower costs). For example, training on various aspects of a planned new product introduction can help the salesman to initiate sales effort on the product more quickly and effectively. Similarly, a planned program of training for new salesmen can greatly compress the time period needed for them to become productive in sales generation and other assigned responsibilities.

---

[8] See Stanton and Buskirk, *Management of the Sales Force*, Chapter 7, for further discussion of sources and approaches to salesmen recruiting.

2. *Selection of personnel to be trained.* Training is expensive. Participants to be trained should be carefully selected. Both new and existing salesmen require various types of training based on an assessment of training objectives and the needs of particular people. For example, a new salesman with prior selling experience in the same industry may require substantially less training than one with no selling experience.

3. *Determination of the content of the training program.* Four main areas cover the possible training needs of salesmen: selling concepts and techniques; time and territory management; product knowledge; and company policies, procedures, and practices. The job description provides a good guide to initial training needs for new salesmen.

4. *Identification of people responsible for providing needed training.* Training can be accomplished by staff personnel (e.g., sales trainers), management and experienced salesmen, and outside specialists. Selection of trainers should be based upon their knowledge of the training areas as well as their capabilities in teaching others. For example, a top performing salesman may be very poor in training others.

5. *Selection of the time and location of training.* New men are typically trained when they enter the organization either on-the-job or at a central location (e.g., home office). Training of existing salesmen may best be handled by assembling them in various areas in the field if the organization is widely dispersed geographically. In a small sales force on-the-job training may be the only feasible alternative. The number and location of people to be trained and type of training required are major determinants as to when and where training should be conducted.

6. *Determination of training methods.* Various training methods are employed in industry including lectures, demonstrations, observation, role playing, seminars or workshops, and self study. Methods should be selected that best accomplish training needs at favorable cost-benefit levels.

7. *Evaluation of training results.* While evaluation of salesman training is admittedly difficult, benchmarks for measuring the benefits of training should be an integral part of the training program. Various criteria for use in assessing program effectiveness include reduced training time, lower turnover, reduced selling costs, and improved salesman performance. Also, tests can be used to monitor the effectiveness of certain types of training (e.g., product knowledge).[9]

---

[9] Detailed discussion of these seven major considerations in the development of a training program is contained in Stanton and Buskirk, *Management of the Sales Force,* Chapters 11 and 12; and Kenneth R. Davis and Frederick E. Webster, Jr., *Sales Force Management* (New York: The Ronald Press Company, 1968), Chapter 9.

Through analysis and planning within the above framework of the major aspects of the training task, an effective program can be developed. Training needs and company size will influence the resulting training effort. Even on-the-job training should be planned to assure proper coverage of training areas and to utilize the time of participants and trainers in an efficient manner. Assignment of a new man to an experienced salesman or supervisor for a few weeks is insufficient unless training needs are analyzed and guidelines for meeting these needs are developed. Assuming that existing salesmen will meet their own training needs without assistance is also inadequate.

Supervision and Motivation

Supervision and motivation of the sales force is one of the most challenging yet perplexing management jobs in the enterprise. In a field organization, people are spread over wide areas and day-to-day contact with management is frequently not possible. Selling can be a frustrating activity and effective motivation is essential to achieving sales objectives. In the following discussion the supervisory task is placed in perspective, the task of motivating salesmen examined, and approaches to salesman compensation are considered.

Supervision in Perspective. The nature of the selling job places special demands upon the supervisor. Depending upon the degree of salesman direction and control that is considered appropriate in a particular firm, geographical dispersion of people, information needs both to and from salesmen (e.g., competitive intelligence), assistance needed by salesmen, and the quality of the sales force various management and supervisory levels must be established. The following functions are typically included in a sales supervisors job:

Creating the work environment. The supervisor is the salesman's main link to the company, and frequently his only contact. The environment created by the supervisor can be a major influence upon salesman performance.

Establishing standards of performance. The salesman looks to his supervisor in developing his concept of the job including performance goals. The supervisor must make his expectations clear to the salesman and have a reasonable basis for believing the salesman can meet performance benchmarks.

Development of sales manpower. Training and development of salesmen is a continuing responsibility of the supervisor. He is in the best position to monitor training and development needs and to see that high priority needs are responded to.

Communication link. Information flows in the sales organization are important to management, salesmen, and customers.[10] Information on prices, products, policies and procedures, customer needs, competitive activity, and other items is continually flowing upward and downward in the sales organization. The supervisor plays a major role in facilitating communications.

Interpreting and enforcing policy and procedures. Various policies and procedures exist in a company and must be complied with. For example, salesmen's expenses are often a major selling cost and must be utilized in the most effective manner. Similarly pricing, credit approvals, collection of bad debts must be coordinated with the salesman and when necessary, interpretation and enforcement must be accomplished by the supervisor.[11]

Motivating Salesmen. The morale of salesmen, like all other employees, can adversely affect job motivation. When salesmen are widely dispersed geographically, maintaining high levels of morale presents supervision with a difficult job. Numerous business factors can contribute to poor morale including poor communications, status and recognition perceptions, unfair treatment and working conditions, weak supervision, pay, job requirements, inequitable territory realignment, and unfair quotas.[12] Various personal factors can also adversely influence a salesman's morale. Various means are used to keep morale high and thus motivate salesmen. Regular discussions with salesmen by supervisors are conducted face-to-face and by phone. Meetings are frequently used to motivate and communicate with salesmen. One of the most significant motivating factors in a sales organization is the compensation plan. "As a general rule the typical salesman is financially motivated far more strongly than is the average employee in his company."[13]

Approaches to Compensation. In the early 1960s a manufacturer of valves and other control devices decided to shift from a factory sales force to independent manufacturer's representatives (they sell a firm's products for a commission on sales).[14] The firm's field managers were given an opportunity to become representatives for their geographical

---

[10] For an interesting study of information flows in a sales organization and the delays, distortions, and losses of information that can occur see Gerald S. Albaum, "Horizontal Information Flow: An Exploratory Study," *Journal of the Academy of Management* (March 1964), pp. 21–33.

[11] The various supervisory functions are examined in greater detail in Davis and Webster, *Sales Force Management,* pp. 564–70.

[12] See Stanton and Buskirk, *Management of the Sales Force,* pp. 478–89.

[13] Smyth and Murphy, *Compensating and Motivating Salesmen,* p. 15.

[14] An analytical approach to determining type of sales force (company, representatives, mixed) is discussed in C. Davis Fogg and Josef W. Rokus, "A Quantitative Method for Structuring a Profitable Sales Force," *Journal of Marketing* (July 1973), pp. 8–17.

areas of responsibility. Several, including one field manager in the Northeast with five salesmen under him, accepted the opportunity. Prior to the change he had received a $12,000 annual salary plus expenses including an automobile. Managers and salesmen were paid a straight salary. During his first year as an independent manufacturer's representative the manager reduced his sales force to three men; moved out of the downtown metropolitan offices he previously insisted were necessary for customer contact; sales were increased by 50 percent over the prior year; and the manager's earnings were substantially higher than when he was an employee of the manufacturer. This example illustrates the influence that compensation can have upon sales force results. Since the design of sales compensation plans is a broad subject it can only be briefly examined.[15]

Compensation alternatives range from a straight salary to a straight commission. There is general agreement that a sales compensation plan should include some type of incentive. The results of a survey of 444 manufacturing companies representing 20 industries are shown below:

Form of Payment	Number of Companies	Percent of Companies
Straight commission	40	9
Straight salary	115	26
Salary plus incentive	289	65
Total	444	100

Thus, in this study nearly 75 percent of the firms compensated their salesmen using other than a straight salary arrangement.[16] Nearly two-thirds utilized a salary plus incentive arrangement.

The particular compensation plan that is used will substantially influence how salesmen direct their efforts, and will determine the degree of management control that can be exercised. For example, salesmen operating on a straight commission tend to be quite independent in channeling their efforts. The starting point in selecting and designing a compensation plan is to analyze the selling job and to determine what objectives the compensation plan should be designed to achieve. This

[15] A good, comprehensive discussion of the design of salesman compensation plans is provided by Smyth and Murphy, *Compensation and Motivating Salesmen.* See also Stanton and Buskirk, *Management of the Sales Force,* Chapters 13 and 14; and Davis and Webster, *Sales Force Management,* Chapter 12. The American Management Association, Inc., through its Executive Compensation Service provides comprehensive salary and benefit data for sales personnel which can be quite useful in establishing salary and incentive ranges; information on training costs, compensation, and selling expenses obtained from the AMA studies is provided in the January 7, 1974, issue of *Sales Management.*

[16] Smyth and Murphy, *Compensating and Motivating Salesmen,* p. 45.

provides a basis for selecting a particular type of compensation plan. The compensation arrangement selected should be based on established salary administration guidelines.

Job Satisfaction. In addition to compensation job satisfaction may contribute substantially to motivation of salesmen. Identification and assessment of factors that are linked to job satisfaction have been examined in a variety of research efforts during the past decade. For example, Churchill, Ford, and Walker have developed and tested an instrument for measuring job satisfaction of industrial salesmen.[17] Based upon their work they indicate that, "The results of this analysis strengthen our conviction that there are job dimensions, such as the behavior of customers, which influence a salesman's job satisfaction and which are unique to the salesman's occupation."[18]

EVALUATION AND CONTROL

A primary sales management responsibility is the evaluation and control of sales operations at all levels (e.g., entire sales organization, region, district, individual salesman, customer). These tasks consume a substantial portion of management resources in an established organization. Evaluation and control activities are examined at the organizational and individual salesman levels to illustrate the types of activities involved in monitoring sales operations.

Control of Selling Operations

Sales management is responsible for monitoring personal selling operations to determine if objectives are being achieved, and taking corrective action when necessary. An illustration of evaluation and control of overall selling activities will be helpful in describing the nature of the function:

Industrial Equipment, Inc. has six major product groups for which total annual sales last year were $7.503-million. As a part of an overall audit of marketing operations, the director of sales has prepared an analysis of sales effort and results by product group. Annual sales, gross profit contribution, estimated market growth, market share, and sales effort for the past year by product group are shown in Table 22–1. After reviewing the analysis the director of sales is appropriately concerned about the allocation of sales effort to the various product groups. Salesmen's effort (based on number of sales calls) has generally been allocated

---

[17] Gilbert A. Churchill, Jr., Neil M. Ford, and Orville C. Walker, Jr., "Measuring the Job Satisfaction of Industrial Salesmen," *Journal of Marketing Research,* 11 (August 1974), pp. 254–60, published by the American Marketing Association.

[18] Ibid., p. 260.

TABLE 22–1

Comparison of Sales Effort and Results by Product Group for Industrial Equipment, Inc.

Product Group	Annual Sales ($1,000s)	Gross Profit* ($1,000s)	Estimated Annual Growth† (percent)	Company Market Share (percent)	Sales Effort (percent of total calls)
A.................	871	217	5	43	17
B‡...............	2,273	1,135	12	16	24
C.................	767	115	−2	28	19
D.................	583	71	1	39	11
E‡...............	1,793	538	8	26	13
F‡...............	1,216	324	7	18	16
Total.............	7,503	2,400	—	—	100

* After deduction of cost of products.
† For the next five years.
‡ The products in these groups are relatively new.

according to product sales volume with apparently limited attention given to gross profit contribution and probable growth in the various product markets. Moreover, nearly half of sales effort has been focused on three older products groups (A, C, and D). Yet, 83 percent of the $2.400 million profit contribution was accounted for by the firm's three newer product groups! There are clear indications that better allocation of sales effort can be made by shifting salesmen's time away from the older products with low profit contribution and low growth potential toward product groups B, E, and F. Current market share for these lines also indicates that further increases may be possible recognizing that competitive strengths must be assessed in each product market.

Given the analysis shown in Table 22–1 sales management is faced with the task of shifting selling effort to achieve higher profit contributions and growth opportunities. Very likely over time new products were added by the firm without specific plans developed for re-allocating selling effort. Since Industrial Equipment, Inc., paid the salesmen on a straight salary there was no incentive for salesmen to make major shifts in selling effort. Using the analysis as an initial basis for action, management should first analyze existing and potential customer requirements for the various product groups to determine the amount of additional selling effort needed for the new products. Since sales and profit contributions for groups B, E, and F have been relatively high major effort shifts may not be appropriate. In this case management should investigate the size of the sales force to assess whether reductions may be needed. Alternatively, if substantial effort shifts appear appropriate, then a plan for accomplishing this should be developed including proper communication with salesmen, possible product training, and consideration of an incentive program based on profit contributions.

Sales effort by product group is one of several sales force evaluation and control areas.[19] Sales effort by size and type of customer is another area that requires continuous monitoring by management. For example, Bliss and Laughlin Industries, Inc. (supplier of electronic and precision tools, construction materials, and other industrial products) has shifted over time to use of mail-order catalogues for several product groups because of relatively small average customer purchases and rapidly increasing costs of sales calls.[20]

Evaluating Salesman Performance

The salesman is a basic unit of management control of the selling effort. A major issue in developing an evaluation and control system for a sales force is how to determine appropriate performance standards (and information on performance) that can be used to make comparisons between salesmen and to assess the overall productivity of the sales force. Several implications concerning evaluation and control of the sales force should be recognized:

In many selling situations the potential impact of the salesmen on work unit results may be overestimated due to the influences of various other factors beyond control of the salesman (e.g., market potential available, competitive strengths, company reputation).

The usefulness of market potential information for adjusting for interwork unit differences should be carefully assessed by management. Since market potential is a measure of the opportunity present, it is likely to be much more useful in sales planning than in control. This may be due to stronger competitive pressure in one work unit compared to another (e.g., two salesmen assigned by a competitive firm to one work unit compared to one in another).

It is normally impossible to arrive at balanced work units in the sense of providing all members of the sales force with equal performance opportunities.[21]

Sales volume is only one criterion of performance in most selling organizations. Profit contribution, new business, and other factors should be considered by management to the extent that they contribute to achieving the objectives assigned to the sales function.

---

[19] A discussion of how to develop reports for use in analyzing field sales operations is provided in Sanford R. Simon, *Managing Marketing Profitability* (New York: American Management Association, Inc., 1969), Chapter 7.

[20] "Marketing Observer," *Business Week* (August 3, 1974), p. 61.

[21] See for example, Harry Deane Wolf and Gerald Albaum, "Inequality in Products, Orders, Customers, Salesmen, and Sales Territories," *Journal of Business*, 35 (July 1962), pp. 298–301.

Because of the difficulty in quantitatively measuring salesman performance, the judgment and experience of sales managers and supervisors should play a central role in the evaluation process, particularly in compensation and promotion decisions.

The development of relative measures of salesman performance is typically more straightforward than attempting to obtain absolute measures. Management can usually identify the very high and very low performing salesman. Yet, it may be difficult to determine whether the firm's top salesmen represent the best sales people available for the job.

While the types of standards used in a given organization will vary, most are linked in some manner to sales, profit contribution, product mix, expenses, or activity (e.g., number of new customers). In certain cases multiple standards may be used. Performance standards, when communicated to the sales force, become a basis for salesman planning. The salesman's portion of the organization's selling job is often designated through assignment by management of a *quota*, which serves as a performance standard. Use of sales quotas for planning and control is widespread. Quotas are used to monitor performance, provide salesmen with goals, and serve as a basis for determination of incentives.[22] In practice quotas are often set based on consideration of market potential, historical sales, and other factors. The result is a judgmentally determined performance standard on the part of management. Quotas are frequently linked to sales volume, although by establishing them for various product groups the relative profitability of different products can be recognized. Management normally incorporates consideration of salesman capabilities in quota determination. Also, in some firms salesmen are involved in the process. A major problem in judgmental quota determination by management is the difficulty of systematically processing the various types of information that should be considered.

The selection of proper criteria to use for performance standards must be largely based on management's experience and judgment. Factors selected should be those that are believed to favorably influence desired operating results. Possible determinants of sales performance where the salesman work unit is a geographic territory are shown in Figure 22–3. Note that several of the determinants are beyond control of the salesman (e.g., market potential, workload). By careful assessment of potential performance determinants, those of major significance in a given organization can be selected. Then, as illustrated below, systematic analysis of these factors can be of substantial value in improving the effectiveness of management judgment and experience.

---

[22] For an expanded discussion of quotas see Stanton and Buskirk, *Management of the Sales Force*, Chapter 22.

FIGURE 22–3

Determinants of Sales Territory Performance

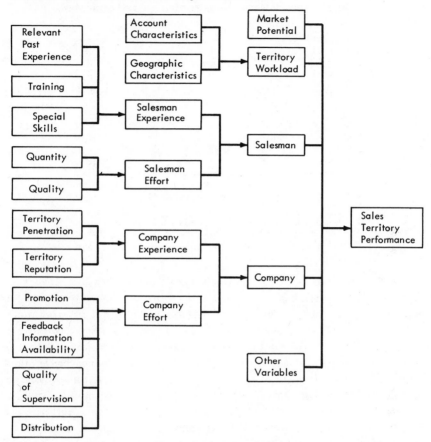

Source: Reproduced by permission of the American Marketing Association from David W. Cravens, Robert B. Woodruff, and Joe C. Stamper, "An Analytical Approach for Evaluating Sales Territory Performance," *Journal of Marketing*, 36 (January 1972), p. 32.

One promising analytical approach to developing performance standards is to investigate the relationship in a given organization between performance targets (criteria) and possible predictors (determinants) of performance.[23] If a relationship describing all work units can be developed by statistical analysis between a performance factor such as sales volume and possible predictors (e.g., market potential, salesman experience, workload, etc.), then standards can be generated for each sales-

---

[23] For an expanded discussion of this approach see David W. Cravens and Robert B. Woodruff, "An Approach for Determining Criteria of Sales Performance," *Journal of Applied Psychology*, 57:3 (1973), pp. 242–47.

TABLE 22–2

Summary of Stepwise Multiple Regression Analysis Using Data Transformed to Logarithmic Values

Step Number	*Variable Entered**	*Multiple R_2*
1........	Length of employment	.730
2........	Average market share	.809
3........	Salesman performance rating	.871
4........	Advertising expenditures	.876
5........	Average workload per account	.878
6........	Number of accounts	.879
7........	Average market share change	.879
8........	Industry sales	.879

* The predictor measures included in the regression relationship at a given step consist of the measure shown for that step plus measures shown for all previous steps.

Source: Copyright 1973 by the American Psychological Association. Reprinted by permission from David W. Cravens and Robert B. Woodruff, "An Approach for Determining Criteria of Sales Performance," *Journal of Applied Psychology*, 57:3 (1973), p. 244.

man work unit. Standards can be developed from the statistical relationship which then provide the salesman a performance benchmark that has been adjusted for factors beyond his control. For example, a preliminary analysis using multiple regression for 25 salesman work units (in this case geographical territories) of an appliance manufacturer is shown in Table 22–2. Sales volume (in dollars) was the performance criterion. A substantial portion of the variation in sales across territories was accounted for by the eight predictor variables thus indicating a reasonably strong relationship. All eight variables except "salesman performance rating" are beyond control of the salesman. A subsequent multiple regression analysis was performed using only length of employment, and average market share (weighed average for prior four years) as predictors; the predicted values of sales for each sales territory were used as performance benchmarks (standards).

A ranking of the 25 territories according to sales, benchmark achievement (predicted/actual sales), management rating of the salesman, and quota achievement is shown in Table 22–3. There is no observable relationship between management's ratings of salesman (Column 4) and assigned quotas, (Column 5). Note there is little consistency in the rankings of Column 4 compared to 5. Yet there is an apparent relationship between benchmark performance (Column 3) and ratings of the salesman (Column 4). Moreover, this relationship was found to be statistically significant.[24]

---

[24] The Spearman rank-correlation coefficient (r_s) for the benchmark relationship was 0.61 (significant at the 0.001 level). The quota relationship was not statistically significant.

TABLE 22–3

Territory Rankings Based on Sales Volume, Benchmark Achievement, Quota Achievement, and Performance Ratings

(1) Territory Number	(2) Sales Volume	(3) Benchmark Achievement	(4) Management Rating	(5) Quota Achievement
1	15	2	4	1
2	6	9	2	16
3	18	7	20	15
4	8	23	17	22
5	2	5	5	17
6	24	17	7	2
7	3	16	6	24
8	12	25	24	18
9	1	4	3	13
10	5	10	21	19
11	19	20	18	9
12	22	15	9	4
13	20	8	8	8
14	21	11	10	6
15	4	1	1	14
16	11	21	14	21
17	9	14	15	20
18	13	3	11	11
19	14	13	13	10
20	10	18	19	25
21	23	22	25	5
22	16	19	16	12
23	25	24	23	3
24	7	6	22	23
25	17	12	12	7

Source: Cravens and Woodruff, "An Approach for Determining Criteria of Sales Performance" p. 245.

If one assumes that sales management can establish reasonable ratings of salesmen, then the results suggest that the analytically determined performance standards are more relevant than the judgmentally determined quotas (which were based largely on market potential). Since the rankings of benchmark performance and management ratings are not similar for all territories (see for example territories 3, 7, 10, and 24), use of an analytical performance standard that adjusts for factors beyond the salesman's control can help management improve salesman evaluation processes. Since it is difficult for management to systematically consider the relevant determinants of performance without some method of processing the information (such as the analytical approach described above), it is not surprising that the rankings of ratings (Column 4) vary somewhat from the rankings of benchmark achievement (Column 3). Management in the firm, after review of the analytically determined performance standards, indicated that the standards appeared to be appropriate gauges of salesman performance. An executive of the appliance firm indicated that the results of the analysis supported management's dissatisfaction with the existing quota system and reinforced their judgment about the performance of various salesmen.

Other performance criteria can be used in this same type of approach. For example, standards can be developed for profit contribution and for various product groups. Personal selling objectives should be linked to performance criteria. Moreover, analytical tools should be used to assist management rather than in place of judgment and experience. The various factors that must be taken into account in evaluating and controlling the sales force can never be completely accounted for in analytical models. Yet use of these tools can substantially increase the effectiveness of management's judgment and experience.

SUMMARY AND CONCLUSIONS

The sales force is a major element of the marketing mix in many organizations. Personal selling along with advertising make up a substantial portion of the marketing manager's budget. The role and scope of the personal selling function is constantly changing throughout American business and industry.[25] The impact upon personal selling practices of communications technology, social change, and other factors will significantly influence the area in the decade ahead. Various trends such as increased customer concentration, centralized purchasing, system selling, and programmed merchandising promise to cause major alterations in the nature of personal selling.[26]

In this and the previous chapter a perspective has been developed toward the personal selling function and the major sales force decision-making areas examined. Sales management decisions consist of an integrated system of actions aimed at achieving the objectives assigned to the selling organization. Estimating sales response is a key guideline for making sales force size and allocation decisions. Based on these decisions (which are typically revised over time due to changing opportunities and conditions) various activities comprise the ongoing salesmen training, supervision and motivation, and evaluation and control tasks.

---

[25] The entire issue of *Sales Management* (February 21, 1972) is devoted to a critical look at the new era of the salesman.

[26] These trends are discussed in greater detail in David T. Kollat, Roger D. Blackwell, and James F. Robeson, *Strategic Marketing* (New York: Holt, Rinehart and Winston, Inc., 1972), pp. 369–72.

EXERCISES FOR DISCUSSION AND REVIEW

The California Tennis Company is a national distributor of tennis racquets, tennis balls, and tennis clothes (shirts, shorts, socks, shoes, and dresses). The firm's products comprise two major lines:

1. Tennis racquets and balls   (Product Line 1)
2. Tennis clothes   (Product Line 2)

The products are sold to two basic classes of customers: (1) sporting goods stores; and (2) tennis club pro shops. The company is currently using three different sales people: Jim, George and Judith. Each salesperson has been assigned to a different geographic area. Various types of information for each of the sales territories are shown on the next page. Questions 1 through 5 below are in reference to the California Tennis Company.

1. Indicate which categories of information in the table should be used to compare the relative performance of the three salespeople. Support your recommendations. Suggest additional types of information that would be helpful in making a more complete assessment of the performance of California Tennis Company's sales force.

2. How would you evaluate the relative performance of the three sales people? What are your recommendations as to possible changes in the deployment of the firm's sales force? Make any reasonable assumptions that are needed in developing your recommendations.

3. Assuming that California Tennis Company's selling price is the same to both sporting goods stores and tennis pro shops make an assessment of the responsiveness of sales to the firm's selling effort in the two types of retail outlets. Based upon your analysis can you suggest possible changes in sales coverage that should be made, or alternatively support the firm's existing practices.

4. The owner of the California Tennis Company has been considering the installation of an incentive plan for the three salespeople. Salespeople are currently compensated on a straight salary basis. Beyond the information contained in the table, what would you need to determine in order to begin development of an incentive plan.

5. Are there possible sales force management problems and/or areas of analysis beyond those considered in questions 1 through 4 that you feel should be investigated based upon your analysis of the information in the above table? Support your points.

6. Prepare a comparative assessment of the task of measurement of advertising effectiveness with sales force effectiveness (both in terms of individual salesmen and the total sales force).

7. Assume you have been asked by the vice president of sales of a pharmaceutical firm to develop a sales force evaluation program. Outline an approach to this assignment, including in your discussion the specific types of information that will be needed and how you would propose to obtain the information.

California Tennis Company Sales Territory Information—Year 1975

	Salesman											
	Jim			Alex			Judith			Totals		
Product Line*	1	2	Total	1	2	Total	1	2	Total	1	2	Total
Total Sales ($)	144,000	96,000	240,000	42,000	92,000	134,000	48,000	56,000	104,000	234,000	244,000	478,000
Sporting goods stores ($)	88,000	64,000	152,000	32,000	64,000	96,000	20,000	32,000	52,000	140,000	160,000	300,000
Tennis pro shops ($)	56,000	32,000	88,000	10,000	28,000	38,000	28,000	24,000	52,000	94,000	84,000	178,000
Calls made (total)			1,000			1,200			900			3,100
Sporting goods stores			400			700			450			1,550
Tennis pro shops			600			500			450			1,550
Orders taken (total)			600			800			800			2,200
Sporting goods stores			300			600			420			1,320
Tennis pro shops			300			200			380			880
Number of days worked			220			240			230			690
Expenses ($)			20,000			15,000			20,000			55,000
Miles traveled			10,000			16,000			7,000			33,000
Market potential total ($)	400,000	300,000	700,000	240,000	480,000	720,000	340,000	100,000	440,000	980,000	880,000	1,860,000
Sporting goods stores ($)	240,000	140,000	380,000	160,000	320,000	480,000	172,000	80,000	252,000	572,000	540,000	1,112,000
Tennis pro shops ($)	160,000	160,000	320,000	80,000	160,000	240,000	168,000	20,000	188,000	408,000	340,000	748,000

* Product Line 1: Tennis racquets and balls; Product Line 2: Tennis clothes.

23

Controlling the Marketing Program

The continuing task of managing the marketing program draws from the concepts and decision approaches developed and examined in the various chapters of this book. These have been grouped into analysis of the marketing environment; analysis of market opportunities; and marketing strategy development, implementation, and control. The marketing manager is faced with myriad decisions associated with controlling the marketing program to minimize the gap between planned and actual results. This on-going management activity should be accomplished within the marketing management framework provided by Figure 1–2 in Chapter 1, and the various decision process frameworks for specific decision areas discussed throughout the book. Illustrative marketing management control activities include the following:

Strategies must be modified to account for changing environmental conditions, competitive actions, and market needs. Consider, for example, the changes that were made in the pricing of handheld calculators which sold for over $200 in 1971 and were available in 1975 for less than $20.

Products' contributions to corporate goals must be periodically evaluated and those found to be unacceptable must be modified and/or eliminated. The Wurlitzer Co.'s announcement in 1974 to phase out of the "jukebox" business in the United States is illustrative of a decision to eliminate a product no longer profitable to the firm.[1]

Controlling existing products may identify new market opportunities which provide inputs into new product development programs. Consider, for example, the test marketing by the Gillette Co. in 1974 of

[1] "Wurlitzer Phases Out U.S. Jukebox Business; Will Continue in Europe," *Vending Time* (April 1974), p. 49.

723

various items for indoor plant care (e.g., planters, potting soil, plant foods) through supermarkets as a part of the firm's overall strategy to diversify its product offerings in consumer markets.[2]

The effectiveness of the marketing program and the various elements of the mix must be assessed on a continuing basis. Hershey Foods, in the 1960s, first began using advertising as an active element of the firm's marketing mix.

In this chapter, to round out our perspective of the marketing management task, certain key aspects of the ongoing management task are considered. We are assuming that the firm has an existing marketing program and is concerned with controlling the performance of this program to achieve operating objectives. The various concepts, approaches to decision analysis, and related discussions of marketing decision making examined in prior chapters provide a basic framework for this task. First a framework for the evaluation and control process is developed. Next, major areas of evaluation of marketing activities are outlined and discussed. Finally, an application of the control process for analysis of possible products or services to be dropped from a firm's line is discussed and illustrated.

THE CONTROL PROCESS

Marketing strategy is rarely constant. Various uncontrollable factors and variations from predicted responses to the marketing mix bring about the need for marketing program modifications. Recall that our definition of marketing management in Chapter 1 included *planning, implementation,* and *control* functions for the marketing decision maker. While control may appear less challenging than planning, it is a crucial activity in marketing management. Moreover, control and planning are closely linked in that "a plan should be the mirror image of a company's control devices."[3] Since the marketing plan indicates the firm's marketing objectives and the strategies to be used for achieving desired results, it provides a basis for comparing actual results to planned results. Control is the means by which the marketing manager assures accomplishment of the marketing plan.

In Chapter 1 the control process was described in terms of the following major groups of activities:

Determination of which aspects of marketing strategy and tactics should be controlled.

---

[2] "Bucking the Trend, Gillette Pushes Plan to Diversify Products," *The Wall Street Journal* (November 8, 1974), p. 1.

[3] Sanford R. Simon, *Managing Market Profitability* (New York: American Management Association, Inc., 1969), p. 180.

Determination of the performance standards against which actual results can be measured.

Development of formal (and informal) information systems to provide the marketing manager with information on the results of marketing strategy actions.

Comparison and evaluation of marketing program results against performance standards.

Determination of needed modifications in marketing strategy and tactics to improve gaps in marketing performance.

Each of the control activities is interrelated to all others in the process. For example, if performance areas to be monitored are not correctly determined and consistent with what marketing strategy is intended to accomplish, then resulting control efforts will be ineffective (and possibly harmful). Consider the following illustration:

> Sales targets were specified as the primary performance criterion for the field sales force of a large manufacturing firm. Upon review of results for the past year the marketing manager found that sales quotas were achieved in all sales regions. Yet the bulk of sales was accomplished in two product lines, both with low profit contribution margins. Sales in the firm's remaining two product lines actually declined compared to sales in the prior year. Thus, through primary emphasis on meeting sales quotas, profitability was adversely affected.

The control process is shown in Figure 23–1. It will be helpful to examine each of the major stages.

What Should Be Controlled. In order to develop an effective control process, those elements of the program that are critical to achieving desired results must be identified and proper mechanisms established for monitoring the activities. The marketing manager must determine the results areas, when successfully completed, that will indicate the degree of success of the marketing program. Also, those managers responsible for particular areas such as advertising and sales force should likewise identify key results areas. In terms of the total marketing program illustrative areas to be monitored include sales, market share, profit contributions, mix of products sold, marketing program costs, and competitive activities. Monitoring of a particular marketing mix area such as the sales force might include assessment of these same areas for the firm's sales regions, districts, or by individual salesmen.

Performance Standards. After key performance areas have been determined, it is necessary to specify appropriate standards against which actual performance can be judged. Objectives that are set for each market target provide an overall framework for determination of marketing program performance standards. These objectives should be expressed if at all possible in quantifiable terms (e.g., 5 percent increase in market

FIGURE 23–1

**Overview of the Marketing
Management Control Process**

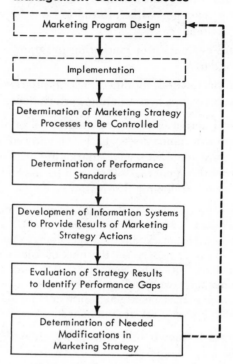

share by the end of 12 months). Working within overall objectives, performance standards can be developed in the detail appropriate for control purposes. Standards should be developed for each level of control (e.g., marketing division, sales department, sales region or district, individual salesman work unit) and for various marketing activities (e.g., advertising).

The management by objectives (MBO) approach to planning and evaluation of marketing activities provides a useful basis for linking plans and results together.[4] The MBO system of management involves a participative approach between superior and subordinate of developing specific results targets and measures to be used to monitor results achievement. Plans and performance standards are generated together, and allow the individual considerable opportunity for setting his or her perform-

---

[4] See for example, Michael J. Etzel and John M. Ivancevich, "Management by Objectives in Marketing: Philosophy, Process, and Problems," *Journal of Marketing*, 38 (October 1974), pp. 47–55.

ance benchmarks. An illustrative performance and action plan for a divisional sales manager is shown in Figure 23–2. Note for example on item 1 that the objective statement (results target) is a 10 percent market penetration. Specific actions intended to facilitate accomplishment of this objective over a one year period are indicated on a quarterly basis. On item 1 the divisional manager is falling somewhat short of the target, but is ahead of targets set for items 2 and 3. This type of plan which includes quantified results targets and means of achieving them provides the superior and his subordinate with a specific basis for both planning and monitoring marketing activities.

Performance standards need to be related to each market target since ultimately results should be tied back to performance in selected market areas.[5] The marketing objectives established for each market target provide a basis for developing performance benchmarks at each level of control and for each major marketing activity area (e.g., advertising, sales force, etc.). For example, advertising program performance should be evaluated in terms of its effectiveness in accomplishing specified results (e.g., increase in level of customer awareness, attitude change, level of exposure, etc.).

Information Planning. Once key results areas and performance standards are specified, they serve to identify the information that is needed to perform the control function. If not already available, information should be planned for and acquired providing the cost-benefits are favorable. It is essential that control information provided to the marketing manager and his staff be matched to needs. An illustrative marketing data base of a consumer specialty food manufacturer is shown in Figure 23–3. A typical marketing data base might include information on internal operations (salesmen's call reports, costs, etc.); customer information; channel information; competitive intelligence; and environmental information (e.g., technological trends, social change, etc.).

Evaluation of Performance. In order for the control process to operate, actual results must be compared to planned levels of performance. Without this evaluation of performance, there is no basis for taking corrective action where needed. Sales and cost trend analysis is one of the most widely used management control tools. Analysis of sales and costs by market target, product line, geographical area, and sales territory should be a regular activity of the marketing manager. Formal budgeting procedures, break even analysis, and return-on-investment are illustrative of the types of marketing programming guidelines that can be developed through sales and cost analysis. An understanding of basic performance and decision oriented accounting principles and practices is an

---

[5] An approach to market segment profitability analysis is provided in Frank H. Mossman, Paul M. Fischer, and W. J. E. Crissy, "New Approaches to Analyzing Marketing Profitability," *Journal of Marketing*, 38 (April 1974), pp. 43–48.

FIGURE 23–2
Sample Planning and Performance Evaluation Form

Performance and Action Plan for John Smith—Divisional Sales Manager

Objective Statement	3 months Pro-jected	3 months Actual	Plan	6 months Pro-jected	6 months Actual	Plan	9 months Pro-jected	9 months Actual	Plan	1 year Pro-jected	1 year Actual
1. Expand in S.W. region and achieve 10% market penetration	1%	.5%	Temporary transfer of salesmen to S.W. territory	4%	3.5%	Increase advertising expenditure 10%	7%	5.5%	Develop sales promotion to counter competition	10%	
2. Increase profit on product line A by 7% over 2 years	.25%	.25%	Continue rate & type of promotion, continue expense reduction	.5%	.6%	Watch other product lines for losses at the expense of this increase	1.5%	2.1%	Consider readjusting goal if performance continues	3%	
3. Select 2 salesmen for territorial sales management positions out of 20 initial candidates	2	20	Rotate candidates with most potential in district mgr.'s office	2	11	Allow each candidate to participate in significant "people" decisions	2	5	Allow each candidate to participate in significant "strategy" decisions	2	

Source: Reprinted by permission from Michael J. Etzel and John M. Ivancevich, "Management by Objectives in Marketing: Philosophy, Process, and Problems," *Journal of Marketing*, 38 (October 1974), p. 51, published by the American Marketing Association.

FIGURE 23–3

Illustrative Marketing Data Base*

Measures of Retail Activity
  Consumer purchases
  Retail prices
  Stores carrying product/s (percent)
  Stores out of stock of product/s (percent)

Measures of Competitive Activity
  Product or package changes
  New products
  Price changes
  Special promotions
  Advertising activities

Measures of Internal Activity and Performance
  Factory sales
  Expenses by type of marketing activity
  Costs of special marketing activities

Measures of Consumer Reaction
  Consumers using product
  Brand awareness and usage
  Attitudes toward brands
  Use habits of brand users
  Product experience
  Brand experience

* See Edward Dalton Company Case in Robert D. Buzzell, Donald F. Cox, and Rex V. Brown, *Marketing Research and Information Systems* (New York: McGraw-Hill Book Co., 1969), pp. 45–50.

essential marketing management capability.[6] Sales and cost analysis is fundamental to effective marketing planning and control. An illustrative sales and cost analysis for a group of field sales districts is shown in Table 23–1. When this information is compared with performance standards such as the desired earnings index for each district, problem areas can be identified. For example, study of the district comparisons in Table 23–1 indicates that Southwest sales area should be examined in greater depth to determine why its earnings performance is relatively low compared to the other districts. Causes of such deviations from the significantly higher performance levels of other districts should be identified

---

[6] An excellent, comprehensive discussion of decision-oriented accounting principles and practices for use by marketing management is provided in Sanford R. Simon, *Managing Marketing Profitability* (New York: American Management Association, Inc., 1969).

TABLE 23–1

THE BADGER LIGHT COMPANY
Statement of Territorial Earnings, Wholesale Division
Year Ended December 31, 1968
(000s omitted)

| | Total Wholesale | | | | | *Districts* | | | |
		New England	Metropolitan New York City	Middle Atlantic	South	Metropolitan Chicago	Midwest	Southwest	West
Gross sales	$20,229	$2,436	$1,407	$4,213	$2,646	$1,417	$2,946	$ 643	$4,521
Profit contribution	7,565	922	520	1,583	1,000	504	1,097	232	1,707
Profit contribution percentage	37.5%	37.9%	37.0%	37.6%	37.8%	35.6%	37.2%	36.1%	37.8%
Specific district expenses	1,606	124	170	192	231	163	171	295	260
District earnings	5,959	$ 798	$ 350	$1,391	$ 769	$ 341	$ 926	$ (63)	$1,447
District earnings–index	0.79	0.87	0.67	0.88	0.77	0.68	0.84	(0.27)	0.85
General district expenses	443								
Wholesale division earnings	$ 5,516								

Source: Reprinted by permission of the publisher from Sanford R. Simon, *Managing Marketing Profitability* (© 1969 by American Management Association), p. 90.

and projections of future trends developed. This information can then be used to guide necessary changes in strategy. For example, the Southwest district appears to have very high expenses compared to gross sales. This is typical of the variety of sales and cost comparisons that provide useful tools for marketing decision makers in strategy design and control.

The identification of gaps in actual performance compared to standards normally does not provide the reason for unsatisfactory performance. Management is alerted to a problem area and must identify and analyze possible causes. Because of the interrelationships of marketing mix elements, it may be necessary to examine several program areas to pinpoint the factors contributing to poor performance. Moreover, external changes, such as adverse economic conditions or increased competitive activity, may be responsible. Information used to monitor marketing program performance can help the marketing manager locate areas where his attention should be directed. These tools cannot perform the essential management function of determining where the real problems exist and what corrective actions are needed. Thus, performance evaluation should be a combination of control information, analysis, and management judgment and experience.

Taking Corrective Action. The final link in the control process is taking corrective action where indicated through performance evaluation efforts. Strategy modifications may be necessary to shift the marketing program in the direction of desired results. Changes in strategy should not necessarily be viewed as the result of poor strategy design. Well designed plans frequently require revision over time as conditions change and as uncertainties are reduced. A perfect plan is rare in practice. Marketing management is a process of human activities and decision makers are faced with estimating market response in a competitive environment. This places a significant responsibility upon the control function in the marketing management process.

Managing the product recall is an example of corrective action taken in response to product performance problems in consumer durable goods industries. One of the perils of the mass production era is the need for recalling faulty products from customers for modification or replacement. Management of the product recall has become a significant element of marketing activities for the existing products of many firms. For example, in 1973 General Motors Corporation identified a motor mount problem and was required by law to notify 6.5 million car owners by certified mail to take their automobiles in for dealer inspection at a postage cost of about $3.5 million.[7] The increasing quality control problems of mass produced consumer products plus expansion of protection actions by government and consumer crusaders are forcing producers to tighten

---

[7] "Managing the Product Recall," *Business Week* (January 26, 1974), p. 46.

their monitoring of product quality and to develop effective systems for recalling products from the marketplace. The recall effort is a complex and expensive management task because of the typically large number of products, problems in locating and communicating with buyers, and overall development of a reverse distribution system. Because of the dangers of adverse consumer reactions associated with poor handling of a product recall, several large firms have designed recall plans for use if needed. Thus, they have developed plans for taking corrective action should the need occur.

AREAS OF EVALUATION

Assessment of marketing activities may occur at three different levels. These include:

Strategy positioning analysis leading to possible modifications in product-market strategy.

Monitoring of marketing program effectiveness for a given strategy position which may identify needed changes in the various elements of the marketing mix.

Assessment of the effectiveness of resource utilization in a particular mix area such as advertising or personal selling.

These three levels of management assessment are interrelated as shown in Figure 23–4. For example, if the firm occupying the balancing strategy position shown in Figure 23–4 decided to develop a market retention strategy by expanding its existing markets, the shift would require major changes in the firm's current marketing program. End users in the expanded markets would need to be made aware of the firm's product through advertising and/or personal selling efforts, new channels of distribution would be required, and pricing policies relative to channel intermediaries and end users would need to be reviewed. The higher level decisions establish a framework for management action at lower levels. To gain further insights into the nature and scope of management evaluation processes, each level will be examined.

Strategy Positioning Analysis

To establish a perspective toward strategy positioning analysis consider a firm with an existing line of products. Recall in Chapter 10 the marketing strategy positions that correspond to an existing product include balancing, market retention, and market development situations. In these positions, the chief marketing executive can link the firm's existing products to existing, expanded, or new markets. Many firms are continually appraising markets to identify expanded as well as totally

FIGURE 23-4

Levels of Evaluation of Marketing Activities

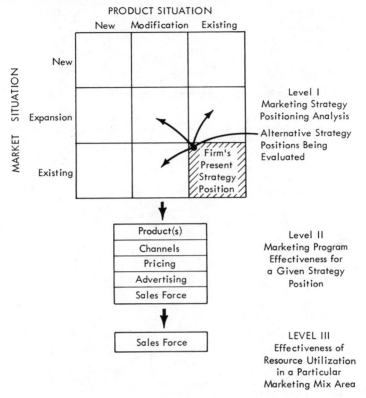

new market opportunities. Thus, a balancing strategy may be modified to facilitate moving into other markets.

Certain implications regarding marketing strategy for existing products should be recognized. Emphasis is upon managing the on-going marketing program. To a large extent, strategy is well established. The major task of the marketing manager is to monitor program performance and modify strategy and tactics to respond to changing opportunities and problems that develop. His function is to narrow the gap between objectives and results, thus achieving performance levels that are so close as possible to marketing objectives. Control is an essential activity of the marketing strategy process for existing products.

Consider for example the strategy implications of the shift in the hosiery market from pantyhose to knee-high as shown in Figure 23-5. The trend in women's fashions from skirts and dresses to slacks and pantsuits in the mid-1970s had a major impact upon hosiery manufacturers:

. . . today's fashion emphasis on pants has left the $1-billion industry bagging at the knees and tugging in all directions to right itself. Women have discovered to their delight that pants will camouflage any runs or tears in their pantyhose, making it unnecessary to buy as many pairs as before. And that the pants permit them to wear knee-length hose, which cost less.[8]

FIGURE 23–5

The Shift in the Hosiery Market: From Pantyhose to Knee-High

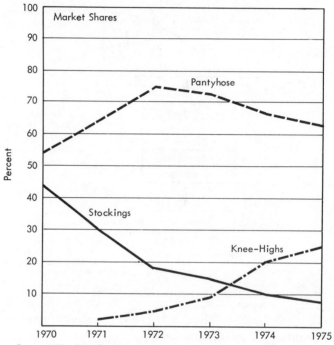

Source: "The New Sag in Pantyhose," *Business Week* (December 14, 1974), p. 98. Data by Market Research Corporation of America.

The decreasing size of the market reduced profit margins, intensified price competition, generated false advertising claims, and stimulated efforts for product differentiation and quality improvements.[9]

Three major areas of assessment in strategy positioning analysis are: (1) environmental monitoring; (2) market opportunity analysis; and (3) product life cycle analysis. Environmental monitoring should seek to identify new opportunities and threats to existing products and markets,

---

[8] "The New Sag in Pantyhose," *Business Week* (December 14, 1974), p. 98.

[9] Ibid., pp. 99–100.

and possible needed changes in strategy positioning. Where changes appear necessary, the means of achieving possible strategy shifts should be identified. The concepts and methods of analysis discussed in Part II of the book provide essential guidelines for managerial analysis of the marketing environment. A fundamental aspect of environmental analysis is obtaining necessary information for use in strategic analysis. King and Cleland recommend that a systematic effort be made to develop environmental information monitoring systems in the areas shown in Figure 23–6.[10] Analysis of these types of information may suggest a need for

FIGURE 23–6

Information Areas for Environmental Monitoring

Image Information: Assessment of the firm's status in the marketplace in terms of its history and its environment with regard to product image and organizational image.

Customer Information: Identification of aggregate market characteristics and probable trends over time.

Potential Customer Information: Determination of potential customer groups for existing and possible new products or services.

Competitive Information: Development of competitor profiles including key personnel, strategies, capabilities, and performance.

Regulatory Information: Identification and monitoring of governmental regulations and constraints that are relevant to the firms industry, markets, and operations.

Intelligence Information: Design of intelligence gathering approaches to provide systematic monitoring of events and trends in the environment.

strategy changes. If so, market opportunity analysis and product life cycle analysis can provide specific guidelines for accomplishing strategy positioning shifts.

Market Opportunity Analysis. Marketing management should continually be assessing the firm's performance in existing markets and also be attempting to identify vacant niches within the product market that existing products can be directed toward. Segmentation analysis plays a key role in strategy positioning for existing products. Identification of market segments where the firm's opportunities and strengths are great-

---

[10] William R. King and David I. Cleland, "Environmental Information Systems for Strategic Marketing Planning," *Journal of Marketing,* 38 (October 1974), pp. 35–40, published by the American Marketing Association.

est can offer important differential advantages over competition. In mature markets for existing products a segmentation strategy is frequently essential due to the strong competitive situations that exist. By establishing priorities in the most promising segments the firm can focus its resources to provide comprehensive coverage of selected segments. The concepts and approaches to market opportunity analysis discussed in Part III provide a systematic basis for regular monitoring of market opportunities.

When a firm chooses to expand into new markets with an existing product, changes in marketing strategy are typically necessary. For example, failure to recognize variations that occur in markets in different geographical areas can adversely affect marketing performance. A marketing mix that works effectively in one region of the country for a particular product may not prove effective in another area due to differences in buyers and prevailing marketing practices. Although the same product is involved, different geographical regions may require changes in distribution relationships, pricing, advertising, and sales force. Recall, for example, the discussion in Chapter 1 of Rheingold's unsuccessful attempt in the 1950s to use a marketing mix on the West Coast identical to that used in New York.[11]

Product Life Cycle Analysis.   Strategy positioning analysis should identify products in the line that have reached the mature stage of their life cycles. Regular monitoring of product life cycles provides vital information for product planning activities, and for guiding needed modifications in the firm's marketing program. New products may be needed to overcome declining profit contribution of older products. Certain products may be candidates for elimination from the enterprise's product line. Alternatively, product modification may be necessary.

Stage in the product life cycle can be used as a frame of reference for determining the competitive value of market share at different stages.[12] Based upon size of market share, competitive factors, and stage of the product life cycle a firm may pursue a marketing strategy designed to (1) increase, (2) decrease, or (3) maintain market share. For example, experience suggests that with mature markets and products attempting to increase market share may present a formidable task and may not yield desired profit levels. Ford, after its unsuccessful venture with the Edsel ended up with an almost identical market share to that held before the introduction of the automobile. The intent of the Edsel strategy was to gain market share from General Motors. In general, increasing

---

[11] Thomas L. Berg, *Mismarketing: Case Histories of Marketing Misfires* (Garden City, N.Y.: Doubleday and Co., 1971), pp. 160–62.

[12] Bernard Catry and Michel Chevalier, "Market Share Strategy and the Product Life Cycle," *Journal of Marketing*, 38 (October 1974), pp. 29–34, published by the American Marketing Association.

market share is a more promising strategy alternative at early stages of a product life cycle, particularly for firms with small market share.[13]

While strategy shifts typically do not occur in a frequent basis, marketing management, in coordination with top management, should, on a periodic basis, examine existing strategy positions for the firm's market targets in seeking to maintain effective strategy positions for existing products and markets, and to realign strategies when appropriate and consistent with the corporate mission.

Marketing Program Effectiveness

The integrative nature of the marketing mix necessitates examining its effectiveness as a total program of efforts aimed at achieving marketing objectives for designated market targets. There are two possible approaches to effectiveness assessment: (1) determination of whether the necessary marketing decision processes are being performed, and how well they are accomplished; and (2) determination of the contribution of the marketing function to the overall performance of the organization. Program effectiveness need not be restricted to one or the other of the two approaches.

The first approach focuses upon whether the marketing function has been planned and executed according to sound marketing management concepts and guidelines. This type of analysis is referred to as an audit of marketing operations. Have appropriate market targets been selected? Have marketing objectives been explicitly stated? Are the marketing tasks being performed? Is an appropriate organizational design being utilized? Has an integrated marketing mix been developed? Are the role and scope of each mix element specified? Has needed information planning been incorporated into marketing management decision processes? Are revenue-cost results in line with projections? These types of questions are illustrative of the marketing program evaluation task.

The second approach essentially rests upon determining the impact of the marketing program upon corporate or organizational performance. For example, mass transit organizations in urban communities have been criticized for failing to develop an innovative marketing program designed to attract ridership and contribute to solving urban problems such as congestion, energy conservation, and automobile pollution. Yet, the nature and magnitude of the impact of the marketing function upon the overall performance of transit organization is difficult to measure with any degree of precision. In most enterprises it is not possible to measure in a quantitative manner the contribution of the marketing

---

[13] See Catry and Chevalier, "Market Share Strategy and the Product Life Cycle," p. 33 for an analysis of possible market share strategies for small, average, and dominant size firms at different product life cycle stages.

function to operating results. (e.g., sales, profit contribution, market share, etc.). In practice, it is normally necessary to judgmentally make this assessment by determining via the first approach the extent to which the marketing function is being accomplished. If the results of this assessment and overall operating results are both favorable, then this suggests that the marketing program is performing in an effective manner.

Consider the case of a firm manufacturing and marketing three major product lines in industrial markets served by the firm and three competing firms.[14] By analyzing marketing program effectiveness in terms of competition considerable insight may be gained as to needed changes in the overall marketing effort. An illustrative competitive analysis is shown in Figure 23–7. The information needed for this type of assessment may be obtained from the firm's marketing personnel, channel intermediaries, and product end users. In addition to internal operating information and judgment and experience inputs, marketing research and intelligence gathering may be necessary (e.g., survey of the firm's distributors). In the Figure 23–7 example, various components of the marketing program have been assessed by management in terms of market share performance and certain key strategic conclusions have been reached concerning product policy, competitive strategy, marketing strategy and service. This type of assessment can be used to evaluate present market standing and to identify appropriate changes in marketing strategy designed to improve performance. In this example market share gain has been used as a criterion of marketing performance.

Mix Component Effectiveness

Considerable attention has been given to the evaluation of mix component effectiveness in the previous chapters. At this level of marketing evaluation the focus is upon the efficiency of resources used for a given element of the mix (e.g., advertising, sales force). The use of resources for every component of the marketing program should be evaluated on a continuing basis. Consider, for example, the sales-call analysis shown in Table 23–2. The information on calls and sales results has been assembled to help evaluate the productivity of the two salesmen assigned to the Buffalo, New York district office. Note the relative allocation of sales effort by Jones and Penn. The bulk of Jones' sales are contributed by five customers whereas most of Penn's sales are from twelve accounts, and his sales are over 50 percent greater than Jones. The break-even level of sales is about $95,000 on an annual basis. The company considers both men to be above average salesmen. Unless future sales gains from low

---

[14] C. Davis Fogg, "Planning Gains in Market Share," *Journal of Marketing* (July 1974), pp. 30–38, published by the American Marketing Association.

TABLE 23–2

Sales-Call Analysis for Salesmen in Buffalo, N.Y., District Office of North Eastern Region

Percent of Calls (current year)	Customer	Sales (in dollars)	
		Last Year	Current Year
Salesman: R. P. Jones			
6.4...................	XYZ Corp.	41,040	43,546
3.6...................	DUP, Inc.	4,262	5,230
8.4...................	ABC Co.	4,373	4,438
3.4...................	IRC, Inc.	1,272	1,254
0.9...................	Atomic, Inc.	888	951
22.7%................	5 accounts	51,835	55,419
77.3%................	68 accounts	14,291	15,735
100.0%................	73 accounts	$ 66,126	$ 71,154
Salesman: C. J. Penn			
15.6...................	CBR Co.	32,374	34,078
19.7...................	LAP, Inc.	22,331	21,948
6.8...................	Washington Corp.	5,429	5,868
0.9...................	MPC, Inc.	790	692
0.6...................	Auto-Engineering	4,420	7,702
1.8...................	Aero, Inc.	5,631	5,840
7.3...................	Chemical Process, Inc.	4,650	4,928
2.6...................	EBC Industries	5,102	4,696
3.2...................	AMC Rubber Co.	2,730	3,040
2.9...................	ACA, Inc.	4,130	4,502
2.1...................	Photo, Inc.	4,805	4,984
0.9...................	EPH Corp.	2,139	2,472
64.4.................	12 accounts	94,531	100,750
35.6.................	29 accounts	8,730	9,700
100.0%................	41 accounts	$103,261	$110,450

producing accounts appear promising, it appears that better use of available sales effort can be made. For example, the most productive accounts of both salesmen could be handled by one person, thus making the other man available for assignment elsewhere.

This example is one of the many aspects of marketing mix component performance monitoring that should be accomplished by the marketing manager and his staff. Several illustrative types of effectiveness assessment are shown in Table 23–3. Management of each mix area should include regular evaluation activities. An essential part of this effort is the design of appropriate information feedback mechanisms to facilitate the monitoring process. The decision process frameworks developed in the prior chapters for product, channels of distribution, price, advertising, and sales force decisions provide a useful basis for identifying information needed for evaluation and control.

FIGURE 23–7

Illustrative Competitive Analysis

Competitive Dimensions	Market Size	Growth per Year	Us	A	B	C	Comments on Data
1. Product Position				Market Share			
Line 1	$15MM	0%	65%	20%	10%	5%	1. Not subject to share gain, manage for cash.
2	$30MM	10%	25%	40%	15%	20%	2. Subject to share gain, A most vulnerable, B, C less so.
3	$20MM	15%	10%	25%	30%	35%	3. Subject to share gain, A, B, C equally vulnerable. Substantial unfilled need for a new product.
2. Pricing Strategy							B and C will be easiest to take share away from on price, and it will be least expensive to maintain share taken away. A is more competitive, will require larger price differentials to gain and maintain share, and it is therefore more costly to take share away.
H = Price for margin	Line 1		C	C	C	H	
C = Price with market	2		C	L	C	C	
L = Price leader or very aggressive	3		C	L	C	C	
3. New Product Policy							Expect new products first from A, monitor market carefully to identify what they're working on—expect A to imitate earliest any new products introduced.
L = Leader	Line 1		L	L	F	F	
F = Follower	2		F	L	F	F	
	3		L	L	L	F	
4. Overall Marketing Strength							A strongest and equal to us. B and C vulnerable to more intensive selling effort offered by us.
No. Representatives	Line 1		5	10	15	15	
No. Distributors	2		40	35	30	30	
No. Salesmen	3		25	20	10	7	
5. Geographic Strength							We may be weak in district G and should consider adding salesmen, otherwise are equal or superior to competition.
No. Salesmen and Reps							
Territory E			9	7	7	6	
F			7	7	6	6	
G			5	8	7	6	
H			9	8	6	4	

6. **Distributor Strength**

No. Distributors

Territory				
E	12	10	8	7
F	10	9	7	8
G	10	9	7	7
H	8	7	6	6

A approximately equal in strength. B and C weaker and definitely vulnerable.

7. *Delivery Norm (weeks)*

Product				
1	6	6	4	7
2	6	3	4	4
3	6	6	7	9

Delivery improvements necessary in 1, 2 to be competitive. Improvement beyond competitive levels will not gain share. Improvement in line 3 will gain advantage against A, B and C according to sales force survey.

8. **Penetration by Account Size %**

$ Market—all products

40 Large	40%	30%	15%	15%
15 Medium	15%	30%	25%	30%
10 Small	10%	30%	20%	40%
$65MM				

We're weak in medium and small accounts, need program to improve penetration and coverage there.

9. **Probable Reaction to:**

- Lower price

  A—Immediate retaliation, continued price reduction to gain share back.

  B, C—Weaker response. Will try to hold large accounts.

  Cost in taking share away from A on price will be high. B and C more vulnerable.

- New product

  A—Will immediately match new product offering.

  C—May match immediately.

  B—Eventually match.

  B and to some extent C vulnerable to new product offering.

- Increased sales coverage

  A—Will match.

  B, C—Some increase.

  B and C vulnerable in some measure to sales coverage, particularly if a new product is launched.

Key Strategic Conclusions

1. *Product Policy:* Focus on lines 2 and 3 where gain is possible by increased penetration and growth with the market and product modification for product 3.

2. *Competitive Strategy:* Focus on taking share away from B and C, who are vulnerable to lower pricing and a new product innovation requested by salesmen. Selectively take business away from competitor A—only up to the point where expensive price retaliation is expected.

3. *Marketing Strategy:* Add three salesmen to territory G and one to F to build strength against key targets—B and C. Shift call pattern and develop mktg. programs for medium to small accounts where penetration is poor. Develop distributor promotion program to capitalize on advantage over B and C.

4. *Service:* Invest in capacity to lower delivery time in product 2 to level competitive with B and C. Maintain competitive standards in other lines.

Source: C. David Fogg, "Planning Gains in Market Share," *Journal of Marketing*, 38 (July 1974), p. 35, published by the American Marketing Association.

TABLE 23–3

Illustrative Marketing Mix Element Effectiveness Assessments

Mix Element	*Illustrative Types of Mix Element Effectiveness Assessments*
Product	Possible additions to product line. Product modification needs. Consideration of dropping product(s) from the line. Evaluation of packaging effectiveness. Assessment of costs of meeting warranty requirements.
Channels	Assessment of field warehouse inventory levels. Evaluation of alternative channel arrangements. Determination of sales and profit contributions of manufacturer representatives. Survey of dealer attitudes and opinions.
Price	Evaluation of the appropriateness of price margins at various levels of the channel of distribution. Consideration of a price reduction to increase sales and profits. Assessment of discount structure for various categories of buyers.
Advertising	Estimation of market potential in target markets reached with media presently utilized. Evaluation of the proportion of sales generated by return of magazine reader reply cards for product information. Assessment of the effectiveness of present outdoor sign locations.
Sales Force	Modification of sales force selection procedures. Establishment of sales force performance standards. Assessment of the effectiveness of an existing sales incentive plan. Quarterly performance discussions of sales manager with salesman.

ELIMINATING PRODUCTS: A CONTROL APPLICATION

The product drop decision is an application of the control process since candidates for elimination from a firm's line are identified as a result of management's regular monitoring of product performance. Examples of the variety of product drop decisions that occur include the following:

RCA's decision in 1971 to discontinue the manufacture and marketing of general purpose computers.

DuPont's termination in 1971 of Corfam production, a synthetic leather substitute for shoes, at a loss of about $100 million.

SCM Corp's elimination of U.S. Shetland-Lewyt canister vacuum cleaner line in 1972 (acquired in 1967) because of the product's continued unprofitability.[15]

Ford Motor Company's widely publicized failure with the Edsel automobile.

---

[15] "SCM Tries a Comeback with Fewer Products," *Business Week* (July 21, 1973), p. 43.

Time, Inc.'s discontinuation of the publication of *Life* magazine in 1972 due to competition from television for both readers and advertising revenues, and increasing production and distribution costs.

All products have limited lives, and thus must be eliminated at some point in the future. The advent of the energy crisis in late 1973 coupled with projections of shortages for the decade through 1985 for various raw materials has shifted the product drop decision from an important to critical position in corporate strategy. Although in the past poor performing products could dampen overall performance, there were adequate materials available to produce the various types and quantities that management determined appropriate in meeting corporate goals. Yet in future years, this option may not exist in many industries and firms. Thus, the product drop decision will become a much more active element of corporate strategy.

Reasons for retaining products presented by the sales force, manufacturing, and other areas of the organization can be very logical. For example, availability of a complete line of products provide a salesman with a strong capability in persuading customers to buy his firm's products. Also, determination of a particular product's contribution to operating results is admittedly difficult due to interrelated sales and costs with other products. Sales of many products are linked to sales of other products such as film for cameras, special purpose paper and supplies used in office equipment, filters for coffee makers, and automobile parts. Nevertheless, acknowledging the complexities of evaluating the performance of existing products the task is substantially less difficult than selecting new products for introduction to the marketplace. Moreover, elimination of a product from the line can yield important profit contributions and free scarce marketing resources to meet higher priority needs when conditions are appropriate for dropping the product.

The analysis related to determining whether or not to drop a product is similar to the management control effort involved in assessing the performance of any element in the marketing mix. Because of the pervasive nature of the product in the firm's operations, it is important that all relevant aspects of the decision situation be assessed. Product performance should be evaluated against expectations on a regular basis as a part of the on-going marketing control process. Product evaluation efforts can lead to three possible actions: (1) continuation of the product with no changes; (2) modification of the product to overcome problems identified in the evaluation process; or, (3) elimination of the product. The decision process leading to these three alternatives is shown in Figure 23–8. In the process of monitoring product performance, there may be no need to modify the product or to consider elimination of most of the firm's products. Once the decision is made to place a product on the

FIGURE 23–8

Evaluation Process for Existing Products

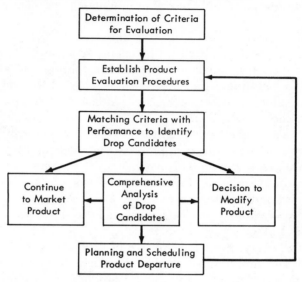

market normally there should be no reason to quickly consider the removal. As discussed in Chapter 15, new product decisions frequently require major resource commitments and these decisions should be based upon comprehensive evaluation in advance of product introduction. Thus, the number of products considered for possible elimination by a firm will be small at any particular point in time. The discussion in the remainder of this section is based on the premise that a continuing activity of product performance monitoring should occur, and when appropriate, a systematic process of product elimination should be initiated.

Criteria for Evaluation

Various criteria for use in evaluating the performance of products have been proposed.[16] These factors generally fall into five groups: per-

---

[16] See for example, David J. Luck, "Product Senility," in *Product Policy and Strategy* (Englewood Cliffs, N.J.: Prentice-Hall, 1972), pp. 71–78; James T. Rothe, "The Product Elimination Decision," *MSU Business Topics,* 18 (Autumn 1970), pp. 45–51; Philip Kotler, "Phasing out Weak Products," *Harvard Business Review* (March–April 1965), pp. 108–18; R. S. Alexander, "The Death and Burial of 'Sick' Products," *Journal of Marketing* (April 1964), pp. 1–7; Conrad Berenson, "Pruning the Product Line," *Business Horizons,* 6 (Summer 1973), pp. 20–26; and D'Orsey Hurst, "Criteria for Evaluating Existing Products and Product Lines," in *Analyzing and Improving Marketing Performance,* Report No. 32 (New York: American Management Association, Inc., 1959), pp. 91–101.

formance, customer, operational, channel participants and suppliers, and competitive. Several illustrative factors for each of these groups are shown in Figure 23–9. Certain of the factors can be quantified; others, such as the impact of a proposed product drop upon channel relationships, must be determined by executive judgment. The selection of a particular set of criteria to be used should be based upon management's assessment of the relevant factors related to product performance in a particular firm. Since these factors may be related to economic, market, and technical performance a team of executives, representing top management and the various functional areas of the firm, may be needed to select the criteria to be used for evaluating product performance. In addition to identifying proper criteria, attention should also be given to establishing the relative importance of different types of factors.

FIGURE 23–9

Illustrative Factors to Be Considered in Product Drop Decision

Performance
  sales and market share trends
  profit contribution
  financial requirements to support product
  costs
  price trends
  stage in product life cycle
Customer
  market impact of drop on firm's other products
  customer needs for product (e.g., social responsibility)
  interrelationships with firm's other products
  product/brand image contributed by product
Operational
  impact on production operations
  impact on marketing activities
  management time demands
  servicing requirements
  alternative uses of resources made available by drop
Channel Participatants and Suppliers
  impact on channel relationships
  sales and profit impact on channel members
  probable reaction of suppliers to drop
Competitive
  advantages drop will provide competition
  competitive product strengths

Evaluation Procedures

Formal procedures should be established for regular monitoring of the performance of a firm's products. In cases where the number of products in the line is large, it may be appropriate to utilize a computer in the evaluation process. Alternatively, an evaluation team made up of representatives of key functional areas in the firm could be used for both selection of performance factors and for evaluation. Procedures that are developed should include provision for periodic evaluation in the future. Depending upon the rate of changes in product life cycle patterns and historical product performance, the frequency of evaluation will vary among firms. An annual review represents a minimum time span; longer intervals may be appropriate depending upon conditions in a given firm. Several of the evaluation methods used to screen new product ideas can be adopted for use in product elimination analysis.

Matching Criteria with Performance Information

Using the criteria determined by management, the performance of existing products should be evaluated. If it is necessary to assess several products, then the performance assessment should be used to screen the group of products to identify possible drop candidates. For example, in the case where a large number of items is carried such as by a wholesale food or drug firm, it would be costly and time consuming to perform a comprehensive analysis. The screening process can be used to sort out products which should receive more detailed study.

Computer models have been developed for use in the screening process when evaluative criteria and performance information can be quantified. The Product Review and Evaluation Subsystem Model (PRESS) can be used by management to identify product deletion candidates.[17] It utilizes standard cost accounting and marketing information, generating product rankings like those shown in Table 23–4. The products with low selection indexes (1.0 or less) are those which have been identified as the most promising for elimination from the firm's line of products. The selection index (SIN) is calculated using the following formula:

$$SIN_i = \frac{CM_i/\Sigma CM_i}{FC_i/\Sigma FC_i} \times (CM_i/\Sigma CM_i)$$

where

---

[17] See, for example, Paul W. Hamelmann and Edward M. Mazze, "Improving Product Abandonment Decisions," *Journal of Marketing*, 36 (April 1972), pp. 20–26, published by the American Marketing Association.

SIN_i = Selection Index Number for Product i

CM_i = Contribution Margin for product i

FC_i = Facilities Costs for product i

ΣCM_i = Summation of contribution margin of all products

ΣFC_i = Summation of facilities costs of all products.[18]

For example, if products A and B have equal contribution margins but A utilizes double the amount of facilities costs compared to B, then A's SIN value will be one-half that of B's. Depending upon the particular evaluation criteria appropriate in a given firm weighing schemes other than facilities costs could be utilized such as shelf space or floor space in a retail firm.

The PRESS model includes additional capabilities that can be used to examine price-volume relationships, sales trends, and product com-

TABLE 23-4

Illustrative Product Rankings Generated by the PRESS Model

Product	Total Contribution Margin ($)	Percent CM	Cost of Facilities Utilization	Percent FU	Selection Index*
810	37065.60	15.45	60.15	4.78	49.94
927	20021.80	8.35	22.16	1.76	39.56
812	24948.10	10.40	95.64	7.60	14.23
801	16909.80	7.05	52.19	4.15	11.98
813	9229.59	3.89	24.33	1.93	7.82
802	14919.10	6.22	62.77	4.99	7.75
815	11767.60	4.91	48.26	3.84	6.27
811	12740.90	5.31	65.27	5.19	5.44
807	12026.60	5.01	58.69	4.66	5.39
808	11315.10	4.72	55.25	4.39	5.07
914	9049.04	3.77	41.90	3.33	4.27
959	9581.52	3.99	55.62	4.42	3.61
951	5275.66	2.20	17.54	1.39	3.47
806	6273.96	2.62	25.59	2.03	3.36
805	5843.32	2.44	25.83	2.05	2.89
960	4635.12	1.93	20.00	1.59	2.35
923	5048.00	2.10	27.41	2.18	2.03
809	5311.16	2.21	34.53	2.74	1.79
814	5392.80	2.25	36.40	2.89	1.75
803	3757.65	1.57	71.73	5.70	.43
926	1325.35	.55	9.05	.72	.42
952	3242.56	1.35	107.88	8.57	.21
917	2602.95	1.09	76.53	6.08	.19
922	837.25	.35	76.63	6.09	.02
804	655.98	.27	86.82	6.90	.01
		100.00%		100.00%	

* Most profitable products have the largest selection indexes.

Source: Reprinted by permission from Paul W. Hamelmann and Edward M. Mazze, "Improving Product Abandonment Decisions," *Journal of Marketing*, 36 (April 1972), pp. 20-26, published by the American Marketing Association.

---

[18] Ibid., p. 23.

plementarity and substitutability, using available subjective and historical data. For example, a form for estimating product complementarity and substitutability is shown in Figure 23–10. This information can then be incorporated into the analysis.

FIGURE 23–10

Product Complementarity and Substitutability

Product No. _____

Product Name _____

If this product is deleted:

1. What product number will be sold instead?

Product Number	Percent of Units of Deleted Product Which This No. Will Replace
a.	
b.	
c.	
d.	

Note: If less than 100 percent is shown, the remainder is assumed to be business which will be lost completely.

2. What tie-in sales on other product numbers will be lost?

Product Number	Percent of Units of Presently Sold Products Which Will be Lost if Above Product is Deleted
a.	
b.	
c.	
d.	
e.	
f.	

Source: Paul W. Hamelmann and Edward M. Mazze, "Improving Product Abandonment Decisions," *Journal of Marketing*, 36 (April 1972), p. 26, published by the American Marketing Association.

Comprehensive Analysis

In cases where only a few products are to be evaluated, a combination of the screening and comprehensive analysis stages may be appropriate. Evaluation teams can be effective in assuring that the assessment process considers the impact of a proposed product drop in various areas of the firm (e.g., production, finance, marketing, and personnel). Since it is impossible to quantify all evaluative criteria, a recommended approach to evaluation is to identify those products which do not meet acceptable standards based only on quantifiable factors (e.g., SIN

assigned for planning the product departure. Moreover, recognition and compensation should be given to those personnel involved in the phasing out process that is comparable to equivalent levels of responsibility.

SUMMARY AND CONCLUSIONS

Evaluation and control of marketing operations are important management activities and comprise a substantial portion of management's time in most firms. These tasks occur at three interrelated levels: strategy positioning analysis; assessment of marketing program effectiveness; and evaluation of individual marketing mix element effectiveness. The central role of evaluation and control has been emphasized and a systematic approach to this management activity was developed. The product drop decision provides an illustration of an important marketing management control area. Our examination of product drop decisions as a continuing marketing management responsibility (shared by other functional areas of the enterprise) recognizes the fact that products should be evaluated on a regular basis. A product or service, once added to the line, should not be assured of a permanent position in the firm. A systematic decision process for evaluating products was developed and approaches to analysis illustrated.

EXERCISES FOR REVIEW AND DISCUSSION

1. You have been asked by the president of a medium size manufacturer of outboard motors, boats, and skimobiles to examine the firm's overall marketing operations and to make appropriate recommendations for improvement. Develop a comprehensive plan of action for conducting the study which will be helpful to you in identifying relevant questions and areas of analysis. The president has told you that there are no apparent problems. Operations are profitable and compare favorably with the industry, but the chief executive feels that improvement can be made. Moreover, recognizing the growth opportunities in the leisure market, management is interested in moving the company toward higher levels of achievement in the decade ahead.

2. Assume a company is currently manufacturing three different products: Product A, Product B and Product C. The company is considering dropping Product A from the line. The following information has been assembled concerning the three products:

	Product A	Product B	Product C	Total
Sales.........................	$100,000	$80,000	$10,000	$190,000
Variable costs...............	$ 80,000	$56,000	$ 6,000	$142,000
Fixed costs				
a. separate...............	$ 15,000	$10,000	$ 1,500	$ 26,500
b. joint but allocated.......	$ 6,000	$10,000	$ 2,000	$ 18,000
Total fixed.................	$ 21,000	$20,000	$ 3,500	$ 44,500

Fixed costs have been divided into categories: *Separable*—They are fixed only in relation to each one of the three products. The fixed costs related to one particular product can be eliminated by dropping that product; *Joint*—Fixed costs are joint fixed costs. Based only on the above information what products (if any) should be dropped? What factors other than sales and costs should be considered in determining whether to eliminate a product from the line?

3. Referring to Exercise 2, assume that A and B are two substitute products and that, if we drop Product A, the sales of Product B would increase by 10 percent. (*a*) Would we still want to keep Product A, or just produce Products B and C? (*b*) What percentage increase would you want in sales of Product B to decide on dropping A?

4. Assume now that the idle facilities made available by dropping Product A would give you the possibility of producing Product D. Cost-revenue estimates for the now Product D are as follows:

$$
\begin{array}{lr}
\text{Sales} & \$50,000 \\
\text{Variable costs} & 35,000 \\
\text{Contribution margin} & 15,000 \\
\text{Separate fixed costs} & 7,000 \\
\end{array}
$$

Should the firm add Product D and drop Product A, or simply keep Products A, B, and C?

5. A food company is currently producing 10 different products. For performance reasons, (the profit contribution margin for these two products is below an acceptable level) the company decides to drop two of these products. What could the impact be of such a decision on (*a*) the customers, (*b*) the channel participants?

6. With existing products, the primary task of the marketing manager is to monitor the performance of the product and modify strategy and tactics in response to changing conditions. Consider the situation of a manufacturer of electro-mechanical adding machines. Describe how marketing mix strategy might be modified during the life cycle of the product up to the time where inexpensive electronic calculators have made major penetrations into the market.

part six

Marketing: A Broader Perspective

24

Nonbusiness Marketing: A New View

Over 20 percent of the U.S. economy is in the nonprofit sector, a sector that is becoming "marketing conscious" if not "marketing oriented."[1] Further, an estimated $3 billion is expended annually on nonprofit advertising, including over one billion dollars by institutional advertisers, $400 million in political ads, $65 million by the federal government, and $80 million by state governments. Marketing activity is clearly visible in the United Fund campaign, Reverend Billy Graham's crusades, volunteer social action programs, and in nonsmoking and drug abuse efforts. Millions of dollars are spent on recruiting the volunteer army, state and local tourism promotion, and on political candidates. Nonbusiness marketing is, in a sense, "big business." Nonprofit groups increasingly employ professional marketers and compete with business in the labor market for marketing expertise.

Although this text is heavily premised on a business oriented, managerial definition of marketing, several nonbusiness examples have been integrated in various chapters. The growing importance of nonbusiness marketing in addition to several unique characteristics of the area together make this chapter essential. This chapter also serves to integrate and summarize many concepts discussed in earlier chapters. In the first section, nonbusiness marketing is placed in historical perspective; secondly, nonbusiness marketing is definitionally distinguished from business and from social marketing; thirdly, uniquenesses of nonbusiness marketing are summarized; and finally, the marketing planning process is applied to selected nonbusiness cases.

---

[1] "Growing Nonprofit Sector, Now 20 Percent of Economy, Becoming Marketing Conscious," *Marketing News*, vol. 7 (January 15, 1974), p. 1. Published by the American Marketing Association.

NONBUSINESS MARKETING IN PERSPECTIVE

Marketing began as an outgrowth of economics at the turn of the century. Viewed as highly related to macroeconomics, the distribution of products became an object of study. In contrast, perhaps the newest statement as to the nature of marketing—called "generic marketing" suggests that "marketing applies to any social unit seeking to exchange values with other social units."[2] Marketing's core idea is limited to "transactions." Critics have suggested that this definition could even encompass kissing!

A longtime scholar of marketing history summarized the evolution of marketing in Figure 24–1. These differing statements vary in basic perspective as well as in scope. Although the final statement (7) uses a managerial perspective, the scope of marketing application is vastly expanded with the addition of the nonbusiness realm. Despite social criticism of the marketing management perspective, treating marketing as a management technology has ironically facilitated applying marketing thought to social and other nonbusiness causes. As long as marketing was equated to, for example, marketing institutions, and was defined as a "thing" rather than a body of techniques and knowledge, it was not readily transferable.

The marketing discipline has in only recent years been primarily viewed from a managerial standpoint. Historically, the marketing process has been studied from the perspectives of different commodities (e.g., agricultural marketing, furniture marketing), of marketing institutions (e.g., different wholesalers and retailers), and as sets of functions (e.g., transporting, grading). Use of the term "marketing" in university course titles appears to have begun around 1905 at the University of Pennsylvania, followed in 1909 at the University of Pittsburg and in 1910 at the University of Wisconsin.[3] These years have been labeled a "period of discovery" with the next decade characterized more by "conceptualization." Beyond this, "The years between 1920 and 1930 marked the coming of age of the discipline of marketing. During that decade not only did all of the branches of the subject attain a general or integrated statement, but two additional areas of specialization appeared—wholesaling and marketing research."[4] Marketing thought was additionally developed during the 1930s, although on much the same structure developed in the previous decade. The 1940s, partially due to World War II, were not as productive as earlier periods although the seeds were sown for a critical

---

[2] Philip Kotler, "A Generic Concept of Marketing," *Journal of Marketing*, vol. 36 (April 1972), p. 53. Published by the American Marketing Association.

[3] This paragraph based on Robert Bartels, *Marketing Theory and Metatheory* (Homewood, Ill.: Richard D. Irwin, Inc., 1970), pp. 29–57.

[4] Ibid., p. 40.

period of "reconceptualizing" in the 1950s, a period encompassing the solidification of the managerial viewpoint and the related development of the marketing concept. As noted in Figure 24–1, later years have encompassed the integration of systems theory and of behavioral concepts (such as the study of consumer behavior). Partially from viewing marketing as an interacting participant in a larger system has come consideration of marketing as a social and a societal process.

When one studies the dramatic transitions evidenced in Figure 24–1, it is tempting to wonder, "Where next?" Have marketing theorists and practitioners finally agreed that the managerial perspective is *the* way to view marketing? Most likely, as the young discipline of marketing continues to mature, several perspectives will become (and remain) equally legitimate from a scholarly standpoint. From the viewpoint of management, whether business or nonbusiness, it is likely that the concepts espoused in this text will remain of first priority. But most importantly, it is essential to not only understand that several viewpoints currently exist, but also that the future will likely hold even additional views.

Business, Nonbusiness, and Social Marketing

Today, the "traditional" conception of marketing holds that marketing is essentially a *business* activity directed toward meeting the needs of *customers* for *goods* and *services*. Marketing, it is argued by some, is intrinsically a business activity, and to expand its meaning beyond business is to dilute marketings' true purpose and effectiveness.[5] Many also confine the "products" with which marketing deals to economic goods and services. In contrast, advocating broadening the concept of marketing, Kotler and Levy instead noted that "the choice facing those who manage nonbusiness organizations is not whether to market or not market, for no organization can avoid marketing. The choice is whether to do it well or poorly, and on this necessity the case for organizational marketing is basically founded."[6] They further proposed that *every* organization produces a "product" including at least physical products, services, persons, organizations, and/or ideas. Equally, every organization has, "consumer groups," broadly defined to include clients (immediate consumers of the product), trustees or directors (who enjoy benefits from the product), active publics (that take a specific interest in

---

[5] See, for example, David Luck, "Broadening the Concept of Marketing—Too Far," *Journal of Marketing*, vol. 33 (July 1969), pp. 53–54; Also, Ben M. Enis, "Deepening the Concept of Marketing," *Journal of Marketing*, vol. 37 (October 1973), pp. 57–62. Published by the American Marketing Association.

[6] Philip Kotler and Sidney J. Levy, "Broadening the Concept of Marketing," *Journal of Marketing*, vol. 33 (January 1969), p. 15. Published by the American Marketing Association.

FIGURE 24–1

Evolution of the Scope of Marketing

1. Distribution of Products

Originally the economic process was conceived as divided between production and distribution, the marketing portion of the process beginning upon completion of production. Marketing was viewed as a technical process, dealing with physical distribution and the economic and legal aspects of transaction. Marketing also was conceived in general terms as concerned with the macro aspects of the distributive process. It dealt with economic variables and with economically motivated market behavior. That was the state of marketing early in this century, when it was an outgrowth of the economics discipline.

2. Economics of Distributive Enterprise

Beginning in the early 1920s, enterprise aspects of marketing became increasingly emphasized. Functions and problems of institutional operation, but not yet the processes of management decision making, were the principal subjects of concern. This interest coincided with the need for mastery of the mathematics of markup and merchandising and of distribution cost accounting in the expanding activities of marketing manufacturers and distributive institutions. Yet marketing remained associated with the discipline of economics and with the distribution of products.

3. Management of the Distributive Process

An evaluation of marketing management occurred during the 1950s, when variables other than the simple mathematics of making ends meet gained attention. Management of the "4Ps" of marketing—products, price, promotion, and place—represented a concept of marketing moved one step more from the macro to the micro and from the general to the specific, yet from the routinely operational to the coordinatively managerial. "The marketing concept" represented an enlargement of the marketing manager's role within the internal organizational structure.

4. Distributive Managerial Decision Making

With the introduction of new managerial concepts into marketing management, emphasis shifted a degree further from macro considerations toward a broadened interdisciplinary concept of management itself. Educational literature and courses reflected this in their incorporation of models, quantitative analysis, electronic data processing, and various methods and techniques of decision making.

Figure 24–1 (continued)

5. A Social [Behavioral] Process

In the late 1950s, increasing interest in behavioral disciplines imbued marketers with greater appreciation of the humanistic aspects of marketing. This constituted a new element, in contrast alike to the economics of distribution, the mathematics of merchandising and the processes of decision making. Roles of marketing participants definable in other than their economic context were identified, and the patterns of their interactions and perceptions of responsibility were explored. As the roles identified were exclusively those of participants in the marketing process, and not those in other social, nonbusiness institutions, the ethics deduced were those relevant to competitors, customers, employees, and the like. This step in broadening the concept of marketing led to the study of consumer behavior, system interactions, and economic social responsibility.

6. A Societal Process

During the 1960s, marketing became increasingly regarded not merely as a social process involving economic participants, but as a societal process, one undertaken by society in which the functions and responsibilities of the marketing segment were viewed as interrelated with all other segments of the social structure. In its relationships with the legal, political, educational, religious, and general community environments marketing was both a dependent and an independent variable. Marketing behavior was seen to be influenced by the nonbusiness values of its participants, and nonbusiness institutions were seen to be influenced by business and the activities of businessmen. In this mutual interdependence was spawned a consciousness of social responsibility, a responsibility to individuals in roles other than that of customer.

7. A Generic Function Applicable to Nonbusiness Institutions

Beyond its relationship to society in general in the distribution of economic goods, marketing in the late 1960s became viewed as a generic process, one applicable to the fulfillment of the needs and goals of all types of institutions. Kotler and Levy in 1969 identified the marketing functions as product development, pricing, distribution, and communication. Thus in preparing and presenting their ideas and programs, government departments, political campaigners, military recruiters, educators, and activists are said to be engaging in "marketing"; and it is the province of professional marketers to provide expertise on their behalf.

Source: Robert Bartels, "The Identity Crisis in Marketing," *Journal of Marketing*, vol. 38 (October 1974), pp. 73–74. Published by the American Marketing Association.

the organization), and the general public (people who may develop attitudes which could affect the organization).

Statements from several specific sources are integrated into Figure 24–2 to delineate business, non-business and social marketing. As illustrated, business marketing normally involves a business organization in pursuit of economic profit (self-serving) by a business organization via the marketing of traditional goods and services. As diagrammed, certain aspects of business marketing encompass part of what is currently called "social marketing." Specifically, social responsibility considerations relating to business marketing decisions are part of social marketing. In addition, business marketers profitably pursuing social markets—such as construction of public housing—and business marketers contributing their expertise to social organizations have significant social consequences (and are part of social marketing). These societal dimensions of marketing are discussed in Chapters 2 and 5.

Of more interest here, however, is the right side of Figure 24–2, non-business marketing. It may be seen that social marketing also subsumes a portion of *non*business marketing and this part is referred to as the

FIGURE 24–2

Social, Nonbusiness, and Business Marketing

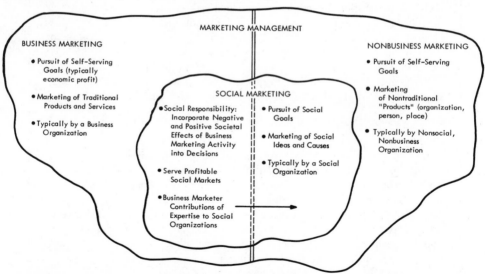

Sources: Adel I. El Ansary and Oscar E. Kramer, Jr., "Social Marketing: The Family Planning Experience," *Journal of Marketing*, vol. 37 (July 1973), p. 1, published by the American Marketing Association; Gerald Zaltman and Ian Vertinsky, "Health Service Marketing: A Suggested Model," *Journal of Marketing*, vol. 35 (July 1971), p. 19, published by the American Marketing Association; William Lazer and Eugene J. Kelley, eds., *Social Marketing: Perspectives and Viewpoints* (Homewood, Ill.: Richard D. Irwin, 1973), pp. ix, 4; William Lazer, "Marketing's Changing Social Relationships," *Journal of Marketing*, vol. 33, no. 1 (January 1969), p. 5, published by the American Marketing Association; Philip Kotler and Gerald Zaltman, "Social Marketing: An Approach to Planned Social Change," *Journal of Marketing*, vol. 35 (July 1971), p. 5, published by the American Marketing Association; Philip Kotler, *Marketing Management: Analysis, Planning and Control*, Second Edition (Englewood Cliffs, N.J.: Prentice-Hall, 1972), pp. 868, 870, 880.

"pursuit of social goals via the marketing of social ideas and causes, typically by a social organization." The part of nonbusiness marketing not encompassed by this is the "pursuit of self-serving goals (but not just economic profit) through the marketing of nontraditional products (organizations, persons, places), typically by a nonbusiness organization." Perhaps the best example to fit this part of nonbusiness marketing is that of a political candidate motivated largely by self-interest, who represents a "product" (person) and is "marketed" by a nonbusiness, yet nonsocial organization (e.g., Committee to Reelect John Doe). A case of nonbusiness, *social* marketing might involve a family planning clinic (social organization), marketing the "idea" of family planning for the purpose of reducing problems associated with large families (social goal). These conceptions recognize that different *goals* (or motives), different *products* as well as different *organizations* may distinguish business, nonbusiness, and social marketing from each other. While recognizing that exceptions to the combinations presented here do exist, Figure 24–2 should encompass the overwhelming majority of cases. By way of integration, *social marketing refers to the interrelationships between marketing and the societal system, including the impacts of business marketing on society as well as the application of marketing tools and concepts to social problems or opportunities. Nonbusiness marketing is the application of marketing tools and concepts to nonbusiness* (not just social) *problems and opportunities.* With the terms defined, let us consider unique aspects of nonbusiness marketing.

Uniqueness of Nonbusiness Applications

It would be a misnomer to characterize nonbusiness marketing as an entirely different area of study than business marketing. The concepts and techniques discussed throughout this text are, with few exceptions, equally applicable to nonbusiness marketing. Marketing in the computer industry is different than marketing food products; but the basic techniques and perspective are the same. This is also true of business versus nonbusiness marketing. Yet creativity and imagination are required to perceive how to apply the same managerial concepts to nonbusiness marketing cases and, indeed, several uniquenesses in application do exist. A small, but growing body of nonbusiness marketing cases allows for a tentative statement of unique factors (discussed later in the chapter):

> Nonbusiness marketing, more often than business, has objectives other than stimulating demand. Mass transit companies may try to reduce demand during certain times of the day and increase it during others.

Nonbusiness organizations are often more dependent on several groups or "publics" whereas business, even today, is usually considered responsible first to stockholders. A state university, for example, must respond to students, legislators, alumni, contributors and many other groups.

    Related, environmental analysis may be even more critical than for business due to high dependence on several groups, and

    Marketing activity may necessarily be directed at several of the nonbusiness organizations' publics. Universities, for example, analyze the needs and "market" themselves to each of the groups noted.

The nature of nonbusiness activity is often more socially sensitive and controversial and, therefore, more subject to environmental constraints such as legislation or social pressure. Abortion clinics, for example, although now legal, face severe local pressure in many communities. Coping with such pressure may involve marketing-type activity.

The sensitive nature of many nonbusiness "products" may make information planning and assembling (e.g., marketing research) more difficult than for business. For example, collection of information for analyzing the environment of abortion clinics or for assessing such a "market opportunity" could easily involve high nonresponse rates and biased answers.

Products are more often intangible than for business—such as the marketing of "ideas." Consider, for example, antismoking and alcoholism campaigns.

Nonbusiness marketing is much more than just nonbusiness or social advertising. Such *advertising* is common, *marketing* is much less evident. *Marketing* requires an analysis of market needs and coordination of product development and other marketing variables to match those needs. Consider, for example, the *advertising* of political candidates, such as in the 1972 presidential campaign.[7]

The "price" of nonbusiness products is often nonmonetary but the concept of the downward sloping demand curve still holds. "Free" health clinics may require incurring travel costs, possible embarrassment, and other "psychic costs" that are very real to potential users.

Channel of distribution components or "middlemen" may be very different than traditional components. Idea "distribution" may substantially overlap with promotional variables in, for example, use of the communications media as "channels of distribution." Dis-

---

[7] "The GOP Admen Have the Edge," *Business Week* (August 5, 1972), p. 20.

tributing "ideas" such as the negative consequences of consuming alcoholic beverages, cigarettes, and marijuana may be primarily through radio and television "outlets."

Performance measures for control purposes may be more difficult to develop given the nebulous nature of some nonbusiness marketing activities and the absence, in many cases, of tangible "sales" data. Mass transit marketing may partially rely on ridership rates and the United Fund on "dollars collected." Others such as drug abuse campaigns are more difficult to measure and evaluate.

Clearly, exceptions exist to this set of generalizations, but it is probable that future studies of nonbusiness marketing will continue to support these statements, at least in degree.

NONBUSINESS MARKETING: ILLUSTRATION

Marketing concepts are increasingly used for marketing the services of the United States Post Office, safe driving, antismoking, the fine arts, and politicians. These are but selected examples of a growing number of available cases. A conference on social marketing in the early seventies provided the first compendium of cases and, more recently, a comprehensive textbook on marketing for non-profit organizations became available.[8]

The following discussion highlights the above uniquenesses within the framework used to structure this text; environmental analysis, market opportunity analysis, marketing strategy design, implementation, and control. The marketing of family planning services as shown in Figure 24–3 will be used to illustrate nonbusiness marketing.[9]

Environmental Analysis

Family planning ideas and techniques are sufficiently sensitive and controversial in Southern Louisiana (Figure 24–3) to make an understanding of the environment very important. With the statement of an organizational mission of "encouraging the use of family planning methods" (to alleviate problems associated with large family size and overpopulation), the relevant parts of the macro and task environment

---

[8] Jagdish Sheth, and Peter L. Wright, eds. *Marketing Analysis for Societal Problems–National Conference on Social Marketing* (Urbana, Ill.: University of Illinois Press, 1974); Philip Kotler, *Marketing for Nonprofit Organizations* (Englewood Cliffs, N.J.: Prentice-Hall, 1975); also see Gerald Zaltman, Philip Kotler and Ira Kaufman, eds. *Creating Social Change* (New York: Holt, Rinehart and Winston, 1972).

[9] Much of the information contained in Figure 24–3 is credited to Adel I. El-Ansary and Oscar E. Kramer, Jr.

FIGURE 24–3

Marketing Family Planning Services

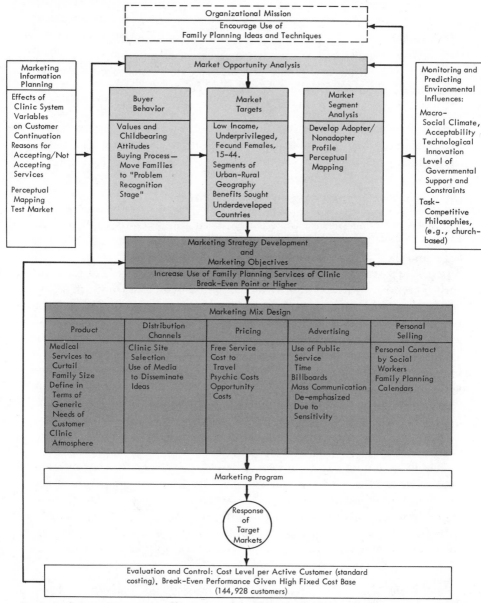

Source: Partially based on Adel I. El-Ansary and Oscar E. Kramer, Jr., "Social Marketing: The Family Planning Experience," *Journal of Marketing*, vol. 37 (July 1973), pp. 1–7; Also see, Julian L. Simon, "A Huge Marketing Research Task—Birth Control," *Journal of Marketing Research*, vol. 5 (February 1968) pp. 21–27; and John U. Farley and Harold J. Leavitt, "Marketing and Population Problems," *Journal of Marketing*, vol. 35 (July 1971), pp. 28–33. Published by the American Marketing Association.

may be identified. Within the macro-environment, the social environment is particularly germane because of the opposition of some groups. If the community is in overwhelming opposition to family planning organizations, there may be little hope of building a viable service program. Social forces may be of such magnitude and occur with such rapidity as to preclude any hope of providing family services. Analysis of the social setting, cultural values and the likelihood of social issues developing is cently, a comprehensive textbook on marketing for nonprofit organiza-essential at the outset. Social resistance to family planning would be even greater in many less developed countries.

The technological environment is also important given that birth control methods have progressed well beyond the "rhythm method" to the IUD and the "pill." Developing effective marketing strategy today is dependent on a low probability of methods becoming obsolete tomorrow. Also, technological innovations that reduce detrimental side effects of specific methods would significantly alter the specific set of services marketed. If, for example, a "morning after" pill became generally marketable, the educational process required to modify behavior (how to take the pill) would be significantly changed.

The governmental environment in different countries and even in different states within the United States may significantly constrain marketing activity. Legal sanctions in the United States have, until recently, prohibited promotion of birth control products in broadcast media. Changing values and life styles of the citizenry undoubtedly contributed to a relaxation of regulation in this area. Government may also actively support and fund family planning services with a given level of support often determining the available resources for marketing activity. Government may be one of several publics on which a family planning organization is dependent. Thus, government may be considered a "target group" to which marketing effort is directed.

Within the task environment, competition and buyers are of immediate concern. Competitive philosophies emanate from sources such as antiabortion groups, church-related statements and racial minority representatives who view population control as a threat to their strength. It is essential that competition be analyzed and considered in developing counterstrategies. "Buyers," as part of the task environment, influence the entire marketing planning process, particularly market opportunity analysis.

Market Opportunity Analysis

Marketing starts with understanding the customer and identifying generic needs, in this case, fulfilled by family planning services (Figure 24–3). For large families with limited incomes, the need may be financially based. For others, such services may simply facilitate more freedom from children and, generally, a preferred lifestyle. Implementing the marketing concept is as important to nonbusiness marketing as to business. Nonprofit groups often ignore this and have an overbearing "product" emphasis with too little attention to their consumers. As shown in Figure 24–4, beginning with the generic need, we may break out additional levels for analysis at the product/service level and brand level. Emphasis is placed in this instance on public family planning clinics.

Understanding the values, perceptions and attitudes of potential clients in various publics as well as how they relate to the "buying process" is also important (Figure 24–3). The major challenge may be to just make potential "customers" *aware* of the services and alternative methods. This is especially true in countries with less developed communication systems than in the United States. Beyond awareness, marketing effort to "move" the consumer into the "problem recognition" stage of the buying process may be the greatest challenge confronting family planning organizations. Until the consumer perceives having additional children as a problem, there is no incentive to search for alternative solutions and continue through the buying process.

It is therefore essential that marketing information be assembled as a basis for marketing decisions (Figure 24–3). The type of information needed must be determined, the value of additional information considered and the extent to engage in formal, primary data collection

FIGURE 24–4

Market Opportunity Analysis: Family Planning

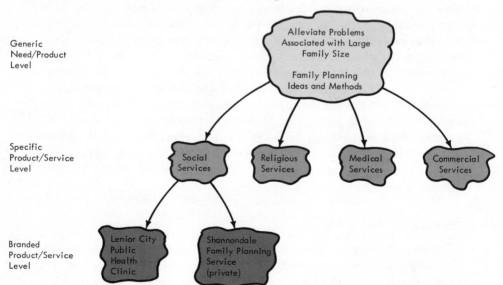

finally decided. Marketing research in the Louisiana case was necessary to determine potential consumer perceptions, to ascertain the reasons for accepting (or not accepting) services and to determine the effect of various clinic variables on customer continuation. Test marketing may also contribute by systematically using different communications, locations and other variables to better assess demand response to alternative marketing approaches. Demographic profiles were also developed for adopters and nonadopters to help describe appropriate market targets.

A public family planning clinic should also "position" itself in the market relative to other services such as those offered by personal physicians. Product and "brand" positioning would likely place a public clinic on the lower end of the consumer socioeconomic scale relative to personal physicians who serve more affluent customers. In Figure 24–3, the characteristics of the target market are cited as low-income, underpriviledged, fecund females of child-bearing age, located in rural areas. These descriptive characteristics of a market segment with an unserved need are useful for effectively developing marketing strategy.

Marketing Objectives and Program

Nonbusiness organizations often operate on very limited budget and are tempted to view marketing as a superfluous activity. A family planning clinic with no clientele, however, would be unable to continue operating. Limited expenditures on a well developed marketing program may generate additional clientele well worth the costs. Marginalism concepts of marketing programming, including analysis of "sales" response at various expenditure levels, apply to nonbusiness cases—both for determining the overall level of expenditure on marketing as well as the allocation of the marketing budget to alternative uses (e.g., another sales representative versus an increased advertising program.) The development of marketing strategy must be based on operational marketing objectives and, probably more often than for business, may not involve the objective of increasing demand. Instead, as shown in Table 24–1, the marketing task is dependent on the demand state. The objective may actually be to decrease demand (demarketing) or, for example, to synchronize demand better with the available supply or capacity. The limited capacity of family planning clinics, for example, could at some point require carefully timed marketing effort.

Product. Nonbusiness organizations are often involved with marketing nontraditional, intangible products. As noted in Figure 24–2, products encompass organizations, persons, places, ideas and causes. Family planning services, compared to many nonbusiness "products" are fairly traditional. They may be simply an extension of other medical services. Yet the product is not really the specific method or technology adopted but

TABLE 24–1

Basic Marketing Tasks

	Demand State	Marketing Task	Formal Name
I.	Negative demand	Disabuse demand	Conversional marketing
II.	No demand	Create demand	Stimulational marketing
III.	Latent demand	Develop demand	Developmental marketing
IV.	Faltering demand	Revitalize demand	Remarketing
V.	Irregular demand	Synchronize demand	Synchromarketing
VI.	Full demand	Maintain demand	Maintenance marketing
VII.	Overfull demand	Reduce demand	Demarketing
VIII.	Unwholesome demand	Destroy demand	Countermarketing

Source: Philip Kotler, "The Major Tasks of Marketing Management," *Journal of Marketing*, vol. 37 (October 1973), pp. 42–49. Published by the American Marketing Association.

rather the whole "idea" of using family planning concepts. For many, a new way of viewing the newborn (and unborn) may even be required and, in any case, new information must be perceived and accepted. The consumer is in a sense "buying" the idea of a smaller family and the advantages (and disadvantages) that accrue. Also, accepting the use of birth control methods is an "idea" much different than that of having a vasectomy or an abortion—the latter requiring difficult marketing strategies.

The orientation must be to match the needs of a group with a "product" for satisfying those needs. Otherwise, it may be "selling" but not marketing. Examples abound of nonbusiness organizations promoting their *products*—but not based on an analysis of market needs. Many other concepts in the earlier product chapters also have application to nonbusiness products. The new product introduction process is essentially the same for family planning and causes and organizations commonly go through product life cycles. Additionally, a family planning clinic has a "product mix" from information to birth control methods to abortion. The same basic ideas apply.

Distribution. The intangible nature of many nonbusiness products contributes to the use of unorthodox distribution channels (Figure 24–3). The distribution of family planning medical services is via family planning clinics, these representing "retail outlets." The *ideas* are distributed less conventionally, actually using promotional media (e.g., television) in addition to distributing information at the clinics. Distributing ideas is difficult to separate from the promotional part of the marketing mix because of the important role of promotional media in communicating messages. Even in selecting media, however, the degree of selectivity must be considered as in distribution (e.g., a selective direct mail campaign versus broad scale coverage in broadcast media) and the distribution strategy must be consistent with other marketing mix variables. The actual distribution of services via clinics involves many of the usual considerations of number of "stores," site selection, number of hours open, clinic design, and other marketing decisions.

Pricing. The price variable is particularly unique in nonbusiness marketing because the product is often "free" in the usual sense. Yet this is seldom true, even for traditional products and services. There is the actual cost of traveling to a shopping center, the value of the consumer's time and the costs of opportunities foregone (Figure 24–3). Additionally, there may be potential costs. Some low-income consumers are reportedly reluctant to shop in department stores because they fear the possible encounter of embarrassing circumstances. Family planning clinics probably hold an even greater threat for most people. Sensitivity of sex-related matters introduces many potential "costs" for consumers even though the services themselves may be free. Also, the opportunity *costs* of not having additional children must be weighed against perceived benefits and, in the case of vasectomies, the potential opportunity costs in the event of remarriage may be very high.

Clearly, lowering the "price" of family planning services calls for attention to client confidentiality, providing a friendly, possibly nonclinical atmosphere, and making services conveniently available. Having an onsite babysitting service could facilitate visits to the clinic and contribute to the number of babies remaining constant! Looking to another example, most who have "kicked the habit" of cigarette smoking would assess a high "price" to the first few days of the process. These nonmonetary factors are very real to the potential consumer although, consistent with the downward sloping demand curve, anything that reduces the intangible (as well as economic) costs to consumers will tend to increase demand. Pricing decisions, as always, must be based on assessing competition, demand, and costs and weighing the intangibles in the analysis process.

Advertising and Personal Selling. In addition to using promotional media as distribution channels for ideas, advertising and personal selling represent an important part of the nonbusiness marketing mix. Social cause *promotion* is not new but social cause *marketing* is new to most nonbusiness organizations. Development of an advertising campaign may itself be productive in developing greater awareness of family planning services or clinic site locations. A campaign could even contribute to more people using birth control measures. But such a program would be more effective if systematically coordinated with overall marketing strategy. Political candidates often use advertising campaigns but less often use marketing. Again, marketing requires attention first to consumer needs and then to the marketing mix variables including product (the candidate). Use of advertising to mislead voters about candidates is certainly as objectionable as misuse by business marketers. Instead, marketing requires that products be responsive to market needs and that advertising be an integral *part* of marketing strategy.

Public service time provided free by the broadcast media represents an opportunity for many nonbusiness organizations. Unfortunately, the time is too often used ineffectively with poorly planned communications. Creative planning is also necessary to generate exposure through publicity. Developing specific communication objectives combined with communications pretesting (Figure 24–3) would vastly improve the programs of most nonbusiness groups. Pretesting advertising copy was an important part of the family planning case and advertising effectiveness measures were also used. As part of the promotional mix, however, advertising in the mass media was deemphasized due to the social sensitivity of family planning services and ideas. Personal selling effort was relied on heavily with social workers acting as selling representatives. Family planning calendars were also used as sales promotional items.

Marketing by nonbusiness groups may rely less on persuasive communications than business marketers so in some instances the term "promotion" may be inappropriate. The term "communications" may be more accurate if the intent is solely to inform, not to influence. In any event, developing objectives and carefully making decisions on such matters as promotional media, messages, and timing is important.

Evaluation and Control

With marketing objectives operationally stated at the outset, evaluating performance becomes largely a matter of measurement. For a family planning clinic, a key measure is the number of active clientele. With a high fixed cost base in facilities and equipment, an important objective is to build the volume of clientele so that the cost level per active customer reaches a reasonable level. If funding is provided on a per client basis, then break-even performance may serve as an objective as in Figure 24–3.

Although the ultimate objective may be "sales," other measures may be required for effective measurement. Monitoring the buying process to determine the level of awareness within a market segment for example, may be a better short-term measure if, say, our current marketing objective is largely to develop awareness of a new family planning clinic location. If performance in a given time frame is below planned levels, determining the problem is required. Family planning service utilization might be down for only two specific clinics. Analyzing *why* is the crux of problem analysis. Once identified, the problem may require simple remedial action or, of course, could be a complex matter of fully analyzing the changing environment, shifting market opportunities and then redesigning marketing strategy as needed.

OTHER CASES

Each nonbusiness case relates to the marketing task in different ways so it is useful to briefly overview two additional examples: March of Dimes fund raising and the recycling of solid waste, as shown in Table 24–2.

The March of Dimes raises funds to use in reducing birth defects. Understandably, young married couples (at the child bearing stage) represent a target group as do groups with notable financial resources. Encouraging volunteer recycling of solid wastes requires attention to each of the target groups that together comprise a reverse channel of distribution. Consumers become de facto producers and are expected to initiate sending such "products" as glass, paper, and soft-drink bottles back through a distribution network. Each of the stages along the way, such as pick-up stations, must accept responsibility until the material is finally reprocessed and marketed (in a conventional sense) as recycled materials.

Carefully defining market targets often requires the use of marketing research (Table 24–2). For example, prior to applying marketing principles to fund raising, little attention had been given to identifying the characteristics of "heavy-givers," similar to the "heavy-half" concept used in segmentation planning. To effectively implement marketing activity to encourage recycling requires research to understand *why* people voluntarily recycle materials, that is, research on motives.

The "product" for both fund raising and recycling is probably best considered "felt satisfaction." Defining the product in terms of the needs it satisfies, engaging in volunteer work or making financial contributions presumably give donors a sense of satisfaction. Perhaps this view assumes human behavior to be overly selfish, but it may be realistic to assume that special attention to increasing the satisfaction "obtained" by donors will facilitate reaching the organization's goals. Also related to the product variable, causes and associations commonly go through product life cycles. The March of Dimes life cycle was temporarily halted with the development of the Salk vaccine although the adoption of a new cause extended its life.

If the fund raising product is "satisfaction," then the volunteers who collect contributions must "deliver" the satisfaction. Training mothers for the "mother's march" to deliver satisfaction was part of the sales-type training they received. Numerous middlemen may exist for recycling as shown in Table 24–2. Alternative channel arrangements exist such as direct to consumer (e.g., fund raising) or via more distant specialists

TABLE 24–2. Nonbusiness Marketing Applications

Nonbusiness Application	Market Target	Product	Promotion Advertising	Promotion Selling	Promotion Other	Price	Distribution	Marketing Research	Effectiveness Measures
Fund raising* March of Dimes (birth defects)	Young marrieds Businesses Others "heavy giver"	Ideas and cause: need to reduce birth defects Satisfaction from giving Self-protection Product life cycle of causes and organizations	Print and broadcast media Determination of interest, distinctiveness, and ability of ad themes	Mother's march-sales training	Brochures	Dollar contributions by donors Setting contribution guidelines	Volunteers collect contributions and "deliver satisfaction" from giving	Develop "heavy-giver" profile Awareness of March of Dimes new cause Information on prior donors Competitive analysis	"Sales" increased by 33 percent, expenses by 14 percent over previous year Measure of awareness of March of Dimes and cause (advertising effectiveness)
Recycling solid waste†	Various people in reverse channel: consumers, middlemen, reprocessors, and reusers Motivate and persuade to recycle Consumers are de facto producers	"Value of recycling"; ideas and cause Resulting services provided by consumers and others Solid waste returned for reuse in present form, energy landfill, fertilizer, metals, glass, etc.	Use of media for ecology education, awareness, and concern promotion	Offering reward for return of merchandise Door-to-door collection campaigns	Packaging— "Don't Be A Litterbug" (pass laws— force to buy)	Consumers who "buy" the cause may: Incur inconvenience by separating waste dollar and opportunity costs of transporting waste to sites	Result of consumer "buying ideas" leads to: reverse channel—start with consumer Reclamation or recycling center Channel varies by "product" and "market" Community group clean-up days as middlemen Store as middleman for returnable bottles Waste disposable specialists	Consumer perceptions and attitudes Research consumer motives Analysis of costs and benefits of recycling	Quantity and value of waste recycled Proportion of usable waste recycled Number of consumers who recycle National resources conserved

Sources: * William A. Mindak and H. Malcolm Bybee, "Marketing's Application to Fund Raising," *Journal of Marketing*, vol. 35 (July 1971), pp. 13–18.
† William G. Zikmund and William J. Stanton, "Recycling Solid Wastes: A Channels of Distribution Problem," *Journal of Marketing*, vol. 35 (July 1971), pp. 34–39.
Published by the American Marketing Association.

(e.g., paper and cloth collectors for recycling). Price may be affected by reduced inconvenience, but for fund raising, the amount contributed is the largest consideration. The promotional variables in Table 24–2 are largely self-explanatory, as are possible effectiveness measures.

CONCLUSION

Although some argue that a broader concept and application of marketing will dilute its effectiveness, others do not share these fears and, in fact believe the overall value of marketing will be greatly heightened. As long as organizations stay focused on the needs being served, marketing should be consistent with societal welfare. It has been noted that, "in the course of evolving, many organizations lose sight of their original mandate, grow hard, and become self-serving. The bureaucratic mentality begins to dominate the original service mentality."[10] But if organizations maintain a consumer orientation rather than a product orientation, it would appear that the extension of marketing to nonbusiness organizations would be a bonus for the larger community. Yet the literature is pervaded with what marketers should direct *toward* the consumer. It seems particularly critical in extending marketing to other organizations and publics, that rather than doing something *to* someone, marketers should think in terms of doing it *with* them. This perspective needs to be integrated into both business and nonbusiness marketing thought. Clearly, for nonbusiness groups "to do marketing well" (as noted at the beginning of this chapter) is not socially desirable if the group's objectives are antisocial or if they are succeeding at the demise of a more deserving "competitor." As more and more nonbusiness groups engage in sophisticated marketing practices, it may become increasingly necessary for government to monitor conflicts and practices.

EXERCISES FOR REVIEW AND DISCUSSION

1. Select a nonbusiness organization with which you are familiar (and/or have access to) and demonstrate the applicability of the marketing planning process as discussed in Chapter 1 (and in this chapter). Using the framework in Figure 24–3 of this chapter, briefly discuss and interrelate (*a*) environmental analysis, (*b*) market opportunity analysis, and (*c*) marketing strategy development. Cite major information needs for each of these tasks as well as the means for controlling the marketing program.

Examples of Appropriate Groups and Organizations

United Fund, Inc.	Volunteer army	Hospital
A church	University	U.S. Post Office
Mass transit company	Abortion clinic	Health maintenance
Student government	Local zoo	organization
		YMCA

---

[10] Kotler, "Broadening the Concept of Marketing," p. 15.

2. Using a specific nonbusiness organization (such as the above), select a specific chapter in this textbook and evaluate the transferability of each major concept to the nonbusiness case that you selected.

3. Review the unique features of nonbusiness marketing as outlined early in this chapter and evaluate each of them in the context of three nonbusiness cases of your choice. Are certain of these "uniquenesses" more defensible than others?

4. Marketing has undergone very significant changes since its beginnings at the turn of the century. Based on a quick review of Chapters 1, 2, 3, as well as this chapter, concisely summarize the differing perspectives represented. With this analysis in mind, what is your definition of marketing?

5. Based on a review of the macro-marketing process in Chapter 2 (Figure 2–2), decide if the evolving nature of marketing can be partially explained by that discussion. If so, how?

Index

*This book has been set in 10 pt. and 9 pt.
Caledonia, leaded 2 points. Part numbers and
part titles are 24 point (small) Helvetica
italic. Chapter numbers are 36 point Scotch
Roman italic and chapter titles are 24 point
(small) Helvetica. The size of the type page
is 27 x 45½ picas.*